SECURITY ANALYSIS AND PORTFOLIO MANAGEMENT

Donald E. Fischer
University of Connecticut

Ronald J. Jordan
University of Bridgeport

PRENTICE-HALL INC., Englewood Cliffs, New Jersey 07632

SECURITY ANALYSIS AND PORTFOLIO MANAGEMENT

2ND EDITION

Library of Congress Cataloging in Publication Data

Fischer, Donald E
    Security analysis and portfolio management.
    Includes bibliographical references and index.
    1. Investments.   2. Securities.   3. Bonds.
I. Jordan, Ronald J   joint author.
II. Title.
HG4521.F58 1979   332.6'7   78-16923
ISBN   0-13-798850-8

Editorial/production supervision by Barbara Alexander
Interior design by Chris Gadekar
Cover design by Chris Gadekar
Manufacturing buyer: Trudy Pisciotti

Security Analysis and Portfolio Management, Second Edition
Donald E. Fischer and Ronald J. Jordan

Printed in the United States of America
10   9   8   7   6   5   4

Prentice-Hall International, Inc., *London*
Prentice-Hall of Australia Pty. Limited, *Sydney*
Prentice-Hall of Canada, Ltd., *Toronto*
Prentice-Hall of India Private Limited, *New Delhi*
Prentice-Hall of Japan, Inc., *Tokyo*
Prentice-Hall of Southeast Asia Pte. Ltd., *Singapore*
Whitehall Books Limited, *Wellington, New Zealand*

To our parents,
and to Mary,
Sheryl and Noah

CONTENTS

CHAPTER SEVEN

INDUSTRY ANALYSIS — 167

CHAPTER EIGHT

COMPANY ANALYSIS: MEASURING EARNINGS — 210

CHAPTER NINE

COMPANY ANALYSIS: FORECASTING EARNINGS — 266

PREFACE

This book is about investing in securities. It is aimed at providing a comprehensive introduction to the areas of security analysis and portfolio management. The text approaches investing as a rational decision-making process in which the investor attempts to select a package or portfolio of securities that meets a predetermined set of goals. These investor goals are usually expressed in terms of return on investment and the degree of uncertainty about the return or risk. More return is desirable; more uncertainty or risk is undesirable.

Special attention has been directed throughout to clarity of exposition. We have tried to make the contents as readable, understandable, and non-mathematical as possible. Only simple algebra and some elementary statistics are used in the book. For those who dread mathematics, even the algebra and the statistics are explained in the most lay terms.

In the past several decades the fields of security analysis and portfolio management have changed from a completely descriptive institutional body of literature to a highly formalized quantitative area of study. We have attempted to blend the best and most relevent pieces from the evolving field of endeavor into a meaningful, cohesive framework of analysis that would be of interest to the student of business and finance, the practitioner in the field, and the informed investor.

The text starts with the premise that the reader has no knowledge of investments but some knowledge of economics and accounting. As such, it should serve for an introductory course in investment analysis at either the undergraduate or graduate level. The material builds in difficulty as the chapters progress. With the exception of Part VI and Chapter 16, the text is designed to be followed in the presented progression. However, some users will prefer to cover Chapters 16-20 early in the course. This can be done without loss in continuity. All chapters end with comprehensive questions and/or problems that apply the material presented in the chapter.

An innovation of this work is the inclusion of a comprehensive continuing illustration of the application of the techniques of security analysis and portfolio management to a *real* stock and a *real* portfolio. Each chapter that presents tools of analysis includes an application of the tools to the Lodging Industry and

Holiday Inns. This way the reader can see the transference of explicated theory to a tangible real-life situation.

The book is divided into six sections. Part I, The Investment Environment, contains three chapters. Chapter 1 surveys alternative investment vehicles, their more salient attributes, and the relative supply and demand for these investment types in the recent past. The functioning of major securities markets or how an investor goes about buying and selling particular security types is also examined (Chapter 2). Finally, the impact of differential taxes and transaction costs is explored, for these costs are a very real part of the investment decision (Chapter 3).

Part II, Framework of Risk-Return Analysis, develops in detail the theoretical tenants that explain what a security is worth and the manner in which *returns* are measured (Chapter 4). Equally important, we examine *risk*: what creates it and techniques for stating risk in explicit quantitative terms (Chapter 5).

In Part III, Common-Stock Analysis, a detailed systematic approach to estimating future dividends and price for common stocks is developed. The framework for the approach is an economic-industry-company analysis (E-I-C). The strong link between economic activity and security prices requires that the investor forecast the direction and degree of change in economic activity (Chapter 6). Key sectors of overall economic activity influence particular industries in different ways. The investor must link forecasts of economic activity to the prediction of relative movements in specific industries and analysis of selected industries (Chapter 7). From the industry level to the level of the firm, the investor must examine and analyze factors at the company level that influence earnings, dividends, and stock prices (Chapters 8-10). The final chapter in Part III (Chapter 11) examines various forms of options that might be purchased or sold. These options represent rights to underlying common shares.

Bonds and preferred stocks represent less exciting but nonetheless important alternatives to common stock investing. The systematic sources of risk affecting bonds, particularly inflation, and changes in the level and structure of interest rates, are key areas in bond analysis that are examined first (Chapter 12). In addition, unsystematic risk and other nonrisk factors that influence required yields on bonds are explored in depth (Chapter 13). The final chapter in Part IV (Chapter 14) presents information on historical return-risk experiences in holding bonds and provides a procedure for estimating return and risk on a bond over a forward holding period.

The approach developed in detail in Parts III and IV is best described as *fundamental analysis*. Considerations of economic-industry-company analysis were linked in order to reach considered estimates of return and risk on individual securities. In Part V we also develop the rationale and explore the methods employed by so called technical analysis (Chapter 15). This approach concentrates on supply and demand relationships in the market and historical price and volume relationships to predict the movement of the market as well as the prices of individual securities. The last segment of Part V is devoted to the idea of efficient markets and the theory of random walk. The efficient market notion questions the validity of technical analysis and raises some questions about fundamental analysis (Chapter 16).

The risk-return output of security analysis is the raw material for portfolio management. Part VI deals systematically with the procedures involved in portfolio management. Using modern methods for analyzing portfolios and packaging securities in such a way as to achieve diversification of risk is the first task to be accomplished (Chapter 17). The selection of the one best portfolio from those available to the investor is stage two of portfolio management (Chapter 18). Following the analysis and selection of a portfolio, the investor must be attentive to revising it as economic conditions and the propects for individual securities change (Chapter 19). The final chapter in the text (Chapter 20) explores the ways in which an investor might place his funds in the hands of professionals for management and how portfolios managed individually or by others might be evaluated for performance over time.

This edition of the text has some significant revisions which are worth noting:

1. Complete updating of the Lodging industry and Holiday Inns, Inc. as an integrating example to illustrate certain analytical aspects of security analysis.
2. New chapter on options. This chapter examines puts and calls (including convertible securities) and discusses widely accepted trading strategies.
3. Rewritten chapters on transaction costs and taxes to incorporate the latest developments in these areas.
4. Expanded chapter on accounting information to expose the reader to the very latest in areas of interest to analysts (e.g. replacement accounting, business segment reporting).
5. Additional materials on fixed income securities to include accepted techniques for active bond portfolio management.
6. Revised and enlarged end-of-chapter questions and problems that have had extensive class testing.
7. Additional aids to instructors in the teachers manual including specifics on setting up and administering a securities trading game.

As in all large undertakings, the principals gain invaluable advice from numerous individuals. We were no exception. The authors are indebted to Professor Michael G. Ferri (University of Kentucky), Professor John K. Ford (Northeastern University), Professor J. Ronald Hoffmeister (University of Wyoming), Professor John S. Cochran (Georgia State University), Professor Robert E. Nelson (Western Kentucky University), Professor Lal C. Chugh (Northeastern University), Professor Alden Olson (Michigan State University), and Dr. Richard A. Fey (Dynamics Associates). Charlotte Schneiter typed various versions of the manuscript with her usual good cheer and efficiency. Finally, we are indebted to the Prentice-Hall staff—principally, Michael Melody, David Hildebrand, and Barbara Alexander—for their special efforts in getting the manuscript into production and for following through to the bound book.

We invite all those who find this book useful to share with us any observations that might serve to improve the substance and employment of the contents.

Donald E. Fischer *and* Ronald J. Jordan

Storrs, Connecticut

Bridgeport, Connecticut

THE INVESTMENT ENVIRONMENT

Before we begin our investigation of the ways and means of analyzing individual securities and constructing portfolios, we must understand the investment environment in which we will operate. This is the purpose of this section.

The array of investment vehicles and the participants in the investment arena represent elements worth understanding. Each type of investment has different risk and return characteristics. The participants in the investment game range from the mighty institutional investors (such as pension funds) with considerable dollar muscle to the small, individual investor of modest means. It is important to assess the shifting role and tastes of market participants across a wide spectrum. Who is in the game, and what characterizes the behavior of these participants?

Knowledge of what is available and who the buyers and sellers are must be followed by attention to how one goes about the business of buying or selling securities. It is important to know the various markets through which stocks, bonds, and options can be purchased or sold. The placing of orders to buy and sell and the markets through which this is accomplished are key decision areas in the investment process.

The final link in the investment environment is investor knowledge of the costs of investing. Investing cannot be conducted without cost. Every investor faces the real impact of transaction costs, such as brokerage commissions, and he/she must be attuned to the ever present differences in the ways in which returns from securities are taxed. Efforts to minimize the burden of transaction costs and taxes occupy much of an investor's time and energy.

Chapter 1 presents a discussion of the differences between investment and speculation, a survey of alternative investment vehicles, and a review of the supply and demand for various security forms during the last several years.

Chapter 2 presents very pertinent information about the function, structure, and operation of the major securities markets in the United States.

Chapter 3, the last chapter in this section, outlines the taxes and other transaction costs that every investor must face and should understand.

CHAPTER ONE

INTRODUCTION TO SECURITIES

This book is about investing in securities. Unfortunately, however, we cannot provide the toll for the easy road to riches. Security analysis and portfolio management are hard work, requiring discipline and patience, and the work is not always rewarded by exceptional returns.

None can deny that handsome returns have been reaped in the market by a variety of methods ranging from sheer genius to the occult. The unfortunate thing about most of these techniques is that they are difficult to duplicate consistently by everyone. Often they just cannot be verbalized in a way that permits systematizing.

Our approach is straightforward and consistent within a well-developed framework for decision making. We propose that investors are interested primarily in eventually selling a security for more than they paid for it. Including the receipt of interest or dividends during the time the security is held, the investor hopes to achieve a higher reward than would have been possible by simply placing the same amount of money in a savings account. This reward, or *return*, must be measured and estimated for each security being considered, with appropriate adjustments for decision-making costs.

But in seeking rewards that exceed those available on savings accounts, every investor, consciously or not, faces the very real risk that his hoped-for return will fall short of his expectations. *Risk* means the variability of returns. This aspect of investing in securities must also be measurable and estimated for each security being considered. The entire process of estimating return and risk for individual securities is known as *security analysis.*

This has not always been the function of security analysis in practice. Traditionally, analysts have attempted to identify undervalued securities to buy, and overvalued securities to sell. Modern-day thinking, strongly influenced by the efficient-markets hypothesis—sometimes popularly called the random-walk theory—questions the validity of or benefit to be derived from traditional security analysis. In fact, the efficient-markets hypothesis sees only indirect benefits emanating from the analyst's risk-return calculations.

Briefly stated, the concept of market efficiency means that stock prices nearly always fully reflect *all* available information. If this is so, it would be exceedingly difficult for the average investor or analyst to earn exceptional returns—particularly on a consistent basis. In fact, the only way for the analyst in such a market to achieve superior performance is by having (1) access to "secret" or "inside" information, (2) superior analytical tools, or (3) superior forecasting abilities. This last item can include everything from being able to forecast earnings per share for some future period to being able to assess the impact of technological and economic developments on the firm's future. We hope that this book will aid the reader in developing analytical ability and useful tools of analysis. For if the domestic stock markets are efficient, it is only through unique insights that the investor can achieve unusually high returns— and then, perhaps only rarely.

Securities that have return and risk characteristics of their own, in combination, make up a *portfolio*. Portfolios may or may not take on the aggregate characteristics of their individual parts. *Portfolio analysis* thus takes the ingredients of risk and return for individual securities and considers the blending or interactive effects of combining securities. *Portfolio selection* entails choosing the one best portfolio to suit the risk-return preferences of the investor. *Portfolio management* is the dynamic function of evaluating and revising the portfolio in terms of stated investor objectives.

Investment vs. Speculation

Because this text deals with investments, we will begin our venture with a clear understanding of just what an investment is and what the investment process entails.

An investment is a commitment of funds made in the expectation of some positive rate of return. If the investment is properly undertaken, the return will be commensurate with the risk the investor assumes.

Generally, investment is distinguished from speculation by the time horizon of the investor, and often by the risk-return characteristics of the investments. The true investor is interested in a *good* rate of return, earned on a rather consistent basis for a relatively long period of time. The speculator seeks opportunities promising *very large* returns, earned rather quickly. The speculator is less interested in consistent performance than is the investor, and is more interested in the abnormal, extremely high rate of return than the normal, more moderate rate. Furthermore, the speculator wants to get these high returns in a short time and then seek greener pastures in other investment outlets. In this text the emphasis will be on investments and investment analysis, although speculative situations will also be considered.

The same stock can be purchased as a speculation or an investment, depending on the motivation of the purchaser. For example, AT&T—American Telephone and Telegraph—is generally considered an investment-grade security. That is, it represents a basic service in our economy, and therefore the firm and the price of its shares should grow pretty much with the economy on average over time. However, if a student of the stock market feels that AT&T, selling at $60 a share, is underpriced and is likely to rise to the mid 60s very quickly, he might buy it as a speculation. He is unconcerned with AT&T's dividend or long-term growth prospects. His only concern is with its potential short-term price appreciation.

Despite his motivations, the speculator adds to the market's liquidity and depth, for he is frequently "turning over" (changing) his portfolio. Thus his presence provides a market for securities (depth) and a wider distribution of ownership of securities (breadth), and enhances the capital markets.

Investment in securities in the *capital markets* (markets for securities with maturities over one year) is a key factor in the U.S. economy. If the economic environment is ripe and corporate management expectations are optimistic, a firm normally wishes to expand. This expansion can take the form of an enlarged physical facility, an increased sales force, or any one of a number of such factors. If conditions are appropriate, all this will eventually lead to higher earnings and higher prices for the firm's outstanding securities. Financing this expansion often comes about by gaining access to the capital markets—namely, through the sale of stocks and bonds. Investors who have earned profits, called *capital gains*, on previous investments in securities or have observed others doing this will be standing ready to finance expansions by providing funds. Thus firms grow, jobs are provided, families prosper, and the economy grows.[1]

**The
Investment
Process**

Now that we have distinguished between investment and speculation and extolled some of the virtues of the capital markets, it becomes necessary to see how one goes about entering the investment arena.

SECURITY ANALYSIS

Traditional investment analysis, when applied to securities, emphasizes the projection of prices and dividends. That is, the potential price of a firm's common stock and the future dividend stream are forecast, then discounted back to the present. This so-called intrinsic value is then compared with the security's current market price (after adjusting for taxes and commissions). If the current market price is below the intrinsic value, a purchase is recommended. Conversely, if the current market price is above this intrinsic value, a sale is recommended.

Although modern security analysis is deeply rooted in the fundamental concepts just outlined, the emphasis has shifted. The more modern approach to common-stock analysis emphasizes return-and-risk estimates rather than mere price and dividend estimates. The return-and-risk estimates, of course, are dependent on the share price and the accompanying dividend stream. Chapter 3 will discuss tax and commission considerations, and Chapters 4 and 5 will establish the framework of analysis for risk and return that we will be utilizing throughout the text.

Any forecast of securities must necessarily consider the prospects of the economy. As we shall see in Chapter 6, the economic setting greatly influences the prospects of certain industries, as well as the psychological outlook of the

---

[1] Obviously, the presence of organized secondary markets, where already-issued securities are traded, facilitates and boosts investor participation; for these markets provide liquidity for the investor. These issues will be discussed in greater detail in Chapter 2.

investment public. Among industries, the impact of the economy will differ, and thus it is incumbent on the analyst to be thoroughly informed about any industry peculiarities. This industry analysis will be the subject of Chapter 7. Even within industries, the outlook for specific firms will differ. A company's outlook will be related to such things as product line, production efficiency, marketing force, finances, and management capability. A recommended procedure for screening firms and their securities will be presented in Chapters 8-14; the analysis in these chapters will yield estimates of risk and return.

THE COMPUTER AND INVESTMENT ANALYSIS

Most of the techniques of security analysis can be applied manually by a limited number of personnel using desk calculators, but this process is feasible only for analyzing a small number of securities. For a large number, the use of a computer becomes a necessity.

Computers can absorb many thousands of pieces of information and can make use of them as the computer program instructs. The analyst informs a programmer as to the given inputs, the required operations, and the desired format of the output. The required calculations, which might take days to perform manually, can be done by the computer in seconds. This kind of quick turnaround is invaluable to the analyst.

The computer also assists in other valuable ways. First, the analyst can vary his assumptions, resubmit the data, and observe what differences arise as a result of the changed assumptions. Second, alternative constructs can be tested on data of various companies merely by applying "canned" (already-existing) programs to data that have been collected and are stored at the computer center.[2] The results of these various constructs can be compared—often within minutes after they have been conceived. This allows the analyst to follow through immediately with various thought processes without interrupting them for several days while the data are being compiled and processed.

These advantages are realized not only by the largest research organization; individuals can lease limited amounts of time on computers, and various data banks as well, for a reasonable cost. The implication is not that all small investors can (or should) run out and lease computer time for mere pennies a day. It does mean, however, that an individual investor with the necessary know-how and a portfolio of above-average size can avail himself of more sophisticated research techniques and systems.

From time to time throughout the text, we will point out areas where computer applications are both efficient and necessary.[3]

---

[2]Services exist that provide pertinent balance-sheet, income-statement, stock-price, trading-volume, and other data on magnetic tape to subscribers. The data are regularly updated.

[3]Before turning to portfolio analysis in Chapter 17, we will examine two alternative explanations of the behavior of stock prices. Chapter 15 will present the essentials of technical analysis—a set of techniques based on a study of the patterns of share prices. Chapter 16 will discuss the theory of random walk, which denies the existence of such patterns.

PORTFOLIO MANAGEMENT

We have already seen that modern security analysis differs in emphasis from traditional security analysis. The former emphasizes risk-and-return estimates; the latter emphasizes the calculation of an intrinsic value. Portfolio management is also characterized by an old and a new way of solving the portfolio problem.

Portfolios are combinations of assets. In this text, portfolios will consist of collections of securities. Traditional portfolio planning called for the selection of those securities that best fit the personal needs and desires of the investor. For example, a young, aggressive, single adult would be advised to buy stocks in newer, dynamic, rapidly growing firms. A retired widow would be advised to purchase stocks and bonds in old-line, established, stable firms, such as utilities.

Modern portfolio theory suggests that the traditional approach to portfolio analysis, selection, and management may well yield less than optimum results— that a more scientific approach is needed, based on estimates of risk and return of the portfolio and the attitudes of the investor toward a risk-return trade-off stemming from the analysis of the individual securities.

The return of the portfolio, as we shall see in Chapter 17, is nothing more than the weighted average of the returns of the individual stocks. The weights are based on the percentage composition of the portfolio. (A stock representing 10 percent of the portfolio receives a weight of .10.) The total risk of the portfolio is more complex. Here we need only point out that securities when combined may have a greater or lesser risk than the sum of their component risks. This fact arises from the degree to which the returns of individual securities move together or interact. Modern portfolio-management techniques will be discussed in Chapters 18 and 20. More traditional timing and management techniques will be the subject of Chapter 19.

Investment Categories

Investments generally involve *real assets* or *financial assets*. Real assets are tangible, material things, like buildings, automobiles, and textbooks. Financial assets are pieces of paper representing an indirect claim to real assets held by someone else. These pieces of paper represent debt or equity commitments in the form of IOUs or stock certificates.

Among the many properties that distinguish real from financial assets, one of special interest to investors is *liquidity*. Liquidity refers to the ease of converting an asset into money quickly, conveniently, and at little exchange cost. Real assets are generally less liquid than financial assets, largely because real assets are more heterogeneous, often peculiarly adapted to a specific use, and yield benefits only in cooperation with other productive factors. In addition, returns on real assets are frequently more difficult to measure accurately, owing to the absence of broad, ready, and active markets. Many of the concepts, techniques, and decision rules applicable to financial assets are applicable to real assets, but our principal concern in this book is with financial assets.

Financial assets can be categorized in a variety of ways. We will examine them according to their source of issuance (public or private) and the nature of the buyer's commitment (creditor or owner).

DEBT INSTRUMENTS

Financial assets often take the form of IOUs, issued by governments, corporations, and individuals. They call for fixed periodic payments, called *interest*, and eventual repayment of the amount borrowed, called the *principal*. Debt instruments provide interest in either of two ways. Interest is paid periodically (for example, every six months), or the securities are sold to the investor on a discount-price basis. In the latter type, the instrument is sold at a price below the eventual redemption price, and the difference between the sale price and the redemption value constitutes interest. Thus, 6 percent interest is received from a debt security due in one year and redeemable for $100 by either (a) paying $100 at the start and receiving $6 interest payments or (b) paying $94.30 at the outset and receiving $100 at redemption.[4] The redemption amount is referred to as the *face, par,* or *maturity value*. The interest payment in dollars, stated as a percentage of the face, par, or maturity value, is referred to as the *nominal* or *coupon rate*. The repayment of principal is either on demand or at some future time. When the principal is paid in the future, it can be in one lump-sum payment or piecemeal payments spread over time. In all cases it is important to remember that debt instruments represent money loaned rather than ownership to the investor.

Institutional Deposits and Contracts

Money and checking and savings accounts all represent fixed-dollar commitments that are debtlike in character. Currency is in reality a government IOU. Checking and savings accounts, referred to as *demand* and *time deposits*, are loans to banks and other financial institutions. Demand deposits bear no interest and are redeemable upon demand. Savings accounts, or time deposits, technically cannot be withdrawn without notice, although institutions normally provide this privilege. Savings accounts draw interest, and some forms, called *certificates of deposit* (CDs), have specified maturities (such as one, two, four, or six years). CDs pay higher interest than do normal savings accounts, and penalties are exacted (for instance, loss of interest) if withdrawal is made before the maturity date.

Certain types of life insurance policies build up what is called *cash surrender value*. This reserve accumulates primarily because premiums paid by policyholders normally exceed death benefits in early years. This difference is placed in reserve for later years, when death benefits exceed premiums paid. A policyholder's share of the reserve is similar to a savings account. A policy can be turned in for its cash surrender value, or money may be borrowed from the insurance company against it.

[4]The $5.70 difference ($100 − $94.30) is 6 percent of $94.30.

Employees who contribute to pension funds in anticipation of retirement can usually withdraw their own contributions if they leave the company before that time. Normally, during the years of employment, both the employer and the employee will contribute to the pension fund. Upon retirement, the employee receives a pension supported partly by his own and his employer's contributions. Leaving the company before retirement does not usually entitle the employee to the share contributed by his employer.

Thus, cash, demand and savings accounts, and reserves built up in insurance policies and pension funds all represent fixed-dollar commitments. Some bear interest, others do not. Maturities may run from demand to several years' duration. In all cases, however, these "investments" originate with some institution (bank, savings and loan association, insurance company, or other corporation) and are transferable to or redeemed by only the issuer. They may not have title transferred to a third party.

Government Debt Securities

Debt securities are issued by federal, state, and local governments. They differ in quality (risk), yield, and maturity. U.S. government securities (USGs) are among the safest and most liquid securities available anywhere. Securities of states and municipalities vary substantially in quality.

Short-Term. Short-term government securities have maturities of one year or less. USGs include Treasury bills offered weekly at a discount, with maturities of 91 days up to three years. Government agencies, such as Federal Home Loan Banks and the Federal National Mortgage Association, frequently sell short-term, interest-bearing obligations.[5] State and local governments frequently sell short-term notes in advance of receipts from taxes and bond issues. These instruments are called *tax* or *bond anticipation notes.*

Long-Term. The U.S. government issues Treasury notes (one- to five-year maturities) and Treasury bonds (maturities in excess of five years), which bear interest. Over 60 percent of the U.S. government securities held by individuals represent savings bonds. These securities are sold at a discounted price and can be acquired via payroll deductions through employers. Federal agencies also sell longer-term issues. States and municipalities sell long-term debt of two types: *general obligations* and *revenue obligations.* General obligations are backed by the taxing powers of the issuer, whereas revenue bonds pay interest and principal from a special revenue source. In the latter case, a toll-road bond would pay interest and principal from toll receipts. It is easy to see that revenue bonds can represent high risks if the revenue source does not meet expectations.

Private Issues

Private debt issues are offered by corporations engaged in mining, manufacturing, merchandising, and financing activities. As a unit, private issues

---

[5]The securities of government agencies are technically not guaranteed by the full faith and taxing powers of the U.S. government.

run the spectrum in quality (risk) and yield, from the high quality of AT&T bonds to the defaulted securities of the Penn Central.

Short-Term. The most common short-term privately issued debt securities are *commercial paper.* Commercial paper is unsecured promissory notes of from 30 to 270 days' maturity. These securities are issued to supplement bank credit and are sold by companies of prime credit standing. *Banker's acceptances* are issued in international trade. They are of high quality, since they carry bank guarantees, and have maturities of from 90 days to one year. Large corporate time deposits in commercial banks are often of certain minimum amounts for a specified time period. Unlike time deposits of individuals, these *certificates of deposit* are negotiable; that is, they can be sold to and redeemed by third parties.

Long-Term. There is a great variety of subclassifications in long-term corporate or private bonds. It may be well to remember that these subclasses merely represent modifications of the two basic promises in a debt contract: (1) to pay regular interest, and (2) to redeem the principal at maturity.

Interest is usually paid on bonds every six months. Failure to make such payments constitutes an act of default, and bondholders may seek relief from default in the courts. All interest on bonds, current and accumulated, must be paid before any dividends are distributed to shareholders. The only exception to this rule is with the *income bond*, on which interest is paid only if earnings are sufficient to permit it. These bonds often result from reorganizations and are infrequently sold to raise new capital because of the residual nature of interest payments.

We normally associate bonds with the fixed return from interest that gives them their basic appeal to investors seeking safety and regular income. However, the *convertible bond* provides the holder with an option to exchange his bond for a predetermined number of common shares at any time prior to maturity. As the cost of this option, convertible bonds usually provide lower interest (yield) than straight bonds do, since at some future time, if converted into shares, the bond might provide more current income; and/or there may be a handsome capital gain as the bond price moves up with the value of the underlying shares. Obviously, the underlying shares can prove a disappointment both in dividends and in price movement.

The promise to redeem bonds at maturity can be altered or modified by what is termed a *call feature*, provided for the benefit of the issuer (borrower). In the event that interest rates decline after the sale of a bond issue, he would want the option to accelerate the maturity (call the bonds) and replace them at a lower interest cost. Issuers are normally required to pay a penalty (premium) of one year's interest for the call privilege. Quite frequently, call privileges are given but deferred (inoperative) for a period of years.

A special form of call feature, called a *sinking fund*, is often found in bond issues for the benefit of investors. Under a sinking fund, bonds are redeemed piecemeal over the nominal maturity, very much as monthly payments amortize a home mortgage. Such payments give the investor peace of mind that the principal will be repaid, an assurance that is not inherent in the promise of a single lump-sum payment at a distant maturity date. Bonds are retired for sinking-fund purposes at a price not greater than par (plus accrued interest). Bonds are retired in the open market if market prices are below par. If market prices exceed par, bonds are redeemed by random lot. An alternative strategy to sinking-fund bonds is the *serial bond*. Serial issues are really several small bond issues carrying many maturity dates rather than a single one. Each series is redeemed as it comes due, usually at par. Rather than a single bond issue with a thirty-year maturity, we might have thirty subissues due one year apart for from one to thirty years.

To protect the return of principal and any unpaid interest in the event of adversity, bond investors often seek a lien against specific assets of the issuer. The advantage is that during liquidation, creditors with specific liens receive proceeds from the sale of those assets, up to a limit of the debt and interest owed. Otherwise, in the absence of any specific asset claim, bondholders become general or unsecured creditors sharing equally in asset distributions (after creditors with liens or secured creditors). The names attached to bonds often indicate the existence of the security and the type. Unsecured bonds are normally referred to as *debentures*. Bonds secured by real property are known as *mortgage bonds*, with first lienholders called *first-mortgage bondholders*, and so on. Personal property usually stands behind *collateral trust bonds* (bonds and stocks of other companies) and *equipment trust certificates* (railroad rolling stock, airplanes).

The types and variations of bonds available are substantial. Every investor should study the *indenture*, or bond contract, which spells out all the details behind the issue. Most investors do not examine the actual indenture, but more likely an abbreviated version found in the offering *prospectus* available for all new issues of securities sold publicly. A prospectus is a document required by law that is issued for the purpose of describing a new security issue.

Short-term or long-term loans to government and business can be bought from or sold to other investors, often via middlemen or "brokers." Thus, unlike the case with savings accounts and contract reserves, investors in these debt securities need not deal exclusively with the original issuer of the claim. This swapping of debt securities for cash and vice versa takes place through well-established markets, or exchanges.

EQUITIES

We have just discussed investment media that represent a debtor position—that is, in which the investor in bonds or in other debt instruments is a creditor of the party issuing the debt. In this section we will discuss investment media that represent an ownership position—that is, in which the investor in stocks or certain options is an owner of the firm and is thus entitled to a residual share of profits.[6] We will divide equity ownership into two main categories, one

---

[6] Admittedly, the holder of an option is often not an owner of the firm until he exercises his option and acquires stock.

representing indirect equity investment through institutions, and the second representing direct equity investment through the capital markets.

Equity Investment via Institutions

Several vehicles permit an equity investment that requires less supervision than does a direct investment in common or preferred stocks. These investments involve a commitment of funds to an institution of some sort that in return manages the investment for the investor. The most common vehicle is shares of an investment company, but we will defer our discussion of this form of professionally managed portfolio to a later chapter. Several other important institutional outlets for investment dollars should be noted.

Variable Annuities. Under current federal tax laws, certain taxpayers are permitted to have certain portions of their salaries withheld by their employers for investment in a variable annuity. The great advantage of this scheme is that the amount invested in the variable annuity is not taxable to the investor until it (along with accumulated earnings on it) is withdrawn from the plan. Generally, this is during retirement, when the taxpayer is in a lower tax bracket. Quite simply, then, the *tax-sheltered variable annuity* is a device for deferring the payment of federal income taxes. Although variable annuities are not always of the tax-sheltered variety (the setup is the same in all cases, though), this is the form usually thought of in discussions of variable annuities.

The equity characteristic is that the organization managing the annuity typically invests the proceeds of all the participants in the plan in a portfolio. It is called *variable* because the amount of the monthly annuity payment can vary, depending on the success of the portfolio's investments, which are mainly equities. Thus, this form of planning for retirement is not only tax-sheltered but also quite aggressive.

Insurance Policies. Purchasing a life insurance policy could well be considered an investment. In fact, if the policy is purchased from a mutual insurance company, the insured becomes an owner of the company. The discussion of adequate life insurance coverage is a specialized area, and we recommend that the interested reader consult any basic life insurance text for further information. In this book we will assume that the investor has already made proper provisions for life insurance, savings accounts, a home, automobile, and other necessities, and is contemplating an investment with other available funds.

Direct Equity Investments

The two main direct equity investments are common stocks and preferred stocks. In addition, several options exist that, when exercised, permit the purchase of one of these types of stocks.

Common Stock. Common stock represents an ownership position. The holders of common stock are the owners of the firm, have the voting power that, among other things, elects the board of directors, and have a right to the earnings of the firm after all expenses and obligations have been paid; but they also run the risk of receiving nothing if earnings are insufficient to cover all obligations.

Common-stock holders hope to receive a return based on two sources—dividends and capital gains. Dividends are received only if the company earns sufficient money *and* the board of directors deems it proper to declare a dividend. Capital gains arise from an advance in the market price of the common stock, which is generally associated with a growth in per-share earnings. Since earnings often do not grow smoothly over time, stock prices have historically been quite volatile over time. This fact points out the need for careful analysis in the selection of securities for purchase and sale, as well as in the timing of these investment decisions, for common stock has no maturity date at which a fixed value will be realized. We advocate the use of fundamental analysis, as outlined in later chapters.

Stock Splits. Often one reads of a firm's declaring a stock split. When this occurs, the firm ends up with more shares outstanding, which sell at a lower price and have a lower par value than the outstanding shares did previous to the split. Stock splits are frequently prompted when the company's stock price has risen to a level that corporate management feels is out of the "popular trading range." If this is so, trading volume in the shares will decrease and investor interest may subside. To overcome this, management may declare a stock split.[7]

For example, suppose ABC Corporation has 1 million shares of common outstanding. The par value is $2 per share and the current market price is $100 per share. Management may rightfully believe that the average investor wishes to deal in lots of 100 shares—round lots—and would like to buy 100 shares of ABC but cannot afford to invest $10,000 at one time. Therefore management decides to declare a 2-for-1 split.[8] Then there will be 2 million shares outstanding, with a par value of $1 per share and a theoretical market price of $50 per share. Thus it would require only $5,000 (ignoring commissions) to purchase 100 shares of ABC for cash. Of course, earnings per share would be proportionately reduced (by half, in this case) because of the split. Splits can occur at any ratio of new-to-old shares. Several popular ratios are 2 for 1, 3 for 2, and 5 for 4.

Stock Dividends. Instead of (and sometimes in addition to) cash dividends, investors can receive dividends in the form of stock. The end result to the investor is the same as from a stock split: He or she receives more shares. Stock dividends are typically stated in percentage terms—such as a 20 percent stock dividend, meaning a 20 percent increase in the number of shares outstanding.[9]

---

[7]Sometimes the price of a firm's stock is very low, and management wishes to raise the prestige of the stock. One way to do this is to declare a *reverse split*. This has the opposite effect of a stock split. Fewer shares will be outstanding, but each will sell at a higher price.

[8]In conjunction with management's desire to bring the price of the stock into a more popular trading range is its desire to improve the stock's liquidity. Since more shares are outstanding after a stock split, there are more shares available for trading, and it is quite likely that there will be a wider distribution of ownership (more stockholders). These events aid in providing a fluid market in the shares of the firm. In addition, certain findings indicate that there may be an increase in price associated with some stock splits. See Eugene F. Fama, Lawrence Fisher, Michael Jensen, and Richard Roll, "The Adjustment of Stock Prices to New Information," *International Economic Review*, January 1969, pp. 1-21.

[9]A 20 percent stock dividend is equivalent to a 6-for-5 split.

The investor previously owning 100 shares of common would own 120 shares after the stock dividend has been paid. Instead of reducing the par value of the stock on the corporate books, as in the stock-split case, the firm in this case transfers amounts from retained earnings to the capital-stock account for par value of the newly issued stock in the case of a large stock dividend (generally over 25 percent), and transfers the market value of the shares from retained earnings to the common-stock and paid-in-capital accounts in the case of a small stock dividend. Frequently firms will have to account for stock splits as large stock dividends. These seemingly arbitrary rules have been set up by the accounting profession.

Let us suppose that our firm, with its 1 million shares of $2-par common, declares a 3-for-2 stock split. But its accountants rule that the announced split does not meet the AICPA definition of a stock split. Therefore the firm must account for the split as a large stock dividend (since a 3-for-2 stock split is equivalent to a 50 percent stock dividend, and 50 percent is greater than 25 percent). The only effect on the balance sheet of the firm is that the retained-earnings account is reduced by $1 million (500,000 shares × $2 par) and the common-stock account is increased by a like amount. Since dividends, both cash and stock, can be paid only out of retained earnings, the payment of a stock dividend reduces the firm's ability to pay future dividends by the amount of par value issued. Stock splits do not have this implication.

As in the stock-split case, earnings, dividends, and theoretical share prices are proportionately reduced by the stock dividend. A 100 percent stock dividend has the same theoretical effect on these values as a 2-for-1 stock split.

Rights, Warrants, and Other Options. Rights, warrants, and other options all represent investment media that the investor can use to acquire common stock. They differ in the lifetime over which they can be exercised, the leverage they provide the investor, and the risks they carry. Since the issues surrounding these options are somewhat intricate, we defer their full treatment to a later chapter.

Preferred Stock. Preferred stock is said to be a "hybrid" security, because it has features of both common stock and bonds. Preferred stock is preferred with respect to assets and dividends. In the event of liquidation, preferred-stock holders have a claim on available assets before the common-stockholders. Furthermore, preferred-stock holders get their stated dividends before common-stock holders can receive any dividends. Preferred dividends are stated in either percentage-of-par or dollar terms. Thus the issue might be known as a $6 preferred or a 6 percent preferred. If the preferred had a $100 par value, this would mean that a 6 percent preferred paid $6-per-share per annum in dividends.

Thus the dividends are fixed for preferred stocks; however, they must be declared before a legal obligation exists to pay them. The fixed characteristic is akin to that of bond interest; the declaration feature is similar to that of common-stock dividends.

Frequently, preferreds are said to be *cumulative* with respect to dividends. This means that if a quarterly dividend is passed (that is, not declared), *all* preferred dividend arrearages must be paid before *any* dividends can be paid to common-stock holders. Most companies provide that if a certain number of preferred dividend payments are missed, the preferred-stock holders may elect representatives to the board of directors in the hope that the new directors will reinstate the dividends. In addition, preferred stock sometimes, although rarely, is *participating*. This means that it can sometimes receive a double dividend— the stated dividend plus an extra dividend bonus after the common has received a dividend. Of course, as in the case of common stock, preferred stock has no maturity date.[10]

Size and Distribution of Investments

Investment, in an economic sense, refers to committing funds to capital assets. Thus, in this sense, investors are users of funds. But in finance, investing refers to the act of acquiring debt and equity instruments with savings. Thus, for us, investors are *suppliers* of funds.

Savings find their way into investments directly or indirectly. Direct investing occurs when business uses its profits to expand plant; individuals invest directly when they acquire debt and equity securities through established markets for their own accounts.

Much of the savings of individuals is invested indirectly, through a complex of institutions that serve as channels through which money flows from savers to users. A common characteristic of these institutions is that they accept funds, issue deposit or contractual liabilities, and invest the funds in financial assets (debt and equity).

Financial institutions include the deposit type—commercial banks, mutual savings banks, and savings and loan associations—and the contractual type— insurance companies and pension funds. Deposit types give savers deposit accounts, and contractual institutions issue contracts as liabilities. Other institutions include investment companies that issue equity shares and, in turn, acquire debt and equity instruments of others.

In the sections that follow, we want to gauge (1) the amount of debt and equity issued and outstanding, and (2) who owns them, directly and indirectly.

SUMMARY OF DEBT AND EQUITY OUTSTANDING

Table 1-1 shows estimates of dollar amounts outstanding in major debt and equity categories at the end of 1972 and 1976. In addition, the relative growth of each segment over the 1972-1976 period is indicated. Note that the broad sweep of change during this period masks the shift in importance that takes place from year to year. In Chapter 12 we shall see the significance of these year-to-year and intrayear flows in forecasting interest rates.

Table 1-1 does not include all sources of debt available but merely concentrates upon those that are more prominent and/or available for direct in-

[10]Other possible provisions of a preferred-stock issue will be discussed in Chapter 11.

vestment by individuals. Loans to consumers and business, while not insignificant, are generally institutionalized. The mortgage debt outstanding runs second only behind corporate stocks at the end of 1976. The vast majority of mortgage money is made available indirectly through financial institutions; individuals rarely invest directly in mortgages, owing to their large dollar size. Mortgages lend themselves particularly well to pooled financing through institutions.

TABLE 1-1

DATA ON OUTSTANDING LONG-TERM INVESTMENT SOURCES
($ IN BILLIONS)

	1972	*1976*	*% Change, 1972-1976*
Mortgages*	$ 458	$ 760	66%
Corporate securities:			
Bonds	216	334	55
Stocks†	1,142	1,051	(8)
U.S. government securities	296	526	78
State and local government securities	174	242	39

*Includes securities of government agencies and excludes amounts held privately. Short-term Treasury bills included in U.S. government total.

†Amounts shown are market values. Between 1972 and 1976, the *decrease* of $91 billion consists of $128 in *decline* in market value and only $37 billion in net new issues. Thus, the percentage change attributable to net new issues is only about 3 percent.

Source: Salomon Brothers, *Prospects for the Credit Markets in 1977,* (New York: Salomon Brothers, 1977).

PRINCIPAL SUPPLIERS OF DEBT AND EQUITY FUNDS

Investors can be classified as individuals, businesses, and government. Further subclassifications are also possible. Table 1-2 indicates the relative roles of investor groups in supporting the debt and equity instruments shown in Table 1-1. Recall that individuals provide investment funds *indirectly* via many institutions.

Commercial banks and the various nonbank institutions play mixed roles in the holding of particular kinds of investments. These differences stem largely from rules and regulations, taxation, structure of finances, and management preferences.[11] The dominant role of indirect or institutional investing is manifest in mortgages and corporate bonds. Individuals play a major role in the market for corporate stocks and securities of federal, state, and local government. In the federal securities area, perhaps 60-65 percent of the holdings of individuals represents savings bonds. The special tax-exempt status of state and local government securities tends to make them attractive to people in high tax brackets.

[11] For an excellent discussion of the sources of differences in investment policies of financial institutions, see Harry Sauvain, *Investment Management* (Englewood Cliffs, N.J.: Prentice-Hall, 1973), Chaps. 22-25; and H. E. Dougall and J. E. Gaumnitz, *Capital Markets and Institutions* (Englewood Cliffs, N.J.: Prentice-Hall, 1975).

TABLE 1-2

SUMMARY OF MAJOR INVESTMENTS HELD, BY TYPE OF INVESTOR
DECEMBER 31, 1976 (ESTIMATED)

	Investment Classification ($ in billions)				
Investor Category	Mortgages*	Corp. Bonds	Corp. Stocks†	U.S. Government Securities‡	State-Local Government Securities
Mutual savings banks	$ 81	$ 20	$ 5	$ 15	$ 2
Savings and loan assns.	322			33	2
Credit unions	2			7	
Life insurance companies	91	119	36	7	5
Property-casualty ins. cos.		14	17	6	35
Private pension funds	2	40	123	16	
State & local pension funds	9	61	37	7	5
Bank trust funds	3	16	121	15	17
Foundations & endowments	1	13	41	3	
Real estate trusts	6				
Investment companies		9	48	4	8
Finance companies	11				
Commercial banks	147	9		133	106
Foreigners		11	67	80	
Households (direct)		57	555	135	61
Total §	$675	$369	$1,051	$526	$242

*Excludes $85 in mortgages held by federal agencies.

†Includes common and preferred stocks.

‡Total treasury and agency debt is $786; $260 is held by government.

§Totals may not add due to excluding minor investor categories and/or rounding.

Source: Salomon Brothers, *Prospects for the Credit Markets in 1977*, (New York: Salomon Bros., 1977).

FLOW OF NEW BONDS AND STOCKS

Table 1-3 indicates net new issuance of corporate bonds and stocks from 1968 through 1977. *Net new issuance* means the difference between brand-new cash

TABLE 1-3

NET NEW ISSUANCE OF CORPORATE BONDS AND STOCKS, BY YEAR, 1968-1977 ($ IN BILLIONS)

	1968	1969	1970	1971	1972	1973	1974	1975	1976	1977 (est.)
Corporate bonds (net issuance):										
Straight debt	$ 9.3	$ 8.9	$21.9	$22.9	$18.6	$14.3	$27.1	$32.4	$27.6	$23.7
Convertible debt	4.7	4.9	1.8	1.8	0.3	(0.8)	0.4	0.3	0.0	0.4
Total	14.0	13.8	23.8	24.7	18.9	13.5	27.5	32.7	27.6	24.1
Corporate stock (common and preferred)*	(0.9)	4.2	6.8	13.5	13.0	9.1	4.3	10.3	13.1	15.8

*Values in brackets mean that retirements exceeded new issuances or that a net decrease occurred in the available supply.

Source: Salomon Brothers, *Supply and Demand for Credit* (1968-77); *Prospects for the Credit Markets in 1977* (New York: Salomon Brothers, 1977).

offerings and issues retired during the year. Bonds are divided between straight debt and convertible debt.

Note how corporate bond financing has exploded, particularly in recent years. Convertible debt financing enjoyed a period of popularity in the late 1960s and then waned. The amount of net new stock financing (common and preferred) in 1969 alone exceeded the aggregate of the preceding seven years. To a very considerable extent, the rise in stock financing, starting in 1969 was necessary to compensate for the abundant harvest of debt financing during the 1960s. It is significant that between 1962 and 1968, net new issuance of stock aggregated a mere $4.5 billion. Yet in four short years (1969-72), the aggregate amount jumped to $38 billion, about a 750 percent increase.

Table 1-1 indicated that between 1968 and 1976 alone, the market value of corporate stocks *declined* about $91 billion. Only $37 billion was from net new issues; the other $128 billion decrease was largely the result of two horrible declines in the stock market in 1973 and 1974.

BEHAVIOR OF INDIVIDUALS AS INVESTORS[12]

The roles of the individual and the institution are evident in the area of investments just as in other areas of life. Table 1-2 showed the dominant role of individuals in total market value of stock holdings and their more modest position in the holding of corporate bonds. However, these data represent accumulated values at December 31, 1976. What is obscured is the relative shifting back and forth over time.

In Table 1-4 we portray the flow of participation by individuals in the market for bonds and stocks over time. The figures indicate a vigorous interest shown

TABLE 1-4

PARTICIPATION OF INDIVIDUALS IN CORPORATE BONDS AND STOCKS, 1968-1977 ($ IN BILLIONS)

	1968	*1969*	*1970*	*1971*	*1972*	*1973*	*1974*	*1975*	*1976*	*1977 (est.)*
Bonds:										
Individuals	2.1	6.8	10.1	7.4	3.3	2.9	6.9	11.7	8.5	6.3
Others	11.9	7.0	13.7	17.3	15.6	10.6	20.6	21.0	19.1	17.8
Total	14.0	13.8	23.8	24.7	18.9	13.5	27.5	32.7	27.6	24.1
Stocks:										
Individuals	−13.9	−10.1	−5.0	−10.6	−10.2	−17.3	−6.4	−7.5	−12.7	−14.2
Others	13.0	14.3	11.8	24.1	23.2	26.4	10.7	17.8	25.8	30.0
Total	−0.9	4.2	6.8	13.5	13.0	9.1	4.3	10.3	13.1	15.8

Note: Negative amounts indicate net liquidation.

Source: Salomon Brothers, *Supply and Demand for Credit* (1968-77); *Prospects for the Credit Markets in 1977* (New York: Salomon Brothers, 1977).

[12]Some of the material in this section draws upon the *Institutional Investor Study Report of the Securities and Exchange Commission, Volume 1,* 92nd Cong., 1st sess., House Document No. 92-64, Part 1 (Washington, D.C.: Government Printing Office, 1971), Chap. 3.

in recent years by individual investors in corporate bonds. More significant, perhaps startling, is the protracted period during which individuals have been, on balance, liquidating holdings of corporate stocks, which have ended up in the hands of institutions. The net aggregate liquidation by individuals totalled about $108 billion from 1968 through 1976. This is one of the bits of information that have led many to talk of the increasing institutionalization of the stock market.

In 1971 a long-awaited study by the Securities and Exchange Commission on institutional investors came to some conclusions about individuals as well. Commenting on household savings and portfolio decisions, the study said:

> . . . In their aggregate portfolio, households have substituted for proprietors' equity, have shifted into short-term claims, and have exhibited preference for intermediated rather than direct holdings of long-term assets. They have also exhibited a willingness to disintermediate, however, if relative yields make this attractive. . . .[13]

In sum, the study is saying that individuals seem more inclined to invest money in businesses run by others than to go into business for themselves; that is, to invest through intermediaries (usually institutions) rather than directly. Further, households will invest directly in debt instruments such as bonds when interest rates become relatively more attractive than those offered by institutional arrangements such as savings accounts.

Of course, we are talking about the aggregate. Differences exist in investment behavior as a function of the age and wealth of the individual. Older and more affluent persons are likely to devote more time, attention, and money to direct stockholding. The less well-to-do will do most of their stockholding through intermediaries, via insurance and pension reserves. National Bureau of Economic Research data for 1962, for example, showed that at that time, more than 80 percent of direct stock ownership was associated with individuals whose total assets exceeded $100,000.[14]

INSTITUTIONS AND THE STOCK MARKET

We have seen that individuals changed from net purchasers to net sellers of corporate shares between the 1950s and the 1960s. A takedown in the total values of shares held directly by the public was the inevitable result. Nonetheless, individuals continue to account for almost 70 percent of the market value of corporate stock. The fact that institutions hold a smaller percentage of stock than individuals do masks the degree of activity, or turnover, of these institutional holdings.

SEC statistics show that between 1960 and 1968, the percentage of the dollar amount of corporate stock outstanding that individuals held stayed relatively constant—around 70 percent—even though they were net sellers

[13]*Ibid.*, p. 89.
[14]*Ibid.*

during much of the period. This seems to indicate that individuals retained or purchased equities that appreciated more rapidly than those held or purchased by institutions. This observation would, in turn, seem to suggest that individuals as a group have done better than the market and better than institutions as a whole over the 1960-68 period.[15]

The SEC study of institutional investors noted a possible explanation for the relative performance of individuals and institutional investors over this period. Because of regulations and management preferences, most institutions prefer to hold the shares of large established companies with large numbers of shares outstanding. Individuals can, and often prefer to, invest in the shares of newer, smaller companies. And during the decade of the 1960s, sales, earnings, and market values of larger companies did not grow as rapidly as those of smaller firms.

The tendency of institutions to concentrate on larger, more established companies can be inferred from data on their holdings of New York Stock Exchange stocks. In 1968 about one-quarter of the market value of all New York Stock Exchange stocks was in the hands of institutions. It is estimated that the total value of the NYSE-listed shares owned by institutions will rise to over 36 percent in 1980 and about 55 percent in the year 2000.[16]

Another factor, at least as important, in the ownership of stocks is the enormous trading activity of institutions. For example, assume that you hold 500 shares of stock and your friend owns only 100 shares. But you hold your 500 shares intact throughout an entire year, and your friend "trades" his shares, by selling and buying 100 shares of various stocks throughout the year. In investment jargon, we would say that your friend has more activity, or "turnover." Thus, while the dollar value of individual ownership of stocks exceeds that of institutions by a factor of 70 to 30 percent (or 2.33 to 1), the real market impact from institutions comes from their moving more actively in and out of the stocks they do hold. In 1972, about 70 percent of the New York Stock Exchange *volume* of trading was created by institutions, while they owned only 28 percent of the market value of shares listed.[17]

RISK AND REWARD IN SECURITIES:
A HISTORICAL PERSPECTIVE

The risks and rewards available from holding various classes of securities over the period 1926 through 1976 are vividly displayed in Figures 1-1 and 1-2.[18]

The graph in Figure 1-1 clearly indicates that among common stocks, govern-

[15]*Ibid.*, p. 124.

[16]G. L. Levy, "Outlook for the Securities Industry," a speech before the Conference of the Financial Analysts Federation, Fall 1972, reprinted in the *Wall Street Transcript,* November 27, 1972, p. 30.

[17]*Ibid.*

[18]This information on returns from various types of securities is presented in R. G. Ibbotson and R. A. Sinquefield, *Stocks, Bonds, Bills, and Inflation: The Past (1926-1976) and The Future (1977-2000)* (Chicago, Ill.: Roger G. Ibbotson and Rex A. Sinquefield, 1977).

FIGURE 1-1

WEALTH INDICES OF INVESTMENTS IN THE U.S. CAPITAL
MARKETS 1926-1976

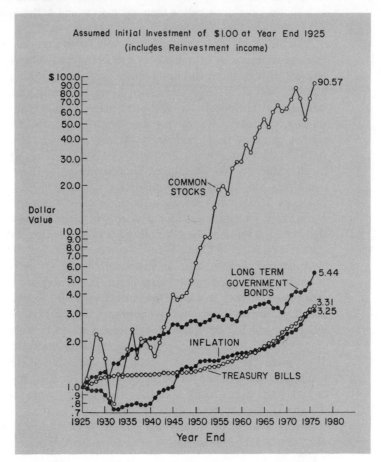

Source: Roger G. Ibbotson and Rex A. Sinquefield, Chicago, Illinois.
Copyright © 1977.

ment bonds, and treasury bills, stocks came out far ahead of the others. That is,
$1.00 invested in common stocks at the end of 1925 (with subsequent dividends
reinvested) would have grown to $90.57 by year-end 1976. Long-term govern-
ment bonds grew to only $5.44.

However, an examination of Figure 1-2 contrasts the annual variation in the
return on stocks and government bonds. Notice that the lower return governments displayed much more stability in terms of annual returns than did stocks.
The average annual return and range of returns for the period 1926-1976 can
be summarized as follows:

Class of Security	Average Return	Range of Returns High-Low
Government bills (short-term)	2.3%	8.0%-0%
Corporate bonds (long-term)	3.9%	18.4%-(8.1)%
Common stocks	11.4%	54.0%-(43.3)%

Notice that there is a strong relationship between risk and return. While the average return on common stocks was 11.4% the range of returns varies from an exciting 54% to a most discouraging −43.3%. It seems clear that risk and return are inseparable!

The data presented here is historical. It may or may not be the pattern of the future. In any case it is important to note the general principle illustrated by the record: the right investment or group of investments for anyone depends upon one's preference for return relative to one's distaste for risk. No specific investment is wrong for everyone.

FIGURE 1-2
VOLATILITY OF ANNUAL RETURNS FROM THE U.S. CAPITAL
MARKETS 1926-1976

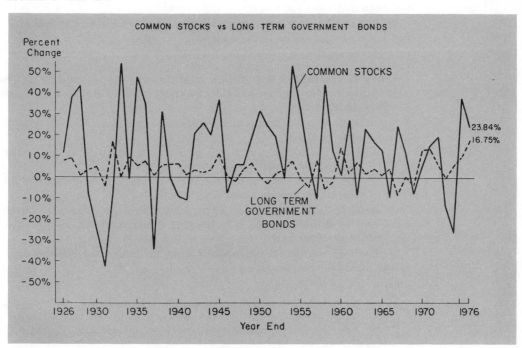

Source: Roger G. Ibbotson and Rex A. Sinquefield, Chicago, Illinois.
Copyright © 1977.

Summary

This chapter provided a broad overview of the nature of security analysis and portfolio management. It was noted that the measurement of return and risk are the main focus of the job of the security analyst and the portfolio manager.

We explored the primary categories of securities—debt and equity instruments. We learned that debt and equity securities include a wide array of variations on the central themes of creditor and ownership interests. Finally, the size of the markets for investments and the relative participation of individuals and institutions were highlighted. The phenomenon of increasing institutionalization of the securities markets emerged quite clearly.

Questions and Problems

1. Distinguish carefully between *investing* and *speculating*. Is it possible to incorporate investment and speculation within the same security? Explain.

2. Compare briefly the traditional and modern approaches to security analysis; to portfolio management.

3. What is liquidity, and why is it so important to the efficient operation of securities markets?

4. What are the two basic promises embodied in debt contracts? Indicate examples of how each of these promises is often modified.

5. Refer to Table 1-2. Why are life insurance companies so heavily committed to mortgages and bonds, and not to common stocks?

6. Refer to Table 1-3. What are the implications of the tremendous surge in new issues of stock in the 1975-77 period?

7. Archway. Inc., stock is selling for $100 per share. At present the company pays $2 per year in cash dividends. At the most recent meeting of the board of directors, it was decided that (a) three new shares would be issued for each two shares currently outstanding, and (b) a quarterly dividend of $.48 on new shares would be declared.

    a. Is the 3-for-2 a stock split or a stock dividend? Does it make a difference what we call it?

    b. What should happen to the price per share after the 3-for-2 split, assuming the dividend was advanced to $1.33 per year?

    c. After the 3-for-2 split and the new $.48 quarterly dividend, what is the effective percentage increase in the dividend?

8. Refer to Table 1-2. Considering the large percentage of the total corporate stock held by individuals, why is there so much fuss about the "institutionalization" of the stock market?

9. List three significant observations about the investment behavior of individuals during the past decade.

CHAPTER
TWO

MARKETS
FOR
SECURITIES

We have examined the broad universe of investment vehicles that are available. Now we are ready to focus upon the mechanism through which securities can be bought and sold.

Securities markets is a broad term embracing a number of markets in which securities are bought and sold. In this chapter the function, structure, and operations of major types of markets will be discussed, including how an individual investor goes about the business of placing an order to buy or sell, how the order is executed, and the process of settling the payment and transfer costs.

Markets and Their Functions

One way in which securities markets may be classified is by the types of securities bought and sold there. The broadest classification is based upon whether the securities are new issues or are already outstanding and owned by investors. New issues are made available in the *primary markets;* securities that are already outstanding and owned by investors are usually bought and sold through the *secondary markets.* Another classification is by maturity: Securities with maturities of one year or less normally trade in the *money market;* those with maturities of more than one year are bought and sold in the *capital market.* Needless to say, the classification system has many variations.

The existence of markets for securities is of advantage to both issuers and investors. As to their benefit to issuers, securities markets assist business and government in raising funds. In a society with private ownership of the means of production and distribution of goods and services, savings must be directed toward investment in industries where capital is most productive. Governments must also be able to borrow for public improvements. Market mechanisms make possible the transfer of funds from surplus to deficit sectors, efficiently and at low cost.

Investors also benefit from market mechanisms. If investors could not resell securities readily, they would be hesitant to acquire them in the first place, and such reluctance would reduce the total quantity of funds available to finance industry and government. Those who own securities must be assured of a fast, fair, orderly, and open system of purchase and sale at known prices.

The classification of markets we are most interested in is the one that differentiates between new and old securities—the primary and secondary markets. In recent years the secondary markets have been further fragmented, creating "third" and "fourth" markets. We will discuss each of these markets in turn. First, let us look at some factors to consider in choosing a broker.

SELECTING A BROKER

The investor's first step in establishing a satisfactory relationship with a broker is to choose a firm that is suitable for his needs and to select a representative of the firm with whom he can work. In practice it is hard to separate the two choices, for if one has chosen a satisfactory firm but is unhappy with the representative, it is embarrassing to shift one's account to another representative within the same firm. The brokerage firm should be a well-known and long-established institution. In selecting a firm an investor can ask for recommendations from his bank or from friends whose opinions he trusts.

Brokerage houses differ enormously in the type of clientele they attempt to build up. Some try to develop a large business with investors of modest means who are primarily interested in buying and selling odd lots; others seek wealthier customers; and still others are interested primarily in soliciting institutional business. These differences are apparent in the public advertising of brokerage firms.

The research reports of certain houses are obviously written for general public reading, while other houses turn out detailed and sophisticated evaluations aimed primarily at analysts for large institutions. Some houses emphasize mutual funds and advertise the New York Stock Exchange's monthly investment plan.

In short, while almost all brokerage firms welcome all types of investors, some houses are keyed to a particular type. In choosing a brokerage firm that will serve his needs best, an investor should try to judge the type of clientele sought by the firm in relation to the type of investor he is.

At first glance it might appear that most brokers offer about the same services. To the average investor, all firms appear equally efficient in executing orders. Differences between firms relate more to the availability of a special service that an investor may or may not want.

Most brokerage firms have research departments. The staff in these departments varies from large groups of full-time, highly competent analysts to relatively uninformed persons who process the analytical work of others and in effect turn out "second-hand" analyses. The measure of professional competence in the security analysis field is the designation "Chartered Financial Analyst" (CFA). Holders of the CFA have passed a series of three rigorous examinations on investment management decision making, and they must have had a minimum of three years' experience as a financial analyst and must possess a bachelor's degree from an accredited academic institution or the equivalent in training. An investor selecting a brokerage firm on the basis of its research department should know the size of the department and the number of CFAs on the staff. Also he should read some of their reports and compare them with similar ones published by other brokerage houses.

Many firms combine their regular brokerage business with a volume of activity as underwriters of new corporate securities. For an investor who is interested in purchasing new issues, such a house is desirable.

Many brokerage offices maintain a research library in which their customers can check on companies that interest them. If such facilities are important to an investor, he should certainly investigate their availability.

The person within the brokerage office with whom an investor will have the most contact is the registered representative. One can evaluate a representative by inquiring into his business and educational background and his investment philosophies and goals. An investor should also determine whether the representative is available at all times during business hours and should make sure that this individual is not so overburdened with other accounts that he will be unable to give the investor sufficient attention. The representative should be able to furnish the investor at all times, on reasonable notice, information on any specific company's securities.

The representative should not be the type who is always trying to sell the investor something. On the other hand, he should be aware of the securities held by the investor and should inform him of any news that is relevant to these holdings. Basically, the function of the representative is to give service and information to the investor so that the latter can make investment decisions and can have them executed properly and swiftly. A share of the responsibility for a mutually satisfactory business relationship between the two lies with the investor, for he must make his own investing philosophies and goals quite clear so that the representative will be able to offer the type of service desired.

PRIMARY MARKETS

Securities available for the first time are offered through the primary securities markets. The issuer may be a brand-new company or one in business for many, many years. The securities offered may be a new type for the issuer or additional amounts of a security used frequently in the past. The key is that these securities absorb new funds for the coffers of the issuer, whereas in the secondary markets, existing securities are simply being transferred between parties, and the issuer is not receiving new funds. After their purchase in the primary market, securities are traded subsequently in the secondary markets.

Role of Investment Bankers

Billions of dollars worth of new securities reach the market each year. The traditional middleman in the primary markets is called an *investment banker*. The investment banker's principal activity is to bring sellers and buyers together, thus creating a market. He normally buys the new issue from the issuer at an agreed-upon price and hopes to resell it to the investing public at a higher price. In this capacity, investment bankers are said to *underwrite*, or guarantee an issue. Usually, a group of investment bankers join together to underwrite a security offering and form what is called an underwriting syndicate. The commission received by the investment banker in this case is the *differential*, or *spread*, between his purchase and resale prices. The risk to the underwriter is that the issue may not attract buyers at a positive differential.

Sales through investment bankers can take the form of a *best-efforts*, or agency, arrangement. In such a case the investment banker does not underwrite the issue but merely uses his best efforts to sell it. Any unsold securities are returned to the issuer. This best-efforts activity is mainly employed in the sale of securities of two types of issuers. New, small companies may represent too much risk for an investment banker to underwrite their securities, so he takes them only on a best-efforts basis. At the other end of the spectrum, many established and popular companies feel that their new issues will be enthusiastically received, so it would be less expensive to use a best-efforts arrangement rather than a more costly, and unnecessary, full underwriting.

Not all new issues are underwritten. Many issuers make direct sales to investor groups, with only some investment-banking services provided. For example, securities are often sold directly to institutions. This is referred to as a *private placement*. The investment banker may act only as a finder; that is, he locates the institutional buyer for a fee. Such private placements are normally restricted to bond and preferred stock isssues. Common stock issues are frequently offered directly to existing shareholders, with the investment banker standing ready to sell any shares not taken by the existing shareholders. This is called a *standby* underwriting.

Thus the investment banker is a middleman. He is paid a fee commensurate with services performed. These services can range from serving merely as a finder to assuming full market risk for the successful sale of an issue (underwriting). As a true intermediary, the investment banker brings buyer and seller together, thus creating a market.

Buying New Issues

In the marketing of goods, we traditionally think of the marketing channel as being made up of the manufacturer, wholesaler, and retailer. In the primary markets for securities, the issuer can be thought of as the manufacturer. The investment banker serves the wholesaling function in the channel of distribution. He will locate and do business with buyers through retail outlets. These retail outlets are what we know as brokerage firms. Many investment bankers also serve as brokers and dealers; that is, they both underwrite and distribute shares to ultimate buyers.

Investors are informed of new issues in a formal way through a *prospectus*, a summary of important facts relative to the company and the securities being offered. The document is intended to ensure that potential investors are fully apprised of all important facts that may bear upon the value of the securities. In an informal sense, new issues are available only through those firms that are a part of the retail distribution group.[1]

---

[1]*Barron's* publishes a list of new securities planned for future offering as well as those being offered, by day, for a week ahead. The name of the principal underwriter is provided. The *New Issues Digest* is a publication that deals with the new-issues market in depth.

Local brokerage firms will have "allotments" of new issues, depending upon, among other things, the size of the total issue, number of retail distributors, and degree of regional or local interest. For example, issues that are awaited with high enthusiasm are widely distributed, and one may find a participating broker in a given town with only several hundred shares available. To obtain part of a new issue locally, an investor may locate the name of the underwriter and then ascertain from him which brokers are retail distributors of that issue. The alternative means is to request that your broker keep you apprised of any new issues his firm participates in selling.

Issues that are in short supply relative to apparent demand have to be rationed by brokers. Suppose a firm has 1,000 shares of a new issue in its office in Portland, Oregon, and customers place orders for 20,000 shares. Something has to give. Quite often another office in, say, Seattle has an allotment of 5,000 shares and orders for only 1,000. The Portland office may request the excess. Commonly, when the demand exceeds available supply, brokers will fill the requests of their best customers first. (A "best" customer is one who provides generous annual commissions.)

Attraction of New Issues

New stock issues of companies whose shares are already publicly traded are normally offered at prices very near those of the companies' existing shares. The area of the new-issues market that generates the most excitement and publicity concerns companies coming to the public market for the first time. Since these companies do not have publicly traded shares, investors and speculators are keen to test their assessment of the value of the new shares against the offering price.

The record is replete with stories of spectacular success, as well as of horror. We hear of the new issue of a fledgling computer-equipment firm that is offered at $10 a share on Monday. By Wednesday it is at $20. Within six months it has rocketed to $65. Similarly, periods of speculative excess in the new-issues market have seen the same kind of stock, risen to $65, fall to $1 almost overnight. The 1969-70 period is an example of collapse in new issues; many feel that small investors may never emotionally recover from that blow.

New issues are attractive to many because no brokerage commissions are charged to investors when these shares are purchased. The brokerage fees consist of the spread between the price paid the issuer by the investment banker and the resale price to the public. Regular commissions, however, are paid upon the sale of these shares.

SECONDARY MARKETS: THE ORGANIZED EXCHANGES

Once new issues have been purchased by investors, they change hands in the secondary market. There are actually two broad segments of the secondary market: the organized exchanges and the over-the-counter market (OTC).

The primary middlemen in the secondary markets are *brokers* and *dealers*. The distinction between the two is important. The technical difference rests upon whether the person acts as an agent (broker) or as a principal (dealer) in a transaction.

Organized exchanges are physical market places where the agents of buyers and sellers operate through the auction process. There are thirteen organized exchanges. Two are truly national marketplaces, and the others are regional.

The largest and best-known national exchange is the *New York Stock Exchange* (NYSE). It accounts for almost two-thirds of the share volume on all organized exchanges. The *American Stock Exchange* (ASE) accounts for another 30 percent of all exchange volume. The National Stock Exchange lists and trades a very small number of stocks. Local exchanges, located in major areas, include the Pacific, Midwest, Philadelphia-Baltimore-Washington, Boston, Detroit, Cincinnati, and Pittsburgh. The local exchanges generally concentrate their efforts on securities of regional or local interest.[2]

The membership, listing activities, and functioning of organized exchanges are somewhat similar. We will focus on the NYSE because of its impact and degree of development.

What Shares Are Traded?

Each exchange lists certain stocks for trading. On the national exchanges, only these shares are traded. The NYSE has long enjoyed a reputation as the place where large, seasoned companies are listed for trading. Its sister exchange, the American, is identified with listing smaller and younger companies than those that qualify for the NYSE, or "Big Board."

Certain strict standards must be met and fees paid for initial and continued listing. The initial listing requirements concentrate on minimum demonstrated earnings, asset size, number of shares outstanding, and number of shareholders. Continued listing is dependent upon number of holders, number of public holders, and aggregate market value of shares.

Not all companies qualify for listing on the NYSE. Some qualify but do not wish to be listed—perhaps because they do not want wider distribution of their shares, or do not want to meet the requirements concerning disclosure of their affairs.

In any event, listing brings certain advantages to companies as well as their shareholders. Investors get reasonably full and timely information on the company, constant price quotations, and all the benefits and safeguards built into exchange requirements for continued listings. And the prestige and publicity associated with listing have an influence on the company's future financing and its products.

Membership on the Exchange

Only members of the exchange may participate in trading its listed securities on the floor exchange. Since 1953 the NYSE has consisted of 1,366 members.

---

[2]Many also list some NYSE and/or ASE shares. This practice is referred to as dual or multiple listing. In addition, many NYSE and ASE issues are traded but not listed on local exchanges.

Being a member is often referred to as having a "seat" on the exchange. Seats, or memberships, are bought and sold each year, and the board of governors of the exchange must approve all such transfers of exchange membership. Over the years, seats have sold for anywhere from as low as $17,000 to a half-million dollars.

Members perform various functions. According to these functions, they are classified as commission brokers, floor brokers, odd-lot dealers, floor traders, and specialists.

Commission Brokers. About one-half the members of the NYSE are commission brokers, primarily concerned with executing customer orders to buy and sell on the exchange. They receive stipulated commissions for such executions. Prominent commission brokers include such firms as Merrill Lynch, Pierce, Fenner & Smith; Blyth Eastman Dillon; and Bache Halsey Stuart and Shields. Many firms have more than one membership.

Floor Brokers. When a commission broker has orders that he cannot execute personally because of their number, or because of the activity of the market, he engages the services of a floor broker. These floor brokers were once referred to as $2 brokers, because at one time they charged a fee of $2 per transaction; today this fee is considerably higher. Commissions are shared on these orders. It is easy to see that smaller commission brokers are especially prone to being swamped by an influx of orders. The floor broker, as a free-lance operator, provides a vital function in ensuring that the exchange's business is conducted rapidly and efficiently.

Odd-Lot Dealers. Trading on the floor of the exchange is conducted in round, or full, lots of 100 shares. Many investors and speculators buy and sell in lots of less than 100 shares, called odd lots. Odd-lot trades must be executed through odd-lot dealers, who supply commission brokers, or buy from them, any number of shares less than a round lot. Odd-lot orders account for over one-third of all orders.

Floor Traders. Some thirty members of the exchange trade for themselves; they do not engage in business for the public or for other members. These floor traders roam the floor of the exchange in search of buying and selling opportunities. One moment they may buy a stock, only to sell it shortly thereafter. A trader's profits depend upon the size and rapidity of his turnover of stock and on the accuracy of his estimate of future price movements. Traders pay no commissions and can afford to take narrower margins than others do. They are subject to a myriad of rules and regulations governing their activities, owing to their special status.[3]

---

[3] In 1964 new rules and regulations were instituted to correct certain practices of traders that had come under criticism. Prior to that time, a trader could buy 100 shares of a $25 stock and sell it the same day at a profit if it rose as much as 8 cents a share. To do as well, the public would require a price rise of 68 cents. See *Report of the Special Study of the Securities Markets of the Securities and Exchange Commission, Parts I and II*, 88th Cong., 1st sess., House Document No. 95 (Washington, D.C.: Government Printing Office, 1963).

Specialists. One-fourth the membership of the exchange function as specialists. Their key role in the market mechanism will be discussed at length later in this chapter.

Types of Market Transactions

One prerequisite to successful investing in stocks is a basic understanding of the operational mechanics of the secondary securities markets. Before a security is purchased or sold, the investor must instruct his broker about the order. This means clearly specifying how the order is to be placed. Much confusion and ill will can be avoided if proper jargon, which has a widely accepted usage, is utilized.

Investors should be concerned that they get the best "execution" in market transactions. This means the best price on the buy or sell. The adroit handling of orders to buy or sell can have an appreciable effect on the rate of return that an investor realizes from the holding of a security.

There are basically two types of stock transactions—buy orders and sell orders. Sell orders can be further classified as either selling long or selling short.

Buy Orders. Buy orders, obviously, are used when the investor anticipates a rise in prices. When he deems the time appropriate for the stock purchase, the investor enters a buy order. As will be seen shortly, there are several other determinations the investor must make besides just instructing his broker to buy XYZ common.

Sell-Long Orders. When the investor determines that a stock he already owns is going to experience a decline in price, he may decide to dispose of it. To do this, he enters a sell-long order (generally just called a sell order). Here also, other determinations must be made to accompany the sell order.

Sell-Short Orders. Short selling, or "going short," is a special and quite speculative variety of selling. Basically, it involves selling shares of a stock that are not owned but borrowed, in anticipation of a price decline. When and if the price declines, the executor of the short sale buys the equivalent number of shares of the same stock at the lower price and returns to the lender the stock he borrowed. On a per-share basis, the short seller profits by the difference between the sale price and the purchase price (minus taxes and commissions).

The procedure just outlined, carried out in the hope of a stock price decline, is probably the most widely used form of short selling. Furthermore, this speculative form of short selling is the stereotype of a sell-short order in the eyes of the general public. Various other possible uses of short selling, as well as a discussion of its technical aspects, will be presented later in this chapter.

Size of Order

All trading in NYSE stocks occurs as either a round-lot order or an odd-lot order.

Round Lots. When an order is considered a round lot, it is for the proper unit of trading for the particular stock, or some multiple of that unit. For most NYSE securities, the unit of trading is 100 shares.[4] Therefore, orders for 100 shares or multiples thereof, such as 300, 500, or 1,000, are considered round-lot orders.

Odd Lots. An order for less than the unit of trading is considered an odd-lot order. Thus an order for 1, 50, or 99 shares is an odd-lot order. An order for, say, 132 shares is treated as both types of orders; the 100 shares is treated as a round lot and the 32 shares as an odd lot. Odd-lot orders carry somewhat higher costs than round lots, as we shall see in the following chapter.

Price Limit of Orders

An investor can have his order executed either at the best prevailing price on the exchange or at a price he determines.

Market Orders. Market orders are executed as fast as possible at the best prevailing price on the exchange. In the case of a buy order, the best price is the lowest obtainable price; in the case of a sell order, the highest obtainable price. When such an order is desired, the investor merely tells his broker to "buy 100 PQR at the market."

The obvious advantage of a market order is the speed with which it is executed. The disadvantage is that the investor does not know the exact execution price until after the fact, when his broker receives confirmation of the order execution. This disadvantage is potentially most troublesome when dealing in either very inactive or very volatile securities.

Limit Orders. Limit orders overcome the disadvantage of the market order—namely, not knowing in advance the price at which the transaction will take place. Thus, limit orders aid in setting the boundaries of dollar risk the investor wishes to assume. When using a limit order, the investor specifies in advance the limit price at which he wants the transaction carried out. In the case of a limit order to buy, the investor specifies the maximum price he will pay for the stock; the order can be carried out only at the limit price or lower. In the case of a limit order to sell, the investor specifies the minimum price he will accept for the stock; the order can be carried out only at the limit price or higher.

Assume that Holiday Inns (symbol HIA) is currently trading at $12 per share. You want to buy the stock soon, but you want to be certain to obtain shares not much higher than the current price. You might place a limit order to buy at 12½. This order will be executed only at 12½ or less. In this fashion you have stated the maximum price ($12.50) you are willing to pay and thus have limited your dollar risk. Conversely, if you wanted to sell HIA or go short, you might desire to specify the minimum sale price you will accept. Therefore your order might be "Sell HIA 11 limit." This order will be carried out only if $11 or more per share can be obtained.

---

[4]Some relatively inactive or high-priced stocks and many preferred stocks have units of trading of 10 shares.

Generally, limit orders are placed "away from the market." This means the limit price is somewhat removed from the prevailing price (generally, above the prevailing price in the case of a limit order to sell, and below the prevailing price in the case of a limit order to buy). Obviously, the investor operating in this manner believes that his limit price will be reached and executed in a reasonable period of time. Therein, however, lies the chief disadvantage of a limit order—that it may never be executed at all. If the limit price is set very close to the prevailing price, there is little advantage over the market order. Furthermore, if the stock is moving sharply upward or downward, to place a limit order very close to the market and risk not getting the trade off is sheer folly. On the other hand, if the limit is considerably removed from the market, the price may never reach the limit—even because of a fractional difference. And because limit orders are filled on a first-come-first-served basis as trading permits, it is also possible that so many of them are in ahead of the investor's limit at a given price that his order will never be executed. Thus, selecting a proper limit price is a delicate maneuver.

Time Limit of Orders

Thus far we have classified orders by type of transaction (buy or sell), by size (round lot or odd lot), and by price (market or limit). Now we examine differences stemming from the time limit placed on the order. Orders can be for either a day, a week, a month, or until called.

Day Orders. A day order is one that remains active only for the trading day during which it was entered. Unless otherwise requested by the customer, brokers enter all orders as day orders. Market orders are almost always day orders, because they do not specify a particular price. One key rationale for the day order is that market, economic, industry, and firm conditions might change markedly overnight, and thus a seemingly good investment move one day might seem considerably less desirable the following day.

Week Orders and Month Orders. Week orders expire at the end of the calendar week during which they were entered—generally, at the close of Friday's trading session. Month orders expire at the end of the last trading session during the calendar month. As the longevity of the order increases, it approaches an open order.

Open Orders. Open orders remain in effect until they are either executed or canceled. Thus they are often referred to as GTC orders, "good-till-canceled." Frequently, open orders are used in conjunction with limit orders. When using an open or GTC order, the investor is implying that he understands the supply and demand conditions of the stock in question, and therefore feels sufficiently confident that, given enough time, his order will be executed on his terms. Open orders are regularly (monthly or quarterly) confirmed by the broker with the investor to ensure that he is aware of their continued existence.

There are several closely similar types of risks associated with open orders. First, there is the substantial risk the situation surrounding the proposed transaction has changed markedly so that the contemplated action is no longer advisable. For example, some very bullish information may be boosting the stock's price so that a limit sell order is reached. However, circumstances may have changed, and a sell order may be inappropriate and unwanted, but the investor may not have time to cancel the open order. Conversely, some very bearish news may have depressed the stock so that an open limit order to buy is activated. However, the buy may have meanwhile become completely unwarranted. Yet because of the open order and an inability to cancel it in time, the now unwanted purchase may be made. A related risk is that the investor may just forget about the open order because considerable time has passed since it was confirmed by the broker. When this occurs, the investor may (1) not want the transaction any more, or (2) be unable to pay for the stock, in the event of an open order to buy. Finally, the open order may be at a limit price just below (in the case of a buy order) or just above (in the case of a sell order) the price the stock reaches before a major move. In this event, a desired transaction is not consummated because of a fraction of a point differential. Under such circumstances, the open order is indeed penny-wise and pound-foolish.

Special Types of Orders

In this section, several key varieties of orders will be discussed and several situations in which these orders may be desired will be outlined. The discussion will represent a number of possible situations and is not meant to be exhaustive. The Appendix at the end of this chapter lists and describes an array of types of orders available to stock traders.

Technical Aspects of a Sell-Short Order. Most neophytes involved in the stock market tend to think that the only way to make money is to buy a stock that is subsequently expected to rise in price. In other words, if stocks in general are expected to decline in price the best way to behave is to stay out of the market. However, astute speculators use the technique of *short selling* to capitalize on *downward* movement in stock prices.

The mechanics of short selling are simple enough as far as the investor is concerned, even for the uninitiated. If the stock is trading at about the level at which he wishes to take a short position, the seller simply tells his broker to short 100 Crazy Corp., or whatever, at the market. The broker does the necessary paper work.

It is of little concern to the short seller, but the broker, in order to make delivery to the buyer, must borrow the 100 shares somewhere, either within his firm or from an outside lender. The money value of the stock is sent by the broker to the lender and held as collateral until the short's position is closed, or "covered," when the borrowed stock is finally repurchased on the open market and returned to the lender. The difference between the proceeds from the original sale and the cost of the subsequent repurchase represents the profit or loss. The buyer of the shorted stock does not know that the shares he purchased were shorted. Nor does he care, for he received delivery of the shares, as well as any dividends paid on the stock. On the other hand, the customer who lent the stock to the broker does not know he has done it. Nor does he care, for he still receives the dividend. The only difference is that the dividend is credited to his account from a different source. Instead of being paid by the company (it now pays the purchaser of the shorted stock), the lender is paid the dividend by the short seller.

Federal regulations govern short sales. One key requirement in executing a short sale is worthy of note for those who sense that short sellers can drive down the price of the stock through successive short sales (which thereby increases the supply of stock). The Securities Exchange Act of 1934 requires that the short sale occur at a price higher than the preceding sale, or at the same price as the preceding sale if that took place at a higher price than a preceding *different* trade price. For example, if the seller wants to go short at 42 and the preceding trade was at 41¾, there is no problem. However, if he wants to go short at 42 and the preceding trade took place at 42, he can do so only if the last preceding *different* trade price before a 42 trade was below 42, such as 41 7/8. Thus the 42 trade was an "uptick." If the previous different price was above 42, such as 42 1/8, no short sale can take place, because the 42 trade was a "downtick." Thus we say that a short can take place only on either an "uptick" or a "zero tick" (no price change) that follows an "uptick"[5] This is called a "zero plus tick" or "zero uptick." This regulation militates against successively lower prices instigated by a series of shorts.

Example. Assume the following are successive prices involving a specific stock. The time sequence is numbered 1-12:

(1)	(2)	(3)	(4)	(5)	(6)	(7)	(8)	(9)	(10)	(11)	(12)
50	50 1/2	51	51	51	48	49	49 1/2	51	50	50	51 1/2

Legitimate short sales may take place at time-sequence points (2), (3), (7), (8), (9), and (12) following the "uptick" rule, and at points (4), and (5) under the "zero plus tick" rule. We cannot tell about price (1), since no prior prices are given.

One other question that may come to mind is, "How long can stocks be borrowed?" or, alternatively, "How long can an investor remain short?" The answer is quite simple. There is no time limit. The investor must merely maintain an adequate level of cash and collateral in his account.[6] It would make sense to remain short as long as the price declined, and buy the stock back to repay the lender (called "covering" the short sale) when this trend was reversed. Furthermore, if after the short position was taken, the stock continued to rise,

---

[5]If a "zero tick" follows a series of "zero ticks," the records must be traced back to determine if a previous trade at a different price was an "uptick" or a "downtick." An "uptick" is required to execute the short sale.

[6]Margin requirements are discussed later in this chapter.

it would make sense to realize one's error, take a loss, and cover the position.

It should be noted that the most that can be lost (ignoring taxes and commissions) on a buy (going long) is the sum paid. The loss is limited to 100 percent of the investment. However, there is no such finite limit on the loss that can be sustained on a short sale, for theoretically, the stock's price can continue to rise indefinitely. As a practical matter, an investor can prevent this occurrence by the judicious use of stop orders, which we will discuss in a later section of this chapter. This also points out the very speculative nature of this form of short-sell order, and why it is recommended for use only by more sophisticated investors.

Several other aspects of short selling should be noted. When an investor institutes a short sale, he must put up the same amount of cash as when he purchases shares. That is, the margin requirements (to be explained later) are the same. The cash serves as collateral for the short position. Furthermore, should the shorted stock rise in price significantly after the short has taken place and before the position is covered, the investor may have to provide additional collateral. This is called *marking to the market.* Generally, investors seek, as shorting prospects, either shares of firms whose future prospects are dim, shares whose prices are volatile, or shares whose prices appear to be too high.[7]

Other Major Uses of Sell-Short Orders. There are several uses of sell-short orders that have come to be called short sales "against the box." These are situations in which the investor going short already has a long position in the same stock. The "box" in the expression refers to the fact that the stock certificate is, so to speak, in his safe deposit box.

Shorting against the box can be used for tax purposes, for hedging or insurance purposes, and for convenience in delivery of the actual shares. In the first instance, the investor may want to avoid earning any more capital gains in a given tax year. By shorting against the box, he can guarantee a certain profit and postpone taxes for a year. For example, assume that you own 100 shares of JKL with a December market price of $30 per share. Your cost was $20 per share; thus your profit (ignoring taxes and commission) is $1,000. However, you would rather earn the $1,000, and be taxed on it, in the following year. So you go short JKL at $30 in December. The following year, perhaps in January, you deliver the JKL shares you own long and close out the short position. Thus both positions (short and long) are closed, the $1,000 profit is retained, and the taxes are deferred to the next year.

Suppose you have a $1,000 profit from a long position in 100 shares of MNO; however, it is December, and for tax reasons you do not wish to take your profit in this calendar year. Assume that MNO is now trading at 60. You can short 100 MNO against the box. If MNO rises to 70 next year, you will profit an additional $1,000 on the long position. Conversely, if MNO drops to 50, your $1,000 profit on the short position will be offset by a loss of the

---

[7]Generally, all securities that can be borrowed from a broker or through a broker can be shorted. There is usually no charge above commissions and dividends for this service.

same amount in the original long position (again ignoring transaction costs). The merit of this technique is simply that your $1,000 profit has remained intact and yet has been transferred into a more favorable tax year.

This technique can also be used to hedge or insure a position about which the investor is unsure and insecure. Suppose you own MNO but feel it may decline from its current level. On the other hand, for some reason you do not want to sell out your position. One way of handling this dilemma is to short the security against the box. If the stock's price declines, as was thought possible, the profit on the short position will exactly offset the loss on the long position (ignoring commission and taxes). Thus you have insured or hedged yourself against the decline. Conversely, if the stock's price rises, the gain on the long position will be offset exactly by the loss on the short (again ignoring commission and taxes). Obviously, if you knew what was going to happen and had no qualms about closing out your position, this technique would not be necessary, for in both cases profits would have been greater without the short. In the former case, an outright sale followed by a new long position at a lower price would have increased profits, and in the latter case, merely maintaining the long position would have increased profits.

Finally, shorting against the box can be used to facilitate delivery of securities.[8] For example, you are out of town on a business trip or vacation and wish to dispose of one of your holdings, but you will be unable to get the stock certificate to your broker within the alloted time. You can call your broker, sell the stock against the box at the current price, thus insuring the desired sale price, and deliver your stock (held long in your safe deposit box) upon return from your trip.

Stop Orders. A stop order may be used to protect a profit or limit a loss. In effect, a stop order is a special type of limit order, but with very important differences in intent and applications. A stop order to sell is treated as a market order when the stop price or a price below it is "touched" (reached); a stop order to buy is treated as a market order when the stop price or a price above it is reached. Thus a stop order to sell is set at a price below the current market price, and a stop order to buy is set at a price above the current market price. A few examples will help clarify the rationale of the stop order.

Suppose you bought 100 shares of a stock at 20 and it is currently selling at 40. Thus, on paper (excluding taxes and commissions) you have a 20-point or $2,000 profit, which you wish to protect as much as possible; however, should the stock's price continue upward, you wish to maintain your long position. One way of achieving this profit protection is to enter a sell stop order at a price below 40—say, 38. Now if the price falls to 38 or below, your stop order becomes a market order, and your position will be sold out in the area of $38 per share at the best obtainable price. Let's say you are "stopped out" at 38. In this case you would realize an 18-point or $1,800 profit (ignoring taxes and

---

[8] This feature can also be used in conjunction with a highly specialized variety of arbitraging—that is, simultaneously carrying on transactions in the same security in different markets.

commissions). On the other hand, should the price decline to 39, then turn around and continue upward, your long position will be maintained.[9] Thus a certain level of profit is maintained. Such profit protection can also be obtained in a short sale, as you can see by thinking through the procedure for protecting a short-sale profit.

Next let us see how a short-position loss can be minimized through the judicious use of a stop order. Suppose you shorted 100 shares of a stock at 50. However, you are a bit leery about your position; you wish to minimize a possible loss resulting from an upward movement in price, but at the same time, if the stock's price moves downward, you wish to maintain your short position. This can be achieved by entering a buy stop order at a price above the current 50 (where you went short)—say, at 52. Now if the price rises to 52 or above, your stop becomes a market order, and your short will be covered at the best obtainable price, say, 52. Then your loss will be two points, or $200, rather than considerably more. On the other hand, if the price goes to 51 and then goes down, or just declines from 50, your short position will remain intact.

There are several possible dangers in the use of stops. First, if the stop is placed too close to the market, the investor might have his position closed out because of a minor price fluctuation, even though his idea will prove correct in the long run. On the other hand, if the stop is too far away from the market, the stop order serves no purpose. Second, because stop orders become market orders only after the proper price level has been reached, it is possible that the actual transaction will take place some distance away from the price the investor had in mind when he placed the order. (One reason may be a prior accumulation of orders.) In summary, then, stop orders may be useful if used wisely by a generally knowledgeable investor; however, they cannot rectify basically bad investment decisions, and, poorly placed, they can close out good investment positions.

Stop-Limit Orders. The stop-limit order is a device to overcome the uncertainty connected with a stop order—namely, that of not knowing what the execution price will be after the order becomes a market order. The stop-limit order gives the investor the advantage of specifying the limit price: the maximum price he will pay in the case of a stop limit to buy, or the minimum price he will accept in the case of a stop limit to sell. Therefore a stop-limit order to buy is activated as soon as the stop price or higher is reached, and then an attempt is made to buy at the limit price or lower. Conversely, a stop-limit order to sell is activated as soon as the stop price or lower is reached, and then an attempt is made to sell at the limit price or higher. For example, suppose you are long in 100 shares of a stock at 40 and wish to protect most of a profit you currently have. You could enter a stop limit to sell at 38. If and when the stock reaches 38 or below, your order is activated, and an attempt is made to sell at 38 or above. But nothing below 38 will be accepted.[10]

---

[9] In such a situation, you might raise your stop to "lock in" a larger profit.

[10] The stop and limit may be placed at different prices. In our example, you could specify 38 stop, 37 limit. This means you will sell at 37 or above.

The obvious danger is that the order may not be executed in a down market because you have quibbled about a small amount and the end result may well be a substantially greater loss. Thus the investor using stop-limit orders must exercise even greater caution than the investor utilizing stop orders. However, if things work out as planned, the stop-limit order to sell will be very effective. The reader should work through the mechanics of a stop-limit order to buy.

Discretionary Orders. As the name implies, the discretionary order permits the broker leeway in the filling of a customer's order. This leeway can be complete, in which case the broker decides everything from the security to the price to the direction of the order—that is, buy or sell. In the case of a limited discretion account, the broker decides only the timing and price of the transaction. This type of order is frequently used when the investor goes on vacation and does not want to follow and worry about his investments. Obviously, an investor giving his broker any type of discretion must have great faith in the broker's ability, his judgment, and the time at his disposal.

Order Execution

Once the investor instructs his broker about his order, a chain of events is set off. Without going into complete detail on every step, let us trace the process. In the discussion, the reader should note the key role played by the specialist in the proper functioning of the NYSE.

First, let us trace a round-lot order to buy 100 shares of Holiday Inns. The investor calls his broker to determine the current price of Holiday Inns stock. In addition, he wants to know the high and low prices for the day, and the price on the last trade. The broker would also give the bid and asked prices. The bid represents the highest offer to buy that the specialist has received, and the asked represents the lowest offer to sell.

The broker checks his stock-quote machine, and he reports back that HIA (Holiday Inns) is quoted at "11 to a quarter." This means that the investor would probably pay 11¼ if he put in a market order immediately. If this seems appropriate, the market order is placed. The written order is then wired to the New York office of the brokerage firm.[11] From there it is phoned to a clerk of the firm on the floor of the NYSE. The clerk notifies a member partner of the firm (only members—those having seats—are entitled to execute orders) via an annunciator board system—huge boards on which each member can be paged via his assigned number. The member then returns to his clerk (or if he is too busy, he sends an exchange employee) to pick up the orders. Next he goes to the location on the floor at which HIA is traded. (Each stock is assigned to a specialist at a particular U-shaped trading post.) There he checks with the specialist to ascertain the current bid and asked prices of HIA, and he executes the buy order at the best obtainable price. This frequently occurs through face-to-face contact with another member partner representing another investor. They "auction" with each other through offers to buy and sell and

---

[11] This procedure would be followed regardless of where the investor was located.

reach a mutually satisfactory transaction price. This is called a *double-auction process*. It should be observed that buyer bought from seller. One party dealt with another party. The NYSE has provided a place and apparatus that allowed agents of buyers and sellers to meet and transact business.

After the trade is consummated, the brokers note the transaction and with whom it was made, an exchange reporter notes the transaction for reporting on the ticker, and the phone clerks reverse the order-placing process so that the investor is notified how his buy of 100 shares of HIA at the market was executed. This entire process (including the appearance of the trade on the ticker) occurs within minutes of the initial phone call by the investor to his broker.

Role of the Specialist. Almost one in four members of the exchange are specialists. They operate in groups, with each group specializing in several listed stocks. Specialists have two jobs. First, they execute limit orders that other members of the exchange may leave with them when the market price is away from the limit price at the time it is received. Specialists act as brokers (agents) in this undertaking. Second, each specialist is expected to maintain fair and orderly markets in stocks assigned to him. Acting as a dealer, the specialist is expected to buy and sell for his own account when there is a temporary disparity between the supply and the demand for a stock.

The specialist is always at the post where his assigned stocks are traded. Limit orders to buy or sell a stock at a price different from (or "away from," as it is often called) the current market price of the stock are given to the specialist for entry in his book. When trading in the stock reaches the price at which these orders can be executed, the specialist takes the appropriate action. He gets a floor broker's commission from the broker who gave him the order.

The responsibility for maintaining a fair and orderly market for a particular stock is given to the specialist in order to avoid erratic price movements. Obviously, if stock prices typically jump several dollars on one transaction only to drop several dollars on the next transaction, most people would be quite reluctant to place any funds at all in the securities markets. Specialists are not expected to *prevent* a stock from declining or appreciating in price. Their job is to keep price rises and declines *fair* and *orderly* for their securities insofar as is *reasonably* practical under the circumstances.

To do all this, the specialist often must risk his capital by buying stock for a price higher than others are willing to pay at the time. He also often has to sell that stock for less than others are willing to sell for at the time. The specialist often makes the best bid or the best offer in the stock for his own account (acting like a dealer). At other times, he makes both the best bid and the best offer. In either case, the "spread" is narrower than it would have been without him. Thus, when the market price trend of the specialist's stock is *upward* (lots of buy orders and few, if any, sell orders), he usually *sells* stock from his inventory or sells short. Downward trends (lots of sell orders and few, if any, buy orders) usually cause the specialist to buy stock for his inventory.

Example. Jane Bliss notes from the ticker tape that the shares of Main Corp. were just traded on the floor of the exchange at 40½. She feels that the stock is attractive at about 41 or 42. She places a market order to buy with her broker, since she is anxious for immediate execution. The broker's representative on the floor gets the order, goes to the post, and notes that since the sale at 40½ there have been no orders to sell the stock and that the best bid is at 41 and the best offer is at 44. The specialist may very well offer 100 shares from his own inventory at 41½, thereby changing the quotation to 41-41½. Ms. Bliss's order is executed at 41½. She has been able to save two and one-half points (44-41½) because of the presence of the specialist.

Most of the orders received by brokers on the floor before the opening of the market are left with the specialist. Using these orders and also dealing for his own account in varying degrees, the specialist arranges the opening price in each of his assigned stocks. He arranges the opening price as near as possible to the preceding close, considering general market conditions and market circumstances in that stock.

SECONDARY MARKETS: THE OVER-THE-COUNTER MARKET

The over-the-counter market (OTC) is not a central physical marketplace but a collection of broker-dealers scattered across the country. This market is more a way of doing business than a place. Buying and selling interest in unlisted stocks are matched not through the auction process on the floor of an exchange but through *negotiated bidding*, over a massive network of telephone and teletype wires that link thousands of securities firms here and abroad.

Scope of Market

The OTC encompasses all securities not traded on national organized exchanges.[12] It is really a group of markets, each tending to specialize in certain securities. The first of these markets deals in the securities of the U.S. Treasury and government agencies. The second encompasses the trading in municipal bonds. The third is not as clear-cut but deals in listed and unlisted corporate bonds, in many preferred stocks, and in bank and insurance stocks. The fourth major market deals in unlisted stocks of manufacturing, merchandising, and miscellaneous companies. The quality of issues traded in these heterogeneous and diffuse markets ranges all the way from the highest (U.S. governments) to the lowest (small, highly speculative stocks).

Many more securities are traded over-the-counter than on the organized exchanges. Perhaps fifty thousand securities, of which a third are actively traded, are traded in the OTC. However, the volume of activity in the OTC is such that only about one-third of all stock-trading activity in the United States takes place there. The OTC remains dominant in number of issues traded and dollar volume of bonds.

[12] Some listed stocks are also traded over-the-counter.

OTC activity is both wholesale and retail in character. The participants are broker-dealers. A wholesale dealer buys and sells for his own account and from or to professionals. These dealers "make markets" by standing ready to buy or sell securities. They maintain an inventory position in many securities and are actively engaged as principals in buying and selling those in which they are interested. The market here is an interdealer market, since the business transacted is only with other securities firms.

Larger OTC firms are linked by private telephone and teletype. These means of communication serve as the vehicle for buying and selling. Traders quote buy and sell prices to other dealers who call, usually without knowing whether the caller wants to buy or to sell.

Individual investors deal with retail firms. For example, should you wish to buy an OTC stock, your brokerage firm might buy the stock from a wholesale dealer for its own account and resell it to you at a slightly higher price. In this case, your firm is functioning as a dealer. The other way your firm could have handled the deal would be to act as your agent in buying the stock from a wholesaler, and it would charge you a commission for its services.

Prices and Quotations

Buyers and sellers of listed stocks meet through brokers on the floor of an exchange and arrive at prices by the *auction* method. OTC transactions are effected within or between the offices of securities houses, prices being arrived at by *negotiation.*

Answering an inquiry as to the market on a particular security, a dealer may quote "20 bid, offered at 21." The prices quoted are "inside," or wholesale, prices at which dealers will sell to each other. The bid is the highest price the dealer will pay for the stock, and the lowest price he will sell it for (offer it) is 21.

The caller frequently asks about the size of the dealer's market. The reply indicates the number of shares the dealer is willing to buy or sell at the quoted prices. Suppose the response is "300 shares either way" (buy or sell). The next move is up to the caller. He has instructions from his customer as to price limits. If the customer wanted 100 shares at a limit of $20.75, the broker may tell the dealer, "I will pay 20½ for 100 shares." He is *negotiating* for the best price for his customer by bidding away from the offering price (21) and below his customer's limit (20¾). The dealer may or may not be willing to make a concession from his offering price of 21. Perhaps he will counter by paring his offering price somewhat, but not all the way to the broker's offer to buy. The dealer may counter with, "I will sell 100 at 20 5/8." The broker may accept this or negotiate further. If he accepts the price of 20 5/8, he has been able to obtain the stock for his customer below the limit and the dealer's first quote.

The ultimate price to the customer will exceed 20 5/8 by the charges he must pay. If his firm acts as his agent (broker), he will pay the 20 5/8 plus the regular commission. In other cases, his firm might sell from its own inventory at a "net" price, at which a markup is involved but buried in the price. In our example above, if the shares came from the firm's inventory rather than purchase from a wholesaler, the net price might still be 20 5/8; however, it would be difficult to ascertain how much the firm marked up its own stock.[13]

NASDAQ. In 1971 a computerized communications network called NASDAQ came into being to provide automated quotations for OTC securities.[14] Securities salesmen can get up-to-date bid and asked prices on OTC securities from a small console that is electronically connected to the NASDAQ computer. They can then contact dealers offering the best prices and negotiate a trade. This rapid centralizing of bid-asked quotes replaced a long-archaic system of "shopping around" by brokers. Under the old system, an investor had no assurance that he was receiving the best price available.

Not all OTC stocks are active enough to be included in the NASDAQ system. Of those in the system, the more widely held and traded are quoted in the *Wall Street Journal* according to bid-asked prices and volume of trading. The latter information was unavailable under the old system. Figure 2-1 is a schematic diagram of the order execution and confirmation process for exchange-listed and OTC stock.

THE BOND MARKET

There are about twenty-two hundred bond issues on the NYSE, representing the debt of U.S. and foreign corporations, the U.S. government, New York City, international banks, foreign governments, and so forth. Because bonds are traded in large amounts and have special characteristics, the rules of the NYSE ordinarily permit transactions to be executed off the floor even though the issue is listed. Accordingly, bonds are handled primarily in the OTC market.

The actual buying and selling of securities is carried on by traders associated with dealer firms or with large institutions. An institutional trader becomes familiar with the dealers who make markets in the securities in which the institution is interested. By keeping close ties, the institutional trader can gauge whether the dealer is long or short, and the side of the market in which the dealer is likely to be aggressive.

An institution may have direct communications lines to the active dealers; the number of lines depends on its size. On the other hand, individual investors place orders with brokers, who transmit them to their traders for execution. The trader will probably explore the market and obtain several quotations before actually effecting a purchase or sale.

Dealer banks play an important role in the market for bonds of the U.S.

---

[13] The National Association of Securities Dealers, which supervises activities of OTC broker-dealers, suggests that a 5 percent markup is reasonable under normal conditions.

[14] This acronym, NASDAQ, stands for National Association of Securities Dealers Automated Quotations.

FIGURE 2-1
SCHEMATIC DIAGRAM OF ORDER EXECUTION
AND CONFIRMATION

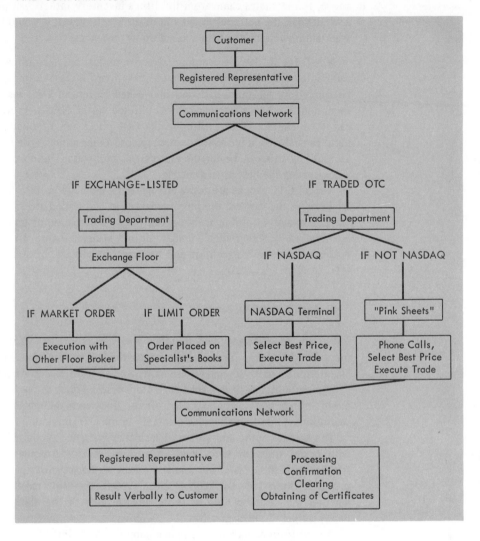

government and federal agencies and for general obligations of state and local governments. In the case of U.S. government bonds, the Federal Reserve Bank of New York, which is the fiscal agent for the U.S. government and the Federal Reserve System, recognizes certain "primary dealers." By agreeing to abide by certain rules, such a dealer becomes entitled to a private line between the reserve bank's trading desk and its own. Without this direct line, which may be withdrawn if its performance is considered unsatisfactory, a dealer would be severely handicapped.

NEED FOR CHANGES

The growth in size and activity of institutional investors has produced increasing pressures on the securities markets. The fixed commission structure, membership requirements, and auction process of the organized exchanges have shown great incompatibility with the nature and needs of institutional investors.

The fact remains that organized exchanges account for two-thirds of all stock-trading activity. Moreover, the NYSE accounts for two-thirds of all exchange share volume. The impact of the NYSE is even more substantial when one considers that the kinds of stocks that are of interest to insitutional investors are virtually monopolized by the NYSE.

The growing size and needs of institutional investors have increasingly come up against exchange rules, regulations, and other rigidities. The result has been the effort of institutional investors to circumvent the floor of the NYSE, primarily to avoid paying the normal commissions.

For many, many years, NYSE commission rates were fixed. Volume discounts were not allowed; the commission on a 5,000-share order was fifty times that of a 100-share order. Institutions bought and sold most stocks they held in large blocks and thus paid high commissions. To overcome these constraints, certain institutional investors employed several strategies. First, because NYSE member firms are prohibited from trading or executing orders off the floor of the exchange except with special permission, the institution began to buy and sell through nonmembers who made markets in listed shares at markups below the NYSE commission schedule. The nonmember firms would accommodate institutions either as dealer-wholesalers or as agents, matching buys and sells between institutions off the floor in much the same way specialists do on the floor. These dealers traded only with big institutions, not with the public. This activity became known as the *"third" market.* It is estimated that some thirteen hundred of the three thousand securities traded on the NYSE and ASE are available in the third market,[15] and that roughly 9 percent of NYSE's annual volume was transacted in the third market in 1972.[16]

The second strategy was for many institutions to try to obtain seats on the NYSE and other exchanges, thus eliminating commissions. Some sought and obtained seats on regional exchanges, but the NYSE forbids institutional membership. Attempts at mergers with member firms were similarly thwarted.

A third strategy developed whereby institutions bought and sold directly with each other, completely bypassing the exchange and broker-dealer services. This is known as *"fourth"-market* activity. Several privately owned fourth-market organizations have developed, each operating differently, in which block traders deal with each other through varied communications networks.

---

[15] R. Martin, "Bargain Brokers," *Wall Street Journal*, January 9, 1972, p. 1.

[16] This compares with only 3 percent as recently as 1966. K. Bacon and R. Rustin, "Public Interest or Self-Interest," *Wall Street Journal*, February 22, 1973, p. 1.

The key is to find one institution to trade with another. The Instinet System, developed by International Networks Corporation, allows subscribers to trade in any listed stock via a cathode-ray-tube display that is connected with a central computer. Subscribers submit limit buy and sell orders for any stock in the system. Orders are thus accessible to all subscribers. The system permits subscribers to communicate anonymously in haggling over price or quantity. Commissions, charged only if a transaction is consummated, average about 30 percent of typical exchange rates.[17] This is but one example of private fourth-market activity.

Institutionalization of the Market

Possibly the most important development in the postwar period has been the gradual domination of the stock market by institutions.

The expanding role of institutions in the securities markets has had several important consequences, including a shift in the site of much trading from the floor of the exchange to the third market and the regional exchanges, the erosion of the minimum commission rate system (discussed in Chapter 3), and the development of special trading patterns.

Fragmentation of the Market

The relatively liberal rules of the regional exchanges and the latitude permitted third-market dealers have attracted institutional business. As a result, the exchange market has been fragmented. The efficiency of the auction system is impaired by the dissipation of orders to different channels.

Fragmentation not only means less business to the NYSE but also causes the floor to become a poorer market. There was and is a real possibility that this deterioration will accelerate. Worsening of the floor as a market and the improvement of other markets would give institutions more reason to execute orders elsewhere. To avert this possibility, the NYSE has sought legislative or SEC sanction to require securities that meet specified standards to trade on the floor. Such a provision is bitterly opposed by the third-market firms, since it would mean the end of their activities.

New Trading Patterns

While the NYSE developed substantially to meet the needs of individual investors, other sectors of the market, especially the block positioners, thrived by responding to the needs of institutional trading. This type of business requires a considerable amount of capital and a willingness to risk it. That willingness, in turn, depends upon the ability of the trader to determine what other blocks of a given stock might appear on the market and who might be interested in accumulating a position.

Some specialists are capable of handling large orders as well as a block posi-

[17] R. R. West, "Institutional Trading and the Changing Stock Market," *Financial Analysts Journal*, May-June 1971, pp. 22-23.

tioner can. Others are less proficient, either because their capital is inadequate or because they are reluctant to commit their capital to risky positions. Institutional traders soon learned that using these less-qualified specialists meant poor executions, and they arranged their transactions off the floor even if the block finally crossed on the floor. Sometimes, to avoid the participation of a specialist, the block was brought to a regional exchange. As a result of the inroads of block positioners, even able specialists found that they were not seeing all the orders, and they began to fear that the appearance of an unexpected block would depress the price of the stock in which they had a position. This situation added to the difficulty of making a good market.

Institutional Membership

The minimum-commission rate system contributed to the fragmentation of the markets and to the drive for a central market. It also abetted institutional interest in stock exchange membership. In part, this interest arose because of the desire of the financial institutions and brokerage firms to diversify. By acquiring a broker-dealer affiliate that did a public business, for example, an insurance company or investment adviser would not only broaden its own activity but also provide a new source of capital to the broker-dealer.

In part, also, the interest reflected a desire to reduce the costs of brokerage. Thus the institution might acquire a so-called shell broker—that is, a broker who became a member of a regional exchange solely to get back some of the brokerage commissions paid by the parent to other brokers. At times, this recapture was effected through a circuitous route whereby the affiliate referred its parent's order to a dual member who executed the transaction on the NYSE, then directed a predetermined amount of commissions on unrelated transactions to the affiliate, which finally rebated part or all of the commissions to the parent.

EFFORTS TOWARD A CENTRAL MARKET

Because of the problems that the securities markets encountered in recent years, a general agreement arose that change was necessary. The SEC was concerned that trading barriers prevented the markets from serving the best interests of the investor; the NYSE saw fragmentation as a threat to its dominance; the regional exchanges wanted freedom to build local impact; and third-market dealers complained about rules that limited their ability to trade with NYSE members. Eventually these conflicting views came together under the concept of a "central market."

The term "central market system" refers to a system of communications by which the various elements of the marketplace, be they exchanges or over-the-counter markets, are tied together. It also includes a set of rules governing the relationships that will prevail among market participants.

The central market is intended to allow investors to buy or sell shares at the then best possible price *wherever* a stock may be traded. The heart of the system is a set of communications linkages consisting of a computer-reporting mechanism, a composite quotation arrangement for displaying the bids and offers of all qualified market makers in listed securities, and a central repository for limit orders. Progress has been slow because of disputes among the interested parties and because of uncertainty regarding the specifics of the new rules.

The SEC has approved a plan designed to provide in one system the latest sale price, volume, and source of transaction. This "consolidated" tape consists of two data streams. One tape shows trades in NYSE stocks on all markets including the NYSE, regional exchanges, the third market, and Instinet. A second tape will show trades in AMEX and selected sole regional issues.

Execution and Clearance

To protect the auction market, the SEC has proposed two basic trading rules. The *auction trading rule* provides that a broker desiring to execute an order may approach any specialist, who, in turn, will have to check all markets to provide the best possible price before executing the order.

The *public preference rule* prevents any member of the system from participating as a principal in any transaction unless his purchase price is higher or his sale price lower than any public bid or offer recorded in the system.

Shifting from present operating methods to the fully automated methods of the future may require the installation of highly complex electronic equipment. Brokers will have access to terminals that permit checking the status of all the markets where a particular security is being traded. The order may electronically be routed to the "best market" or, in the case of limit orders, to a consolidated book that will also be kept electronically. Through the computer system the trade is arranged, verified, and "locked in" for instantaneous transmission to the member firms involved, the consolidated ticker, and the clearing system.

Clearing the order is normally the last part of a securities transaction. It involves final settlement by delivery of certificates and receipt of payment. At one time, a clearinghouse merely served as a conduit for brokers to settle trades with each other. Under the current method, the brokerage firm deals directly with the clearinghouse which stands on either side of every transaction. If a firm fails to deliver stock on the settlement day, the clearinghouse records the stock's market value and the firm is required to mark to the market daily, thereby eliminating the risk of price fluctuation. A major advantage of this procedure is that a broker need make only one delivery of securities daily.

Despite the improvement in clearing methodology, the use of a certificate remains archaic. To immoblize this instrument, the NYSE developed the Depository Trust Co. (DTC). The DTC holds stock certificates for brokerage firms, banks, and other stock markets' clearinghouses and depositories. The major exchanges and the NASD have been working on the development of a national clearance and depository system. Eventually these national systems will be integrated into a single automated system, so that executed trades would be cleared and settled electronically without the use of certificates.

MARGIN TRADING

Securities purchased can be paid for in cash, or a mix of cash and some borrowed funds. The principal reason for buying on margin is to stretch your money. For the same amount of cash, you can control more shares on margin than if you put up the entire purchase price from you own funds.

In stock-market parlance, the cash paid by the customer is the *customer's margin.*[18] Thus, if an investor buys shares worth $10,000 and advances $7,000 cash, his margin is $7,000, or 70 percent of the value of the shares purchased. At all times the customer's margin can be calculated as:

$$\% \text{ Margin} = \frac{\text{Customer's equity}}{\text{Market value of securities}}$$

The Federal Reserve System establishes margin requirements for the minimum amount of equity a purchaser of listed securities is required to deposit. The NYSE has additional requirements. The Federal Reserve requirements have varied between 40 and 100 percent. At present, margin requirements are 50 percent for stocks and 50 percent for convertible bonds. Margins on regular bonds are less than those on stocks and vary according to the bond's overall quality.

Example. A hypothetical example will help illustrate the mechanics and implications of buying stocks with other people's money. Assume that an investor with $10,000 of capital has discovered a stock that he feels confident will rise 10 percent in price over the next few weeks. If the investor's expectations are realized, buying the stock for $10,000 in cash and selling it within a month for $11,000 would return a profit of $1,000, or 10 percent on the original investment, all within a month or less. By margin trading, he could do much better. Suppose the margin requirement is 50 percent. By borrowing to the limit, the investor can purchase $20,000 in stock—$10,000 from his own funds and $10,000 borrowed from a bank or his broker. If the expected 10 percent rise materializes, he will be able to sell the shares for $22,000, repay the $10,000 loan plus interest, and make a profit larger than the $1,000 he would otherwise have made. Ignoring interest and commissions, the profit before taxes would be $2,000 on the original cash investment of $10,000, double the profit in dollars and percentage terms.

Earning the additional profit does not come without added risk. A wrong guess can lead to an unhappy outcome. Suppose the transaction ends with the stock moving *down* 10 percent. A cash transaction would have involved a loss of $1,000. In the margined trade, the shares the investor bought for

---

[18] Margin is also used on short sales. Requirements are basically the same as in purchases, but the effects are reversed, as price rises work against the investor and price declines are in his favor.

$20,000 would be sold for $18,000. After paying off the $10,000 loan, assuming no interest, he would be left with only $8,000 of his original capital— a loss of $2,000. In short, supplementing capital with borrowed money is a two-edged sword that magnifies both profits and losses.

The extent of the magnification of profits and losses can be quantified. The magnification factor is the reciprocal of the margin, or 1/margin (%):

Margin (%)	Magnification Factor
100	1.00
80	1.25
75	1.33
60	1.67
55	1.82
50	2.00
40	2.50
33	3.00
25	4.00

In our example, the 50 percent margin requirement and the 10 percent rise and fall in price saw the profit or loss *doubled* as compared with an all-cash trade, since the magnification factor was 2.00.

Requirements

A customer who wishes to use borrowed funds to finance security transactions usually opens a margin account with his broker. NYSE rules require that a minimum down payment of $2,000 be made into the account before margin trading can take place. Each brokerage firm has its own additional rules, such as higher down payments and not permitting margin transactions in low-priced shares.

The Federal Reserve requires an *initial margin* that applies only on the day of purchase; after the day of the transaction, a *maintenance margin* applies to the account. The maintenance margin set by the Federal Reserve is about 25 percent, although many brokers impose higher maintenance margins. Whenever the customer's equity in a margin account falls below the maintenance-margin percentage, he must put up additional equity. Such a request by a broker is called a *margin call*.

The changing status of the investor's margin account can be visualized through a simplified balance sheet for the investor:

Securities (at market)	$10,000	Borrowed funds	$5,000
		Equity	$5,000

The key factor to bear in mind is that, in the absence of any payments, the borrowed funds are a fixed, contractual obligation of the borrower. Any change in market value of the securities held creates a change of the same amount in the investor's equity.

Consider the impact of the following market values of the securities in our example:

(A) Market Value of Securities	(B) Borrowed Funds	(C) Equity	(C/A) Margin (%)
$15,000	$5,000	$10,000	67
12,000	5,000	7,000	58
10,000	5,000	5,000	50
8,000	5,000	3,000	37½
5,000	5,000	0	0
2,000	5,000	(3,000)	negative

What happens to the investor's status if his margin rises above or falls below the 50 percent limit? If the securities rise in value to, say, $15,000, only $7,500 is required in equity to preserve the 50 percent margin requirement. The customer has $2,500 more in equity than he needs ($10,000 − $7,500). He may withdraw this in cash or buy up to $5,000 worth of additional securities with it.

When securities fall below $10,000 in market value, the margin percentage dips below 50 percent. The account becomes restricted as limitations are imposed on additional transactions. Once the margin percentage falls below the maintenance-margin requirement, the account is said to be *undermargined*. If the maintenance margin was set at 35 percent, when market values fell below about $7,700 a call would be made for more margin.[19] That is, the broker would request more margin or equity. Should the customer be unable to provide additional margin, the broker could sell the securities to cover the value of the loan. Any money left over after settlement of the loan belongs to the customer.

In any case, margin trading is not a device for the fainthearted or unsophisticated investor who is unwilling or unable to assume this added risk of owning securities. Such trading can be done more or less prudently, inasmuch as margin requirements set *maximum* borrowing limits only. Margin trading can be conducted at lower levels of borrowing to reduce the added risks of using other people's money.

[19] In effect, the maintenance margin on long accounts is reached when:

$$\text{Market value of securities} = \frac{\text{Amount of loan}}{1 - \text{Maintenance margin \%}}$$

In our example, the maintenance level is reached at (1/.65)($5,000), or about $7,700. For short sales the maintenance margin is reached when:

$$\text{Market value of securities} = \frac{\text{Initial proceeds + Initial margin (\$)}}{1 + \text{Maintenance margin \%}}$$

DELIVERY

Securities transactions end with funds passing to the seller and securities to the buyer. The custom is to settle funds and securities transfers by the fifth business day (that is, Saturdays, Sundays, and holidays excluded) following the day of the trade. For example, a transaction that takes place on Wednesday would be settled by Wednesday of the following week. These settlements are called *regular-way* settlements.

Two other settlement forms are used frequently. *Cash contracts* are used when the seller requires his money quickly, or with the expiration of tax years, conversion options, and rights. Cash contracts call for same-day delivery, and the price will probably be less than the regular-way price. In the case of expiration of a tax year, an investor might wish to use this settlement option on, say, December 30 to take advantage of a tax loss before year-end. *Seller's option* gives the seller, at his option, up to sixty days to deliver.

Summary

In this chapter we have explored the securities markets, both their nature and mode of operation. We reviewed the distinction between primary and secondary markets and discussed in some depth the inner workings of the main secondary market, the New York Stock Exchange, as well as the OTC markets. In the process, we explored the various types of orders available to an investor and their advantages and disadvantages, as well as the mechnics of paying for and receiving stocks.

Questions and Problems

1. Why is it necessary to maintain a liquid secondary market in securities in the United States?

2. Discuss the functions of commission brokers, floor brokers, and odd-lot dealers.

3. The New York Stock Exchange is often used as an example of a competitive market because of the direct confrontation of buyers and sellers. Discuss this statement.

4. How does the OTC market differ from the organized exchanges?

5. It has been said that short selling is an uncomfortable maneuver for most investors, whereas they are quite comfortable going long. Why should this be so?

6. Under what circumstances would you be inclined to place a limit order to buy?

7. What are some possible disadvantages of limit orders?

8. Suppose you have a friend who says that when he finds a stock he would like to buy, he selects an appropriate price and places an open or GTC order. What advice, if any, would you give him?

9. Suppose you are generally bearish on the market. In particular you feel that the craze over home insulation (due to the energy crisis) has caused the price of Sterling Fiberglas to move ahead too far to $60.

    a. If you shorted 100 shares of Sterling, what sort of order(s) might it be appropriate to use? Why?

    b. Suppose you shorted 100 shares of Sterling in March at $60 using the margin limit (cost of borrowing, 10%):

        (1) Would your order be executed if the immediate last price of the stock was $60? Why?

        (2) At what price on the stock would a 25 percent maintenance margin be reached?

        (3) If you "covered" four months later at $51, how much better (worse) would you do being on 50 percent margin as opposed to 100 percent margin?

    c. Suppose you owned 100 shares of the stock "long" at a cost of $55. What are two reasons why you might go "short" at $60?

10. The following represents a consecutive series of prices (hypothetical) during part of a trading day in IBM shares:

A	B	C	D	E	F	G	H	I	J	K	L
250	250.5	251	251	250	248	249	249.5	252	250	250	251

    a. Indicate by letter reference those prices at which short sales would be permitted (ignore "A").

    b. Why would someone "long" 100 shares of IBM consider shorting 100 shares at, say, $251?

11. What are three possible uses of "shorting against the box"?

12. Answer each question below, given the following information: You have $100,000 to invest in a single stock. The initial margin limit is 40 percent. The maintenance margin is set at 25 percent. Funds can be borrowed from your broker at 10 percent per annum (ignore commissions and taxes).

    a. How many dollars in securities could you buy if margined to the limit?

    b. Suppose you bought $20,000 of Disney stock, borrowing $10,000 from your broker. You sell Disney at the end of six months for $22,000. What is the annual rate of return on your equity?

13. How is a stop order different from a limit order?

14. How can an investor use a stop order to protect a short-sale profit?

15. Since each stock is assigned to only one specialist on the NYSE, the specialist has a monopoly; therefore, the specialist function as it currently exists cannot be efficient. Do you agree?

16. How does the operation of the OTC differ from the operation of the NYSE with respect to order execution?

17. Is trading on margin a good idea?

18. If margin requirements are 40 percent and an investor has $6,000 on deposit with his broker, how much stock can he purchase?

19. Suppose you used $10,000 to purchase $15,000 in stocks (non-dividend payers). The $5,000 needed is borrowed from a broker at 10 percent. Six months later you sell out at $20,000 (debt has not been reduced). Demonstrate the effect of margining on your rate of return.

**Types of
Orders**   *Market order.* An order to buy or sell at the most advantageous price obtainable after the order is represented in the trading crowd.

Limit, limited, or limited price order. An order to buy or sell a stated amount of a security at a specified price, or at a better price, if obtainable after the order is represented in the trading crowd.

All or none order. A market or limited price order that is to be executed in its entirety or not at all.

Alternative or either/or order. An order to do either of two alternatives—e.g., sell (buy) at a limit price or sell (buy) on stop.

At the close order. A market order to be executed at or as near the close as practicable.

At the opening order. A market or limited price order to be executed at the opening of the stock or not at all.

Buy "minus" order. A market or limited price order to buy a stated amount of a stock provided that the price is not higher than the last sale if the last sale was a "minus" or "zero minus" tick, and is not higher than the last sale minus the minimum fractional change in the stock if the last sale was a "plus" or "zero plus" tick.

Day order. An order to buy or sell which, if not executed, expires at the end of the trading day on which it was entered.

Do not reduce (DNR) order. A limited order to buy or a stop limit order to sell a round lot or odd lot or a stop order to sell an odd lot that may not be reduced by the amount of an ordinary cash dividend on the ex-devidend date.

Fill or kill order. A market or limited price order to be executed in its entirety as soon as it is represented in the crowd and if not so executed is to be treated as canceled.

Good till canceled (GTC) or open order. An order to buy or sell that remains in effect until executed or canceled.

Immediate or cancel order. A market or limited price order to be executed in whole or in part as soon as such order is represented in the trading crowd; the portion not executed is to be treated as canceled.

Not held order. A market or limited price order marked "not held," "disregard tape," "take time," or any such qualifying notation.

Order good until a specified time. A market or limited price order to be represented in the trading crowd until a specified time, after which such order or any portion not executed is to be canceled.

Percentage order. A market or limited price order to buy (sell) a stated amount of a specified stock after a fixed number of shares in that stock have traded.

Scale order. An order to buy (sell) a security specifying the total amount to be bought (sold) and the amount to be bought (sold) at specified price variations.

Sell "plus" order. A market or limited price order to sell a stated amount of a stock provided that the price is not lower than the last sale if the last sale was a "plus" or "zero plus" tick, and is not lower than the last sale plus the minimum fractional change in the stock if the last sale was a "minus" or "zero minus" tick.

Stop order (odd lots only). An order to buy (sell) which becomes a market order when a transaction in the security occurs at or above (below) the stop price after the order is represented in the trading crowd.

Stop limit order. A buy (sell) order executable at the limit price or better when a transaction in the security occurs at or above (below) the stop price after the order is represented in the trading crowd.

Switch or contingent order. An order for the purchase (sale) of one stock and the sale (purchase) or another stock at a stipulated price difference.

Time order. An order that will become a market or limited price order at a specified time.

CHAPTER
THREE

COSTS
OF INVESTING
IN SECURITIES

Investment and speculation are not carried on without cost. There are *direct costs*, such as commissions, interest paid on borrowed funds, and taxes, and *indirect costs*, such as federal estate and gift taxes. Finally, there are *implicit costs*, such as the investor's time in seeking out and evaluating investment opportunities (and worrying about them after purchase) and deciding what to sell, as well as the implicit cost of money tied up in an investment.[1]

These various transaction costs are the topic of this chapter. We shall attempt to provide general relationships between tax law, commission structure, and the investment process. Investors and speculators should appreciate the complexities of the transaction-cost environment and know when to seek expert advice—or at the very least, take transaction costs into account when contemplating an investment or speculative action.

Direct Commissions and Transfer Taxes

When an investor buys and sells securities, his transaction costs involve direct costs stemming from the transaction—brokerage commissions and transfer taxes—and costs stemming from the completion of a transaction cycle—a buy and a sell order in the same security. These latter costs will be discussed in conjunction with the personal income tax, in a later section of this chapter. First, we will consider the brokerage costs and transfer taxes associated with stock transactions.

Direct transaction costs can cut deeply into profits. In fact, if the profit (in either dollars or percentage) is relatively small, these costs can change it into a net loss. Such a situation is most likely to occur with a speculator who is constantly switching positions in order to capitalize on minor price fluctuations.

---

[1] It has been vividly noted elsewhere that frequent buying and selling—high turnover—is expensive not only in dollars but also in undermining the quality of decisions. The more frequent the buy and sell decisions, the greater the strain on the quality of analysis and the judgment in making choices. Hence, transaction costs come in many forms. See C.D. Ellis, *Institutional Investing* (Homewood, Ill.: Dow Jones-Irwin, 1971), Chap. 7.

REGULAR COMMISSIONS

Prior to March 1972 all investors in the stock market would pay a standard commission per "round" lot, that is, lots of 100 shares. In March 1972 this commission structure was changed. The new structure required all investors to continue to pay the same commission per round lot on dollar amounts up to $300,000; but on amounts above $300,000, the commission would be reached by negotiation. This commission structure continued until May 1, 1975, when all fixed commission rates were abolished. All commissions became negotiated commissions on May 1, 1975.

The idea behind a competitive or negotiated rate structure was to increase competition among the brokerage houses. However, an SEC study has shown that the actual brokerage rates for small investors actually rose by 2 percent from April 1975 to March 1976. During the same period the commission rates for the large institutions operating in the market decreased by 23 percent. In fact, some big institutions have been able to negotiate discounts of as much as 85 percent. It has been reported that the typical small investor pays a regular commission of about 51 cents per share while large institutions pay a commission of between 10 and 12 cents per share.[2]

DISCOUNT BROKERS

With the new era of fully negotiated commissions, the discount broker assumed a role in the stock market. Discount brokers do not charge the same commissions as the larger retail brokerage firms such as Merrill Lynch, Pierce, Fenner & Smith or Bache Halsey Stuart. These discount commission brokers provide fewer services than do the better-known, larger firms. For example, the discount brokers frequently provide no research support or little if any investment advice. The customer merely phones the discount broker and places an order. In other words, the discount broker is best for an investor who makes his own investment decisions about *what* to buy or sell and *when* to buy or sell it. The discount brokers are not set up to give investment advice to the customer. The discounts offered can range anywhere from 10 to 50 percent off the commissions that the better-known retail brokerage firms would charge. In fact, the discount might even be greater than 50 percent for a very large order.[3] Table 3-1 compares typical commission rates for the purchase of 50 shares and 100 shares, respectively, of a $30 stock; and for 50 shares or 100 shares, respectively, of a $50 stock. One can very readily see how large the discounts can be. It should be pointed out that these discount houses, aside from not providing investment advice, often quote rates based upon a required minimum amount of business per year. They often charge extra for such services as delivery of stock certificates, placing limit orders, or placing an order on one of the major stock exchanges.

---

[2]"What You Should Know about Discount Stock Brokers," *Consumer Reports*, October 1976, pp. 588-91.

[3]The discounters claim that this can be as much as 80 percent. See "Discount Brokers Do What They Advertise, Three 'Investors' "Find," *Wall Street Journal*, April 5, 1977, p. 1.

TABLE 3-1

WHAT IT COSTS TO TRADE STOCKS

The table below compares the commission rates charged for four typical stock trades by three of the country's largest brokerage houses and by eight discount brokers. New York State transfer tax and SEC fee are not included. Commission prices, rounded to the nearest dollar, are as of mid-August.

	$30 Stock		$50 Stock	
	Commission on 50 Shares	Commission on 100 Shares	Commission on 50 Shares	Commission on 100 Shares
Big Brokers				
Merrill Lynch, Pierce, Fenner & Smith (Regular)	$38	$59	$52	$80
Merrill Lynch, Pierce, Fenner & Smith (Sharebuilder)	26	47	42	68
Bache Halsey Stuart	40	58	53	80
Dean Witter & Co.	38	59	54	82
Discounters				
Source Securities, New York City*	25	35	33	35
Quick & Reilly, New York City†	30	35	30	43
StockCross, Boston‡	29	34	29	34
Kulak, Voss & Co., Springfield, Va.	25	40	35	54
Daley, Coolidge & Co., Cleveland	26	43	37	57
Burke, Christensen & Lewis Securities, Chicago§	23	23	23	23
Letterman Transaction Services, Newport Beach, Calif.	24	36	40	60
Charles Schwab & Co., San Francisco	24	40	40	60

*For a person who generates $250 or less in commissions per year; lower rates for people who trade more.

†For market orders; limit orders cost slightly more.

‡Orders must be accompanied by 20 percent collateral in cash or securities. Limit orders cost $10 more.

§For orders executed on Midwest Stock Exchange, or third market; orders executed on New York Stock Exchange will probably cost more.

Source: Copyright © by Consumers Union of United States, Inc., Mount Vernon, N.Y. 10550. (Reprinted)(Excerpted) by permission from *Consumer Reports*, (October, 1976).

ODD-LOT DIFFERENTIAL

Odd lots generally consist of orders for fewer than 100 shares. Such transactions are carried out through odd-lot brokers on the floor of the exchange. Because of the involvement of this additional middleman, the cost of executing odd-lot orders is more expensive than the cost of round-lot orders.

Odd-lot brokers charge a fee known as an odd-lot differential for their service. For New York Stock Exchange securities, this differential is 12½ cents per share, or one-eighth of a "point" (dollar) for stocks selling below $55 per share. For stocks selling above $55, the charge is one-fourth of a point, or 25 cents per share. This per-share charge is added to the actual purchase price of the stock in the case of a buy order, and subtracted from the actual sales price in the case of a sell order. Thus, if an odd lot is purchased at $12 per share, the investor will pay 12 1/8 in addition to the normal brokerage commissions. Conversely, if an odd lot is sold at $12 per share, the investor will receive 11 7/8 minus normal brokerage commissions and transfer taxes.

TRANSFER TAXES

The state of New York imposes a tax on the *seller* of stocks. It varies according to the price of the stock and the place of residence of the seller; however, the maximum rate is only 5 cents per share. Thus the state transfer tax generally does not play a material role in the investment decision, but it is a cost nonetheless.

The federal government has not imposed a stock transfer tax since 1965, but the SEC does assess a fee on *securities sold*, also levied only on the seller. This fee is 1 cent for each $500 or fraction thereof of transaction value. Thus, if 100 shares of a $9 stock are sold, the SEC fee would be 2 cents in total.

After the direct transaction costs have been paid, the investor must still face up to paying federal taxes on his profits, although he gets tax relief on any losses sustained. Federal taxes are the next topic to be examined.

Federal Personal Income Tax

Our major concern in discussing federal taxes will be their impact upon individuals as investors. First, let us briefly note the general procedure for tax calculations; then we shall see how the amount of tax is affected by dividends, capital gains provisions, and various tax shelters that are available under the current tax laws.[4]

TAX RETURN PROCEDURE

The first step in calculating the tax liability is to derive *gross income*—wages, salaries, interest, rent, net capital gains, and so on. Interest on municipal bonds, social security benefits, and other such items are specifically excluded from gross income. The second step is to arrive at *adjusted gross income*, determined by subtracting from gross income such items as business expenses and moving expenses. Adjusted gross income is then reduced by allowable deductions— medical expenses, charitable contributions, state and local taxes, and interest paid, or else a "standard deduction." The standard deduction is the greater of $2,100 or 16 percent of adjusted gross income up to a maximum of $2,800 if the taxpayer is married. If the taxpayer is single, the standard deduction is the greater of $1,700 or 16 percent of adjusted gross income up to a maximum of $2,400.[5] In addition to the standard or itemized deduction, taxpayers are allowed to claim personal exemptions for dependents. For each taxpayer and those persons supported financially by the taxpayer, a personal deduction of $750 is allowable. Thus for a married couple with three dependent children, the total allowable personal deduction is $3,750 ($750 × 5) on a joint tax return.

[4]The provisions outlined in this chapter are based on the U.S. tax laws as of mid-1977. Unfortunately, tax laws change frequently by congressional action or are applied and interpreted differently based on recent court decisions.

[5]As this chapter is being written, there is legislation to change the standard deduction to a flat dollar amount.

Let us assume that a married couple with two children are attempting to calculate their taxable income. The husband earns $30,000 in salary and the wife $11,000. There is no other income. Itemized deductions total $2,000. Taxable income would be calculated as follows (assuming a joint return):

Adjusted gross income	$41,000
Less:	
Standard deduction	−2,800
Personal exemptions	−3,000
Taxable income	$35,200

Notice that the standard deduction was used, since it exceeded the amount derived by itemizing. Further, 16 percent of gross income would suggest a standard deduction of $6,560 (16 percent of $41,000). However, the maximum amount allowable under the standard deduction method is $2,800 for married taxpayers.

The income tax owed is based on taxable income. Table 3-2 contains the income tax rates that prevailed for various types of taxpayers with taxable incomes in excess of $20,000 in 1976. For example, if a married couple had taxable income of $35,200 and filed a joint return, their tax liability would be $10,004. This is calculated by taking $8,660 found in the table as the tax on

TABLE 3-2
INDIVIDUAL INCOME TAX RATE SCHEDULES

SCHEDULE X—Single Taxpayers Not Qualifying for Rates in Schedule Y or Z

Taxable Income Over—	But not over—	Tax	of the amount over—
$20,000	$22,000	$5,230+38%	$20,000
$22,000	$26,000	$5,990+40%	$22,000
$26,000	$32,000	$7,590+45%	$26,000
$32,000	$38,000	$10,290+50%	$32,000
$38,000	$44,000	$13,290+55%	$38,000
$44,000	$50,000	$16,590+60%	$44,000
$50,000	$60,000	$20,190+62%	$50,000
$60,000	$70,000	$26,390+64%	$60,000
$70,000	$80,000	$32,790+66%	$70,000
$80,000	$90,000	$39,390+68%	$80,000
$90,000	$100,000	$46,190+69%	$90,000
$100,000	....	$53,090+70%	$100,000

SCHEDULE Y—Married Taxpayers and Qualifying Widows and Widowers

Married Taxpayers Filing Joint Returns and Qualifying Widows and Widowers

Taxable Income Over—	But not over—	Tax	of the amount over—
$20,000	$24,000	$4,380+32%	$20,000
$24,000	$28,000	$5,660+36%	$24,000
$28,000	$32,000	$7,100+39%	$28,000
$32,000	$36,000	$8,660+42%	$32,000
$36,000	$40,000	$10,340+45%	$36,000
$40,000	$44,000	$12,140+48%	$40,000
$44,000	$52,000	$14,060+50%	$44,000
$52,000	$64,000	$18,060+53%	$52,000
$64,000	$76,000	$24,420+55%	$64,000
$76,000	$88,000	$31,020+58%	$76,000
$88,000	$100,000	$37,980+60%	$88,000
$100,000	$120,000	$45,180+62%	$100,000
$120,000	$140,000	$57,580+64%	$120,000
$140,000	$160,000	$70,380+66%	$140,000
$160,000	$180,000	$83,580+68%	$160,000
$180,000	$200,000	$97,180+69%	$180,000
$200,000	....	$110,980+70%	$200,000

Married Taxpayers Filing Separate Returns

Taxable Income Over—	But not over—	Tax	of the amount over—
$20,000	$22,000	$6,070+48%	$20,000
$22,000	$26,000	$7,030+50%	$22,000
$26,000	$32,000	$9,030+53%	$26,000
$32,000	$38,000	$12,210+55%	$32,000
$38,000	$44,000	$15,510+58%	$38,000
$44,000	$50,000	$18,990+60%	$44,000
$50,000	$60,000	$22,590+62%	$50,000
$60,000	$70,000	$28,790+64%	$60,000
$70,000	$80,000	$35,190+66%	$70,000
$80,000	$90,000	$41,790+68%	$80,000
$90,000	$100,000	$48,590+69%	$90,000
$100,000	....	$55,490+70%	$100,000

SCHEDULE Z—Unmarried (or legally separated) Taxpayers Who Qualify as Heads of Household

Taxable Income Over—	But not over—	Tax	of the amount over—
$20,000	$22,000	$4,800+35%	$20,000
$22,000	$24,000	$5,500+36%	$22,000
$24,000	$26,000	$6,220+38%	$24,000
$26,000	$28,000	$6,980+41%	$26,000
$28,000	$32,000	$7,800+42%	$28,000
$32,000	$36,000	$9,480+45%	$32,000
$36,000	$38,000	$11,280+48%	$36,000
$38,000	$40,000	$12,240+51%	$38,000
$40,000	$44,000	$13,260+52%	$40,000
$44,000	$50,000	$15,340+55%	$44,000
$50,000	$52,000	$18,640+56%	$50,000
$52,000	$64,000	$19,760+58%	$52,000
$64,000	$70,000	$26,720+59%	$64,000
$70,000	$76,000	$30,260+61%	$70,000
$76,000	$80,000	$33,920+62%	$76,000
$80,000	$88,000	$36,400+63%	$80 000
$88,000	$100,000	$41,440+64%	$88,000
$100,000	$120,000	$49,120+66%	$100,000
$120,000	$140,000	$62,320+67%	$120,000
$140,000	$160,000	$75,720+68%	$140,000
$160,000	$180,000	$89,320+69%	$160,000
$180,000	....	$103,120+70%	$180,000

Source: *Federal Tax Course*, Prentice-Hall Editorial Staff (Englewood Cliffs, N.J.: Prentice-Hall, 1977).

$32,000 for married taxpayers filing a joint return, and adding 42 percent of the $3,200 excess over $32,000.

SPECIAL FEATURES OF THE TAX LAWS FOR INVESTORS

Investors receive favorable tax treatment in a number of their investment dealings. In this section we will explore the main areas of preferential tax treatment. If the investor is aware of these areas, he is better able to plan his investment policies and management decisions so that, if possible, his taxes may be minimized.

Corporate Dividends

An investor is permitted to exclude from gross income the first $100 in dividends he has received during the year.[6] In the case of a joint return, if both parties had dividend income, *each* can exclude up to $100, for a maximum exclusion of $200. However, if the wife earned $40 in dividends and the husband earned $160, only $140 could be excluded on a joint return (the wife's $40 plus the husband's $100); the husband is not entitled to his wife's unused $60 of dividend exclusion.

To ensure maximum exclusion, a husband and wife (1) should hold some stock jointly, or (2) should divide ownership of their stock in such a way that each earns at least $100 in dividends. Dividends earned above the $100-per-person exclusion are taxed as ordinary income.

Regulated Investment Company Dividends

Dividends received from regulated investment companies, more commonly called mutual funds, also qualify for special treatment. If they pay out at least 90 percent of their investment income, these funds are not taxed on these earnings, and they can avoid corporate taxation. The advantage to the investor is that the distributions he receives are treated for his tax purposes as though *he*, not the fund, actually made the transaction. Thus, if part of the distribution of mutual-fund investment income stems from long-term capital gains earned by the fund, the investor can treat that portion of his dividend as a long-term capital gain. (We shall see shortly that this is quite a boon to the investor.) Furthermore, that portion (if any) of the distribution the investor receives that is not the result of a long-term gain still often qualifies for the $100-per-person dividend exclusion. Of course, any gain or loss realized on the price of the mutual-fund shares themselves is treated as a capital gain or loss upon sale of the shares.

---

[6] This statement applies to cash dividends. Stock dividends are generally taxable not when received but rather when they are sold (if sold at a gain). (See the capital gains section of this chapter.) In addition, some dividends received from public utilities and mutual funds are tax-free and thus need not be counted toward the dividend exclusion.

Interest on Government Bonds

Interest received on municipal bonds is free of federal income taxes and is therefore not included in gross income. Thus many wealthy individuals invest in municipal bonds, receive regular interest payments, and pay no federal income taxes on them.[7]

Series E, F, and J bonds of the U.S. government are sold on a discounted basis. Thus, for example, a Series E bond purchased for $75 will be worth $100 at maturity. The $25 difference is interest earned. Normally, taxpayers report their income on a cash basis; that is, income is reported for tax purposes as received. But taxpayers investing in U.S. government bonds of Series E, F, and J have an option in reporting the interest earned on these bonds. They can elect to wait until maturity and then report the total increase in value—in our example, $25—in that year as interest income; or they can elect to report each year's increase in value (interest) as it is earned. Electing one method or the other depends on the expected future tax bracket.

Series H bonds are current-income bonds; the interest is paid to the investor semiannually, rather than accumulated. Income tax must be paid on this interest in the year it is received. Therefore the Series E, F, and J bonds have a tax advantage over Series H.

Capital Gains and Losses

Current capital gains provisions in U.S. tax law furnish individual taxpayers with a number of ways of being taxed at lower rates than those shown in our tax table. Generally, capital gains stem from the increased value of capital (property). To the investor, this could mean anything from a rise in the price of a stock to the sale of cattle above the purchase price. After outlining the general framework of the capital gains tax provisions, we will show specific investment situations that can qualify for this favorable treatment.

Transactions qualify for either long-term or short-term capital gains treatment. In the case of securities, the criterion is a twelve-month holding period, after which the gain is considered long term. Short-term capital gains are treated as ordinary income; long-term capital gains are taxed in either of two ways, whichever results in the lower tax.[8]

1. One-half the capital gain is *added* to other *income* and regular tax rates are applied.
2. Twenty-five percent of the entire capital gain is *added to* the *tax* on the taxpayer's ordinary income.

Example. If a married taxpayer has long-term capital gains of $20,000 and ordinary income of $20,000, the tax on his ordinary income is $4,380. Now, if

---

[7]Some states, however, levy taxes on interest earned on municipal bonds.

[8]The long-term capital gain provisions discussed here apply only to the first $50,000 of gain. Another procedure is followed for computing the tax on capital gains in excess of $50,000. The maximum effective tax rate on this excess is 35 percent (one-half the maximum marginal tax rate).

we use step 1 to handle the capital gains portion, his taxable income would be $30,000 ($20,000 ordinary income plus half of $20,000 long-term capital gains). The total tax bill would be $7,880. Under procedure 2, the total tax bill would be $9,380 (the $4,380 on the ordinary income plus one-fourth of $20,000 long-term capital gains). Option 1 would be elected because it results in the lower tax liability. This option is the method usually selected by a married taxpayer filing a joint return if his taxable income (before long-term capital gains) is less than $52,000.

When capital losses are incurred, they may be offset against capital gains of the same tax year. If there are more short-term losses than short-term gains, the excess short-term capital loss may be offset against ordinary income up to a limit of $3,000. But excess *long-term* losses can be offset against ordinary income only on a two-for-one basis. That is, it takes $2,000 of excess long-term capital loss to offset $1,000 of ordinary income. However, the total capital loss (long-term plus short-term) may not exceed $3,000 in a given year. Any unused losses may be carried forward any number of years, and the losses retain their original character; that is, short-term capital loss carryforwards are treated as short-term capital losses in future tax years, and long-term capital loss carryforwards remain long-term capital losses in future tax years.

Example. An investor who earns $10,000 sells one stock held for fifteen months for a $2,000 profit. He sells another stock held for one month for $3,000 profit. Overall, $4,000 is added to his income. This is calculated as follows:

50% of long-term gain	$1,000
100% of short-term gain	3,000
Added to income	$4,000

Example. An investor who earns $20,000 sells one stock held for a year and a half for a $3,000 profit, and sells another stock held for two months for a $2,000 loss. In this case, $500 is added to his income, calculated as follows:

Long-term gain	$3,000
Minus short-term loss	2,000
Excess long-term gain	$1,000
Minus 50% of long-term gain	500
Added to income	$ 500

If the short-term loss had been $5,000, the excess short-term loss would have been $2,000. All of this amount could be used to reduce ordinary income in the current year.

Example. If an investor realized a net short-term gain of $4,000 and a net long-term loss of $5,000, $500 would be deducted from ordinary income. This is calculated as follows:

Short-term gain	$4,000
Minus long-term loss	5,000
Net long-term loss	$1,000

But since only 50 percent of long-term loss is deductible from ordinary income, the deduction would be $500. Also, there is no carryforward. If the long-term loss had been $3,000 in the above example, $1,000 (net short-term gain) would be added to ordinary income.

If an investor incurred net short-term losses of $4,500 and net long-term losses of $800, he would first deduct $3,000 of net short-term loss, the maximum loss that can offset income in a given year. The remaining $1,500 of short-term loss and $800 of long-term loss would be carried forward, retaining their identity.

Figure 3-1 summarizes the process for determining the net amount of capital gains and losses for the tax year. In addition, the tax treatment of the net amount of short- and/or long-term capital gains (losses) is specified.

FIGURE 3-1
INVESTMENT MANAGEMENT, INDIVIDUAL PORTFOLIOS

TAXATION OF CAPITAL GAINS AND LOSSES

SHORT-TERM	LONG-TERM
Gain (++)	Gain (+)
‾Loss (−−)	‾Loss (−)
= net $\overline{(++)}$ $\underline{(−−)}$	= net $\oplus$ $\ominus$

OUTCOME OF NETTING   TAX TREATMENT

$\oplus$ Add one-half to income.

$\ominus$ Deduct one-half from income ≤ $3,000. Carry over remainder.

$(++)$ Add all to income.

$(−−)$ Take all from income ≤ $3,000. Carry over remainder.

$\oplus , (++)$ Add one-half long-term gain to income; add all short-term gain to income.

$\oplus , (−−)$ Loss exceeds gain: deduct all from income ≤ $3,000. Carry over remainder.
     Gain exceeds loss: add one-half to income

$(++), \ominus$ Loss exceeds gain: deduct one-half of loss from income ≤ $3,000. Carry over remainder.
     Gain exceeds loss: add all to income.

$\ominus , (−−)$ Offset up to $3,000 in this order:
     (a) Apply to short-term loss (−−)
     (b) Then apply to long-term loss (−)
     (c) Carry over remainder with separate identification

Corporate Securities. If corporate securities are held for more than twelve months, they qualify for long-term capital gain (or loss) treatment. Thus, if corporate management follows a policy of paying little or no dividends, it aids the investor in minimizing his tax burden. This is so because dividends (above the $100 exclusion) are taxed as ordinary income, whereas profits from increased share prices are taxed as capital gains. And these increased share prices usually result from increasing company earnings, which in turn follow from, among other sources, reinvestment of earnings that were not paid out as dividends. If the stock has been held for more than twelve months, this means that the investor receives a tax shelter in the form of a long-term capital gain.[9]

Short Sales. In the normal stock transaction, the investor buys a security in the hope that its price will advance. When he sells, if his hope is realized, he has a profit. If the stock has been held for more than twelve months, the profit is taxed as a long-term capital gain. If the stock has been held for less than twelve months, the profit is taxed as a short-term capital gain. However, recall that in a short sale the procedure is reversed. First the investor or speculator sells, hoping the stock's price will decline, then he buys. If he is right, the purchase will be at a lower price than the sale and he will make a profit. From a tax standpoint, he has not held the stock at all, irrespective of the minimum of twelve months. Therefore any gains from short selling are taxed as short-term capital gains, and losses are treated as short-term capital losses.

Wash Sales. Investing is a risky business. Occasionally investors make mistakes. That is, stocks purchased long occasionally decline rather than advance in price. When this occurs, if the stock has not yet been sold, unrealized losses, or "paper losses" as they are often called, result. If the investor still believes in the stock's potential, he wants to maintain his position; but at the same time, he would like to get the tax benefit resulting from a capital loss. The way of solving this dilemma is to sell the stock, thereby establishing a tax loss, and at the same time buy a like amount of the same stock at the same price, thereby maintaining a position. Unfortunately, current tax law would disallow the loss on such a transaction—which is called a "wash sale." In fact, if "substantially identical" stock is purchased within thirty days of the sale (before or after), the tax loss will not be allowed. Normally, "substantially identical" means the stock of the same company, or a security convertible into the stock. Sale of a stock in one industry and the purchase of a stock of a different firm in the same industry within thirty days does not constitute a wash sale. Thus the sale of Ramada Inns and the purchase of Holiday Inns shares would not be a wash sale.

Put and Call Options. Later in this text we will devote a chapter to options. Here, it is our purpose only to point out the main tax implications of put and call options.

A *call option* is an option to purchase shares at a given price from the option

[9] Small Business Investment Corporation stocks (SBIC's) provide an even greater boon to investors. Gains on SBIC shares are taxed as capital gains, but losses on such shares are fully deductible without limit as ordinary losses (against ordinary income).

writer. A *put option* is an option to sell shares at a given price to the option writer. The tax problem with options can be summarized rather briefly. The buyer of an option realizes a short-term or long-term gain or loss just as with stocks if he sells the option or lets it expire. If a call is exercised, the price he paid for it is added to the exercise price to determine the cost of the stock he acquires. His holding period on the stock begins on the day he exercises, and the holding period of the call is not added to the holding period of the stock.

The writer of an option receives a premium. This premium is "held in suspense" until the option transaction is consummated. The termination of the option, by expiration, causes the premium to be subject to treatment as a short-term capital gain. Termination by repurchase results in a short-term gain or loss. Exercise of the option results in a short-term or long-term gain or loss depending upon how long the writer has held the stock. If the option position is terminated with a closing purchase, the profit or loss realized is the difference between the premium of the option sold and the price paid for the closing option. Such profit or loss is reported as a short-term capital gain or loss. This rule does not apply to options written by broker-dealers in the ordinary course of their trade or business. Gain or loss from such transactions is to be treated as ordinary gain or loss.

Federal Estate and Gift Taxes

The Tax Reform Act of 1976 made sweeping changes in existing estate and gift tax laws. The changes are extremely complex. Our purpose in this chapter is merely to present a cursory introduction to this new area of taxation. Under current law the estate and gift taxes have been combined into one tax table. The new unified rates range from 18 percent to 70 percent. Since these rates are highly progressive, it is important for investors of some means to consider estate planning in their total investment picture.

INTRODUCTION TO MAJOR ESTATE AND GIFT TAX PROVISIONS

Under previous tax law, the federal gift tax was levied on gifts made by an investor or grantor during his lifetime. In addition, a federal estate tax was levied on property that was transferred upon the death of the taxpayer. The gift tax rate was pegged at three-quarters of the corresponding estate tax rate. After 1976, however, a new unified rate schedule was applied to cumulative transfers during the taxpayer's life and at his death. We have already mentioned that this new unified rate schedule ranges from 18 percent to 70 percent. The entire rate schedule is given in Table 3-3.

The amount of tax payable under the new law is determined by applying a new unified rate schedule to the cumulative lifetime taxable transfers and then subtracting the taxes payable on gifts made for past tax periods. Taxable gifts

TABLE 3-3

UNIFIED ESTATE AND GIFT TAX RATE SCHEDULE

Taxable Transfers		Tax =		Of Excess
From	To	This Amount	+, %	Over
$ 0	$ 10,000	$ 0	18	$ 0
10,000	20,000	1,800	20	10,000
20,000	40,000	3,800	22	20,000
40,000	60,000	8,200	24	40,000
60,000	80,000	13,000	26	60,000
80,000	100,000	18,200	28	80,000
100,000	150,000	23,800	30	100,000
150,000	250,000	38,800	32	150,000
250,000	500,000	70,800	34	250,000
500,000	750,000	155,800	37	500,000
750,000	1,000,000	248,300	39	750,000
1,000,000	1,250,000	345,800	41	1,000,000
1,250,000	1,500,000	448,300	43	1,250,000
1,500,000	2,000,000	555,800	45	1,500,000
2,000,000	2,500,000	780,000	49	2,000,000
2,500,000	3,000,000	1,025,800	53	2,500,000
3,000,000	3,500,000	1,290,800	57	3,000,000
3,500,000	4,000,000	1,575,800	61	3,500,000
4,000,000	4,500,000	1,880,800	65	4,000,000
4,500,000	5,000,000	2,205,800	69	4,500,000
5,000,000	....	2,550,800	70	5,000,000

that were made prior to 1977 must be included in determining a taxpayer's cumulative lifetime taxable transfers. The reduction for taxes previously paid is based upon the new rate schedule.

The term *cumulative transfers* means that a taxpayer must keep track of all gifts made during his lifetime as well as property that passes upon his death. The new estate tax is calculated by applying the unified rate schedule to the total cumulative transfers during life and upon death and then subtracting the gift taxes payable on the lifetime transfers.

PROCEDURE FOR CALCULATING THE TAXABLE TABLE

Under previous law, there was a $60,000 estate tax exemption as well as a $30,000 gift tax exemption. These exemptions reduced the amount of taxable gift and estate. Under the new law, a single unified tax credit was provided for estate and gift taxes after 1976. This new credit has a phase-in period consisting of five years. In 1981 the credit will be $47,000. Table 3-4 gives the amount of unified credit that applies during the phase-in period and also lists the equivalent exemption of this new credit.

The procedure for calculating the estate tax is as follows:

1. Subtract debts and expenses (such as funeral expenses, medical expenses from the last illness, and administrative costs) from the gross estate to obtain the *adjusted gross estate*.

2. From the adjusted gross estate, subtract the marital deduction and add prior taxable gifts to arrive at the amount of taxable estate.[10]

3. Calculate the tax on this taxable estate.

Let us assume the following set of facts to illustrate the gift and estate tax calculations: Mr. Smith gives property valued at $500,000 to his wife and at his death leaves the remaining estate of $500,000 to his wife. Computations of the combined gift and estate taxes under the new law are as follows:

Gift tax:		
Gift	$ 500,000	
Annual exclusion*	(3,000)	
Marital deduction	(248,500)	
Taxable gift	$ 248,500	
Tax		$ 70,320
Unified credit (after 1980)		(47,000)
Gift tax payable		$ 23,320
Estate tax:		
Value of estate	$ 500,000	
Marital deduction	(250,000)	
Taxable estate	$ 250,000	
Prior taxable gifts	248,500	
	$ 498,500	
Tax		$ 155,290
Prior gift tax paid		(23,320)
Unified credit		(47,000)
Estate tax payable		$ 84,970
Combined gift and estate taxes		$ 108,290

*Annual gifts of $3,000 per donee may be made without incurring any gift tax.

TABLE 3-4
UNIFIED CREDIT DURING PHASE-IN

	Unified Credit	*Equivalent Exemption*
1977	$30,000	$120,667
1978	34,000	134,000
1979	38,000	147,333
1980	42,500	161,563
1981 and thereafter	47,000	175,625

Note—The $30,000 credit applies for estate tax purposes for the entire year 1977 and for gift tax purposes after June 30, 1977. The gift tax credit for gifts made from January 1, 1977 through June 30, 1977 is limited to $6,000.

[10] Estates can deduct $250,000 as a marital deduction or 50 percent of the adjusted gross estate if this is greater.

Our discussion of taxes has undoubtedly convinced the reader that this subject is no easy one to master. However, it was our intention to expose the investor to key aspects of our federal tax system—factors affecting personal income tax, estate tax, and gift tax—in order that he may be better able to plan with tax considerations in mind and to know when to seek competent tax advice.

Other Costs of Investing

Other costs of investing are often overlooked by investors. First, there are opportunity costs. Investors spend time analyzing possible investments and then spend time monitoring and worrying about them after they are made. These are very real opportunity costs, because the investor is sacrificing the satisfaction he could receive or money he could earn in alternative activities that he could engage in if he were not investing or worrying. Furthermore, when money is committed to an investment, the investor with limited capital (which is most of us!) forgoes alternative returns that he would earn elsewhere, such as interest earned on a savings-bank account. In addition, when securities are bought on margin, interest is paid on the borrowed funds. Even though the interest is deductible on the investor's income tax return—subject to limitations— this too should be treated as a very real cost of investing.

Summary

In this chapter we have examined the various transaction costs that must be considered in any investment decision. These include brokerage costs, transfer taxes, personal income taxes, and federal estate and gift taxes. We observed that all these will reduce the return an investor realizes—particularly an investor with a short time horizon (less than twelve months). In the next chapter, these costs will be incorporated explicitly into a generalized framework for security analysis with the emphasis on common stocks.

Questions and Problems

1. A married couple receives $170 in corporate dividends. Assuming that the husband owns stock representing $90 of the dividends, his wife owns stock representing $80 of the dividends, and the couple files a joint return, how much of the dividends can the couple exclude from their income?

2. If an investor receives $10,000 in interest on municipal bonds and files his tax return as a single person, how much of this interest will be subject to income taxes?

3. A married investor earned $60,000 and had $20,000 of long-term capital gains. Calculate his taxes (assume no deductions), using both capital gains computational methods and the tax-rate schedule.

4. If an investor has a $1,600 long-term loss, how much can he offset against his regular income? Is there a carryforward? If so, how much?

5. If an investor has a $1,600 short-term loss, how much can be offset against his regular income? Is there a carryforward? If so, how much?

6. If an investor has a $1,600 long-term gain, how much is added to his regular income? If he has a $1,600 short-term gain, how much is added to his regular income? If he has both these gains, how much is added to his regular income?

7. If an investor has a $2,000 long-term gain and a $500 short-term loss how much is added to his regular income?

8. If an investor has a net short-term gain of $2,000 and a net long-term loss of $4,000, how much would be deducted from ordinary income? Is there a carryforward?

9. It is near the end of the 1978 tax year. Each item listed below represents the result of security transactions already completed in 1978. For each case, indicate what type(s) of "paper" gains or losses might be turned into "realized" gains or losses in order to minimize taxes. Indicate your reasons in each case. (Treat each case separately.)

    a. Realized long-term gain

    b. Realized long-term loss (no short-term gains available)

    c. Realized net short-term gain and net long-term loss

    d. Realized short-term loss

10. For each of the following, state the amount of the *tax paid* by a single person in the 30 percent tax bracket (treat each separately): (1) $1,000 capital gain from a short sale (stock bought on 4/1/78 and sold on 1/4/79); (2) $180 received in dividends: $90 from common stocks, $90 from preferred stocks; (3) $500 in interest from Toledo, Ohio, Sewer Bonds; (4) 5 percent stock dividend on Revlon shares (added shares held by investor rather than sold).

11. Ms. Quinn is figuring taxes for 1978. She discovered that she lost $4,000 on Xerox shares held for four months. In addition, she has a profit of $7,000 on IBM shares held from February until December 1978, and a loss of $10,000 on Chrysler common sold this year and purchased in 1976. These transactions have already been completed in 1978. She now has her eye on a paper profit of $6,000 on Disney which was purchased just three months ago.

    a. Is it better to take the profit on Disney now for tax purposes? Why?

    b. What would be added to (subtracted from) her taxable income for 1978 if Disney were sold now, given the other completed transactions?

12. Following are a series of hypothetical security transactions:

Code	Security	Date Bought	Date Sold	Gain (Loss)
A	Dow Chemical	9/78	10/78	$(6,000)
B	Xerox	4/77	6/78	(8,000)
C	General Motors	1/76	5/78	6,000
D	IBM	6/69	2/78	6,000
E	Xonics	3/70	4/78	2,000

For any *two* cases below, fill in the required information:

Transactions	Which?: "Net" Gain (Loss)	Short-Term? or Long-Term?	Amount Added to (+) or Deducted from (−) Taxable Income	Amount of Carryover
(1) A + B				
(2) B + C				
(3) A + E				
(4) A + B + C				

13. Assume that auto stock prices have suffered recent setbacks, and Investor C wants to take a tax loss he has on General Motors. However, he feels this industry is due for a large rebound. What should he do?

14. Under the new unified rate schedule for estates and gifts, how will taxable gifts be treated upon the death of the donor?

APPENDIX

**Year-End
Tax
Strategies**

This Appendix provides a series of steps that might be helpful in planning year-end tax savings strategy. But you should remember that the investment incentive for holding or selling a stock is a crucial matter and that saving on taxes is an extra and not the end point of investing.

Near the end of the tax year you should consider what have been your realized gains and losses from completed transactions. Next check to see what your "paper" gains and losses are. Then you might consider the following transactions if your completed security transactions show:

Long-term gain. You might avoid taking any losses this year and pay capital gains tax on these gains. If you want to realize losses, sell securities giving long-term losses.

Short-term gain. You might realize losses to offset these gains that would be taxed at ordinary income tax rates. Sell securities giving long-term losses to offset these gains.

Long-term loss. You might consider realizing gains that would be offset by these losses. Sell securities giving short-term gain. Net long-term capital losses in excess of short-term capital gain are subject to this limitation: Only 50 percent of the net long-term loss is deductible from up to $3,000 of ordinary income. Therefore, to take full advantage of the loss, it is advisable to realize short-term gains. If you do not have short-term gains, you might consider selling a stock having a paper long-term gain with an immediate repurchase of the stock. The gain is offset by the loss; on the repurchase, you get an increased tax basis. Wash sale rules do not apply to profitable sales.

Short-term loss. You might consider realizing short-term gains, to offset these losses. In planning the extent of your sales, note that short-term losses up to $3,000 may be deducted in full from ordinary income.

Net short-term gain and net long-term gain. You might sell securities giving short-term loss not in excess of the short-term gain.

Net long-term gain and net short-term loss. You might sell securities giving short-term gain up to the amount of short-term loss.

Net short-term gain and net long-term loss. If the long-term loss is equal to the short-term gain, you might consider no further transactions, as the loss eliminates the gain. If short-term gain exceeds the net long-term loss, you might sell securities to realize long-term loss to the extent of the excess. If the long-term loss exceeds the short-term gain, you might sell securities to realize short-term gain up to the extent of the excess loss.

FRAMEWORK
OF RISK-RETURN
ANALYSIS

There are many motives for investing. Some people invest in order to gain a sense of power or prestige. Often the control of corporate empires is a driving motive. For most investors, however, their interest in investments is largely pecuniary—to earn a return on their money. However, selecting stocks exclusively on the basis of maximization of return is not enough.

The fact that most investors do not place available funds into the one, two, or even three stocks promising the greatest returns suggests that there must be other considerations besides return in the selection process. Investors not only like return, they dislike risk. Their holding of an assortment of securities attests to that fact.

To say that investors like return and dislike risk is, however, simplistic. To facilitate our job of analyzing securities and portfolios within a risk-return context, we must begin with a clear understanding of what risk and return are, what creates them, and how they should be measured.

Chapter 4 examines the theoretical tenets that explain what determines the value of a security, or what it is worth, and also explores the matter in which return is measured.

Chapter 5 looks into what creates risk, and it provides a quantitative measure of risk. We examine those forces that are largely uncontrollable, external, and broad in their effect upon securities—risks referred to as systematic in nature—and the controllable, internal factors somewhat peculiar to certain industries and/or firms—referred to as elements of unsystematic risk. Our search for a suitable quantification of risk will encompass the notion of risk premiums and the notion that risk refers to the variation in rates of return. The chapter concludes with a historical look at return-and-risk measures for individual stocks as well as for broad groups of stocks and bonds.

SECURITY
VALUATION AND
RETURN

The ultimate decisions to be made in investments are (1) what securities should be held, and (2) how many dollars should be allocated to each. These basic decisions are normally made in two steps. First, estimates are prepared of the return and risk associated with available securities over a forward holding period. This step is known as *security analysis*. Second, return-risk estimates must be compared in order to decide how to allocate available funds among these securities on a continuing basis. This step is composed of *portfolio analysis, selection,* and *management.* In effect, security analysis provides the necessary inputs for analyzing and selecting portfolios. Parts II through V of this text cover security analysis, and Part VI examines portfolios.

Security analysis is built around the idea that *investors are concerned with two principal properties inherent in securities: the return that can be expected from holding a security, and the risk that the return that is achieved will be less than the return that was expected.* The primary purposes of this chapter are to explore the notion of security values and to focus upon return and how it is measured. Chapter 5 will examine risk in holding securities—what risk is and how it is measured.

Approaches to Valuation

There are essentially three main schools of thought on the matter of security value and the behavior of security prices. Advocates are normally classified as (1) fundamentalists, (2) technicians, and (3) random-walk theorists[1] —although few people would fit neatly into any one of the three categories. Let us try to compare these different perspectives in summary form before going into detail on them in the subsequent text.

Fundamentalists argue that, at any time, the price of a security is equal to the

[1] Representative examples of these philosophies can be seen in Benjamin Graham et al., *Security Analysis* (New York: McGraw-Hill, 1962); G. W. Bishop, Jr., *Charles H. Dow and the Dow Theory* (New York: Appleton-Century-Crofts, 1960); and E. F. Fama, "Random Walk in Stock Market Prices," *Financial Analysts Journal*, 21 (September-October 1965), 55-59.

discounted value of the stream of income from the security; that in the main, the price is a function of a set of anticipated returns and anticipated capitalization rates corresponding to future time periods. Prices change as anticipations change, and a major source of altered anticipation is new information. Where we have something less than complete dissemination of information, the actual price of a security is generally away from its theoretical value. Fundamentalists would buy the stock if its market price is below its theoretical value, or sell the stock if the price exceeds underlying value. For so-called fundamentalists, such matters as earnings, dividends, asset values, and management are the basic ingredients in determining underlying security values.

Technical analysis stands on the assumption that the value of a stock is primarily dependent upon supply and demand, having very little to do with such things as earnings and dividends. Underlying supply and demand are influenced by rational and irrational forces. Information, moods, opinions, and guesses (good and bad) as to the future all intermix. The result is price movement that follows trends for appreciable lengths of time. Changes in trend represent shifts in the supply-demand balance. However caused, these shifts are detectable sooner or later in the action of the market itself.

Technicians assess supply-demand strength through a variety of tools, generally in the form of charts wherein price and volume relationships are compared. Consensus and reinforcement from varied indicators serve as the basis for price predictions.

Random-walk theorists are directly at odds with the technician.[2] They argue that one cannot forecast future stock prices on the basis of past history alone. To random-walk theorists, technical analysis borders on the occult, and technicians enjoy the same stature as palmists or tea-leaf readers. Random-walk advocates contend that securities markets are perfect, or at least, not too imperfect. In such a market, security prices should reflect all the information available to market participants and all price changes should be independent of any past history about a company that is generally available to the public. The major complaint is aimed at the technician who tries to predict future price movements solely from the historical record.

In sum taken in their strongest forms, fundamentalists say that a security is worth the present value (discounted) of a stream of future income to be received from the security; technicians contend that price-trend data should be studied for their own sake, independent and regardless of the underlying data; random-walk theorists say that a share of stock is generally worth whatever it is selling for.

Chapters 4 through 14 deal with the approach normally associated with modern fundamental security analysis. Chapters 15 and 16 will compare and contrast the ideas of technical analysis and random walk.

---

[2]Certain strong forms of the random-walk theory challenge fundamental analysis also. These issues will be discussed in Chapter 16.

Investments provide satisfaction to the holder in both financial and nonfinancial ways. A person may own a house and some paintings because they give him pleasure. Someone may own stock for prestige and/or control. The importance of nonmonetary motives is undeniable, but such benefits are very difficult to measure accurately. *Satisfaction* and *return* in this chapter refer to money motives.

Security returns come from two sources: (1) regular receipts in the form of dividends or interest, and (2) changes in capital invested. Individual securities differ in the total amount of return afforded, as well as in the relative amounts provided from the two sources.

VALUE AND TIME

Money has a "time value." A dollar now is worth more than a dollar a year from now, since we could put the dollar now in a bank at 5 percent interest, and have $1.05 in a year. For different securities, future benefits may be received at different times. Even when the amount of future payments is the same, differences in the speed of their receipt may create differences in value. The time value of money suggests that earlier receipts are more desirable than later receipts, even when both are equal in amount and certainty, because earlier receipts can be reinvested to generate additional returns before later receipts come in. The force operating is the principle of compound interest.

An initial investment or input of any kind can grow over time. The terminal value V_n, can be seen in general as:

$$V_n = P(1 + g)^n \tag{4.1}$$

where:

V_n = ending or terminal value
n = number of compounding periods
g = rate of compounding (%)
P = initial value

Thus, for example, a dollar placed in the bank at 5 percent interest will grow to $1.05 at the end of a year, since $V_n = \$1(1 + .05)^1 = \$1.05$. At the end of two years, we will have $1.1025,

$$V_n = \$1(1 + .05)^2 = 1.1025$$

since the $1.05 earned in the first year will earn an additional $.0525 in interest. We can deal quite easily with amounts other than $1.00. Suppose we place $6.22 in the bank today at 5 percent interest. What will the terminal value be at the end of three years?

$$V_n = \$6.22(1 + .05)^3$$

$$= \$6.22(1.1576)$$

$$= \$7.20$$

(For convenience and simplicity in illustration, we are assuming that the *frequency* of compounding is once per period, at the end of each period. Therefore, annual compounding is used rather than quarterly or shorter periods.)[3]

Present values can be thought of as the reverse of compounding or future values. The formulation for present value can be achieved from Equation 4.1 by (1) dividing both sides of the equation by $(1 + g)^n$, and (2) dropping the subscript n from V_n:

$$P = \frac{V}{(1 + g)^n} \qquad (4.2)$$

For example, how much should we deposit in the bank today at 5 percent interest in order to have $2 one year hence?

$$P = \frac{\$2}{(1 + .05)^1}$$

$$= \$1.9048$$

Referring back to compounding, let us see whether $1.9048 will indeed grow to $2 in one year at 5 percent.

$$V_n = \$1.9048\,(1 + .05)^1$$

$$= \$2.00$$

Equations 4.1 and 4.2 describe the future and present values of *single sums.* In other words, we can determine from Equation 4.1 the future value of a single lump sum invested initially and permitted to compound for a number of periods. Similarly, Equation 4.2 tells us the present value of a single sum to be received at some terminal point in the future. Tables 4-1 and 4-2 summarize future and present values of a single payment of $1 for various values of g and n.

---

[3] For other than annual compounding, the more general formula is $V_n = P[1 + (g/m)]^{mn}$, where m = number of times per year compounding occurs. For example with monthly compounding, the terminal value of $1 at 6 percent would be:

$$V_n = \$1\left(1 + \frac{.06}{12}\right)^{12 \cdot 1}$$

$$= \$1(1.005)^{12} = \$1.067$$

Single, annual compounding would give $1.06.

TABLE 4-1
COMPOUND SUM OF $1

Year	1%	2%	3%	4%	5%	6%	7%
1	1.010	1.020	1.030	1.040	1.050	1.060	1.070
2	1.020	1.040	1.061	1.082	1.102	1.124	1.145
3	1.030	1.061	1.093	1.125	1.158	1.191	1.225
4	1.041	1.082	1.126	1.170	1.216	1.262	1.311
5	1.051	1.104	1.159	1.217	1.276	1.338	1.403
6	1.062	1.126	1.194	1.265	1.340	1.419	1.501
7	1.072	1.149	1.230	1.316	1.407	1.504	1.606
8	1.083	1.172	1.267	1.369	1.477	1.594	1.718
9	1.094	1.195	1.305	1.423	1.551	1.689	1.838
10	1.105	1.219	1.344	1.480	1.629	1.791	1.967
11	1.116	1.243	1.384	1.539	1.710	1.898	2.105
12	1.127	1.268	1.426	1.601	1.796	2.012	2.252
13	1.138	1.294	1.469	1.665	1.886	2.133	2.410
14	1.149	1.319	1.513	1.732	1.980	2.261	2.579
15	1.161	1.346	1.558	1.801	2.079	2.397	2.759
16	1.173	1.373	1.605	1.873	2.183	2.540	2.952
17	1.184	1.400	1.653	1.948	2.292	2.693	3.159
18	1.196	1.428	1.702	2.026	2.407	2.854	3.380
19	1.208	1.457	1.754	2.107	2.527	3.026	3.617
20	1.220	1.486	1.806	2.191	2.653	3.207	3.870
25	1.282	1.641	2.094	2.666	3.386	4.292	5.427
30	1.348	1.811	2.427	3.243	4.322	5.743	7.612

Year	8%	9%	10%	12%	14%	15%	16%
1	1.080	1.090	1.100	1.120	1.140	1.150	1.160
2	1.166	1.188	1.210	1.254	1.300	1.322	1.346
3	1.260	1.295	1.331	1.405	1.482	1.521	1.561
4	1.360	1.412	1.464	1.574	1.689	1.749	1.811
5	1.469	1.539	1.611	1.762	1.925	2.011	2.100
6	1.587	1.677	1.772	1.974	2.195	2.313	2.436
7	1.714	1.828	1.949	2.211	2.502	2.660	2.826
8	1.851	1.993	2.144	2.476	2.853	3.059	3.278
9	1.999	2.172	2.358	2.773	3.252	3.518	3.803
10	2.159	2.367	2.594	3.106	3.707	4.046	4.411
11	2.332	2.580	2.853	3.479	4.226	4.652	5.117
12	2.518	2.813	3.138	3.896	4.818	5.350	5.936
13	2.720	3.066	3.452	4.363	5.492	6.153	6.886
14	2.937	3.342	3.797	4.887	6.261	7.076	7.988
15	3.172	3.642	4.177	5.474	7.138	8.137	9.266
16	3.426	3.970	4.595	6.130	8.137	9.358	10.748
17	3.700	4.328	5.054	6.866	9.276	10.761	12.468
18	3.996	4.717	5.560	7.690	10.575	12.375	14.463
19	4.316	5.142	6.116	8.613	12.056	14.232	16.777
20	4.661	5.604	6.728	9.646	13.743	16.367	19.461
25	6.848	8.623	10.835	17.000	26.462	32.919	40.874
30	10.063	13.268	17.449	29.960	50.950	66.212	85.850

There are cases in which *periodic* sums are invested or received. Such periodic sums, or series of payments, are called *annuities*. Figure 4-1 shows a graphic illustration of the future value of an annuity. Notice that we are now dealing

TABLE 4-2
PRESENT VALUE OF $1

Year	1%	2%	3%	4%	5%	6%	7%	8%	9%	10%	12%	14%	15%
1	.990	.980	.971	.962	.952	.943	.935	.926	.917	.909	.893	.877	.870
2	.980	.961	.943	.925	.907	.890	.873	.857	.842	.826	.797	.769	.756
3	.971	.942	.915	.889	.864	.840	.816	.794	.772	.751	.712	.675	.658
4	.961	.924	.889	.855	.823	.792	.763	.735	.708	.683	.636	.592	.572
5	.951	.906	.863	.822	.784	.747	.713	.681	.650	.621	.567	.519	.497
6	.942	.888	.838	.790	.746	.705	.666	.630	.596	.564	.507	.456	.432
7	.933	.871	.813	.760	.711	.665	.623	.583	.547	.513	.452	.400	.376
8	.923	.853	.789	.731	.677	.627	.582	.540	.502	.467	.404	.351	.327
9	.914	.837	.766	.703	.645	.592	.544	.500	.460	.424	.361	.308	.284
10	.905	.820	.744	.676	.614	.558	.508	.463	.422	.386	.322	.270	.247
11	.896	.804	.722	.650	.585	.527	.475	.429	.388	.350	.287	.237	.215
12	.887	.788	.701	.625	.557	.497	.444	.397	.356	.319	.257	.208	.187
13	.879	.773	.681	.601	.530	.469	.415	.368	.326	.290	.229	.182	.163
14	.870	.758	.661	.577	.505	.442	.388	.340	.299	.263	.205	.160	.141
15	.861	.743	.642	.555	.481	.417	.362	.315	.275	.239	.183	.140	.123
16	.853	.728	.623	.534	.458	.394	.339	.292	.252	.218	.163	.123	.107
17	.844	.714	.605	.513	.436	.371	.317	.270	.231	.198	.146	.108	.093
18	.836	.700	.587	.494	.416	.350	.296	.250	.212	.180	.130	.095	.081
19	.828	.686	.570	.475	.396	.331	.276	.232	.194	.164	.116	.083	.070
20	.820	.673	.554	.456	.377	.312	.258	.215	.178	.149	.104	.073	.061
25	.780	.610	.478	.375	.295	.233	.184	.146	.116	.092	.059	.038	.030
30	.742	.552	.412	.308	.231	.174	.131	.099	.075	.057	.033	.020	.015

Year	16%	18%	20%	24%	28%	32%	36%	40%	50%	60%	70%	80%	90%
1	.862	.847	.833	.806	.781	.758	.735	.714	.667	.625	.588	.556	.526
2	.743	.718	.694	.650	.610	.574	.541	.510	.444	.391	.346	.309	.277
3	.641	.609	.579	.524	.477	.435	.398	.364	.296	.244	.204	.171	.146
4	.552	.516	.482	.423	.373	.329	.292	.260	.198	.153	.120	.095	.077
5	.476	.437	.402	.341	.291	.250	.215	.186	.132	.095	.070	.053	.040
6	.410	.370	.335	.275	.227	.189	.158	.133	.088	.060	.041	.029	.021
7	.354	.314	.279	.222	.178	.143	.116	.095	.059	.037	.024	.016	.011
8	.305	.266	.233	.179	.139	.108	.085	.068	.039	.023	.014	.009	.006
9	.263	.226	.194	.144	.108	.082	.063	.048	.026	.015	.008	.005	.003
10	.227	.191	.162	.116	.085	.062	.046	.035	.017	.009	.005	.003	.002
11	.195	.162	.135	.094	.066	.047	.034	.025	.012	.006	.003	.002	.001
12	.168	.137	.112	.076	.052	.036	.025	.018	.008	.004	.002	.001	.001
13	.145	.116	.093	.061	.040	.027	.018	.013	.005	.002	.001	.001	.000
14	.125	.099	.078	.049	.032	.021	.014	.009	.003	.001	.001	.000	.000
15	.108	.084	.065	.040	.025	.016	.010	.006	.002	.001	.000	.000	.000
16	.093	.071	.054	.032	.019	.012	.007	.005	.002	.001	.000	.000	
17	.080	.060	.045	.026	.015	.009	.005	.003	.001	.000	.000		
18	.069	.051	.038	.021	.012	.007	.004	.002	.001	.000	.000		
19	.060	.043	.031	.017	.009	.005	.003	.002	.000	.000			
20	.051	.037	.026	.014	.007	.004	.002	.001	.000	.000			
25	.024	.016	.010	.005	.002	.001	.000	.000					
30	.012	.007	.004	.002	.001	.000	.000						

with compound sums; early payments are compounding and then compounding again. Thus the future or terminal value of $1 deposited each year for three years (rather than once only at the beginning) at 6 percent is $3.184. Since the third payment is made at the end of the third year, it does not earn interest. In contrast, the future (compounded) value of $1 invested one time only at 6 percent will in three years equal $1(1 + .06)^3$, or $1.191.

FIGURE 4-1
GRAPHIC REPRESENTATION OF COMPOUND SUM OF ANNUITY

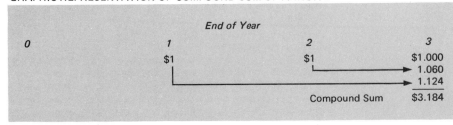

Figure 4-2 shows the present value of an annuity.[4] The present value of a series of payments of $1 received each at the end of each of the next three years at a rate of 6 percent is $2.673. This contrasts with the present value of a single payment at the end of the third year at 6 percent, which is $P = \$1/(1 + .06)^3 = \$.840$. Tables 4-3 and 4-4 show future and present values of annuities of $1 where g and n are varied.

We now have the rudiments for talking about the future or present value of a single lump-sum payment or a series of payments.

**Bond
Valuation**   The powerful tools of compounding and discounting can assist us in building a theoretical framework of valuation for bonds and stocks. Bond values are reasonably easy to determine. As long as a bond is not expected to go into

FIGURE 4-2
GRAPHIC REPRESENTATION OF PRESENT VALUE OF ANNUITY

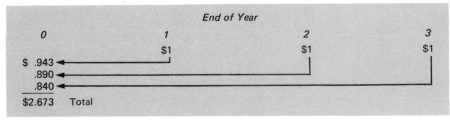

[4]The mathematically inclined will note that the future value of an annuity (sum of an annuity) is described as:

$$\frac{(1 + i)^n - 1}{i} \times \text{Amount}$$

and the present value of an annuity is described as:

$$\frac{1 - (1 + i)^{-n}}{i} \times \text{Amount}$$

TABLE 4-3

SUM OF AN ANNUITY OF $1 FOR *N* YEARS

Year	1%	2%	3%	4%	5%	6%
1	1.000	1.000	1.000	1.000	1.000	1.000
2	2.010	2.020	2.030	2.040	2.050	2.060
3	3.030	3.060	3.091	3.122	3.152	3.184
4	4.060	4.122	4.184	4.246	4.310	4.375
5	5.101	5.204	5.309	5.416	5.526	5.637
6	6.152	6.308	6.468	6.633	6.802	6.975
7	7.214	7.434	7.662	7.898	8.142	8.394
8	8.286	8.583	8.892	9.214	9.549	9.897
9	9.369	9.755	10.159	10.583	11.027	11.491
10	10.462	10.950	11.464	12.006	12.578	13.181
11	11.567	12.169	12.808	13.486	14.207	14.972
12	12.683	13.412	14.192	15.026	15.917	16.870
13	13.809	14.680	15.618	16.627	17.713	18.882
14	14.947	15.974	17.086	18.292	19.599	21.051
15	16.097	17.293	18.599	20.024	21.579	23.276
16	17.258	18.639	20.157	21.825	23.657	25.673
17	18.430	20.012	21.762	23.698	25.840	28.213
18	19.615	21.412	23.414	25.645	28.132	30.906
19	20.811	22.841	25.117	27.671	30.539	33.760
20	22.019	24.297	26.870	29.778	33.066	36.786
25	28.243	32.030	36.459	41.646	47.727	54.865
30	34.785	40.568	47.575	56.085	66.439	79.058

Year	7%	8%	9%	10%	12%	14%
1	1.000	1.000	1.000	1.000	1.000	1.000
2	2.070	2.080	2.090	2.100	2.120	2.140
3	3.215	3.246	3.278	3.310	3.374	3.440
4	4.440	4.506	4.573	4.641	4.770	4.921
5	5.751	5.867	5.985	6.105	6.353	6.610
6	7.153	7.336	7.523	7.716	8.115	8.536
7	8.654	8.923	9.200	9.487	10.089	10.730
8	10.260	10.637	11.028	11.436	12.300	13.233
9	11.978	12.488	13.021	13.579	14.776	16.085
10	13.816	14.487	15.193	15.937	17.549	19.337
11	15.784	16.645	17.560	18.531	20.655	23.044
12	17.888	18.977	20.141	21.384	24.133	27.271
13	20.141	21.495	22.953	24.523	28.029	32.089
14	22.550	24.215	26.019	27.975	32.393	37.581
15	25.129	27.152	29.361	31.772	37.280	43.842
16	27.888	30.324	33.003	35.950	42.753	50.980
17	30.840	33.750	36.974	40.545	48.884	59.118
18	33.999	37.450	41.301	45.599	55.750	68.394
19	37.379	41.446	46.018	51.159	63.440	78.969
20	40.995	45.762	51.160	57.275	72.052	91.025
25	63.249	73.106	84.701	98.347	133.334	181.871
30	94.461	113.283	136.308	164.494	241.333	356.787

default, the expected return is made up of annual interest payments plus the principal amount to be recovered at maturity or sooner.

Let us take an example of a five-year bond with a principal value of $1,000,

TABLE 4-4
PRESENT VALUE OF AN ANNUITY OF $1

Year	1%	2%	3%	4%	5%	6%	7%	8%	9%	10%
1	0.990	0.980	0.971	0.962	0.952	0.943	0.935	0.926	0.917	0.909
2	1.970	1.942	1.913	1.886	1.859	1.833	1.808	1.783	1.759	1.736
3	2.941	2.884	2.829	2.775	2.723	2.673	2.624	2.577	2.531	2.487
4	3.902	3.808	3.717	3.630	3.546	3.465	3.387	3.312	3.240	3.170
5	4.853	4.713	4.580	4.452	4.329	4.212	4.100	3.993	3.890	3.791
6	5.795	5.601	5.417	5.242	5.076	4.917	4.766	4.623	4.486	4.355
7	6.728	6.472	6.230	6.002	5.786	5.582	5.389	5.206	5.033	4.868
8	7.652	7.325	7.020	6.733	6.463	6.210	5.971	5.747	5.535	5.335
9	8.566	8.162	7.786	7.435	7.108	6.802	6.515	6.247	5.985	5.759
10	9.471	8.983	8.530	8.111	7.722	7.360	7.024	6.710	6.418	6.145
11	10.368	9.787	9.253	8.760	8.306	7.887	7.499	7.139	6.805	6.495
12	11.255	10.575	9.954	9.385	8.863	8.384	7.943	7.536	7.161	6.814
13	12.134	11.348	10.635	9.986	9.394	8.853	8.358	7.904	7.487	7.103
14	13.004	12.106	11.296	10.563	9.899	9.295	8.745	8.244	7.786	7.367
15	13.865	12.849	11.938	11.118	10.380	9.712	9.108	8.559	8.060	7.606
16	14.718	13.578	12.561	11.652	10.838	10.106	9.447	8.851	8.312	7.824
17	15.562	14.292	13.166	12.166	11.274	10.477	9.763	9.122	8.544	8.022
18	16.398	14.992	13.754	12.659	11.690	10.828	10.059	9.372	8.756	8.201
19	17.226	15.678	14.324	13.134	12.085	11.158	10.336	9.604	8.950	8.365
20	18.046	16.351	14.877	13.590	12.462	11.470	10.594	9.818	9.128	8.514
25	22.023	19.523	17.413	15.622	14.094	12.783	11.654	10.675	9.823	9.077
30	25.808	22.397	19.600	17.292	15.373	13.765	12.409	11.258	10.274	9.427

Year	12%	14%	16%	18%	20%	24%	28%	32%	36%
1	0.893	0.877	0.862	0.847	0.833	0.806	0.781	0.758	0.735
2	1.690	1.647	1.605	1.566	1.528	1.457	1.392	1.332	1.276
3	2.402	2.322	2.246	2.174	2.106	1.981	1.868	1.766	1.674
4	3.037	2.914	2.798	2.690	2.589	2.404	2.241	2.096	1.966
5	3.605	3.433	3.274	3.127	2.991	2.745	2.532	2.345	2.181
6	4.111	3.889	3.685	3.498	3.326	3.020	2.759	2.534	2.339
7	4.564	4.288	4.039	3.812	3.605	3.242	2.937	2.678	2.455
8	4.968	4.639	4.344	4.078	3.837	3.421	3.076	2.786	2.540
9	5.328	4.946	4.607	4.303	4.031	3.566	3.184	2.868	2.603
10	5.650	5.216	4.833	4.494	4.193	3.682	3.269	2.930	2.650
11	5.938	5.453	5.029	4.656	4.327	3.776	3.335	2.978	2.683
12	6.194	5.660	5.197	4.793	4.439	3.851	3.387	3.013	2.708
13	6.424	5.842	5.342	4.910	4.533	3.912	3.427	3.040	2.727
14	6.628	6.002	5.468	5.008	4.611	3.962	3.459	3.061	2.740
15	6.811	6.142	5.575	5.092	4.675	4.001	3.483	3.076	2.750
16	6.974	6.265	5.669	5.162	4.730	4.033	3.503	3.088	2.758
17	7.120	6.373	5.749	4.222	4.775	4.059	3.518	3.097	2.763
18	7.250	6.467	5.818	5.273	4.812	4.080	3.529	3.104	2.767
19	7.366	6.550	5.877	5.316	4.844	4.097	3.539	3.109	2.770
20	7.469	6.623	5.929	5.353	4.870	4.110	3.546	3.113	2.772
25	7.843	6.873	6.097	5.467	4.948	4.147	3.564	3.122	2.776
30	8.055	7.003	6.177	5.517	4.979	4.160	3.569	3.124	2.778

bearing a nominal rate of interest (coupon) of 8 percent. Our concepts of present value of a single sum and of a series of payments can assist us in determining the value of the bond. Let us assume that the investor wishes to purchase this bond for a required rate of 8 percent. What should he be willing to pay for a series of five $80 interest payments (annuity) and a single sum of $1,000 at the end of the fifth year?

The present value of the interest-payment stream of $80 per year for five years is as follows:

$$P = \frac{\$80}{(1 + .08)} + \frac{\$80}{(1 + .08)^2} + \frac{\$80}{(1 + .08)^3} + \frac{\$80}{(1 + .08)^4} + \frac{\$80}{(1 + .08)^5} = \$319$$

The present value of the principal at maturity (end of year 5) is $1,000/(1 + .08)^5 = \$681$. Thus the total value of the bond is $319 + $681, or $1,000. In other words, a $1,000 bond is worth $1,000 today if the nominal rate and the required rate of interest are equal. The $1,000 value is a composite of $319 of interest payments and $681 of principal.

In general, the value of a bond can be determined from:

$$V = \left(\sum_{n=1}^{N} \frac{I_n}{(1 + i)^n} \right) + \frac{P_N}{(1 + i)^N} \tag{4.3}$$

where

V = value of bond
I = annual interest ($)
i = required rate of interest (%)
P = principal value at maturity
N = number of years to maturity

It is easy to see that while bonds carry a promise to maintain a constant dollar interest payment to maturity, I, and pay a fixed principal at maturity, P, the number of years to maturity, N, and the required rate of interest, i, can vary.

Table 4-5 contains extracts from a book of bond tables. Bond-yield tables are used by analysts to determine exact yield or return, according to Equation 4.3. The tables are constructed for a given coupon rate—in this case, 6 percent—and indicate the return corresponding to particular combinations of time to maturity and coupon rate. From the table, one can determine a bond's value, or the price (V) necessary to achieve a particular required return (i), or, given a price in the market, the associated return.

For example, a required rate of return of 8% for a five year, 6 percent, $1,000 bond suggests a price of 92.[5] Using the table of present values to solve for the price of 92:

$$V = \frac{\$60}{(1 + .08)} + \frac{\$60}{(1 + .08)^2} + \frac{\$60}{(1 + .08)^3} + \frac{\$60}{(1 + .08)^4} + \frac{\$60}{(1 + .08)^5} + \frac{\$1000}{(1 + .08)^5}$$

$$= \$55.56 + \$51.42 + \$47.64 + \$44.10 + \$40.86 + \$681.00$$

$$= \$920.58$$

[5]92 means 92% of par. For a $1,000 par bond, price is thus $920.

TABLE 4-5
TABLES OF BOND YIELDS

6%   **6%**

MATURITY PRICE	1/4 YEAR	1/2 YEAR	3/4 YEAR	1 YEAR	1 1/4 YEARS	1 1/2 YEARS	1 3/4 YEARS	2 YEARS
85	76.30	42.35	29.67	23.72	20.13	17.83	16.16	14.95
85 1/2	73.56	40.94	28.77	23.05	19.60	17.39	15.78	14.62
86	70.86	39.53	27.88	22.39	19.08	16.96	15.41	14.29
86 1/2	68.18	38.15	26.99	21.74	18.56	16.53	15.04	13.97
87	65.54	36.78	26.12	21.09	18.05	16.10	14.67	13.65
87 1/2	62.92	35.43	25.25	20.45	17.54	15.67	14.31	13.32
88	60.34	34.09	24.40	19.81	17.03	15.25	13.95	13.01
88 1/2	57.78	32.77	23.55	19.18	16.53	14.83	13.59	12.69
89	55.25	31.46	22.71	18.55	16.03	14.41	13.23	12.38
89 1/2	52.75	30.17	21.87	17.93	15.54	14.00	12.88	12.06
90	50.27	28.89	21.05	17.32	15.05	13.59	12.52	11.76
90 1/2	47.83	27.62	20.23	16.71	14.56	13.19	12.18	11.45
91	45.41	26.37	19.42	16.10	14.08	12.78	11.83	11.14
91 1/2	43.01	25.14	18.61	15.50	13.60	12.38	11.49	10.84
92	40.64	23.91	17.82	14.91.	13.13	11.98	11.14	10.54
92 1/2	38.30	22.70	17.03	14.31	12.65	11.59	10.81	10.24
93	35.98	21.51	16.24	13.73	12.19	11.20	10.47	9.95
93 1/2	33.68	20.32	15.47	13.15	11.72	10.81	10.13	9.65
94	31.41	19.15	14.70	12.57	11.26	10.42	9.80	9.36
94 1/2	29.17	17.99	13.94	12.00	10.80	10.04	9.47	9.07
95	26.94	16.84	13.18	11.43	10.35	9.66	9.15	8.78
95 1/4	25.84	16.27	12.81	11.15	10.12	9.47	8.98	8.64
95 1/2	24.74	15.71	12.44	10.87	9.90	9.28	8.82	8.49
95 3/4	23.65	15.14	12.06	10.59	9.68	9.09	8.66	8.35
96	22.56	14.58	11.69	10.31	9.45	8.91	8.50	8.21
96 1/4	21.48	14.03	11.33	10.03	9.23	8.72	8.34	8.07
96 1/2	20.41	13.47	10.96	9.76	9.01	8.54	8.18	7.93
96 3/4	19.34	12.92	10.59	9.48	8.79	8.35	8.02	7.79
97	18.27	12.37	10.23	9.21	8.57	8.17	7.86	7.65
97 1/4	17.22	11.83	9.87	8.94	8.35	7.98	7.70	7.51
97 1/2	16.16	11.28	9.51	8.66	8.13	7.80	7.54	7.37
97 3/4	15.11	10.74	9.15	8.39	7.91	7.62	7.39	7.23
98	14.07	10.20	8.79	8.12	7.70	7.43	7.23	7.09
98 1/4	13.03	9.67	8.44	7.85	7.48	7.25	7.07	6.95
98 1/2	12.00	9.14	8.08	7.59	7.27	7.07	6.92	6.81
98 3/4	10.97	8.61	7.73	7.32	7.05	6.89	6.76	6.68
99	9.95	8.08	7.38	7.05	6.84	6.71	6.61	6.54
99 1/4	8.93	7.56	7.03	6.79	6.62	6.53	6.45	6.41
99 1/2	7.92	7.04	6.68	6.52	6.41	6.35	6.30	6.27
99 3/4	6.91	6.52	6.33	6.26	6.20	6.18	6.15	6.13
100	5.91	6.00	5.98	6.00	5.99	6.00	5.99	6.00
100 1/4	4.91	5.49	5.64	5.74	5.78	5.82	5.84	5.87
100 1/2	3.92	4.98	5.30	5.48	5.57	5.65	5.69	5.73
100 3/4	2.93	4.47	4.96	5.22	5.36	5.47	5.54	5.60
101	1.95	3.96	4.62	4.96	5.16	5.30	5.39	5.47
101 1/2		2.96	3.94	4.45	4.74	4.95	5.09	5.20
102		1.96	3.27	3.94	4.33	4.60	4.79	4.94
102 1/2		.98	2.61	3.44	3.92	4.26	4.49	4.68
103			1.95	2.93	3.52	3.92	4.20	4.42
103 1/2			1.29	2.44	3.12	3.58	3.91	4.16
104			.64	1.94	2.72	3.25	3.62	3.90
104 1/2			.00	1.45	2.32	2.91	3.33	3.65
105				.96	1.93	2.58	3.04	3.39
105 1/2				.48	1.54	2.25	2.76	3.14
106				.00	1.15	1.92	2.47	2.89

MATURITY PRICE	2 1/4 YEARS	2 1/2 YEARS	2 3/4 YEARS	3 YEARS	3 1/2 YEARS	4 YEARS	4 1/2 YEARS	5 YEARS
75	20.38	19.03	17.89	16.98	15.53	14.45	13.61	12.95
76	19.69	18.41	17.32	16.45	15.07	14.05	13.25	12.62
77	19.02	17.79	16.77	15.94	14.63	13.65	12.90	12.29
78	18.35	17.19	16.22	15.44	14.19	13.26	12.55	11.97
79	17.70	16.60	15.68	14.94	13.76	12.88	12.20	11.66
80	17.06	16.02	15.15	14.45	13.34	12.51	11.86	11.35
81	16.42	15.45	14.63	13.97	12.92	12.14	11.53	11.05
82	15.80	14.88	14.11	13.49	12.51	11.77	11.20	10.75
83	15.19	14.33	13.60	13.03	12.10	11.41	10.88	10.45
84	14.58	13.78	13.11	12.57	11.70	11.06	10.56	10.16
85	13.99	13.24	12.61	12.11	11.31	10.71	10.24	9.87
86	13.40	12.71	12.13	11.66	10.92	10.36	9.93	9.59
87	12.82	12.19	11.65	11.22	10.54	10.02	9.63	9.31
88	12.25	11.67	11.18	10.79	10.16	9.69	9.33	9.04
89	11.69	11.16	10.72	10.36	9.79	9.36	9.03	8.76
90	11.14	10.66	10.26	9.94	9.42	9.03	8.74	8.50
90 1/2	10.86	10.41	10.03	9.73	9.24	8.87	8.59	8.36
91	10.59	10.17	9.81	9.52	9.06	8.71	8.45	8.23
91 1/2	10.32	9.92	9.58	9.31	8.88	8.55	8.30	8.10
92	10.05	9.68	9.36	9.11	8.70	8.40	8.16	7.97
92 1/2	9.79	9.44	9.14	8.90	8.52	8.24	8.02	7.84
93	9.52	9.20	8.92	8.70	8.35	8.08	7.88	7.71
93 1/2	9.26	8.96	8.70	8.50	8.17	7.93	7.74	7.59
94	9.00	8.72	8.49	8.30	8.00	7.77	7.60	7.46
94 1/2	8.74	8.49	8.27	8.10	7.83	7.62	7.46	7.33
95	8.48	8.25	8.06	7.90	7.66	7.47	7.32	7.21
95 1/4	8.35	8.14	7.95	7.81	7.57	7.39	7.26	7.15
95 1/2	8.22	8.02	7.85	7.71	7.49	7.32	7.19	7.08
95 3/4	8.10	7.91	7.74	7.61	7.40	7.24	7.12	7.02
96	7.97	7.79	7.63	7.51	7.32	7.17	7.05	6.96
96 1/4	7.84	7.68	7.53	7.42	7.23	7.09	6.99	6.90
96 1/2	7.72	7.56	7.42	7.32	7.15	7.02	6.92	6.84
96 3/4	7.59	7.45	7.32	7.22	7.06	6.94	6.85	6.78
97	7.47	7.34	7.22	7.13	6.98	6.87	6.78	6.72
97 1/4	7.34	7.22	7.11	7.03	6.90	6.80	6.72	6.66
97 1/2	7.22	7.11	7.01	6.94	6.81	6.72	6.65	6.60
97 3/4	7.09	7.00	6.91	6.84	6.73	6.65	6.59	6.53
98	6.97	6.88	6.80	6.75	6.65	6.58	6.52	6.47
98 1/4	6.85	6.77	6.70	6.65	6.57	6.50	6.45	6.41
98 1/2	6.72	6.66	6.60	6.56	6.49	6.43	6.39	6.35
98 3/4	6.60	6.55	6.50	6.47	6.40	6.36	6.32	6.30
99	6.48	6.44	6.40	6.37	6.32	6.29	6.26	6.24
99 1/4	6.36	6.33	6.30	6.28	6.24	6.21	6.19	6.18
99 1/2	6.24	6.22	6.20	6.19	6.16	6.14	6.13	6.12
99 3/4	6.12	6.11	6.10	6.09	6.08	6.07	6.06	6.06
100	5.99	6.00	6.00	6.00	6.00	6.00	6.00	6.00
100 1/4	5.87	5.89	5.90	5.91	5.92	5.93	5.94	5.94
100 1/2	5.75	5.78	5.80	5.82	5.84	5.86	5.87	5.88
100 3/4	5.64	5.67	5.70	5.72	5.76	5.79	5.81	5.82
101	5.52	5.57	5.60	5.63	5.68	5.72	5.74	5.77
102	5.04	5.14	5.21	5.27	5.37	5.44	5.49	5.54
103	4.58	4.71	4.82	4.91	5.05	5.16	5.24	5.31
104	4.12	4.30	4.44	4.56	4.75	4.89	5.00	5.08
105	3.66	3.88	4.06	4.21	4.44	4.62	4.75	4.86
106	3.21	3.47	3.68	3.86	4.14	4.35	4.51	4.64

Since the $60 interest payments are similar to a five-year *annuity*, and the principal value of the bond at maturity is a *single sum*, we can see that bond tables are themselves built by using Tables 4-2 and 4-4. Thus:

Present value of single sum of $1,000 principal received at the end of five years
at 8% (Table 4-2) = $1,000 (.681) = $681.00

Present value of annuity of $60 per year for five years at 8% (Table 4-4)
= $60 (3.993) = $239.58

Present value of bond $920.58

The same 8 percent required return for a 25-year maturity suggests a price of

TABLE 4-5 (cont.)

6%

MATURITY PRICE	13½ YEARS	14 YEARS	14½ YEARS	15 YEARS	16 YEARS	17 YEARS	18 YEARS	19 YEARS
75	9.29	9.21	9.15	9.08	8.97	8.88	8.79	8.72
76	9.13	9.06	9.00	8.94	8.83	8.74	8.65	8.58
77	8.97	8.91	8.85	8.79	8.69	8.60	8.52	8.45
78	8.82	8.76	8.70	8.65	8.55	8.46	8.39	8.33
79	8.67	8.61	8.55	8.50	8.41	8.33	8.26	8.20
80	8.52	8.47	8.41	8.36	8.28	8.20	8.14	8.08
81	8.38	8.32	8.27	8.23	8.15	8.07	8.01	7.96
82	8.23	8.18	8.14	8.09	8.02	7.95	7.89	7.84
83	8.09	8.05	8.00	7.96	7.89	7.83	7.77	7.72
84	7.95	7.91	7.87	7.83	7.76	7.70	7.65	7.61
85	7.82	7.78	7.74	7.70	7.64	7.58	7.54	7.49
86	7.68	7.65	7.61	7.58	7.52	7.47	7.42	7.38
87	7.55	7.52	7.48	7.45	7.40	7.35	7.31	7.27
88	7.42	7.39	7.36	7.33	7.28	7.24	7.20	7.17
89	7.29	7.26	7.24	7.21	7.17	7.13	7.09	7.06
90	7.17	7.14	7.12	7.09	7.05	7.02	6.98	6.96
90½	7.11	7.08	7.06	7.04	7.00	6.96	6.93	6.91
91	7.04	7.02	7.00	6.98	6.94	6.91	6.88	6.85
91½	6.98	6.96	6.94	6.92	6.88	6.85	6.83	6.80
92	6.92	6.90	6.88	6.86	6.83	6.80	6.78	6.75
92½	6.86	6.84	6.82	6.81	6.78	6.75	6.72	6.70
93	6.80	6.78	6.77	6.75	6.72	6.70	6.67	6.65
93½	6.74	6.72	6.71	6.69	6.67	6.64	6.62	6.61
94	6.68	6.67	6.65	6.64	6.61	6.59	6.57	6.56
94½	6.62	6.61	6.59	6.58	6.56	6.54	6.52	6.51
95	6.56	6.55	6.54	6.53	6.51	6.49	6.47	6.46
95¼	6.53	6.52	6.51	6.50	6.48	6.46	6.45	6.44
95½	6.51	6.49	6.48	6.47	6.46	6.44	6.43	6.41
95¾	6.48	6.47	6.46	6.45	6.43	6.41	6.40	6.39
96	6.45	6.44	6.43	6.42	6.40	6.39	6.38	6.37
96¼	6.42	6.41	6.40	6.39	6.38	6.36	6.35	6.34
96½	6.39	6.38	6.37	6.37	6.35	6.34	6.33	6.32
96¾	6.36	6.35	6.35	6.34	6.33	6.31	6.30	6.30
97	6.33	6.33	6.32	6.31	6.30	6.29	6.28	6.27
97¼	6.31	6.30	6.29	6.29	6.27	6.27	6.26	6.25
97½	6.28	6.27	6.26	6.26	6.25	6.24	6.23	6.23
97¾	6.25	6.24	6.24	6.23	6.22	6.22	6.21	6.20
98	6.22	6.22	6.21	6.21	6.20	6.19	6.19	6.18
98¼	6.19	6.19	6.18	6.18	6.17	6.17	6.16	6.16
98½	6.17	6.16	6.16	6.16	6.15	6.14	6.14	6.13
98¾	6.14	6.13	6.13	6.13	6.12	6.12	6.12	6.11
99	6.11	6.11	6.10	6.10	6.10	6.10	6.09	6.09
99¼	6.08	6.08	6.08	6.08	6.07	6.07	6.07	6.07
99½	6.05	6.05	6.05	6.05	6.05	6.05	6.05	6.04
99¾	6.03	6.03	6.03	6.03	6.02	6.02	6.02	6.02
100	6.00	6.00	6.00	6.00	6.00	6.00	6.00	6.00
100¼	5.97	5.97	5.97	5.97	5.98	5.98	5.98	5.98
100½	5.95	5.95	5.95	5.95	5.95	5.95	5.95	5.96
100¾	5.92	5.92	5.92	5.92	5.93	5.93	5.93	5.93
101	5.89	5.89	5.90	5.90	5.90	5.90	5.91	5.91
102	5.78	5.79	5.79	5.80	5.81	5.81	5.82	5.82
103	5.68	5.69	5.69	5.70	5.71	5.72	5.73	5.74
104	5.57	5.58	5.59	5.60	5.62	5.63	5.64	5.65
105	5.47	5.48	5.50	5.51	5.53	5.54	5.56	5.57
106	5.37	5.38	5.40	5.41	5.43	5.45	5.47	5.49

6%

MATURITY PRICE	20 YEARS	21 YEARS	22 YEARS	23 YEARS	24 YEARS	25 YEARS	30 YEARS	CURRENT YIELD
75	8.65	8.59	8.54	8.49	8.45	8.41	8.27	8.00
76	8.52	8.46	8.41	8.37	8.33	8.29	8.15	7.89
77	8.39	8.34	8.29	8.25	8.21	8.17	8.04	7.79
78	8.27	8.22	8.17	8.13	8.09	8.06	7.93	7.69
79	8.14	8.10	8.05	8.01	7.98	7.95	7.83	7.59
80	8.02	7.98	7.94	7.90	7.87	7.84	7.72	7.50
81	7.91	7.86	7.82	7.79	7.76	7.73	7.62	7.41
82	7.79	7.75	7.71	7.68	7.65	7.62	7.52	7.32
83	7.68	7.64	7.60	7.57	7.54	7.52	7.42	7.23
84	7.56	7.53	7.50	7.47	7.44	7.42	7.33	7.14
85	7.45	7.42	7.39	7.36	7.34	7.32	7.23	7.06
86	7.35	7.31	7.29	7.26	7.24	7.22	7.14	6.98
87	7.24	7.21	7.18	7.16	7.14	7.12	7.05	6.90
88	7.14	7.11	7.08	7.06	7.04	7.03	6.96	6.82
89	7.03	7.01	6.99	6.97	6.95	6.93	6.87	6.74
90	6.93	6.91	6.89	6.87	6.86	6.84	6.78	6.67
90½	6.88	6.86	6.84	6.82	6.81	6.80	6.74	6.63
91	6.83	6.81	6.79	6.78	6.76	6.75	6.70	6.59
91½	6.78	6.76	6.75	6.73	6.72	6.71	6.66	6.56
92	6.73	6.72	6.70	6.69	6.67	6.66	6.62	6.52
92½	6.69	6.67	6.65	6.64	6.63	6.62	6.58	6.49
93	6.64	6.62	6.61	6.60	6.58	6.57	6.54	6.45
93½	6.59	6.58	6.56	6.55	6.54	6.53	6.49	6.42
94	6.54	6.53	6.52	6.51	6.50	6.49	6.45	6.38
94½	6.50	6.48	6.47	6.46	6.45	6.45	6.42	6.35
95	6.45	6.44	6.43	6.42	6.41	6.40	6.38	6.32
95¼	6.43	6.41	6.41	6.40	6.39	6.38	6.36	6.30
95½	6.40	6.39	6.38	6.38	6.37	6.36	6.34	6.28
95¾	6.38	6.37	6.36	6.35	6.35	6.34	6.32	6.27
96	6.36	6.35	6.34	6.33	6.33	6.32	6.30	6.25
96¼	6.33	6.33	6.32	6.31	6.31	6.30	6.28	6.23
96½	6.31	6.30	6.30	6.29	6.28	6.28	6.26	6.22
96¾	6.29	6.28	6.27	6.27	6.26	6.26	6.24	6.20
97	6.27	6.26	6.25	6.25	6.24	6.24	6.22	6.19
97¼	6.24	6.24	6.23	6.23	6.22	6.22	6.20	6.17
97½	6.22	6.21	6.21	6.21	6.20	6.20	6.18	6.15
97¾	6.20	6.19	6.19	6.18	6.18	6.18	6.17	6.14
98	6.18	6.17	6.17	6.16	6.16	6.16	6.15	6.12
98¼	6.15	6.15	6.15	6.14	6.14	6.14	6.13	6.11
98½	6.13	6.13	6.13	6.12	6.12	6.12	6.11	6.09
98¾	6.11	6.11	6.10	6.10	6.10	6.10	6.09	6.08
99	6.09	6.08	6.08	6.08	6.08	6.08	6.07	6.06
99¼	6.07	6.06	6.06	6.06	6.06	6.06	6.05	6.05
99½	6.04	6.04	6.04	6.04	6.04	6.04	6.04	6.03
99¾	6.02	6.02	6.02	6.02	6.02	6.02	6.02	6.02
100	6.00	6.00	6.00	6.00	6.00	6.00	6.00	6.00
100¼	5.98	5.98	5.98	5.98	5.98	5.98	5.98	5.99
100½	5.96	5.96	5.96	5.96	5.96	5.96	5.96	5.97
100¾	5.94	5.94	5.94	5.94	5.94	5.94	5.95	5.96
101	5.91	5.92	5.92	5.92	5.92	5.92	5.93	5.94
102	5.83	5.83	5.84	5.84	5.84	5.85	5.86	5.88
103	5.75	5.75	5.76	5.76	5.77	5.77	5.79	5.83
104	5.66	5.67	5.68	5.69	5.69	5.70	5.72	5.77
105	5.58	5.59	5.60	5.61	5.62	5.63	5.65	5.71
106	5.50	5.51	5.53	5.54	5.54	5.55	5.59	5.66

Source: *Bond Yield Tables*, publication no. 254 (Boston: Financial Publishing Co., copyright 1971), pp. 52-53.

between 78 and 79. An appreciation for the availability of these tables develops quickly when one attempts the long way of calculation for a bond with a long maturity.

Figure 4-3 shows the sensitivity of maturity to changes in the required rate of interest. The long-term bond is a 6 percent perpetuity;[6] the short-term bond is a five-year, 6 percent issue (see Table 4-5). Notice that the longer the maturity of a bond, the greater its price change relative to a given change in the required rate of interest. This differential response between long- and short-term bonds always

[6] A perpetuity is a bond that never matures. Such a bond pays interest indefinitely.

holds true. Historically, short-term interest rates have fluctuated more frequently and to a greater magnitude than long-term rates; however, Figure 4-3 suggests that long-term bond prices fluctuate to a greater extent than do short-term bond prices.

FIGURE 4-3
VALUE OF LONG-TERM AND SHORT-TERM BOND AT VARYING
INTEREST RATES

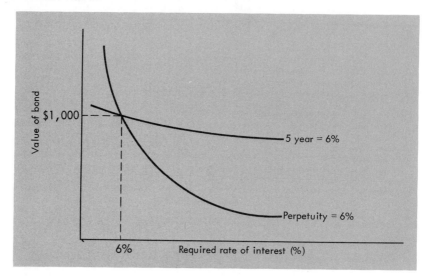

Preferred-
Stock
Valuation

When the term to maturity approaches infinity, as it would in the case of a perpetuity (a security that never matures), interest is paid indefinitely. Equation (4.3) becomes:

$$V = \frac{I}{i} \tag{4.4}$$

Since most preferred stocks entitle their owners to regular fixed dividends similar to interest payments, they are in fact like perpetuities. Although preferreds are often retired, this is not the usual case. The value of a preferred stock can thus be thought of in terms of Equation 4.4, where $I = D$, D signifying annual dividend payments rather than interest payments. Suppose a preferred stock paying annual dividends of $6 was sold in 1955. This preferred today, given market conditions, should be yielding 10 percent. What is it worth today?

$$V = \frac{D}{i}$$

$$= \frac{\$6}{.10} = \$60$$

The absence of a maturity in preferred stock lends perpetuity aspects to this security form. The result is greater value or price fluctuation in preferreds vis-à-vis bonds as a class.

Substituting price in the market for value, it is possible to determine the yield or return. Assume that a $6 preferred stock is selling in the market for $75. The yield or return is:

$$\$75 = \frac{\$6}{i}$$

$$.080 = i$$

Thus, given the annual income flow, it is possible to determine value given the required yield or return; or it is possible to determine the yield or return given the market price.

Common-Stock Valuation

The use of present-value theory by bond and preferred-stock investors is well established. The valuation task is relatively straightforward, because benefits are generally constant and reasonably certain. Perpetuities, or infinite life securities with constant dividend receipts, are the normal case in dealing with straight preferred stock. Bonds represent constant income flows with a finite, measurable life.

Common-stock valuation is different, because earnings and dividend streams are uncertain as to the timing of receipt and the amount of the dividend. The value of a common stock at any moment in time can be thought of as the discounted value of a series of uncertain future dividends that may grow or decline at varying rates over time. The more theoretical present-value approach to common-stock valuation will be compared with the more traditional and pragmatic capitalization or multiplier approach in the next several sections.

PRESENT-VALUE APPROACH

One-Year Holding Period

It is easiest to start with common-stock valuation where the expected holding period is one year. The benefits any investor receives from holding a common stock consist of dividends plus any change in price during the holding period. Suppose we buy one share of the Olsen Co. at the beginning of the year for $25. We hold the stock for one year. One dollar in dividends is collected, and the share is sold for $26.50. The rate of return achieved is the composite of dividend yield and change in price (capital gains yield). Thus, we get:

$$\text{Dividend yield} = \frac{D}{P} = \frac{\$1}{\$25} = .04$$

$$\text{Capital gains yield} = \frac{(\$26.50 - \$25.00)}{\$25} = .06$$

The total rate of return achieved is .04 + .06 = .10, or 10 percent. How might we express this same notion in terms of present values?[7] Thus:

$$V_0 = \frac{D_1}{(1+r)} + \frac{P_1}{(1+r)} \tag{4.5}$$

where:

V_0 = value of stock today (0)
D_1 = dividend to be received at the end of year 1
r = investor's required rate of return or discount
P_1 = selling price at the end of year 1

Therefore:

$$\$25 = \frac{\$1.00}{(1+r)} + \frac{\$26.50}{(1+r)}$$

Will r = .10 balance the equation? At a required rate of return of 10 percent, the dividend is worth $0.909 today (see Table 4-2);[8] the selling price has a present value of $24.091 ($26.50 × .909). The combined present value is $.909 + $24.091 = $25.00.

Should a rate of return of 15 percent have been required, the purchase price would have been too high at $25. (The $1 dividend is assumed fixed, and the selling price of $26.50 remains constant.) To achieve a 15 percent return, the value of the stock at the *beginning* of the year would have had to be:

$$V_0 = \frac{\$1.00}{(1+.15)} + \frac{\$26.50}{(1+.15)}$$

$$= \$0.87 + \$23.04$$

$$= \$23.91$$

An alternative approach would be to ask the question, At what price must we be able to sell the stock at the *end* of one year (if the purchase price is $25 and the dividend is $1) in order to attain a rate of return of 15 percent?

---

[7]Present-value models of stock price determination have a long and abundant history in the literature, from the early thoughts of J. B. Williams, *The Theory of Investment Value* (Amsterdam: North Holland Publishing Company, 1964), to an excellent and critical summary by Michael Keenan, "The State of the Finance Field Methodology Models of Equity Valuation: The Great SERM Bubble,"*Journal of Finance*, 25, No. 2 May (1970), 243-73.

[8]Dividends are generally received quarterly. Our example assumes receipt once each year, at the end of the year.

$$\$25 = \frac{\$1.00}{(1 + .15)} + \frac{P_1}{(1 + .15)}$$

$$\$25 = \$0.87 + .87P_1$$

$$\$24.13 = .87P_1$$

$$\$27.74 = P_1 \text{ (selling price)}$$

Multiple-Year Holding Period

Consider holding a share of the Olsen Co. for five years. In most cases the dividend will grow from year to year. To look at some results, let us stipulate the following:

g = annual expected growth in earnings, dividends and price = 6%
e_0 = most recent earnings per share = $1.89
d/e = dividend payout (%) = 50%
r = required rate of return = 10%
P = price per share
P/E = price-earnings ratio = 12.5
T = holding period in years

Given these stipulations, the present value of a share of stock can be determined by solving the following equation:

$$P = \left(\sum_{t=1}^{T} \frac{[(e_0)(d/e)] \, (1 + g)^t}{(1 + r)^t} \right) + \left(\frac{(P/E)[(e_0)(1 + g)^T]}{(1 + r)^T} \right) \tag{4.6}$$

This imposing formula says, "Sum the present value of all dividends to be received over the holding period, and add this to the present value of the selling price of the stock at the end of the holding period to arrive at the present value of the stock."

Let us write out the string of appropriate numbers. Since the current earnings per share (e_0) are $1.89 and the dividend payout (d/e) is 50 percent, the most recent dividend per share is e_0 times d/e, or $1.89 times 50 percent, or $.943. This was stipulated in the beginning of the problem. After one year, the dividend is expected to be $.943 times $(1 + g)^1$, where $g = .06$. So the first year's dividend will be $1. The process is repeated for years 1 through 5 as follows:

Dividend Year 1	Dividend Year 2	Dividend Year 3	Dividend Year 4	Dividend Year 5
$.943(1.06)^1$	$.943(1.06)^2$	$9.43(1.06)^3$	$.943(1.06)^4$	$.943(1.06)^5$
$1.00	$1.06	$1.12	$1.19	$1.26

The values of $(1.06)^t$ are found conveniently in Table 4-1. The next step is to discount each dividend at the required rate of return of 10 percent. Thus:

$$\frac{\$1.00}{(1.10)^1} + \frac{\$1.06}{(1.10)^2} + \frac{\$1.12}{(1.10)^3} + \frac{\$1.19}{(1.10)^4} + \frac{\$1.26}{(1.10)^5}$$

The values for the string $(1.10)^t$ can also be found in Table 4-1. The string of fractions reduces to:

$$\frac{\$1.00}{1.10} + \frac{\$1.06}{1.21} + \frac{\$1.12}{1.333} + \frac{\$1.19}{1.464} + \frac{\$1.26}{1.611}$$

The sum of the numbers above is:

$$\$.909 + \$.876 + \$.844 + \$.813 + \$.783 = \$4.225$$

Thus the present value of the stream of dividends is equal to $4.225 over the five-year period if the required rate of return is 10 percent and the dividends grow at a rate of 6 percent per year. Although the number of dollars of dividends is $5.63, their present value is only $4.225 as indicated, since the dividends grow at only 6 percent and the investor requires a 10 percent rate of return.

The price of the stock at the end of the holding period (year 5) is the last part of our equation. The current earnings per share (e_0) are $1.89, and the price-earnings ratio (P/E) is 12.5. Holding P/E at 12.5, the current earnings, expected to grow at 6 percent per year for five years, should amount to $1.89 N $(1.06)^5$ at the end of the fifth year. Thus:

$$\begin{aligned} \text{Selling price at the} \\ \text{end of year 5} \quad &= (12.5)[(\$1.89)(1.06)^5] \\ &= \$31.61 \end{aligned}$$

The present value of the selling price is $31.61/(1.10)^5$, or $19.63. Adding the present value of the stream of dividends to the present value of the expected selling price of the stock yields $4.22 + $19.63, or $23.85.

Notice that throughout this explanation, the variables g, d/e and P/E are estimated by the analyst or investor. The current price of the stock (P) and current earnings (e_0) are observed. Equation 4-6 is solved for the rate of return (r). Let's illustrate our efforts up to now with a real-world example.

Example: Holiday Inns Stock. Let us estimate the return on Holiday Inns stock as an investment to be held for five years. Holiday Inns operates the largest motel system in the country. Assume that its common stock can be purchased at the end of 1976 for $12. A thoroughgoing analysis of expected future earnings, dividends, and price-earnings ratio (P/E) has provided the following predictions:

Year	Earnings per Share	Dividends per Share*
1977	$1.55	$ .47
1978	1.70	.51
1979	1.86	.56
1980	2.03	.61
1981	2.25	.68
		$2.83

*About 30 percent of earnings are paid in dividends each year ($d/e = .30$).

It is estimated that at the end of 1981, the stock will sell for 9 times 1981 earnings. Given the estimated earnings in 1981 of $2.25, the forecast selling price at the end of the fifth year is $20.25 ($2.25 × 9P/E).

What rate of return would equate the flow of dividends and the terminal price shown above back to a current market price of $12? Alternatively stated, what yield or return is required on an investment of $12 in order that an investor may withdraw dividends each year as indicated above and be able to remove a final balance of $20.25 at the end of five years?

In effect, we want to find the rate of return that will solve the following:

$$\$12 = \frac{\$0.47}{(1+r)} + \frac{\$0.51}{(1+r)^2} + \frac{\$0.56}{(1+r)^3} + \frac{\$0.61}{(1+r)^4} + \frac{\$0.68}{(1+r)^5} + \frac{\$20.25}{(1+r)^5}$$

where r is the rate of return. Calculating the rate that will solve the equation is a somewhat tedious task, requiring trial-and-error computation using Table 4-2. One rate is tried, and if it fails to work, we must try others. Let us turn the equation into columnar form and try some discount rates.

Year	Receipt	12% Present-Value Factor (Table 4-2)	Present Value
1	$ 0.47	.893	$ 0.42
2	0.51	.797	0.41
3	0.56	.712	0.40
4	0.61	.636	0.39
5	0.68	.567	0.38
5	20.25	.567	11.48
			$13.48

At 12 percent, this stream of receipts has a present value of $13.48, not the $12 the market is asking. This suggests that the discount rate is more than 12 percent. In order to achieve lower present values of the stream of payments, Table 4-2 suggests higher discount rates. Using 14 percent, the present value results are:

Year	Receipt	14% Present Value	Present Value
1	$ 0.47	.877	$ 0.41
2	0.51	.769	0.39
3	0.56	.675	0.38
4	0.61	.592	0.36
5	0.68	.519	0.35
5	20.25	.519	10.51
			$12.40

We are very close! The yield is really about 15 percent per annum. The investor must decide if 15 percent is a satisfactory return for him, given his alternative investment opportunities and his attitude toward risk in holding Holiday Inns stock.

THE CAPITALIZATION OR MULTIPLIER APPROACH

Judging from current practice, the capitalization or multiplier approach to valuation still holds the preeminent position. A recent survey of practicing analysts indicated that 75 percent of them preferred simple multiplier techniques.[9] Present-value techniques were preferred by only about 6 percent. The underlying reasons for ignoring present-value formulas seem to lie in (1) severe earnings-forecasting limitations, and (2) the influence of sharply increased competition on short-range performance.

The multiplier is a short-cut computation to find the present value. The analyst estimates earnings per share for the year ahead. He divides this figure into the current market price of the stock, and the result is an earnings multiplier. The terms *multiplier* and *price-earnings ratio* are used interchangeably. Thus:

$$\text{Earnings multiplier} = \text{P/E ratio} = \frac{\text{Current market price}}{\text{Estimated earnings per share}}$$

The multiplier, or P/E, is primarily determined by the riskiness of the firm and the rate of growth in its earnings. High multipliers are associated with high earnings growth. The Dow Jones Industrial Average might sell in the 9-11 P/E range. It represents a cross-section of stocks with average risk and growth prospects. McDonald's may sell at a P/E of 16, because of its high rate of earnings growth. American Telephone and Telegraph Co. may sell at a P/E of 9, because of average growth.

The analyst seeks various rules of thumb for selecting an appropriate price-earnings ratio that can be applied to a company's earnings to determine value for its shares. The resulting price is compared with current market prices to

[9]R. A. Bing, "Survey of Practitioners' Stock Evaluation Methods," *Financial Analysts Journal*, 26, No. 2 (May-June 1971), 55-60.

assess bargains or overpriced stocks. For example, if Standard Oil of California is expected to earn $6 per share next year and normally sells at a P/E of 8, the analyst might conclude that a fair price at present is $48. If the stock is currently selling for $40, it is undervalued; if it is selling for $55, it is over-priced (overvalued).

The determination of the current P/E on a stock must be followed by a standard of comparison, taken from the historical record of the stock in question. The analyst may ascertain the median or mean P/E for a stock, as well as its range over time. More weight can be given to the recent past. This provides boundaries within which the P/E should fall (range) and indicates whether the stock is tending to sell at the upper limits of expectation (high end of P/E range) or lower limits. Industry P/E's provide some guidelines; however, different companies in the same industry frequently carry quite different P/E's.

OUR MEASUREMENT OF RETURN

One of our principal tasks throughout the remainder of the text will be to estimate return and risk for both securities and portfolios over a forward holding period. The holding period, or elapsed time between the purchase and sale of a security, could be any amount of time, from one hour to a decade, or longer. The *holding-period yield* will be defined as the percentage dividend or interest yield plus percentage capital-appreciation yield over the holding period—or:

$$\text{Stock HPY} = \frac{D_1 + (P_1 - P_0)}{P_0} \qquad (4.7)$$

$$\text{Bond HPY} = \frac{I_1 + (P_1 - P_0)}{P_0} \qquad (4.71)$$

where:

HPY = expected holding-period yield
D_1 = expected dividends over holding period
I_1 = expected interest over holding period
P_0 = current security price
P_1 = expected security price, end of holding period

These equations say that the holding-period yield is the sum of the dividend or interest yield and the capital-appreciation yield.

Frequently, return will be expressed as holding-period yield plus unity, or HPY + 1. Thus an HPY of 20 percent would be expressed as .20 + 1.00, or 1.20. This suggests return as a relative or ratio of original investment. Therefore an HPY of 1.20 means that $1.20 is earned for each $1.00 invested (or $12 for $10, and so on), or that $1 yields 20 cents in return. The advantage of using *holding-period return* (HPY + 1) is in dealing with negative yields. An HPY of −.20 or −20 percent, when translated into holding-period-return terms, becomes (−.20 +

1.00), or .80. The advantage comes in certain mathematical transformations such as the use of logarithms, where it is not possible to take the log of a negative number.

Holding-period return (HPR) can also be determined by:

$$\text{Stock HPR} = \frac{D_1 + P_1}{P_0} \tag{4.8}$$

$$\text{Bond HPR} = \frac{I_1 + P_1}{P_0} \tag{4.81}$$

Assume that a stock is purchased for $25 and is expected to be sold for $27.50 after one year. Dividends of $1.25 are anticipated at the end of the holding period. Holding-period yield (HPY) and holding-period return (HPR) become:

$$\text{HPY} = \frac{\$1.25 + (\$27.50 - \$25.00)}{\$25.00} \qquad \text{HPR} = \frac{\$1.25 + \$27.50}{\$25.00}$$

$$= \$3.75/\$25.00 \qquad\qquad = \$28.75/\$25.00$$

$$= .15, \text{ or } 15\% \qquad\qquad = 1.15, \text{ or } 115\%$$

Thus, HPR is equal to HPY plus unity (1.00).

Referring back to our present-value discussion, for the one-year case the HPY is equivalent to the required rate of return (r) necessary to discount the dividend of $1.25 and the price of $27.50 back to the prevailing market price of $25, or:

$$V_0 = \frac{D_1}{(1+r)} + \frac{P_1}{(1+r)} \tag{4.5}$$

$$\$25 = \frac{\$1.25}{(1+r)} + \frac{\$27.50}{(1+r)}$$

$$\$25 = \frac{\$1.25}{1.15} + \frac{\$27.50}{1.15}$$

$$\$25 = \$1.08 + \$23.92$$

Since we shall rely heavily upon a one-year holding period throughout most of our discussions in the remainder of the book it is easy to see that the HPY and HPR formulas (Equations 4.7 and 4.8) are shortcuts that yield identical results to present-value calculation and also facilitate risk measurement in securities.

Summary

This chapter focused upon the fundamental approach to the determination of the value of a security, and how to calculate return on a security. The central idea that a security is worth the discounted present value of all future income that flows from it enabled us to discuss the theory behind what a stock or a bond *should* sell for. The value of a preferred stock or a bond is easier to calculate than the value of a common stock, since the latter is likely to provide income flows whose timing and amount are more uncertain. Bond interest and preferred dividends are fixed by contract. Bond tables were introduced to facilitate the valuation process.

We saw the method for determining the present worth or value of a share of common stock when the holding period is one year or a number of years. The multiplier or P/E approach to stock valuation was explored briefly, since it is preeminent in use today by practicing security analysts.

The notion of return on a security or an investor's required rate of return was explored in depth, as we learned how to calculate holding-period yield (HPY) and holding-period return (HPR).

**Questions
and
Problems**

1. a. At an annual rate of compounding of 8 percent, how long does it take a given sum to double? triple? quadruple?

b. How do you explain the results in (a) above?

2. Which amount is worth more at 16 percent: $1,000 today or $2,100 after five years?

3. How much should you be willing to pay today for an annual cash payment of $10,000 to be received forever if your required rate of return is 9 percent?

4. Duker Electronics has a 6 percent, $100 par value bond outstanding that is due in ten years. The firm also has a $6 preferred stock outstanding.

a. What is the present value of each security if the required rate of return on these securities in the marketplace is 8 percent?

b. How do you account for the differences in value determined in (a) above?

5. Why is it more difficult to determine the value of a common stock as opposed to finding the value of a bond?

6. Tasty Fast Foods, Inc., stock is currently selling for $35 per share. The stock is expected to pay a $1 dividend at the end of the next year. It is reliably estimated that the stock will sell for $37 at the end of one year.

a. Assuming that the dividend and price forecasts are accurate, would you pay $35 today for the stock to hold it for one year if your required rate of return were 12 percent?

b. Given the present price of $35 and the expected dividend of $1, what would the price have to be at the end of one year to justify purchase today if your required return were 15 percent?

7. Consult *Value Line, Moody's,* or other investment services to determine price and dividend data for American Telephone and Telegraph Company and McDonald's Corporation. If you had purchased each stock at the average of its high and low prices in 1974 and sold each stock at the average price in 1978 what rate of return would you have earned on each stock (before transaction costs and taxes)? Assume dividends paid each year are collected in one payment at the end of the year.

8. You have just made some forecasts for Standard Oil Company of Ohio. It is determined that you want to buy 450 shares today with the intention of selling out at the end of five years (at which time you will retire to Bermuda). You estimate that SOHIO will pay $1.35 per share in dividends each year into the foreseeable future and that, at the end of the five-year holding period, the shares could be sold for $55. What would you be willing to pay today for these shares if your required return is 10 percent per annum?

9. My-Lady, Inc., a manufacturer of women's high-fashion apparel, is expected to earn $1.00 per share next year and pay a dividend of $0.25 per share. Earnings and dividends are expected to grow into the foreseeable future at 10 percent per annum. Investors are judged to require a return of 15 percent per annum on the company's stock.

    a. What is the theoretical *value* of this stock?

    b. What would the theoretical *price-earnings ratio* be for this stock if, other things equal, required returns by investors were only 12 percent?

Other things equal, (1) indicate whether each of the following events (treat each separately) would tend to cause the price of My-Lady, Inc., stock to *rise, fall,* or remain *unchanged,* and (2) state *why.*

    c. Increase in total debt relative to equity financing?

    d. A merger with Hi-Scent Flavors & Fragrances, a large maker of men's cosmetics?

    e. Decline in the dividend from $0.25 to $0.20?

APPENDIX

Infinite Case

The natural extension of our discussion of common-stock valuation is the case in which growth rates are constant and the flows or dividends are infinite. This assumption is consistent with the infinite nominal life of common shares. Theoretically, a share of stock can be sold at any point in time for a price equivalent to the present value of all dividends from that point to infinity.[10] This *perpetual, constant* growth case represents the most abstract and theoretical notion of common-stock value. Sparing the mathematical proof, suffice it to say that for this infinite case, where N is very large and approaches infinity, Equation 4.5 becomes:[11]

$$V_0 = \frac{D_1}{r - g} \tag{4.9}$$

Our Olsen Co. share (see page 91) under the infinite case would be worth:

[10]The notion of infinity is less startling in reality in these cases. Value added after fifty years under present-value techniques is quite small. For example, at 8 percent, the present value of $1 received at the end of fifty years is 2.1 cents.

[11]Note that when growth is zero, we have the formula for a perpetuity.

$$V_0 = \frac{\$1.00}{.10 - .06}$$

$$= \frac{\$1.00}{.04}$$

$$= \$25.00$$

Examine Equation 4.9. Given the level of dividend, D, any narrowing of the differential between r and g indicates increases in value; that is, lowering of required return, r, or increase in growth rate, g. For example, suppose we held other factors constant and caused r to drop to .08. Then:

$$\frac{1.00}{.08 - .06} = \frac{1.00}{.02} = \$50$$

Similarly, other things equal, permit g to expand to .09. Then:

$$\frac{\$1.00}{.10 - .09} = \frac{\$1.00}{.01} = \$100$$

Similarly, widening the spread between r and g suggests lower values. Changes in D, the dividend, are not independent of the growth rate. So we cannot, for the time being, assume that large increases in the dividend per share will lead to higher values. We will explore this relationship more closely in Chapter 9.

There are certain implied key preconditions and assumptions behind Equation 4.9. First, r must be greater than g, or resulting values are negative prices. Second, the dividend must be greater than zero, or we end up with zero price. Finally, the relationship between r and g is assumed constant and perpetual.

This dividend-discounting formulation raises questions of how the equation accommodates stocks that pay no dividends at the present time. How can we value the dividend stream or speak about its growth? It is, of course, true that most companies paying no dividends still command positive stock prices. These prices exist because it is expected that the lack of dividends will not last forever. Suppose a stock is expected to pay a dividend from the start of the eleventh year until infinity. In present-value terms, the stock is worth the present value of the dividends from year 11 to infinity, discounted at some required rate of return. Thus, at a required rate of return of 20 percent, a perpetuity is worth $5 ($V = \$1/.20$). Without any growth in dividends from year 11 on, the value of an annuity from year 11 through infinity is $.081 ($5.00 minus $4.193—see Table 4-4).

At a required rate of 10 percent, the stock is worth $3.855. Taking into account growth in the dividends over time would lead to different results but would still explain a positive price in the absence of current dividends.

It is not too difficult to realize that the rate and duration of growth in earnings and/or dividends are neither constant nor infinite. The rate of growth is likely to decline gradually as the advantages enjoyed by the firm melt away because of competition, expiring patents, the appearance of substitute products, and so on.

In most situations, earnings and dividends grow at different rates for varying durations. For example, a stock could grow at 10 percent for ten years and then at only 5 percent for the next fifty years. The transition period from $g = .10$ to $g = .05$ may take one or several years, and the rate of decay in g may assume differing configurations.

The practical application of present-value ideas to common stocks has been greatly facilitated by tables composed of numerous combinations of underlying factors, such as earnings and dividend growth rates, growth duration, and required rate of return.[12] In the early 1960s sets of tables were introduced by Soldofsky and Murphy and by Molodovsky, May, and Chottiner. We will look at these tables now.

Soldofsky and Murphy used *dividend* growth rates and constructed so-called one-step and two-step growth yield tables.[13] The one-step table is based upon the assumption of one growth period of a constant dividend growth rate. The two-step table is based upon two growth periods of constant but different dividend growth rates. Figures in the body of the tables are *price-dividend* ratios. Table 4-6 is taken from their work.

A simple example will help to illustrate the use of two-step tables. Suppose that to a given investor a stock has the following attributes: Dividends are expected to grow at 15 percent per year for the next ten years, and then continue to grow at 10 percent for five more years, and subsequently not at all. Assume that this investor has a required rate of return of 9 percent. What is a reasonable price for the stock? It is possible to go through the extensive labor of calculating the present value, but the Soldofsky-Murphy tables provide a rapid answer. Look at the bottom half of Table 4-6, "Growth Rates 15%, 10%," and at the far left columns. We estimated the initial growth period of ten years and the second period of five years, for a total of fifteen years. The left columns marked "10-5-15," traced across to the required-return column of 9 percent, yields the number 42.23. This number tells us that the value of the stock is 42.23 times the current dividend; a current dividend of $1.00 makes the stock worth $42.23.

The calculations of Molodovsky, May, and Chottiner represent a variant on the work of Soldofsky and Murphy.[14] The former use price-earnings in their

[12] Among the earliest stock tables were those of S. E. Guild, *Stock Growth and Discount Tables* (Boston: Financial Publishing Company, 1931), p. 163. Other tables not discussed here are those of W. S. Bauman, *Estimating the Present Value of Common Stocks by the Variable Rate Method* (Ann Arbor: Bureau of Business Research, University of Michigan, 1963).

[13] R. M. Soldofsky and J. T. Murphy, *Growth Yield on Common Stock—Theory and Tables* (Iowa City: Bureau of Business and Economic Research, State University of Iowa, 1964).

[14] Nicholas Molodovsky, Catherine May, and Sherman Chottiner, "Common Stock Valuation: Theory and Tables," *Financial Analysts Journal*, 20, (March-April 1965), 104-23.

TABLE 4-6

MULTIPLIERS FOR EACH DOLLAR OF MOST RECENT PERIOD
PAYMENTS ON A COMMON STOCK GIVEN A CERTAIN GROWTH
YIELD (DISCOUNT RATE) AND DIFFERING RATE OF GROWTH
FOR EACH OF TWO PERIODS INDICATED AND A ZERO
PERPETUAL RATE OF GROWTH THEREAFTER

Growth Periods—Years

First Period	Second Period	Total	Dividend Growth Yields*					
			6½%	6¾%	7%	8%	9%	10%
Growth Rates 15%, 6%†								
5	5	10	35.55	34.08	32.71	28.10	24.53	21.70
5	10	15	42.08	40.20	38.45	32.60	28.12	24.59
10	5	15	58.49	55.70	53.13	44.52	37.96	32.82
5	15	20	48.45	46.10	43.93	36.70	31.24	26.99
10	10	20	68.06	64.57	61.35	50.68	42.64	36.43
15	5	20	92.11	87.04	82.38	66.99	55.50	46.71
5	20	25	54.66	51.78	49.14	40.43	33.94	28.99
10	15	25	77.39	73.12	69.19	56.28	46.71	39.44
15	10	25	106.14	99.88	94.15	75.41	61.62	51.22
5	30	35	66.60	62.53	58.82	46.90	38.35	32.03
10	25	35	95.32	89.26	83.74	66.01	53.33	44.00
15	20	35	133.09	124.15	116.04	90.03	71.56	58.08
20	15	35	181.90	168.92	157.16	119.70	93.37	74.36
5	45	50	83.22	77.09	71.60	54.55	43.00	34.91
10	40	50	120.31	111.15	102.94	77.50	60.33	48.33
15	35	50	170.64	157.05	144.89	107.30	82.08	64.59
25	25	50	328.42	299.39	273.52	194.49	142.58	107.43
Growth Rates 15%, 10%†								
5	5	10	40.89	39.13	37.51	32.03	27.80	24.46
5	10	15	55.01	52.36	49.92	41.75	35.54	30.70
10	5	15	66.31	63.03	60.00	49.90	42.23	36.26
5	15	20	71.58	67.71	64.15	52.40	43.64	36.94
10	10	20	87.00	82.20	77.77	63.20	52.34	44.06
15	5	20	103.57	97.66	92.22	74.34	61.09	51.01
5	20	25	91.02	85.51	80.46	64.06	52.11	43.18
10	15	25	111.29	104.43	98.15	77.76	62.93	51.85
15	10	25	133.90	125.42	117.67	92.53	74.30	60.74
5	30	35	140.50	130.03	120.58	90.80	70.24	55.66
10	25	35	173.08	160.02	148.24	111.15	85.57	67.43
15	20	35	211.07	194.86	180.23	134.23	102.58	80.20
20	15	35	254.56	234.54	216.49	159.86	121.04	93.72
5	45	50	250.51	226.25	204.84	140.93	100.59	74.31
10	40	50	310.47	280.19	253.48	173.76	123.47	90.73
15	35	50	382.66	344.93	311.65	212.43	149.91	109.29
25	25	50	570.70	512.64	461.48	309.45	214.28	152.96

*Growth yields for rates up to and including 4% are based upon discounting the expected income stream for 200 years. A 100-year income stream was used in determining growth yields beginning with 4¼% through 10% and a 50-year stream was used for 12% and above. In all cases, however, at least 99% of the value of a perpetuity is included at each growth yield. In most cases much of the final 1% of the value of a perpetuity is included despite the foreshortening of the discount period.

†The first of these two growth rates applies to the first period; the second growth rate applies to the second growth period.

Source: R.M. Soldofsky and J.T. Murphy, *Growth Yield on Common Stock: Theory and Tables* (Iowa City, Iowa. Bureau of Business and Economic Research, 1961).

calculations and they use a built-in relationship between the growth rate and dividend payout ratio, determined through statistical analysis. The pattern of growth assumed is shown in Figure 4-4. Notice a high but constant growth rate for the initial period (Segment A), followed by a transitional period during which the growth rate will decline to zero (Segment B). Zero growth is then extended infinitely (Segment C). The tables here are really three-step rather than two-step like those of Soldofsky and Murphy, which lacked any transition period (and were price-dividend in construction).

FIGURE 4-4
PATTERN OF EARNINGS GROWTH EVALUATED BY
MOLODOVSKY-MAY-CHOTTINER TABLES

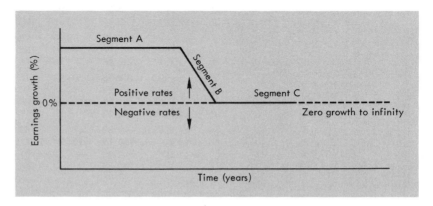

Referring to Table 4-7, which is an extract from the Molodovsky-May-Chottiner tables, let us use an example. RST Co. earnings are expected to grow at 10 percent a year for the next ten years. Thereafter, the rate of growth will decline to zero over a twenty-year period. Earnings will then stabilize at zero growth (from year 31 on). The investor seeks a 9 percent rate of return. On Table 4-7, the initial growth rate of 10 percent is found in the right-hand column. Finding 10 in the "Years Constant Growth" column, read across to the column marked "20" for years of diminishing growth. The table number is 22.9. The interpretation is that if current earnings are $3.00, the stock is worth about $68.70 ($3 X 22.9).

The tables we have analyzed are attempts to put present-value theory into operational form. The main difficulty in application lies in the problems inherent in forecasting (a) rates, (b) duration, and (c) pattern of growth of earnings or dividends of a stock for a long period ahead. These obstacles create doubts in the minds of many investors who look to more direct, short-focused, and pragmatic approaches to the question of valuation.

TABLE 4-7
INVESTMENT VALUES OF NORMAL EARNINGS OF $1 AT 9% RETURN

Projected Earnings Growth Rate — 5.0%
Years Diminishing Growth

Years Constant Growth	2	4	6	8	10	12	14	16	18	20
2	8.6	8.9	9.2	9.5	9.8	10.0	10.2	10.4	10.6	10.8
4	9.4	9.7	9.9	10.2	10.4	10.7	10.9	11.1	11.3	11.4
6	10.1	10.3	10.6	10.8	11.0	11.3	11.5	11.6	11.8	12.0
8	10.7	11.0	11.2	11.4	11.6	11.8	12.0	12.2	12.3	12.5
10	11.3	11.5	11.8	12.0	12.2	12.3	12.5	12.7	12.8	13.0
12	11.9	12.1	12.3	12.5	12.7	12.8	13.0	13.1	13.3	13.4
14	12.4	12.6	12.8	13.0	13.1	13.3	13.4	13.6	13.7	13.8
16	12.9	13.1	13.2	13.4	13.5	13.7	13.8	14.0	14.1	14.2
18	13.3	13.5	13.7	13.8	13.9	14.1	14.2	14.3	14.4	14.5
20	13.7	13.9	14.0	14.2	14.3	14.4	14.6	14.7	14.8	14.9
22	14.1	14.3	14.4	14.5	14.7	14.8	14.9	15.0	15.1	15.2
24	14.5	14.6	14.7	14.9	15.0	15.1	15.2	15.3	15.4	15.4
26	14.8	14.9	15.0	15.2	15.3	15.4	15.5	15.5	15.6	15.7
28	15.1	15.2	15.3	15.4	15.5	15.6	15.7	15.8	15.9	16.0
30	15.4	15.5	15.6	15.7	15.8	15.9	16.0	16.0	16.1	16.2

Projected Earnings Growth Rate — 9.0%
Years Diminishing Growth

Years Constant Growth	2	4	6	8	10	12	14	16	18	20
2	9.3	9.9	10.5	11.1	11.7	12.3	12.8	13.3	13.9	14.4
4	10.6	11.2	11.8	12.4	13.0	13.5	14.1	14.6	15.1	15.6
6	11.9	12.5	13.1	13.7	14.2	14.8	15.3	15.9	16.4	16.9
8	13.1	13.7	14.3	14.9	15.5	16.1	16.6	17.1	17.7	18.2
10	14.4	15.0	15.6	16.2	16.8	17.3	17.9	18.4	18.9	19.4
12	15.7	16.3	16.9	17.5	18.0	18.6	19.1	19.7	20.2	20.7
14	16.9	17.5	18.1	18.7	19.3	19.9	20.4	20.9	21.5	22.0
16	18.2	18.8	19.4	20.0	20.6	21.1	21.7	22.2	22.7	23.2
18	19.5	20.1	20.7	21.3	21.8	22.4	22.9	23.5	24.0	24.5
20	20.7	21.3	22.0	22.5	23.1	23.7	24.2	24.7	25.3	25.8
22	22.0	22.6	23.2	23.8	24.4	24.9	25.5	26.0	26.5	27.0
24	23.3	23.9	24.5	25.1	25.6	26.2	26.7	27.3	27.8	28.3
26	24.5	25.1	25.8	26.3	26.9	27.5	28.0	28.5	29.1	29.6
28	25.8	26.4	27.0	27.6	28.2	28.7	29.3	29.8	30.3	30.8
30	27.1	27.7	28.3	28.9	29.4	30.0	30.5	31.1	31.6	32.1

6.0%
Years Diminishing Growth

Years Constant Growth	2	4	6	8	10	12	14	16	18	20
2	8.8	9.2	9.5	9.9	10.2	10.5	10.8	11.1	11.4	11.6
4	9.7	10.1	10.4	10.8	11.1	11.4	11.6	11.9	12.1	12.4
6	10.6	10.9	11.3	11.6	11.9	12.1	12.4	12.7	12.9	13.1
8	11.4	11.7	12.1	12.3	12.6	12.9	13.1	13.4	13.6	13.8
10	12.2	12.5	12.8	13.1	13.3	13.6	13.8	14.1	14.3	14.5
12	12.9	13.2	13.5	13.8	14.0	14.3	14.5	14.7	14.9	15.1
14	13.7	13.9	14.2	14.4	14.7	14.9	15.1	15.3	15.5	15.7
16	14.3	14.6	14.8	15.1	15.3	15.5	15.7	15.9	16.1	16.2
18	14.9	15.2	15.4	15.6	15.9	16.0	16.2	16.4	16.6	16.8
20	15.5	15.8	16.0	16.2	16.4	16.6	16.8	16.9	17.1	17.2
22	16.1	16.3	16.5	16.7	16.9	17.1	17.3	17.4	17.6	17.7
24	16.6	16.8	17.0	17.2	17.4	17.6	17.7	17.9	18.0	18.2
26	17.1	17.3	17.5	17.7	17.9	18.0	18.2	18.3	18.4	18.6
28	17.6	17.8	18.0	18.1	18.3	18.4	18.6	18.7	18.8	19.0
30	18.1	18.2	18.4	18.6	18.7	18.8	19.0	19.1	19.2	19.3

10.0%
Years Diminishing Growth

Years Constant Growth	2	4	6	8	10	12	14	16	18	20
2	9.5	10.2	10.9	11.6	12.3	12.9	13.6	14.2	14.8	15.4
4	11.2	11.9	12.6	13.3	14.0	14.7	15.3	16.0	16.6	17.3
6	13.0	13.7	14.4	15.1	15.8	16.5	17.2	17.8	18.5	19.1
8	14.8	15.5	16.2	16.9	17.7	18.3	19.0	19.7	20.4	21.0
10	16.6	17.3	18.1	18.8	19.5	20.2	20.9	21.6	22.3	22.9
12	18.4	19.2	19.9	20.7	21.4	22.1	22.8	23.5	24.2	24.9
14	20.3	21.1	21.9	22.6	23.4	24.1	24.8	25.5	26.2	26.9
16	22.2	23.0	23.8	24.6	25.3	26.1	26.8	27.5	28.2	28.9
18	24.2	25.0	25.8	26.6	27.3	28.1	28.8	29.6	30.3	31.0
20	26.1	27.0	27.8	28.6	29.4	30.2	30.9	31.7	32.4	33.1
22	28.2	29.0	29.8	30.7	31.5	32.3	33.0	33.8	34.5	35.3
24	30.2	31.1	31.9	32.8	33.6	34.4	35.2	36.0	36.7	37.5
26	32.3	33.2	34.1	34.9	35.7	36.6	37.4	38.2	38.9	39.7
28	34.5	35.4	36.2	37.1	37.9	38.8	39.6	40.4	41.2	42.0
30	36.6	37.6	38.4	39.3	40.2	41.0	41.9	42.7	43.5	44.3

7.0%
Years Diminishing Growth

Years Constant Growth	2	4	6	8	10	12	14	16	18	20
2	9.0	9.4	9.9	10.3	10.7	11.1	11.4	11.8	12.1	12.5
4	10.1	10.5	10.9	11.3	11.7	12.1	12.5	12.8	13.1	13.4
6	11.1	11.6	12.0	12.4	12.7	13.1	13.4	13.8	14.1	14.4
8	12.2	12.6	13.0	13.4	13.7	14.1	14.4	14.7	15.0	15.3
10	13.2	13.6	13.9	14.3	14.7	15.0	15.3	15.6	15.9	16.2
12	14.1	14.5	14.9	15.2	15.6	15.9	16.2	16.5	16.8	17.0
14	15.1	15.4	15.8	16.1	16.4	16.7	17.0	17.3	17.6	17.9
16	15.9	16.3	16.6	17.0	17.3	17.6	17.9	18.1	18.4	18.6
18	16.8	17.1	17.5	17.8	18.1	18.4	18.6	18.9	19.2	19.4
20	17.6	18.0	18.3	18.6	18.9	19.1	19.4	19.7	19.9	20.1
22	18.4	18.7	19.0	19.3	19.6	19.9	20.1	20.4	20.6	20.8
24	19.2	19.5	19.8	20.1	20.3	20.6	20.8	21.1	21.3	21.5
26	19.9	20.2	20.5	20.8	21.0	21.3	21.5	21.7	22.0	22.2
28	20.6	20.9	21.2	21.5	21.7	21.9	22.2	22.4	22.6	22.8
30	21.3	21.6	21.9	22.1	22.4	22.6	22.8	23.0	23.2	23.4

11.0%
Years Diminishing Growth

Years Constant Growth	2	4	6	8	10	12	14	16	18	20
2	9.7	10.5	11.3	12.1	12.8	13.6	14.4	15.1	15.9	16.6
4	11.6	12.5	13.3	14.1	14.9	15.7	16.5	17.2	18.0	18.8
6	13.6	14.5	15.3	16.2	17.0	17.8	18.6	19.5	20.3	21.1
8	15.7	16.6	17.5	18.4	19.2	20.1	20.9	21.8	22.6	23.4
10	17.9	18.8	19.7	20.6	21.5	22.4	23.3	24.1	25.0	25.9
12	20.1	21.1	22.0	23.0	23.9	24.8	25.7	26.6	27.5	28.4
14	22.4	23.4	24.4	25.4	26.3	27.3	28.2	29.2	30.1	31.0
16	24.9	25.9	26.9	27.9	28.9	29.9	30.9	31.8	32.8	33.8
18	27.4	28.4	29.5	30.5	31.5	32.6	33.6	34.6	35.6	36.6
20	29.9	31.0	32.1	33.2	34.3	35.4	36.4	37.5	38.5	39.5
22	32.6	33.8	34.9	36.0	37.1	38.2	39.3	40.4	41.5	42.6
24	35.4	36.6	37.8	38.9	40.1	41.2	42.4	43.5	44.6	45.7
26	38.3	39.5	40.8	42.0	43.2	44.3	45.5	46.7	47.8	49.0
28	41.3	42.6	43.8	45.1	46.3	47.6	48.8	50.0	51.2	52.4
30	44.4	45.7	47.0	48.3	49.6	50.9	52.2	53.4	54.7	55.9

8.0%
Years Diminishing Growth

Years Constant Growth	2	4	6	8	10	12	14	16	18	20
2	9.1	9.7	10.2	10.7	11.2	11.7	12.1	12.5	13.0	13.4
4	10.4	11.0	11.5	12.0	12.4	12.9	13.4	13.8	14.2	14.6
6	11.7	12.2	12.7	13.2	13.7	14.1	14.6	15.0	15.4	15.8
8	13.0	13.5	14.0	14.5	14.9	15.4	15.8	16.2	16.6	17.0
10	14.2	14.7	15.2	15.7	16.1	16.5	17.0	17.4	17.8	18.1
12	15.4	15.9	16.4	16.8	17.3	17.7	18.1	18.5	18.9	19.3
14	16.6	17.1	17.6	18.0	18.4	18.9	19.3	19.7	20.0	20.4
16	17.8	18.3	18.7	19.2	19.6	20.0	20.4	20.8	21.1	21.5
18	18.9	19.4	19.8	20.3	20.7	21.1	21.5	21.9	22.2	22.6
20	20.1	20.5	21.0	21.4	21.8	22.2	22.6	22.9	23.3	23.6
22	21.2	21.6	22.0	22.5	22.9	23.2	23.6	24.0	24.3	24.7
24	22.2	22.7	23.1	23.5	23.9	24.3	24.7	25.0	25.4	25.7
26	23.3	23.7	24.2	24.6	24.9	25.3	25.7	26.0	26.4	26.7
28	24.4	24.8	25.2	25.6	26.0	26.3	26.7	27.0	27.4	27.7
30	25.4	25.8	26.2	26.6	27.0	27.3	27.7	28.0	28.3	28.6

12.0%
Years Diminishing Growth

Years Constant Growth	2	4	6	8	10	12	14	16	18	20
2	9.9	10.8	11.7	12.5	13.4	14.3	15.2	16.1	17.0	17.9
4	12.0	13.0	13.9	14.9	15.8	16.7	17.7	18.6	19.5	20.5
6	14.3	15.3	16.3	17.3	18.3	19.3	20.3	21.3	22.2	23.2
8	16.7	17.8	18.8	19.9	20.9	22.0	23.0	24.1	25.1	26.2
10	19.3	20.4	21.5	22.6	23.7	24.8	25.9	27.0	28.1	29.2
12	22.0	23.2	24.3	25.5	26.6	27.8	29.0	30.1	31.3	32.5
14	24.8	26.1	27.3	28.5	29.7	31.0	32.2	33.4	34.7	35.9
16	27.8	29.1	30.4	31.7	33.0	34.3	35.6	36.9	38.2	39.5
18	31.0	32.4	33.7	35.1	36.5	37.8	39.2	40.6	42.0	43.3
20	34.4	35.8	37.2	38.7	40.1	41.6	43.0	44.5	45.9	47.4
22	37.9	39.4	40.9	42.5	44.0	45.5	47.0	48.6	50.1	51.6
24	41.6	43.2	44.8	46.4	48.1	49.7	51.3	52.9	54.5	56.1
26	45.6	47.3	49.0	50.7	52.4	54.1	55.8	57.5	59.2	60.9
28	49.7	51.5	53.3	55.1	56.9	58.7	60.5	62.3	64.1	65.9
30	54.1	56.0	57.9	59.8	61.7	63.6	65.5	67.4	69.3	71.2

Source: Nicholas Molodovsky. "Common Stock Valuation: Theory and Tables," *Financial Analysts Journal*, 20, No. 2 (March-April, 1965), 122.

CHAPTER
FIVE

RISK
IN HOLDING
SECURITIES

Risk in holding securities is generally associated with the possibility that *realized* returns will be less than the returns that were *expected*. The source of such disappointment is the failure of dividends (interest) and/or the security's price to materialize as expected.

Our goals in this chapter are (1) to examine what it is that creates risk, and (2) to provide a quantitative measure of risk.[1]

What Creates Risk?

Forces that contribute to variations in return—price or dividend (interest)—constitute elements of risk. Some influences are external to the firm, cannot be controlled, and affect large numbers of securities. Other influences are internal to the firm and are controllable to a large degree. In investments, those forces that are uncontrollable, external, and broad in their effect are called sources of *systematic* risk. Conversely, controllable, internal factors somewhat peculiar to industries and/or firms are referred to as elements of *unsystematic* risk.

Systematic risk refers to that portion of total variability in return caused by factors affecting the prices of all securities. Economic, political, and sociological changes are sources of systematic risk. Their effect is to cause prices of nearly all individual common stocks and/or all individual bonds to move together in the same manner. For example, should it become apparent that the economy is moving into a recession and that corporate profits will shift downward, stock prices may decline across a broad front. Nearly all stocks listed on the New York Stock Exchange move in the same direction as the New York Stock Exchange Index. On the average, 50 percent of the variation in a stock's price can be explained by variation in the market index.[2] In other words, about one-half the total risk in an average common stock is systematic risk.[3]

---

[1] The words "risk" and "uncertainty" are used interchangeably. Technically, their meanings are different. Risk suggests that a decision maker knows the possible consequences of a decision and their relative likelihoods at the time he makes that decision. Uncertainty, on the other hand, involves a situation about which the likelihood of the possible outcomes is not known.

[2] B. F. King, "Market and Industry Factors in Stock Price Behavior," *Journal of Business,* January 1966, pp. 139-90. Since King's study, other researchers have found that the market effect has declined in importance. However, King's work did pick up this approaching trend.

[3] Systematic risk/Total risk = Systematic risk %.

Unsystematic risk is the portion of total risk that is unique to a firm or industry. Such factors as management capability, consumer preferences, labor strikes, and the like cause unsystematic variability of returns in a firm. Unsystematic factors are largely independent of factors affecting securities markets in general. Since these factors affect one firm, they must be examined for each firm.

Firms with high systematic risk tend to be those whose sales, profits, and stock prices follow the level of economic activity and the level of the securities markets closely. These companies include most firms that deal in basic industrial goods and raw materials. In the industrial chain, we might find that industries related to automobile manufacture take on high systematic risk (steel, rubber, glass, and so on).

Higher proportions of unsystematic risk are found in firms producing nondurable consumer goods. Examples include suppliers of basic necessities such as telephone, light and power, and foodstuffs. Sales, profits, and stock prices of these companies do not depend as much upon the level of economic activity or the stock market.

Systematic and unsystematic risk can be subdivided. Systematic risk for bonds as a group is normally identified with interest-rate risk; for stocks, with market risk. For securities in general, purchasing-power risk is pervasive. Unsystematic risk, or risk unique to an industry or firm, includes business and financial risks.

Systematic Risk MARKET RISK

It is not uncommon to find stock prices falling from time to time while a company's earnings are rising, and vice versa. The price of a stock may fluctuate widely within a short span of time even though earnings remain unchanged. The causes of this phenomenon are varied, but it is mainly due to a change in investors' attitudes toward equities in general, or toward certain types or groups of securities in particular. Variability in return on most common stocks that is due to basic sweeping changes in investor expectations is referred to as *market risk.*

Market risk is caused by investor reaction to tangible as well as intangible events. Expectations of lower corporate profits in general may cause the larger body of common stocks to fall in price. Investors are expressing their judgment that too much is being paid for earnings in the light of anticipated events. The basis for the reaction is a set of real, tangible events—political, social, or economic.

Intangible events are related to market psychology. Market risk is usually touched off by a reaction to real events, but the emotional instability of investors acting collectively leads to a snowballing overreaction. The initial decline in the market can cause the fear of loss to grip investors, and a kind of herd instinct builds as all investors make for the exit. These reactions to reactions frequently culminate in excessive selling, pushing prices down far out of line with fundamental value. With a trigger mechanism such as the assassination of a president, virtually all stocks are adversely affected. Stocks in a particular industry group can be hard hit when the industry goes "out of fashion."

This discussion of market risk has emphasized adverse reactions. Certainly, buying panics also occur as reactions to real events. However, investors are not likely to think of sharp price advances as risk.

Two other factors, interest rates and inflation, are an integral part of the real forces behind market risk and are part of the larger category of systematic or uncontrollable influences. Let's turn our attention to interest rates. This risk factor has its most direct effect on bond investments.

INTEREST-RATE RISK

Interest-rate risk refers to the uncertainty of future market values and of the size of future income, caused by fluctuations in the general level of interest rates.

The root cause of interest-rate risk lies in the fact that as the rate of interest paid on U.S. government securities rises or falls, there is a rise or fall in the rates of return demanded on alternative investment vehicles, such as stocks and bonds issued in the private sector. In other words, as the cost of money changes for nearly risk-free securities (U.S. governments), the cost of money to more risk-prone issuers (private sector) will also change.

Investors normally regard U.S. government securities (USGs) as coming closest to being risk-free. The interest rates demanded on USGs are thought to approximate the "pure" rate of interest, or the cost of hiring money at no risk. Changes in rates of interest demanded on USGs will permeate the system of available securities, from corporate bonds down to the riskiest common stocks.

Interest rates on USGs shift with changes in the supply and demand for government securities. For example, a large operating deficit experienced by the federal government will require financing. Issuance of added amounts of USGs will increase the available supply. Potential buyers of this new supply may be induced to buy only if interest rates are somewhat higher than those currently prevailing on outstanding issues. Should rates on USGs advance from, say, 5 to 5¼ percent, investors holding outstanding issues that yield 5 percent will notice a decline in the price of their securities. Since the rate of 5 percent is fixed by contract on these "old" USGs, a potential buyer would be able to realize the competitive 5¼ percent rate only if the present holder "marked down" the price. As the rate on USGs advances, they become relatively more attractive and other securities become less attractive. Consequently, bond purchasers will buy governments instead of corporates. This will cause the price of corporates to fall and the rate on corporates to rise. Rising corporate bond rates will eventually cause preferred and common stock prices to adjust downward as the chain reaction is felt throughout the system of security yields. (The exact nature and extent of this markdown process and the relationships between rates, prices, and maturity will be explored in Chapter 14.)

Thus there is a rational structure of security yields that is highly inter-connected. Shifts in the "pure" cost of money will ripple through the structure. The direct effect of increases in the level of interest is to cause security prices to fall across a wide span of investment vehicles. Similarly, falling interest rates precipitate price markups on outstanding securities.

In addition to the direct, systematic effect on all security prices, there are indirect effects on common stocks. First, lower or higher interest rates make the purchase of stocks on margin (using borrowed funds) more or less attractive. Higher interest rates, for example, may lead to lower stock prices because of a diminished demand for equities by speculators who use margin. Ebullient stock markets are at times propelled to some excesses by margin buying when interest rates are relatively low.

Second, many firms finance their operations quite heavily with borrowed funds. Others, such as financial institutions, are principally in the business of lending money. As interest rates advance, firms with heavy doses of borrowed capital find that more of their income goes toward paying interest on borrowed money. This may lead to lower earnings, dividends, and share prices. Advancing interest rates can bring higher earnings to lending institutions whose principal revenue source is interest received on loans. For these firms, higher earnings could lead to increased dividends and stock prices.

PURCHASING-POWER RISK

Market risk and interest-rate risk can be defined in terms of uncertainties as to the amount of current dollars to be received by an investor. *Purchasing-power risk* is the uncertainty of the purchasing power of the amounts to be received. In more everyday terms, purchasing-power risk refers to the impact of inflation or deflation on an investment.

If we think of investment as the postponement of consumption, we can see that when a person purchases a stock, he has forgone the opportunity to buy some good or service for as long as he owns the stock. If, during the holding period, prices on desired goods and services rise, the investor actually loses purchasing power. Rising prices on goods and services are normally associated with what is referred to as *inflation*. Falling prices on goods and services are termed *deflation*. Both inflation and deflation are covered in the all-encompassing term *purchasing-power risk*.

Generally, purchasing-power risk has come to be identified with inflation (rising prices); the incidence of declining prices in most countries has been slight. The most widely recognized sources of inflation are rising costs of production and excess demand for goods and services relative to their supply. In the vocabulary of economics, these types of inflation are called *cost-push* and *demand-pull*.

Demand-pull inflation is traceable to unfilled demand when the economy is at a full-employment level of operations. At this level, supply cannot be readily increased in the short run until the labor force or production expands. With demand high and increasing, available goods and services are allocated by price increases that bring supply and demand into equilibrium by forcing out some of the demand.

Cost-push inflation stems from increasing costs of production. As raw material and wage costs rise, producers attempt to pass along these increased costs through higher prices. In an environment where many labor contracts are up for renewal and workers feel their wages are lagging in comparison to prices, a spiral can be set off—wage increases followed by price increases, and so on.

Since we described purchasing-power risk as generally associated with price changes on goods and services, the question remains as to what specific price changes we should be concerned with as a measure of inflation (or deflation). The most common measure used on the level of prices on goods and services is the *consumer price index.* This index uses a "market basket" of goods and services for an average American family—including food, shelter, and a variety of services from medical to laundry—and prices them on a continuous basis. The *wholesale price index* measures the general price level associated with raw materials used in the manufacture of finished products. The record of inflation in recent years according to these indexes is shown in Table 5-1.

Rational investors should include in their estimate of expected return an allowance for purchasing-power risk, in the form of an expected annual percentage change in prices. If a cost-of-living index begins the year at 100 and ends at 103, we say that the rate of increase (inflation) is 3 percent $[(103 - 100)/100]$. If from the second to the third year, the index changes from 103 to 109, the rate is about 5.8 percent $[(109 - 103)/103]$. Referring to Table 5-1 we note that a market basket of goods and services that cost the average consumer $100 in 1967 rose to $170 in 1976. Using compound interest tables, we can see that the annual compound rate of inflation was about 6 percent between 1967 and 1976.

The necessity to adjust expected return for anticipated price changes can be seen in a simple example. Suppose you lend $100 today for a promise to be repaid $105 at the end of the year. The rate of interest is 5 percent. However,

TABLE 5-1
PRICE INDEXES

Year	Wholesale Price Index (1967 = 100)	Consumer Price Index (1967 = 100)
1967	100.0	100.0
1968	102.5	104.2
1969	106.5	109.8
1970	110.4	116.3
1971	112.9	121.2
1972	119.8	125.3
1973	134.7	133.1
1974	160.1	147.7
1975	174.9	161.2
1976	182.9	170.5

Source: *Federal Reserve Bulletin.*

assume that prices over the next year are expected to advance 6 percent (index from 100 to 106). The $105 received at the end of the year has a purchasing power of only 94 percent of $105, or $98.70. You must charge a rate of 11 percent in the beginning (5 percent, plus 6 percent expected inflation) to allow for this.

Just as changes in interest rates have a systematic influence on the prices of all securities, both bonds and stocks, so too do anticipated purchasing-power changes manifest themselves. If annual changes in the consumer price index or other measure of purchasing power have been averaging steadily around 3 percent, and it appears that prices will spurt ahead by 4½ percent over the next year, required rates of return will adjust upward. This process will affect government and corporate bonds as well as common stocks.

Market, purchasing-power, and interest-rate risk are the principal sources of systematic risk in securities; but we should also consider another important category of security risks—unsystematic risks.

Unsystematic Risk

Unsystematic risk is that portion of total risk that is unique or peculiar to a firm or an industry, above and beyond that affecting securities markets in general. Such factors as management capability, consumer preferences, labor strikes, and so on can cause unsystematic variability of returns for a company's stock. Since these factors affect one industry and/or one firm, they must be examined separately for each company.

The uncertainty surrounding the ability of the issuer to make payments on securities stems from two sources: (1) the operating environment of the business and (2) the financing of the firm. These risks are referred to respectively as *business risk* and *financial risk*. They are strictly a function of the operating conditions of the firm and the way in which it chooses to finance its operations. Our attention here will be directed to the broad aspects and implications of business and financial risk. In-depth treatment will be the principal goal of later chapters on analysis of the economy, the industry, and the firm.

BUSINESS RISK

Business risk is a function of the operating conditions faced by a firm and the variability these operating conditions inject into operating income and expected dividends. In other words, if operating earnings are expected to increase 10 percent per year over the foreseeable future, business risk would be higher if operating earnings could grow as much as 14 percent or as little as 6 percent than if the range were from a high of 11 percent to a low of 9 percent. The degree of variation from the expected trend would measure business risk.

Business risk can be divided into two broad categories: external and internal. *Internal business risk* is largely associated with the efficiency with which a firm conducts its operations within the broader operating environment imposed upon it. Each firm has its own set of internal risks, and the degree to which it is successful in coping with them is reflected in operating efficiency.

To a large extent, *external business risk* is the result of operating conditions imposed upon the firm by circumstances beyond its control. Each firm also faces its own set of external risks, depending upon the specific operating environmental factors that it must deal with. The external factors, from cost of money to defense-budget cuts to higher tariffs to a downswing in the business cycle, are far too numerous to list in detail, but the most pervasive external risk factor is probably the business cycle. The sales of some industries (steel, autos) tend to move in tandem with the business cycle, while the sales of others move countercyclically (housing). Demographic considerations can also influence revenues through changes in the birthrate, or the geographical distribution of the population by age group, race, and so on. Political policies are a part of external business risk; government policies with regard to monetary and fiscal matters can affect revenues through the effect on the cost and availability of funds. If money is more expensive, consumers who buy on credit may postpone purchases, and municipal governments may not sell bonds to finance a water-treatment plant. The impact upon retail stores, TV manufacturers, and producers of water purification systems is clear.

Among other things, the nature of general economic conditions will influence the level of revenues. This is an external influence or risk. But, from an internal-risk standpoint, how can a firm adjust to the business cycle? If we segregate costs of operation into fixed and variable costs, we see that as revenues change, if fixed costs absorb a large percentage of total costs, the firm will have difficulty curtailing expenses and production during declines in the economy; and it may also be sluggish to respond as demand surges upward. Such a firm would have large internal business risks relative to its ability to respond to changing business conditions. On the other hand, if total revenues come from a diversified list of products, it is possible that the products are not equally vulnerable to the business cycle to the same degree or at the same time. To this extent, internal risk is reduced by spreading the cycle effects over multiple products or product lines.

The extent to which a change up or down in total revenues leads to more or less than proportionate changes in earnings before interest and taxes (EBIT) is an indication of internal business risk. If a decline in revenue from one product line can be offset by an increase in another, leaving total revenue virtually unchanged, the firm is using product diversification to protect it against business risk. Downward pressures on revenues can also be minimized in EBIT via cost and production cutbacks and other evidences of operating skill on the part of management.

FINANCIAL RISK

Financial risk is associated with the way in which a company finances its activities. We usually gauge financial risk by looking at the capital structure of a firm. The presence of borrowed money or debt in the capital structure creates fixed payments in the form of interest that must be sustained by the firm. The presence of these interest commitments—fixed interest payments due to debt or fixed dividend payments on preferred stock—causes the amount of residual earnings available for common-stock dividends to be more variable than if no interest payments were required. Financial risk is avoidable risk to the extent that managements have the freedom to decide to borrow or not to borrow funds. A firm with no debt financing has no financial risk.

By engaging in debt financing, the firm changes the characteristics of the earnings stream available to the common-share holders. Specifically, the reliance on debt financing, called *financial leverage*, has at least three important effects on common-stock holders.[4] Debt finance (1) increases the variability of their returns, (2) affects their expectations concerning their returns, and (3) increases their risk of being ruined.

Let us assume we have two identical companies, in the very same line of business and selling to the same types of customers, differing only with respect to the mix of their financing. One company, Careful, Inc., is financed entirely with 1 million shares of common stock, sold initially at $20 per share. The other company, Daring Co., is financed half with common stock (500,000 shares sold at $20 per share) and half with debt ($10 million) bearing interest at 5 percent. Each company has $20 million in assets, expected to yield earnings of $1 million, or 5 percent of total assets. We will assume that there are no corporate income taxes.

The earnings of $1 million can easily be converted into a per-share figure for each company. Careful, Inc., earns $1 per share on 1 million shares. Daring pays $500,000 in interest ($10 million × 5 percent), and the remaining $500,000 provides $1 in earnings for each of the 500,000 shares outstanding. At this point, both firms enjoy earnings per share of $1. There appear to be no effects of financial leverage on the stockholders' returns.

Let us consider the effects on both companies of a very good year for business and a very bad year for business, when earnings go up 50 percent in one case and down 50 percent in the other, as in Table 5-2.

Recall that originally each company earned $1 per share. Thus a 50 percent rise in earnings (from $1 million to $1.5 million) causes a 50 percent rise in earnings per share for Careful, Inc., and a 100 percent rise for Daring Co. In the latter case, the effect is magnified because the bondholders receive only 5 percent on their money no matter how well or how poorly the company does. Thus the shareholders of a levered company like Daring get a good deal of

TABLE 5-2
EARNINGS UNDER ALTERNATIVE RETURN ON ASSET ASSUMPTIONS

	Good Year	Bad Year
Assumed rate of return on assets	7½%	2½%
Operating earnings	$1.5 million	$0.5 million
Earnings per share:		
Careful, Inc.	$1.50	$0.50
Daring Co.	2.00	0.00

[4]Debt financing is also referred to as *trading on the equity*, because by its use the company is able to acquire a larger amount of assets than equity contributed by owners.

action from even small changes in operating earnings. Conversely, a 50 percent decrease in earnings (from $1 million to $500,000) causes the earnings per share of Careful to fall 50 percent (from $1 to $0.50), but Daring's earnings per share fall from $1 to zero, a 100 percent drop. It should be easy to see that when operating earnings fall to $500,000, there is only a 2½ percent return on assets, and since bondholders still get their 5 percent, the difference is, in effect, taken from the pockets of shareholders. Leverage is a two-edged sword!

The significance is that not only does this fixed-return borrowed capital enhance the return to shareholders or reduce it substantially but the variation in returns for the owners of shares in companies with borrowed funds (levered firms) exceeds the variation for stockholders in unlevered firms. This variance in returns is what we refer to when we discuss financial leverage or financial risk. To the extent that firms have the freedom to choose how they will be financed, we say that financial leverage or financial risk is an *avoidable* risk, within the power of management to control.

The risk of shareholders' being ruined can be seen quite simply. Should even small negative rates of return on assets persist for a number of years in a row, stockholders' equity can be wiped out. Careful, Inc., shows a positive earnings per share of $.50 when the rate of return on assets is 2½ percent, but Daring shows zero earnings per share at this level. Then what happens if the rate of return on the assets is zero percent? Careful earns zero on a per-share basis, whereas Daring *loses* $.50 per share, or $500,000 (the amount of interest owed).

Negative rates of return can have even more dramatic effects than those already suggested. For example, a negative 4 percent return on assets is magnified into a negative 22 percent loss for Daring Co. A few years like this and equity can be literally wiped out. The risk of bankruptcy is an increasing function of the degree of financial leverage or financial risk.

Thus we think of business risk as concerned with that zone of the income statement between revenues and EBIT; financial risk can be seen in that zone between EBIT and EBT (earnings before taxes).

If the underlying revenue, cost, and EBIT pattern of a firm is somewhat erratic (that is, has some degree of business risk), then the use of borrowed funds (financial risk) may magnify the impact of the eventual earnings and dividends carried through to the shareholders. In the example above, borrowed money has caused underlying volatility of rate of return on equity to be magnified or intensified. Such magnification can be disastrous in bad years like 1972, or beneficial in good years like 1971. To the extent that borrowed funds in the capital structure inject such magnification, real or imagined, bondholders and stockholders perceive greater risk (financial risk) atop existing business risk. As a result, interest payments, earnings, and, therefore, dividends take on a greater degree of uncertainty.

There are other, more exact measures of leverage and financial risk, as well as insights into its impact, which will be explored later in our examination of analysis of the firm. Suffice it to say here that all the risks we have mentioned combine to cause returns from securities to vary. The separate risk forces may move in tandem or at cross-currents in causing variations in returns for individual securities or classes of securities. For example, while rising interest rates are depressing the price of bonds and stocks in general, favorable developments in business risk may tend to cushion the blow in specific industries and companies. Now let's take a look at some ways of quantifying risk.

ASSIGNING RISK ALLOWANCES (PREMIUMS)

One way of quantifying risk and building a required rate of return (r) would be to express the required rate as being made up of a riskless rate plus compensation for individual risk factors previously enunciated, or as

$$r = i + p + b + f + m + o$$

where:

  i = real interest rate (riskless rate)
  p = purchasing-power-risk allowance
  b = business-risk allowance
  f = financial-risk allowance
  m = market-risk allowance
  o = allowance for "other" risks

The first step would be to determine a suitable riskless rate of interest. Unfortunately, no investment is risk-free. The return on U.S. Treasury bills or an insured savings account, whichever is relevant to an individual investor, can be used as an approximate riskless rate. Savings accounts possess purchasing-power risk and are subject to interest-rate risk of income but not principal. U.S. government bills are subject to interest-rate risk of principal. The riskless rate might be from 5 to 6 percent.

Using the rate on U.S. government bills and assuming that interest-rate-and-risk compensation is already included in the USG bill rate, Figure 5-1 depicts the process of building required rate of return for alternative investments.

To quantify the separate effects of each type of systematic and unsystematic risk would be next to impossible, because of overlapping effects and the sheer complexity involved. In the remainder of the chapter we shall examine some proxies for packaging into a single measure of risk all those qualitative risk factors taken together that perhaps cannot be measured separately.

STATING PREDICTIONS "SCIENTIFICALLY"

Security analysts cannot be expected to predict with certainty whether a stock will increase or decrease in price, and by how much. The amount of dividend income may be subject to more or less uncertainty than price in the estimating process. The reasons are simple enough. There is not enough understanding of

FIGURE 5-1
BUILDING A REQUIRED RATE OF RETURN

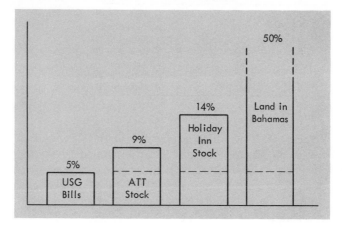

political and socioeconomic forces to permit predictions that are beyond doubt or error.

This existence of uncertainty does not mean that security analysis is valueless. It does mean that analysts must strive to provide not only careful and reasonable estimates of return but also some measure of the degree of uncertainty associated with these estimates of return. Most important, the analyst must be prepared to quantify the risk that a given stock will fail to realize its expected return.

The quantification of risk is necessary to ensure uniform interpretation and comparison. Verbal definitions simply do not lend themselves to analysis. A decision on whether to buy stock A or stock B, both of which are expected to return 10 percent, is not made easy by the mere statement that there is only a "slight" or "minimal" likelihood that the return on either will be less than 10 percent. This sort of vagueness should be avoided. Although whatever quantitative measure of risk is used will be at most only a proxy for true risk, such a measure provides analysts with a description that facilitates uniform communication, analysis, and ranking.

Pressed on what he meant when he said that stock A would have a return of 10 percent over some holding period, an analyst might suggest that 10 percent is, in a sense, a "middling" estimate or a "best guess." In other words, the return could be above, below, or equal to 10 percent. He might express the degree of confidence he has in his estimate by saying that the return is "very likely" to be between 9 and 11 percent, or perhaps between 6 and 14 percent.

A more precise measurement of uncertainty about these predictions would be to gauge the extent to which actual return is likely to differ from predicted return—that is, the dispersion around the expected return. Suppose stock A, in the opinion of the analyst, could provide returns as follows:

Holding-Period Yield	Likelihood
7%	1 chance in 20
8	2 chances in 20
9	4 chances in 20
10	6 chances in 20
11	4 chances in 20
12	2 chances in 20
13	1 chance in 20

This sounds a little like weather forecasting. We have all heard the phrase "a two-in-ten chance of rain." This likelihood of outcome can be stated in fractional or decimal terms. Such a figure is referred to as a *probability*. Thus a "two-in-ten chance" is equal to 2/10, or .20. A likelihood of "four chances in twenty" is 4/20, or .20. When individual events in a group of events are assigned probabilities, we have a *probability distribution*. The total of the probabilities assigned to individual events in a group of events must always equal 1.00 (or 10/10, 20/20, and so on). A sum less than 1.00 indicates that events have been left out. A sum in excess of 1.00 implies incorrect assignment of weights or the inclusion of events that could not occur. Let us recast our "likelihoods" into "probabilities."

Holding-Period Yield	Probability
7%	.05
8	.10
9	.20
10	.30
11	.20
12	.10
13	.05
	1.00

Based upon his analysis of economic, industry, and company factors, the analyst assigns probabilities subjectively. The number of different holding-period yields to be considered is a matter of his choice. In this case, the holding-period yield (HPY) of 7 percent could mean "between 6½ and 7½ percent." Alternatively, the analyst could have specified 6½ to 7 and 7 to 7½ percent as two outcomes, rather than just 7 percent. This fine tuning provides greater detail in prediction.

Security analysts use the probability distribution of HPYs to specify expected *return* as well as *risk*. The expected return is the weighted average of the HPYs. That is, if we multiply each HPY by its associated probability and add the results together, we get a weighted-average HPY, or what we will call the expected average HPY.

(1) Holding-Period Yield	(2) Probability	(1) × (2)
7%	.05	.35
8	.10	.80
9	.20	1.80
10	.30	3.00
11	.20	2.20
12	.10	1.20
13	.05	.65
	1.00	10.00%

The expected average HPY is 10 percent. The expected return lies at the center of the distribution. Most of the possible outcomes lie either above or below it. The "spread" of possible HPYs about the expected return can be used to give us a proxy for risk. It is possible for two stocks to have identical expected HPYs but quite different "spreads" or dispersions, and thus different risks. Consider stock B:

(1) Holding-Period Yield	(2) Probability	(1) × (2)
9	.30	2.7
10	.40	4.0
11	.30	3.3
	1.00	10.0%

Stocks A and B have identical expected average HPYs of 10 percent. But the spread for stocks A and B is not the same. For one thing, the range of outcomes from high to low HPY is wider for stock A (7 to 13). For B, the range is only 9 to 11. However, a wider range of outcomes does not necessarily imply greater risk; the range as a measure of dispersion ignores the relative probabilities of each of the outcomes.

The spread or dispersion of the probability distribution can also be measured by the degree of variation around the expected HPY. The deviation of any outcome from the expected HPY is:

$$\text{Outcome} - \text{Expected HPY}$$

Since outcomes do not have equal probabilities of occurrence, we must weight each difference by its probability:

$$\text{Probability} \times (\text{Outcome} - \text{Expected HPY})$$

For purposes of computing a *variance*, we will square the deviations or differences before multiplying them by the relative probabilities:

$$\text{Probability} \times (\text{Outcome} - \text{Expected HPY})^2$$

The value of the squaring can be seen in a simple example. Assume three HPYs—9, 10, and 11 percent—each equally likely to occur. The expected HPY is thus $(9\%) \, .33 + (10\%) \, .33 + (11\%) \, .33 = .10$. Since 10 percent is the expected HPY, the other values must lie equally above and below it. If we took an average of the deviations from 10 percent, we would get:

$$\text{Weighted deviation} = .33 \times (9 - 10) = -.33$$
$$= .33 \times (11 - 10) = +.33$$

The sum of the deviations or differences, multiplied by their respective probabilities, equals $+.33 + (-.33)$, or zero. Squaring the differences eliminates the plus and minus signs to give us a better feel for the deviation. The variance is the weighted average of the squared deviations, with each weighted by its probability.

Table 5-3 shows the calculation of the variance for stocks A and B. The larger variation about the expected HPY for stock A is indicated in its variance relative to stock B (2.1 vs. .6). Also shown is the standard deviation, the square root of the variance. Its usefulness will be examined shortly.

If we pause to reflect upon the significance of Table 5-3, we might notice that variance measures variability in *both* directions around the expected HPY. However, it might be more meaningful to think of risk from the mean downward. That is, can we really feel there is risk associated with HPYs *above* the

TABLE 5-3
CALCULATION OF VARIANCE AND STANDARD DEVIATION
FOR TWO STOCKS, A AND B

	Stock A				Stock B		
(1) HPY minus Expected HPY	*(2)* Difference Squared	*(3)* Probability	*(4)* (2)×(3)	*(5)* HPY minus Expected HPY	*(6)* Difference Squared	*(7)* Probability	*(8)* (6)×(7)
7 − 10 = −3	9	.05	.45				
8 − 10 = −2	4	.10	.40				
9 − 10 = −1	1	.20	.20	9 − 10 = −1	1	.30	.30
10 − 10 = 0	0	.30	.00	10 − 10 = 0	0	.40	.00
11 − 10 = +1	1	.20	.20	11 − 10 = +1	1	.30	.30
12 − 10 = +2	4	.10	.40				
13 − 10 = +3	9	.05	.45				
		1.00	2.10			1.00	.60
Variance			2.10				.60
Standard deviation			1.45				.77

expected HPY of 10 percent? Using only the negative deviations from the mean would give us what is called the semivariance. But wait. The deviations on either side of the mean are symmetrical, or balanced. The semivariance would be half the variance, for the probability distribution and the deviations below the mean are the mirror image of those above the mean. Hence, where there is this symmetry, the variance serves just as well as the semivariance. Let's compute the semivariance for stock A and see if it is half the variance, or 1.05.

Whereas the variance was calculated by squaring each difference from the mean, multiplying the answer by the related probability, and summing the resulting amounts, the semivariance performs the same manipulations only for differences *below* the mean:

(1) HPY minus Expected HPY	(2) Difference Squared	(3) Probability	(4) (2) X (3)
7 − 10 = −3	9	.05	.45
8 − 10 = −2	4	.10	.40
9 − 10 = −1	1	.20	.20
Semivariance			1.05

The semideviation would be the square root of the semivariance. However, few distributions of HPYs are sufficiently different from symmetrical to warrant use of the semivariance or semideviation. Further, our assumption of advance predictions is that expected HPYs will turn out to be approximately symmetrically distributed. Therefore we will use the variance and standard deviations as risk surrogates throughout this text in all cases. The expected return and variance or standard deviation will be used in forming estimates for all securities.

In general, the expected HPY, variance, and standard deviation of outcomes can be shown as:

$$E = \sum_{i=1}^{m} P_i O_i$$

$$V = \sum_{i=1}^{m} P_i (O_i - E)^2$$

$$\sigma = \sqrt{V}$$

where:

E = expected HPY
V = variance of HPYs
σ = standard deviation of HPYs
P = probability
O = outcome
m = total number of different outcomes

The variability of return around the expected average is thus a quantitative description of risk. Moreover, this measure of risk is simply a proxy or surrogate for risk, since other measures could be used. Throughout the remainder of the text, we shall use variance and standard deviation of returns as a risk measure.

The total variance is the rate of return on a stock around the expected average this includes both systematic and unsystematic risk. In Chapter 17 we will see how it is possible, using somewhat more refined statistical tools to partition total variance into the amount attributable to systematic risk on the one hand and unsystematic risk on the other. This partitioning exercise is a very vital undertaking when packaging individual securities into portfolios.

**Historical
Risk-Return
Relationships
on Common
Stocks
and Bonds**

The past is not always a good indicator in investments. However, it might be well to look at some historical risk-return relationships for (1) a sample of individual stocks, and (2) broad groups of stocks and bonds in general. We will begin our exploration with an example of the detailed mechanics of making risk-return calculations for an individual stock.

RISK-RETURN MEASUREMENT: HOLIDAY INNS STOCK

Holiday Inns operates the largest motel system in the country. Shown in Table 5-4 is the historical information on annual dividend payments and closing stock prices at the end of June and December for the period 1967 through 1976. Our purpose in presenting the data is to illustrate *historical* return and risk computations using the mean-variance approach. Return is calculated assuming one-year holding periods: The stock is assumed to be purchased in June of one year and sold in June of the next year, and also purchased in December of one year and sold in December of the next. This process of buy and sell could have been repeated for a vast number of one-year periods between 12/67 and 12/76.

There is nothing sacred about the one-year holding periods or the starting and ending dates in each case. The principal reason for using one-year HPYs is our emphasis on this time horizon in much of the analysis that will appear throughout the remainder of the text.

What does Table 5-4 tell us? First, the horrendous collapse in the stock market subsequent to December 1972 (which was precipitated in large part by the energy crisis) had a devastating effect upon the market price of Holiday Inns shares. The fact that Holiday Inns' business is so critically dependent upon the availability of fuel suggests that this company was hit much harder than most by the rising awareness of problems with energy sources. For example, an investor who purchased Holiday Inns shares at the end of June 1972 at $52.75 per share and held them as of December 1973 would have seen the price of the shares drop to about 13 1/8. In other words, Holiday Inns shares lost two-thirds of

TABLE 5-4

HOLIDAY INNS, INC., SELECTED DIVIDEND AND PRICE DATA,
1967-1976

Month-Year Ending	Dividends* per Share	Price† per Share	HPY‡
12-67	$.06	$26.62	+.377
6-68	.076	33.69	+.237
12-68	.082	36.50	+.139
6-69	.094	41.50	−.323
12-69	.100	41.38	−.064
6-70	.104	27.88	+.735
12-70	.112	38.50	+.195
6-71	.119	48.13	+.101
12-71	.125	45.75	−.071
6-72	.131	52.75	
12-72	.138	42.25	
6-73	.144	18.13	−.376
12-73	.150	13.13	−.585
6-74	.156	11.00	+.224
12-74	.162	5.13	+1.872
6-75	.169	13.13	+.124
12-75	.176	14.39	−.061
6-76	.188	14.39	
12-76	.200	13.13	

*Semiannual dividend.

†Closing price, end of quarter (rounded to nearest cent).

‡December to December, June to June, etc.: e.g., 12/73-12/74 =

$$\frac{\$0.318 + (\$5.13 - \$13.13)}{\$13.13} = (0.585)$$

Source: *Wall Street Journal*, © Dow Jones & Company, Inc. All rights reserved.

their market value in an eighteen-month period! Based upon a small sample of nine one-year holding periods between 1968 and 1972, an investment in Holiday Inns common stock would have provided the holder an average return of 14.7 percent before commissions and taxes. However, the dispersion around this average is such that returns ranged from as high as +74 percent to as low as −32 percent. If we calculate the standard deviation, it is 30.1 percent. Were the distribution of the returns "normal," then one would expect that over 95 percent of the returns would lie between plus and minus two standard deviations of the mean return, or roughly between 14 percent plus 60 percent and 14 percent minus 60 percent. This band is from −45 percent to +75 percent.

Since the value of Holiday Inns shares fell so precipitously after December 1972, a second small sample of six one-year holding periods from June 1973 through December 1976 was calculated. The average one-year return is 20 percent before commissions and taxes. The dispersion around this average suggests a range of +187 percent to −58 percent. The standard deviation of these returns is 87 percent. Risk in holding Holiday Inns stock (measured by the standard deviation) was quite high in the 1967-72 and the 1973-76 period.

Soldofsky and Miller conducted a study of the risk-return for a broad spectrum of securities for the period 1950-66.[5] As part of their study they examined 75 common stocks and calculated HPYs for one-year holding periods. Stocks were assumed to be purchased on the first day of each year, held one year and sold, purchased the first day of the next year, and so on. Table 5-5 lists the results of their risk-return calculations for the individual stocks studied. The purpose of examining the particular stocks listed was to meet several criteria; the most important was that they be stocks that differed in price volatility, as judged subjectively by rating agencies. Notice the tendency for stocks that have high yields (returns) to generally experience high risk, and vice versa. In a few cases, however, extremes of low yield-high risk are in evidence, such as J. I. Case and Congoleum-Nairn.

A significant recent study of rates of return on common stocks and bonds was conducted by Roger G. Ibbotson of the University of Chicago and Rex A. Sinquefield of the American National Bank and Trust Company of Chicago.[6]

They concluded that the annual compounded rate of return and the risk (standard deviation of returns) for selected investment vehicles over the period 1926-1976 was as follows:

Investment	Return (Compounded, Annually)	Risk (Standard Deviation)
Common stocks	9.2%	22.4%
Corporate bonds	4.1	5.6

The Ibbotson and Sinquefield data vividly displays the link between return and risk. While common stocks outperformed bonds, their returns were clearly more volatile. The return on corporate bonds is not even one-half the return on stocks, but observe the significantly lower standard deviation on bonds versus stocks.

These authors utilized the Standard and Poor's (S & P) Composite Index to determine the returns on common stocks. This Index includes 500 of the largest stocks (in terms of market value) in the United States. Prior to March, 1957 the Index consisted of ninety of the largest stocks in the United States.

Table 5-6 shows annual rates of return on two popular stock-market averages between 1957 and 1975. The returns are calculated under the assumption of purchasing the average at the start of the year, collecting annual dividends at the end of the year, and selling out at year-end. The average annual HPYs for the Dow Jones and Standard & Poor's indexes were 8.3 and 8.5 percent respectively.

[5] R. M. Soldofsky and R. L. Miller, "Risk-Premium Curves for Different Classes of Long-Term Securities, 1950-1966," *Journal of Finance,* 24, No. 3 (June 1969), 429-45.

[6] R. G. Ibbotson and R. A. Sinquefield, *Stocks, Bonds, Bills, and Inflation: The Past (1926-2000) and The Future (1977-2000)* (Chicago, Ill.: Roger G. Ibbotson and Rex A. Sinquefield, 1977).

TABLE 5-5

YIELD-RISK MEASUREMENTS OF PERFORMANCE OF
75 CLASSIFIED COMMON STOCKS, 1951-1966

Name of Corp.	Performance Measurement		Name of Corp.	Performance Measurement	
	Yield*	Risk†		Yield*	Risk†
Avon Products	31.3%	59.5%	Union Oil of Calif.	15.7%	22.2%
Amer. Tel. & Tel.	9.4	14.8	Hiram Walker	12.4	18.3
Campbell Soup	8.4	23.8	ABC Consolidated	14.8	43.1
Corn Products	14.1	19.6	Amer. Distilling	11.5	31.2
Amer. Home Prod.	21.3	32.0	Ashland Oil Corp.	17.1	20.2
Eastman Kodak	17.7	31.3	Beckman Instruments	14.9	40.7
Gen. Electric	10.5	31.8	Chic. Pneumatic Tool	15.5	31.2
Gen. Foods	15.5	20.2	Deere & Co.	15.7	21.7
Int. Bus. Machines	25.7	29.2	Grand Union	11.2	36.5
Kellogg Co.	11.3	35.3	Greyhound	13.9	32.3
Merck & Co.	18.8	26.1	Maytag	22.1	56.0
Minn. Mining & Mfg.	15.7	23.3	Peabody Coal	12.0	48.4
Sears, Roebuck & Co.	14.1	26.4	Raybestos-Manhattan	13.9	16.2
Smith, Kline & French	20.0	35.5	Rockwell Standard	15.8	28.3
Brown Shoe	13.4	16.5	Stewart Warner	16.6	22.8
Caterpillar Tractor	17.8	35.4	Union Tank Car	12.4	19.4
Columbia Broadcasting	23.1	25.8	Warren (S.D.) & Co.	25.5	48.8
R. R. Donnelley & Sons	18.6	40.9	American Bank Note	10.7	22.1
Dun & Bradstreet	21.3	20.5	Cooper Industries	15.3	36.1
General Motors	16.2	30.7	Walt Disney	22.8	56.8
Ralston Purina	20.9	39.2	Divco-Wayne Corp.	13.0	33.8
Tampax, Inc.	21.5	34.7	Gen. Steel Castings	12.7	23.3
Time, Inc.	20.4	27.8	Interco, Inc.	4.5	12.6
Winn-Dixie Stores	20.6	30.8	Melville Shoe	9.0	20.0
Federated Dept. Stores	15.4	26.2	Stanley Warner Corp.	18.7	51.5
Amer. Hosp. Supply	22.7	30.3	United Eng. & Foundry	5.0	22.0
Baxter Laboratories	21.1	35.8	Warner & Swasey	16.5	36.2
Cont. Corp. of Amer.	14.1	24.6	Brown Co.	6.6	37.1
Dana Corp.	12.8	26.1	Congoleum-Nairn	5.0	46.4
Elec. Storage Battery	10.6	24.9	J. I. Case	0.0	42.6
Max Factor	21.5	46.9	Crucible Steel	7.1	47.4
Gen. Cable Corp.	25.4	30.8	Dayco	11.6	37.5
Int. Nickel of Canada	14.7	28.4	Detroit Steel	3.9	49.5
Lorillard & Co.	14.3	40.6	General Baking	7.1	22.1
Moore Corp., Ltd.	18.8	14.9	Lowenstein & Sons	4.2	37.2
Pepsico, Inc.	17.0	19.5	Rheem Mfg.	2.4	47.7
Square D. Co.	21.5	31.2	Sharon Steel	2.7	48.6
Lavington	9.7	20.1			

*Geometric mean.

†Standard deviation around the geometric mean.

Source: Robert M. Soldofsky, "Yield-Risk Performance Measurements," *Financial Analysts Journal*, 24, No. 5 (September-October 1968), 132.

Standard deviation of returns was 3.5 percent for the DJIA and 3.4 percent for the S&P 500. The similarity between the return measures on these indexes and the Ibbotsen-Sinquefield efforts is the reason why many investment people, when asked about the kinds of returns an average investor can achieve in the stock market over the long run, will quote numbers in the 8-9 percent range.

TABLE 5-6
ANNUAL HPYs ON TWO POPULAR STOCK—MARKET INDEXES

Year	S&P 500	Dow Jones Industrials
1957	−.105	−.084
1958	.424	.386
1959	.118	.200
1960	.003	−.062
1961	.266	.224
1962	−.088	−.076
1963	.225	.206
1964	.163	.187
1965	.123	.142
1966	−.100	−.157
1967	.237	.190
1968	.108	.077
1969	−.083	−.116
1970	.035	.088
1971	.142	.098
1972	.189	.185
1973	−.147	−.133
1974	−.263	−.235
1975	.371	.448
For 19 one-year holding periods:		
Mean HPY	.085	.083
Variance	.034	.035
Standard deviation	.184	.187

RISK-RETURN ON CORPORATE BONDS

Recent studies of returns on bonds between 1926 and 1968 present some interesting contrasts with returns on common stocks.[7] Estimates of one-year-holding-period returns of a portfolio of 4 percent, twenty-year AAA bonds over the period showed a mean (average) return over the entire period of 3.9 percent. Over the period 1925-65, the bond return averaged 3.7 percent compounded annually, compared with the 9.2 percent on stocks found in the Ibbotson-Sinquefield studies cited earlier.

The bond results suggest further that long-term bonds have provided not only a lower average return than a well-diversified portfolio of common stocks but a more than proportionately lower dispersion. In other words, bonds return less than stocks but bear risk that is more than proportionately lower.

A test of annual rates of return on stocks and on bonds during market swings

[7]Roman L. Weil, "Realized Interest Rates and Bondholders' Returns," *American Economic Review,* 60, No. 3 (June 1970) 502-11; and Lawrence Fisher and Roman L. Weil, "Coping with the Risk of Interest-Rate Fluctuations: Returns to Bondholders from Naive and Optimal Strategies," *Journal of Business,* 44, No. 4 (October 1971), 408-31.

from mid-1965 to early 1973 indicated that bonds increased at an annual rate of return about equal to that of stocks in bull markets, and declined at an annual rate substantially less than stocks in bear markets. The study found that the annual rate of return during rallies was 32 percent for stocks compared with 25-32 percent for bonds, depending upon the type of bond portfolio chosen. In bear markets, the overall rate of decline in total return was 15 percent for stocks, compared with 4-8 percent for bonds. These comparisons were made between the Standard & Poor's 500 Composite Stock Index and three different groups of high-quality public utility bonds. The rates of return quoted are annualized rates of total return during bull and bear markets, and they do not reflect the overall performance of the stock and bond markets for investors who bought securities in mid-1965 and held them through early 1973. For the full 7½-year period, the holding-period yield was over 40 percent for stocks, as compared with 15 percent for bonds.[8]

Salomon Bros., a large bond house in New York, has developed an index that measures total return over various time periods for the long-term corporate bond market. The relevant "market" is basically all industrial and utility bonds originally publicly offered with a maturity of 1985 or later, of high quality, and an outstanding par amount of at least $25 million.

Table 5-7 shows the results of investing in a portfolio of these bonds between 1969 and 1976. For example, an investment in the bond portfolio at the start of the first quarter of 1969 that was held to the end of the quarter would have resulted in an annualized rate of return of −8.77 percent. An investor would have received 6.33 percent in interest from the portfolio (annualized), but the principal value would have declined 15.11 percent (annualized).

The Ibbotson and Sinquefield study referred to earlier notes some interesting risk and return relationships from the Salomon Bros. Bond Index.[9] As previously noted, long-term corporate bonds returned 4.1 percent per year compounded annually over the period 1926-76 period. Long-term bonds had positive returns in forty-one out of the fifty-one years examined. Returns ranged from 18.7 percent in 1976 to −8.1 percent in 1969.

Summary

The risk associated with holding common stocks is really the likelihood that expected returns will not materialize. Should dividends or price appreciation fall short of expectations, the investor is disappointed. The principal sources behind dividend and price-appreciation uncertainties are forces and factors that are either controllable or not subject to control by the firm.

Uncontrollable forces, called sources of systematic risk, include market, interest-rate, and purchasing-power risks. Market risk reflects changes in investor attitudes toward equities in general that stem from tangible and intangible

---

[8]R. I. Johannsen, Jr., "Stock and Bond Performance During Market Swings Since 1965," *Memorandum to Portfolio Managers* (New York: Salomon Brothers, July 10, 1973).

[9]Salomon Bros., *High Grade Corporate Bond Total Rate-of-Return Index* (New York: Salomon Bros., various dates, 1970-77), pp. 59-60.

TABLE 5-7
HIGH GRADE CORPORATE BOND INDEX
TOTAL RATE OF RETURN FOR COMPOSITE
CORPORATE PORTFOLIO

Holding Period Covered	Principal Return	Coupon Return	Principal Plus Coupon Return
1st Qtr. 1969	−15.11%	6.33%	−8.77%
2nd Qtr.	−1.11	6.58	5.47
3rd Qtr.	−17.28	6.60	−10.67
4th Qtr.	−26.24	7.21	−19.03
1st Qtr. 1970	12.49	7.72	20.21
2nd Qtr.	−23.93	7.64	−16.29
3rd Qtr.	24.29	8.12	32.42
4th Qtr.	26.87	7.69	34.56
1st Qtr. 1971	9.05	7.20	16.26
2nd Qtr.	−18.64	7.04	−11.59
3rd Qtr.	9.36	7.39	16.74
4th Qtr.	14.33	7.22	21.55
1st Qtr. 1972	−3.06	6.97	3.90
2nd Qtr.	−1.89	7.02	5.13
3rd Qtr.	−1.72	7.06	5.33
4th Qtr.	6.77	7.09	13.86
1st Qtr. 1973	−6.42	6.97	.54
2nd Qtr.	−8.43	7.08	−1.35
3rd Qtr.	1.05	7.23	8.29
4th Qtr.	−10.30	7.21	−3.09
1st Qtr. 1974	−21.25	7.41	−13.85
2nd Qtr.	−28.38	7.82	−20.56
3rd Qtr.	−20.70	8.42	−12.28
4th Qtr.*	7.08	2.22	9.30
1st Qtr. 1975	2.71	2.07	4.78
2nd Qtr.	1.54	2.02	3.55
3rd Qtr.	−5.25	1.99	−3.26
4th Qtr.	7.07	2.10	9.17
1st Qtr. 1976	2.13	2.06	4.19
2nd Qtr.	−1.72	2.01	0.29
3rd Qtr.	3.48	2.05	5.53
4th Qtr.	5.47	1.98	7.45

*Non-annualized percentage returns subsequent to September 1974.
Source: Salomon Bros., *High Grade Corporate Bond Total Rate-of-Return Index* (New York: Salomon Bros., 1978).

events. Tangible events might include expectations of lower corporate profits; intangible events might be overreaction to lower expected profits and the resultant panic selling. Interest-rate risk and purchasing-power risk are associated with changes in the price of money and other goods and services. Increases in interest rates (the price of money) cause the prices of all types of securities to be marked down. Rising prices of goods and services (inflation or purchasing-power changes) have an adverse effect on security prices, since the postponement of consumption through any form of investment means less "real" buying power in the future.

The principal sources of unsystematic risk affecting the holding of common stocks are business risk and financial risk. Business risk refers to changes in the operating environment of the firm and how the firm adapts to them. Financial risk is related to the debt-and-equity mix of financing in the firm. Operating profits can be magnified up or down, depending upon the extent to which debt financing is employed and under what terms.

The various sources of risk in holding common stocks must be quantified so that the analyst can examine risk in relationship to measures of return employed in Chapter 4. A reasonable surrogate of risk is the variability of return. This proxy measure in statistics is commonly the variance or standard deviation of the returns on a stock around the expected return. In reality, the variation in return *below* what is expected is the best measure of risk, but we saw that since the distribution of returns on stocks is nearly normal in a statistical sense, the semideviation or semivariance below the expected value need not be calculated.

Questions and Problems

1. Identify the risks normally associated with the following terms: (a) investor panic, (b) cost-of-living, (c) labor strikes, (d) increased debt/equity ratios, (e) product obsolescence.

2. Of those risks normally associated with the holding of securities, (a) what three risks are commonly classified as systematic in nature? (b) what risks are most prevalent in holding common stocks?

3. Show in tabular form a frequency distribution of the sums obtained by tossing a pair of dice.

4. Show a simple example using probabilities where two securities have equal expected returns but unequal variances or risk in returns.

5. A stock costing $100 pays no dividends. The possible prices that the stock might sell for at the end of the year and the probability of each are:

End-of-Year Price	Probability
$ 90	.1
95	.2
100	.4
110	.2
115	.1

a. What is the expected return?

b. What is the standard deviation of the expected return?

c. What is the semideviation of the expected return?

6. Ignoring the interactive effect of combining securities, graph the calculated risk and return for the securities in Table 5-5. Which stocks dominate, in the sense that they have a higher return than another stock for the same or lower risk, or lower risk for the same or higher return?

7. Cite recent examples of political, social, or economic events (market risk) that have excited (a) the stock market, and (b) stocks in a specific industry, to surge ahead or plummet sharply.

8. Mr. Calvert has analyzed a stock for a one-year holding period. The stock is currently selling for $10, but pays no dividends, and there is a fifty-fifty chance that the stock will sell for either $10 or $12 by year-end. What is the expected HPY and risk if 250 shares are acquired with 80 percent margin? Assume the cost of borrowed funds is 10 percent. (Ignore commissions and taxes.)

9. What is the significance to an investor of a stock with the following specifications: expected return = .10, variance = .10, semivariance (below the mean) = .01?

10. Stocks Q and R do not pay dividends. Stock Q currently sells for $50 and R for $100. At the end of the year ahead there is a fifty-fifty chance that Q will sell for either $61 or $57 and R for either $117 or $113. Which stock, Q or R, would you prefer to purchase now? *Why?*

11. Determine dividends paid and the high and low prices on shares of IBM from *Value Line, Moody's Handbook of Common Stocks*, or other sources. Assuming the IBM was bought and sold each year from 1972 through 1978 at the average of the high-low price and that dividends for the year were collected, calculate, for the years 1972 through 1978, (a) the average annual holding-period yield, and (b) the standard deviation of the annual HPYs.

12. An investor has a normal required rate of return of 9 percent, which includes expectations of an annual rate of inflation of 4 percent. How much should he be willing to pay for a stock that pays no dividends and is expected to sell for $30 at the end of the year, if he intends to hold the stock until year-end? What if inflation expectations change to 3 percent?

13. Russo Corporation has been in the business of distributing national brands of swimming pools for many years. Recently the owner's son has been encouraging his father to increase the size of the business by 50 percent through distributing a complete line of ski equipment and accessories. In what ways would the expansion alter the business risk associated with the operation of Russo Corporation as merely a swimming-pool distributor?

14. Financial risk or leverage in the case of individuals is normally associated with margin trading, or increasing one's ability to purchase securities by borrowing money. Investor A has analyzed a stock for a one-year holding period. There is a 50-50 chance that the stock, currently selling at $10, will sell for $9 or $12 by year-end. The investor can borrow on 50 percent margin from his bank at 9 percent per annum. (Ignore taxes and transaction costs.)

    a. What are the investor's expected holding-period yield and risk if he buys 100 shares and does not borrow from his bank?

    b. What are expected yield and risk if he buys 200 shares, paying half the cost with borrowed funds at 9 percent per annum?

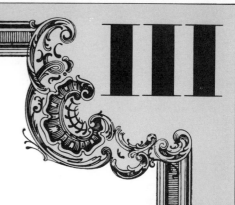

COMMON-STOCK ANALYSIS

The primary motive for buying a stock is to sell it subsequently at a higher price. In many cases, dividends will be expected also. Dividends and price changes are the principal ingredients in what investors regard as return or yield.

If an investor had impeccable information and insight about dividends and stock prices over subsequent periods, he would be well on his way to great riches. But the real world of investing is full of political, economic, social, and other forces that we do not understand sufficiently to permit us to predict anything with absolute certainty. Forces intermix and flow at cross-currents. Nothing is static.

For the security analyst, what primary influences will determine the dividends to be paid on a stock in the future and what the stock price will be in the future are the ultimate questions to be answered. A logical, systematic approach to estimating future dividends and stock price is indispensable.

The framework we will be using is the economic-industry-company approach, or the E-I-C framework.

ECONOMIC AND INDUSTRY ANALYSIS

King observed that, on the average, over half the variation in a stock's price could be attributed to a market influence that affects all stock-market indexes, such as the Dow Jones Industrial Average or the Standard & Poor's 500 Stock Index.[1] But stocks are also subject to an industry influence, over and above the influence common to all stocks. King noted that this industry influence explained, on the average, about 13 percent of the variation in a stock's price. In sum, about two-thirds of the variation in the prices of stocks observed in King's study was the result of market and industry influences or factors. King actually examined only about sixty companies, so it is dangerous to extrapolate from this small sample to a generalization about *all* stocks. However, although the amount of variation in a stock's price attributable to the market may be more or less than the percentage observed by King, the impact of a common market influence is obviously something to be contended with.

---

[1] B. F. King, "Market and Industry Factors in Stock Price Behavior," *Journal of Business,* 39 (January 1966), 139-90.

The significance of these conclusions seems to be that in order to estimate stock price changes, an analyst must spend more than a little time probing the forces operating in the overall economy, as well as influences peculiar to industries he is concerned with. A failure to examine overall economic and industry influences is a naive error, that of assuming that individual companies follow their own private paths in a vacuum.

It is important to predict the course of the national economy because economic activity affects corporate profits, investor attitudes and expectations, and ultimately security prices. An outlook of sagging economic growth can lead to lower corporate profits, a prospect that can engender investor pessimism and lower security prices. Some industries might be expected to hold up better, and stock prices of companies in these industries may not decline as much as securities in general. The key for the analyst is that overall economic activity manifests itself in the behavior of stocks in general—or the stock market, if you will. This linkage between economic activity and the stock market is critical.

Investing is a business of relative changes. When the economic outlook is assessed, along with the direction of change in the overall market for stocks, the analyst must realize that even though industry groups and/or individual companies may find it difficult to "buck the trend," they do not necessarily respond to the same degree. For example, it is widely assumed that heavy-goods industries fare worse in economic recessions than do consumer-goods industries. Heavy-goods industries include automobiles (and related industries such as rubber, steel, glass) and machinery. Consumer-goods and service industries include utilities (telephone, power), food, and banks. Recessions or expansions in economic activity may translate into falling or rising stock markets with different *relative* price changes among industry groups.

For the analyst, industry analysis demands insight into (1) the key sectors or subdivisions of overall economic activity that influence particular industries, and (2) the relative strength or weakness of particular industry or other groupings under specific sets of assumptions about economic activity.

Chapter 6 considers how the analyst goes about forecasting the direction and degree of change in economic activity. Chapter 7 links the forecast of economic activity to the prediction of *relative* movements in specific industries and analysis of selected industries.

COMPANY ANALYSIS

Estimating dividends and price changes for individual stocks must be preceded by sound economic and industry analysis. Without these, the King study shows, an analyst is looking at only a third of the story.

The most immediately recognizable effect of economic and industry influences on a specific company is probably the impact on revenues. The sales of some industries (steel, autos) tend to move in tandem with the business cycle; others (food, telephone, utilities) are relatively immune from the cycle; still others (such as housing) move countercyclically. From the viewpoint of the individual company, adjustments to changes in the general business cycle can be different from those of the industry in general. Product mix and pricing peculiar to specific firms can cause total revenues to respond more or less to broad economic and industry impact. Diversified product lines, for example, make it possible for a company to spread cyclical effects.

Revenue changes in firms in the same industry with identical product mix and pricing policies may lead to different relative changes in costs. As we saw in Chapter 5, a company in which fixed costs absorb a large percentage of total costs may have difficulty curtailing expenses during economic declines, and responding as demand increases. A firm with a large proportion of its total costs variable may respond better, both up and down. In the end, the latter firm may show better earnings (revenue minus costs). The relationship of revenues and expenses to economic and industry changes, and the resulting earnings, is the focal point of company analysis.

Earnings and Stock Price Changes

Many factors are responsible for producing revenue and in turn converting revenue into earnings. However, in the final analysis, stock price changes and dividends paid are to some degree governed by what happens to earnings. This connection between earnings and stock price is very much analogous to the connection between what a piece of equipment is worth and the earnings it is expected to produce. The exact nature of the earnings-stock price relationship is somewhat complex, and other factors affect the price of a stock. Chapters 8, 9, and 10 will examine factors at the company level influencing stock prices and dividends. For the time being we want to paint some broad strokes.

The current price of a stock will, in some measure, reflect market expectations of earnings. Stocks of companies with prospects for superior earnings growth will sell at higher prices relative to earnings than will those of slower-growing companies. For example, companies G and H are in the same industry. Both have just reported earning $1 per share. Stock G sells for $15 and stock H for $30. Investors are paying $15 in price for each $1 of current earnings for G; they are paying $30 in price for each $1 of current earnings for H. Analysts often refer to this relationship as the price-earnings ratio, or simply the "P/E."

The principal reason for the differences in P/E ratios (15 for G and 30 for H) can be traced to the fact that investors *expect* earnings to grow more rapidly for H than for G. Unanticipated changes in earnings should result in an adjustment of the stock price. Should earnings exceed expectations, stock prices should rise. Prices should fall if earnings are below expectations. Numerous studies have been made on why stocks sell at different P/E ratios. The results tend to suggest that at any moment in time, P/E ratios differ between firms according to differences in projected earnings growth and variations in the rate of earnings growth. Higher P/E's are associated with more rapid earnings growth and less variation (greater stability) in the rate of that growth over time.

Knowledge of what determines P/E's is essential. We can use this information to determine an expected selling price for a stock at the end of the holding period. In effect, applying an estimated P/E to a forecast of earnings at the end of the holding period allows the analyst to determine the expected selling price:

$$P_1 = (P/E)_1 \, (E_1)$$

where:

P_1 = stock price, end of holding period
$(P/E)_1$ = price-earnings ratio, end of holding period
E_1 = estimated earnings, end of holding period

The P/E ratio used at the end of the holding period will embody expectations of *future* earnings growth and stability, beyond the holding period. In subsequent chapters we will explore P/E ratios and alternative means for estimating end-of-holding-period price.

Earnings and Dividends

The remaining element of return an analyst must estimate is the dividend. Stocks pay all kinds of dividends, from $0 on up. However, it is possible that three stocks paying $0, $1, and $2 in current dividends will all sell for $40. This suggests that dividends being paid *now* are not all that is important to investors.

It is quite common to speak of the percentage of its reported earnings that a company pays in dividends. The *dividend payout ratio* is calculated by dividing annual dividends by current annual earnings. Hence a company that earns $3.00 per share and pays $1.20 in dividends is said to have a 40 percent payout ratio ($1.20/$3.00). Companies sometimes pay dividends in excess of current earnings. Although this practice cannot be sustained for long, it can occur if the firm expects the earnings picture to improve in the near future. In such cases the payout ratio exceeds 100 percent. Dividend payments when earnings are zero or below provide payout ratios that lack quantitative significance.

The dividend paid by a company in a given quarter or year is strongly tied to earnings. However, the dividend paid in absolute dollar terms or relative to current earnings does not necessarily reflect current earnings alone, but past and expected future earnings as well.

Many corporations recognize two fairly clear notions about the reaction of investors to dividends. First, absolute dollar levels, once established, are reduced only when it is clear that declining earnings will not recover. Second, declining stock prices are associated with reductions in absolute dollar dividends.

The most positive effects on stock price seem to lie in maintaining a "target" payout ratio over time. Over time, companies will display payout patterns that can assist the analyst in making predictions of holding-period dividends. By and large, the payout ratio that emerges over the years depends to a large extent upon the expected return on new investment opportunities generated in the firm and the need for earnings retention as a source of financing these opportunities.

Auto and rubber are examples of industries that pay out a low percentage of earnings. Their earnings are typically unstable, and their reluctance to use borrowed money to any great extent means that they must rely heavily upon equity financing. Earnings retention provides a big assist in this area. The air-transport and office-equipment industries are also known for low dividend payouts, but for other reasons. Their rate of expansion of assets is so great that they retain earnings to support the use of debt. Air-transport companies face the double problem of cyclical growth. This means that while earnings trend upward over time, nonetheless they fluctuate widely. Often these companies use stock dividends instead of cash dividends in the face of heavy internal cash needs and unstable earnings.

Relatively high payout industries include in their ranks those whose rate of return on reinvested earnings is low. In other words, they are not expanding dramatically, and/or the amount of expansion they engage in does not require that large proportions of earnings be retained. The tobacco and paper industries are examples of high-payout industries.

The analyst's job is particularly difficult in those situations where a company does not follow a regular dividend policy. This subject will be pursued again in Chapter 10. Let us now begin our analysis of common stocks with the economic analysis.

CHAPTER SIX

ECONOMIC ANALYSIS

Timing is of critical importance in the investment process. It is not enough to know *what* to buy or sell; one must also know *when*. In order to facilitate a logical approach to the overall investment decision-making process (which includes knowing both *what* to buy and *when* to buy), in the next few chapters we will examine the role of the economic, industry, and company factors. Our purpose is to see how this information is relevant to the investment decision. However, first it is necessary to see how this economy-industry-company (E-I-C) approach fits into the framework established in Chapters 4 and 5.

We have noted that an investor in common stocks should be concerned with the return-and-risk characteristics of the securities under consideration. The expected return for a holding period of one year is determined by adding the price change that the investor expects to occur during the year to the dividends to be received, and dividing this sum by the price at the beginning of the year. A useful risk surrogate, we found, is the standard deviation of previous one-year-holding-period returns. The E-I-C framework provides a useful, logical means for arriving at the dividend and price change.

In brief, the analyst focuses first on the broad picture—the expected future economic environment during his one-year time horizon—in order to detect any probable emerging patterns. Such variables as the forecast of gross national product (GNP) and its key components, personal consumption, investment, government expenditures, and net exports, must be understood. In addition, monetary and fiscal policy, the outlook for corporate profits, and interest rates would be considered. From this analysis, the security analyst attempts to forecast which industries are likely to perform best in such an economic environment.[1] With this base, the E-I-C analysis continues to explore in depth the selected "good performers" among the universe of all domestic industries. After the industry analysis, the companies that the analyst feels will do best in the industries are explored in great detail. Company analysis culminates in a forecast of terminal price and dividends.

[1] Frequently the analyst or investor has in mind an industry that he is seriously considering as an investment opportunity. Here, the E-I-C framework is of value. The approach here is to determine first which economic variables are critical to the success of the industry. After forecasting these variables, he proceeds to the industry and company analyses. Both approaches will be utilized in a comprehensive example at the end of this chapter.

Before an investor commits funds in the market, he must decide if the time is right to invest in securities at all; and if so, he must then decide which type of security to purchase under the circumstances.[2] Thus he must decide whether to purchase common stocks, options, preferred stocks, bonds, or some combination thereof. In this chapter we will explore the relevance of broad economic variables such as national income and defense expenditures to the investor or analyst considering the purchase of common stocks. In the process, we will place major emphasis on the techniques most frequently employed by business economists as they go about their business of short-term economic forecasting. These are important for the security analyst or investor to know, because he will be utilizing much of the output of the economists' efforts as a basis for his own opinion about the impending economic environment. In this respect, the analyst can better evaluate economic forecasts if he has at least some knowledge of alternative economic forecasting tools—not only the techniques but also their advantages and shortcomings. The techniques we will examine and evaluate include the use of surveys, key economic indicators, diffusion indexes, econometric model building, and the opportunistic model building. First, let's discuss the relationship of economic forecasting to the stock-investment decision more fully.[3]

Economic Forecasting and the Stock-Investment Decision

If an investor purchases the stock of an automobile manufacturer that is selling near an all-time high, and shortly thereafter the automobile workers go on strike for a long period of time, the investor will surely suffer a large paper loss on his investment. Certainly if the investor had waited until the strike was close to being settled, other things being equal, his purchase price would have been considerably lower and his potential capital gains greatly enhanced. In analyzing the economy, a careful analyst would have considered the potential impact of an impending automobile workers' strike.

However, there is yet another important reason for considering the economic environment before taking an investment action. As we have seen, research has discovered that approximately half the variability in stock prices is explained by the movement of the overall market. In investment jargon, this common or

[2]Obviously, timing (which we consider to include both the *what* and *when* issues) is of critical importance not only in a purchase decision but also in the sell decision; however, in order to ease the explanation of the relevant factors, we will restrict our discussion to the purchase question, and leave it to the reader to adapt the methodology discussed in the text to the sell decision.

Furthermore, as an adjunct to the timing issue, the economic forecast of the analyst can be compared with the overall market's behavior as reflected in stock prices. If the analyst's expectations are markedly different from the apparent consensus market forecast, an investment action may be warranted. The reader should recall that if one accepts the efficient-market hypothesis, this will occur only in rare instances—and then for the good only if the investor analyst is particularly astute and skillful.

[3]Throughout this chapter we should keep in mind that the exact cause-and-effect relationships between macroeconomic variables and the stock market are not known. However, we know that they are related, and thus the economic environment must be considered.

market effect is known as systematic risk. Furthermore, it is intuitively appealing to reason that the total market or some index of market performance is related to overall economic performance. That is, the success of the economy will ultimately include the success of the overall market.[4] For without a positive and healthy economic environment, corporations in general will find it difficult to flourish over time, and investors' holding-period returns will suffer. This in turn will adversely affect an index of overall stock-market performance.

Above and beyond these broad, general relationships, we should observe that future prospects of many specific industries and firms will be tied to future developments in specific economic series, because profits are based on key economic factors. For example, labor-intensive industries will be tied to labor costs and conditions, most firms involved with transforming material and producing a final product will be tied to the costs of raw materials, savings and loan associations will be affected by the course of interest rates and the demand for mortgages, and leisure-products firms will be affected by the availability of leisure time and consumer disposable income.

Thus we see the importance of relating economic phenomena to security price movements. To better equip the security analyst and investor for this undertaking, we will, in the next few sections, discuss several commonly used forecasting techniques, with major emphasis on the sources of this information, their potential usefulness to the analyst, and their limitations.

**Forecasting
Techniques** SHORT-TERM VERSUS LONG-TERM
ECONOMIC FORECASTS

First, let us define some terms in the manner in which a business forecaster uses them. When he speaks of a *short-term forecast*, he is generally referring to one covering a period of up to three years, although frequently he means a much shorter period, such as a quarter or several quarters. An *intermediate forecast* refers to a three- to five-year period ahead. And finally, a *long-term forecast* refers to a period more than five years, and frequently ten or more years, in advance. These definitions are those of the business forecaster; but we must understand the different usage generally employed by a security analyst.

To a security analyst, a *short-term forecast* is related to the current U.S. tax law, which says that assets held for less than twelve months are liable for short-term tax treatment, and the *long-term forecast* with those assets held for twelve months and a day or more, which are treated as long-term assets for tax purposes. The next logical step is to reconcile these very different definitions of

---

[4]Notwithstanding this, we will observe shortly that an index of 500 common-stock prices is classified as a leading indicator, with a median lead time of four months. However, it is still possible for individual economic components, such as disposable income, population, expenditures on defense, and income distribution by age group, to lead corporate sales, earnings, and the stock prices of certain industries and companies. Furthermore, if business conditions can be forecast far enough ahead, even in a general fashion, they will lead stock prices, thus *leading a leading indicator.*

the economist and the analyst and show how they in fact fit together very nicely.

We noted in an earlier chapter that one of the differences between investment and speculation is the time horizon of the individual in question. That is, the speculator is interested in very short-term holds of securities (short-term in both a tax sense and a forecasting sense) in order to realize quick capital gains; on the other hand, the investor is interested in situations that will yield adequate returns in both dividends and capital gains for their risk class over a period of several years. However, we also observed earlier that even in the true investment situation, the investor or analyst must constantly review each security's performance both in an absolute sense and in a relative sense—relative to the market. Furthermore, he must regularly observe the state of the stock market, the money and capital markets, and the economy in general in order to ascertain if basic economic conditions have changed sufficiently to warrant his changing his investment strategy. This is another reason for viewing the macroeconomic picture—namely, to detect the relatively most attractive industries at a given moment. Thus, even for the pure investor with a long time horizon, we see that this long period is broken into several short-term periods. In other words, his initial long-term forecast can be broken down into a series of short-term forecasts that are constantly reviewed and revised. Therefore we will focus on a one-year horizon throughout our analysis.

In this chapter we will discuss only short-term forecasting techniques, realizing that when these various short-term forecasts are put side by side, they constitute a check for consistency with an independently arrived-at long-term forecast.[5]

ALTERNATIVE TECHNIQUES OF SHORT-TERM BUSINESS FORECASTING

Central to all forecasting techniques is an understanding of the national income and product accounts, which summarize both the receipts and the expenditures of all segments of the economy, whether government, business, or personal. These macroeconomic accounts taken together measure the total of economic activity in the United States over some specified period of time. By definition, the total of the final expenditures must equal the total of the receipts in the economy. This total quantity is known as the *gross national product*, or GNP for short. Thus, to give it a formal definition, GNP is the *total market value of the final output of goods and services produced in the economy.* The various approaches we are about to discuss are used in conjunction with forecasting GNP for short periods in advance, as well as for forecasting various components of GNP over similar periods of time.

It would be of no small interest to an analyst to have knowledge in advance of impending moves, particularly in those components of GNP that are most closely related to the industry or firm he is investigating. For example, if the

[5]For a discussion of an approach to long-term forecasting, see John P. Lewis and Robert C. Turner, *Business Conditions Analysis* (New York: McGraw-Hill, 1967).

analyst were considering a defense-oriented company or the defense industry, he would be much interested in a forecast of federal expenditures for defense. If he were examining a consumer-oriented firm, he would undoubtedly be very interested in a forecast of disposable personal income and per capita real GNP. (Real GNP is GNP adjusted for price-level changes.) Certainly forecasts of the rate of population growth, the rate of GNP growth, and thus the rate of growth in per capita GNP would also be important to a consumer-oriented firm's future prospects.

Figure 6-1 depicts the economy's historical performance as reflected by the actual levels of GNP obtained versus the potential levels of GNP obtainable by the economy.[6] Information such as that contained in the chart is useful as a broad gauge of the economy's performance and can thus be used most directly in analyzing basic industries in the economy, and also as a benchmark in evaluating whether progress is being made on schedule toward an intermediate or long-term forecast level of GNP. When actual GNP is below potential GNP, such as in 1970-72, this period represents an underutilization of capacity probably brought on by unemployment in excess of 4 percent. If the forecaster or analyst has predicted an upturn in economic activity, then in time the gap between actual and potential GNP should begin to close. If this does not happen, perhaps it is time for the analyst to reconsider his forecast! In Figure 6-1 it can be seen that this gap closed almost entirely during 1973.

The matter of business forecasting is rather complex and quite specialized. As a result, it is not likely that the security analyst or investor will be called upon to make his own complete forecast of the entire economy, or for that matter a complete forecast of any individual sector in the economy. Nonetheless, it will undoubtedly be necessary for him to use, in his decision-making process concerning securities, economic forecasts or information that a business forecaster uses as a starting point; and thus, it is a prerequisite to knowledgeable and successful investing that he be able to understand and evaluate economic inputs and forecasts that are furnished to him.

To this end, we will next turn our attention to a brief review of major reputable approaches to short-term business forecasting. Our purpose will not be to turn the reader into a professional forecaster, but rather to equip him with the knowledge of the sources of this type of information and to help him understand the value, advantages, and limitations of these approaches.

Anticipatory Surveys

Perhaps the most logical place to start a forecast is to ask prominent people in government and industry what their plans are with respect to construction, plant and equipment expenditure, and inventory adjustments, and to ask consumers what their future spending plans are. To the extent that these various entities plan and budget for expenditures in advance and adhere to their intentions,

---

[6]Potential GNP is defined as the level of GNP the economy could obtain assuming a 4 percent unemployment rate.

FIGURE 6-1
ACTUAL AND POTENTIAL GROSS NATIONAL PRODUCT

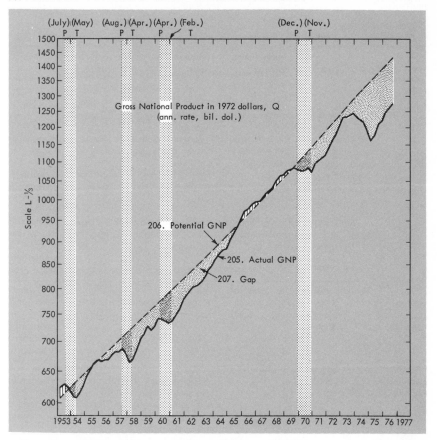

Current data for these series are shown on page 95. [1]Trend line of 3.5 percent per year (intersecting actual line in middle of 1955) from 1st quarter 1952 to 4th quarter 1962, 3.75 percent from 4th quarter 1962 to 4th quarter 1965 and 4 percent from 4th quarter 1965 to 3rd quarter 1975. See special note on page 95.

Source: U.S. Department of Commerce, *Business Conditions Digest,*
Oct., 1976.

surveys of intentions constitute a valuable input in the forecasting process.[7] Table 6-1 contains a summary of the sources, uses, and timing of key forecasting information, including the sources of key survey results. These sources provide valuable insights to the analyst from people who ought to know.

Inasmuch as we are living in a decentralized economy (that is, an economy in which economic decisions are made by individual entities rather than dictated to them by a centralized government), it is necessary that a survey of intentions be based upon elaborate statistical sampling procedures. Furthermore, adequate

---

[7]For a more complete discussion of the survey approach to forecasting, see Morris Cohen, "Surveys and Forecasting," in William F. Butler, Robert A. Kavesh, and Robert B. Platt, eds., *Methods and Techniques of Business Forecasting* (Englewood Cliffs, N.J.: Prentice-Hall, 1974).

TABLE 6-1

SOURCES AND USES OF KEY FORECASTING INFORMATION

Component of GNP	Type of Information	Source and Date	Uses of the Information
Federal government spending	1. President's budget message to Congress.	Newspapers carry summaries in January. Also published by government.	Provides the most important information on federal expenditures for the next fiscal year, starting on July 1. Is subject to revision by Congress.
	2. Summary of the budget message.	*The Budget in Brief* (Government publication in January).	Presents a summary of the budget message.
	3. Review of the economic situation with emphasis on the federal budget.	President's *Economic Report* (Government publication in late January).	Presents an interpretation of the budget and its economic implications.
	4. Review of the economic situation with emphasis on the federal budget.	*Midyear Budget Review* (Government publication in August).	Presents a review of the federal spending program for the current fiscal year, reflecting congressional revisions of the budget.
	5. Reports on congressional action on presidential spending plans.	Newspapers and weekly magazines throughout the sessions of Congress.	Provides information on the success or failure of the President's program in Congress, as well as predictions of future plans both of the President and Congress.
State and local government spending	1. Data on the levels of state and local government spending in recent periods.	The national income accounts in the *Survey of Current Business* (monthly).	The usual procedure is to extrapolate the recent trend into the future, with possible revisions based on newspaper reports on expedited programs or on financial difficulties.
Investment in plant and equipment	1. Surveys of intentions to invest.	McGraw-Hill Book Company (*Business Week* in November); also Department of Commerce and SEC (*Survey of Current Business*, November, March, and other issues).	These surveys provide excellent information in business investment plans for the coming year (or quarter). The past record of these surveys is good for most periods.
	2. New orders for durable goods.	*Survey of Current Business* (monthly).	Since orders usually lead actual production and sales, this series provides suggestions on future changes in investment.
	3. Nonresidential construction contracts (F. W. Dodge Index).	*Survey of Current Business* (monthly) and *Business Conditions Digest* (monthly).	Since construction awards should normally lead actual construction, this series suggests potential changes in the building of factories, office buildings, stores, etc.
Residential construction	1. Family formation.	Intermittent projections by the Bureau of the Census.	Provides information of a key segment of the potential market for new housing.
	2. Residential construction contracts awarded or housing starts.	*Survey of Current Business* (monthly) and *Business Conditions Digest* (monthly).	Provides an indication of potential changes in housing construction before those changes take place.

TABLE 6-1 (cont.)

Component of GNP	Type of Information	Source and Date	Uses of the Information
	3. Mortgage terms and ease of securing loans (down payments, interest rates, monthly payments).	Newspapers provide intermittent reports. *Federal Reserve Bulletin* (monthly).	Information on the terms on FHA, VA, and regular mortgages indicates the financial restraints on the purchase of new homes.
	4. Vacancy rate.	Bureau of Labor Statistics.	Indicates the extent of saturation of the housing market.
	5. Home-building survey.	*Fortune* magazine (monthly).	Indicates developments in residential construction.
Inventory investment	1. Ratios of inventories to sales on the manufacturing, wholesaling, and retailing levels (requires computations involving series on inventories and series on sales).	*Survey of Current Business* (monthly).	Indicate whether inventories are high or low in relation to a "normal" ratio. Must be interpreted with caution in the light of recent changes in final sales and the attitude of businessmen toward inventories.
	2. Manufacturers' inventory expectations.	*Survey of Current Business* (monthly)	Indicate extent to which businessmen expect to expand or contract inventories.
	3. Inventory surveys.	*Fortune* magazine (monthly).	On the basis of sales expectations and assumed inventory-sales ratios, estimates amount of inventory change.
Consumer durable goods	1. Surveys of consumers' intentions to spend and save (including intention to buy automobiles).	Survey Research Center, University of Michigan and Federal Reserve Board. *Federal Reserve Bulletin* (quarterly).	Indicates intentions to purchase durable goods. There is considerable correlation between these intentions and actual purchases.
	2. Rate of housing construction.	*Survey of Current Business* (monthly).	The building of new houses has an important influence on sales of furniture and appliances.
	3. Installment credit outstanding (in relation to the disposable personal income).	*Federal Reserve Bulletin* (monthly).	A high level of installment credit already outstanding may mean a lower willingness to incur new debt or a lower willingness to lend.
	4. Buying-plan surveys.	National Industrial Conference Board *Business Record*.	Suggests potential changes in the purchase of consumer goods.
	5. Projected consumer outlays on durable goods and housing.	*Consumer Buying Indicators* (quarterly).	Covers surveys of plans of consumers to purchase automobiles, appliances, furniture, and housing.
Nondurable consumer goods and services	1. Regression lines relating the past consumption of nondurable goods and services to the past disposable personal income.	Past issues of the *Survey of Current Business* provide the necessary data. Special articles in the *Survey of Current Business* review findings on such relationships.	Past relationships to disposable personal income show considerable stability, though the rate of sales to income rises in recession.
Comprehensive collection of indicators	1. Charts covering most of the best known indicators.	*Business Conditions Digest* (monthly).	A compact collection of charts covering indicators of income, production, prices, employment, and monetary conditions.

Source: W. W. Haynes, *Managerial Economics: Analysis and Cases* (Dallas: Business Publications, Inc., 1969), pp. 131-33.

facilities must be provided for the processing and tabulation of the results of the questionnaires. As a result, the use of surveys in forecasting is of recent vintage when compared with several of the other approaches we will discuss shortly; and because of this lack of history of performance, each forecaster must decide for himself the relative usefulness of the various surveys for his purposes. That is, the analyst must decide which surveys overestimate and which underestimate the actual observed results, so that he can determine how the survey results need to be adjusted before inclusion in his individual forecast. This leads us to a most important point—that survey results should not be thought of as forecasts in themselves, but rather as a consensus that the forecaster can use in framing his own forecast.

Perhaps the greatest shortcoming of intention surveys is that the forecaster has no guarantee that the intentions will be carried out into final action. For this reason, the survey approach is most reliable for short-term forecasts that are continually monitored. External shocks such as strikes, political turmoil, or government action can cause sudden changes in intentions. But to the extent that intentions do become translated into final action, this survey approach provides a most valuable insight to the business investor.

Despite the shortcomings of anticipatory surveys, a great plus is their abundance and easy availability even to a noninstitutional investor. To name only three (see Table 6-1), *Fortune, Business Week,* and the *Survey of Current Business* are key sources of survey results and are publications that many investors either subscribe to or can easily consult at a local library.

Barometric or Indicator Approach

Another forecasting tool is the barometric or indicator approach.[8] It has its foundations in work pioneered by Wesley C. Mitchell, Arthur F. Burns, and Geoffrey H. Moore, at the National Bureau of Economic Research (NBER). Currently the U.S. Department of Commerce, following the NBER, has published in its *Business Conditions Digest* data on over 100 cyclical indicators, classified according to cyclical timing and economic process. In Table 6-2 we see a cross-classification of these indicators by economic process and timing. For example, there are ten series dealing with production and income of which two are leading indicators of business cycle peaks and eight are coincident indicators.

Table 6-2 demonstrates that the cyclical-timing classification is either leading, roughly coincident, or lagging. The leading indicators are those time series of data that historically reach their high points (peaks) or their low points (troughs) in advance of total economic activity; the roughly coincident indicators reach their peaks or troughs at approximately the same time as the economy; and finally, the lagging indicators reach their turning points after the economy has already reached its own. The NBER has painstakingly examined historical data

---

[8]For a fuller treatment of this complex subject, see Julius Shiskin and Leonard H. Lempert, "Indicator Forecasting," in Butler, Kavesh, and Platt, *Methods and Techniques of Business Forecasting.* Shiskin and Lempert cite a number of excellent NBER sources of information.

TABLE 6-2
CROSS-CLASSIFICATION OF CYCLICAL INDICATORS BY ECONOMIC PROCESS AND CYCLICAL TIMING

A. Timing at Business Cycle Peaks

Economic Process / Cyclical Timing	I. EMPLOYMENT AND UNEMPLOYMENT (18 series)	II. PRODUCTION AND INCOME (10 series)	III. CONSUMPTION, TRADE, ORDERS, AND DELIVERIES (13 series)	IV. FIXED CAPITAL INVESTMENT (18 series)	V. INVENTORIES AND INVENTORY INVESTMENT (9 series)	VI. PRICES, COSTS, AND PROFITS (17 series)	VII. MONEY AND CREDIT (26 series)
LEADING (L) INDICATORS (62 series)	Marginal employment adjustments (6 series) Job vacancies (2 series) Comprehensive employment (1 series) Comprehensive unemployment (3 series)	Capacity utilization (2 series)	New and unfilled orders and deliveries (6 series) Consumption (2 series)	Formation of business enterprises (2 series) Business investment commitments (5 series) Residential construction (3 series)	Inventory investment (4 series) Inventories on hand and on order (1 series)	Stock prices (1 series) Commodity prices (1 series) Profits and profit margins (7 series) Cash flows (2 series)	Money flows (3 series) Real money supply (2 series) Credit flows (4 series) Credit difficulties (2 series) Bank reserves (2 series) Interest rates (1 series)
ROUGHLY COINCIDENT (C) INDICATORS (23 series)	Comprehensive employment (1 series)	Comprehensive output and real income (4 series) Industrial production (4 series)	Consumption and trade (4 series)	Backlog of investment commitments (1 series) Business investment expenditures (5 series)			Velocity of money (2 series) Interest rates (2 series)
LAGGING (Lg) INDICATORS (18 series)	Duration of unemployment (2 series)			Business investment expenditures (1 series)	Inventories on hand and on order (4 series)	Unit labor costs and labor share (4 series)	Interest rates (4 series) Outstanding debt (3 series)
TIMING UNCLASSIFIED (U) (8 series)	Comprehensive employment (3 series)		Trade (1 series)	Business investment commitments (1 series)		Commodity prices (1 series) Profit share (1 series)	Interest rates (1 series)

B. Timing at Business Cycle Troughs

Economic Process / Cyclical Timing	I. EMPLOYMENT AND UNEMPLOYMENT (18 series)	II. PRODUCTION AND INCOME (10 series)	III. CONSUMPTION, TRADE, ORDERS, AND DELIVERIES (13 series)	IV. FIXED CAPITAL INVESTMENT (18 series)	V. INVENTORIES AND INVENTORY INVESTMENT (9 series)	VI. PRICES, COSTS, AND PROFITS (17 series)	VII. MONEY AND CREDIT (26 series)
LEADING (L) INDICATORS (47 series)	Marginal employment adjustments (3 series)	Industrial production (1 series)	New and unfilled orders and deliveries (5 series) Consumption and trade (4 series)	Formation of business enterprises (2 series) Business investment commitments (4 series) Residential construction (3 series)	Inventory investment (4 series)	Stock prices (1 series) Commodity prices (2 series) Profits and profit margins (6 series) Cash flows (2 series)	Money flows (2 series) Real money supply (2 series) Credit flows (4 series) Credit difficulties (2 series)
ROUGHLY COINCIDENT (C) INDICATORS (23 series)	Marginal employment adjustments (2 series) Comprehensive employment (4 series)	Comprehensive output and real income (4 series) Industrial production (3 series) Capacity utilization (2 series)	Consumption and trade (3 series)	Business investment commitments (1 series)		Profits (2 series)	Money flow (1 series) Velocity of money (1 series)
LAGGING (Lg) INDICATORS (40 series)	Marginal employment adjustments (1 series) Job vacancies (2 series) Comprehensive employment (1 series) Comprehensive and duration of unemployment (5 series)		Unfilled orders (1 series)	Business investment commitments (2 series) Business investment expenditures (6 series)	Inventories on hand and on order (5 series)	Unit labor costs and labor share (4 series)	Velocity of money (1 series) Bank reserves (1 series) Interest rates (8 series) Outstanding debt (3 series)
TIMING UNCLASSIFIED (U) (1 series)							Bank reserves (1 series)

Source: U.S. Department of Commerce, *Business Conditions Digest,* June 1977.

going back in some cases as far as 1870, in order to ascertain which economical variables have led, lagged after, or moved together with the economy. In order to facilitate the use of the indicator approach, the NBER has developed a "short list" of indicators, consisting of twelve leading, four roughly coincident, and six lagging indicators. This short list is summarized graphically in Figure 6-2. The reader is urged to study Figure 6-3 so that he can fully appreciate the vast amount of information contained in Figure 6-2, which is representative of the kind of material contained in a typical issue of *Businss Conditions Digest.* For example, indicator 1, the average workweek in manufacturing, is recorded in hours and plotted on an arithmetic scale, "Scale A." The workweek dropped to a low during 1960, rose to nearly 42 hours a week during 1966, trended downward until 1970, started upward again, and then started declining in 1974.

Perhaps an explanation of the economic rationale behind the indicator approach will be helpful. For example, the rationale for the average workweek of production workers in manufacturing being expressed in hours is that before aggregate business activity picks up, the length of the workweek of production workers will increase. That is, before a company goes out and hires new workers, they will offer overtime to their present workers and thus utilize them more intensively. So we see that a leading indicator may be leading because it measures something that foreshadows a change in productive activity.

Figure 6-4 shows the relationship between leading indicators and industrial production, as well as the percent of leading indicators expanding. The ability of the leading indicators to signal changes in production well in advance is particularly in evidence in early 1974 and again in early 1975.

The indicator approach is most valuable in suggesting the *direction* of a change in aggregate economic activity; however, it tells us nothing of the magnitude or duration of the change. Table 6-3 contains a summary of the performance of the "short list" of indicators. The ratings can take on a value of 0 to 100, based on the six major criteria contained in the table. Notice that the highest score of the leading indicators was 81, stock prices. Most other scores among the leading indicators were in the 60s. This would indicate that forecasting based solely on leading indicators is a hazardous business.

There are several other difficulties with these techniques, which are excellently summarized by Professors Lewis and Turner:

> Even with respect to indicating direction of change, the National Bureau's barometric technique encounters some difficulties. The leading series are subject to a number of wiggles, and many of the turns in them prove after the fact to have been false signals of turns in general business activity. Thus, it requires, in addition to the month or so needed to collect data, at least another two or three months' confirmation time before an apparent change of course in the leading series can be regarded as significant, and this, of course, greatly diminishes the one unique advantage the technique has. Moreover, there are frequent differences among the leading series themselves. Some signal a turn, then others do not.[9]

In order to overcome the last objection Lewis and Turner mention, the diffusion-index approach has been developed.

[9] Lewis and Turner, *Business Conditions Analysis*, p. 376.

FIGURE 6-2

I
A

CYCLICAL INDICATORS

COMPOSITE INDEXES AND THEIR COMPONENTS—Con.

Chart A2. Leading Index Components

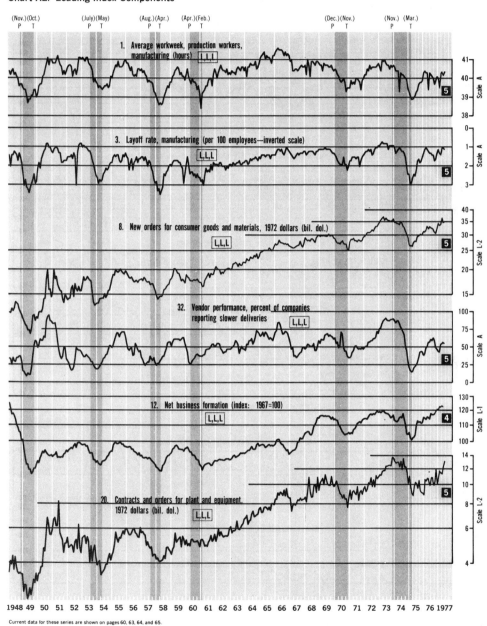

Current data for these series are shown on pages 60, 63, 64, and 65.

Source: U.S. Department of Commerce, *Business Conditions Digest,*
June, 1977.

FIGURE 6-2 (cont.)

I A CYCLICAL INDICATORS

COMPOSITE INDEXES AND THEIR COMPONENTS—Con.

Chart A2. Leading Index Components—Con.

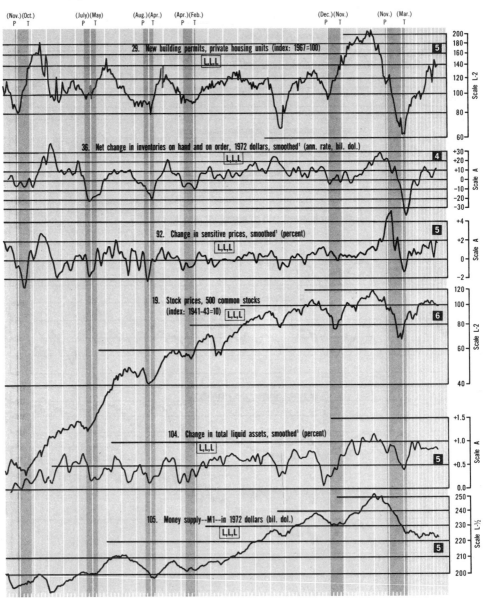

[1] This series is a weighted 4-term moving average (with weights 1.2.2.1) placed on the terminal month of the span.

FIGURE 6-2 (cont.)

I A CYCLICAL INDICATORS

COMPOSITE INDEXES AND THEIR COMPONENTS—Con.

Chart A3. Coincident Index Components

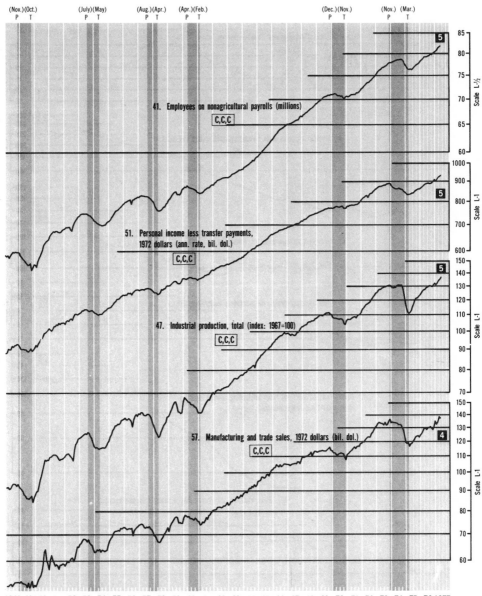

Current data for these series are shown on pages 61, 62, and 64.

FIGURE 6-2 (cont.)

I / A CYCLICAL INDICATORS

COMPOSITE INDEXES AND THEIR COMPONENTS—Con.

Chart A4. Lagging Index Components

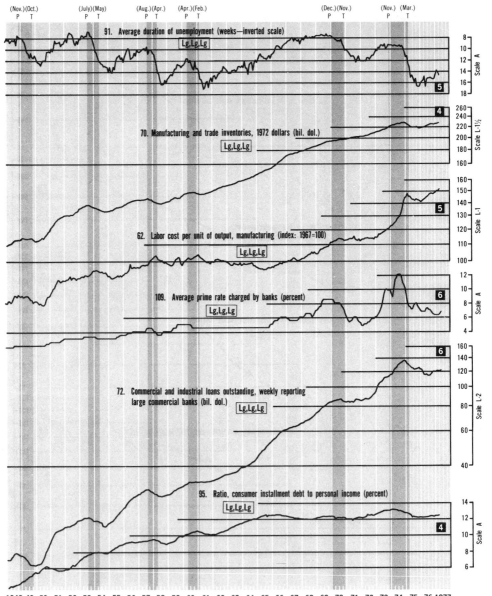

Current data for these series are shown on pages 61, 67, 69, and 72.

152

FIGURE 6-3

HOW TO READ CHARTS

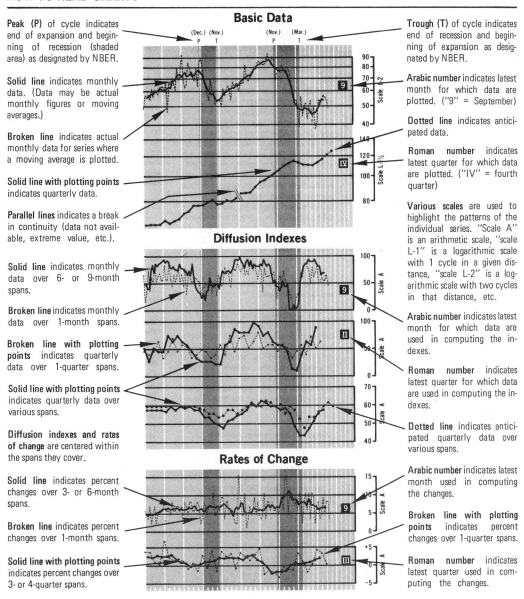

Peak (P) of cycle indicates end of expansion and beginning of recession (shaded area) as designated by NBER.

Solid line indicates monthly data. (Data may be actual monthly figures or moving averages.)

Broken line indicates actual monthly data for series where a moving average is plotted.

Solid line with plotting points indicates quarterly data.

Parallel lines indicates a break in continuity (data not available, extreme value, etc.).

Solid line indicates monthly data over 6- or 9-month spans.

Broken line indicates monthly data over 1-month spans.

Broken line with plotting points indicates quarterly data over 1-quarter spans.

Solid line with plotting points indicates quarterly data over various spans.

Diffusion indexes and rates of change are centered within the spans they cover.

Solid line indicates percent changes over 3- or 6-month spans.

Broken line indicates percent changes over 1-month spans.

Solid line with plotting points indicates percent changes over 3- or 4-quarter spans.

Trough (T) of cycle indicates end of recession and beginning of expansion as designated by NBER.

Arabic number indicates latest month for which data are plotted. ("9" = September)

Dotted line indicates anticipated data.

Roman number indicates latest quarter for which data are plotted. ("IV" = fourth quarter)

Various scales are used to highlight the patterns of the individual series. "Scale A" is an arithmetic scale, "scale L-1" is a logarithmic scale with 1 cycle in a given distance, "scale L-2" is a logarithmic scale with two cycles in that distance, etc.

Arabic number indicates latest month for which data are used in computing the indexes.

Roman number indicates latest quarter for which data are used in computing the indexes.

Dotted line indicates anticipated quarterly data over various spans.

Arabic number indicates latest month used in computing the changes.

Broken line with plotting points indicates percent changes over 1-quarter spans.

Roman number indicates latest quarter used in computing the changes.

HOW TO LOCATE A SERIES

1. See ALPHABETICAL INDEX—SERIES FINDING GUIDE at the back of the report where series are arranged alphabetically according to subject matter and key words and phrases of the series titles, or—

2. See TITLES AND SOURCES OF SERIES at the back of the report where series are listed numerically according to series numbers within each of the report's sections.

Source: U.S. Department of Commerce, *Business Conditions Digest*

TABLE 6-3
SHORT LIST OF INDICATORS: SCORES AND TIMING CHARACTERISTICS

Classification and Series Title (1)	First Business Cycle Turn Covered (2)	Average Score (3)	Scores, Six Criteria						Timing at Peaks and Troughs				
			Economic Significance (4)	Statistical Adequacy (5)	Conformity (6)	Timing (7)	Smoothness (8)	Currency (9)	Business Cycle Turns Covered (10)	Leads (11)	Rough Coincidences* (12)	Lags (13)	Median Lead (−) or Lag (+) in Months (14)
Leading indicators (12 series)													
1. Avg. workweek, prod. workers, mfg.	1921	66	50	65	81	66	60	80	19	13	4(2)	2	−5
30. Nonagri. placements, BES	1945	68	75	63	63	58	80	80	10	8	4(0)	1	−3
38. Index of net business formation	1945	68	75	58	81	67	80	40	10	8	3(1)	0	−7
6. New orders, durable goods indus.	1920	78	75	72	88	84	60	80	20	16	7(1)	0	−4
10. Contracts and orders, plant and equipment	1948	64	75	63	92	50	40	40	8	7	2(0)	1	−6
29. New building permits, private housing units	1918	67	50	60	76	80	60	80	22	17	5(1)	1	−6
31. Change in book value, mfg. and trade inventories	1945	65	75	67	77	78	20	40	10	9	2(1)	0	−8
23. Industrial materials prices	1919	67	50	72	79	44	80	100	21	13	9(4)	2	−2
19. Stock prices, 500 common stocks	1873	81	75	74	77	87	80	100	44	33	14(2)	5	−4
16. Corporate profits after taxes, Q	1920	68	75	70	79	76	60	25	20	13	11(4)	2	−2
17. Ratio, price to unit labor cost, mfg.	1919	69	50	67	84	72	60	80	21	17	10(1)	3	−3
113. Change in consumer installment debt	1929	63	50	79	77	60	60	40	14	11	4(0)	1	−10
Roughly coincident indicators (7 series)													
41. Employees in nonagri. establishments	1929	81	75	61	90	87	100	80	14	6	12(6)	2	0
43. Unemployment rate, total (inv.)	1929	75	75	63	96	60	80	80	14	4	8(3)	6	0

154

	Year											
50. GNP in constant dollars, expenditure estimate, Q	1921	73	75	75	91	58	80	50	17	7	9(3)	3	-2
47. Industrial production	1919	72	75	63	94	38	100	80	21	9	13(9)	3	0
52. Personal income	1921	74	75	73	89	43	100	80	19	10	12(2)	5	-1
816. Mfg. and trade sales	1948	71	75	68	70	80	80	40	8	4	6(4)	0	0
54. Sales of retail stores	1919	69	75	77	89	12	80	100	21	5	7(1)	6	0
Lagging indicators (6 series)													
502. Unempl. rate, persons unempl. 15+ weeks (inv.)	1948	69	50	63	98	52	80	80	8	1	5(1)	6	+2
61. Bus. expend., plant and equip., Q	1918	86	75	77	96	94	100	80	20	2	16(5)	13	+1
71. Book value, mfg. and trade inventories	1945	71	75	67	75	66	100	40	10	2	7(0)	8	+2
62. Labor cost per unit of output, mfg.	1919	68	50	70	83	56	80	80	21	0	1(0)	14	+8
72. Comm. and indus. loans outstanding	1937	57	50	47	67	20	100	100	12	1	6(0)	7	+2
67. Bank rates, short-term bus. loans, Q	1919	60	50	55	82	47	80	50	21	2	5(1)	15	+5

*Rough coincidences include exact coincidences (shown in parentheses) and leads and lags of 3 months or less. Leads (lags) include leads (lags) of 1 month or more. The total number of timing comparisons, which can be less than the number of business cycle turns covered by the series, in the sum of the leads, exact coincidences, and lags. Leads and lags of quarterly series are expressed in terms of months.

Source: Geoffrey H. Moore and Julius Shiskin, *Indicators of Business Expansions and Contractions* (New York: National Bureau of Economic Research, 1967), p. 68.

FIGURE 6-4

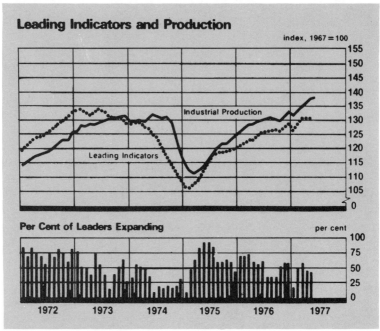

Leading Indicators and Production

index, 1967 = 100

Industrial Production

Leading Indicators

Per Cent of Leaders Expanding

per cent

1972 1973 1974 1975 1976 1977

All data are seasonably adjusted.
Source: Board of Governors of the Federal Reserve System, U.S. Department of Commerce, Harris Bank.

Diffusion Indexes

There are two main categories of diffusion indexes.[10] The first and broadest category is of those that combine several indicators into one measure in order to measure the strength or weakness in the movements of these particular time series of data. Therefore this type of diffusion index is a composite or consensus index. A diffusion index of the short list of leading indicators is an example of this type. Since there are twelve leading indicators, the diffusion index would be stated as a percentage of the total. For example, if four of the twelve series move up in one month, the diffusion index would be .333, or 33 percent. If, in the next month, six series moved up, the index would be .50, or 50 percent. The forecaster would need to interpret the index relative to levels of the index in the past. Certainly a move from 30 to 50 percent in the index of leading indicators would be a good indication of the future. If, in the next month, the diffusion index rose again, this would be an even stronger confirmation of a period of economic advance.

The second and more narrow type of diffusion index has been constructed by the National Bureau of Economic Research in order to measure the breadth of

[10]For a more complete discussion of this topic, see Albert T. Sommers, "Diffusion Indexes," in William F. Butler and Robert A. Kavesh, *How Business Economists Forecast* (Englewood Cliffs, N.J.: Prentice-Hall, 1966).

the movement within a particular series. Specifically, an indicator, whether leading, lagging, or coincident, is a summary measure compiled from statistics representing a cross section of the economy, so that in one figure is summarized the results of many different occurrences—for example, if an indicator refers to all production, it is a summation of many different industries. The more narrow diffusion index examines under a microscope the data going into the series, so that the forecaster can get a feel for the inner workings of the particular indicator. To follow through with the example just cited, the diffusion index will tell the forecaster how many industries within the indicator had experienced upturns, how many had had downturns, and how many had not changed at all.

The diffusion indexes have another important attribute. They tend to lead the indicator that is being analyzed by the index (although, unfortunately, the lead times of the various diffusion indexes are variable); and thus the diffusion indexes themselves can be thought of as a special kind of leading indicator.[11]

Unfortunately, these diffusion indexes are not without their problems. First, they are complex, in a statistical sense, to calculate; and second, even though they tend to eliminate some of the irregular moves evidenced in the indicators themselves, they are unable to eliminate them entirely. Nonetheless, the combination of the indicator approach, diffusion indexes, and judgment becomes an extremely powerful tool in the hands of a skillful forecaster.

Money and Stock Prices

In recent years the monetarist notion of economics has grown increasingly more popular.[12] Although not universally accepted, this monetary theory in its simplest form states that fluctuations in the rate of growth of the money supply are of utmost importance in determining GNP, corporate profits, interest rates, and, of interest to us, stock prices. Monetarists contend that changes in the growth rate of the money supply set off a complicated series of events that ultimately affect share prices. In addition, they maintain that these monetary changes lead stock price changes: ". . . changes in monetary growth lead changes in stock prices by an average of about 9 months prior to a bear market and by about 2 or 3 months prior to bull markets."[13] These lead times are averages and are based on historical data. It cannot be said whether these average relationships can and will persist for future periods.

Research in the area of monetary theory has led many analysts, both economic and security, to consider changes in the growth rate of the money supply when preparing their forecasts.

Econometric Model Building

Econometrics is the field of study that applies mathematical and statistical techniques to economic theory. As such, it is the most precise and scientific of

---

[11] David H. McKinsley et al., *Forecasting Business Conditions* (New York: American Bankers Association, 1969).

[12] This section draws from Beryl W. Sprinkel, *Money and Markets: A Monetarist View* (Homewood, Ill.: Richard D. Irwin, 1971).

[13] *Ibid.*, p. 221.

the approaches we have discussed thus far, because, in applying this technique the user is forced to specify in a formal mathematical manner the precise relation between the independent and dependent variables. Thus, in using econometrics, the forecaster must quantify precisely the relationships and assumptions he is making. Naturally, one of the key advantages of this approach is that the forecaster must think through clearly all the interrelationships of the economic variables; and for his reward he is yielded a forecast that gives him not only direction but magnitudes. In short, his method yields him a precise figure; even so, however, his forecast is not better than his underlying understanding of economic theory, his application of it, the quality of his data input, and the validity of his assumptions.[14]

Econometric model building involves the specification of a system of simultaneous equations containing both endogenous and exogenous variables. *Endogenous variables* are those determined by the system of equations; *exogenous variables* are those determined outside the system of equations. Therefore, at least one equation is needed to determine a forecast value of each endogenous variable. Values of the exogenous variables are predetermined.

Generally speaking, the well-known econometric models, such as the FRB-MIT (Federal Reserve Board-Massachusetts Institute of Technology), the Michigan, the Pennsylvania, and the Brookings models, are extremely complex; that is, they contain many equations. Their results, both new and revised, are reported regularly in the financial press, such as the *Wall Street Journal.*

Some of the problems with the econometric approach are these: (1) Large computer facilities and vast amounts of clerical and programming support are needed to maintain and update the system. (2) Frequently the overall forecast is more reliable than the individual components of the forecast. (This is because errors tend to cancel themselves out in the overall forecast.) (3) Because of the vast amounts of data that must be collected, processed, and prepared for inclusion in the model, there are delays in making the results available to the public. Needless to say, this time lapse is potentially more troublesome to the security analyst than to the business forecaster. (4) Generally, these models are useful only for very short-term forecasts.

However, as stated earlier, the beauty of this approach is that it yields a blueprint of the economic system that is based on precisely stated factors that can then be used to yield a definite forecast figure.

Opportunistic Model Building

Opportunistic model building (or GNP model building, sectoral analysis, or any other of the often-used titles for this approach) refers to the most eclectic

---

[14]For a fuller treatment of this approach, the reader is urged to read John G. Myers, "Statistical and Econometric Methods Used in Business Forecasting," in Butler, Kavesh, and Platt, *Methods and Techniques of Business Forecasting*; and Daniel B. Suits, "Forecasting and Analysis with an Econometric Model," *American Economic Review*, March 1962.

and perhaps most widely used forecasting method.[15] The forecaster using this approach draws from any and all of the methods already discussed in his quest for an accurate economic forecast. Its similarity to other approaches lies in its use of the national accounting framework to achieve a short-term forecast; its difference arises from its great flexibility and reliance on informed judgments. Perhaps this method can best be appreciated by understanding how it is applied in practice.

Initially the forecaster must hypothesize total demand, and thus total income, during the forecast period. Obviously, this will necessitate assuming certain environmental decisions, such as war or peace, political relationships among various groups in the economy, any imminent tax changes, the rate of inflation, and the level of interest rates. After this work has been done, the forecaster begins building a forecast of the GNP figure by estimating the levels of the various components of GNP. That is, he must fill in the numbers for consumption expenditures, gross private domestic investment, government purchases of goods and services, and net exports.

Generally, the forecaster will begin with the easiest figure to come by and work toward the most complex. He usually begins with an estimate for the government sector, broken down into federal expenditures and state and local expenditures, with the federal portion being further broken down into defense and nondefense expenditures. The various government publications, including the federal budget itself and the *Annual Economic Report of the President*, provide very useful sources of information for the forecaster. Further insight can be gained in conversations with key government employees. State and local expenditures can be arrived at rather simply, merely by extrapolation of past data, because they have risen by a fairly stable percentage year after year.

Gross private domestic investment is broken down into business expenditures for plant and equipment, residential construction, and changes in the levels of business inventories. Many of the sources of both corporate and consumer surveys cited earlier in Table 6-1 are very useful starting points in forecasting each of these three figures. The most difficult to forecast accurately is the change in business inventories; this figure changes drastically over the business cycle.

The next sector to be forecast is that of net exports. This is a particularly hard number to come by, for the forecaster must consider not only domestic but also international, political, and foreign economic problems.

The last sector to forecast in opportunistic model building is the personal consumption factor. Traditionally, this sector is subdivided into three components: durable goods minus automobiles, automobiles, and nondurable goods and services. This sort of breakdown allows the forecaster to find any stable re-

---

[15]Much of the material in this section parallels the discussion contained in two classics in this area of study: William F. Butler and Robert A. Kavesh, "Judgmental Forecasting of the Gross National Product," in Butler, Kavesh, and Platt, *Methods and Techniques of Business Forecasting*; and Lewis and Turner, *Business Conditions Analysis*, particularly Chaps. 17-24. The interested reader is encouraged to refer to these works for a fuller treatment of this fascinating subject.

lationships between economic variables, such as between disposable income and expenditures on nondurables. Inasmuch as durables and automobiles tend to fluctuate vigorously over the business cycle, it is best for the forecaster to analyze these components separately. Here too, the surveys mentioned in Table 6-1 provide a valuable source of information.

After the forecaster has acquired totals for these four major categories, he adds them together to come up with his GNP forecast. However, his work is not yet completed, for he must then test this total for consistency with an independently arrive-at *a priori* forecast of GNP, as well as test the overall forecast for internal consistency. The former consistency check might necessitate his retracing some of his steps in order to bring the two forecasts into line with each other. Thus he may have to approximate successively the various subcategories, as well as the final estimate of GNP. The internal consistency check arises because of the interrelatedness of the GNP accounts. For example, consumption by individuals implies a level of savings that affects business investment, which further affects productive activity and thus incomes, which will once again affect savings. While these circular effects take place, other factors such as interest rates, unemployment, and inflation will be affected. Thus it is necessary for the forecaster to ensure in the light of all these relationships that both his total forecast and his subcomponent forecast make sense and fit together in a reasonable economic fashion.[16]

In short, opportunistic model building employs all the aforementioned techniques, plus a vast amount of judgment and ingenuity, in what has been described as

> ... an effort to build a view of the short-run business outlook that is comprehensive, that is as quantitiatively precise as the state of our knowledge permits, that is internally consistent, that draws upon rather than sidesteps all the pertinent insights of modern aggregative economics but, at the same time, does not make a fetish of theoretical rigor. Instead, the technique seeks to exploit any and all evidences of business prospects that may come to hand. It is particularly distinguished from pure econometric model building by its heavy use of data concerning the advance plans and commitments of certain spending groups, and it retains a sizable place for judgment and freehand adjustments.[17]

This versatile approach to forecasting is at once the greatest asset to opportunistic model building and its greatest liability, for with the advantages that accrue to the economist by mobilizing a variety of forecasting tools and adding judgment come the aforementioned weaknesses of these techniques. Unfortunately, although the weaknesses can be lessened through selective combination, they cannot be entirely eliminated. Notwithstanding the possible shortcomings of business forecasting, the analyst must still consider and incorporate economic data in his investment decision-making process. Several key sources that sum-

---

[16]Another method of checking for this internal consistency is to forecast what the distribution of incomes will be—between wages, interest, salaries, etc.—under his forecast level of GNP and the various subclassifications, and check to see if these relationships make economic sense.

[17]Lewis and Turner, *Business Conditions Analysis,* p. 571.

marize forecasts of key research organizations, banks, and economists are the Federal Reserve Bank of Philadelphia's "Predictions for 19-," published in January of each year, and the Federal Reserve Bank of Richmond's "Business Forecasts," published in February of each year. In addition, the *New York Times* and the *Wall Street Journal*, among others, publish many forecasts as they are released.

ACCURACY OF SHORT-TERM ECONOMIC FORECASTS

It is interesting to see how short-term forecasters have fared in their undertaking. The NBER has studied this issue and has discovered that shorter-term forecasts of three to six months are more accurate than forecasts approximately one year in advance. In other words, forecast errors go up as the length of the prediction period increases. In addition, their studies indicate that the total forecasts tend to be more accurate than the subcomponent forecasts.[18]

By now, at least two key points are apparent about economic forecasting: (1) It is an extremely arduous and difficult process, even for specialists; and (2) because of this, an analyst must critically evaluate such forecasts and not accept them blindly. To point out the degree of success achieved recently by some forecasters, Table 6-4 contains a comparison of several forecasts and actual results.

An Illustration of an Economic Analysis

In order to understand more clearly the E-I-C framework, in the next several chapters we will apply the techniques discussed in these chapters to the same continuous example. For analysis purposes, we will examine the lodgings industry and Holiday Inns, because this industry and company should prosper in the year ahead. Furthermore, the company is widely known and contains a variety of areas of analytical interest. In this section we will attempt to analyze economic

TABLE 6-4
COMPARISON OF ACTUAL VS. FORECAST GNP ($ IN BILLIONS)

Source	*1976*	*1975*	*1974*	*1973*	*1972*
The Conference Board	1,677	1,480	N/A	1,262	1,148
RCA	1,636	1,507	N/A	1,259	N/A
U.S. Trust	1,627	N/A	1,403	N/A	1,157
MAPCAST, General Electric	N/A	1,526	1,383	1,267	1,151
Wharton EFA	N/A	1,525	1,388	1,261	1,150
Actual	1,692	1,516	1,413	1,307	1,152

[18]Victor Zarnowitz, *Appraisal of Short-Term Economic Forecasts* (New York: NBER, Occasional Paper 104, 1967); and Jacob Mincer, ed., *Economic Forecasts and Expectations* (New York: NBER, Studies in Business Cycles, No. 19, 1969).

data relevant to this industry in order to ascertain if the expected economic environment will be favorable for the leisure-time industry in general and for the lodgings industry in particular.

The forecasts of business conditions of any given year are by themselves difficult to construct. But the year 1977 presented even more problems because of the energy crisis and the uncertainty surrounding future actions by the Arab oil-exporting countries, as well as possible energy conservation measures that might be taken by the administration in Washington: the continuing worries about the rate of inflation; uncertainty as to the future course of interest rates; the international monetary situation; prospects of a large federal budget deficit; fears of possible formal or informal wage and price controls imposed by the government; and uncertainty about changes in the federal personal and corporate tax structure, particularly as these changes affect the taxation of capital gains (as was discussed in our Chapter 3).

DISPOSABLE INCOME AND CORPORATE PROFITS

Most forecasts of GNP for 1977 (such as those provided by major banks and econometric models) call for $1,870 billion to $1,890 billion in current dollars. Inasmuch as consumer expenditures on goods and services will be predominantly made out of disposable income, it is important to forecast this key figure. We expect that personal disposable income will be approximately 70 percent of GNP; this would place it between $1,309 billion and $1,323 billion, using the GNP forecasts cited above.

However, knowing disposable-income figures is not enough, for the distribution of this income is of great importance to the lodgings industry. That is to say, if income is highly concentrated among a relatively small segment of the population, total expenditures on this lodgings segment of the leisure-time industry will be very different from what can be expected when income is fairly well distributed. Why? Because if income is fairly well distributed, more families will be able to travel and use lodgings facilities than if only a relatively small group of families can afford to travel. Even a wealthy person needs only one bed to sleep in!

It is estimated that 75 percent or more of all hotel-motel users have an income of $10,000 a year or more.[19] Since the economic outlook for 1977 is fairly optimistic, more families in the United States than ever before should reach this level of income. Thus there exists the potential for a significant increase in

---

[19] The reader may wonder where the security analyst would get this information. The answer lies in *research*. The security analyst specializing in an industry must be intimately familiar with all available trade publications, research projects, and statistical agencies that compile information of interest to him. (Other, more general sources were mentioned in an earlier chapter.) A key source of information to a lodgings-industry analyst is *Trends in the Hotel-Motel Business*, published annually by Harris, Kerr, Forster, and Company.

the demand for the lodgings industry in the consumer sector.[20] More people who can afford to travel need more rooms.

As for the business sector, most economists look for the expansion of corporate profits continuing at least through the end of 1977. Corporate profits, and consequently the outlook for corporate profits, are a key economic variable for forecasting the demand for lodgings facilities from the business sector; studies have indicated that hotel-motel occupancy rates (that is, the proportion of available rooms that are utilized) are closely related to corporate profits, because businesses tend to cut back on expense accounts and travel when company profits are level or down. And since it is estimated that approximately 60 percent of hotel-motel business is derived from businessmen, it can easily be seen that an accurate forecast of corporate profits, or at least the direction of corporate profits, is essential to a good forecast of the lodgings-industry demand.[21]

OTHER ECONOMIC FACTORS

Two somewhat related factors that must be considered, particularly regarding industries that are building new physical facilities (such as the hotel-motel industry), are construction costs and interest rates. These can be significant influences in expanding industries, because they cut into profits and therefore affect earnings per share, dividends, and share prices. Inflationary pressures could continue to increase construction costs in terms of material used in construction and in terms of the wages of workers in the construction trades, which are highly unionized. Should construction costs continue to rise, and should firms in the industry still want to expand their physical plant, these additional costs will affect future profits. Forecasts for 1977 also show considerable concern that interest rates will begin moving upward again. To the extent that this occurs, this will have an adverse effect on the lodgings industry. Why? The reason is that business setbacks can have a very adverse effect on the lodgings industry because of the reduction in the business portion of income in sales in the lodgings industry. This decline in revenue is greatly magnified in net income because so many of the hotel's costs are fixed—that is, expenses such as depreciation and property taxes.

Travelers or would-be travelers need more money in order to travel. They also need time. Fortunately for the lodgings industry, the trend has been to more leisure time. For one thing, the government has instituted five national three-day weekends with the passage of the Federal Monday Holiday Law. Also,

---

[20] We use the word *potential* because consumers need not necessarily spend their income. They can save or invest a portion of it. This decision will depend in part on their expectations of future economic developments.

[21] This assumes that this past relationship persists at a significant level—namely, that firms will continue to spend more on travel when corporate profits are on the upturn.

many companies have begun switching to four-day workweeks. Finally, workers have been receiving more vacation time per production hour more quickly. That is, companies are increasing the amount of vacation time awarded to workers. These factors look particularly good for firms in the lodgings industry prepared to cater to the vacation traveler. It should also be noted that U.S. expenditures for travel have been growing, with increased expenditures on foreign travel. In fact, expenditures on domestic travel as well as expenditures on foreign travel have increased recently, particularly in conjunction with charter tours and package tours. This is true of both bus and airline packages. Thus, U.S. firms in the lodgings industry, particularly those with interests abroad, should benefit in a substantial fashion.

Since we are interested in focusing our analysis on Holiday Inns, and since Holiday Inns is essentially a motel operation, it would be helpful to examine one factor that is highly correlated with motel occupancy rates—namely, automobile purchases. It is estimated that 70 percent of all motel business arrives by automobile; furthermore, 40 percent of the motel industry's revenues are from the pleasure traveler. Putting these two facts together, it certainly appears that automobile purchases and motel revenues are highly correlated. Economists project continued growth in automobile sales. If the sales forecast should materialize, the effects could portend well for the motel industry.[22]

The only real dampening national effect on the lodgings industry would be the petroleum-related problems. If gasoline prices were to suddenly increase drastically above 1976 levels, there would be a sizable lapse in the amount of pleasure travel and in the distance that vacationers would travel by automobile. To the extent that this materializes, the lodgings industry—which caters to the vacation traveler—will be adversely affected. However, we feel that if gasoline prices inch their way up gradually, this factor will not have too much of an adverse effect on the industry. On the other hand, if the Administration in Washington enacts stringent gasoline measures, this could have a negative effect on the industry. To offset these possible effects is the fact that personal disposable incomes are continuing to rise, unemployment continues to go down, and Americans are traveling more, not less. This secular rise in pleasure travel could also possibly be impeded if inflation should get out of hand, because then the consumer might be faced with the necessity of spending a larger portion of his income on necessities. But once again, the new discount airline fares and the more attractive travel packages are attempts by the industry to combat inflation and encourage travel.

On balance, 1977 looks like a good year for the economy, corporate profits, and the leisure-time industries, particularly the lodgings industry. In the next chapter we will examine this industry in some detail, as we continue toward our goal of price, dividend, and risk estimates of Holiday Inns, Inc.

---

[22] However, the increased popularity of recreational vehicles, camping, and second homes may somewhat dampen the potential of the hotel-motel industry.

Summary

In this chapter we assessed the importance of short-term economic forecasting in the decision-making process surrounding the purchase of common stocks. In order to understand and appreciate the forecasting task, we discussed and critically evaluated several major economic forecasting techniques—anticipatory surveys, indicators, diffusion indexes, econometric models, and opportunistic model building. All these techniques have distinct advantages as well as disadvantages, but on balance they have been successful for forecasts up to a few quarters in advance. For the security analyst or investor, the anticipated economic environment, and therefore the economic forecast, is important for making decisions concerning both the timing of an investment and the relative investment desirability among the various industries in the economy.

In the next chapter we will continue our efforts to forecast price and dividend information for our holding-period-return calculations by discussing and applying useful techniques of industry analysis.

Questions and Problems

1. Compare and contrast the survey, indicator, and econometric approaches to short-term forecasting.

2. Of what importance is the concept of "potential GNP"? What industries do you suppose would be most affected by the gap between actual and potential GNP? Why?

3. What is *opportunistic model building?*

4. Would you suppose that GNP forecasts for next year prepared by major universities, banks, and research organizations would be quite similar? Why, or why not? Get three major GNP forecasts for next year and see.

5. What economic factors do you think most directly affect defense-oriented industries and thus would be most important to forecast properly?

6. What economic factors would you be most interested in forecasting if you were an analyst investigating major consumer durable-goods sales for next year?

7. If you were told that more families than ever before would have second cars next year and that the expected lives of cars had increased, which industries do you suppose would benefit most?

8. It has often been said that common stocks are a good "hedge against inflation." Why do you suppose people think this way? Are you inclined to agree or disagree with this sentiment?

9. What does indicator 19 in Figure 6-2 mean to you?

10. If you were designing an equation to forecast corporate capital spending for an econometric model, what variables do you suppose would be useful in explaining the level of corporate capital spending?

11. How might one classify industries within a business cycle framework?

12. a. What are three examples of key leading economic indicators (excluding stock prices)?

b. What is the rationale for the use of diffusion indexes to accompany forecasts using leading indicators?

13. What is the significance of a diffusion index with a large, positive reading?

14. The "cumulative" nature of business cycles suggests that various sectors of the economy react to changes in economic conditions to produce revivals and recessions in aggregate economic activity. Suppose Congress passed a public works program totaling $4 billion. This program would create a net addition to government spending with no offsetting increase in taxes or decrease in other previously scheduled government spending. Assuming that the economy is in the *initial* stages of recovery, indicate the sectors of the economy and the components of GNP that would be most *immediately* affected and describe their reaction.

CHAPTER SEVEN

INDUSTRY ANALYSIS

The analyst with an economic forecast that he has developed from scratch, or a set of figures that he has developed from forecasts prepared by others, is now ready to apply this information to an appropriate industry. Before demonstrating this, however, let us look at some definitions of an industry.

**Alternative
Industry
Classification
Schemes**

Webster's Dictionary defines an *industry* as "a department or branch of a craft, art, business, or manufacture." And more specifically:

> [A] group of productive or profit-making enterprises or organizations that have a similar technological structure of production and that produce or supply technically substitutable goods, services, or sources of income.[1]

Although at first glance these definitions seem neat and clear-cut, this is not so in reality. First, it may seem desirable to break industries down by their products; however, defining a product is no easy chore.

INDUSTRY CLASSIFICATION BY PRODUCT

Are glass containers in the same industry as metal containers? Is steel in the same industry as aluminum? Is a fast-food chain in the same industry as a chain of restaurants?

In one sense, a container is a container, and the substance from which it is constructed should not cause the product to appear in a separate industry for an industry analysis; however, the firms producing these different products might be very dissimilar in the other products that they produce.[2] Between the steel and aluminum industries, the economics, technology, and refinements are so substantially different that it is advisable to analyze them as separate industries.

---

[1] *Webster's Third New International Dictionary* (Springfield, Mass.: Merriam, 1966), pp. 1155-56.

[2] In an antitrust case, the Supreme Court prevented the merger of Continental Can (metal containers) with Hazel-Atlas Glass (glass containers), on the grounds of a possible lessening of competition. Thus a key issue in this case was the delineation of the container industry.

And there are also substantial differences between the mode of operation in a limited-menu, fast-food, take-out type of restaurant and that of a limited-menu, sit-down type or a legitimate full-menu restaurant.

By now it should be clear that pinpointing an industry is not easy, and the investigator needs to have a clear goal in mind so that he can properly classify firms into industries for his specific purpose. For example, if the goal were to reach an estimate of sales for the industry, the analyst might want to consider similar products and products that could be substituted for the item in question (glass containers for metal, or aluminum containers for steel). But if he were calculating comparative costs of the industry, he might consider only those firms with similar manufacturing processes, for only such a comparison would be meaningful. For instance, the analyst might compare the costs of one candy producer with those of another candy producer but not with those of a toy manufacturer.

Industry classification by product does not present a terribly acute problem for the astute analyst when he is classifying firms with basically one product or a homogeneous group of products. The problem does worsen considerably, however, when he deals with a firm that has a diversified product line. Unfortunately, in this day and age the latter case is the rule rather than the exception. Our illustration later in this chapter will serve to highlight this problem.

SIC CLASSIFICATION

In order to provide an organized reporting framework for the vast amount of data collected by the federal government, the Standard Industrial Classification (SIC) was developed. The following passage from the *Census of Manufacturers* describes the organization of this system:[3]

> Structure of the Standard Industrial Classification.—The basic classification system employed in the economic censuses is the Standard Industrial Classification (SIC). The SIC was developed for use in the classification of establishments by type of activity in which engaged. It covers the entire field of economic activities subdivided as follows:

Industrial Division		Major Groups
A	Agriculture, forestry, and fisheries	01-09
B	Mining	10-14
C	Contract construction	15-17
D	Manufacturing	19-39
E	Transportation, communication, electric, gas, and sanitary services	40-49
F	Wholesale and retail trade	50-59
G	Finance, insurance, and real estate	60-67
H	Services	70-89
I	Government	91-94
J	Nonclassifiable establishments	99

[3] *Census of Manufacturers* (Washington, D.C.: Government Printing Office).

Below the major-group level, the SIC provides for three-digit groups and finally for four-digit industries:

> Structure of the SIC Manufacturing Division.—For the manufacturing division, the 21 2-digit SIC Major Groups (19 to 39) are subdivided into 149 3-digit SIC Groups (191 to 399) and into 422 4-digit industries (1911 to 3999).[4]

For example, under "Manufacturing," major group 20 is "Food and kindred products," industry group 202 is "Dairy products," and industry 2023 is "Condensed and evaporated milk."

A sample page of the Census of Manufacturers is shown in Figure 7-1. This table contains comparative data on industry classifications regarding the number of firms, number of employees, number of production workers, value of shipments, new capital expenditures, and so on. This information is useful in detecting changing industrial patterns and developments over time, such as expansion or contraction.

Although the Census provides valuable information to the industry analyst, it is not without its drawbacks. For example, the methodology employed in classifying firms into the various categories is not consistent over the entire spectrum of the U.S. economy.[5]

INDUSTRY CLASSIFICATION ACCORDING TO BUSINESS CYCLE

Another way of classifying industries is in a cyclical framework; that is, by how they react to upswings and downswings in the economy. The general classifications in this framework are growth, cyclical, defensive, and cyclical-growth.

Growth industries are generally characterized by expectations of abnormally high rates of expansion in earnings, often independent of the business cycle. Frequently, this type of situation is associated with a major change in the state of technology or an innovative way of doing or selling something. In the early part of the twentieth century, industries such as automobiles and airplane manufacturing were considered the growth groups. In the 1940s, 1950s, and 1960s, the growth industries were associated with photography, color television, computers, drugs, office equipment, and sophisticated communications equipment. In recent years the growth industries have dealt with such things as mobile homes, soft contact lenses, the Wankel engine, and a warehouse-retail-showroom type of marketing strategy.

Cyclical industries are considered to be those most likely to benefit from a period of economic prosperity, and most likely to suffer from a period of economic recession. We shall see later in this chapter that consumer and manufacturer durables, such as refrigerators and drill presses, are the type of products

---

[4]*Ibid.*

[5]The discussion surrounding these issues is highly complex and beyond the realm of this text; however, the interested reader is referred to a fine treatment of the material in Joe S. Bain, *Industrial Organization* (New York: John Wiley, 1968), pp. 129-49.

that characteristically benefit most, relatively, from an economic boom and suffer most in a recession. This is because their purchase can be postponed until personal financial or general business conditions improve. These industries, then, are considered cyclical.

Defensive industries are those, such as the food-processing industry, hurt least in periods of economic downswing. We will see later that consumer nondurables and services, which in large part are those items necessary for people's existence—like food and shelter—are products in defensive industries. Defensive industries often contain firms whose securities an investor might hold for income. Defensive stocks might even be considered countercyclical, because their earnings might very well expand while the earnings of cyclical stocks are declining.

The investment press and brokerage firms have coined yet another classification, that of *cyclical-growth industries*. Obviously, these possess characteristics of both a cyclical industry and a growth industry. An example in this classification would be the airline industry. Airlines, according to some, grow tremendously, then go through periods of stagnation and perhaps even decline, and then resume their growth—often because of changes in technology, such as the introduction of a new type of aircraft, like the B747 or the DC10.

The Economy and the Industry Analysis

In the preceding chapter we saw how various techniques could be brought to bear upon the investment decision. Specifically, we observed how various approaches could be used to forecast components of GNP, and we noted that for the investment decision it was often as significant to predict the direction of any change in these sectors as it was to predict their actual level. Perhaps an example or two would help to highlight this concept.

When the GNP is growing, unemployment is relatively low (4-5 percent), and the general economic climate is optimistic, an economic forecast based upon any of the approaches already discussed would probably show high and increasing levels of expenditures on consumer durables, inventory, and plant and equipment. Since business is buoyant and it is generally expected that this will continue, businessmen accumulate inventory in anticipation of still higher sales levels, and they also increase their capacity through plant and equipment expenditures. At the same time, on the consumer's side of the market, individual households are experiencing high levels of personal discretionary income (income available for luxuries), and they are free to spend some of this money on such things as residential housing, automobiles, and other consumer durables. Indeed, if prior economic periods had been far less booming than those just described, expenditures on various durables, having been postponed, could now become exaggerated.

It would be desirable at such a time to buy securities of firms in industries most likely to benefit from these purchasing patterns. As you will recall in the opportunistic-model-building approach, the forecaster would arrive at specific estimates of the broad categories we have just mentioned. It is easy to see how

FIGURE 7-1

General Statistics for Establishments, by Industry Specialization and Primary Product Class Specialization: 1972

This table presents selected statistics for establishments according to their degree of specialization in products primary to their industry. The measures of plant specialization shown are (1) industry specialization—the ratio of primary product shipments to total product shipments, primary plus secondary, for the establishments; and (2) product class specialization—the ratio of the largest primary product class shipments to total product shipments.

primary plus secondary, for the establishment. See the appendix for method of computing these ratios. Statistics for establishments with specialization ratios of less than 75 percent are included in total lines but are not shown as a separate class. In addition, data may not be shown, for some industries, product classes, or specialization ratios for various reasons: e.g. to avoid disclosure of individual company data

Industry or product class code	Industry or product class by percent of specialization	Establish- ments	All employees		Production workers			Value added by manufac- ture	Cost of materials	Value of shipments	Capital expendi- tures, new
			Number	Payroll	Number	Man-hours	Wages				
(number)		(number)	(1,000)	(million dollars)	(1,000)	(millions)	(million dollars)	(million dollars)	(million dollars)	(million dollars)	(million dollars)
3991	BROOMS AND BRUSHES										
	ENTIRE INDUSTRY	450	17.5	118.5	14.2	26.8	79.5	235.5	204.9	438.3	13.0
	ESTABLISHMENTS WITH 75% OR MORE SPECIALIZATION	425	14.5	99.4	11.7	22.2	65.5	191.8	180.9	370.3	10.9
39911	BROOMS										
	(PRIMARY PRODUCT CLASS OF ESTABLISHMENT)	65	2.7	14.2	2.2	3.9	10.1	28.0	28.5	56.5	1.0
	ESTABLISHMENTS WITH 75% OR MORE SPECIALIZATION	46	1.7	8.6	1.3	2.2	6.2	15.2	15.8	31.2	.4
39912	PAINT AND VARNISH BRUSHES										
	(PRIMARY PRODUCT CLASS OF ESTABLISHMENT)	45	4.2	30.7	3.4	6.5	19.8	65.5	65.0	128.3	4.9
	ESTABLISHMENTS WITH 75% OR MORE SPECIALIZATION	39	3.8	28.0	3.0	5.9	18.0	59.4	57.5	114.5	4.7
39913	OTHER BRUSHES										
	(PRIMARY PRODUCT CLASS OF ESTABLISHMENT)	102	9.2	65.3	7.5	14.3	43.9	124.7	95.7	220.1	5.9
	ESTABLISHMENTS WITH 75% OR MORE SPECIALIZATION	86	6.9	48.4	5.6	10.7	32.0	84.8	78.1	162.4	4.1
3993	SIGNS AND ADVERTISING DISPLAYS										
	ENTIRE INDUSTRY	3 287	49.8	415.9	37.5	68.3	261.9	760.8	447.0	1 198.0	29.8
	ESTABLISHMENTS WITH 75% OR MORE SPECIALIZATION	3 246	47.6	400.3	35.8	65.4	252.1	744.0	413.0	1 147.6	28.6
39931	LUMINOUS TUBING AND BULB SIGNS										
	(PRIMARY PRODUCT CLASS OF ESTABLISHMENT)	298	10.3	98.6	7.4	14.0	64.1	167.2	87.4	250.8	7.2
	ESTABLISHMENTS WITH 75% OR MORE SPECIALIZATION	243	9.1	87.8	6.6	12.4	57.0	150.6	79.7	226.8	6.2
39932	NONELECTRIC SIGNS AND ADVERTISING DISPLAYS										
	(PRIMARY PRODUCT CLASS OF ESTABLISHMENT)	627	20.0	172.0	14.9	28.0	105.7	292.1	202.7	490.3	10.7
	ESTABLISHMENTS WITH 75% OR MORE SPECIALIZATION	549	17.1	147.6	12.7	24.0	91.1	258.5	159.7	414.6	9.1
39933	ADVERTISING SPECIALTIES										
	(PRIMARY PRODUCT CLASS OF ESTABLISHMENT)	167	7.3	54.4	5.5	10.0	34.2	106.1	65.3	169.9	3.1
	ESTABLISHMENTS WITH 75% OR MORE SPECIALIZATION	144	6.5	48.5	4.9	8.8	30.7	94.6	59.4	152.6	2.4
3995	BURIAL CASKETS										
	ENTIRE INDUSTRY	515	14.8	109.3	11.8	22.6	72.0	210.3	183.7	391.9	8.8
	ESTABLISHMENTS WITH 75% OR MORE SPECIALIZATION	510	14.7	108.1	11.7	22.4	71.4	208.4	181.6	387.9	8.8

Item	Establishments									
39951 METAL CASKETS, COFFINS, LINED, TRIMMED (ADULT)										
(PRIMARY PRODUCT CLASS OF ESTABLISHMENT)	148	8.6	64.2	6.7	12.9	40.3	127.4	109.8	236.1	5.2
ESTABLISHMENTS WITH 75% OR MORE SPECIALIZATION	75	5.3	40.9	4.1	7.6	24.9	91.0	68.4	158.9	3.7
39952 WOOD CASKETS, COFFINS, LINED, TRIMMED (ADULT)										
(PRIMARY PRODUCT CLASS OF ESTABLISHMENT)	68	2.5	17.4	2.0	4.0	12.2	31.2	28.5	59.0	.9
ESTABLISHMENTS WITH 75% OR MORE SPECIALIZATION	21	1.2	8.4	1.0	2.0	6.2	13.9	9.6	22.9	.5
39933 OTHER CASKETS AND COFFINS AND METAL VAULTS										
(PRIMARY PRODUCT CLASS OF ESTABLISHMENT)	42	2.1	17.7	1.8	3.4	13.0	30.9	26.5	57.1	1.5
ESTABLISHMENTS WITH 75% OR MORE SPECIALIZATION	35	1.9	16.2	1.6	3.0	11.9	28.3	24.3	52.2	1.4
3996 HARD SURFACE FLOOR COVERINGS										
ENTIRE INDUSTRY	20	5.8	59.4	4.6	9.7	44.7	212.0	135.2	342.3	14.0
ESTABLISHMENTS WITH 75% OR MORE SPECIALIZATION	19	(D)	(D)	(D)	(D)	(D)	(D)	(D)	(D)	(D)
3999 MANUFACTURING INDUSTRIES, NEC										
ENTIRE INDUSTRY	3 368	65.3	432.1	51.6	94.9	281.1	900.3	654.0	1 539.9	40.3
ESTABLISHMENTS WITH 75% OR MORE SPECIALIZATION	3 270	55.5	357.6	44.6	81.7	236.8	768.4	559.2	1 311.7	33.8
39991 CHEMICAL FIRE EXTINGUISHING EQUIPMENT AND PARTS										
(PRIMARY PRODUCT CLASS OF ESTABLISHMENT)	25	4.2	40.4	2.7	5.4	24.5	83.8	84.6	163.2	3.3
ESTABLISHMENTS WITH 75% OR MORE SPECIALIZATION	22	(D)	(D)	(D)	(D)	(D)	(D)	(D)	(D)	(D)
39992 COIN-OPERATED AMUSEMENT MACHINES										
(PRIMARY PRODUCT CLASS OF ESTABLISHMENT)	10	3.0	22.9	2.7	5.2	17.0	42.8	28.6	69.6	.9
ESTABLISHMENTS WITH 75% OR MORE SPECIALIZATION	9	(D)	(D)	(D)	(D)	(D)	(D)	(D)	(D)	(d)
39993 MATCHES										
(PRIMARY PRODUCT CLASS OF ESTABLISHMENT)	20	3.7	26.2	3.1	6.3	20.5	57.9	25.0	81.9	2.4
ESTABLISHMENTS WITH 75% OR MORE SPECIALIZATION	20	3.7	26.2	3.1	6.3	20.5	57.9	25.0	81.9	2.4
39994 CANDLES										
(PRIMARY PRODUCT CLASS OF ESTABLISHMENT)	65	5.4	30.9	4.2	7.5	19.4	57.5	50.7	106.7	3.3
ESTABLISHMENTS WITH 75% OR MORE SPECIALIZATION	58	4.4	24.9	3.5	6.3	16.7	42.5	43.8	85.7	2.4
39995 LAMP SHADES										
(PRIMARY PRODUCT CLASS OF ESTABLISHMENT)	54	2.2	12.4	1.8	3.5	8.7	19.2	16.7	35.6	.3
ESTABLISHMENTS WITH 75% OR MORE SPECIALIZATION	52	(D)	(D)	(D)	(D)	(D)	(D)	(D)	(D)	(D)
39996 FURS, DRESSED AND DYED										
(PRIMARY PRODUCT CLASS OF ESTABLISHMENT)	83	2.1	14.6	1.8	3.2	11.3	24.4	18.2	42.4	.4
ESTABLISHMENTS WITH 75% OR MORE SPECIALIZATION	83	2.1	14.6	1.8	3.2	11.3	24.4	18.2	42.4	.4
39997 UMBRELLAS, PARASOLS, AND CANES										
(PRIMARY PRODUCT CLASS OF ESTABLISHMENT)	29	1.3	8.5	.9	1.7	4.6	16.6	26.0	40.9	.3
ESTABLISHMENTS WITH 75% OR MORE SPECIALIZATION	27	(D)	(D)	(D)	(D)	(D)	(D)	(D)	(D)	(D)
39999 OTHER MISCELLANEOUS FABRICATED PRODUCTS, NEC										
(PRIMARY PRODUCT CLASS OF ESTABLISHMENT)	504	23.5	164.3	18.4	34.7	103.0	384.6	253.8	632.3	17.6
ESTABLISHMENTS WITH 75% OR MORE SPECIALIZATION	460	19.9	139.7	15.7	29.1	88.1	331.6	220.1	545.2	15.6

(D) Withheld to avoid disclosing figures for individual companies.

Source: *Census of Manufacturers* (Washington, D.C.: Government Printing Office).

such an economic forecast can be helpful, not only in selecting industries that will benefit in a period of general economic prosperity but also in selecting those that will benefit in periods when only certain sectors of the economy are expanding. Examples of the latter type would be defense industries in a period when the federal government is boosting the economy through large national-defense expenditures, and also those industries that will be hurt least during a period of economic downswing—such as those producing food, something that is always necessary.

Another way of gauging the economy's performance with special regard to specific industry classifications is to examine regularly the statistics contained in the monthly *Federal Reserve Bulletin.* By examining the behavior of the various series over time, the analyst can gain insights to important economic developments in many industries and important industry subsectors. For example, in the table from the *Federal Reserve Bulletin* that is reproduced in Figure 7-2, note the relative growth in consumer goods versus equipment since the base year of 1967. During the period from 1967 to November 1976, the index for consumer goods grew from 100 to 138.9, a 38.9 percent increase. During the same period, the equipment index grew only from 100 to 116.6, a 16.6 increase. In addition, the pace of construction contracts has grown tremendously since 1967. The possible benefit of investment in consumer-oriented industries and construction-related industries during the late 1960s and through the mid-1970s can be seen even from this superficial kind of supplemental analysis.[6]

Key Characteristics in an Industry Analysis

In an industry analysis, there are any number of key characteristics that should be considered at some point by the analyst. In this section we will enumerate and discuss several of these key characteristics: past sales and earnings performance, the permanence of the industry, the attitude of government toward the industry, labor conditions within the industry, the competitive conditions as reflected in any barriers to entry that might exist, and stock prices of firms in the industry relative to their earnings.

PAST SALES AND EARNINGS PERFORMANCE

One of the most effective steps in forecasting is assessing the historical performance of the industry in question. Certainly, two factors with a central role in the ultimate success of any security investment are sales and earnings; therefore, in order to gain a perspective from which to forecast, it is helpful to look at the historical performance of sales and earnings.

One important factor the analyst might uncover is that the history of the industry is very short. This finding alone might make him more cautious about a commitment in this industry, because the industry may not have proved its

---

[6]Meaningful analysis of much of the information contained in the *Federal Reserve Bulletin* requires comparison with earlier time series and great familiarity with the behavior of these series.

FIGURE 7-2

SELECTED BUSINESS INDEXES

(1967 = 100, except as noted)

Period	Industrial production — Total	Market Products Total	Market Products Final Total	Market Products Final Consumer goods	Market Products Final Equipment	Market Products Intermediate	Market Materials	Market Manufacturing	Industry	Capacity utilization in mfg. (per cent of 1967 output)	Construction contracts	Nonagricultural employment—Total[1]	Manufacturing[2] Employment	Manufacturing[2] Payrolls	Total retail sales[3]	Prices[4] Consumer	Prices[4] Wholesale commodity
1955	58.5	56.7	55.4	59.0	50.4	61.6	61.3	58.2		87.0	......	76.9	92.9	61.1	59	80.2	87.8
1956	61.1	59.9	58.6	61.2	55.3	64.4	62.9	60.5		86.1	......	79.6	93.9	64.6	61	81.4	90.7
1957	61.9	61.2	60.4	62.7	57.5	64.4	62.8	61.2		83.6	......	80.3	92.2	65.4	64	84.3	93.3
1958	57.9	58.7	57.6	62.1	51.5	62.9	56.6	56.9		75.0	......	78.0	83.9	60.3	64	86.6	94.6
1959	64.8	64.5	63.2	68.1	56.5	69.5	65.3	64.1		81.6	......	81.0	88.1	67.8	69	87.3	94.8
1960	66.2	66.3	65.3	70.7	58.0	69.9	66.1	65.4		80.1	68.6	82.4	88.0	68.8	70	88.7	94.9
1961	66.7	67.0	65.8	72.2	57.3	71.3	66.2	65.6		77.3	70.2	82.1	84.5	68.0	70	89.6	94.5
1962	72.2	72.3	71.4	77.1	63.7	75.7	72.1	71.5		81.4	78.1	84.4	87.3	73.3	75	90.6	94.8
1963	76.5	76.4	75.5	81.3	67.5	79.9	76.7	75.8		83.5	86.1	86.1	87.8	76.0	79	91.7	94.5
1964	81.7	80.9	79.8	85.8	71.4	85.2	82.9	81.0		85.7	89.4	88.6	89.3	80.1	83	92.9	94.7
1965	89.8	88.2	87.6	92.6	80.7	90.6	92.4	89.7		89.5	93.2	92.3	93.9	88.1	90	94.5	96.6
1966	97.7	95.9	95.9	97.3	94.0	96.2	100.7	97.9		91.1	94.8	97.1	99.9	97.8	97	97.2	99.8
1967	100.0	100.0	100.0	100.0	100.0	100.0	100.0	100.0		86.9	100.0	100.0	100.0	100.0	100	100.0	100.0
1968	106.3	106.2	106.2	105.9	106.5	106.3	106.5	106.4		87.0	113.2	103.2	101.4	108.3	109	104.2	102.5
1969	111.1	110.3	109.6	109.8	109.3	112.9	112.5	111.0		86.2	123.7	106.9	103.2	116.6	114	109.8	106.5
1970	107.8	106.9	105.3	109.0	100.1	112.9	109.2	106.4		79.2	123.1	107.7	98.1	114.1	119	116.3	110.4
1971	109.6	108.5	106.3	114.7	94.7	116.7	111.3	108.2		78.0	145.4	108.1	94.2	116.7	130	121.2	113.9
1972	119.7	118.0	115.7	124.4	103.8	126.5	122.3	118.9		83.1	165.3	111.9	97.6	131.5	142	125.3	119.8
1973	129.8	127.1	124.4	131.5	114.5	137.2	133.9	129.8		87.5	179.5	116.8	103.2	149.2	160	133.1	134.7
1974	129.3	127.3	125.1	128.9	120.0	135.3	132.4	129.4		84.2	169.7	119.1	102.1	157.1	171	147.7	160.1
1975	117.8	119.3	118.2	124.0	110.2	123.1	115.5	116.3		73.6	166.0	116.9	91.4	151.0	186	161.2	174.9
1975—Nov	123.5	123.8	122.3	131.1	110.0	129.3	123.1	122.7		}76.8	148.0	117.8	92.4	158.9	192	165.6	178.2
Dec	124.4	124.9	123.5	132.3	111.5	129.9	123.3	123.6			137.0	118.1	93.0	162.3	198	166.3	178.7
1976—Jan	125.7	126.0	123.9	133.1	111.2	133.6	125.3	125.2			183.0	118.7	94.0	165.9	197	166.7	179.3
Feb	127.3	127.4	125.3	134.9	112.1	135.3	127.3	127.0		}79.0	170.0	119.0	94.3	165.4	201	167.1	179.3
Mar	128.1	128.1	126.4	136.1	112.9	134.9	128.2	127.9			185.0	119.4	94.9	167.4	204	167.5	179.6
Apr	128.4	128.0	126.3	136.1	112.9	134.7	129.2	128.5			189.0	119.9	95.5	166.1	205	168.2	181.3
May	129.6	128.9	127.3	137.4	113.5	135.0	130.6	129.6		}80.2	205.0	119.8	95.4	170.7	202	169.2	181.8
June	130.1	129.5	127.6	137.8	113.8	135.9	131.1	130.2			187.0	119.9	95.3	171.6	206	170.1	183.1
July	130.7	129.8	127.6	136.8	114.9	137.6	132.2	131.0			184.0	120.2	95.2	173.2	205	171.1	184.3
Aug	131.3	130.3	128.3	137.5	115.7	137.8	133.0	131.6		}80.8	162.0	r120.4	r95.2	175.9	209	171.9	183.7
Sept	130.9	130.0	127.5	136.2	115.5	139.0	132.4	130.7			164.0	120.8	96.1	177.7	207	172.6	184.7
Oct	130.4	129.6	127.3	136.5	114.7	138.3	131.7	129.9			237.0	120.6	95.0	175.9	209	173.3	185.2
Nov	132.0	131.5	129.5	138.9	116.6	139.2	133.0	131.7				121.0	95.6	179.3	212	......	185.6

▲ Revised data for 1955–62, comparable to the revised data beginning 1963 shown below, will be published later.
1 Employees only: excludes personnel in the Armed Forces.
2 Production workers only. Revised back to 1973.
3 F.R. index based on Census Bureau figures.
4 Prices are not seasonally adjusted. Latest figure is final.
NOTE.—All series: Data are seasonally adjusted unless otherwise noted.

Capacity utilization: Based on data from Federal Reserve, McGraw-Hill Economics Department, and Dept. of Commerce.
Construction contracts: McGraw-Hill Informations Systems Company, F.W. Dodge Division, monthly index of dollar value of total construction contracts, including residential, nonresidential, and heavy engineering.
Employment and payrolls: Based on Bureau of Labor Statistics data; includes data for Alaska and Hawaii beginning with 1959.
Prices: Bureau of Labor Statistics data.

Source: *Federal Reserve Bulletin,* December 1976.

ability to weather a variety of economic growth prospects, the opportunity of getting in on the ground floor might be a paramount consideration.

The historical record of the industry is crucial for yet another reason—namely, the calculation of both average levels and stability of performance in both sales and earnings, including growth-rate calculations. Even though past average levels or past variability may not be repeated in the future, the analyst needs to know how this industry has reacted in the past. With knowledge and understanding of the reasons behind past behavior, he is better able to assess the relative magnitudes of performance in the future.[7]

A related factor that the analyst must also consider is the cost structure of the industry—that is, the relation of fixed to variable costs. The higher the fixed-cost component, the higher the sales volume necessary to achieve the

---

[7]We saw in Chapter 5 how the mean and variance forecasts are important outputs of security analysis and inputs to portfolio analysis. Briefly, the analyst forecasts the future level and stability of the firm's earnings, prices, and return. We will use the mean and standard deviation of return to reflect the anticipated level and stability of the security's performance.

firm's breakeven point. Conversely, the lower the relative fixed costs, the easier it is for a firm to achieve and surpass its breakeven point.

PERMANENCE

Another important factor in an industry analysis is the relative permanence of the industry. Permanence is a phenomenon related to the products and technology of the industry, whereas the historical record just discussed deals with the behavior of the numbers without regard to the factors that underlie them. If the analyst feels that the need for this particular industry will vanish in an extremely short period of time, it would seem foolish to invest funds in the industry. Sometimes an industry fades from the scene because of a replacement industry that eliminates or diminishes the need for the original industry. Certainly the rise of the automobile caused a decline in the importance of the carriage and the buggy whip, the growth of popularity of margarine hurt the demand for butter, and so on. In this age of rapid technological advance, the degree of permanence of an industry has become an ever more important consideration in industry analysis.

THE ATTITUDE OF GOVERNMENT TOWARD THE INDUSTRY

It is important for the analyst or prospective investor to consider the probable role government will play in the industry. Will it provide support—financial or otherwise? Or will it restrain the industry's development through restrictive legislation and legal enforcement? For example, if the government feels that foreign competition is too severe for a particular domestic industry, it can impose restrictive import quotas and/or tariffs that would tend to assist the domestic industry. Conversely, if the government feels the domestic industry is becoming too independent, it can remove any barriers currently existing and thus aid foreign competition. Furthermore, government can aid selected industries through favorable tax legislation, such as the investment tax credit, which especially aids industries with large capital output.

As government becomes more influential in attempting to regulate business and to advocate consumer protection, the permanence of the industry might well be affected—not in that government interference will necessarily drive it out of business, but in that profits of the industry can be substantially lessened. Sometimes an industry declines in importance because of legal restrictions that are placed upon it.

LABOR CONDITIONS

As unions grow in power in our economy, the state of labor conditions in the industry under analysis becomes ever more important. That is, if we are dealing with a very labor-intensive production process or a very mechanized capital-intensive process where labor performs crucial operations, the possibility of a strike looms as an important factor to be reckoned with. This is particularly true in industries with large fixed costs, for fixed costs such as rent and insurance continue even when production is curtailed. Should a strike occur in such an industry, the large fixed costs would cut deeply into profits earned before and after the strike. An example of such an industry would be steel manufacturing.

In a labor-intensive industry, the variable costs would undoubtedly dominate the fixed costs; however, even here, the loss of customer goodwill during a long strike would probably more than offset the possible advantages of low fixed costs. That is, customers would find other suppliers, and even the low fixed costs might be difficult for the firm to cover.

COMPETITIVE CONDITIONS

Another significant factor in industry analysis is the competitive conditions in the industry under study. One way to determine the competitive conditions is to observe whether any barriers to entry exist. Professor Bain speaks of three general types of barriers: (1) a product-differentiation edge that forestalls the entry of competition, (2) absolute-cost advantages, and (3) advantages arising from economies of scale.[8]

Product-differentiation advantages generally arise when buyers have a preference for the products of established firms or industries, such as in patent medicines and breakfast cereals. Because existing firms or industries have such an advantage, a new entrant is not likely to be able to charge as high a price as they do. Furthermore, a new entrant would probably have to expend large sums of money on sales and promotion expenses in order to procure an acceptable sales level.

By absolute-cost advantages, we refer to the fact that established firms or industries are able to produce and distribute their products at any level of production or distribution at a lower cost than any new entrant can. These advantages arise from such things as patents, ownership of resources or other key raw materials, and easier access to necessary equipment, funds, or management skills. With this combination of circumstances, it can be seen that the established firms are likely to have considerably wider profit margins than their newer competition.

Economics of scale are found in industries in which it is necessary to attain a fairly high level of production in order to obtain economically feasible levels of cost—such as in producing automobiles. A firm attempting to break into such an industry would, under normal circumstances, have to obtain a significant share of the market if it expects to have a competitive cost structure relative to existing firms.

The investment implication when examining an industry that has significant barriers to entry should be clear to the reader. An analyst or prospective investor would like to see that the industry in which he is considering investment seems

[8] Bain, *Industrial Organization*, p. 255.

to be well protected from the inroads of new firms; if the industry were protected by product differentiation, not only would it be difficult for new firms
to enter it but it would also be exceedingly difficult for new industries to
develop in competition with the market currently owned by the existing industry.

INDUSTRY SHARE PRICES RELATIVE
TO INDUSTRY EARNINGS

Having evaluated the various characteristics of past sales and earnings, industry
permanence, government attitude, labor conditions, and industry competitive
conditions, the analyst must ultimately reach a considered investment decision.
However, even if all indications are that the industry has very favorable future
prospects, this does not necessarily imply that funds should be committed to it
immediately. A decision to purchase is not made based only on the current
status and future prospects, but also on the current prices of securities in the
industry, their risk, and the returns they promise.

At this point we will refer to only the price consideration. If the price is very
high relative to future earnings growth, these securities might not be a wise
investment. Conversely, if future prospects are dim but prices are low relative to
a fairly level future pattern of earnings, the stocks in this industry might well be
an attractive investment. Frequently, when an industry develops because of
technology or some other such reason, investors become overzealous in their
desire to purchase securities of firms in this new industry. Thus, these share
prices are bid to very high levels, with the consequence that the P/E ratio soars.
So it can be seen that the "market psychology" can be a crucial factor in both
raising prices to exorbitant levels and depressing prices to unreasonable levels,
depending on how the market evaluates the industry's future prospects.

**Lodgings
Industry
Example**

Following the order of presentation, let's determine the key characteristics of
the lodgings industry.

1. *Past sales and earnings performance:* One key source of U. S. domestic
industry data is a publication of Harris, Kerr, Forster & Company, entitled
Trends in the Hotel-Motel Industry. Table 7-1 contains data extracted from
this source.

It can be seen that gross annual income of the industry has grown drastically
since 1948. Even more drastic, however, has been the growth in the motel sector
of the industry—from 1.4 percent of total revenues in 1948 to 52.6 percent of
the total in 1975. From these figures we can ascertain that the lodgings industry
has undergone substantial growth in sales. The only questionable figures are the
overall decline in the percentage-occupancy rates, the percentage of available
rooms that are actually occupied, from 89 percent in 1948 to 60 percent in
1975. But digging beneath these figures, we find that there has been a large
drop in the occupancy rates of hotels, and a rise in the occupancy rates of

TABLE 7-1

PAST SALES AND EARNINGS PERFORMANCE

	1948	1960	1965	1970	1975
Gross annual income (in billions)	$2.18	$3.87	$5.93	$8.33	$11.44
Number of establishments	22,835	36,740	37,550	37,435	37,825
% Occupancy	89%	69%	66%	63%	60%
Motel-motor hotel revenues as % of total	1.4%	33.7%	44.4%	50.9%	52.6%

Source: Harris, Kerr, Forster & Company, *Trends in the Hotel-Motel Business.*

motels, indicating that the motel type of operation has been expanding, while the hotel type has been contracting. However, the industry as a whole is suffering from overexpansion of available rooms during the 1960s and 1970s.

2. *Permanence of the industry:* Innkeeping has existed since the beginning of recorded time. The lodgings industry itself, however, as pertaining to the stock market, is fairly new. Most of the companies listed on the NYSE have had their greatest growth within the last twenty years.

As long as businessmen and others travel, the lodgings industry will continue to prosper, because people will continue to need a place to stay. However, this growth is not likely to be the same for all sectors of the industry. As cities deteriorate in all ways, business headquarters are likely to move to the suburbs; people visiting cities will prefer to stay in less-congested areas; so hotels and hotel chains are likely to suffer, and motel and motel chains are likely to prosper. As foreign travel picks up, those firms with foreign operations may well benefit. At the same time, as the number of trailers, campers, mobile homes, and second homes increases, vacationers will have less need for lodgings industry facilities.

3. *The attitude of government:* There has been little government intervention in the industry when compared with most industries. Periodically, national campaigns are instituted to encourage everyone to travel in the United States and "See America First."

There are also motions on the part of government to encourage foreign travel to the United States—primarily to help the U. S. balance-of-payments situtation. These efforts certainly benefit the lodgings industry. Few other American industries benefit so directly from such governmental advertising support. Foreign currency realignments will have an effect on industry earnings because of the influence of FASB *Statement No. 8*, as discussed in our Chapter 8. These foreign currency evaluations and realignments are reflected in earnings per share. However, in addition to this effect, changes in the relative value of foreign currency and the U.S. dollar will influence the cost of travel of foreigners to the United States and of U.S. citizens abroad. This effect would be more pronounced with those members of the industry who have foreign operations. Those members of the industry who do not have extensive foreign operations will only have the one-sided effect—namely, the extent of foreign travel in the United States.

4. *Labor conditions.* Labor costs are high, usually 30-35 percent of sales; the

higher percentage is indicative of establishments with restaurant facilities. Working conditions are excellent, but wage rates are notoriously low. A boost in the minimum federal wage rates could hurt some establishments, especially those in the South. Because of the high proportion of fixed costs in this industry, a prolonged labor strike could be costly.

5. *Competitive conditions:* Between 1965 and 1970, the ten leading chains increased their share of the hotel-motel market from 7 to 16 percent. Also during this period, the net increase in rooms was 205,000, of which Holiday Inns, Howard Johnson, and Ramada Inns accounted for 145,000—nearly 75 percent of the total.

Fairly recently, approximately 75 to 80 percent of all new motel construction was either chain-affiliated or chain-controlled. This trend toward consolidation has sprung from the many barriers to entry of the lodgings industry. The chains enjoy the following characteristics that make it difficult for the small or medium-sized firm to compete:

a. *Computerized reservation system.* This takes some of the uncertainty out of traveling for the pleasure traveler. Holiday Inns has the largest advance reservation system, and plans to use it overseas also. The other large chains belong to the American Express Space Bank. This brings the cost of a confirmed reservation from $5.00 to $1.50, or in Holiday Inns' case, $.50. The computer is also valuable in forecasting, management duties, accounting, and other areas. It is a big step forward in increasing the technology of hotel-motel management.

b. *Product differentiation.* One of the main benefits of enjoying the hospitality of a large lodgings chain is the guarantee of uniform quality. All the chains insist on high standards, which are rigorously enforced in both company-owned and franchised properties.

c. *Economies of scale.* The well-managed chains can save money on purchases and on managerial technology. Their large size enables them to employ a sophisticated staff, skilled in planning, market research, construction, accounting, and financial management. Some companies have integrated vertically, and own subsidaries that supply everything from construction to furnishings to supplies and provisions.

One other benefit for a large firm is the ability to tap capital markets. This can assure them a steady supply of financing at a cost lower than that of the independent hotel-motel owner.

It is estimated that by 1980, at least half of all available rooms will be chain-associated. One big factor in the growth of the chain organizations has been the franchising possibilities. A franchise can be purchased for a minimum fee of $15,000. However, some of the large chains are leaning away from this method of expansion in the future, because profits are greater when the property is company-operated.

6. *Industry share prices relative to industry earnings:* The industry enjoyed rapid growth and high P/E multiples during the 1960s. For example, during the period 1966-71 the compound earnings growth rate per annum for the better known motel chains was in the 15 to 25% range. P/E ratios hovered in the 25-35 range. This pace has faded rapidly since 1972.

TABLE 7-2
KEY SHARE PRICE DATA ON SELECTED FIRMS IN THE LODGING INDUSTRY

| Company | October, 1977 | | | Earnings Per Share | | | | Actual Growth Rate 1972-1976 | Forecasted Growth Rate 1975-1981 |
	Stock Price 10/77	P : E Ratio	Divi-dend Yield	1974	1975	1976	1977E		
Hilton Hotels	$19.0	7.2	5.5	$1.09	$1.41	$2.21	$2.60	16.0%	8.5%
Holiday Inn	13.0	8.4	3.9	1.06	1.37	1.28	1.55	(0.5)	11.0
Howard Johnson	11.0	7.6	3.3	.81	1.11	1.31	1.40	13.0	11.5
Marriott Corp.	9.6	8.8	nil	.74	.65	.88	.99	14.5	13.5
Ramada Inns	3.3	10.3	3.6	.35	.04	.20	.30	(13.5)	22.0
Value Line 900 In-dustrials		8.6	4.4					11.5	11.0

Table 7-2 contains pertinent data on selected lodging industry firms as well as an industry-composite benchmark. As you can see, the industry composite (*Value Line*) had a P/E of 8.6 in late 1977 that was very much in line with the multiples afforded the companies listed. Note that the estimated growth rates of earnings per share for the participant companies is generally in line with the *Value Line* 900 Industrials. Note further that differences in the P/E ratios afforded individual companies appears to be strongly related to differences in expected earnings growth. Marriott and Ramada have P/E's that exceed the 900 Industrials and their projected earnings growth rates are similarly higher. Holiday Inns, Inc. sports a P/E and earnings growth rate projection in line with the 900 Industrials.

These trends in the lodgings industry would indicate attractive investment opportunities in selected large lodgings chains. This estimate is reinforced by:

1. Professional management of the publicly owned companies.
2. High entry costs.
3. High failure rate of small operators.
4. Small additions to capacity. New chain-controlled rooms are mainly re-placements of old, retired properties.

Industry Life Cycle

Thus far in this chapter, we have discussed a number of pertinent factors that should be considered in an industry analysis. A framework within which we can place many of these considerations is known as the industry life-cycle theory.[9]

[9]This theory is generally attributed to Julius Grodinsky. See Grodinsky, *Investments* (New York: Ronald Press, 1953), pp. 64-89.

FIGURE 7-3
INDUSTRIAL LIFE CYCLE

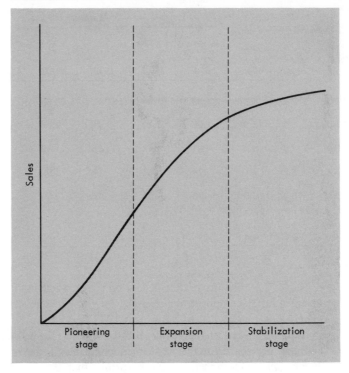

The life of an industry can be separated into the pioneering stage, the expansion stage, the stagnation stage, and the decay stage.[10] These stages are illustrated graphically in Figure 7-3.

PIONEERING STAGE

The pioneering stage is typified by rapid growth in demand for the output of the industry. In fact, in this earliest stage, demand not only grows but grows at an increasing rate. As a result there is a great apparent opportunity for profits, and thus venture capital comes into the industry. As large numbers of firms attempt to capture their share of the market, there arises a high business mortality rate; many of the weaker firms that are attempting to survive in this new industry are eliminated, and a lesser number of firms survive the initial phases of the pioneering stage. Firms are eliminated in part because of price competition, heavy losses resulting from start-up costs, and generally hard nonprice competition stemming from such things as attempts to develop a

---

[10]For convenience, we will combine the stagnation and decay stages and refer to them as the stabilization stage.

brand name, a differentiated product, or a market edge as a result of product image that has been created.

Many firms are lured into the industry as a result of profit opportunities, and they compete vigorously with each other. The result is a constant shifting of the relative positions of the firms in the industry. Thus it is difficult at this stage for the analyst to select those firms that will remain on top for some time to come. Even if the analyst has the ability to recognize an emerging industry in the pioneering stage, he will probably not invest at this point in the industry's development, because of the great risks involved and because of the tremendous difficulty in selecting the survivors. However, the astute analyst will not even consider investment in the industry in the pioneering stage but will rather observe the industry's maturity and will wait for the expansion stage before he commits funds.

EXPANSION STAGE

The expansion stage is characterized by the appearance of the firms surviving from the pioneering stage. These few companies continue to get stronger, both in share of the market and financially. Their competition in the expansion stage usually brings about improved products at a lower price. These firms continue to expand, but at a more moderate rate of growth than the one they experienced in the pioneering stage. As a result, these now stronger, steadier, more efficient firms become more attractive for investment purposes. While they are still growing, they have the aura of stability about them. In fact, in the expansion stage, many companies establish the precedent of paying dividends, making them an even more desirable investment.

STABILIZATION STAGE

The growth of the industry, which had moderated in the expansion stage, begins at some point to moderate even further, and perhaps even begins to stagnate. In other words, the ability of the industry to grow appears to have been lost. Sales may be increasing at a slower rate than that experienced by competitive industries or by the overall economy. Grodinsky refers to a possible explanation of this transition as "latent obsolescence":

> Latent Obsolescence—While an industry is still expanding, economic and financial infection may develop. Though its future is promising, seeds of decay may have already been planted. These seeds may not germinate, and the industry may remain strong. If the seeds do germinate, the latent decay becomes real. These seeds may be described as "latent obsolescence," because they may not become active, and they are the earliest signs of decline. Such factors must be examined and interpreted by the investor.[11]

[11]Grodinsky, *Investments*, pp. 71-72.

Symptoms of "latent obsolescence" include changing social habits, high labor costs, changes in technology, and stationary demand.

The investment implication as these events take place is to dispose of one's holdings as soon as the industry begins to pass from the expansion stage to the stabilization stage, for after the transition becomes general knowledge, the stock's price may be depressed. However, an industry may only stagnate intermittently before resuming a period of growth (for example, airlines, in the view of some analysts)—thus starting a new cycle by, say, the introduction of a technological innovation or a new product. Thus it is crucial for the investor or analyst to monitor industry developments constantly.

Although our exposition of the industry life-cycle theory seems to imply that it is easy to detect which stage of development an industry is in at any point in time, this is not necessarily so, for often the transition from one stage to the next is slow and unclear, making it detectable only by careful analysis. Nonetheless, this approach is useful in a somewhat crude way, and at the same time it gives the analyst insight into the apparent merits of investments in a given industry at a given time. In fact, one investment advisory service states, "In judging the probable future trend of an individual stock it is therefore more important to project the trend of its industry group than to project the trend of the general market. . . ."[12]

Despite the intuitive attractiveness of the industry life-cycle framework, it should be noted that it is only a *general* framework, and therefore, exceptions to the stereotype presented here will be met in practice. The analyst must be careful not to attempt to force all situations encountered in practice into the pioneering, expansion, and stabilization molds as outlined here. Furthermore, the investment-policy implications mentioned in conjunction with the foregoing analysis serve as only a general guideline. Due heed must be paid to the current price of the security relative to its future earnings prospects.

Techniques for Evaluating Relevant Industry Factors

Thus far in this chapter, we have discussed the role of relevant industry factors in the investment decision-making process. At this point we should turn our attention to the techniques for analyzing this information and to the readily available sources of it.[13]

---

[12]George A. Chestnutt, Jr., *Stock Market Analysis: Facts and Principles* (Greenwich, Conn.: Chestnutt Corporation, 1971), p. 12.

[13]One key input to the analyst is gained from visits with managements of firms in the industry under study. Sometimes this involves traveling to the various corporate headquarters; sometimes the company officials come to the analysts, via talks to groups of analysts at regularly scheduled luncheons of Financial Analysts societies, held in major cities across the United States. Information gained from exposure to management is extremely valuable to the analyst. The sources of information discussed in this section supplement such personal contacts and are often the only sources available to the analyst or investor.

END-USE AND REGRESSION ANALYSIS

End-use analysis, or product-demand analysis, as it is sometimes called, refers to the process whereby the analyst or investor attempts to diagnose the factors that determine the demand for the output of the industry. Determining such demand is clearly crucial, since, in a single-product firm, units demanded multiplied by price will equal sales revenue. In the process, the analyst hopes to uncover the relationships that "explain" demand, thereby enabling him to forecast industry sales more accurately. Frequently, such variables as GNP, disposable income, per capita consumption, price elasticity of demand, and per capita income are powerful *explanatory variables*. If this is the case and certain basic assumptions are upheld, linear regression analysis and correlation analysis can be useful techniques.[14]

FIGURE 7-4
SCATTER DIAGRAM

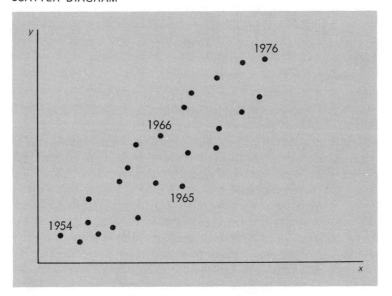

Briefly stated, simple linear regression analysis mathematically fits a line to a series of points on a scatter diagram, and correlation analysis permits us to measure the "goodness of the fit." Perhaps a simple illustration will help clarify the advantages of these techniques. Figure 7-4 shows a hypothetical scatter diagram, and Figure 7-5 shows this same scatter diagram with three regression lines, *AB, CD,* and *EF,* fitted to the data.

---

[14]For a detailed treatment of the assumptions underlying regression analysis and correlation analysis, see any comprehensive statistics or econometrics text, such as J. Johnston, *Econometric Methods* (New York: McGraw-Hill, 1963).

FIGURE 7-5

SCATTER DIAGRAM WITH A "FITTED" REGRESSION LINE

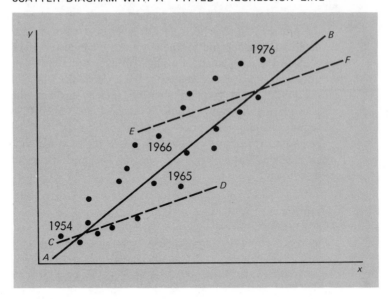

Merely "eyeballing" the data contained in Figure 7-4 is not a very scientific way of analyzing it. Actually, two different persons might interpret the significance of the data quite differently. The next step up in sophistication would perhaps be to fit a line freehand to the data; however, this too is subjective and lacks the necessary rigor. Fortunately, there exists a technique known as the "method of least squares," which allows us to base the fitted line on the simple equation $y = a + bx$, the equation of a straight line.[15] You will recall that y is generally the dependent variable, x is the independent variable, a is the y intercept, and b is the slope of the line. For example, y might be machine production or sales, and x might be industrial production. Each point would represent the figures for both variables for a particular period, such as a year.

Most computer installations own "canned" (ready-to-use) regression programs for the interested user. These programs normally furnish the user at least such output as a, b, the mean of the independent and dependent variables, and some correlation measures of the "goodness of fit" and the "explanatory" powers of the independent variable.

We can undoubtedly imagine many uses of this statistical technique in industry analysis, such as regressing industry sales against time; industry sales against a key macroeconomic variable like GNP, personal income, or disposable income; and industry earnings over time. Figure 7-6 is an excerpt from a Standard & Poor's *Industry Surveys*; specifically, a portion of a basic analysis of the machinery industry. It contains a diagram with a fitted regression line. In this case,

[15]The reader interested in the mechanics of this technique, as well as in correlation analysis, should read one of the many statistics texts available.

the *y*, or dependent variable, is machinery production, and the *x*, or independent variable, is U.S. industrial production as measured by the Federal Reserve Board Index of Industrial Production. Such an application of regression analysis is common in industry analyses.

Sometimes the analyst will not be satisfied with the results of a simple linear regression analysis and will feel that two, three, or more variables would much better be able to "explain" the variability of the dependent variable. In such an instance, the analyst will use multiple regression analysis (an extension of simple linear regression analysis). In this technique, the dependent variable is regressed against several independent variables. For example, if we were attempting to forecast the sales of the power-lawnmower industry, we might use disposable income, expected rainfall, and the number of single-unit residential homes as independent variables.

Problem Areas in Regression Analysis[16]

First, we can observe three distinct regression lines that have been fitted to the data contained in Figure 7-5. There are three because three different time periods were used to calculate the least-squares regression line—the period 1954-65 for line *CD*, the period 1966-76 for line *EF*, and the period 1954-76 for line *AB*. Thus the selection of beginning and end points is critical in determining the line that will be fitted to the data. This fact is always true when any determinants underlying the variables themselves change significantly over time. In the example, some sort of underlying shift occurred during 1965-76 that affected this industry—such as a change in consumer tastes, technology, or economic or tax environment. In selecting beginning or end points, it is important that basic conditions were similar in the base and end-point years, as well as in the interim.[17]

A second problem area involves the nature of the relationship the analyst is measuring. The technique we are discussing here assumes a *linear* relationship as opposed to a nonlinear one, such as a curvilinear relationship, in which the points lie along a curve rather than a straight line. To the extent that this is not a valid assumption, the results of the regression analysis may at best be somewhat misleading, and at worst they will be totally meaningless.

The third and last problem to be discussed here involves the interpretation of the results of the adjunct correlation analysis. It is possible for two series of data to be highly correlated—that is, to go up and down pretty much together—and yet to be not at all causally related. For example, it is possible that for some time period, rainfall and the stock market might be highly correlated; however, we would be wrong in asserting that rainfall caused the market to go up and a drought spelled disaster for the market. If this were true, the best training for

---

[16]The reader should be cautioned that these are not the only potential problem areas.

[17]Frequently, in an effort to partially overcome this problem of the appropriate time period, analysts forecast from a base period to an end period rather than from a discrete point to a discrete point. That is, to continue the example, the period average for 1954-56 would be used as the base and the period 1974-76 as the end period. However, even this is only a minimum compensation and does not completely overcome the problem. That can be achieved only by selecting a stable, but meaningful, period.

security analysis would be to study meteorology! Therefore the analyst should not just blindly strive for high correlation. The variables should appear to be related in a significant *economic* sense as well as in a *statistical* sense before he jumps to conclusions about probable causation.

INPUT-OUTPUT ANALYSIS

Input-output analysis can be thought of as a way of getting inside demand analysis or end-use analysis. This technique, which is reflected in an input-output table, reflects the flow of goods and services through the economy, including intermediate steps in the production process as the good proceeds from the raw-material stage through final consumption. Thus input-output analysis observes patterns of consumption at all stages—not just the consumption of final goods—in order to detect any changing patterns or trends that might indicate the growth or decline of industries.

Basically, an input-output table is a matrix consisting of rows and columns of identically coded industries. Reading down a column tells us what the required

FIGURE 7-6
ANALYSIS OF THE MACHINERY INDUSTRY

With the economy extending an upturn that began in the spring of 1975, concern is mounting that the continuing lag in capital spending could restrict a more sustained recovery. Consideration is also being given to a possible re-emergence of shortages of industrial capacity and basic materials, similar to those that occurred in 1973 and early 1974. Such shortages would, of course, likely lead to a rekindling of inflation.

The latest Commerce Department survey on plant and equipment spending projects a 6.5% increase in 1976 outlays, a gain that would be more than offset by higher prices. The most recent MCGRAW-HILL Economics Department survey of business indicates that spending will advance 13% in 1976 and that businessmen expect a 9% increase in capital goods prices, resulting in a 4% pickup in the real volume of plant and equipment spending. Other independent estimates point to gains in real outlays on the order of 3% to 5%. The MCGRAW-HILL study pointed out that some 50% of planned 1976 expenditures of $127.3 billion were slated for expansion, with the remainder going for modernization. While such outlays for expansion represent a larger share of investment dollars, compared with 1975, the significant spending on modernization (including safety and environmental requirement outlays) indicates a cautious concern for overexpansion.

With U.S. industry operating at less than 75% of capacity in the 1976 first quarter, there would appear to be considerable slack yet to be taken up before additional facilities are required. This idle capacity, much of it representing obsolete or otherwise unusable equipment, is expected to fall to 20% by year end, a level that usually triggers a surge in spending. Further, the continuing abatement in the rate of inflation, coupled with the growing strength of the consumer sector, could well provide the necessary impetus for businessmen to step-up their spending plans before too long.

Additional encouragement should come from the healthier prospects for financing investment. Recent increases in corporate cash flow—profits plus depreciation—have been substantial; many businesses could finance much higher capital spending rates internally.

Industrial production, earnings, and capital expenditures						
	Indexes of Production			Corp. Profits	Cap. Consumption Allow.	Total Profits & Allow.
	Industrial	Durable Mfrs.	Machinery			
Year	1967=100			Billions of Dollars		
1975	113.7	105.7	112.8	71.2	78.3	149.5
R1974	124.8	120.7	128.1	79.5	78.3	157.8
1973	125.6	122.0	125.8	R68.7	R69.0	R137.7
1972	115.2	108.4	107.5	R54.7	R65.4	R120.1
1971	106.8	99.4	96.2	R44.3	R60.6	R104.9
1970	106.6	101.4	100.3	R37.0	R55.1	R92.1
1969	110.7	110.0	106.8	R43.8	R49.4	R93.2
1968	105.7	105.5	101.9	R46.2	R44.4	R90.6
1967	100.0	100.0	100.0	46.6	R40.4	R87.0
1966	97.9	99.0	98.6	49.9	36.7	R86.6

R = Revised.
Sources: Department of Commerce, Federal Reserve Board.

Source: Standard & Poor's *Industry Surveys* (New York: Standard & Poor's Corporation).

FIGURE 7-6 (cont.)

Outside capital costs are lower, although still above historical averages, and the increased cash flow should restrict interest rate increases, as fewer firms have to borrow. Finally, the surge in stock prices has made the equity market an attractive capital source.

Should a major improvement in capital spending lag behind the consumer sector of the economy by more than the usual 18 months or so, a form of cushion exists now that was not available to soften the capacity and material shortages of a few years ago. With the economies of most major European countries recovering at a much slower pace than that of the U.S., it is possible that domestic shortages could be eased by imports.

Orders expected to rise

New orders for nonelectrical machinery should be up substantially in 1976, with the bulk of the gain coming in the second half. According to MCGRAW-HILL, machinery orders spurted 27% in the first quarter of 1976, versus the comparable year-earlier period. While the domestic orders index after the first quarter was one-third ahead of the year-earlier level and the export orders index was up 22%, at 209 the total index was still some 5% below the August 1974 peak of 220. Nonetheless, the broadening recovery, combined with modest rates of price increases, suggests a significant advance in over-all profits this year and a more rapid rise in capital investment.

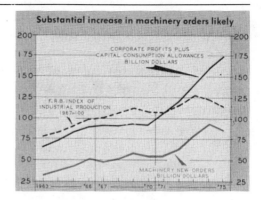

For individual components of the broad machinery category, outlays for pollution control equipment and services are expected to be maintained at relatively high levels. Construction and material handling equipment manufacturers should benefit from the stepped-up economic pace, with increased housing starts sparking a mild recovery in smaller equipment sales, offsetting a possible decline in shipments to energy-related areas. Indications are that electric utilities will be advancing new plant additions, boding well for power equipment producers.

Expenditures for new equipment by U.S. business
(In millions of dollars)

Industry	1966	1967	1968	1969	1970	1971	1972	1973	1974	1975	E1976
Manufacturing	26,990	26,690	28,370	31,680	31,950	29,990	31,350	38,010	46,010	47,950	51,850
Durable goods industries	13,990	13,700	14,120	15,960	15,800	14,150	15,640	19,250	22,620	21,840	22,930
Primary iron and steel	2,170	2,310	2,270	2,130	2,000	1,700	1,570	2,050	2,120	3,030	2,750
Primary nonferrous metals	860	900	1,090	1,100	1,240	1,080	1,180	1,670	2,330	2,280	2,180
Electrical machinery & equip.	1,190	1,240	1,780	2,030	2,270	2,140	2,390	2 840	2,970	2,310	2,530
Machinery, except electrical	2,860	2,950	2,840	3,440	3,470	2,800	2,900	3,420	4,420	4,500	5,090
Motor vehicles & equipment	1,930	1,660	1,360	1,650	1,590	1,510	1,830	2,280	2,700	2,060	2,410
Transportation equipment, excluding motor vehicles	1,090	1,090	1,120	1,110	840	620	700	853	800	920	800
Stone, clay & glass products	910	730	860	1,070	990	850	1,200	1,490	1,440	1,420	1,600
*Other durable goods	2,980	2,830	2,820	3,440	3,410	3,450	3,870	4,960	5,100	4,380	4,550
Nondurable goods industries	13,000	13,000	14,250	15,720	16,150	15,840	15,720	18,760	23,390	26,110	28,920
Food and beverage	1,390	1,410	2,210	2,590	2,840	2,690	2,550	3,110	3,250	3,260	3,920
Textile	1,130	890	530	630	560	610	730	770	840	660	760
Paper & allied products	1,500	1,640	1,320	1,580	1,650	1,250	1,380	1,860	2,580	2,950	3,330
Chemical & allied products	2,990	2,880	2,830	3,100	3,440	3,440	3,450	4,460	5,690	6,250	6,670
Petroleum and coal	4,420	4,650	5,250	5,630	5,620	5,850	5,250	5,450	8,000	10,510	11,630
Rubber	420	490	980	1,090	940	840	1,080	1,560	1,470	1,000	1,120
†Other nondurable goods	1,140	1,040	1,130	1,100	1,110	1,150	1,270	1,560	1,550	1,480	1,490
Mining	1,470	1,420	1,630	1,860	1,890	2,160	2,420	2,740	3,180	3,790	3,880
Railroad	1,980	1,530	1,450	1,860	1,780	1,670	1,800	1,960	2,540	2,550	2,080
Transportation other than rail	3,440	3,880	4,150	4,190	4,260	3,260	3,920	4,070	4,120	5,020	4,150
Public utilities	8,410	9,880	10,200	11,610	13,140	15,300	17,000	18,710	20,550	20,140	23,240
‡Commercial, communications, and other	18,360	18,250	21,970	24,350	26,690	28,820	31,960	34,250	36,010	33,340	34,860
††Total	60,630	61,660	67,760	75,560	79,710	81,210	88,440	99,740	112,400	112,780	120,060

Note: Data exclude expenditures of agricultural business and outlays charged to current account. *Includes fabricated metal products, lumber products, furniture & fixtures, instruments, ordnance, and miscellaneous manufacturers. †Includes apparel & related products, tobacco, leather & leather products, and printing & publishing. ‡Includes trade-service, finance, and construction. ††—Detail may not add to totals because of rounding. E−Estimated.
Sources: Securities & Exchange Commission, Department of Commerce.

inputs for the industry in the column head were from all the industries. Conversely, reading across a row tells us what the output (from the industry in the left-hand column) to each industry was, including intraindustry sales.

Table 7-3 is an excerpt from an actual input-output table. We can see in row 1 that the livestock and livestock-products industry sold $26,322 million worth of goods in 1958. The inputs to this industry can be read by going down column 1. We see that most of the raw material comes from the livestock and livestock-products industry itself and from the other-agricultural-products group (see rows 1 and 2). Note that the row total must equal the column total for a given industry classification—in this case, $26,322 million.

This technique, because of technical difficulties, is more appropriate for an intermediate or long-term forecast than for a short-term forecast. However, despite these shortcomings of the input-output technique, it has been said that "the system presents the most incisive look at an economy's industrial structure yet accomplished. . . ."[18]

**External
Sources of
Information
for
Industry
Analysis**

FEDERAL GOVERNMENT

Figures 7-1 and 7-2 showed examples of information published by the government that can be useful during the industry phase of the analysis. It is well worth the time to thumb through the *Census of Manufacturers, Federal Reserve Bulletins,* and *Survey of Current Business* in order to appreciate more fully the wealth of information, helpful in the economic as well as industry analysis, available in these government sources. Many private services use these government-furnished data as an input to their own security-analysis efforts.

INVESTMENT SERVICES

There are many investment services available to furnish the investor or analyst with valuable industry and corporate information. The ones we shall single out in this section are perhaps the best known.[19]

Standard & Poor's

Standard & Poor's regularly covers a number of different industries in two ways—a basic analysis and a current update of the basic analysis. The basic

---

[18]Howard B. Bonham, Jr., "The Use of Input-Output Economics in Common Stock Analysis," *Financial Analysts Journal,* January-February 1967, p. 27. For a fuller treatment of input-output analysis, see this article, and also D. A. Hodes, "Input-Output Analysis: An Illustrative Example," *Business Economics,* Summer 1965, p. 37; Wassily W. Leontief, "The Structure of the U.S. Economy," *Scientific American,* April 1965, pp. 26-32; and Anne P. Carter, The Economics of Technological Change," *Scientific American,* April 1966, pp. 25-31.

[19]The *Wall Street Journal, Barron's,* the *Commercial and Financial Chronicle,* and *Predicasts* are among other key sources of investment information.

TABLE 7-3
INPUT-OUTPUT TABLE

Interindustry Transactions, 1958
(In millions of dollars at producers' prices)

For the distribution of output of an industry, read the row for that industry.
For the composition of inputs to an industry, read the column for that industry.

	1 Livestock and live-stock products	2 Other agricultural products	Intermediate outputs, total	Personal consumption expenditures	Gross private fixed capital formation	Net inventory change	Net exports[3]	Federal Government purchases	State and local government purchases	Total final demand	Total
1. Livestock & Livestock Products	4,153	1,705	23,565	2,111		601	38	-3	11	2,758	26,322
2. Other Agricultural Products	6,600	703	17,624	2,429		428	1,813	1,073	27	5,770	23,395
3. Forestry & Fishery Products	---	---	1,257	281		19	30	-137	(*)	104	1,451
4. Agricultural, Forestry & Fishery Services	493	878	1,563	---		20	3	45	-68	18	1,564
5. Iron & Ferroalloy Ores Mining	---	---	1,227	---		-23	41	---	---	18	1,245
6. Nonferrous Metal Ores Mining	---	1	1,155	---		-32	4	192	---	163	1,319
7. Coal Mining	6	---	2,120	201		-22	332	---	61	831	2,752
8. Crude Petroleum & Natural Gas	---	---	10,865	---		-40	28	---	-12	-12	10,852
9. Stone and Clay Mining and Quarrying	1	67	1,583	17		4	23	10	-12	41	1,624
10. Chemical & Fertilizer Mineral Mining	---	28	485	1		-1	55	11	12	78	563
11. New Construction	---	---	---		36,957		2	3,388	12,069	52,416	52,410
12. Maintenance & Repair Construction	234	377	12,455				---	1,081	3,339	4,420	16,875
13. Ordnance & Accessories	---	---	2,136	158		84	17	2,270	4	2,533	4,669
14. Food & Kindred Products	2,964	3	17,536	45,759		248	1,298	53	272	47,620	65,165
15. Tobacco Manufactures	---	---	1,284	4,250		-26	436	---	(*)	4,661	5,945
16. Broad & Narrow Fabrics, Yarn & Thread Mills	---	7	10,008	712		-104	210	50	9	878	10,886
17. Miscellaneous Textile Goods & Floor Coverings	6	27	1,690	743		-27	46	4	1	812	2,502
I. Intermediate Inputs, Total	17,298	11,573	---	* * *	* * *	* * *	* * *	* * *	* * *	* * *	* * *
V.A. Value Added	9,024	11,822	---	* * *	* * *	* * *	* * *	* * *	* * *	* * *	* * *
T. Total	26,322	23,395	---	290,069	62,392	-1,491	2,206	53,594	40,564	447,334	447,344

Source: U.S. Government Printing Office.

analysis provides an in-depth report on all facets of the industry and the firms comprising the industry. A revised basic analysis is published approximately every year. The current update, entitled *Current Analysis and Outlook,* is published roughly every quarter. An index to the Standard & Poor's *Industry Surveys* is reproduced in Figure 7-7. As can be seen, the index contains the dates of the latest current and basic analyses, as well as page references.

Figure 7-6 showed part of a basic analysis. Standard & Poor's also publishes the *Security Price Index Record,* containing indexes of the Standard & Poor's groupings, which are helpful when performing an industry analysis.

The Value Line

The Value Line also publishes industry data, but in a considerably more condensed form than does Standard & Poor's. Figure 7-8 is a typical *Value Line* industry report. Such a report is followed by separate pages of data for each major firm in the industry. Note that along with descriptive material, the report contains a summary of mutual-fund activity in the shares of firms in the industry, and a graph of the relative strength of the industry's share prices compared to the *Value Line* index of 1,500 stocks.

On a weekly basis, *The Value Line* ranks the probable market performance of industries over the next twelve months, and in the case of individual stocks, their probable performance over the next twelve months and the next three to five years. Figure 7-9 contains *Value Line*'s industry rankings in August 1977.

Forbes

The early-January issue of *Forbes* contains its "Annual Report on American Industry." This report includes a number of rankings of profitability, growth, and stock-market performance of over 700 U.S. corporations. Of interest here are its rankings of major industry groupings, from which the analyst can see the industry groups that appear to be on the move.

Trade Publications

Virtually every major U.S. industry has at least one trade association, which in its publications reports much data pertaining to the industry it represents. The analyst can locate these sources, as well as references to various industries in other publications, by checking the *Business Periodicals Index* and the *Science and Technology Index,* as well as secondary sources already mentioned in this chapter.

Chestnutt Corporation

The Chestnutt Corporation provides an excellent service that compiles a number of interesting barometers of industry performance, as well as the performance of individual securities. Among the interesting data reported by Chestnutt are graphs and commentaries such as those contained in Figure 7-10. These very strongly point up the importance of sound industry analysis.

FIGURE 7-7

index to surveys

STANDARD & POOR'S INDUSTRY SURVEYS
Standard & Poor's is a subsidiary of McGraw-Hill, Inc.

Dates of Latest Surveys

IN VOLUME 1

	Current Analysis	Basic Analysis
A Aerospace	12-23-76	11-25-76
Air Transport	1-13-77	4-15-76
Apparel (incl. Footwear)	10-14-76	6-24-76
Autos-Auto Parts	2-10-77	8-12-76
B Banking (incl. Finance & Personal Loans)	3-24-77	7-8-76
Beverages	3-10-77	10-28-76
Building	3-17-77	9-16-76
C Chemicals	2-17-77	12-30-76
Communication	3-31-77	10-14-76
Containers	12-16-76	3-24-77
E Electronics-Electrical	2-24-77	9-23-76
F Food Processing	2-3-77	4-29-76
H Health Care, Drugs, and Cosmetics	12-30-76	7-29-76
Home Furnishings	12-9-76	2-10-77
I Insurance	1-6-77	3-10-77
Investment	1-27-77	11-4-76
L Leisure-Time	1-13-77	11-11-76

IN VOLUME 2

	Current Analysis	Basic Analysis
M Machinery (incl. Rail Equip.)	3-31-77	5-27-76
Metals-Nonferrous	12-23-76	11-18-76
O Office Equipment	1-27-77	8-19-76
Oil	3-3-77	6-10-76
Oil-Gas Drilling & Services	3-3-77	10-7-76
P Paper	2-10-77	9-9-76
R Railroads	2-17-77	6-3-76
Retailing (Department, Mail Order, Variety, and Drug Chains)	12-30-76	8-5-76
Retailing-Food (Supermarkets, Restaurants, and Food Service)	1-20-77	12-16-76
Rubber Fabricating	12-23-76	10-21-76
S Steel-Coal	2-3-77	9-2-76
T Telephone	12-2-76	12-23-76
Textiles	2-17-77	5-20-76
Tobacco	3-10-77	5-6-76
Trucking	1-6-77	3-25-76
U Utilities-Electric	1-20-77	7-22-76
Utilities-Gas	1-13-77	3-17-77

Subject Guide

VOLUME 1 CONTAINS PAGES A THROUGH L
VOLUME 2 CONTAINS PAGES M THROUGH U

A
	Page
Accident Insurance	I-19, I-22
Acids, Mineral	C27
Additives	C30, C32
Advertising	C69, C74, C78
Advertising Outlays	
Automobile	A153
Beverage	B73
Cigarette	T113
Advertising Agencies	C78
Aerosol Containers	C124
Aerospace	A9
Aggregates	B124
Agricultural Chemicals	C33
Agricultural Machinery	M28
Air Conditioning	B119, E21, E31
Air Freight	A80, T140
Air Pollution Control	A145, M15, M179, M190, P24, U18
Air Transport	A63
Aircraft	A9, A18, A82
Airlines	A63
Airports	A82
Alkalies	C28
Alloy Steels	S49, S57
Aluminum	C123, M169
Amtrak	R34
Amusements	L7
Analog Computers	O14
Anthracite Coal	S58
Apparel	A99
Appliances, Electrical	E19
Asbestos	B121
Atomic Energy	
Electronics	E26
Power Equipment	M22
Utility Plants	M190, O72, U15
Audio Visual	C64
Auto Insurance	I-22
Auto Parts	A148
Auto Safety	A146
Automobiles	A137
Avionics	A26, E27, E33

B
	Page
Bags, Grocers'	C119
Bakery Products	F32
Bank Deposits	B22
Bank Investments	B22
Bank Loans	B21
Banking	B9
Batteries (Automotive)	A150, M179
Bauxite	M172
Bearings, Ball & Roller	A150
Bedding	H60
Beer	B62
Beet Sugar	F20
Beryllium	M192
Beverages	B59
Bicycles	L13
Bitum'nous Coal	S58
Boating	L12
Boats, Service	O121
Boilers	M22
Bond Funds	I-62
Book Clubs	C68
Book Publishing	C63
Bottles	C119
Plastic	C126, B72
Bottling Plants	B72
Bowling	L14
Boxboard	P18
Brakes, Auto	A149
Brass Mills	M178
Breakfast Cereals	F31
Breeder Reactors	E31, U13
Brewers	B62
Broadcasting	C74
Broadcasting Equipment	E23
Brokerage Firms	I-55
Building	B105
Electrical Equip.	E28
Government Programs	B112, B117
Building Materials	B118
Burley Tobacco	T112
Bus Production	A142
Business Forms	O28

C
	Page
CAB	A21, A67
CATV	C77, E14
Calculators	E16, O26

	Page
Camping	L14
Cane Sugar	F20
Candy	F32
Canning	F27
Cans	B64, C122
Carbon Steel	S49
Carpets	H56, T39
Carriers, Motor	T135
Casualty Insurance	I-21
Catalog Businesses	R133
Catalytic Converters	A145, M180, M188
Caustic Soda	C28
Cement	B122
Cereals (Breakfast)	F31
Certificates of Deposit	B23
Chemicals	C21
(See also: Synthetic Fibers)	
Chewing Gum	F33
Chewing Tobacco	T111
Chlorine	C28
Chromium	M189
Cigarettes	T106
Cigars	T109
Citizens Band Radios	E14
Cleansers	C35
Closed-End Investment Cos.	I-60
Closures	C127
Clothing	A99
Coal	O72, S58, U14, U68
Coatings	C32
Cocoa	F32, S14
Coffee	F30
Coke	S50, S62
Color Television	E12
Commercial Loans	B21
Communication	E23, C59
Communications Satellites	T18
Components, Audio	E18
Components, Electronic	A146, E35
Compressors, Air	O126
Computer Leasing	O21
Computers	A145, E22, O12
Confectionery	F32
ConRail	R34
Construction	B105
Construction Machinery	M25
Construction-Maintenance & Repairs	B118
Construction, Marine	O118
Consumer Electronic Products	E12
Consumer Spending	B32
Containerboard	C116, P17
Containers	B64, B72, C113
Convenience Stores	R171
Converted Flexible Packaging	C126
Copper	M173
Copper Fabricating	M178
Copying Equipment	O22
Copyrights	C63
Corn Refining	F18
Corn Syrup	F18
Corrugated Cartons	C118, P17
Cosmetics	H25
Crude Oil	C35, O66
Cyclamates	B69

D
	Page
Dairy Products	F22
Dental Equipment	H23
Department Stores	R128
Detergents	C32
Dictating Machines	O27
Diesel Engines	A145, M24
Diesel Locomotives	M33
Digital Computers	O14
Digital Watches	E17
Disc Drives	O20
Discount Stores	R131
Discrete Components	E37
Disposables, Paper	P16
Distilled Spirits	B65
Drug Stores	R135
Drugs	H13
Dual-Purpose Funds	I-63
Duplicating Equipment	O23

E
	Page
Earthmoving Machinery	M25
Educational Construction	B117
Educational Equipment	E25
Educational Publishing	C63

Source: "Index to Surveys," Standard & Poor's *Industry Surveys* (New York: Standard & Poor's Corporation, April 30, 1977).

FIGURE 7-7 (cont.)

FIGURE 7-8

This year's unusual weather pattern has stirred fears that sharply rising food' prices might feed the fires of inflation, upsetting the U.S. economic applecart. In general, we find that the commodity price outlook is favorable for the food processing industry. Despite some uncertainty over the weather, this year's crop prospect favors plentiful stocks of corn and wheat, and an improved soybean supply.

It took the food processing industry 1975 and most of 1976 to fully recover from the impact of the increase in commodity costs that took place in 1972-74, and industry profit margins are about back to normal. This year's earnings gains will be well off the unusually vigorous pace set during the past two years.

Very few food stocks look interesting from a near-term performance perspective, but several offer above-average dividend yields. Many lower yielding stocks also have interesting long-pull dividend growth potential. Although this industry has traditionally been thought of as defensive from an investment standpoint, there are only a handful of stocks in the group that still fit that description.

COMPOSITE STATISTICS: FOOD PROCESSING INDUSTRY

1972	1973	1974	1975	1976	1977	L. Arnold Bernhard & Co. Inc.	79-81 E
58637	71196	88548	93903	106000	11900	Sales ($mill)	160000
8.8%	8.7%	8.0%	8.1%	9.0%	9.0%	Operating Margin	8.8%
1144	1297	1408	1488	1690	1900	Depreciation ($mill)	2550
1965	2411	2487	2697	3530	3925	Net Income ($mill)	4840
46.0%	46.6%	48.6%	48.2%	48.2%	48.7%	Income Tax Rate	50.0%
3.4%	3.4%	2.8%	2.9%	3.3%	3.3%	Net Income Margin	3.0%
9358	11097	12748	13906	15900	17850	Working Cap'l ($mill)	24000
5404	5907	6984	7347	9985	11935	Long-Term Debt ($mill)	16475
16187	18223	19965	21348	23225	25515	Net Worth ($mill)	33300
9.9%	10.8%	10.1%	10.4%	11.5%	11.5%	% Earned Total Cap'l	11.0%
12.1%	13.2%	12.5%	12.6%	15.0%	15.0%	% Earned Net Worth	14.5%
7.1%	8.5%	7.8%	8.0%	9.5%	9.5%	Earn'gs Plowback Ratio	8.5%
44%	39%	39%	39%	37%	38%	% All Div'ds to Net Inc	43%
13.9	11.7	9.4	9.6	76-77 italic figures		Avg Ann'l P/E Ratio	12.0
3.1%	3.2%	4.1%	4.0%	are VL estimates		Avg Ann'l Div'd Yield	3.5%

Everybody's Talking About the Weather . . .

. . . and its effect on food prices. This has been a most unusual year, weatherwise. Freezing temperatures wiped out a large part of the Florida citrus and vegetable crops in mid-January, pushing fruit and vegetable prices higher and stirring fears that food prices (which comprise the largest component of the consumer price index) would set off a new round of double-digit inflation. These fears are probably groundless; for the most part, vegetable prices peaked in the first quarter, turning lower in April and May.

The drought in California and the Pacific Northwest is a potentially more dangerous problem from the standpoint of food price inflation. California is the largest U.S. agricultural state, accounting for significant production of a wide variety of food products. (For example, California farmers produce well over half the country's lettuce, tomatoes, barley, grapes, almonds, peaches, strawberries, and several other fruits.) This has been the second consecutive dry winter out West, and the reservoirs which are the primary source of irrigation water are uncomfortably low. This condition has potentially negative implications for 1978 as well as this year. It will take above-normal rainfall this summer to replenish the reservoirs. Meanwhile, produce prices will probably remain well above last year's lows.

Perhaps the most serious weather-related condition at present is the lack of subsoil moisture which exists throughout much of the Midwest corn belt. Here again,

back-to-back years of below-average precipitation are at the root of the problem. The region affected is the source of nearly half of U.S. corn production and a large portion of domestic soybean output. Although this year's plantings are ahead of expectations, the depleted underground water level makes crop yield projections conjectural at this juncture. We'll have to watch this situation closely over the next few months, but the final verdict won't be known until the harvest is brought in this fall.

The Commodity Price Prospect

In general, the current commodity situation is favorable for the food processing industry, with few exceptions. In particular, wheat, corn, and sugar are well below last year's price levels; in the case of each of these key commodities global supply far exceeds current demand. Although fresh fruit and vegetable prices are high as a result of the western drought, this is generally having more impact on the supermarket industry than on food processors. (Of course, the inflating effect on the consumer price index has negative implications for the economy as a whole, which affects demand for all food products.) With the exception of the vegetable canners— *Del Monte, Green Giant,* and *Stokely-Van Camp*—fresh vegetables don't represent a major food processing cost input. Besides fresh produce, the most troublesome components of the food price index are coffee, cocoa, soybeans, and the two primary soy by-products, oil and meal. In the case of each of these items, world inventories are unusually thin relative to demand, and prices are distressingly high. Tuna fish prices are heading higher in the U.S. due to restrictions governing the killing of porpoises incidental to the netting of tuna. On a positive note, most livestock prices have remained comfortably low 'for longer than we had expected, largely due to a large overhanging supply of hogs and poultry. We're still looking for higher meat prices over the next 12 months, but the timing of the turn is not yet clear.

Commodity Table

	Cash Prices June 2 Close	% Change vs. Year Ago
Corn, bushel	2.46	− 16%
Wheat, bushel	2 41	− 35
Soybean, bushel	9 64	+ 66
Soybean meal, ton	263.00	+ 50
Soybean oil, lb.	.32	+102
Beef, lb.	.64	− 3
Pork, lb.	.85	− 11
Broilers, lb.	.44	+ 3
Sugar, lb.	.17	− 19
Coffee, lb.	2.90	+100

Source: Wall Street Journal

According to the U.S. Department of Agriculture, corn planting intentions are surprisingly strong this year. For the most part, sowing is well ahead of schedule, which usually would indicate an abundant fall harvest. The chief uncertainty is the weather. If this summer is not unusually dry, the corn crop will probably be another bin-buster. That would keep corn prices favorably low, which has positive implications for almost all the food processing companies we review.

The wheat situation is even better from a supply standpoint. As of July 1st, combined U.S. and Canadian wheat stocks will total over 1½ billion bushels. This huge carryover, along with prospects for another healthy crop this year, is strong assurance that wheat and flour prices will remain depressed over the next 12 months. This is particularly good news for the baking companies, which include *American Bakeries, Campbell Taggart, Entenmann's,* and *Nabisco.* Even a mediocre wheat crop this year wouldn't put pressure on prices, in our opinion.

Soybean planting intentions are up about 10% this
(Continued on next page)

Source: *Value Line Investment Surveys* (New York: Arnold Bernhard & Co., June 10, 1977), pp. 1451-52.

FIGURE 7-8 (cont.)

(Continued from preceding page)

year, but we think there's a good chance the current high price for this crop will encourage additional sowings. Last year's harvest was disappointingly below expectations, and current soybean inventories are about as low as they can get. Bean prices topped $10 a bushel earlier this year, before receding to their present $9+ level. A healthy crop this fall will take some of the pressure off, but we're still going to look for soybean prices in the $5 a bushel range next year. Lower soybean prices would be a breath of fresh air to *Anderson, Clayton, Archer Daniels, Central Soya, Ralston Purina,* and *Staley.*

Early prospects for 1977-78 world agricultural production are generally favorable. Weather conditions in most parts of the world were promising for the spring planting season. There are spotty weather problems in parts of China and South Asia, but its too early to judge the potential impact on crop yields. With normal foreign production following last year's large grain supluses, we expect export demand for U.S. crops to be on the moderate side, But, as always, we caution that the weather is an unpredictable factor which can throw our expectations off the mark.

Implications for the Industry

The food processing industry weathered a very challenging period in 1972-74. Profit margins were squeezed between sharply rising commodity costs on one side, and price controls followed by consumer resistance to higher prices, on the other. The decline in commodity prices that started in 1975 and continued through last year permitted profit margins to return to normal. The industry in the aggregate logged unusually strong earnings gains in 1975 and 1976. In 1977, we expect the industry to turn in its first "typical" performance in some time; that is, profit growth will be well off the pace of the past two years.

It must be pretty clear that stability in the commodity market is the key to the long-term profit growth potential of this industry. As farm prices skyrocketed in the early Seventies, food processors were forced to cut back on non-essential activities, including advertising and new product development, in order to bolster their profitability. Higher material costs also inflated inventories and receivables, draining cash positions and requiring costly short-term financing. Now that the cost pressure is off, most companies have resumed their advertising and promotional efforts, and the flow of new products is mounting. In addition, as a result of belt tightening a few years ago, many companies find their corporate treasuries brimming with cash. In general, management is sharing this wealth with common stockholders in the form of higher dividends.

Investment Perspective

Not many food stocks are of interest for performance-minded investors at present. While average industrial company profits are rising an estimated 14% or so in 1977, the typical food processor will probably report an earnings gain only in the 9%-11% range. Several stocks that are ranked Average for year-ahead relative market performance offer above-average dividend yields. These include: *ConAgra, General Host, Green Giant, Pet, Staley, Tootsie Roll,* and *Unilever NV.*

In general, we expect common dividends to grow faster over the next few years than they've been doing over the past few. Accordingly, some lower yielding foods stocks may interest income-oriented investors, provided that they offer the possibility of above-average dividend expansion through 1980. In the table we include the projected annual dividend growth rate along with the current estimated yield and Safety rating for each of the stocks in the industry.

Traditionally, food processing stocks have been thought of as defensive investments—that is, because of their predictable, steadily rising profits they tend to outperform falling stock markets. In our opinion, many of the stocks in this industry can no longer be categorized as defensive. The most conservative long-term investments in the group are the big, multi-product, diversified companies that have little direct commodity exposure. These would include *Beatrice Foods, Campbell Soup, Carnation, Heinz,* and *General Mills.* L.K.

Stock	Safety Rank	Estimated Dividend Yield	Projected Div'd Growth Rate
American Bakeries	4	7.5%	27.5%
American Maize	3	5.1	11.5
Anderson, Clayton	3	4.4	22.0
Archer Daniels	3	1.4	25.0
Beatrice	2	3.9	12.0
Borden	2	4.5	10.0
CPC International	2	5.1	8.0
Campbell Soup	2	4.1	12.0
Campbell Taggart	3	3.8	13.5
Carnation	2	2.9	15.5
Castle & Cooke	3	5.5	11.5
Central Soya	3	5.8	11.0
Chock Full O'Nuts	5	Nil	NMF
ConAgra	4	6.0	NMF
Consolidated Foods	2	5.9	8.0
Cook Industries	5	Nil	NMF
DeKalb	3	1.8	36.5
Del Monte	2	6.0	9.5
DiGiorgio	3	4.1	17.0
Esmark	3	5.7	14.5
Fairmont	3	6.9	10.5
General Foods	2	5.0	9.0
General Host	5	6.7	10.5
General Mills	2	3.3	15.0
Gerber	3	4.2	10.5
Green Giant	3	6.2	5.5
Heinz	2	4.1	15.5
Hershey	2	6.1	17.5
International Multifoods	2	5.3	11.5
Kellogg	2	4.6	14.0
Kraft	1	5.1	9.0
Nabisco	2	4.9	8.0
Norton Simon	3	3.6	19.5
Peavey	3	6.0	12.0
Pet Inc.	2	5.8	9.0
Peter Paul	3	6.5	7.5
Pillsbury	2	3.3	14.5
Pioneer	3	2.8	22.0
Quaker Oats	3	4.5	15.0
Ralston Purina	2	2.8	16.5
Russell Stover	4	5.4	13.5
Smucker	2	4.9	12.0
Staley	3	6.4	20.5
Standard Brands	1	5.2	10.5
Stokely-Van Camp	4	6.0	10.0
Tootsie Roll	3	6.1	9.5
Tropicana	4	2.2	NMF
United Brands	5	Nil	NMF
Unilever Ltd.	3	4.1	8.5
Unilever N.V.	2	6.5	10.0
Ward Foods	4	Nil	NMF
Wrigley	2	4.8	9.0

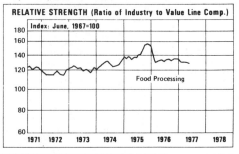

RELATIVE STRENGTH (Ratio of Industry to Value Line Comp.)

Index: June, 1967=100

Food Processing

FIGURE 7-9

THE ◈ VALUE LINE
Investment Survey

Published Weekly by ARNOLD BERNHARD & CO., INC., 5 East 44th St. New York, N.Y. 10017.
For the confidential use of subscribers/Reprint by permission only.
Copyright 1977 by Arnold Bernhard & Co., Inc.

**Part 1
Summary
&
Index**

August 12, 1977

File at the front of the Ratings & Reports binder. Last week's Summary & Index should be removed.

TABLE OF SUMMARY-INDEX CONTENTS

The Median of **PRICE-EARNINGS RATIOS** of all stocks with earnings	The Median **ESTIMATED YIELDS** (next 12 months) of all dividend paying stocks under review	The Estimated Median **APPRECIATION POTENTIAL** of all 1650 stocks in the hypothesized economic environment 3 to 5 years hence
7.5	**4.7%**	**95%**

26 Weeks Ago*	Market Low 12-23-74*	Market High 12-13-68*	26 Weeks Ago*	Market Low 12-23-74*	Market High 12-13-68*	26 Weeks Ago*	Market Low 12-23-74*	Market High 12-13-68*
8.1	4.7	19.0	4.3%	7.8%	2.7%	85%	234%	18%

*Estimated medians as published in The Value Line Investment Survey on the dates shown.

ANALYSES OF INDUSTRIES IN ALPHABETICAL ORDER WITH PAGE NUMBER
Numeral in parentheses after the industry is rank for probable performance (next 12 months).

PAGE	PAGE	PAGE	PAGE
Advertising (2) 1807	Dual Fund (34) 1982	Machine Tool (40) 1371	REIT (59) 669,1232,1972
Aerospace/Diversified (18) 101	Electrical Equipment (20) 1001	Maritime (3) 291	Recreation (11) 1751
Agricultural Equipment (57) 797	Electric Utility-Cent. (78) 701	Meat Packing (29) 382	Retail-Special Lines (46) 1562
Air Transport (22) 251	Electric Utility-East (79) 201	Medical Services (1) 1827	Retail Store (52) 1655
Aluminum (64) 1151	Electric Utility-West (88) 1697	Metal Fabricating (30) 271	Savings & Loan (5) 1216
Apparel (50) 1601	Electronics (21) 1040	Metals & Mining-Gen'l (70) 1151	Securities Brokerage (86) 371
Auto & Truck (33) 126	Fast Food Service (47) 325	Mobile Home (58) 1579	Shoe (73) 1260
Auto Parts-OEM (43) 804	Finance (37) 1990	Multiform (49) 1740,1389	Silver (82) 1151
Auto Parts-Replacement (55) 135	Food Processing (66) 1451	Natural Gas (51) 449	Soft Drink (7) 1515
Bank (61) 1901	Gold Mining (48) 1151	Newspaper (10) 1798	Steel-General (83) 610
Bank-Midwest (80) 678	Grocery (54) 1534	Office Equipment (32) 1076	Steel-Integrated (90) 1193
Brewing (44) 1883	Health Care/Hosp. Sup. (60) 2004	Oilfield Services (26) 1349	Steel-Specialty (72) 2020
Broadcasting (15) 506	Home Appliance (39) 1424	*Packaging & Cont. (56) 957	Sugar (87) 1140,1506
*Building (25) 851	Household Products (67) 1523	*Paper & Forest Prods. (75) 930	Telecommunications (76) ..2039,753
*Cement (23) 916	Ind'l Gases/Fertilizer (68) 2028	Personal Services (9) 1815	Textile (74) 1632
Chemical-Basic (81) 551	Industrial Services (28) 352	Petroleum-Integrated (27) 401	Tire & Rubber (17) 154
Chemical-Specialty (45) 1243	Insurance-Diversified (4) 1861	Petroleum-Producing (36) 1846	Tobacco (53) 648
Coal & Uranium (62) 1835	Insurance-Life (12) 1121	Precision Instrument (42) 167	Toiletries/Cosmetics (38) 624
Copper (89) 1151	Insurance-Property/Cas. (8) 529	Publishing (31) 1777	Toys & School Supplies (13) 787
Distilling (84) 343	Investment Company (41) 1948	Railroad Equipment (69) 833	Travel Services (19) 517
Drug-Ethical (71) 595	Lead, Zinc, Minor Mtls (77) 579	Railroad-East (24) 638	Trucking & Bus Lines (16) 301
Drug-Proprietary (85) 1208	Machinery (14) 1301	Railroad-West (6) 1181	
Drug Store (63) 770	Machinery-Const. (65) 818	Real Estate (35) 658	*Reviewed in this week's edition.

In three parts: This is Part I, the Summary & Index. Part II is Selection & Opinion. Part III is Ratings & Reports. Volume XXXII, No. 45.

Source: *Value Line Investment Surveys* (New York: Arnold Bernhard & Co., August 12, 1977).

FIGURE 7-10

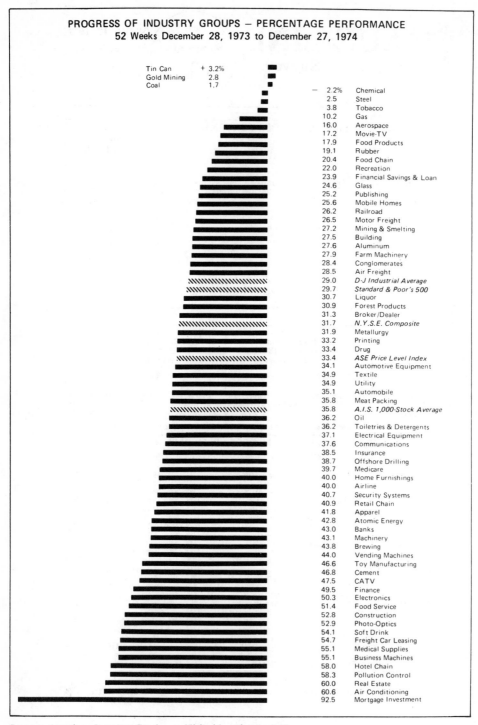

PROGRESS OF INDUSTRY GROUPS — PERCENTAGE PERFORMANCE
52 Weeks December 28, 1973 to December 27, 1974

Tin Can	+ 3.2%
Gold Mining	2.8
Coal	1.7

— 2.2%	Chemical
2.5	Steel
3.8	Tobacco
10.2	Gas
16.0	Aerospace
17.2	Movie-TV
17.9	Food Products
19.1	Rubber
20.4	Food Chain
22.0	Recreation
23.9	Financial Savings & Loan
24.6	Glass
25.2	Publishing
25.6	Mobile Homes
26.2	Railroad
26.5	Motor Freight
27.2	Mining & Smelting
27.5	Building
27.6	Aluminum
27.9	Farm Machinery
28.4	Conglomerates
28.5	Air Freight
29.0	*D-J Industrial Average*
29.7	*Standard & Poor's 500*
30.7	Liquor
30.9	Forest Products
31.3	Broker/Dealer
31.7	*N.Y.S.E. Composite*
31.9	Metallurgy
33.2	Printing
33.4	Drug
33.4	*ASE Price Level Index*
34.1	Automotive Equipment
34.9	Textile
34.9	Utility
35.1	Automobile
35.8	Meat Packing
35.8	*A.I.S. 1,000-Stock Average*
36.2	Oil
36.2	Toiletries & Detergents
37.1	Electrical Equipment
37.6	Communications
38.5	Insurance
38.7	Offshore Drilling
39.7	Medicare
40.0	Home Furnishings
40.0	Airline
40.7	Security Systems
40.9	Retail Chain
41.8	Apparel
42.8	Atomic Energy
43.0	Banks
43.1	Machinery
43.8	Brewing
44.0	Vending Machines
46.6	Toy Manufacturing
46.8	Cement
47.5	CATV
49.5	Finance
50.3	Electronics
51.4	Food Service
52.8	Construction
52.9	Photo-Optics
54.1	Soft Drink
54.7	Freight Car Leasing
55.1	Medical Supplies
55.1	Business Machines
58.0	Hotel Chain
58.3	Pollution Control
60.0	Real Estate
60.6	Air Conditioning
92.5	Mortgage Investment

Source: *American Investors Service,* published by Chestnutt Corp.,
Box 2500, Greenwich, Ct. 06830

FIGURE 7-10 (cont.)

PROGRESS OF INDUSTRY GROUPS — PERCENTAGE PERFORMANCE
December 27, 1974 to December 26, 1975

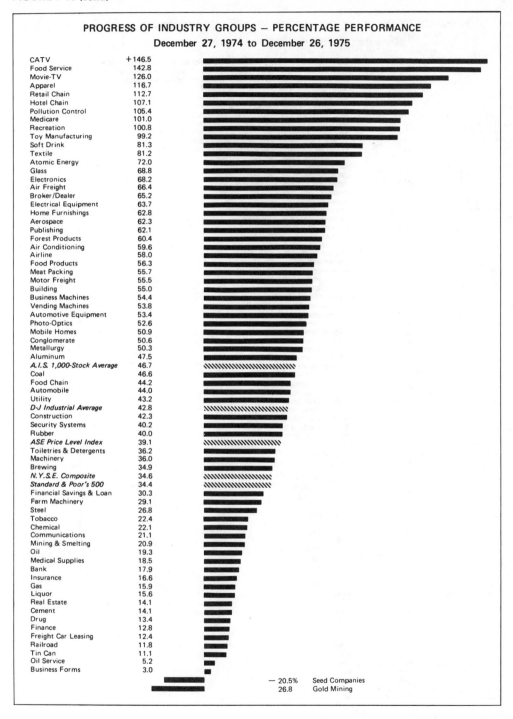

CATV	+146.5
Food Service	142.8
Movie-TV	126.0
Apparel	116.7
Retail Chain	112.7
Hotel Chain	107.1
Pollution Control	105.4
Medicare	101.0
Recreation	100.8
Toy Manufacturing	99.2
Soft Drink	81.3
Textile	81.2
Atomic Energy	72.0
Glass	68.8
Electronics	68.2
Air Freight	66.4
Broker/Dealer	65.2
Electrical Equipment	63.7
Home Furnishings	62.8
Aerospace	62.3
Publishing	62.1
Forest Products	60.4
Air Conditioning	59.6
Airline	58.0
Food Products	56.3
Meat Packing	55.7
Motor Freight	55.5
Building	55.0
Business Machines	54.4
Vending Machines	53.8
Automotive Equipment	53.4
Photo-Optics	52.6
Mobile Homes	50.9
Conglomerate	50.6
Metallurgy	50.3
Aluminum	47.5
A.I.S. 1,000-Stock Average	46.7
Coal	46.6
Food Chain	44.2
Automobile	44.0
Utility	43.2
D-J Industrial Average	42.8
Construction	42.3
Security Systems	40.2
Rubber	40.0
ASE Price Level Index	39.1
Toiletries & Detergents	36.2
Machinery	36.0
Brewing	34.9
N.Y.S.E. Composite	34.6
Standard & Poor's 500	34.4
Financial Savings & Loan	30.3
Farm Machinery	29.1
Steel	26.8
Tobacco	22.4
Chemical	22.1
Communications	21.1
Mining & Smelting	20.9
Oil	19.3
Medical Supplies	18.5
Bank	17.9
Insurance	16.6
Gas	15.9
Liquor	15.6
Real Estate	14.1
Cement	14.1
Drug	13.4
Finance	12.8
Freight Car Leasing	12.4
Railroad	11.8
Tin Can	11.1
Oil Service	5.2
Business Forms	3.0

— 20.5%   Seed Companies
  26.8   Gold Mining

FIGURE 7-10 (cont.)

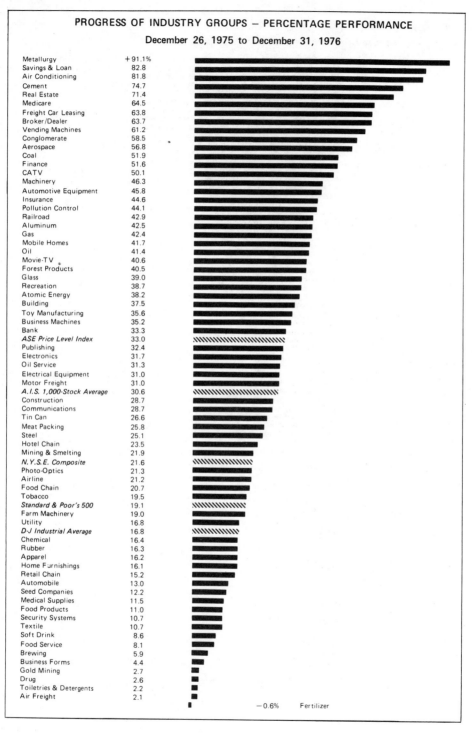

PROGRESS OF INDUSTRY GROUPS — PERCENTAGE PERFORMANCE

December 26, 1975 to December 31, 1976

Metallurgy	+91.1%
Savings & Loan	82.8
Air Conditioning	81.8
Cement	74.7
Real Estate	71.4
Medicare	64.5
Freight Car Leasing	63.8
Broker/Dealer	63.7
Vending Machines	61.2
Conglomerate	58.5
Aerospace	56.8
Coal	51.9
Finance	51.6
CATV	50.1
Machinery	46.3
Automotive Equipment	45.8
Insurance	44.6
Pollution Control	44.1
Railroad	42.9
Aluminum	42.5
Gas	42.4
Mobile Homes	41.7
Oil	41.4
Movie-TV	40.6
Forest Products	40.5
Glass	39.0
Recreation	38.7
Atomic Energy	38.2
Building	37.5
Toy Manufacturing	35.6
Business Machines	35.2
Bank	33.3
ASE Price Level Index	33.0
Publishing	32.4
Electronics	31.7
Oil Service	31.3
Electrical Equipment	31.0
Motor Freight	31.0
A.I.S. 1,000-Stock Average	30.6
Construction	28.7
Communications	28.7
Tin Can	26.6
Meat Packing	25.8
Steel	25.1
Hotel Chain	23.5
Mining & Smelting	21.9
N.Y.S.E. Composite	21.6
Photo-Optics	21.3
Airline	21.2
Food Chain	20.7
Tobacco	19.5
Standard & Poor's 500	19.1
Farm Machinery	19.0
Utility	16.8
D-J Industrial Average	16.8
Chemical	16.4
Rubber	16.3
Apparel	16.2
Home Furnishings	16.1
Retail Chain	15.2
Automobile	13.0
Seed Companies	12.2
Medical Supplies	11.5
Food Products	11.0
Security Systems	10.7
Textile	10.7
Soft Drink	8.6
Food Service	8.1
Brewing	5.9
Business Forms	4.4
Gold Mining	2.7
Drug	2.6
Toiletries & Detergents	2.2
Air Freight	2.1
Fertilizer	−0.6%

It should be observed how drastically the stock prices of certain industries fluctuate from year to year—large numbers of industries doing poorly in 1974, and large numbers doing well in 1975 and 1976. To see the changes that can occur within one industry, let us trace the tobacco group. It declined 4 percent in 1973, advanced 22 percent in 1975, and advanced 20 percent in 1976. Similarly, toy manufacturing declined 47 percent in 1974, and advanced 100 percent and 36 percent respectively in 1975 and 1976. Thus, being invested in the right industries at the right time at the right price is a winning formula!

Funk and Scott Index

The Funk and Scott Index of Corporations and Industries provides a valuable indexing service for the investor or analyst seeking published industry and company information. This service, published monthly, lists articles appearing in more than seven hundred trade and business publications. Funk and Scott index this information by Standard Industrial Classification (SIC) and by company name. The researcher can then consult the various cited articles and obtain information on the industry, company, or competition of the firm under investigation.

Other Observations on Industry Analysis

Throughout this chapter we have enumerated a number of relevant quantifiable and nonquantifiable factors, and have alluded to others, that should be considered when performing an industry analysis. Now let us point out several additional considerations: the composition of the industry's population, the distribution of income and wealth among the population, any evolving buying habits of consumers, and foreign and domestic production competition. These pieces of information are not always easy to come by, but the analyst who takes the trouble to develop *all* necessary information will find it worth his efforts.

We observed earlier that the market psychology is an important, if at times seemingly irrational, factor that must be dealt with in an industry analysis. That is to say, within a short period of time, an industry's relative attraction as an investment opportunity can change from an extremely desirable, conservative, undervalued situation to a highly risky, potentially overpriced situation. As a recent example of the market's enthusiasm—an enthusiasm that developed almost overnight—take the industries and companies connected with the Wankel engine. This was so evident that the *Wall Street Journal* featured a story on the "hot" Wankel stocks. It started by saying:

> Here are four ways to make your corporation's stock bound up. 1. Rename your company "The Wankel Works." 2. Announce you have just received a contract to make a screw that might be used in Wankel engines. 3. Announce that you have just hired scientists to look into Wankel engine research. 4. Announce that the clerk in your shipping room has a brother-in-law who is thinking about buying a car that has a Wankel engine.[20]

[20]*Wall Street Journal,* June 15, 1972, p. 1.

When this kind of fervor hits the market, it takes a cool analyst to discern whether the potential growth prospects of the industry have been fully discounted or whether the growth warrants purchase in the midst of such an uproar. In other words, even the best of growth situations can be bought at too high a price and thus bring a low or negative return to the investor. And even low- or no-growth industries, when bought at a very low price, can bring respectable returns. This situation arises because the market seems to value highly industries on the verge of tremendous growth in earnings, and to value low those industries that have already achieved their growth and have stabilized. That is, stocks on the verge of growth generally sell at high P/E ratios, and stocks that have come to the end of their growth pattern generally sell at low P/E ratios.

Table 7-4 shows the proportions of securities held by investment companies in various industries at various dates. Note that seven industries represented about 80 percent of the dollar value of the "favorite fifty" securities at the end of 1976. Observe too that the importance of motor holdings declined over the five-year period reported in the table, and the oil and natural gas industry holding grew in importance over the same period.

TABLE 7-4

SUMMARY OF FAVORITE FIFTY BY INDUSTRY (DOLLAR VALUE
OF STOCKS BY INDUSTRY TO TOTAL DOLLAR VALUE OF
FAVORITE FIFTY)

	12-31-76	*9-30-76*	*12-31-75*	*12-31-71*
Oil & natural gas	25.3%	25.1%	22.9%	14.9%
Office equipment	20.4	20.4	18.7	17.4
Chemicals & drugs	11.6	14.7	16.2	7.9
Leisure	6.0	6.5	7.6	8.3
Utilities	7.2	6.5	5.4	4.8
Motors	5.7	5.5	4.4	8.0
paper & printing	3.7	2.5	2.6	0.0
Miscellaneous	20.1	18.8	22.2	38.7
	100.0%	100.0%	100.0%	100.0%

Source: *Vickers Guide to Investment Company Portfolios.*
Copyright © 1977 by Vickers Associates, Inc. REPRODUCTION HEREOF PERMITTED ONLY ON WRITTEN PERMISSION FROM VICKERS ASSOCIATES, INC., THE COPYRIGHT OWNERS. As reprinted in *Barron's*, (March 7, 1977), p. 9.

Before we continue our illustration of the application of industry-analysis techniques, it is necessary to place the importance of an industry analysis in the proper perspective. Its benefits can be fully realized only if it occurs along with a properly conceived economic analysis and company analysis.

A good economic analysis informs the investor about the propriety of a current stock purchase, regardless of the industry in which he might invest. If the economic outlook suggests purchase at this time, the economic analysis along with the industry analysis will aid the investor in selecting the proper industry in which to invest. Nonetheless, knowing when to invest and in which industry to invest is not enough. It is also necessary to know which companies in which industries should be selected. We turn our attention to this topic in the ensuing three chapters.

End-Use or Demand Analysis for the Lodgings Industry

One of the main objectives of industry analysis is an understanding and fore-cast of demand for the industry's output. In our illustration, we are interested in determining the demand for a special kind of service—the provision of a place to sleep, and possibly to eat. As previously, a good starting point is the relation-ships that have existed in the past. Table 7-5 contains data on occupied rooms, rooms available, and occupancy rates for the entire lodgings industry for selected years.

TABLE 7-5
DEMAND FOR TOTAL LODGINGS INDUSTRY

Year	Occupied Rooms/Night (thousands)	Rooms Available (thousands)	Occupancy Rate
1948	1,007	1,127	89%
1960	1,054	1,532	69%
1965	1,141	1,739	66%
1970	1,185	1,882	63%
1975	1,215	2,026	60%

Source: Harris, Kerr, Forster & Company; U.S. Census Bureau.

One fairly surprising observation is that actual physical demand for lodgings (occupied rooms per night) has remained relatively unchanged since 1948. Furthermore, since the number of available rooms has expanded greatly while demand has leveled off, overall industry occupancy rates have dropped.

Other interesting insights to demand can be obtained by focusing on the reasons for travel of lodgings users, and their means of travel. For if we know why people travel, we can attempt to forecast the future levels of these stimuli, and if we know how they travel, we know more about their economic status and the kinds of services they are likely to demand. Tables 7-6 and 7-7 give us some of this information.

These two tables illustrate that the majority of trips taken in the United States are by automobile and for pleasure, and that motels get more of this auto-travel business than hotels do. But upon further investigation—looking at the numbers behind the percentages—it can be found that motels still do not accom-modate the majority of this auto-travel group. This is because half of all pleasure travelers stay with relatives or friends, about one-third in a hotel or motel, and the remainder in tents, trailers, boats, or other facilities. Therefore, motel chains that can appeal to this segment of pleasure travelers, and perhaps lure away airline travelers from hotels, are likely to do very well in future periods.

TABLE 7-6
DEMAND BY PURPOSE OF TRAVEL

Reason for Travel	Hotel Users	Motel Users	Total Industry	All Trips Taken by U.S. Population
Business	52%	56%	54%	21%
Convention	18	5	11	—
Pleasure	28	35	32	61
Other	2	4	3	18
	100%	100%	100%	100%

Source: *The Commercial Lodging Market*, Michigan State University.

TABLE 7-7
DEMAND BY MEANS OF TRAVEL

Means of Travel	Hotel	Motel	All Trips Taken by U.S. Population
Airline	49%	25%	5%
Automobile	33	69	84
Railroad	7	1	3
Bus	4	1	4
Other	7	4	4
	100%	100%	100%

Source: *The Commercial Lodging Market,* Michigan State University.

DEMAND ELASTICITY

We must also consider the different *elasticities of demand* (responsiveness of demand to changes in income and price) involving each segment of the lodgings market—business, convention, and pleasure. Lodgings are a necessity to a businessman; demand is relatively inelastic in terms of personal income as well as price, since he views his expenses as part of the cost of doing business and is usually reimbursed by his company for his expenditures. The businessman's patronage is closely related to general business conditions. Expense accounts for travel are cut back swiftly during recessions. It is because of a weakened business outlook that occupancy levels were depressed in 1975.

Many people consider the cost of conventions as a business expense, so the demand elasticity of this group tends to be low. Demand is elastic for the pleasure traveler, since it can be a function of level of income, leisure time, desire to travel, and the relative costs of substitute goods or services.

AGE

It would also be helpful to determine if there is any correlation between the population of a certain age group and the demand for lodgings facilities. If so, this would indicate that one segment of the population is more mobile than the others. The 20-39 age group has been shown to be the most mobile. Some attribute the demand in the lodgings industry between 1948 and 1970 (Table 7-5) to the population mix, since the number of people in the most mobile age group, 20-39, remained static during the period 1948-65, and increased moderately from 1966 to 1970, paralleling the growth of the demand for hotel-motel rooms. Using U.S. census projections, in 1977 the number of people in this age group should be 65 million; in 1980, there should be 77 million.

The over-59 age group will also affect demand. The mobility of this group is rapidly increasing, owing to early retirement, increased government benefits, and the greater prevalence of company pension plans. The younger retirement age also indicates a healthier, more mobile retiree.

INCOME

Lodging demand is also a function of the level of income. Table 7-8 illustrates the fact that about 80 percent of commercial-lodgings users have an annual household income of at least $10,000.

TABLE 7-8
DEMAND BY INCOME

Annual Household Income	Proportion of U.S. Households		1967 Commercial Lodgings User
1967 dollars	*1967*	*1980E*	
Less than $10,000	70.1%	50.0%	20.9%
$10,000-15,000	19.4	25.5	27.7
$15,000 and over	10.5	24.5	51.4
	100.0%	100.0%	100.0%

Source: *The Consumer of the Seventies,* The Conference Board;
The Commercial Lodging Market, Michigan State University.

In 1967 approximately 60 million people (30 percent of 200 million) belonged to a household that had an income of $10,000 or more. By 1980, 50 percent of the population, or 115 million people, will be in this category. This indicates a compound growth rate of 5½ percent a year (60 million in 1967, 115 million in 1980, factor of 1.91). This would seem to indicate a growing potential market for the lodgings industry (ignoring inflation effects).

The prime market is the $15,000-and-over category. The approximate numerical size of this category is expected to grow from 21 million in 1967 (.105 × 200 million) to 56 million in 1980 (.245 × 230 million). However, the lodgings industry must compete with alternate forms of accommodations for this group, such as second homes, boats, and recreational vehicles.

TIME

Demand is a function of leisure time, or time to travel. The average workweek declined to 38 hours by 1970. The trend now indicates a 35-hour, four-day workweek in the early 1980s. Vacation weeks and holidays have increased, the passage of the Federal Monday Holiday Law providing five three-day weekends a year; this also provides more time in which to travel. All this points to a probable increase in the demand for lodgings facilities.

OPERATING AND FINANCIAL LEVERAGE

Any discussion about the lodgings industry would be incomplete without a comment on occupancy rates. Because of the high degree of fixed costs, taxes, and capital charges, the operating leverage in the lodgings industry is very great. It can cause profits to increase rapidly, and to decrease just as rapidly. All this is related to the occupancy rate. An increase in occupancy from 70 to 75 percent will increase revenues 7.1 percent, expenses 6.8 percent, and profit before interest and taxes 13.8 percent. (See Table 7-9.)

TABLE 7-9
EFFECT OF OPERATING LEVERAGE

	Occupancy Levels		%
	70%*	75%	Increase
Total sales and income:			
Rooms	$ 578	$ 619	
Food and beverages	385	412	
Other	37	40	
Total	$1,000	$1,071	7.1
Departmental wages and expenses:			
Rooms	$ 159	$ 170	
Food and beverages	318	340	
Other	34	36	
Total	$ 511	$ 546	6.8
Gross operating income	$ 489	$ 525	
Other expenses (real estate taxes, insurance, etc.)	300	310	3.3
Profit before interest and taxes	$ 189	$ 215	13.8

*Average figures for 1970, from Harris, Kerr, Forster & Co. (Basis: per $1,000 total revenues at 70% occupancy.)

Financial leverage works in the same manner. (See Table 7-10.) Interest payments have the same effect as fixed charges. Most hotel-motel properties are highly mortgaged, so the occupancy rate is very important in determining profitability. This was clearly illustrated to the industry in 1975. Therefore, it is critical for the analyst to forecast occupancy rates as well as possible.

TABLE 7-10

EFFECT OF FINANCIAL LEVERAGE

	Leveraged Occupancies		% Increase	Unleveraged Occupancies		% Increase
	70%	75%		70%	75%	
Profit before interest and taxes	$189	$215	13.8	$189	$215	13.8
Less: Interest	80	80		0	0	
Pre-tax profit	$109	$135		$189	$215	
Income tax	50	63		90	103	
Net profit	$ 59	$ 72	22.0	$ 99	$112	13.1

*Average figures for 1970, from Harris, Kerr, Forster & Co. (Basis: per $1,000 total revenues at 70% occupancy.)

FUTURE TRENDS

Because the profits of the hotel-motel industry closely follow the business cycle, 1975 was not a very profitable year. Some managers coped better than others, however, and managed to earn some profit.

The business conditions of 1975 severely affected the profitability of the industry as a whole. However, there were additional factors impeding the continuing progress of the industry. Substantially higher operating costs were present, and we saw in Tables 7-9 and 7-10 how this can drastically affect the bottom line of the industry because of the great operating and financial leverage the industry enjoys. Thus the higher-cost situation coupled with the lower occupancy rates caused 1975 to be a bad year for the lodgings industry.

In addition, there are those who say that the lodgings industry during the 1960s and early 1970s created an oversupply condition—that is, an overabundance of rooms. It is felt that this condition is now apparent to the major operators in the industry and will cause a marked decline in the expansion of capacity—that is, the rate of growth in available rooms will not increase and perhaps will only remain at a constant level. This is caused not only by the oversupply condition but also by the increasing difficulty the industry will find in raising the necessary financing through creditors. We anticipate that in the next few years the rate of new construction in the industry will be about 2-3 percent per year. This rate of new construction, when coupled with the normal rate of retirement of old rooms, will only maintain the total supply of available rooms in the industry at a constant level. However, if the economy maintains its strength and the secular increase in the pleasure segment of the economy continues to increase, this should have a very positive effect on the industry. Because with limited new construction at ever-higher costs, more control of operating costs by the industry, and higher room rates and higher occupancy levels, the industry should fare well in the immediate future, at least in our opinion.

In order for the lodgings industry to cope with the new combination of factors we have just outlined, it will be necessary for hotel-motel managers to rely on sources other than increased room capacity alone for growth in the future.

Some of the trends that managers in this industry will undoubtedly look to will be:

1. *Increased utilization of properties.* It should be possible to use properties both in season and out of season. Also, the properties should be capable of different functional uses—such as conventions and weddings. This would ensure complete use of all facilities regardless of day of the week or time of the year.

2. *Development of new profit centers.* Food and beverage service is a very likely candidate. This can also attract nonguest customers.

3. *Development of new markets.* The suburban market has often been neglected. The absence of good-quality entertainment has been noted by many hotels and motels.

4. *Development of new marketing techniques.* In the past, hotel-motel managers have been primitive in their marketing campaigns. Improvement in this area could boost occupancy and/or public-room sales. This is also important because stiff competition exists for the leisure-time dollar.

5. *Development of the budget motel.* With construction costs rising every month, there is a dire need for a low-cost motel room. A few companies have formulated a system for constructing and operating a motel at a lower cost, resulting in an average room rate of from $8 to $10. This new concept relies on efficiency and good management. It provides for the basic needs of the businessman or traveler, with no unnecessary frills or services. A few of the larger chains are investigating the possibility of entering this field.

Unfortunately, after all these factors are considered, it is impossible to substitute these figures into a simple formula in order to forecast an occupancy rate for the motel industry. The analyst must subjectively estimate what effect these factors will have overall on the total industry, and then arrive at his forecast figure.

We forecast a 68 percent occupancy rate for the motel industry in 1977, primarily because of the more favorable economic environment forecast for that time—that is, GNP and its components, such as consumer spending and corporate profits. In addition, the factors discussed in this chapter suggest continued growth for the entire lodgings industry in 1977.

Summary

In this chapter we first discussed alternative industry-classification schemes, observing that different schemes are appropriate for different purposes. Next, we observed how the economic analysis could best be meshed with the industry analysis. Key characteristics of the industry that the analyst needs to consider include the past sales and earnings performance of the industry, its permanence, the attitude of government toward the industry, labor conditions prevalent in the industry, industry competitive conditions, and the industry P/E levels. We illustrated this part of the analysis with an extended example using the lodgings industry. The concepts of an industry life cycle, end-use analysis, regression analysis, and input-output analysis were explained. Finally, we noted some sources of industry information and then continued our lodgings industry analysis.

Questions and Problems

1. If you were attempting to forecast the sales of the candy industry, what classification scheme would you use?

2. What is a cyclical industry?

3. Of what value is the past sales and earnings performance of an industry in forecasting the future prospects of the industry?

4. What domestic industries do you suppose will decline in importance in the next decade? Why?

5. Why do you suppose only four automobile manufacturers in the United States almost completely dominate the auto industry?

6. How high would industry share prices have to go relative to industry earnings before you would decide that the shares were overpriced for investment purposes? Explain.

7. Of what use is the industry-life-cycle approach to an industry analyst?

8. How would you go about forecasting the sales of domestically produced beer next year? What variables are most important in determining the demand for beer?

9. Based on the latest Standard & Poor's *Basic Analysis* of the aerospace industry, would you recommend stock purchases in the group? Why?

10. What industries were most widely held by mutual funds as of the end of 1976?

11. The analysis of sales growth is generally the starting point in estimating earning power potential for an industry (and firms therein). Further, on a perspective basis, it is common to look at an industry from an industrial-life-cycle point of view.

> a. Assume that two companies in an industry have identical rates of sales growth. Why might an analyst nevertheless consider the sales record of one superior to that of the other?
>
> b. Which stage of the industrial life cycle is the most attractive from an investment point of view?,

12. What are the three most critical variables one might "track" in forecasting the outlook for the lodgings industry?

13. What are two major problem areas in using regression analysis for evaluating relevant industry factors in investment decision making?

CHAPTER EIGHT

COMPANY ANALYSIS: MEASURING EARNINGS

We are now ready to translate economic and industry assessments into judgments about holding-period yields for specific companies. The next three chapters will demonstrate how an analyst estimates return and risk for specific stocks. This chapter examines the nature and sources of relevant information about companies that is required to make judgments about return and risk. Chapters 9 and 10 will demonstrate how to translate that information into expectations about holding-period yields.

Introduction

Many pieces of information influence investment decisions. Investors need to know the characteristics of various investment alternatives and must keep informed on the institutions and markets where they are available. Up-to-date information is required on the status of and trends in the economy, particular industries, and firms.

The United States is a nation known for an abundance of widely available and rapidly disseminated information of almost every sort imaginable. This flood of information creates problems for the investor; he must continuously sample, sift, and sort messages and events for "good" information. Success in investing will be largely dependent upon (1) discovering new and credible information rapidly and in more detail than others do, and (2) applying superior judgment so as to ascertain the relevance of the information to the decision at hand. *The true test of an analyst's worth lies in his or her ability to develop a system of security analysis that couples original insight and unique ways of forming expectations about the prospects for individual companies.* Varied public and private sources of information must be analyzed.

Superior judgment comes from the capacity to take information and (1) see given relationships more clearly, or (2) perceive more interrelationships. Judgment depends pretty much upon one's store of knowledge and experiences. The task of security analysis is largely a matter of sifting, sorting, and rearranging data on markets, the economy, industries, and firms. Applying various tools of analysis to the data, the investor formulates expectations and judgments about the alternatives open to him.[1]

[1]R. G. E. Smith, "Uncertainty, Information and Investment Decision," *Journal of Finance,* March 1971, pp. 73-77.

This chapter is concerned with two broad categories of information: internal and external. Internal information consists of data and events made public by firms concerning their operations. It mainly takes the form of interim and annual reports to shareholders, and public and private statements of the officers and managers of the firm. The principal information sources generated internally by a firm are its financial statements. The analyst does not, of course, limit inquiry to information provided by accountants; ingenious and competent analysts sample widely from many kinds of information.

External sources of information are those generated independently outside the company. They provide a supplement to internal sources by (1) overcoming some of the bias inherent in company-generated information, and (2) providing information simply not found in the materials made available by companies themselves.

THE KEY ROLE OF FINANCIAL STATEMENTS

An overwhelming weight is placed by analysts and investors on the information contained in the financial statements of firms. One critical reason for this reliance lies in the vouchsafed nature of the statements, since their form and content is controlled under a variety of rules, regulations, and statutes.[2] The vast majority of these statements are attested to by independent auditors. In sum, investors tend to accept financial statements as the closest thing to complete credibility in information available to them. In the private and public statements of company officers, there is little chance of corroborating what is said. Very often the true significance of such pronouncements is clouded by some degree of enthusiasm and loyalty.

FINANCIAL STATEMENTS AS PROXIES OF REAL PROCESSES

Accounting is a proxy that has been developed for representing *real* processes and *real* goods. Accounts and statements are devices created to summarize certain types of information about real corporate goods and processes.[3]

As such, these statements, to a large extent, form the basis for action by investors, potential investors, creditors, and potential creditors of the corporation. Because of this, it is critical for analysts to understand in a general way how these statements are prepared so that they can better interpret the statements' true meaning. A good beginning point for investment analysis and

[2]For an excellent short monograph on accounting, written for analysts, see J. A. Mauriello, *Accounting for the Financial Analyst,* rev. ed., C.F.A. Monograph Series (Homewood, Ill.: Richard D. Irwin, 1971).

[3]Michael Keenan, "The State of the Finance Field Methodology Models of Equity Valuation: The Great SERM Bubble," *Journal of Finance,* May 1970, pp. 257-58.

ultimately investment decision making is to be aware of the historical record of the firm in a financial sense. This historical record of the firm's earnings and financial position can often give the analyst insight into the inner workings of the firm and thus assist him in projecting the future. This investigation of the past is a vital first step taken by the investment analyst.

Someone once said, however, that accounting statements are liké the tips of icebergs: What you see is interesting, but what you don't see is significant! A good investment analyst must judge financial statements as they meet the tests of (1) correctness, (2) completeness, (3) consistency, and (4) comparability.

Correctness, or accuracy, is normally established through the presence or absence of an "unqualified" auditor's certification. Nearly all public corporations retain public accounting firms to audit and certify the fairness of financial statements. Unaudited statements are not necessarily inaccurate or fraudulently prepared; they simply lack the intrinsic credibility of audited statements accompanied by the signed opinion of a CPA.

Completeness is a matter of disclosure. Inasmuch as accounting is only a proxy of real goods and processes, it cannot and does not pretend to tell everything. Many, many bits of information about a business were never intended to be incorporated in established financial reports and statements. The Securities and Exchange Commission (SEC), the American Institute of Certified Public Accountants (AICPA), and the Financial Accounting Standards Board (FASB) have worked together, and at times at odds, in dealing with the matter of fuller disclosure. The vital emphasis placed upon financial statements by analysts and investors, always hungry for more and better information, is creating increasing pressure for making more and more information available in different forms.[4]

Auditors are charged with the primary responsibility of ensuring that changes in reporting over time are justified and brought to the attention of the public. *Consistency* is vital in making comparisons of the performance of a firm over time. Data constructed differently at various points in time lack meaningful continuity unless reconciled prior to analysis.[5]

No area of accounting information has created more debate and difficulties for the analyst than *comparability*. Using audited financial statements for a firm, most of the time an analyst can work toward more complete and consistent information on his own. However, investment decision making involves comparing alternatives—or, as it were, *comparing the data derived from the financial statements of different firms.* The problem: Are the financial statements of different

---

[4]Many have suggested that the form of the income statement should be changed to assist analysis. Traditional expense breakdowns do not explain dynamic changes in costs as volume changes. Fixed and variable cost division would be more informative for marginal analysis. Other cost segregations used by managements could also help investors. For an interesting and stimulating book on financial reporting, see Arthur Andersen & Co., *Objectives of Financial Statements* (New York: Arthur Andersen & Co., 1972).

[5]A discussion of the treatment of accounting changes is found in U.S. General Accounting Office, *Outline of Opinions of the Accounting Principles Board* (Washington, D.C., 1971) pp. 81-91. This pamphlet is an excellent summary of Accounting Principles Board Opinions on various accounting subjects. See also recent pronouncements of the Financial Accounting Standards Board.

firms prepared under the same ground rules? Is it valid to make choices between two companies on the basis of financial information if the information is not generated on a uniform basis?

Accounting for revenue, costs, and profits is not done under a set of rigid rules whereby each event and transaction, regardless of the firm, is handled in one way only. To the extent that accounting provides options in handling certain transactions, comparability diminishes.

One set of accounting rules in the name of uniformity is perhaps an unrealistic ideal. Highly flexible accounting practices have grown up over the years, to recognize the wide diversity of circumstances within American business. However, from an analyst/investor point of view, the need for uniformity is obvious, since investment decisions are the product of comparative analysis of data for the determination of relative values.

In the following pages we shall examine the principal financial statements made public by corporations. Our goal is neither to teach accounting nor to cover every one of the many areas of interest in financial reporting. We do want to focus on critical problem areas—the sources of an analyst's difficulties in interpreting financial statements. A good analyst must train himself to understand the kinds of flexibility permitted in accounting and the effects of this flexibility on his interpretation of what he sees. Further, an analyst must learn to rely upon the *total* impact of all financial statements taken as a unit over time. The auditor's opinion is a critical part of the financial statements, as are the notes to the statements. In short, the prudent analyst will look at the statements "taken as a whole" and will understand how the major statements are interrelated. There is danger in looking at single figures on individual statements in an isolated year. Finally, and perhaps most important, reported financial data (especially reported earnings) need to be examined carefully and to be interpreted in the light of other generally available information.

The results of our exploration into financial statements should enable the analyst to work with the interrelationships contained in the various statements in forming expectations about earnings, dividends, and stock prices.

OPERATING RESULTS: THE INCOME STATEMENT

Three major financial statements make up the backbone of internal information available to the analyst: the statement of income and retained earnings, the balance sheet, and the statement of changes in financial position. Accompanying notes to these statements are also crucial and are no less important than the statements themselves.

In the early 1900s, security analysts placed primary emphasis on the evaluation of the corporation's balance sheet. In fact, it would not be unfair to say that emphasis was almost exclusively placed on the financial strength or weakness of the company. As the years went by, this emphasis on the evaluation of the balance sheet began to shift toward an emphasis on the income statement. This shift continued until the early 1970s. Again it would not be unfair to say that in these years major emphasis was placed on earnings and earnings per share as reflected in the income statement. The growth rate of these earnings was also of vital importance to the analyst. However, in the mid-1970s it became apparent that looking at the income statement and the earnings figures to the detriment of the balance sheet was not a prudent thing to do any longer. And so, today analysts look very closely at both the balance sheet and the income statement as well as the statement of changes in financial position. This last statement is becoming increasingly popular to the analyst because it very nicely connects the income statement and balance sheet.

In the sections that follow we will discuss each of these statements—namely, the statement of income and retained earnings, the balance sheet, and the statement of changes in financial position. Our discussion will point out certain trouble spots which the security analyst should be aware of when examining these various statements. Since these trouble spots are often very complex to analyze—even for a trained accountant—we strongly feel that an analyst should realize that these problem areas exist so that he will at least proceed with caution and will be aware of potential pitfalls in any analysis. With this general warning, let us proceed with our analysis of these statements.

Income-Statement Format

The Accounting Principles Board has suggested the format shown in Table 8-1 for a statement of income and a statement of retained earnings. The income statement provides an analysis of significant factors that have contributed to and affected the earnings for the period. The statement of retained earnings bridges the gap between the income statement and the position statement (balance sheet), in the sense that the net income on the income statement is reflected in the retained-earnings part of the stockholders' equity on the balance sheet. The usual changes in retained earnings are the net income or loss for the period, dividends declared, and corrections of net income for prior periods.

The income statement is a key financial statement by which analysts judge management's performance. It is used perhaps more than any other statement in attempting to assess the future. Past earnings reported on the income statement are very often used as a base for predicting future performance. Thus a major job for the analyst is to probe principal areas of the income statement to assess their impact on earnings.

The nature of a company is a principal determinant of the extent to which a particular item is likely to have significance with respect to earnings. For example, the choice of depreciation method has considerable impact upon the earnings of an airline, which has almost all its assets in equipment. The choice of depreciation method is less significant, although not unimportant, for a bank, since most bank assets are in securities and loans. The analyst is forced to examine almost every item of revenue, expense, and resulting earnings on the income statement. Elements of the statement of retained earnings, particularly charges for prior periods, should be investigated. Let us address ourselves to some *major problem areas* on the income statement and statement of retained earnings.

TABLE 8-1

ILLUSTRATIVE COMPARATIVE STATEMENT OF INCOME AND
STATEMENT OF RETAINED EARNINGS*

Statement of Income
Years Ended December 31, 19X0 and December 31, 19X1

	19X0	19X1
Net sales (net of trade discounts, returns, and allowances)		
Other income (e.g., rents, interest, dividends, royalties)		
Costs and expenses:		
Cost of goods sold (cost of merchandise sold during period)		
Selling expenses (creating sales, storing goods, and delivery, including depreciation)		
Administration and general expenses (administering overall activities, including depreciation)		
Financial management expenses (interest on borrowed money)		
Other deductions (items extraneous to primary operations)		
Income tax (federal, state, and local)		
Income before extraordinary items (per share: 19X0 19X1:)		
Extraordinary items, less applicable income tax (per share: 19X0: ; 19X1:) (usually nonrecurring and not related to primary operating activity of the business.		
Net income (per share: 19X0: ; 19X1:		

Statement of Retained Earnings
Years Ended December 31, 19X0 and December 31, 19X1

	19X0	19X1
Retained earnings at beginning of year:		
As previously reported (on prior-period balance sheet)		
Adjustments (corrections of income reported in prior periods; e.g., settlements of law and tax suits, and for carelessness or imprudence in valuing assets at end of earlier periods)		
As restated		
Net income (last line of statement of income)		
Cash dividends on common and preferred stock (shown separately)		
Retained earnings at end of year		

*At this writing, it appears that there will be changes in what is properly classified as an extraordinary item. See "Accounting Unit Votes Changes in Adjusting Prior-Period Reports," *Wall Street Journal*, July 1, 1977, p. 12.

Earnings from Regular Operations

The analyst must recognize that earnings from regular, normal operations reflect the major thrust of a business, and so these earnings should be segregated from earnings (or losses) resulting from infrequent, unusual, or nonrecurring events. Since earnings from these regular, normal operations are more apt to be continuing for some reasonable period, their separate disclosure is important to the analyst in judging and forecasting the future. Obviously, the assumption is made that these recurring types of transactions are a better base on which to build or forecast than nonrecurring or infrequent types of transactions. However, as can be seen in Table 8-1, so-called extraordinary gains or losses do sometimes occur in the operations of a business. Fortunately, however, the accounting profession has specifically defined how these items are to be treated in the financial statements.[6]

Extraordinary items need to arise from material transactions that are both unusual in nature and occur infrequently in the operating environment of the business. The *environment* of the business would include such things as the characteristics of the industry in which the firm operates, the geographic location of the facilities of the corporation, and the role of governmental regulations in this corporation's affairs. As can be seen, this definition very narrowly defines what can properly be called an extraordinary item. For example, a loss resulting from an earthquake in certain sections of California might not be considered an extraordinary item; however, damage caused by an earthquake in Connecticut would be considered an extraordinary item. As was shown in Table 8-1, the extraordinary item would be listed separately and would be listed net of any income tax affects.

Accounting Principles Board (APB) *Opinion No. 30* also deals with the problem of properly disclosing information related to disposals of certain major segments of the business. Any income or loss from such discontinued operations must also be separately disclosed in the financial statements. If a corporation in the same year had normal operations, had extraordinary items, and disposed of a segment of its business, there would be three different income figures disclosed in the income statement. The first would probably be labeled "income from continuing operations." Then there would probably be a separate section for the discontinued operations, which would lead to another income figure labeled "income before extraordinary items." Lastly there would be a section for disclosing the extraordinary items, which would lead to a final figure labeled "net income." Therefore the analyst must be careful to select the proper income figure to use as a basis for any forecast.

The Matching Principle

Accounting is based upon many "rules of the road" called *generally accepted accounting principles.* An important rule applied to income statements that concerns the analyst is what accountants call the *matching principle.* In simple terms, the matching principle requires that expenses be reflected in the same period as the revenues to which they are related. Various accounting methods have been devised, some rather scientific and others somewhat arbitrary, for matching costs and revenues. The utility of accounting information to the investment analyst is impaired if (1) expenses and revenues are improperly matched, or (2) methods employed are switched over time.

The process of matching costs and revenues is only approximate and often yields to expediency. Do we really know the rate at which a machine depreciates? In what order did inventory really flow out of the plant? Will a

---

[6] Accounting Principles Board, *Opinion No. 30,* "Reporting the Results of Operations—Reporting the Effects of Disposal of a Segment of the Business, and Extraordinary, Unusual and Infrequently Occurring Events and Transactions," AICPA (New York, 1973).

particular expenditure benefit this period alone, or several future periods? If several periods, how many? Judgment in prorating expenses and recognizing revenues is needed within clearly drawn guidelines. Let us examine some key statement areas in which the matching problem creates difficulties in analysis.

Intangibles.   Many assets are developed or purchased that lack a physical or tangible character. Some, such as patents, copyrights, and franchises, have limited life by law. Others, such as goodwill, trademarks, and secret processes or formulas, have an indeterminate life. In the past, some companies have written off intangibles immediately; others have set them up with no amortization; still others have written them off over lives determined by expediency.

Accounting Principles Board (APB) *Opinion No. 17* has helped to clarify the ground rules for recording and amortizing intangibles. In essence, it says that purchased intangibles are to be set up at cost and amortized on a straight-line basis over *estimated* useful lives not to exceed forty years. And the *Opinion* specifies certain factors to consider in estimating useful life.

Pension Costs.   Every company pension plan requires accounting for past, present, and future costs. Prior to the publication of APB *Opinion No. 8*, accounting for pension costs could be utilized to smooth profits. Some companies would treat pension costs on a cash rather than an accrual basis; that is, they would make annual contributions into the fund based upon profits. Low profits would call for modest pension-fund contributions, and vice versa. Under *Opinion No. 8*, an accrual rather than a cash basis is required for pension-fund accounting.

However, accountants still differ on how pension costs are to be computed. This argument centers on determination of the amount of contribution and accrual necessary to account properly for past, present, and future service costs. Accounting for pension costs is still in transition, and the analyst is advised to probe notes to financial statements and other sources to uncover details on a company's pension-accounting policies.

Implications of Inventory Costing Methods

Two areas that deserve special attention are accounting for inventories and fixed assets. For the majority of businesses, these items amount to a major slice of total expenses during an accounting period.

Goods available for sale during the year either are sold or remain in inventory. Accountants generally subtract a value for ending inventory from goods available for sale in order to arrive, indirectly, at the cost of what was sold.

Accounting convention permits placing a value upon inventory in any of a number of ways. The most widely known methods are LIFO (last-in, first-out) and FIFO (first-in, first-out). LIFO assumes that the last units produced are the first sold; FIFO assumes that older units are sold first. There are no problems created by either method when prices remain the same, period to period. The difficulty arises when prices change.

LIFO assesses recent costs against sales and includes earlier costs in inventory. During periods of rising prices, the effect is to diminish profits and create a low carrying value for inventory. The result is deferral of income taxes. FIFO assesses sales with costs in the order of their origin. The cost of earlier units is charged against sales, and inventory includes recent purchases. Inventory is valued near current market value. When prices rise, profits are higher than with LIFO. The result is that taxes are paid as profits are reported, unlike LIFO, where taxes are deferred until inventory is liquidated.

Consider the following example: Grinnell Co. buys a product at the prevailing market price and sells it at a price 10 cents higher. The purchase price remains constant during the year. Assume that no expenses other than the cost of goods sold are incurred during the year. Let us see the effects of LIFO and FIFO inventory valuation upon (1) reported earnings, and (2) the position statement:

		LIFO	FIFO
Units of beginning inventory (cost = $.50)	1,000		
Units purchased during year (cost = $.75)	1,000		
Units sold (@ $.85)	1,000		
Sales		$850	$850
Cost of sales:			
Beginning inventory		$ 500	$ 500
Purchases		750	750
Goods available for sale		$1,250	$1,250
Less: Ending inventory:			
LIFO: (1,000 @ $.50)		$ 500	
FIFO: (1,000 @ $.75)			$ 750
Total cost of sales		$750	$500
Pre-tax profits		$100	$350
Taxes (50%)		$ 50	$175
Ending inventory		$500	$750

Rising purchase prices caused profits to be three and one-half times larger under FIFO, and on the position statement, FIFO inventory is 50 percent larger. The resulting numbers would be altered if prices and/or total sales were changed.

Most analysts would agree that during periods of advancing prices, LIFO provides a more conservative statement of income, with earnings less distorted and patterns more easily identified, whereas FIFO tends to overstate earnings. Conversely, during periods of falling prices, the effects on the position and income statements would be the opposite.

So choice of inventory valuation method is important to the analyst, depending as it does upon the movement of prices and the nature of the industry. Firms that have large proportions of total assets devoted to inventories can affect reported earnings through the inventory method chosen. Other things being equal, firms prefer smoothed profits rather than fluctuating profits. Smoothed profits tend to produce level share prices. LIFO permits smoothing of income, while FIFO accentuates ups and downs. The analyst should be aware of the quite different effects of LIFO and FIFO on earnings, taxes, and the carrying value of inventory as price levels change.

If the results for Grinnell Co. under FIFO and LIFO depicted results for two different firms with equal operating results and dissimilar inventory valuation methods, it is easy to see that the company using FIFO enjoys three and one-half times the pre-tax profits of its counterpart. However, the LIFO company pays less than one-third the taxes of the FIFO company. Which company is economically better off?

Depreciation Accounting

Net income reported on the financial statements can be affected by depreciation accounting. Depreciation recognizes that an asset will be exhausted at some point. In general, fixed assets are charged off against revenues they help create. From an analytical point of view, a problem arises in the rate at which a fixed asset is written off. Moreover, in the same firm, not all assets are depreciated on the same basis, and shifts in rate of charge-off take place over time.

The amount of annual charge for depreciation depends primarily upon the original cost of the asset, its estimated useful life, and its estimated salvage value at the end of its useful life. Fixed assets are depreciated under accounting convention on the basis of use or the basis of time. When depreciation is based upon the passage of time, so-called straight-line and/or accelerated bases of depreciation can be employed.

The straight-line method writes off depreciation uniformly over the useful life. The accelerated method recognizes that assets do not depreciate equally year by year. More likely, the value of services from a fixed asset declines at an irregular rate. In other words, accelerated depreciation would permit the charge-off to be larger in the beginning and become progressively smaller.

Among the more significant benefits of this kind of charge-off is the delay in tax payments. For example, larger write-offs in the beginning reduce taxable income and, correspondingly, taxes. In later years the smaller depreciation charges result in higher taxable income, and therefore higher taxes, than with the straight-line method. Unless tax rates change appreciably over time, the *total* tax bill is the same under both methods of depreciation. However, considering the "time value" of money, accelerated depreciation affords a relative advantage over straight-line because tax payments are postponed.

In the straight-line method, the annual charge for depreciation would be calculated as

$$\text{Straight-line depreciation} = \frac{\text{Original cost} - \text{Estimated salvage}}{\text{Estimated useful life}}$$

Accelerated methods do not permit the firm to write off any more depreciation in the aggregate than does the straight-line; the rate of write-off is simply accelerated. A popular method is the declining-balance method.[7] Double-

---

[7]Sum-of-the-years'-digits is another popular accelerated method. The digits in the estimated useful life are added together to get a denominator (e.g., 5 years is $1 + 2 + 3 + 4 + 5 = 15$). First year's charges are 5/15, second year's are 4/15, and so on.

declining balance allows a charge-off of twice the straight-line rate the first year. In the second year, this doubled rate is repeated, not on original cost but on the "declining balance" (original cost less first year's depreciation), and so on. By this method, the asset is never completely written off, but the tax laws permit switching to straight-line whenever the company wishes. The only limitation is that total depreciation may not exceed the original cost of the asset.

Let us see the impact of using normal and accelerated depreciation in a common example. A company acquires $300,000 in new equipment with an estimated life of five years and no salvage value. Annual depreciation under straight-line would be 1/5, or 20 percent. Declining-balance would permit 2/5, or 40 percent of undepreciated original cost each year:

Year	Straight-Line Depreciation	Double-Declining-Balance Depreciation
1	$ 60,000	$120,000
2	60,000	72,000*
3	60,000	43,200
4	60,000	32,400†
5	60,000	32,400
Total	$300,000	$300,000

*40% ($300,000 − $120,000) = $72,000.
†The company reverts to straight-line depreciation here. During the fourth year, accelerated depreciation would be $25,920. Reversion to straight-line provides larger depreciation.

The different effects upon pre-tax profits should be obvious. If tax rates remain unchanged, taxes will be the same in the aggregate; however, they are postponed under accelerated depreciation (declining-balance).

Not all companies use the same method of computing depreciation, nor are estimates of useful life and salvage value uniform. All this is further complicated by frequent changes in depreciation guidelines by Congress and the tax authorities. The result is great difficulty for the analyst in comparing data for a single company over time, as well as in comparing companies.

Provision for Income Taxes

The matching principle requires that income taxes be offset against related income, or that tax savings be offset against a related loss. Thus, in Table 8-1, income taxes related to operating income are shown separate from taxes related to extraordinary items. Just as ordinary and extraordinary income are offset by appropriate taxes, ordinary and extraordinary losses would be offset by taxes that are refundable.

During years when a loss is shown and no prior-year income is available, the tax savings could be utilized in offsetting possible income in future years. Such tax savings are, however, contingent upon future earnings and are noted in footnotes to the financial statements rather than being carried as contingent assets. Should future periods produce net income, this income is reduced by appropriate taxes, and the carryover savings from prior years is shown in the income statement as extraordinary income. This procedure avoids clouding the true picture of earnings.

Certain items are treated differently on the financial statements and in the tax returns of companies. The tax expense shown on the income statement conforms to the income reported on the statements, rather than to the income reported to the tax authorities. For example, it is both legal and quite common to use accelerated depreciation on tax returns and straight-line on the financial statements. The result is that tax savings now from accelerated depreciation will be offset by higher taxes in later years. It is customary to set up a long-term or deferred tax liability for the savings, which is converted into a current liability in the future period in which the later tax is due.

Referring to our earlier example involving depreciation, recall that we contrasted depreciation under straight-line and declining-balance for new equipment costing $300,000 with a useful life of five years and no salvage value. Let us see what the tax effects would be:

Year	(A) Straight-Line Depreciation on Statements	(B) Declining-Balance Depreciation on Tax Return	(C) Added Taxes or (Savings) @ 50% Rate Using (B)
1	$ 60,000	$120,000	($30,000)
2	60,000	72,000	(6,000)
3	60,000	43,200	8,400
4	60,000	32,400	13,800
5	60,000	32,400	13,800
Total	$300,000	$300,000	

Assume that net income before depreciation and taxes in year 1 was $500,000. The tax rate is 50 percent. Using accelerated depreciation on the tax return results in a tax bill of $190,000 [½($500,000 − $120,000)]. Straight-line depreciation on the income statement for stockholders reporting would result in taxable income of $220,000 [½(500,000 − $60,000)]. To "normalize" the effect of the difference between the tax expense shown ($220,000) and taxes actually owed ($190,000), a $30,000 deferred liability would be shown on the balance sheet. In year 2, the difference between tax expense and taxes owed would be $6,000. The deferred tax liability account at the end of year 2 would be $36,000 ($30,000 + $6,000). Between year 3 and the end of year 5, the deferred tax liability would reduce to zero.

Earnings per Share

In order to determine earnings per share, the analyst must first calculate the number of common shares outstanding, as follows: First, the number of shares issued is reduced by the number of treasury shares; these are common stock sold at one time but subsequently repurchased by the company, often with the intention of reissue. Second, a weighted average is used when stock transactions involving asset accounts have taken place during the period. For example, if 1 million shares are outstanding at the beginning of the period, and 200,000 shares are sold July 1 (midyear) for cash (an asset), the weighted-average number of shares would be 1.1 million [1 million + ½(200,000)] .[8]

Third, when stock transactions take place that do *not* involve assets, such as stock dividends or splits, the new number of shares is treated as being effective from the beginning of the year. For example, 1 million shares are outstanding. In November a 20 percent stock dividend is declared. The weighted-average number of shares at year-end would still be 1.2 million.

Once we have determined the number of common shares outstanding, it is customary to translate net income after taxes into a per-share-of-ownership equivalent, in order to compare firms on a common size basis. Firms A and B may each have earnings of $1 million. However, if A has 1 million shares outstanding and B has only 500,000, firm A would have earnings per share of $1, and B of $2.

The increasing use of securities that are convertible into common shares and of stock options through warrants creates the overhang, or contingent creation of new common shares, as conversion privileges, warrants, or other options are exercised. The existence of such contingent shares is now being recognized in financial reporting by the calculation of two supplementary earnings-per-share figures. One is called *primary earnings* per share, the other *secondary* or *fully diluted earnings* per share. Primary earnings per share reflects the assumption that all options and warrants are exercised, but reflects convertible securities *only* if at the time of issuance their value by the market was mostly due to the conversion privilege. For example, if a convertible bond issue is sold at a price that yields investors 6 percent to maturity while similar bonds without conversion rights are selling to yield 10 percent, it might be said that the convertible bonds were purchased more for their option feature than as straight bonds. The other EPS figure, fully diluted or secondary earnings per share, assumes that *all* options, warrants, and convertibles were turned into stock. In effect, secondary earnings would represent the most conservative statement of EPS and would be less than or equal to primary earnings per share.

For the analyst, it is important to recognize (1) that there are multiple earnings-per-share figures, and (2) that secondary earnings per share represent the most reasonable statement of earnings, taking into account all contingent shares. Below are shown abbreviated statements for 197X for a company with convertible bonds and preferred stock outstanding. Regular earnings per share are shown.

Income Statement		*Balance Sheet*	
Operating income	$4,200,000	4% convertible bonds (convertible	
Interest expense	400,000	into 500,000 shs. of common)	$10 million
Earnings before taxes	$3,800,000		
Taxes (50%)	1,900,000	5% preferred (convertible into	
Net income	$1,900,000	500,000 shs. of common)	$ 5 million
Preferred dividends	250,000		
Earnings to common	$1,650,000	Common (1,600,000 shares)	$ 8 million
EPS	$1.03		

[8]200,000 shares sold April 15 would be outstanding for 8½ months, or about 7/10 of a year. Weighted-average total shares would be 1 million plus 140,000, or 1,140,000.

If we assume that the preferred at the time of issue was *not* sold mainly because of the conversion option but the bonds were, then primary earnings per share would be:

Operating earnings		$4,200,000
Taxes (50%)		2,100,000
Net income		2,100,000
Preferred dividends		250,000
Earnings to common		1,850,000
Shares:		
Bonds	500,000	
Common	1,600,000	2,100,000 shares
EPS		$.88

Fully diluted or secondary earnings per share (all convertibles assumed converted) would be:

Operating earnings		$4,200,000
Taxes (50%)		2,100,000
Earnings to common		2,100,000
Shares:		
Bonds	500,000	
Preferred	500,000	
Common	1,600,000	2,600,000 shares
EPS		$.81

Interim Earnings Reports

Quarterly reports to stockholders are an effort to provide disclosure of the continuous nature of corporate developments. The Financial Analysts Federation surveys reveal that the majority of investment analysts regard interim data of equal or greater importance than annual data. In the main, quarterly reports are used by analysts to update and adjust projections of future performance. However, there are problems in using these reports.

Quarterly reports are generally not audited. This creates problems with respect to outside, independent control over proper matching of revenues and expenses. Income can be "managed" by not segregating nonrecurring income, or by cutting off sales and related costs at different times. The brief time period involved in quarterly reports creates problems of proper estimation and proration of many items that are difficult enough to assess on an annual basis. Shortened time periods lead to more arbitrary period allocations. Further, interim reports do not contain information on changes in accounting methods and retroactive adjustments.

The usual interim or quarterly financial report is a very abbreviated earnings statement and balance sheet. The analyst would no doubt have more confidence in interim data if full and complete statements (including a funds statement) were provided, with an auditor's certification.[9]

[9]See L. J. Seidler and W. Benjes, "The Credibility Gap in Interim Financial Statements," *Financial Analysts Journal,* 23 (September-October 1967), 109-15.

Other Topics

There are several other key areas in income statement analysis with which the analyst should be familiar. However, these topics also have a profound influence on the balance sheet, and we will therefore defer the discussion of these recent developments in financial statement analysis and deal with them in a separate section later in this chapter. The topics that will be discussed include accounting for foreign currency transactions, reporting the financial results of various segments of a business enterprise, reporting replacement cost data, and, finally, reflecting changing price levels in the financial statements. Let us now turn our attention to the balance sheet.

FINANCIAL POSITION: THE BALANCE SHEET

The level, trend, and stability of earnings are powerful forces in the determination of security prices. This *flow* of earnings is depicted on the income statement. The *stock* of assets and the claims to those assets that provide the fuel for those earnings are shown on the balance sheet. The balance sheet shows, at a given point in time, the assets, liabilities, and owners' equity in a company. It is the analyst's primary source of information on the financial strength of a company.

Assets include properties and rights to properties, both tangible (such as buildings) and intangible (such as patents and goodwill). Liabilities are debts that are payable on demand or over specified future periods. They are evidenced by simple invoices or rather lengthy legal documents, such as mortgages. The equity of stockholders represents the excess of assets over liabilities at the balance-sheet date.

Modern accounting principles dictate the basis for assigning values to assets. Liability values are set by contracts. When assets are reduced by liabilities, the "book value" of stockholders' equity can be determined. This book value invariably differs from current value in the marketplace, since market value is dependent upon the earning power of assets, and not their cost or value in the accounts.

The Cost Principle

For the most part, the accounting concept of conservatism requires that assets be carried at original or historical cost when they are first acquired. During subsequent time periods, they may be valued at cost or market, whichever is lower.

Income-statement and reported-earnings problems can stem from the rate at which assets are written off against related revenues, a matter we discussed under inventory and depreciation accounting. In addition, the framework of historical cost does not make reference to the changing purchasing power of the dollar. When inflation occurs, historical-dollar accounting can be unrealistic and deficient.

First, the income statement fails to express all items in dollars of the same purchasing power. For example, revenues closely represent current dollars, whereas FIFO inventory costing would represent "old" dollars. Needless to say, over time interperiod comparability is destroyed.

Second, assets and stockholders' equity reflect an admixture of items shown in dollars of different purchasing power. For example, FIFO inventory procedures might tend to show inventories in near-current dollars, but fixed assets may be worth many times their carrying value. These distortions in asset groups are similarly reflected in the stockholders'-equity section of the balance sheet. The erosion of the purchasing power of the dollar affects measurements using the balance sheet and influences "real" earning power.

Balance-Sheet Format

Table 8-2 illustrates a balance-sheet format. It is in *account form*, with assets on the left side of the page and liabilities and stockholders' equity on the right side. Total assets equals total liabilities plus stockholders' equity.[10]

Discussion of other problems the analyst faces in using the balance sheet will be explored in the analysis of fixed-income securities in Chapter 13.

TABLE 8-2
BALANCE SHEET

December 31, 19X0 and December 31, 19X1

Assets	*Liabilities and Equity*
Current assets:	Current liabilities:
Cash and securities	Accounts payable
Receivables	Accrued wages
Inventories	Taxes payable
Prepaid expenses	Long-term liabilities:
Permanent investments:	Long-term notes
Investments in other companies	Bonds payable
Realty held for investment	Stockholders' equity:
Fixed tangible assets:	Capital stock
Buildings	Additional paid-in capital
Land	Retained earnings
Machinery and equipment	
Furniture and fixtures	
Fixed intangible assets:	
Goodwill	
Patents	
Deferred charges to expense:	
R&D expenses	
Organization costs	
Total assets	Total Liabilities and Equity

[10]The *report form* lists assets, deducts liabilities, and establishes stockholders' equity. The increasingly popular *modified report form* lists current assets and deducts current liabilities to establish working capital; long-term assets are added and long-term liabilities deducted from working capital to ascertain equity.

Most accounting statements deal with rather arbitrary cutoff points in time.[11] Thus *accounting statements cannot be considered complete* without parenthetical references and notes that not only clarify the data in the body of the statements but also introduce new information not conveniently admissible within the statements proper.

Quite often, valuation bases for assets are shown next to the item caption or in footnotes. Parenthetical references should be examined to note where assets have been pledged and the related liability secured.

Footnotes to the balance sheet often show many of the following items of importance to the analyst.[12]

1. Contingent liabilities for taxes, dividends, and pending lawsuits.
2. Particulars on options outstanding, leases, loans, and other financing arrangements.
3. Changes in accounting principles and techniques, including bases of valuation, and the dollar effect on income.
4. Facts of importance occurring between the balance-sheet date and date of submission of statements that might have a material effect on the statements. Examples include refinancing, proposed mergers, and changes in capitalization.

The analyst will find a wealth of information in these parenthetical references and footnotes that can shed light on the company under analysis.

STATEMENT OF CHANGES IN FINANCIAL POSITION

This statement discloses all important aspects of a company's financing and investing activity between the beginning and the end of the accounting period. It is a condensation of how activities have been financed and how the financial resources have been used.

The basic ingredients for the statement of changes in financial position come from the balance sheet, income statement, statement of retained earnings, and certain other supplementary data. Table 8-3 shows very simple income and position statements, and Table 8-4 is a statement of changes in financial position prepared from Table 8-3 for the Douglas Corporation. Certain detail on transactions not found directly in the income statement or balance sheet is required to prepare the statement of changes in financial position. This information is shown in Table 8-4 but cannot be traced directly to Table 8-3.

The statement of changes in financial position displays changes in working capital, as well as changes traced to noncurrent assets, long-term liabilities, and stockholders' equity. Let us examine Table 8-4. There are two main subdivisions in the statement: sources (of financing) and applications (investing activity). The first major source of financing is income for the period. Notice that ordinary and extraordinary income are shown separately (items A and K). Net losses would be

---

[11] Calendar and fiscal years are based upon custom and operating convenience.
[12] Mauriello, *Accounting for the Financial Analyst*, p. 35.

TABLE 8-3
SIMPLIFIED INCOME AND COMPARATIVE BALANCE SHEETS
(IN THOUSANDS OF DOLLARS)

Douglas Corporation
Income Statement
Year Ended 12/31/X1

Net sales	$1,000
Expenses (including taxes)	775
Net income	$ 225
Dividends paid	100
Transferred to retained earnings	$ 125

Douglas Corporation
Comparative Balance Sheets
December 31, 19X0 and December 31, 19X1

	19X1	19X0	Change
Assets:			
Current assets:			
Cash	$ 150	$ 120	+30
Receivables	150	200	−50
Inventories	200	180	+20
Total current assets	$ 500	$ 500	
Tangible fixed assets:			
Plant and equipment	$1,935	$1,700	+235
Less: Accumulated depreciation	(500)	(350)	+150
Net tangible fixed assets	$1,435	$1,350	+ 85
Total assets	$1,935	$1,850	
Liabilities and stockholders' equity:			
Current liabilities:			
Accounts payable	$ 150	$ 125	+25
Accrued taxes and wages	35	105	−70
Total current liabilities	$ 185	$ 230	
Long-term liabilities:			
Nonconvertible bonds	$ 300	$ 295	+ 5
Convertible bonds	150	200	−50
Total long-term liabilities	$ 450	$ 495	
Stockholders' equity:			
Capital stock	$ 170	$ 150	+ 20
Additional paid-in capital	580	550	+ 30
Retained earnings	550	425	+125
Total stockholders' equity	$1,300	$1,125	
Total liabilities and stockholders' equity	$1,935	$1,850	

applications, not sources. Next, added back to (item B) or deducted from (item G) operating income are items that did not use (or provide) working capital or cash during the period. Depreciation and amortization are the principal income-statement items not requiring cash outlay in the current period that are added back to income before extraordinary items. Working-capital changes not consti-tuting a use of cash during the current period can be determined by comparing the changes in each current asset and current liability account (components of working capital) between the present and prior balance sheets. In general, to income before extraordinary items:

Add:	*Subtract:*
Decreases in current-asset accounts (item E)	Increases in current-asset accounts (item H)
Increases in current-liability accounts (item F)	Decreases in current-liability accounts (item I)
Extraordinary gains (net of tax) (item K)	Extraordinary losses (net of tax) (item K)

The effects of other financing and investing activities, in addition to working capital or cash provided from operations, include:[13]

1. Outlays for purchase and receipts from sale of long-term assets (items (P, M)
2. Conversion of debt or preferred stock to common stock (items O, Q)
3. Issuance, redemption, assumption, and repayment or repurchase of long-term debt or stock (item N)
4. Dividends or other stockholder distributions (except stock dividends or splits) (item R)

In general, proceeds received from these types of activities are "sources"; outlays are called "applications." A conversion of debt or preferred to common stock would be shown as both a source and an application, in order to cancel one event against the other.

Use of Statement by Analyst

The statement of changes in financial postion discloses clearly and individually the significant financing and investing activities of the company during an accounting period, giving the analyst an overall view of the financial management of a company and its policies. Some of the questions the statement may help to answer are:[14]

1. Where did profits go?
2. Why were dividends not larger (or smaller)?
3. How were dividends possible in the face of a net loss for the period?
4. Why are current assets down and net income up?
5. How did the company finance plant expansion?
6. How was debt retirement accomplished?
7. What became of the proceeds of the new bond issue?
8. How was the increase in working capital financed?

---

[13]Accounting Principles Board, *Opinion No. 19.* See *Outline of Opinions of the Accounting Principles Board,* pp. 76-80.

[14]Mauriello, *Accounting for the Financial Analyst,* p. 90.

TABLE 8-4

DOUGLAS CORPORATION: STATEMENT OF CHANGES IN
FINANCIAL POSITION (IN THOUSANDS OF DOLLARS)

Item				
	Sources:			
	Operations:			
A	Income before extraordinary items			$225
B	Add: Income-statement items not requiring outlay of cash in current period:			
C	Depreciation	$150		
D	Changes in working-capital elements that constitute a *source of cash* in current period:			
E	Decrease in receivables	$ 50		
F	Increase in accounts payable	25	$225	
G	Less: Changes in working-capital elements that constitute *use of cash* in current period:			
H	Increase in inventories	$ 20		
I	Decrease in accrued wages	70	90	$135
J	Cash provided from operations of the period exclusive of extraordinary items			$360
K	Gain or loss associated with extraordinary items (net of applicable income tax)			0
L	Cash provided from operations			$360
M	Proceeds from sale of fixed assets			100
N	Proceeds from issuance of bonds			5
O	Issuance of common stock through conversion of bonds			50
				$515
	Applications:			
P	Purchase of fixed assets			$335
Q	Conversion of bonds to common stock			50
R	Payment of dividends			100
				$485
S	Net increase in cash during year			$ 30

NOTES:

1. *Sources* of cash normally identified with decreases in asset accounts and increases in liabilities and equities. *Uses* of cash are: + assets and − liabilities and equity.

2. Working capital equals current assets minus current liabilities. Working capital, 19X0 = $500 − $230 = $270; 19X1 = $500 − $185 = $315. Change in working capital is +45 ($315 − $270).

Comparing statements over the past provides insight into patterns that may or may not be followed in the years ahead. The statement of changes in financial position is a valuable supplement to the balance sheet and income statement. The analyst should probe it thoroughly.

CONSOLIDATED FINANCIAL STATEMENTS

Very often, certain operating units of a parent company are not owned 100 percent. That is, the voting common stock is shared with third parties, often other companies. Where 50 percent or more of the voting common stock is held by the parent company, the company held is referred to as a *subsidiary*. Less than 50 percent control results in an *affiliated* company. An *associated* company is a company owned jointly by two other companies.

A holding company may own anywhere from a small fraction up to 100 percent of another company. Where the percentage of ownership exceeds 50 percent, accountants strongly recommend that company statements be consolidated. Although there are certain refinements in the process, consolidation means adding the statements of the companies together. The portion of the equity that is not owned by the consolidator, or holding company, is shown as a "minority-interest" liability on the balance sheet. Net income on the statement of income is reduced by the portion accruing to minority interests.

Where ownership of voting common stock is between 20 and 50 percent, the accounting profession adopts the view that the holding company has effective control of dividend policy of the subsidiary. Thus the initial cost of the investment in the subsidiary stock is shown separately as a long-term investment under Assets on the holding company's balance sheet. As time passes, the investment account is adjusted upward for the holding company's share of subsidiary profits, and downward for its share in subsidary losses and for dividends received. This is referred to as the *equity method* of accounting for subsidiaries. For ownership of less than 20 percent, if it can be shown that the holding company and the affiliate are two separate units and that effective control is not exercised by the holding company, then the *cost method* of accounting for subsidiaries is permitted. The investment in affiliate shares is shown at cost on the balance sheet. Dividends received are treated as income.

The essential difference between the cost and equity methods is that the former does not generally adjust the investment up and down for profits and losses, less dividends. More significantly, on the income statement only dividends received are shown, and not the parent's portion of total income. This latter provision can lead to abuses, by which dividend declarations by subsidiaries or affiliates can be regulated to affect the parent's earnings. The following example illustrates the use of the *equity method* of accounting for subsidiaries.

Example. The Melicher Co. purchased 40 percent of the voting common stock of the Rush Corp. one year ago, at a cost of $5 million. At that time, Melicher's balance sheet showed "Investments in affiliates, $5,000,000." During the past year, Rush had after-tax earnings of $250,000. It declared dividends on common shares of $100,000. The holding company's share of profits and dividends is $100,000 and $40,000 respectively. Melicher would show the net difference between its share of profits and dividends received, $60,000, as an addition to its investment account. The account would now show a total of $5,060,000. The reason for netting profits and dividends received can be seen in another way. Rush Corp. will show an increase in its assets and retained earnings of $150,000, or after-tax earnings of $250,000 less dividends of $100,000 paid. Melicher's share of these assets and retained earnings is 40 percent, or $60,000.

Investors and investment analysts look to an independent certified public accounting firm to attest to the financial statements we have been discussing. The CPA after he has conducted his examination, renders an opinion on the financial statements. An example of the general wording of a typical "unqualified" auditor's opinion follows:

> We have examined the balance sheet of RJJ Corporation as of December 31, 198X, and the related statements of income and retained earnings and changes in financial position for the year then ended. Our examination was made in accordance with generally accepted auditing standards, and accordingly included such tests of the accounting records and such other auditing procedures as we considered necessary in the circumstances.
>
> In our opinion, the aforementioned financial statements present fairly the financial position of the RJJ Corporation and the results of its operations and the changes in its financial position for the year then ended, in conformity with generally accepted accounting principles applied on a basis consistent with that of the preceding year.

This unqualified opinion, which would generally be addressed to the board of directors of the corporation, often is mistakenly taken as a *guaranty* from the CPA that the statements are 100 percent accurate. This is *not* true. You will note that the third word in the opinion is "examined." This simply means that the auditor has reviewed the content of the statements rather than that he has prepared or guaranteed these statements. Furthermore, the opinion goes on to say that the examination was conducted in accordance with certain prescribed auditing standards and that the auditor performed those tests he considered necessary. Thus the reader is made aware of the existence of specific rules that auditors must follow, and the fact that the auditor *does* exercise subjective opinion in judgment. Nonetheless, the fact that the auditor does issue this type of opinion should give some consolation to the reader that these statements and notes have been subjected to stringent external review.

When circumstances do not permit the issuance of such an unqualified opinion as that discussed in the preceding paragraph, the auditor has a number of other types of opinions he can issue. The board of directors of the corporation or its auditing committee, however, would usually prefer that the auditor issue an unqualified opinion, and they therefore tend to cooperate with the auditor in every way possible so that he can issue this type of opinion.[15]

We have already discussed many key accounting conventions or *generally accepted accounting principles.* These rules become "generally accepted" in two main ways: (1) by authoritative pronouncements from such bodies as the Financial Accounting Standards Board (FASB) and the Securities and Exchange Commission (SEC), and (2) by widespread usage and custom among respected certified public accountants.

---

[15]The reader who is interested in learning more about the other types of possible opinions should consult *Statements on Auditing Standards*, AICPA (New York, 1977), or any basic auditing textbook.

We will now discuss some new reporting requirements which the accounting profession feels are necessary in order to better inform the investment community.

KEY RECENT CHANGES IN GENERALLY ACCEPTED ACCOUNTING PRINCIPLES AFFECTING INVESTMENT ANALYSIS

In the sections that follow we will briefly describe several major recent developments and changes in generally accepted accounting principles. The reader should understand that these are merely some of the changes that have occurred that affect the financial statements. However, we believe we have selected those specific changes whose effect will be most widely felt in the investment community.

Accounting for Foreign Currency

In 1975 the Financial Accounting Standards Board developed standards of financial accounting and reporting for the translation of foreign currency transactions and foreign currency financial statements.[16] The FASB felt that because of the U.S. dollar devaluations in 1971 and 1973 and the institution of "floating" exchange rates, there was a need for the development of standards reflecting these financial dealings. Furthermore, the FASB felt that:

> the expansion of international business activities, extensive currency realignments—including two U.S. dollar devaluations—that followed the recent major revision of the international monetary system, and the acceptance in practice of significantly different methods of accounting have highlighted problems concerning currency translation. . . .
>   This statement establishes standards of financial accounting and reporting for foreign currency transactions in financial statements of a reporting enterprise. . . . It also establishes standards in financial accounting and reporting for translating foreign currency financial statements incorporated in the financial statements of an enterprise by consolidation, combination, or the equity method of accounting. . . .[17]

FASB *Statement No. 8* requires that gains and losses arising from currency translations be reported in income in the accounting period in which they arise. Furthermore, FASB *No. 8* requires that financial statements for previous periods be restated, if practicable, to conform to this statement. These rules are effective for fiscal years beginning on or after January 1, 1976. FASB *No. 8* has effects that are reflected in the corporation's balance sheet as well as its income statement.

According to FASB *No. 8*, current exchange rates, that is, exchange rates in

[16] Financial Accounting Standards Board, *Statement of Financial Accounting Standards No. 8, Accounting for the Translation of Foreign Currency Transactions and Foreign Currency Financial Statements,* FASB (Stamford, Conn., 1975).

[17] *Ibid,*, p. 1.

effect at the balance-sheet date, are to be used to translate receivables, payables, and cash, as well as other assets and liabilities that would be carried on the statements at current prices. It further requires that historical exchange rates be applied to those accounts whether they be assets, liabilities, revenues, or expenses that are being carried on the books of the company at historical cost. Other revenues and expenses may be translated on the basis of some average exchange rate. Therefore FASB *No. 8* has profound effects for corporations doing business abroad. In fact, the larger the extent of foreign operations, the larger the effect FASB *No. 8* has on the corporation's financial statements.

Financial Reporting for Segments of the Business Enterprise

In December 1976 the Financial Accounting Standards Board issued its *Statement of Financial Accounting Standards No. 14, Financial Reporting for Segments of a Business Enterprise.*[18] The FASB recognized that businesses have continually broadened their base of operations into various industries, foreign countries (as noted in the preceding section), and various markets within countries. The FASB felt that it was necessary for financial statements to include information about the corporation's business as it occurred in different industries, in different countries, and to various major customers when the firm issues a *complete* set of statements that present financial position, and so forth. *Statement No. 14*, perhaps more than any other statement that the FASB has issued to date, reflects the accounting profession's growing awareness of the need for various types of information for various reasons—particularly among the investment community. It is of considerable interest to students of the securities markets to note the wording the FASB used in explaining why it had issued *No. 14*:

> . . . Financial statement users point out that the evaluation of risk and return is the central element of investment and lending decisions—the greater the perceived degree of risk associated with an investment or lending alternative, the greater is the required rate of return to the investor or lender. If return is defined as expected cash flows to the investor or creditor, the evaluation of risk involves assessment of the uncertainty surrounding both the timing and the amount of the expected cash flows to the enterprise, which in turn are indicative of potential cash flows to the investor or creditor. Users of financial statements indicate that uncertainty results, in part, from factors unique to the particular enterprise in which an investment may be made or to which credit may be extended. Uncertainty also results, in part, from factors related to the industries and geographic areas in which the enterprise operates and, in part, from national and international economic and political factors. Investors and lenders analyze factors at all of those levels to evaluate the risk and return associated with an investment or lending alternative.
>
> Information contained in an enterprise's financial statements constitutes an important input to that analysis. Financial statements provide information about conditions, trends, and ratios that assist in

---

[18]Financial Accounting Standards Board, *Statement of Financial Accounting Standards No. 14, Financial Reporting for Segments of a Business Enterprise* (Stamford, Conn., 1976).

predicting cash flows. In analyzing an enterprise, a financial statement user often compares information about the enterprise with information about other enterprises, with industrywide information, and with national or international economic information in general. Those comparisons are helpful in determining whether a given enterprise's operations may be expected to move with, against, or independently of developments in its industry and in the economy within which it operates.

The broadening of an enterprise's activities into different industries or geographic areas complicates the analysis of conditions, trends, and ratios and, therefore, the ability to predict. The various industry segments or geographic areas of operations of an enterprise may have different rates of profitability, degrees and types of risk, and opportunities for growth. There may be differences in the rates of return on the investment commitment in the various industry segments or geographic areas and in their future capital demands.[19]

The principal disclosure requirements of *Statement No. 14* are sales and revenue, operating profit or loss, and identifiable assets. Information relating to these specific items must be identified with specific industry segments. This required information must be presented in the body of the financial statement, or in its footnotes, or in a separate schedule that is clearly an integral part of the financial statements. The following example is taken from FASB *No. 14* and indicates what this new information and notes for this new information should look like.[20]

To be identified as a recordable segment, an industry segment must be significant to the business as a whole. An industry segment must be recorded separately if it satisfies one or more of the following tests:

a) Its revenue (including both sales to unaffiliated customers and intersegment sales or transfers) is 10 percent or more of the combined revenue (sales to unaffiliated customers and intersegment sales or transfers) of all of the enterprise's industry segments.
b) The absolute amount of its operating profit or operating loss is 10 percent or more of the greater, in absolute amount, of:
  (i) The combined operating profit of all industry segments that did not incur an operating loss, or
  (ii) The combined operating loss of all industry segments that did incur an operating loss.
c) Its identifiable assets are 10 percent or more of the combined identifiable assets of all industry segments.[21]

Clearly, the impact of FASB *No. 14* on financial statement users will be monumental. This new information will greatly assist analysts not only in examining and understanding the past performance of the business as a whole but also in forecasting the future. While consolidated information is important, understanding the makeup of this consolidated information as defined in FASB *No. 14* will greatly benefit the investment community.

[19]*Ibid.*, pp. 27-28.
[20]*Ibid.*, pp. 53-56.
[21]*Ibid.*, p. 10.

EXHIBIT A

X COMPANY
CONSOLIDATED INCOME STATEMENT
YEAR ENDED DECEMBER 31, 1977

Sales		$4,700
Cost of sales	$3,000	
Selling, general, and administrative expense	700	
Interest expense	200	3,900
		800
Equity in net income of Z Co. (25% owned)		100
Income from continuing operations before income taxes		900
Income taxes		400
Income from continuing operations		500
Discontinued operations:		
Loss from operations of discontinued West Coast division (net of income tax effect of $50)	70	
Loss on disposal of West Coast division (net of income tax effect of $100)	130	200
Income before extraordinary gain and before cumulative effect of change in accounting principle		300
Extraordinary gain (net of income tax effect of $80)		90
Cumulative effect on prior years of change from straight-line to accelerated depreciation (net of income tax effect of $60)		(60)
Net income		$ 330

Replacement Cost Data and Accounting for Price-Level Changes

Throughout this chapter we have noted that accountants typically report information based upon historical cost. This means that the cost—particularly of items like fixed assets—is evidenced by purchase orders, contracts, and canceled checks. This objectively verifiable information is part of the data that allows the CPA to present an opinion such as that illustrated earlier in this chapter. Nonetheless, in the face of continued inflation, accountants, investors, and others have become troubled by the exclusive use of historical costs. This is particularly so with respect to the reporting of depreciation. If a firm depreciates based on historical cost, some contend that the firm will be understating expenses and overstating income. Why? Because the replacement cost of the asset is considerably higher than the book value of the asset. Therefore the firm's financial position and earnings are not adequately reflected merely by reporting historical cost.

To overcome this objection, the Financial Accounting Standards Board in 1974 attempted to establish a supplementary set of financial information to accompany historical basis statements. The supplementary set was to reflect changes in the general purchasing power of the dollar. But, as of this date, this has not become a generally accepted accounting principle.[22]

[22]*Financial Accounting Standards Board, Financial Reporting in Units of General Purchasing Power*, exposure draft (Stamford, Conn., 1974).

EXHIBIT B
X COMPANY
INFORMATION ABOUT THE COMPANY'S OPERATIONS IN
DIFFERENT INDUSTRIES YEAR ENDED DECEMBER 31, 1977

	Industry A	Industry B	Industry C	Other Industries	Adjustments and Eliminations	Consolidated
Sales to unaffiliated customers	$1,000	$2,000	$1,500	$ 200		$ 4,700
Intersegment sales	200		500		$(700)	
Total revenue	$1,200	$2,000	$2,000	$ 200	$(700)	$ 4,700
Operating profit	$ 200	$ 290	$ 600	$ 50	$ (40)	$ 1,100
Equity in net income of Z Co.						100
General corporate expenses						(100)
Interest expense						(200)
Income from continuing operations before income taxes						$ 900
Identifiable assets at December 31, 1977	$2,000	$4,050	$6,000	$1,000	$ (50)	$13,000
Investment in net assets of Z Co.						400
Corporate assets						1,600
Total assets at December 31, 1977						$15,000

See accompanying note.

NOTE

The Company operates principally in three industries, A, B, and C. Operations in Industry A involve production and sale of (describe types of products and services). Operations in Industry B involve production and sale of (describe types of products and services). Operations in Industry C involve production and sale of (describe types of products and services). Total revenue by industry includes both sales to unaffiliated customers, as reported in the Company's consolidated income statement, and intersegment sales, which are accounted for by (describe the basis of accounting for intersegment sales).

Operating profit is total revenue less operating expenses. In computing operating profit, none of the following items has been added or deducted: general corporate expenses, interest expense, income taxes, equity in income from unconsolidated investee, loss from discontinued operations of the West Coast division (which was a part of the Company's operations in Industry B), extraordinary gain (which relates to the Company's operations in Industry A), and the cumulative effect of the change from straight-line to accelerated depreciation (of which $30 relates to the Company's operations in Industry A, $10 to Industry B, and $20 to Industry C). Depreciation for Industries A, B, and C, respectively, was $80, $100, and $150. Capital expenditures for the three industries were $100, $200, and $400, respectively.

The effect of the change from straight-line to accelerated depreciation was to reduce the 1977 operating profit of Industries A, B, and C, respectively, by $40, $30, and $20.

Identifiable assets by industry are those assets that are used in the Company's operations in each industry. Corporate assets are principally cash and marketable securities.

The Company has a 25 percent interest in Z Co., whose operations are in the United States and are vertically integrated with the Company's operations in Industry A. Equity in net income of Z Co. was $100; investment in net assets of Z Co. was $400.

To reconcile industry information with consolidated amounts, the following eliminations have been made: $700 of intersegment sales; $40 relating to the net change in intersegment operating profit in beginning and ending inventories; and $50 intersegment operating profit in inventory at December 31, 1977.

Contracts with a U.S. government agency account for $1,100 of the sales to unaffiliated customers of Industry B.

Source: Copyright © by Financial Accounting Standards Board, High Ridge Park, Stamford, Connecticut 06905, U.S.A. Reprinted with permission. Copies of the complete document are available from the FASB.

However, the Securities and Exchange Commission felt that even though generally accepted accounting principles did not require disclosure of price-level adjusted statements or the recasting of historical cost figures, this information was still necessary for readers of financial statements. Therefore in 1976 the SEC, in its *Accounting Series Release 190,* required disclosure of the replacement cost of fixed assets, inventories, and certain other selected accounts. These figures, together with the explanation of how these amounts were arrived at, must be included in the 10-K report which is filed annually with the SEC. This supplementary report must be filed by approximately one thousand of the largest corporations in the United States.

In general, the affected corporations are quite averse to this additional required filing.[23] The accounting profession has recently issued a statement of auditing standards for this "unaudited" replacement cost information.[24]

PUBLISHED FINANCIAL FORECASTS

In recent years, analysts and regulatory agencies have been pressing to have accounting statements and annual reports provide greater utility to investors. It has been suggested, for instance, that companies provide forecasts of future operations in annual reports, alongside traditional historical information. The primary item, of course, that investors would like projected or forecast are earnings for the year ahead.[25] The merits, legalities, and ethics of such a move will no doubt take some time to resolve.

OFFICIALLY FILED INFORMATION

Public companies are required to file certain information with the Securities and Exchange Commission. In the main, public companies are those listed on the

[23] See "Inflation Accounting in SEC-Ordered Test, Irks Many Companies," *Wall Street Journal,* May 23, 1977, p. 1.

[24] AICPA, *Statement on Auditing Standards, No. 18, Unaudited Replacement Cost Information* (New York, 1977).

[25] The 1972 Annual Report of Fuqua Industries, Inc., was one of the earliest attempts to incorporate forecasts of future operations into an annual report.

organized securities exchange and traded over-the-counter that meet certain size tests (assets and number of shareholders). These filings take the form of periodic reports, proxies, financial statements, and other information.

Three periodic reports must be filed with the SEC: Form 8-K reports various events as they occur—acquisition and disposition of assets, changes in securities (amounts), defaults on senior securities, issuance of options, revaluation of assets, and other material events. Form 10Q is a quarterly report containing financial information in summary form. Form 10-K is an annual report containing certified financial statements and certain detailed supporting schedules not normally seen in annual reports provided to the public. These financial statements include notes on the basis for computing depreciation and certain details on leases, funded debt, management stock options, and inventory classification, among other items.

These periodic reports provide expanded information for analysts and investors. They are available from private firms that have reproduced the reports on microfilm or microfiche, and from the SEC itself. Reproduction, handling, and postage costs must be considered.[26]

External Information

External sources that the analyst can turn to for basic company information are prepared by investment services and brokerage firms. Three of the major services, to which even the novice investor will often turn for valuable information, are Standard & Poor's, Moody's, and *The Value Line.*

Figure 8-1 is taken from a portion of a Standard & Poor's *Current Analysis of the Office Equipment, Systems, and Services Industry.* Note that it contains paragraphs on several of the industry participants, as well as a summary of key financial data. These current analyses update and supplement the S&P basic analysis of the industry. Figure 8-2 is a report taken from the Standard & Poor's *Stock Reports.* This report concerns a firm on the New York Stock Exchange, but S&P also publishes similar reports on all American Stock Exchange firms and selected over-the-counter securities. These reports contain a recommendation, a report on the firm's operation and recent developments, information on the firm's financing, and pertinent share-price data, as well as other financial data. New reports are issued for this loose-leaf service at frequent intervals.

Moody's *Handbook of Common Stocks*, published quarterly, contains approximately the same type of information as the S&P *Stock Reports.* A reproduction from Moody's is shown in Figure 8-3.

The Value Line Investment Survey, in conjunction with the *Industry Reports*, lists excellent one-page summary sheets of member firms. As can be seen in Figure 8-4, these reports are abundant in extremely valuable information. Along with information similar to that contained in Moody's and Standard & Poor's (although contained in a different format), *The Value Line* projects key income-statement data several years in advance, computes betas (the measure of

---

[26]For example, a complete 10-K report may be fifty pages in length and cost anywhere from 10 to 25 cents per page, excluding postage and other handling charges.

FIGURE 8-1

Prospects for eight issues vary

DATA GENERAL (DGN)

Data General is the third-largest factor in the minicomputer industry, but is generally regarded as the fastest-growing company. DGN was one of the first to offer customers a full-systems approach and is attempting to maintain traditionally wide profit margins by integrating vertically. Sales for the fiscal year to end September 30 are expected to advance more than 40% from the $161.1 million of the prior year, even excluding a moderate-size acquisition. Shipments of the new *MicroNova* and *Eclipse* lines are expected to be especially heavy. Margins may narrow slightly because of the costs of acquisitions and higher new plant start-up charges. On the increased volume, however, earnings for fiscal 1977 are expected to advance some 35% or so from the $1.98 of fiscal 1976. Initiation of cash dividends is not contemplated. **Although the speculative shares (44, NYSE) have been under pressure recently, we would use periods of market weakness to accumulate them for longer-term growth.** ■

DIGITAL EQUIPMENT (DEC)

This company is the dominant factor in the minicomputer market and was the first company to offer a full-systems approach to minicomputer customers. Revenues for the fiscal year ending June 30 are expected to advance close to 40% from the record $736.3 million of the prior year as a result of strong backlogs for both smaller data communications and larger time-sharing computers. Margins are expected to be well maintained, as benefits from the higher volume and proportionately smaller increases in administrative expenses offset the costs of further additions to the workforce and new plant start-up. With more average shares outstanding, share earnings may rise 30%–35% from the $1.98 of fiscal 1976. Payment of cash dividends is not expected in the current fiscal year. **The speculative shares (48, NYSE) have been declining recently; such periods of weakness can be used to purchase the stock as a vehicle for possible capital gains.** ■

ADDRESSOGRAPH-MULTIGRAPH (AIN)

Addressograph makes an extensive line of duplicating, copying, repetitive writing, transaction processing, composition, and micrographic machines, and provides related services and supplies. The duplicator business faces increasing competition from high-speed plain paper xerographic copiers. Sales for the fiscal year ending July 31 should moderately exceed the $573 million of fiscal 1976. Business equipment sales should benefit from improved economic activity, although demand for duplicators will be restricted by increased competition from high-speed plain paper copiers. Poor returns from international operations and competitive conditions in the domestic market should restrict over-all margins. On balance, earnings for fiscal 1977 could exceed the depressed $0.80 a share of fiscal 1976. Any resumption of quarterly dividends would probably be conservative; a $0.10 special dividend was paid November 9. **The shares (13, NYSE) are speculative.** ■

DENNISON MANUFACTURING (DSN)

Dennison Manufacturing makes a broad line of paper products and related items. In 1975, retail systems accounted for 12% of revenues and 19% of earnings; stationery products and systems for 40% and 45%, respectively; technical papers for 15% and 9%; industrial systems for 17% and 33%; and office systems for 16% and a loss equal to 6% of the total. Earnings for 1976 are estimated at $3.30 a share, up from the reduced $2.47 of the prior year. For 1977, a good gain in sales is expected as the economy continues to expand. Demand for stationery products and systems and retail systems is expected to improve, and sales of industrial systems should increase. Margins should be fairly well maintained on the prospective rise in volume, and a good gain in earnings is expected for 1977. Dividends should continue at a minimum of $0.25 quarterly. **The shares (24, NYSE) merit retention.** ■

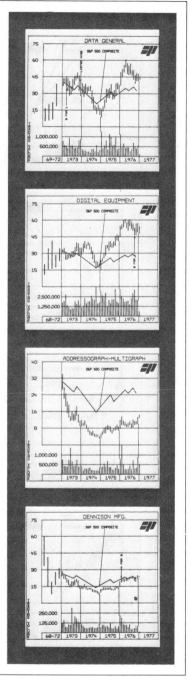

Source: *Current Analysis of the Office Equipment, Systems, and Services Industry* (New York: Standard & Poor's Corporation, April 30, 1977).

FIGURE 8-1 (cont.)

Comments on other issues

A. B. DICK is a leading manufacturer and distributor of duplicating, printing and copying equipment, and related supplies. New product developments include plain paper copiers, word processing, and micrographics. Earnings for 1976 are expected to be reported below the reduced $0.86 a share of 1975. A gain in sales is expected for 1977, aided by increased economic activity. In the duplicator market, there should be increased competition from high-speed plain paper copiers, and pricing likely will remain competitive. Depressed margins could improve somewhat, and some recovery in earnings is possible for 1977. **The shares are speculative.■**

DICTAPHONE is a leading manufacturer of electronic dictating and transcribing equipment, provides office supplies and services and, through the October 1976 acquisition of Data Documents, is a significant factor in data processing cards, business forms, and labels. Earnings for 1976 should be reported significantly above the $0.70 a share (to be restated to $0.65) of 1975. Sales will be significantly higher in 1977 as a result of the full-year inclusion of Data Documents. Demand for dictation equipment and systems should improve. The gain in volume and a contribution from Data Documents should permit earnings to advance in 1977. **The shares are worth retaining.■**

SAVIN BUSINESS MACHINES—Revenues for the fiscal year ending April 30 should show a strong gain from the $64.8 million of fiscal 1976 as a result of full-year sales of the new Savin *750* plain paper copier and an expanded marketing effort. Sales of the line of electrostatic products are expected to decline, since plain paper copier sales will be emphasized. Because of increased placements of the *750* plain paper copier, earnings for fiscal 1977 are expected to easily surpass the $0.87 a share (excluding a $0.10 special tax loss carryforward credit) of fiscal 1976. Increased demand for the new plain paper copier augurs well for fiscal 1978 earnings, but competition may be a limiting factor. Earnings over the long term will depend on the success of new products in the competitive plain paper copying and word-processing fields. **The shares are a speculation on continued earnings improvement.■**

NASHUA CORP. is a leading producer of electrostatic copy paper and xerographic toners and developers, markets office copying machines abroad, makes graphic and coated adhesive products, and provides photofinishing services. Earnings for 1976 should be reported well above the depressed $0.31 a share (before a $0.29 special credit) of 1975. A further gain in revenues seems likely in 1977, aided by moderately higher demand for coated and printed products. In the office copy products group, sales of plain paper products could improve, while demand for electrostatic equipment and supplies may be soft. Margins should be helped by the prospective increase in sales and cost-reduction efforts, although there are uncertainties surrounding the computer products operation. Some improvement in earnings is tentatively projected for 1977. **The shares are a speculation on continued earnings recovery.■**

*STATISTICAL POSITION OF COMMON STOCKS IN THE OFFICE EQUIPMENT INDUSTRY

Italicized entry shows addition or name change since last issue.	No. of Months	INTERIM OR ANNUAL OPERATING DATA §Sales 1975	§Sales 1976	§Net Inc. 1975	§Net Inc. 1976	Earns. $ Per Sh. 1975	Earns. $ Per Sh. 1976	[9]FINANCIAL POSITION Mil. $ Cash & Equiv.	Curr. Assets	Curr. Liabs.	**ANNUAL EARNINGS Year Ends	$ Per Share 1974	$ Per Share 1975	$ Per Share E1976	$ DIVS. PER SH. [4]Paid 1976	¶Indic. Rate	1976-77 Price Range	1-20-77 Price	†Price Earns. Ratio	‡Yield %
COMPUTER MANUFACTURERS																				
■ Burroughs Corp.	12 Dec.	1,702.1	1,901.8	164.41	185.90	4.14	4.62	106.00	1,217.0	706.0	Dec.	3.66	4.14	P4.62	0.66	0.68	108½ - 78	79½	17.2	0.9
■ Control Data	9 Sept.	891.6	970.8	29.06	36.08	1.71	2.08	12.40	702.0	461.0	Dec.	0.09	2.39	2.90	Nil	Nil	27⅛ - 17⅝	25¾	8.9	Nil
■ Data General	12 Wks.	29.0	47.1	3.50	5.33	0.37	0.56	[15]39.50	[15]108.0	[15]29.4	Sept.	1.22	1.51	P1.98	Nil	Nil	60¾ - 37⅜	44¼	22.3	Nil
■ Digital Equipment	3 Sept.	140.5	204.5	11.39	16.71	0.95	1.29	[11]201.00	[11]648.0	[11]149.0	June	1.27	1.28	A1.98	Nil	Nil	60⅞ - 45⅛	48¼	24.4	Nil
■ Electronic Associates	9 Sept.	22.9	17.9	1.25	d1.41	0.47	d0.53	N.A.	18.9	5.5	Dec.	[7]d4.27	0.63	...	Nil	Nil	5⅛ - 2	3	...	Nil
■ Honeywell Inc.	9 Sept.	1,642.1	1,757.2	43.63	65.27	2.23	3.20	[11]263.00	[11]1,155.0	[11]676.0	Dec.	3.74	3.89	4.75	1.50	1.60	56⅛ - 32¾	45⅞	9.7	3.5
■ Int'l. Bus. Machines	12 Dec.	14,436.5	16,304.3	1,989.88	2,398.09	13.35	15.94	[10]4,768.0	[10]8,115.0	[10]3,363.0	Dec.	12.47	13.35	P15.94	8.00	9.00	288½ - 223⅜	273	17.1	3.3
■ NCR Corp.	9 Sept.	1,517.0	1,596.9	48.65	51.16	2.01	2.03	243.00	1,386.0	645.0	Dec.	3.67	2.72	3.25	0.72	0.72	38⅜ - 23⅝	34⅞	10.7	2.1
■ Sperry Rand	6 Sept.	1,529.2	1,564.2	69.11	72.33	1.99	2.08	[11]38.10	[11]1,530.0	[11]796.0	Mar.	3.81	4.19	4.50	0.88	0.92	51¾ - 38⅜	39	8.7	2.4
★ Systems Engineer Labs.	13 Wks.	2.8	6.0	d0.59	0.02	d0.23	0.01	N.A.	14.7	3.9	June	d1.96	d0.17	Ad0.05	Nil	Nil	10⅜ - 4⅞	6⅞	def.	Nil
★ Wang Laboratories	6 Dec.	42.2	56.2	2.16	3.07	0.42	0.60	[11]3.06	[11]61.4	[11]19.8	June	0.96	0.64	A1.21	0.08½	0.12	17½ - 8¼	14⅜	11.9	0.8
PERIPHERAL EQUIPMENT AND SUBSYSTEMS																				
★ Calif. Computer Prods.	3 Sept.	26.7	30.5	d3.22	0.27	d0.96	0.08	N.A.	54.0	31.8	June	1.76	d3.83	Ad1.20	Nil	Nil	6¾ - 3⅝	4¾	def.	Nil
■ Centronics Data Comp.	6 Dec.	24.4	27.2	4.80	5.92	1.00	1.22	[11]7.37	[11]37.6	[11]9.3	June	1.65	1.52	A2.02	0.30	0.80	36⅛ - 19¼	26¼	13.0	3.0
★ Dataproducts Corp.	9 Dec.	61.7	84.9	4.83	9.11	0.71	1.28	[15]12.40	[15]55.8	[15]21.2	Mar.	0.86	1.03	...	Nil	Nil	14⅝ - 4⅝	11¾	...	Nil
■ Milgo Electronic	3 Dec.	9.1	13.0	0.53	1.24	0.30	0.71	[18]0.83	[18]25.8	[18]9.7	Sept.	2.13	2.50	P1.35	Nil	Nil	22¾ - 15	21⅝	16.0	Nil
■ Mohawk Data Sciences	6 Oct.	80.6	74.0	1.20	1.22	0.18	0.16	[19]4.74	[19]70.0	[19]27.7	Apr.	d3.47	0.30	...	Nil	Nil	9⅞ - 3	7⅛	...	Nil
Recognition Equipment	12 Oct.	59.3	65.3	2.20	3.60	0.37	0.60	[19]N.A.	[19]27.6	[19]10.1	Oct.	0.08	0.37	P0.60	Nil	Nil	10⅞ - 5¾	9⅜	15.6	Nil

FIGURE 8-2

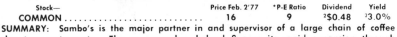

Sambo's Restaurants

1977M

Stock—	Price Feb. 2'77	*P-E Ratio	Dividend	Yield
COMMON	16	9	[2]$0.48	[2]3.0%

SUMMARY: Sambo's is the major partner in and supervisor of a large chain of coffee shop-type restaurants. The company has helped finance its rapid expansion through selling 50% interests in its units to key corporate personnel, including unit managers. Recent emphasis on improving unit volume along with further rapid growth of new units should contribute to continued strong earnings gains.

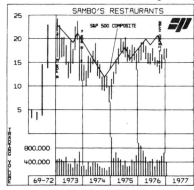

REVENUES (Million $)

Quarter:	1976	1975	1974	1973	1972
March	38.70	28.94	20.71	13.00	3.50
June........	44.96	33.99	23.90	15.41	4.18
Sept........	53.02	38.24	27.37	20.21	4.72
Dec.		37.77	28.89	19.41	[4]28.41

Revenues for the nine months ended September 30, 1976 advanced 35% from those of the year-earlier period. The increase primarily reflected the opening of 104 new restaurants and full-period inclusion of the 125 units opened in 1975. A 7% gain in comparable-unit sales (mostly due to menu price increases) was also helpful. Margins were penalized by rising costs for certain food and supply items which were not fully passed on and by sharply higher advertising expenditures, especially for regional television; operating income was ahead 26%. Substantially higher depreciation charges pared the gain in profits before taxes to 25%. After taxes at 38.8%, versus 44.6%, net income was up 38%. Earnings equaled $1.37 per share, compared with $1.08 in the prior-year interim.

PROSPECTS

Near Term—Revenues for 1976 are placed at $185 million, up from 1975's $139 million. Share earnings are estimated at $1.85, compared with the $1.48 of the prior year.

For 1977, revenues should show another worthwhile advance, aided by further rapid expansion of new unit openings and continued emphasis on improving unit volume.

Margins could be maintained, benefiting from the higher per unit sales, relatively stable food costs, and an improved product mix stressing more higher-margined items. Although operating costs, particularly for advertising and utilities, will be rising, earnings for 1977 are expected to post a good gain. Quarterly dividends have been raised to $0.12, from $0.08, effective with the March 29, 1977 payment.

Long Term—Continued rapid expansion of new restaurants, rising unit volume, and increased consumer expenditures for eating out should contribute to higher sales and earnings.

RECENT DEVELOPMENTS

Expansion plans for 1977 call for opening some 160 restaurants, up from the 140 units placed into operation during 1976.

In October, 1976 the company obtained a $20,000,000 17-year loan commitment at 9⅝% from Prudential Insurance Co. of America. Earlier in 1976 the company completed a $22,000,000 long-term loan package with institutional lenders with take downs in 1976 and 1977 in connection with the company's plans to retain ownership in a portion of the property of new restaurants.

The company's common shares began trading on the New York Stock Exchange on October 13, 1976; the shares will continue to be traded on the American Stock Exchange.

DIVIDEND DATA

Payments in the past 12 months were:

Amt. of Divd. $	Date Decl.	Ex-divd. Date	Stock of Record	Payment Date
0.08...	May 6	May 25	Jun. 1	Jun. 27'76
0.08...	Aug. 16	Aug. 26	Sep. 1	Sep. 27'76
0.08...	Oct. 11	Nov. 24	Dec. 1	Dec. 27'76
0.12...	Jan. 31	Feb. 23	Mar. 1	Mar. 29'77

[3]COMMON SHARE EARNINGS ($)

Quarter:	1976	1975	1974	1973	1972
March	0.41	0.32	0.23	0.16	0.10
June........	0.44	0.38	0.27	0.19	0.12
Sept........	0.52	0.38	0.30	0.22	0.16
Dec.		0.40	0.29	0.19	[4]0.16

[1]Listed N.Y.S.E.; also listed American & Pacific S.Es. & traded Philadelphia S.E. [2]Indicated rate. [3]Based on com. shs. & com. sh. equivalents (stk. options); adj. for 5-for-4 split paid in Jan. 1974. [4]Incl. M & F Packing for 12 mos. *Based on latest 12 mos. earns.

Source: *Standard N.Y.S.E. Reports*, Vol. 44, No. 27 (New York: Standard & Poor's Corporation, February 8, 1977).

FIGURE 8-2 (cont.)

1977M

SAMBO'S RESTAURANTS, INC.

[1]INCOME STATISTICS (Million $) AND PER SHARE ($) DATA

Year Ended Dec. 31	Total Revs.	% Total Inc. of Revs.	Total Inc.	Depr.	Net Bef. Taxes	Net Inc.	—[2]Common Share ($) Data— Earns.	Divs. Decl.	Price Range	Price-Earns. Ratios HI LO
1977--	-----	---	----	---	----	----	---	0.12	---------	-----
1976--	-----	---	----	---	----	----	---	0.32	19⅜-12¾	-----
1975--	138.94	26.0	36.10	4.75	30.68	17.64	1.48	0.15	20¼- 7¼	14- 5
1974--	100.87	27.0	27.27	3.41	23.54	12.85	1.09	0.10	19 - 6⅝	17- 6
1973--	68.03	27.2	18.49	2.23	16.00	8.91	0.76	0.08	24¼-11¼	32-15
1972--	40.81	31.0	12.64	1.41	10.90	6.00	0.54	0.053	23 -13⅞	43-26
1971--	11.88	71.3	8.46	0.82	7.18	3.68	0.35	0.024	14½- 3¾	41-11
1970--	8.09	70.9	5.74	0.58	4.82	2.42	0.23	0.022	5¼- 2⅝	23-11
1969--	5.92	71.8	4.25	0.41	3.65	1.79	0.17	Nil	5⅛- 3¼	30-19
1968--	3.31	65.6	2.17	0.25	1.76	0.90	0.12	---	---------	-----
1967--	2.27	66.1	1.50	0.15	1.21	0.69	0.09	---	---------	-----
1966--	1.91	71.8	1.37	0.07	1.25	0.75	0.10	---	---------	-----

[1]PERTINENT BALANCE SHEET STATISTICS (Million $)

Dec. 31	Gross Prop.	Capital Expend.	Cash Items	Inven-tories	Receiv-ables	——Current—— Assets	Liabs.	Net Workg. Cap.	Cur. Ratio	[3]Long Term Debt	Share-hldrs. Equity	[2]($) Book Val. Com. Sh.
1975--	78.44	42.51	14.28	6.74	7.67	28.97	15.06	13.91	1.9-1	10.15	83.40	6.49
1974--	57.80	23.37	6.44	3.84	10.63	21.07	14.46	6.61	1.5-1	4.89	51.81	4.38
1973--	37.15	13.30	11.26	2.46	5.89	19.81	10.31	9.50	1.9-1	2.95	39.80	3.38
1972--	24.42	10.35	12.27	1.90	3.84	18.28	7.22	11.06	2.5-1	2.87	30.54	2.65
1971--	13.97	4.74	5.62	Nil	2.10	8.01	5.88	2.12	1.4-1	4.56	11.08	1.06
1970--	11.38	5.66	2.28	Nil	1.08	3.53	2.78	0.76	1.3-1	5.03	7.41	0.71
1969--	7.31	3.42	1.17	Nil	1.27	2.54	2.39	0.15	1.1-1	3.05	5.22	0.50
1968--	4.28	----	1.07	Nil	0.94	2.07	1.41	0.66	1.5-1	2.04	3.15	0.41

[1]Data for 1973 & thereafter as originally reported; data for each yr. prior to 1973 as taken from subsequent yr.'s Annual Report; incl. M & F Packing aft. 1971. [2]Adj. for splits of 5-for-4 decl. in 1973, 3-for-2 decl. in 1972, 3-for-2 decl. each in Nov. & July 1971, 10% stk. div. decl. in 1970, 5-for-4 split decl. in Dec. 1969 & 350-for-1 split in Mar. 1969. [3]Incl. lease deposits.

Fundamental Position

Sambo's Restaurants is primarily engaged in developing, operating and managing a chain of coffee shops. As of December 31, 1976 there were 713 units in operation in 40 states, with the heaviest concentration in California. Other important states are Florida, Texas and Washington.

In 1975 food and restaurant supply sales accounted for about 61% of revenues (53% to affiliates and 8% to others), company's share of restaurant earnings 11%, lease and rental income 11%, fees for management, supervision and purchasing services 8%, sale of interests in restaurants 5%, insurance premiums written and earned 3%, and other income 1%.

The restaurants are designed to provide moderately priced dining in a family atmosphere and most are open 24 hours a day. Each unit operates with a standard menu and ranges from 100 to 250 seats, with the buildings averaging 4,000 square feet. The average capital expenditure for a typical 130-seat unit is some $450,000, of which about $130,000 is for equipment, furnishings, signs and landscaping. Unit volume averaged $498,000 in 1975, up from $463,000 in 1974.

The company usually retains a 50% to 60% interest in each restaurant (which is operated as a joint venture) and sells the remaining interest at a cash price of $5,000 for each 5% interest to the manager of the restaurant and other key corporate personnel. The manager of a particular unit purchases a 10% to 20% interest and the remaining interest is normally purchased by one or more joint venture groups organized by the company for the sole purpose of purchasing these remaining interests. Each group consists of cash investors who are exclusively restaurant managers, district supervisors, officers, or other key company employees.

The company by written agreements with each restaurant joint venture provides management control and administrative services (i.e. advertising, supervisory, and accounting) for which it receives a fee. It also arranges for property, casualty and health insurance, of which a portion is reinsured through a wholly-owned subsidiary.

Most of the food and related products are provided by the company to all restaurants from central meat processing, food handling and warehousing facilities in California and Kentucky operated by M&F Packing Co. (wholly-owned).

Cash dividends, initiated in 1970, averaged 10% of earnings in the five years through 1975.

Employees: 29,200. Shareholders: 13,222.

Finances

Rent expense for 1975 totaled $16,640,000; sub-rentals received were $18,984,000. At 1975 year-end, minimum annual rentals for the five years through 1980 approximated $16,029,600.

In November, 1975 the company marketed 1,250,000 common shares (250,000 sold by stockholders) at $17 per share.

CAPITALIZATION

LONG TERM DEBT: $10,948,449.
COMMON STOCK: 12,841,518 shs. (no par); some 16% owned by officers and directors.
OPTIONS: To purchase 243,261 shares at $16.50 to $18.06 each.

Incorporated in Calif. in 1961. **Office**—3760 State St., Santa Barbara, Calif. 93105. **Tel**—(805) 687-6777. **Pres**—S. D. Battistone. **VP-Secy**—G. D. McKaig. **VP-Treas**—O. G. Johnston. **Dirs**—S. Battistone, Sr. (Co-Chrmn), F. N. Bohnett (Co-Chrmn), D. V. Angeloff, S. D. Battistone, W. Becker, G. A. Cavalletto, R. L. Hild, R. Jallow, O. G. Johnston, W. L. Wagner, Sr. **Transfer Agents and Registrars**—Bradford Trust Co., NYC; United California Bank, Los Angeles.

relative responsiveness of the stock's price to the market, to be examined in Chapter 18), and provides an insider index (which measures insiders' decisions to buy the stock relative to their decisions to sell), historical growth rates, and *Value Line* ratings on performance, income, and safety. The use and significance of these ratings are explained by *Value Line* in Figure 8-5.

In addition to these easily accessible services (most libraries subscribe to them), there is another source that all interested investors can obtain in some form from a stockbroker: Standard & Poor's *Stock Guide* and *Bond Guide.* Both these guides are published monthly and contain key skeletal information on all listed stocks and bonds and many unlisted securities. The *Stock Guide* provides a brief statement of the nature of the firm's business, selected accounting information, and selected price data on the stock. The *Bond Guide* contains many other items of interest-information on the firm's business, key bond provisions, investment-times-interest-earned ratios, the amount of debt outstanding, the S&P bond rating, and price data on the various bond issues of the firm. Figures 8-6 and 8-7 contain examples of the pages from these guides that contain data on Holiday Inns.

Certainly an investment decision should not be based on such sketchy data. Their use is primarily to act as a screening device for the investor. He may decide that the firm is so unappealing to him that it's not even worth a trip to the library for more research information. On the other hand, the security may look interesting, and worthy of some research. At the library, after consulting the sources already mentioned, the investor may decide to probe still further. To aid him, we recommend the use of the *Wall Street Journal Index,* the *Business Periodicals Index,* and the *Funk and Scott Index of Corporations and Industries.*[27]

The annual *WSJ Index* contains an alphabetical listing of firms mentioned in the *Wall Street Journal* during the year. Under the firm's name are listed key words from the title of the story, plus documentation concerning the issue, page, and column in which the story appeared. The interested investor can then go to the sources and read up on the company.

The *Business Periodicals Index* provides an alphabetical listing by key word, industry, and company of all stories carried by major business publications that are covered by the index. From it, researchers can readily locate much information on the industry, firm, and firm's products in which they are interested, for they can track down the stories and read up on almost all published data they need to know.

The *F&S Index* provides a similar but more specific kind of service. It indexes data on companies, products, and industries from over 750 publications—many of them specialized trade journals. Furthermore, this information is accessible numerically by SIC classification as well as alphabetically by company name. The SIC classification is useful because researchers will find references to all firms in that particular classification in one place. Using the alphabetical listing, they can zero in on firms of particular interest to them, regardless of the SIC classification.

[27] All three indexing services publish monthly supplements to their annual volumes.

FIGURE 8-3

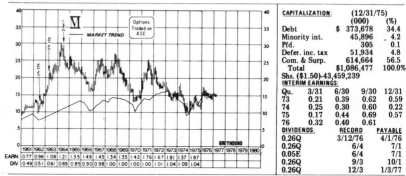

GREYHOUND CORPORATION

LISTED	SYMBOL	INDICATED DIV.	RECENT PRICE	PRICE RANGE (1976)	YIELD
NYSE	G	$1.09	15	18 - 13	7.3%

MEDIUM GRADE. REVENUES REFLECT EXPANSION INTO FOOD AND LEASING. ACQUISITION OF ARMOUR ADDS A CYCLICAL FACTOR.

CAPITALIZATION: (12/31/75)

	(000)	(%)
Debt	$ 373,678	34.4
Minority int.	45,896	4.2
Pfd.	305	0.1
Defer. inc. tax	51,934	4.8
Com. & Surp.	614,664	56.5
Total	$1,086,477	100.0%

Shs. ($1.50)-43,459,239

INTERIM EARNINGS:

Qu.	3/31	6/30	9/30	12/31
73	0.21	0.39	0.62	0.59
74	0.25	0.30	0.60	0.22
75	0.17	0.44	0.69	0.57
76	0.32	0.40	0.61	

DIVIDENDS:

	RECORD	PAYABLE
0.26Q	3/12/76	4/1/76
0.26Q	6/4	7/1
0.05E	6/4	7/1
0.26Q	9/3	10/1
0.26Q	12/3	1/3/77

	1961	1962	1963	1964	1965	1966	1967	1968	1969	1970	1971	1972	1973	1974	1975
EARN.	0.77	0.96	1.08	1.21	1.35	1.49	1.43	1.34	1.35	1.42	1.76	1.67	1.81	1.37	1.87
DIV.	0.49	0.51	0.61	0.69	0.85	0.90	0.98	1.00	1.00	1.00	1.00	1.01	1.04	1.09	1.04

BACKGROUND:

Greyhound became a holding company at the start of 1964 to facilitate diversification and now has more than 100 subsidiaries in transportation, food, finance, food service, consumer products and pharmaceutical. In recent years, about 20% of Greyhound's sales dollars and 50% of income came from transportation activities. Operations of Armour and Co. include manufacture and distribution of meat and poultry products and consumer goods such as grocery and household products. All food service firms are coordinated by Greyhound Food Management. Company's subsidiaries include Greyhound Leasing and Financial Corp., 74% owned, Greyhound Computer Corp., General Fire and Casualty Co. and Traveler's Express Co.

RECENT DEVELOPMENTS:

Net income in the third quarter of 1976 fell 11% to $26.4 million as revenues slipped 5% to $951.9 million. The drop in revenues was primarily caused by lower prices of meat and meat products sold by the Company's Armour Food subsidiary. During the quarter, however, all product groups were profitable. Greyhound bus operations continued to turn in below average performance, partly as a result of inadequate fare increases. Consumer products and pharmaceutical operations both posted improved earnings in the quarter.

PROSPECTS:

Continued recovery is anticipated for the Company's consumer products and pharmaceutical products groups. Competitive fares, relative to other modes of transportation, and increased consumer travel should encourage greater use of Greyhound's bus services. Recent and proposed fare increase should help this operation achieve a better level of profitability. Moreover, many problems that occurred in recent years have been partially resolved. A lower level of interest rates should continue to benefit the Company's financial and computer leasing operations.

STATISTICS:

YEAR	GROSS REVS. ($ MILL.)	OPER. PROFIT MARGIN %	NET INCOME ($ 000)	WORK CAP. ($ MILL.)	SENIOR CAPITAL ($ MILL.)	SHARES (000)	EARN. PER SH. $	DIV. PER SH. $	DIV. PAY. %	PRICE RANGE	P/E RATIO	AVG. YIELD %
67	574.1	11.9	45,449	22.7	83.3	31,450	1.43	0.98	69	$25\frac{7}{8}$ - $16\frac{2}{8}$	14.7	4.7
68	613.6	11.5	43,233	36.7	112.8	31,989	1.34	1.00	75	$26\frac{1}{4}$ - 19	17.4	4.3
69	682.8	11.1	43,929	17.8	239.2	32,310	1.35	1.00	74	$25\frac{1}{4}$ - 16	15.4	4.8
g70	2,753.2	3.8	55,460	202.8	399.7	39,066	1.42	1.00	70	$18\frac{7}{4}$ - $13\frac{1}{4}$	11.1	6.3
71	2,506.6	4.0	70,542	99.8	309.9	40,250	1.76	1.00	57	$25\frac{7}{8}$ - $15\frac{1}{8}$	11.9	4.8
72	2,912.4	4.1	h70,104	186.3	300.5	42,166	h1.67	1.01	60	$23\frac{7}{8}$ - $16\frac{1}{8}$	12.0	5.0
73	3,421.4	4.3	76,408	154.0	278.9	42,153	1.81	1.04	58	$18\frac{5}{8}$ - $13\frac{7}{8}$	8.9	6.5
74	3,469.3	3.9	57,955	211.1	356.4	42,203	1.37	1.09	80	$18\frac{5}{8}$ - $9\frac{6}{8}$	10.4	7.7
75	3,748.2	9.9	81,220	220.8	374.0	43,459	1.87	1.04	56	$15\frac{3}{8}$ - $10\frac{4}{8}$	6.9	8.1
76								1.09		$17\frac{5}{8}$ - 13		7.1

a-Incl. securities convertible into common. g-Incl. Armour & Co. h-Excl. special items $3.3 mill. (8c a sh.) loss.

INCORPORATED: Sept. 20, 1926—Del.	**TRANSFER AGENT:** Morgan Guaranty Trust Co., N.Y. Continental Ill. Natl. Bk & Tr., Chic. Crocker National Bank San Francisco, Calif.	**OFFICERS**
PRINCIPAL OFFICE: Greyhound Tower Phoenix, Arizona, 85077		G.H. Trautman, Chmn. R.F. Shaffer, Pres.
ANNUAL MEETING: Second Tuesday in May	**REGISTRAR:** Citibank, N.Y.	G.T. Christie, Secy. F.E. Lake, Treas.
NUMBER OF STOCKHOLDERS: 166,287	**INSTIT. HOLDINGS:** NO.: 81 SHS.: 2,349,548	

Source: *Moody's Handbook of Common Stocks,* April 1977 Edition
(New York: Moody's Investor Service, Inc., 1977).

FIGURE 8-4

Source: "Holiday Inns," *Value Line Investment Surveys*, July 22, 1977
(New York: Arnold Bernhard & Co., 1977).

FIGURE 8-5

HOW TO SELECT STOCKS FOR YOUR PORTFOLIO

To select a suitable common stock by the Value Line Method, proceed as follows:

FIRST: Decide on the degree of risk you are willing to assume All stocks involve risk But some are safer, that is to ˏsay, less risky, than others.

Risk is measured by the characteristic volatility of the stock's price around its own long term trend The narrower the band of fluctuation around trend, the safer the stock, the wider the band, the less safe, or the riskier

Stocks ranked 1 (highest) for Safety are relatively the least volatile

Stocks ranked 2 (above average) are less safe than the 1's but safer than stocks ranked 3 (average), 4 (below average) or 5 (lowest)

Stocks ranked 5 (lowest) are the riskiest, or least safe

Stocks ranked 4 are riskier than average but not so risky as those ranked 5 (lowest)

Those ranked 3 are of average safety (i e , risk)

SECOND: Pick out from among the stocks with acceptable Safety Ranks those whose current dividend yields appear attractive to you You can select by referring to the weekly Summary Index of this Service where all 1550 stocks monitored by Value Line are listed in alphabetical order together with their recent prices, dividend yields, Safety Ranks and Performance Ranks On the first page of the Summary Index you will find the average yield of all dividend-paying stocks It will serve as a reference point

Dividend yield may be desirable for some persons, not for others Where there is a division of interest, as in a trust which may distribute only the dividend income to beneficiaries, reserving capital growth for the remaindermen, dividends obviously are important Furthermore, many conservative investors shrink as a matter of habit from "invading principal", including appreciation of principal For them, dividend income is the only true income On the other hand, to the investor in a high tax bracket, as well as the investor who looks to "total return" (which is the sum of dividend payments and capital appreciation) dividend yield may appear to be the less important portion of return High dividend yields generally signal low appreciation potential because they indicate that the market foresees relatively little further dividend growth in the future For the vast majority of stocks over a long period of years, capital appreciation has far outweighed the dividend as a factor in total return

THIRD: Having picked a list acceptable in terms of safety and current yield, cull out from that list the stocks ranked 1 (highest) and 2 (above average) for Performance in the next 12 months Select one of these and hold it until its rank falls to 3 (average) or lower (4 or 5) Then sell and replace it with another stock ranked 1 or 2 culled from a list that then also offers an acceptable Safety Rank and yield The policy of selling as soon as a stock falls to a Performance rank of 3 or lower may be too rigidly aggressive for all accounts Capital gains tax liability and brokerage expense should be taken into account; and where stocks sell extremely low in relation to their 3 to 5 year appreciation potentiality, performance within the next 12 months might reasonably be assigned a lesser weight in the judgment of some investors Still the general rule is worth observing when buying, concentrate on stocks ranked 1 or 2 for Performance in the next 12 months; when selling take aim at stocks ranked 4 or 5 for Performance When a stock falls to a rank 3 (average) for Performance in the next 12 months, bear in mind that in the coming year it will probably perform no better, but no worse either, than the average of all 1550 stocks

---

Source: "How to Select Stocks for Your Portfolio," *Value Line Investment Surveys,* Vol. 29, No. 19, February 15, 1974 (New York: Arnold Bernhard & Co., 1974).

FIGURE 8-6
STANDARD & POOR'S *STOCK GUIDE*

108 Hol-Hou **STANDARD & POOR'S CORPORATION**

INDEX	Ticker Symbol	STOCKS NAME OF ISSUE (Call Price of Pfd. Stocks)	Market	Earns & Div Ranking	Par Val.	Inst. Hold Cos	Inst. Hold Shs. (000)	PRINCIPAL BUSINESS	PRICE RANGE 1960-74 High	1960-74 Low	1975 High	1975 Low	1976 High	1976 Low	Sep. Sales in 100s	September, 1976 Last Sale Or Bid High	Low	Last	% Div. Yield	P-E Ratio
1	HIA	**Holiday Inns**	NYS,Bo,Ci,MW,Ph,PS	A—	1½	79	2288	Own some Inns,most licensed	55⅝	1⅜	16½	5⅛	20	11⅝	8027	13⅜	11¾	12	3.3	9
2	A	**[51]Stk Div Cv Spl Stk A ([52]105)vtg**	NYS	. . .	1⅛	1	1	bus transp,steamship	82½	9¾	26	11⅜	30	21	26	23⅞	22½	22¼B	s. . .	. .
3	HOL.A	**Hollinger Mines Cv'A'**	ASE,MS,TS	B+	5	18	1263	Iron ore in Canada: invests	50½	18¼	30	22	39¼	27½	2	38	37	31B	♦5.8	12
4	HOC	**Holly Corp**	ASE	B	50¢	. . .	. . .	Oil refinery & pipelines	8½	⅝	3⅜	1⅛	3¼	2	358	2⅞	2½	2⅝	. . .	4
5	HLY	**Holly Sugar**	NYS	B	5	2	14	Large US beet sugar prod'r	39⅜	10⅝	33¾	22½	46¾	32⅜	941	39½	35⅜	35¾	†12.3	3
6	HMA	**Hollymatic Corp**	MW	B	No	. . .	. . .	Food portion'g: mixer-grind'r	31⅝	3¾	5½	3⅛	4¾	2½	130	3	2½	2⅞	. . .	6
7	HLS	**Holly's, Inc**	MW	B+	2	1	3	Restaurants, motor inns	12	2⅞	6¾	2¾	4¼	2¾	20	4	3⅝	4	5.0	4
8	HTRF	**Hollywood Park**	OTC	B+	1	. . .	. . .	Horse racing track	46⅝	9⅜	15	11½	16	12	78	13¾	13¼	13¼B	7.5	13
9	HOLO	**Holobeam, Inc**	OTC	NR	10¢	1	12	Electro-optical eq: laser:lamp	35½	1⅛	2¾	1	2½	⅞	305	1⅞	1½	1⅝B	. . .	d
10	HOM	**Homasote Co**	Ph,Bo	B	20¢	. . .	. . .	Fiberboard:dist bldg supplies	12⅞	⅞	7	4⅛	7½	5	2	6½	6½	6½	e4.9	6
11	HBENB	**Home Beneficial Cl B[55]**	OTC	. . .	2½	4	90	Hldg:life,accident,health	49	12½	22¾	14¾	26¼	17¼	47	25¼	25	25B	4.6	5
12	HG.A	**Home Oil,Cl'A'[56]**	ASE,Bo,PS,MS,TS,VS	B+	No	47	916	Crude oil & natural gas	84½	6¾	30	16¾	34¾	26⅜	56	28½	26¾	26¾B	♦1.9	8
13	HG.B	**Class B**	ASE,Bo,PS,MS,TS,VS	BBB	No	12	268	Canada: pipeline systems	81	6⅜	26¼	18½	30½	22½	7	25	23⅝	22B	♦2.3	7
14	HM	**Homestake Mining**	NYS,Bo,MW,Ph,PS,Sp	B+	1	35	338	Lgst US gold prod'r:lead/zinc	69⅝	8	55½	31½	44⅛	24⅞	6011	33⅜	26	31¾	e3.1	14
15	HWOD	**Homewood Corp**	OTC	NR	25¢	. . .	. . .	Land development & constr'n	28	3	7	3	7½	4	44	5¾	5½	5¾B	. . .	7
16	HONI	**HON Indus**	OTC	A—	1	4	155	Metal office furn: mtl hdl eq	19½	2$\frac{5}{16}$	13	7¾	17¾	11¾	277	17½	16¼	17¼B	†3.5	9
17	HONDY	**Honda Motor[57]**	OTC	. . .	j50	2	3523	Motorcycles,autos,trucks	64⅜	5½	45¼	29½	53	44	107	47¾	44	45½B	1.1	46
18	HON	**Honeywell, Inc**	NYS,Bo,Ci,MW,Ph,PS	A—	1½	160	2349	Computer/ind'l control sys	170¾	17½	40½	20⅞	56⅛	32¾	9367	48¼	44⅛	45⅞	3.5	11
19	HOOK	**Hook Drugs**	OTC	B+	No	10	179	Drug stores,food sv,Indiana	27½	⅞	16½	10¾	17	10½	210	11¾	11	11¾B	6.8	10
20	HBB	**Hoover Ball/Bearing**	NYS	B+	1	2	6	Bearing, auto hdwre, spring	31½	5¼	15¾	8½	24½	14	518	23⅛	21⅝	21⅝	4.6	7
21	HOOV	**Hoover Co**	OTC	A—	2½	16	1459	Vacuum cleaner: appliances	41½	1¾	15	8⅞	14⅝	10¾	1512	13⅛	12	12⅜B	6.1	16
22	HZN	**Horizon Corp**	NYS,Bo,Ph	NR	1¢	1	100	Land develop: Ariz, NM, Tex	44¼	1	4½	1¼	3¾	1⅜	1267	1⅞	1⅜	1⅜	. . .	d
23	HRES	**Horizons Research**	OTC	NR	No	. . .	. . .	Research & devel: film mfr	34	2½	6½	¾	1¾	¾	42	1	¾	1B	. . .	d
24	HRL	**Hormel (Geo A)& Co**	ASE	B+	1⅞	1	70	Meat packing: canned food	30	6¼	17⅞	15⅜	20	16¾	109	19¾	19¼	19½	5.1	8
25	HOR	**Horn & Hardart Co(NY)**	ASE,Ph	C	1	1	.1	Restaurants: gift mail order	53	2⅝	8½	3¼	8⅜	4⅛	257	7⅜	6½	6½B	. . .	30
26	HAF	**Hospital Affil Int'l**	NYS	B+	40¢	6	271	Owns hospitals: medical svs	28⅜	4⅜	17⅜	7¼	14¾	11⅜	775	14¾	12⅜	14¼	s1.7	7
27	HSP	**Hospital Corp Amer**	NYS,Bo,MW	B+	1	64	2898	Owns, operates hospitals	45½	5⅝	26¾	8⅝	28½	20¼	3504	25⅞	22¾	25⅝	1.2	9
28	HMG	**Hospital Mtge Gr**	ASE	. . .	1	2	4	Real estate investment trust	24¾	2⅛	7	3⅜	8¼	5¼	119	6⅝	5⅝	5⅞	10.2	23
29	WS	**Wrrt (Purch 1 SBI at $25)**	ASE	. . .	. . .	. . .	. . .	medical facilities	3¾	⅛	½	⅛	⅜	⅛	192	⅛	⅛	⅛	. . .	. .
30	HTCO	**Hospital Trust**	OTC	. . .	1	3	35	Bank hldg,Rhode Island	47½	16	24	17¼	25	18½	47	24	23	23½B	8.2	8
31	HMN	**Hospitality Motor Inns**	ASE	NR	No	8	245	Motor inns & food services	41½	3½	11⅛	3¾	11⅜	6¾	959	9¼	6¾	8⅝	. . .	39
32	HII	**Host Int'l**	NYS,PS	B+	2½	21	1459	Restaurants & gift shops	48	2⅜	13⅞	5⅞	16	9½	1081	10⅛	9½	9½	4.2	6
33	HOT	**Hotel Investors SBI**	ASE	. . .	1	1	10	Real estate investment trust	28¼	5½	12¼	7⅛	14	11¼	185	13½	12⅜	13¼	10.6	9
34	HH	**Houdaille Indus**	NYS,MW,Ph	B+	75¢	9	555	Constr material/contract'g	25⅞	4⅛	10¾	7¼	17¾	10¼	1736	17¾	16⅛	16⅛	†5.9	6
35	Pr	**$2.25 cm Pr Pfd (50)**	NYS,MW	BBB	50	10	27.2	auto/ind'l parts,mach tools	46	20⅛	26	22	27	23½	9	26¼	26	25¾B	8.7	. .
36	HTN	**Houghton Mifflin**	NYS,Bo	B+	1	6	189	Publ trade books, textbooks	41¼	6	15⅛	6	16⅛	11½	374	14⅜	12⅛	14⅛	5.1	6
37	HF	**House of Fabrics**	NYS,PS	B+	No	29	1286	Retails fabrics, notions, etc.	29⅞	½	12	3¾	13⅝	7⅞	2085	9	7⅞	8	3.5	6
38	HRO	**House of Ronnie**	ASE	B+	10¢	1	3	Mfr lingerie & sportswear	17⅜	1⅝	5¼	2⅛	8⅛	4¼	95	5⅛	4⅜	4½	6.7	4
39	HOV	**House of Vision**	ASE	B	1	1	45	Dispensing optician: mfr eq	24⅝	3⅛	6⅞	3⅝	7¾	4½	71	5⅛	4½	4⅝	6.9	7
40	HFC	**Household Finance**	NYS,Bo,MW,Ph	A—	1	116	4149	Consumer finance:mdsg:mfg	40	9	18½	11⅞	21⅜	15¾	14607	21⅜	19¾	20¼	5.9	6
41	Pr B	**$2.375 cm Cv Pfd([65]51.42½)vtg**	NYS,Bo	NR	No	10	46	car & truck rental/leasing	89⅝	23	42	26¾	47½	35½	100	47½	44	44½B	5.3	. .
42	Pr C	**$2.50 cm Cv Pfd ([66]52)vtg**	NYS	NR	No	30	238	variety,food,furn stores	64½	24½	34	25½	37	29¾	172	37	35	35¼	7.1	. .
43	HOU	**Houston Ltg & Pwr**	NYS,Bo,Ci,MW,Ph,PS	A	No	188	4206	Utility: south cent'l Texas	57⅜	16½	26½	18	28⅞	20¼	11600	28⅞	26	27⅞	5.6	7

Uniform Footnote Explanations—See Page 1. Other: [51]$1.70 in stk at com mkt val. [52]Cash or stk. [53]In com stk ($0.85). [54]®$0.40,'75. [55]Non-vtg. [56]Non-voting. [57]ADRs outstg equal to 20 com. [58]Approx. [59]12 Mo Feb'76,Fiscal Aug'75 $0.86. [60]®$3.54,'75. [61]Accum on Pfd. [62]△$1.31,'72. [63]®$1.51,'75. [64]®$2.20,'75. [65]To 4-1-77,scale to $50 in'79. [66]To 12-31-76,scale to $50 in'80.

Source: *Stock Guide* (New York: Standard & Poor's Corporation, Oct. 1976).

FIGURE 8-6 (cont.)

COMMON AND PREFERRED STOCKS

N D E X	Some Divs. Ea. Yr. Since	DIVIDENDS						FINANCIAL POSITION				CAPITALIZATION				E n d e d	— $ Per Shr.—EARNINGS—$ Per Shr.						Last 12 Mos.	INTERIM EARNINGS OR REMARKS $—Per Share—$			N D E X
		—Latest Payment—		Ex. Div.	So Far 1976	Paid 1975	Total Ind. Rate	Cash& Equiv.	Mil-$ Curr. Assets	Curr. Liabs.	Balance Sheet Date	Long Term Debt Mil-$	—Shs. 000— Pfd.	Com.			1972	1973	Years— 1974	1975	1976		Period	1975	1976	
		Pfe s	Date																							
1	1963	Q0.10	11-1-76	9-20	0.38%	0.34%	0.38%	n/a	183.	141.	7-2-76	279.		29497	Dc	1.37	1.49	0.89	1.37	E1.35	1.27	6 Mo Jun	0.56	0.46	1
2	1912			9-20		0.40	0.40	Conv into 1.5 shrs common																	2
3		gQ0.45	11-1-76	7-28	g1.35	1.80	Stk	51.6	5.00	5.00				688	Dc	1.49	2.40	1.45	2.73		2.59	6 Mo Jun	0.96	0.82	3
4		h.	8-31-76	5-16		g1.65	Nil	41.9	51.6	58.3	12-31-75		†4920	Dc	*0.05	*0.13	0.29	*0.44		0.63	9 Mo Jun	0.29	0.48	4
5	1941	Q0.85	9-30-76		†3.55	4.40	4.40	3.89	26.8	58.1	3-31-76	5.29		8200	Jl	1.70	3.41	19.17	13.65		13.65	9 Mo Apr			5
6	1969	Q0.05	5-28-76	5-10	0.10	0.40	Nil	0.62	12.2	4.75	9-30-75	4.36		852	Sp	1.21	1.18	0.84			0.47	9 Mo Jun	0.42	0.05	6
7	1965	Q0.25	10-15-76	9-27	0.10	0.10	0.20	1.30	1.88	1.71	10-31-75	5.07	7	447	Dc	0.93	1.19	1.35	1.03		1.04	9 Mo Jul	0.63	0.64	7
8	1945	Q0.25	9-15-76	8-26	0.75	1.00	1.00	15.5	17.4	16.1	6-30-76	2.32		1966	Mr	2.32	1.14	1.47	1.20		1.76	3 Mo Jun	1.59	1.59	8
9			None Paid			Nil	Nil	n/a	2.74	0.28	6-30-76	0.63		997	Sp	△1.86	0.01	*0.03	1.07		d0.74	3 Mo Jun	*0.47	d0.14	9
10	1940	Q0.08	9-15-76	8-25	0.22	†0.32	†0.18	2.26	4.14	0.84	12-31-75	0.15		825	Dc	0.92	1.49	0.66	0.73		0.10	6 Mo Jun	0.20	0.57	10
11	1906	Q0.29	9-10-76	8-16	0.85	1.16	1.02	Book Value $41.68			12-31-75	69.1		†3200	Dc	△3.80	△4.23	△4.17	△4.60		4.82	6 Mo Jun	△2.05	△2.27	11
12	1956	gS0.25	7-1-76	6-14	g0.50	g0.50	0.50	36.2	64.0	28.5	13-31-76			†8161	Dc	0.96	1.90	2.14	3.26		3.37	6 Mo Jun	□1.52	△1.63	12
13	1963	gS0.25	7-1-76	6-14	g0.50	g0.50	0.50							2573	Dc	0.96	1.90	2.14	2.14		3.32	6 Mo Jun	1.52	△1.63	13
14	1946	Q0.25	9-13-76	6-14	0.75	c1.00	c1.00	52.9	83.9	12.6	12-31-75	11.6		11333	Dc	*0.64	*2.00	0.95	0.65		2.03	6 Mo Jun	0.43	0.54	14
15		0.02	12-31-74	12-24		†1.25	Nil	Equity per shr $8.22			12-31-75			1216	Dc	1.95	1.60			E2.25	0.84	6 Mo Jun	0.35	1.02	15
16	1955	Q0.14	8-12-76	8-12	0.34	0.60	†0.35	7.28	9.53	3.20	7-3-76	9.44	3	3519	Dc	0.88	1.35	1.47	1.62		1.93	6 Mo Jun	0.71		16
17	1949	Q0.25	8-24-76	8-24	*0.504	0.504	0.511	343.	1102	83.9	2-29-76	382.		24350	Fb	1.82	1.86	1.93	0.99		0.99	6 Mo Jun			17
18	1928	Q0.40	9-13-76	8-23	1.10	1.60	1.40	263.	1255	676.	6-30-76	435.		†24350	Dc	*4.08	4.79	3.29	*3.89	*E4.00	4.72	6 Mo Jun	*0.64	*1.47	18
19	1935	Q0.20	10-29-76	10-8	0.80	0.80	0.80	30.3	27.5	12.7		0.96		2885	Dc	1.04	1.21	1.47	1.24		1.19	6 Mo Jun	0.56	0.51	19
20	1935	Q0.25	10-29-76	10-5	0.953	1.00	0.88	41.2	117.	55.6	7-31-76	27.7		5888	Jl	1.93	2.36	1.83	1.95	P3.04	3.04	6 Mo Jun			20
21	1943	Q0.19	9-10-76	8-12	0.55	0.76	0.74	75.8	296.	118.	12-31-75	129		13189	Dc	2.23	2.50	0.66	0.90	d1.40	0.79	6 Mo Jun	0.41	0.30	21
22			None Since Public			Nil	Nil	Equity per shr $0.78			5-31-76	2.88		4468	My	2.19	1.51	1.01	0.08		d1.40	9 Mo Jun	d0.12	*0.14	22
23	1928	Q0.01	12-18-74	11-15			0.92	0.07	1.57	0.94	5-31-76	2.88	372	1114	My	*0.11	d0.20	*0.07	d0.47		0.21	9 Mo Jul	1.94	1.66	23
24		Q0.25	11-15-76	10-18	1.00	1.00		18.4	136.	71.7	10-25-75	25.9		4803	Oc	1.63	1.54	3.62	2.78		2.50	9 Mo Jul			24
25		Q0.15	6-1-66	5-10		†Nil		n/a	87.	8.61	3-27-76	8.69	23	700	Dc	d0.52	*0.63	d2.45	Nil		0.22	6 Mo Jun	d0.42	d0.20	25
26	1976	Q0.06	10-8-76	9-21	s0.12	0.24	4% Stk	6.91	36.1	19.1	12-31-75	71.2		2452	Dc	1.02	1.18	1.38	*1.69	E2.10	1.90	6 Mo Jun	0.91	1.12	26
27	1973	Q0.08	10-29-76	9-24	0.28	0.32	0.26	19.7	99.7	69.8	6-30-76	300.		*10065	Dc	1.13	1.35	1.73	2.25	E2.70	2.56	6 Mo Jun	1.21	0.34	27
28	1972	Q0.08	10-28-76	10-8	0.60	0.60	0.55	Equity per shr $22.85			5-31-76			1178	Fb	1.67	2.08	0.94	0.56		0.25	6 Mo Aug	0.65		28
29			Terms&trad. basis should be checked in detail					Warrants expire Feb 16, 1977						1178	Fb										29
30	1909	Q0.48	8-16-76	7-27	1.44	1.92	1.92	Book Value $33.86			6-30-76	5.00		2000	Dc	△3.74	3.05	△2.01	△2.63		2.87	6 Mo Jun	△1.27	□1.51	30
31			None Since Public			Nil	Nil	2.78	6.40	4.28	12-31-75	20.6		1430	Dc	1.31	1.34	0.93	0.13		0.22	6 Mo Jun	0.07	0.02	31
32	1944	Q0.10	9-30-76	9-9	0.29	0.40	0.36	n/a	49.0	25.5	6-30-76	45.0		5463	Au	1.13	1.26	1.41	d0.09	E1.70	d0.03	6 Mo Jun	0.61	0.67	32
33	1971	Q0.35	10-1-76	9-9	1.05	1.40	1.57	Equity per shr $18.30			6-30-76	54.8	190	1545	Au	1.48	2.24	1.50	1.27		1.40	9 Mo May	1.00	1.13	33
34	1947	Q0.22½	10-1-76	9-9	0.62½	0.95	0.85	40.3	138.	37.5	6-30-76	24.4	190	8371	Dc	67.39	90.68	95.71	91.37	E2.75	2.62	12 Mo Jun	1.94	2.62	34
35	1946	Q0.56¼	10-1-76	9-9	0.56¼	2.25	2.25																		35
36	1908	Q0.18	8-25-76	8-5	0.54	0.72	0.60	20.2	64.8	20.1	12-31-75	5.07		3382	Dc	1.34	*1.74	1.64	2.05	E2.25	1.91	6 Mo Jun	0.04	d0.10	36
37	1974	Q0.07	11-26-76	10-26	0.26	0.28	0.28	1.40	49.4	8.86	7-31-76	2.95		5701	Ja	0.53	0.71	0.75	1.03	E1.25	1.13	6 Mo Jul	0.38	0.48	37
38	1973	Q0.07½	10-1-76	9-3	0.27½	0.30	0.32	0.31	13.1	8.80	6-30-75	1.52		1756	Je	0.74	0.88	0.68	0.57	P1.11	1.11	6 Mo Jun			38
39	1957	Q0.08	9-24-76	8-30	0.24	0.32	0.32	0.34	5.49	4.46	12-31-75	1.20		1305	Dc	0.71	0.54	0.60	0.79		0.63	6 Mo Jun	0.38	0.22	39
40	1917	Q0.30	10-15-76	9-24	1.12½	1.20	1.02½	Equity per shr $18.85			12-31-75	1875	4247	43229	Dc	2.42	0.96	2.41	*2.42	E3.40	3.18	6 Mo Jun	0.83	1.59	40
41	1969	Q0.59½	10-15-76	9-24	2.37½	2.37½	2.37½	Conv into 2.25 shrs common			7-31-76		2268		Dc	19.67	9.79	20.33	23.04		3.77	12 Mo Aug	2.53	3.77	41
42	1920	Q0.62½	10-15-76	9-24	2.50	2.50	2.50	Conv into 1.5 shrs common					2361		Dc	20.70	10.30	21.40	24.25	E3.80					42
43	1922	Q0.39	10-15-76	9-24	1.17	1.56	1.56	10.9	162.	274.		865	1647	26752	Dc	3.10	3.05	2.92	2.92						43

◆ Stock Splits & Divs By Line Reference Index. [19]5-for-1, '72. [20]3-for-1, '73. [21]2-for-1, '74. [22]2-for-1, '72.5-for-2, '76. [23]3-for-1, '72.
[24] Adj to 4%, '76. [25]25%, '72. [26]2-for-1, '73. [27]2-for-1, '72. [28]4-for-3, '72. [29]Adj to 5%, '73. Adj to 2%, '73. [30]2-for-1, '72; adj to 2%, '73. [31]2-for-1, '73. [32]2-for-1, '72; 5-for-2, '72. [33]3-for-2, '72.

FIGURE 8-7
STANDARD & POOR'S *BOND GUIDE*

CORPORATE BONDS

Har-Hol 63

Title-Industry Code & Co. Finances (In Italics) / Individual Issue Statistics Exchange	Ind / Interest Dates	*Chgs. 1973* / S&P Quality Rating	Eligible	*Times Earn. 1974* / Bond Form	*1975 Yr. End* / Legality C M N N N t a H J Y	*Cash &Eqv* / Redemption Provisions Refund Earliest/Other	*Current Assets* / Call Price For S.F.	*Liabs Date* / Call Price Regular	*L. Term Debt (Mil $)* / Out-st'd'g (Mil $)	*Debt % Prop* / Underwriter Firm	Year	*Interim Times Earn. Period* / Price Range 1960-74 High	1960-74 Low	*1975* / 1975 High	*1976* / 1975 Low	1976 High	1976 Low	Mo. End Price Sale(s) or Bid	Curr Yield	Yield to Mat.
Hart El 1st Ser'75 11½s '95	aO	BBB	X	R	✓- ✓✓✓	[1]108.12	[1]100	‡110.83	30.0	F2	'75	....	....	106	100	109	103	108¼	10.62	10.48
Hartford Natl Corp	*10*	*1.16*		*1.10*	*0.67 Dc*				*29.5*			*6 Mo Jun*		*1.12*	*1.07*					
•SF Deb 8½s '96	Mn15	N/R		R	- - - - -	....	[2]100	[2]104¼	20.0	E1	'71	106½	73⅞	85	73½	88⅜	77	86	9.88	10.15
Hawaiian Electric	*72a*	*2.15*		*2.06*	*2.05 Dc*	*3.56*	*36.1*	*37.8 6-76*	*233*	*46.0*		*12 Mo Jun*		*2.12*	*2.00*					
1st F 3s '77	Mn	A	X	CR	✓- ✓✓✓	....	....	:100¼	5.00	D4	'47	86⅞	67¾	92⅝	86⅝	97⅛	92⅝	97⅛	3.09	8.17
1st J 4.70s '87	Ms15	A	X	CR	✓- ✓✓✓	....	....	:102.40	7.00	D4	'57	105½	58¼	67¼	61½	73⅛	67¼	73⅛	6.43	8.66
1st K 4¾s '89	Ms15	A	X	CR	✓- ✓✓✓	....	....	:102.77	10.0	D4	'59	106	55¾	64½	58¾	70⅜	64⅜	70⅜	6.75	8.69
1st L 4.65s '91	Ao	A	X	CR	✓- ✓✓✓	....	....	:102.87	12.0	D4	'61	104¾	52⅝	61⅜	55½	67	61⅛	67	6.94	8.69
1st O 5¾s '97	Ms	A	X	CR	✓- ✓✓✓	....	....	:103¾	13.0	D4	'67	101	57⅛	66¾	60	72	65¾	72	7.99	8.70
•1st Q 9s 2000	aO	A	X	R	✓✓✓✓✓	....	....	:106.74	23.0	D4	'70	112	76	98⅛	86½	101	96⅛	s100½	8.96	8.94
•1st R 8.20s 2001	jD	A	X	R	✓✓✓✓✓	....	....	:106.79	14.0	D4	'71	106	70	87	71	90½	85	93¼	8.79	8.87
•1st S 7⅝s 2002	jD	A	X	R	✓✓✓✓✓	[3]106.06	....	:106.31	10.0	D4	'72	101	85	No Sale		85	81⅛	88⅜	8.63	8.76
•1st T 8.35s 2003	jD	A	X	R	✓✓✓✓✓	[4]106.91	....	:107.49	16.0	D4	'73	101½	83⅞	85	79⅛	91	83	94⅜	8.85	8.90
•1st U 11¼s 2004	jD	A	X	R	✓- ✓✓✓	[5]107.37	....	:110.47	35.0	D4	'74	104	100	109	102	111	106½	111¼	10.11	10.04
Hawaiian Telephone Co.	*67c*	*2.13*		*2.18*	*2.45 Dc*	*1.17*	*24.8*	*25.8 6-76*	*206*	*44.0*		*12 Mo Jun*		*2.23*	*2.69*					
1st R 5⅝s '97	Ao15	AA	X	R	✓✓- ✓✓	....	....	:103.70	16.0	K2	'67	101	56	65½	58¾	72	64½	72	7.81	8.53
1st S 6¾s '98	Ao	AA	X	R	✓✓- ✓✓	....	....	:104.14	20.0	P1	'68	102¾	65⅛	75⅝	68	82⅜	74⅜	82⅜	8.19	8.55
1st T 8¾s 2000	mS	AA	X	R	✓✓- ✓✓	....	....	:106.34	35.0	P1	'70	109⅝	79⅜	92	83½	100½	90¼	100½	8.71	8.69
1st U 8s 2001	mS	AA	X	R	✓✓- ✓✓	....	....	:107¼	20.0	d1	'71	104⅝	74¼	85⅝	77⅛	94	84	94	8.51	8.58
1st V 8½s 2006	Ao	AA	X	R	- - - ✓✓	[2]106.21	z100	‡107½	35.0	P1	'76	....	....	....	....	99	94⅜	98	8.67	8.68
Deb A 8s '94	jJ	A	X	R	- - - ✓✓	....	‡101.44	‡106.82	22.0	S1	'69	104⅛	76	86⅞	78⅞	92½	85½	92½	8.65	8.84
Heinz (H.J.) Co.	*27b*	*△3.73*		*△3.15*	*△4.23 Ap*	*162*	*762*	*319 7-76*	*142*	*42.1*		*3 Mo Jun*		*3.40*	*4.74*					
•SF Deb 7¼s '97	fA	A	X	R	- ✓- - -	[6]103.65	[7]100	105.80	50.0	M9	'72	104	77	84⅝	80	88⅝	84	89⅜	8.11	8.33
[8]***Heller (Walter E.) & Co.***	*26*	*1.20*		*1.20*	*-1.25 Dc*	*74.1*		*12-75*	★*431*											
•Sr Notes 7⅞s '80	mN	A	X	R	- - - - -	....	....	[9]100	50.0	S1	'73	100⅞	83	97	85⅞	100	96	99½	7.91	8.02
•Sr Deb 9½s '89	jD	A	X	R	- - - - -	z‡103¼	....	[9]104½	28.3	S1	'69	113	85¾	101½	91⅛	105	96½	s102⅝	9.26	9.15
•Sr Deb 7¾s '92	Ao	A	X	R	- - - - -	z[3]102.58	....	[6]103.32	40.0	S1	'72	101¾	66	81½	72	87	73⅞	86½	8.96	9.42
•Sr Deb 7¾s '93	Ao	A	X	R	- - - - -	z[4]102.58	....	[7]103.32	40.0	S1	'73	100⅛	72¼	80½	70	84	78	84⅜	9.19	9.66
•Sub Deb 9⅛s '91	Jj	BBB	X	R	- - - - -	z‡‡103.36	[6]100	[2]104.32	20.0	S1	'71	110	68	93	80¾	100½	91¼	97	9.41	9.51
•Sub Deb 10⅛s '91	jJ	BBB	X	R	- - - - -	z[2]103¼	[6]100	[10]102.89	25.0	S1	'76	....	....	....	....	105½	100	s105½	9.60	9.42
•Sub Deb 8s '93	Ao	BBB	X	R	- - - - -	z[4]102.67	[5]100	[7]103.43	20.0	S1	'73	99¼	93½	71	68	83⅝	76	s83⅛	9.62	10.12
•Sub Deb 8½s '93	mN	BBB	X	R	- - - - -	z[4]103.13	[5]100	[7]104.03	25.0	S1	'73	100	62	83⅞	76⅞	83⅜	82	85¼	9.97	10.35
•Jr Sub Nts 10½s '86	jJ	BB	Y	R	- - - - -	z[2]102.33	[6]100	NC	20.0	S1	'76	....	....	....	....	104	100	s103⅞	10.11	9.87
Hercules, Inc.	*14*	*6.58*		*4.13*	*1.85 Dc*	*53.3*	*561*	*291 6-76*	*346*	*47.0*		*6 Mo Jun*		*1.22*	*3.51*					
•Notes 8¾s '83	Ao	A	X	R	- - - - -	....	....	[2]100	100	L4	'75	....	....	103¼	99	105¼	101	104	8.41	7.95
Hershey Foods	*27h*	*3.54*		*7.85*	*.... Dc*	*N/A*	*144*	*32.1 6-76*	*29.4*	*25.3*										
•SF Deb 7¼s '97	mN	A	X	R	- - ✓- -	[6]103.62	[4]100	105.80	25.4	G2	'72	103⅜	83	87	80	No Sale		88½	8.19	8.42
[11]***Hertz Corp.***	*7*	*1.68*		*1.60*	*1.79 Dc*	*23.2*		*12-75*	★*306*	*42.2*										
•SF Deb 8⅞s 2001	Ao	A	X	R	- - - - -	[10]104.437	[6]100	‡108⅞	50.0	L4	'76	....	....	....	....	103	96½	102	8.70	8.67
Heublein Inc	*11b*	*8.29*		*6.50*	*4.60 Je*	*40.4*	*417*	*200 6-75*	*204*	*90.3*										
•Notes 8⅜s '85	Fa15	A	X	R	- - - - -	....	....	[7]100	90.0	G2	'75	....	....	100⅜	95¾	102¾	99⅞	102	8.21	8.04
Hocking Valley Ry.	*54*	*Assumed by Ches & Ohio Ry.:see*																		
•1st Con 4½s '99	jJ	AA	X	CR	✓✓✓✓✓	....	....	NC	15.8	0	'99	100	47	56	51⅞	59½	53⅝	58⅝	7.68	8.70
Holiday Inns	*33*	*2.94*		*1.93*	*2.54 Dc*	*N/A*	*183*	*141 6-76*	*279*	*42.7*										
•xw 1st Mtge 9½s '95	jD15	BBB	X	R	- - - - -	[1]105	[12]100	‡107	30.0	S6	'70	113¾	76	95	83½	101¼	94⅜	100¼	9.48	9.47

Uniform Footnote Explanations—See Page 1. Other: [1]From 1980. [2]From 1981. [3]From 1977. [4]From 1978. [5]From 1984. [6]From 1982. [7]From 1983. [8]Subsid of Heller(W.E.)Int'l. [9]From 1979. [10]From 1986. [11]Subsid.of RCA Corp. [12]From 12-15-76.

Source: *Bond Guide* (New York: Standard & Poor's Corporation, Oct. 1976).

Summary

Armed with economic and industry forecasts, the analyst is ready to look at the shares of specific companies.

Company information is generated internally and externally. The principal source of internal information about a company is its financial statements. The analyst must screen quarterly and annual reports of income, financial position, and changes in financial position, in order to assure himself that such statements are correct, complete, consistent, and comparable. The use of accounting reports can be influenced by options to treat certain transactions in different ways. Further, accounting statements taken as a whole over time can reveal critical information to the trained eye that are not seen by casual analysis of specific statements in isolation, or for only a single year.

Our examination of financial statements highlighted the income statement, statement of retained earnings, balance sheet, and statement of changes in financial position. We saw the continuing importance attached to the income statement as the most prominent source of evidence regarding management performance, particularly in reference to earnings.

Many popular and widely circulated sources of information about companies emanate from outside, or external, sources. These sources provide supplements to company-generated information by overcoming some of its bias, such as public pronouncements by its officers. External information sources also provide certain kinds of information not found in the materials made available by companies themselves.

Questions and Problems

1. What four major tests must financial statements meet to have utility for investment analysis?

2. What advantages and disadvantages would probably accompany a move toward complete uniformity in accounting, where every transaction, regardless of the firm, is handled in one way only?

3. In what ways will a company behave differently with respect to its accounting if it chooses to concentrate upon (a) maximizing earnings, or (b) minimizing taxes?

4. Prepare a table similar to the one shown on page 222, using sum-of-the-years'-digits depreciation. How do you account for any differences in the pattern of added taxes or savings? Which method would you advocate, declining-balance or SYD?

5. Distinguish between primary and secondary earnings per share. Why is such a distinction important to a common-stock investor?

6. With all the concern shown for the income statement, of what significance to an investor is the book value of assets and the amount of debt on the balance sheet?

7. Refer to the financial statements of Holiday Inns, Inc., in the Appendix to this chapter. What specific insights into company operations are offered by examining the consolidated statement of changes in financial position for the year ended December 31, 1976, that are not readily seen on the balance sheet and income statement for the same period?

8. The Rush Co. example in the text highlighted accounting for a subsidiary in which Melicher Corp. held only 40 percent of the voting stock. What changes would occur on the balance sheet of Melicher if it owned 70 percent of the stock of Rush?

9. What are some significant bits of investment information about a company that are not normally found in standard financial statements?

10. What does an "unqualified" auditor's opinion really mean?

11. In what ways, if any, will FASB *No. 14* prove useful to investors or security analysts?

APPENDIX

**Holiday
Inns, Inc.—
Financial
Review**

The following pages show financial highlights, statements, and historical statistics for Holiday Inns., Inc., and its consolidated subsidiaries. This information is provided so that the reader may note key items on the statements that were mentioned in Chapter 8. Further, these statements and statistics will serve as part of the basic data for use in subsequent chapters.

Holiday Inns, Inc. and Consolidated Subsidiaries

Statements of Consolidated Income

Fifty-Two Weeks Ended December 31, 1976
And January 2, 1976

	1976	1975
	(In Thousands, except per share amounts)	
Revenues	$965,626	$916,973
Costs and Expenses		
Operating Costs, excluding items below	819,074	774,008
Depreciation and Amortization of		
Property and Equipment	53,522	53,830
Interest, Net of Interest Capitalized		
of $78,000 and $173,000	24,930	26,892
Foreign Currency Translation Loss (Gain)	3,076	(5,867)
	900,602	848,863
Income From Continuing Operations Before Income Taxes	65,024	68,110
Provision for Income Taxes	25,359	26,663
Income From Continuing Operations	39,665	41,447
Discontinued Operations, Less Income Taxes	(400)	447
Net Income	$ 39,265	$ 41,894
Income Per Common and Common Equivalent Share		
Continuing Operations	$ 1.29	$ 1.36
Discontinued Operations	(.01)	.01
Net Income	$ 1.28	$ 1.37

The accompanying Financial Comments are an integral part of these statements.

Source: *Holiday Inns, Inc., Annual Report, 1976* (Memphis, Tennessee: Holiday Press, 1976).

FIGURE 8-8 (cont.)

Holiday Inns, Inc. and Consolidated Subsidiaries

Consolidated Statements of Changes in Financial Position

Fifty-Two Weeks Ended December 31, 1976
And January 2, 1976

	1976	1975
	(In Thousands of Dollars)	
Source of Funds		
Net Income	$ 39,265	$ 41,894
Add Expenses Not Requiring Current Outlay of Working Capital:		
Depreciation, Amortization and Allowances for		
Property Dispositions	57,814	60,061
Other	9,163	(1,523)
Working Capital Provided from Operations	106,242	100,432
Proceeds from Financing	15,312	8,391
Depreciated Cost of Property Dispositions	25,079	23,869
Total Sources	146,633	132,692
Application of Funds		
Additions to Property and Equipment	70,379	57,076
Payment of Mortgages and Notes	50,313	43,244
Payment of Dividends	11,810	10,366
Increase in Investments and Long-Term Receivables	10,410	5,431
Increase in Statutory Capital Construction Fund	2,201	9,668
Other	7,747	360
Total Applications	152,860	126,145
Increase (Decrease) in Working Capital	$ (6,227)	$ 6,547
Changes in Components Which Increased (Decreased) Working Capital:		
Cash and Temporary Cash Investments	$ 441	$ 14,712
Receivables	7,517	(16,244)
Inventories	(7,531)	(4,599)
Other Assets	2,426	5,779
Long-Term Debt Due Within One Year	(251)	(3,525)
Accounts Payable and Other Current Liabilities	(6,073)	13,535
Accrued Federal and State Income Taxes	(2,756)	(3,111)
Increase (Decrease) in Working Capital	$ (6,227)	$ 6,547

The accompanying Financial Comments are an integral part of these statements.

FIGURE 8-8 (cont.)

Holiday Inns, Inc. and Consolidated Subsidiaries
Consolidated Balance Sheets

	December 31, 1976	January 2, 1976
	(In Thousands of Dollars)	
ASSETS		
Current Assets		
Cash	$ 18,345	$ 26,033
Temporary Cash Investments, at cost	43,257	35,128
Receivables, Less Allowance for Doubtful Accounts		
of $6,031,000 and $5,045,000	88,448	80,931
Inventories	25,276	32,807
Other Current Assets	9,020	8,818
	184,346	183,717
Less Deposits to be Made to Statutory Capital		
Construction Fund	3,761	5,985
Total Current Assets	180,585	177,732
Statutory Capital Construction Fund,		
Including Above Deposits	25,010	22,809
Investments and Long-Term Receivables		
Nonconsolidated Subsidiaries and Less Than Majority		
Owned Affiliates	20,151	21,963
Notes Receivable and Other Investments	31,021	18,846
	51,172	40,809
Property and Equipment, at cost		
Land, Buildings, Improvements and Equipment	979,366	972,404
Less Accumulated Depreciation and Amortization	322,960	305,892
	656,406	666,512
Deferred Charges and Other Assets	22,626	21,826
	$935,799	$929,688

FIGURE 8-8 (cont.)

	December 31, 1976	January 2, 1976
	(In Thousands of Dollars)	
LIABILITIES AND STOCKHOLDERS' EQUITY		
Current Liabilities		
Long-Term Debt Due Within One Year	$ 24,909	$ 24,658
Notes Payable—Banks	3,771	5,138
Accounts Payable	29,387	23,572
Accrued Federal and State Income Taxes	16,606	13,850
Accrued Expenses and Other Taxes	44,630	44,885
Other Current Liabilities	18,045	16,165
Total Current Liabilities	137,348	128,268
Long-Term Debt Due After One Year	264,945	296,160
Deferred Credits	15,404	18,468
Deferred Income Taxes	46,453	42,742

Commitments and Contingencies—See Pages 29, 30 and 31.

Stockholders' Equity		
Capital Stock		
Special Stock: authorized 5,000,000 shares;		
Series A; $1.125 par value; issued 760,358		
and 760,509 shares; convertible into common	855	855
Common: authorized 60,000,000 shares;		
$1.50 par value; issued 29,883,825 and 29,878,599 shares	44,826	44,818
Capital Surplus	114,759	114,350
Retained Earnings	319,199	292,914
	479,639	452,937
Capital Stock in Treasury, at cost	(6,331)	(6,712)
Unissued Deferred Compensation Shares	(1,659)	(2,175)
	471,649	444,050
	$935,799	$929,688

The accompanying Financial Comments are an integral part of these statements.

FIGURE 8-8 (cont.)

Holiday Inns, Inc. and Consolidated Subsidiaries

Statements of Stockholders' Equity

| | Capital Stock | | | | | |
	Special Series A $1.125 Par Value	Common $1.50 Par Value	Capital Surplus	Retained Earnings	Treasury Stock	Unissued Deferred Compensation Shares
			(In Thousands of Dollars)			
Balance—January 3, 1975	$ 856	$ 44,816	$114,338	$262,562	$ (6,252)	$ (2,672)
Net Income	—	—	—	41,894	—	—
Dividend on Special Stock—Series A; 124,377 Shares of Common from Treasury	—	—	(10)	(1,147)	1,157	—
Treasury Stock Acquired	—	—	—	—	(1,283)	—
Cash Dividends Declared On:						
Preferred Stock	—	—	—	(46)	—	—
Common Stock, $.35 Per Share	—	—	—	(10,320)	—	—
Other	(1)	2	22	(29)	(334)	497
Balance—January 2, 1976	$ 855	$ 44,818	$114,350	$292,914	$ (6,712)	$ (2,175)
Net Income	—	—	—	39,265	—	—
Dividend on Special Stock—Series A; 78,612 Shares of Common from Treasury	—	—	383	(1,170)	781	—
Cash Dividends Declared On Common Stock, $.40 Per Share	—	—	—	(11,810)	—	—
Other	—	8	26	—	(400)	516
Balance—December 31, 1976	$ 855	$ 44,826	$114,759	$319,199	$ (6,331)	$ (1,659)

The accompanying Financial Comments are an integral part of these statements.

FIGURE 8-8 (cont.)

Financial Comments

Basis of Consolidation

The consolidated financial statements include the accounts of the Company and its subsidiaries. The accounts of insurance and finance subsidiaries are recorded at equity, as are investments in 20%-50% owned companies.

International Operations

Assets and liabilities of all non-U.S. entities, except for property and equipment and related depreciation and amortization accounts, are translated into U.S. dollars at the rates of exchange in effect at year-end (current rate). Property and equipment, depreciation and amortization accounts are translated at rates of exchange in effect at acquisition dates (historical rate). Income and expense items, except depreciation and amortization, are translated at average rates prevailing during the year.

The consolidated financial statements include the following amounts applicable to operations outside the United States:

	1976	1975
	(In Thousands of Dollars)	
Consolidated Assets	$108,320	$105,030
Consolidated Equity	61,548	37,206
Revenues	72,695	74,144
Pre-Tax Loss (Excluding Translation Loss or Gain)	7,175	6,047

Amortization of Deferred Charges and Deferred Credits

Unamortized deferred charges of $9,263,000 at December 31, 1976, and $9,819,000 at January 2, 1976, include the net cost of purchased companies not allocable to specific assets (amortized over five to forty years); costs incurred in preparing inns for opening (amortized over one to five years); and costs incurred in obtaining long-term financing (amortized over the life of the related loans).

Delta Steamship Lines, Inc., a consolidated subsidiary, was purchased at less than book value. The excess of book value at acquisition over the purchase price is being amortized through 1982 by annual credits to income of $1,228,000.

Income per Share

Income per share of common stock is computed using the weighted average number of shares outstanding during each year, adjusted for common stock equivalents. The principal common stock equivalent is the Special Stock—Series A, which is convertible into one and one-half shares of common stock. The average number of common and common equivalent shares outstanding for 1976 and 1975 was 30,657,000 and 30,606,000, respectively.

Inventories

Inventories are stated at the lower of average cost or market and include material, labor and overhead, where applicable.

FIGURE 8-8 (cont.)

Agreement Under Merchant Marine Act

Delta Steamship Lines, Inc. (Delta) operates under an operating differential subsidy agreement in which the United States Government compensates Delta for portions of certain vessel operating expenses that are in excess of those incurred by its foreign competitors. Subsidies for 1972 through 1976 have been accrued on the basis of estimated rates. Management is of the opinion that the amounts of subsidies, when finally determined, will at least equal the amounts accrued.

Under terms of an agreement with the U.S. Government, which expires December 31, 1995, Delta is required to make deposits of certain fixed amounts to a statutory Capital Construction Fund for the replacement of vessels, acquisition of related equipment and retirement of present vessel debt. Delta is also required to maintain a conservative dividend policy.

Discontinued Operations

In 1975, the Company adopted a plan to divest all manufacturing operations, including food processing. At December 31, 1976, the divestiture of these operations was substantially completed. Operating results of these discontinued businesses prior to the date of adoption of the plan of disposition, and the ultimate losses upon disposal, are classified as discontinued operations in the statements of consolidated income and summary of operations.

Income Taxes

The provision for income taxes for continuing operations is composed of:

	1976	1975
	(In Thousands of Dollars)	
Federal		
Current	$ 15,782	$ 19,759
Deferred, resulting from—		
Accelerated depreciation	4,131	3,798
Litigation payment	—	2,250
Provision for possible loss on disposition of properties	(1,359)	(2,078)
Other timing differences (net)	2,487	266
State and Foreign Taxes	4,318	2,668
	$ 25,359	$ 26,663

The difference between the statutory Federal income tax rate of 48% of income from continuing operations and the actual tax expense is as follows:

	1976		1975	
	Amount	% of Pre-Tax Income	Amount	% of Pre-Tax Income
	(In Thousands of Dollars)			
Computed expected tax expense	$31,212	48.0	$32,693	48.0
Increases (decreases) in tax resulting from:				
Investment tax credit available	(2,228)	(3.4)	(2,942)	(4.3)
Earnings of Delta deposited in Capital Construction Fund	(5,068)	(7.8)	(4,786)	(7.0)
State and Foreign Taxes (Net of Federal tax benefit)	2,245	3.4	1,387	2.0
Other (net)	(802)	(1.2)	311	.4
Actual Tax Expense	$25,359	39.0	$26,663	39.1

Earnings deposited in the Capital Construction Fund of Delta are not subject to Federal income tax unless withdrawn for general Corporate purposes. Accordingly, at December 31, 1976, no provision for taxes has been made for approximately $24,970,000 deposited in the Fund. Withdrawals of deposits for the purposes for which the Fund was established reduce the depreciable tax basis of vessels for Federal income tax purposes. The reduced tax basis decreases allowable depreciation, but the effect of the reduction is offset by deposits to the Fund. At December 31, 1976, the book basis of vessels exceeded the tax basis by $32,688,000.

FIGURE 8-8 (cont.)

Long-Term Debt

Long-term debt is represented by:

	1976	1975
	(In Thousands of Dollars)	
Construction Loans and Land Purchase Contracts (5½%-8%), Maturities to 1990 Upon Conversion to Mortgage Debt	$ 2,359	$ 2,735
Mortgages (5%-10%), Including $13,817,000 and $26,282,000 payable in foreign currencies (principally German Marks), Maturities to 2006	189,425	201,519
United States Government Insured Merchant Marine Bonds (5½%-7¾%), Sinking Fund Payments of $2,622,000 From Statutory Capital Construction Fund Due Annually to 1986, with reduced deposits thereafter to 1998; Secured by First Preferred Ship Mortgage	46,521	49,067
Sinking Fund Notes (7%-7½%), Maturities to 1983	6,400	7,600
Notes Payable—Secured (6%-8¼%), Maturities to 1982	434	2,112
Notes Payable—Unsecured (5%-8¾%), Including $5,421,000 and $13,872,000 payable in foreign currencies (principally German Marks), Maturities to 1989	11,155	18,451
Debentures (5%-10%), Including $18,360,000 and $22,368,000 payable in Dutch Guilders, Maturities to 1985	29,020	33,278
Equipment Obligations (5%-11¼%), Maturities to 1985	4,540	6,056
	289,854	320,818
Less Long-Term Debt Due Within One Year	24,909	24,658
	$264,945	$296,160

Annual principal requirements for the four years subsequent to 1977 are as follows:

Year	Amount
1978	$25,604,000
1979	24,759,000
1980	18,791,000
1981	16,469,000

Certain loan agreements restrict the payment of cash dividends on common stock. Under the most restrictive agreement approximately $268,000,000 of retained earnings are available for cash dividends at December 31, 1976.

The weighted average interest rate applicable to short-term borrowings at the end of 1976 and 1975 was 10.6% and 7.8%, respectively. The average short-term borrowings outstanding and the effective interest rates during 1976 and 1975 were $4,272,000 at 12.2% and $8,160,000 at 9.9%. The highest amount outstanding at any period-end was $5,512,000 in 1976 and $15,149,000 in 1975.

As of December 31, 1976, unused lines of credit totaled $68,311,000. No material compensating balance arrangements or other restrictions exist with regard to these lines of credit. Generally, these credit lines are available to the Company at the prime interest rate. Extension has generally been provided for on an annual basis.

Leases

The Company has entered into leases for both real estate and equipment, some of which provide for contingent rentals in excess of a specified minimum based on percentages of revenue. The average remaining term for these leases extends approximately 15 years. Leases generally contain favorable renewal options. No material restrictions or guarantees exist in the Company's lease obligations.

Total rental expense for all leases amounted to:

	1976	1975
	(In Thousands of Dollars)	
Financing		
Minimum	$ 7,483	$ 7,421
Contingent	4,353	3,398
	11,836	10,819
Non-Financing		
Minimum	10,358	7,374
Contingent	21,368	21,939
	31,726	29,313
	$ 43,562	$ 40,132

FIGURE 8-8 (cont.)

The future minimum rental commitments as of December 31, 1976, for noncancelable leases are as follows:

| | Financing Leases | | Non-Financing Leases | | |
	Real Estate	Equipment	Real Estate	Equipment	Total
			(In Thousands of Dollars)		
1977	$ 6,223	$1,196	$ 4,515	$255	$12,189
1978	6,218	1,115	4,025	110	11,468
1979	6,177	1,100	3,590	43	10,910
1980	6,006	1,071	3,188	43	10,308
1981	5,746	1,021	2,804	35	9,606
1982-86	24,028	4,008	10,881	23	38,940
1987-91	15,158	2,395	8,775	—	26,328
1992-96	6,111	250	7,865	—	14,226
Remaining Balance	20,044	—	21,380	—	41,424

The rentals to be received from existing noncancelable subleases are not material.

The present values of minimum rental commitments for noncapitalized financing leases are summarized below:

	Dec. 31, 1976	Jan. 2, 1976
	(In Thousands of Dollars)	
Real Estate	$ 47,655	$ 51,784
Equipment	7,903	8,446
	$ 55,558	$ 60,230

The weighted average interest rate based on the present value of noncapitalized financing leases is 6.9% for 1976 and 6.8% for 1975, and the range of interest rates is 5%-10% for 1976 and 1975.

If all financing leases were capitalized, rather than current payments being expensed, the impact upon net income would be less than three percent of the average net income for the most recent three years.

Property and Equipment

A major portion of the real estate and equipment is pledged to secure mortgages and other long-term debt. Property and equipment consists of the following:

| | Cost | | Estimated Useful |
	1976	1975	Life in Years
	(In Thousands of Dollars)		
Land and Land Rights	$ 54,350	$ 53,579	—
Buildings, Improvements and Other	447,109	444,668	10-50
Furniture, Fixtures and Equipment	233,230	226,213	3-15
Buses	136,563	139,527	9
Vessels	108,114	108,417	25
	979,366	972,404	
Less Accumulated Depreciation and Amortization	322,960	305,892	
	$656,406	$666,512	

Depreciation and amortization are calculated on the straight-line method.

The Company follows a policy of capitalizing interest cost incurred during construction of property and equipment and depreciating the cost over the life of the property and equipment. Manage- ment believes this policy permits a better matching of revenues and costs. Had the Company used the alternative practice of expensing construction interest when incurred, the effect on net income for both 1976 and 1975 would have been immaterial.

FIGURE 8-8 (cont.)

Capital Stock

At December 31, 1976, shares of common stock were reserved for:

Conversion of Special Stock-Series A	1,032,250
Stock Purchase Options	
Outstanding and Unexercised	477,627
Reserved for Future Grants	331,607
Stock Purchase Warrants at $24.75 per share expiring 1977 (Issued with 9½% First Mortgage Bonds)	219,585
Conversion of 8% Convertible Subordinated Guaranteed Debentures Due 1985 at $35.00 per share	295,724
Deferred Compensation Plan	5,880
	2,362,673

A small number of common stock shares will be required to meet the semi-annual dividend requirements for the outstanding Special Stock-Series A.

There are 150,000 shares of 5%, $100 par value, cumulative preferred stock authorized; none were outstanding at December 31, 1976, or January 2, 1976.

Employee Benefit Plans

A majority of the Company's employees are covered under various pension and profit sharing plans. Pension cost of $7,520,000 and $5,563,000 in 1976 and 1975, respectively, primarily covered current service cost plus amortization of prior service cost over periods of either 30 or 40 years. The Company's policy is to fund pension cost accrued.

At December 31, 1976, the actuarially computed value of vested benefits exceeded the total of the pension fund and balance sheet accruals by approximately $15,652,000. The aggregate unfunded prior service liability at December 31, 1976 is approximately $41,025,000.

Contingencies

Certain litigation has been initiated against the Company alleging, among other things, violations of antitrust laws and contracts. In the opinion of outside counsel, it is quite unlikely that any decisions finally rendered will result in a material adverse effect on the financial position of the Company.

Two additional lawsuits have recently been filed against the Company. One action alleges breach of franchisor-franchisee relationship and the other action alleges security law violations in connection with a secondary offering in 1976. The Company believes that these actions are without substantial merit and intends to vigorously defend against them.

Replacement Cost Data (Unaudited)

The Company has compiled the estimated replacement cost of property and equipment as of December 31, 1976, together with the estimated depreciation for the year then ended on the basis of current replacement cost. This data is required by the Securities and Exchange Commission in the Form 10-K Annual Report (a copy of which is available on request).

Over the years the cumulative impact of inflation has resulted in higher cost for replacement property and equipment. However, the Company has been able to partially offset the impact of inflation by selective price increases and by emphasis on cost and expense control.

Because of the imprecise nature of the replacement cost data, the fact that all properties will not be replaced simultaneously and the possibility of offsetting a portion of the impact of inflation by price increases and improved productivity, the financial statements should not be adjusted to reflect the replacement cost data.

FIGURE 8-8 (cont.)

Holiday Inns, Inc. and Consolidated Subsidiaries

Summary of Operations

	1976	1975	1974	1973	1972
	(In Thousands, except per share amounts)				
Revenues					
Hospitality	$539,400	$525,753	$502,300	$466,960	$419,997
Products	137,232	116,185	139,868	140,398	118,433
Transportation					
Bus	234,722	210,723	202,770	174,570	160,414
Steamship	81,063	82,816	77,843	41,314	30,981
Other	5,378	4,774	4,482	6,942	6,044
	997,795	940,251	927,263	830,184	735,869
Elimination of Products					
Intersegment Revenues	(32,169)	(23,278)	(22,158)	(21,422)	(17,637)
	$965,626	$916,973	$905,105	$808,762	$718,232
Income From Continuing Operations Before Corporate Expense, Interest, Foreign Currency Translation and Income Taxes					
Hospitality	$ 66,898	$ 58,618	$ 49,682	$ 61,749	$ 64,400
Products	1,713	890	8,995	11,924	8,193
Transportation					
Bus	15,148	19,865	25,458	21,331	19,462
Steamship	17,585	18,100	12,472	5,719	5,333
Other	2,015	2,360	3,059	4,538	4,009
	103,359	99,833	99,666	105,261	101,397
Elimination of Products					
Intersegment Income	(1,129)	(953)	(996)	(1,046)	(1,234)
	102,230	98,880	98,670	104,215	100,163
Corporate Expense	(9,200)	(9,745)	(14,161)	(9,361)	(6,902)
Interest, net of interest capitalized	(24,930)	(26,892)	(28,427)	(23,195)	(17,894)
Foreign Currency Translation (Loss) Gain	(3,076)	5,867	(8,614)	(7,402)	303
Income From Continuing Operations Before Income Taxes	65,024	68,110	47,468	64,257	75,670
Provision For Income Taxes	25,359	26,663	20,961	24,520	34,645
Income From Continuing Operations	39,665	41,447	26,507	39,737	41,025
Discontinued Operations, Less Applicable Income Taxes	(400)	447	956	1,997	1,367
Net Income	$ 39,265	$ 41,894	$ 27,463	$ 41,734	$ 42,392
Income Per Common and Common Equivalent Share					
Continuing Operations	$ 1.29	$ 1.36	$ .86	$ 1.27	$ 1.33
Discontinued Operations	(.01)	.01	.03	.06	.04
	$ 1.28	$ 1.37	$ .89	$ 1.33	$ 1.37

NOTE: The summary of operations for 1975 and prior years has been reclassified to comply with Statement of Financial Accounting Standards No. 14. The reclassification includes allocation of certain employee benefits from Corporate Expense to operating groups, elimination of interest expense from operating groups and presentation of steamship operations as a separate line of business.

FIGURE 8-8 (cont.)

Management's Discussion and Analysis of the Summary of Operations

Revenues increased $48,653,000 or 5.3 percent in 1976 and $11,868,000 or 1.3 percent in 1975. Pre-tax income from continuing operations declined $3,086,000 or 4.5 percent during 1976 and increased $20,642,000 or 43.5 percent during 1975. The decline in pre-tax income from continuing operations for 1976 and the increase for 1975 was attributable in large part to the impact of the translation of foreign currencies to the U. S. dollar. Compared to the prior year, the decrease in pre-tax income resulting from foreign currency translation in 1976 amounted to $8,943,000 and the increase in 1975 amounted to $14,481,000.

1976 COMPARED TO 1975
Hospitality Group

The Hospitality Group reported a revenue increase of $13,647,000 or 2.6 percent in 1976 from the same period of 1975. The revenue improvement was primarily due to occupancy gains and room rate increases that offset a slight decline in the number of Company-operated rooms available. The average rate per occupied room increased 6.3 percent in 1976 from the prior year. Occupancy at Company-operated rooms for 1976 increased 3.0 percentage points from the same period of 1975. Royalty payments also increased in 1976 due in large part to room rate adjustments and improved occupancy levels at licensed properties.

Operating income for the Hospitality Group increased $8,280,000 or 14.1 percent in 1976 as profit margins increased primarily due to improved occupancy levels, cost controls and room rate increases. In addition, occupancy improvements and room rate increases contributed to an increase in royalty payments from licensed inns.

Products Group

The Products Group reported an increase in gross revenues of $21,047,000 or 18.1 percent in 1976 from the same period of 1975. The revenue improvement during 1976 resulted from strengthening demand for furnishings and equipment sales due primarily to refurbishing projects. The improvement in gross revenues includes an increase of $8,891,000 in intersegment sales to Company-operated units.

Operating income for the Products Group increased $823,000 or 92.5 percent in 1976. The increase in operating income was attributed to margin improvement that more than offset the losses incurred during the first three quarters as the construction operations were being phased out. The improvements in operating income for the Products Group includes an increase of $176,000 in 1976 from intersegment income principally as a result of increased volume.

Bus Operations

Revenues for the bus operations increased $23,999,000 or 11.4 percent in 1976 from the same period of 1975. Improved charter and package express operations, the acquisition of Tamiami Trails and rate increases were primary contributors to bus revenue improvement.

Operating income for the bus operations declined $4,717,000 or 23.7 percent in 1976 as increased labor and other operating expenses rose more rapidly than revenues. An increase in the estimated salvage value of buses, as of the beginning of 1976, decreased depreciation charges by $2.6 million when compared to prior salvage values. The bus operations also experienced an 18-day work stoppage at five operating companies in the Southeast.

Steamship Operations

Revenues for the steamship operations decreased $1,753,000 or 2.1 percent in 1976 from the corresponding period of 1975. The slight decline in revenues in steamship operations was due to a slight reduction in tonnage carried, fewer voyages completed and a decline in rate-per-ton that more than offset increased revenues resulting from the deployment of a vessel on charter.

FIGURE 8-8 (cont.)

Operating income levels for the steamship operations declined $515,000 or 2.8 percent as the improvement in operating margins due to a significant increase in tonnage carried per voyage was more than offset by the absence of a $2.6 million special subsidy adjustment received in 1975.

Other Factors Affecting Net Income

Corporate expenses declined $545,000 or 5.6 percent in 1976 due to a reduction in legal expenses and bad debt allowances that more than offset the increase in staff expenses. Interest expense declined $1,962,000 or 7.3 percent in 1976 due to the reduction in the amount of long-term debt.

A foreign currency translation loss of $3,076,000 or $.06 per share was recognized in 1976, compared to a gain of $5,867,000 or $.12 per share in 1975. The strength of the Deutsche mark and the Dutch guilder relative to the U. S. dollar was the primary source of the translation losses in 1976. The effective tax rate for 1976 was 39 percent, the same as in 1975.

1975 COMPARED TO 1974

A brief summary of the major elements of change between 1975 and 1974 is given below:

Operating income for the Hospitality Group increased $8,936,000 or 18.0 percent in 1975 from the depressed levels of 1974. The increase was primarily due to increased royalty payments from licensed inns, cost reduction efforts at Company-operated inns and a gain from inn dispositions in 1975 compared to a loss in 1974.

Gross revenues from Products Group continuing operations declined by $23,683,000 or 16.9 percent in 1975 and operating income decreased $8,105,000 or 90.1 percent in 1975. Revenues declined principally as a result of a reduced volume of furnishings and equipment sales for new construction and refurbishing projects which remained depressed in 1975. Operating income declined as volume weakened without a corresponding reduction in operating costs and expenses.

Operating income for the bus operations declined $5,593,000 or 22.0 percent in 1975. Bus passenger miles decreased in 1975 as compared to a material increase recorded in 1974 when many travelers switched to intercity bus transportation as a result of the energy shortage during that period.

Operating income for the steamship operations increased $5,628,000 or 45.1 percent in 1975 due to a favorable subsidy adjustment of $2,591,000 and an improved mix of cargo.

General corporate expense declined by $4,416,000 or 31.2 percent in 1975. This change is primarily attributable to the inclusion in 1974 of a provision for possible loss from litigation of $4,500,000. A foreign currency translation gain of $5,867,000 or $.12 per share was recognized in 1975, compared to a loss of $8,614,000 or $.20 per share in 1974. The strengthening of the dollar in 1975 relative to the Deutsche mark and the Dutch guilder was the primary source of translation gain in 1975.

The provision for income taxes in 1975 increased by $5,702,000 or 27.2 percent as a result of higher operating income. However, the 1975 provision for income taxes reflects a lower effective tax rate than the 1974 provision primarily as a result of an increase in tax-deductible deposits to the statutory funds made possible by higher steamship earnings.

Comment on Introduction of LASH Vessels in 1974

In 1974, the steamship operations benefited by the introduction of three highly productive LASH/Container vessels which significantly increased revenues and operating income levels.

CHAPTER NINE

COMPANY ANALYSIS: FORECASTING EARNINGS

Chapter 8 introduced us to the primary sources of information, internal and external, about firms. We discovered that the principal sources of internal information about a firm were its financial statements. However, the analyst must be aware that there is more to financial statements than meets the eye. More than anything else, it is essential that a good analyst understand the impact of different acceptable methods of accounting for items on the position statement and the statement of income.

The income statement is perhaps used more than any other to assess the future of the firm, and earnings per share has become a key figure on this statement. There is strong evidence that earnings have a direct and powerful effect upon dividends and share prices, so the importance of forecasting earnings cannot be understated. A study of Niederhoffer and Regan suggests that stock prices are strongly dependent upon earnings changes, both absolute and relative to analysts' estimates. They discovered that the common characteristics of the companies registering the best price changes included a forecast of moderately increased earnings and a realized profit gain far in excess of analysts' expectations. The worst-performing stocks were those characterized by severe earnings declines, combined with unusually optimistic forecasts.[1] The accuracy of earnings forecasts is of enormous value in stock selection.

The present chapter has two aims: First, using financial statements, we will examine the "chemistry" of earnings. The various ingredients in the financial statements can be related in such a way that the analyst is able to visualize the critical aspects of a firm's operations that dictate the level, trend, and stability of earnings. Second, we shall take a look at traditional methods employed by analysts in assessing the outlook for revenues, expenses, and earnings in the firm over a forward holding period, given the economic and industry outlook. The methods that will be explained are (1) the return-on-investment or ROI approach, (2) the market-share-profit-margin approach, and (3) an independent, subjective approach of the forecast of revenues and expenses.

In Chapter 10 we will examine some newer techniques used in forecasting revenues, expenses, and ultimately earnings; and we will take up the forecasting of dividends and the market price of a share of stock at the end of the holding period.

---

[1]Victor Niederhoffer and Patrick J. Regan, "Earnings Changes, Analysts' Forecasts, and Stock Prices," *Financial Analysts Journal,* 28, No. 3 (May-June 1972), 65-71.

Let us begin this journey through the next two chapters by taking a look at the ingredients that produce earnings in the firm.

One of the most effective ways of getting "inside" earnings is to explore the financial statements for all possible explanations of a change, or lack of change, in earnings. Changes in reported earnings can result from changes in methods of accounting, as we saw in Chapter 8. Beyond this, they result from changes (1) in the operations of the business, and/or (2) in the financing of the business—that is, changes in productivity or in the resource (asset) base.

The efficiency or profitability with which a firm uses its assets is a key influence on earnings levels and growth. Better-managed companies typically have higher profits (net income) per dollar of assets than do poorly managed firms. The other key to earnings levels and growth lies in how fast a firm increases its asset base and the sources it uses for financing expansion. Debt and equity sources each have a unique effect upon earnings growth.

Our task of earnings analysis will be greatly facilitated by using a simple accounting model to focus on (1) what effect a change in a specific variable will have on earnings, and (2) whether or not each variable can be expected to cause a sustainable influence on earnings over long periods.

ASSET PRODUCTIVITY AND EARNINGS

Every firm has an aggregate of invested capital in the form of assets. These assets are utilized by management to generate revenues and net income. The funds necessary to acquire assets come from debt and equity sources of financing. Firms strive to operate in such a way as to provide shareholders the best possible return per dollar invested.

In balance-sheet terms, firms seek to maximize the return on total funds provided (assets). Should all financing be provided from equity money (no debt financing), the return on assets and equity are the same. To the extent that borrowed money is used to provide assets, return to equity will depend upon the relationship between return on total capital and the cost of borrowed funds.

Separation of the investment and financing activities of the firm makes the problem a bit clearer. Shown below are an income statement and a balance sheet in abbreviated form:

Income Statement		*Balance Sheet (in millions)*	
Sales	$ 100 million	Assets $50	Liabilities $25
— Costs	88		Equity 25
= EBIT	12		
— Interest	2		
= EBT	10		
— Taxes	4		
= EAT	6		
÷ No. of shares	5		
= EPS	$1.20		
DPS	.84		

We have used some shorthand to distinguish earnings at various stages:

EBIT = earnings before interest and taxes
EBT = earnings before taxes
EAT = earnings after taxes
EPS = earnings per share
DPS = dividend per share

Let us set aside the effects of taxes and financing for the moment. The productivity of total assets can be seen as:

$$\text{Return on assets} = \frac{\text{EBIT}}{\text{Assets}} = \frac{12}{50} = 24\%$$

The $50 million provided the firm (without reference to source of funds—debt or equity) generated a 24 percent return before considering distribution of these earnings to the tax collector, creditors, and shareholders. In general, the greater the return on assets, the higher the market value of the firm, other things being equal.

The return on assets, however, is only the end product of a mixture of events within the firm. If we think of the normal operating cycle of a company as analogous to the functioning of a wheel, we are better able to dissect the forces that contribute to the return on assets. Figure 9-1 shows the ordinary operating cycle for a firm, starting with placing cash into inventories. These inventories are then sold to create revenues. Deducting operating costs from revenues (sales) provides a profit. Thus, each time the operating cycle or wheel goes around, a profit (or loss) results. The key to overall return on funds committed to the enterprise is (1) the number of times per year the wheel spins around, and (2) the profits that emerge with each spin. Thus a refinement of the return-on-assets concept is to say that it is the product of the turnover of assets into sales (number of spins of the operating wheel), or intensity of utilization of assets in creating sales, and the margin of profit from each spin, or the profit productivity of sales. In the lexicon of finance, we say that the return on assets is the product of the *turnover* of assets and the *margin* of profit:

FIGURE 9-1
OPERATING CYCLE FOR A FIRM

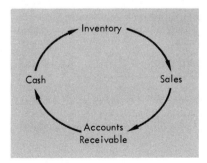

$$\text{Return on assets} = \underbrace{\frac{\text{Sales}}{\text{Assets}}}_{\text{(Turnover)}} \times \underbrace{\frac{\text{EBIT}}{\text{Sales}}}_{\text{(Margin)}}$$

or, as before:

$$\text{Return on assets} = \frac{\text{EBIT}}{\text{Assets}}$$

It is quite possible to find two firms in the same or even different industries earning comparable returns on assets. However, they may have totally different (1) turnover of assets, and/or (2) profit margins on sales. For example, consider the basic character of a jewelry store and a supermarket. They may enjoy similar returns on assets, but jewelry stores turn over their goods very slowly, while supermarkets enjoy an operating cycle that is quite rapid. Yet supermarkets enjoy only modest profit margins, and jewelry-store margins are much higher. So it is conceivable that the following relationship might apply:

	Return on Assets	=	Turnover	×	Margin
Jeweler	.15	=	.5	×	.30
Supermarket	.15	=	15.0	×	.01

Within the same industry, firms with slightly different product mixes and/or operating characteristics might earn competitive returns on assets through skillful compensations for deficiencies in margin or turnover. For example, take two jewelers who differ in the type of merchandise they offer for sale. Jeweler A deals in expensive jewelry, watches, and precious stones; Jeweler B specializes in costume jewelry. Jeweler A might have a higher margin but lower turnover than B, but both may enjoy equal returns on assets. Thus:

	Return on Assets	=	Turnover	×	Margin
Jeweler A	.15	=	.5	×	.30
Jeweler B	.15	=	1.0	×	.15

In sum, the productivity of total funds provided the firm is the product of the management's ability to (1) generate sales and revenues in relation to this package of funds or its intensity of utilization of assets, and (2) increase the profitability that results from each dollar of sales created.

In our hypothetical company, the return on assets is broken down as follows:

$$\text{Return on assets } (R) = \text{Turnover } (T) \times \text{Margin } (M) \qquad (9.1)$$

$$
\begin{array}{ccccc}
R & = & T & \times & M \\
.24 & = & \dfrac{100}{50} & \times & \dfrac{12}{100} \\
.24 & = & 2 & \times & .12
\end{array}
$$

So far, so good. But we have sidestepped taxes and distinctions in the sources of financing.

EARNINGS AND THE ROLE OF FINANCING

The sources of funds available to firms are numerous. In the main, they are either borrowed money or equity funds. Some borrowed money is essentially cost-free—for instance, tax and wage accruals, and trade credit paid on time. Other borrowed money, such as bank loans and bond issues, has a readily identifiable dollar interest cost. Equity funds have explicit and implicit costs. The most readily identifiable explicit cost of equity money is the dividend paid. Of course, we know by now that shareholders expect capital gains in addition to dividends when they purchase common shares. However, capital gains must be thought of more as an implicit cost of equity money. For the time being at least, it may help to think of the requirements of those who provide equity money as stated in the form of an earnings return per dollar of equity capital employed by the firm.

DEBT FINANCING AND EARNINGS

Among the many reasons for debt financing, the most important is the leverage provided to common shareholders. In Chapter 5 the notion of financial risk or financial leverage taught us a simple axiom: If you can earn more on borrowed money than you have to pay for it, you come out ahead—provided you borrow within prudent limits. If you borrow money from your banker at 10 percent and place the funds in another bank to earn 5 percent interest on a savings account, your road to ruin is assured. It would be far better if you had the same deal at a 4 percent cost of borrowing.

The *productivity* of funds was called *return on assets*. The *cost* of borrowed funds is called the *effective interest rate:*

$$\text{Effective Interest Rate } (I) = \frac{\text{Interest expense}}{\text{Total liabilities}} \qquad (9.2)$$

$$= \frac{2}{25} = 8\%$$

The firm in our example has total liabilities of $25 million. The company may have $5 million in debts with no explicit interest cost and a $20 million bond issue outstanding that bears a rate of interest of 10 percent. The weighted-average or "effective" cost of borrowed money is, thus, 8 percent, since some debt bears no direct cost and the remainder costs 10 percent ($0\% \times \$5$ million $+ 10\% \times \$20$ million $= \$2/\$25$ million $= 8\%$).

Relating the return on assets to the effective cost of funds indicates whether the firm is able to earn more than its direct cost of borrowing funds. Now, let us relate the productivity of borrowed funds to their effective cost:

Benefits of borrowed money = Return on assets − Effective interest rate

OR

Benefits of borrowed money = $R - I$

In our example:

$$R - I = .24 - .08 = .16, \text{ or } 16\%$$

The borrowing of money at a fixed cost and the use of these funds to earn a return on assets is known as employing *leverage*. Leverage can also be employed with preferred stock or any form of fixed-cost financing. So long as $R - I$ is a positive difference, leverage is being used to the firm's advantage. The importance of maximizing the difference between R and I is obvious. The necessity to avoid $R < I$ is equally apparent. Less obvious, however, is a reasonable answer to a simple question: If a firm enjoys a positive difference of $R - I$, why not push the mix of total funds acquired to the maximum limit of debt funds and minimize the financing that is done through equity sources? More simply, if you can borrow funds at an effective cost of 8 percent and earn 24 percent on money, why not borrow as much as you possibly can in order to enhance the return on your own funds (equity)?

First, as borrowed funds increase relative to equity funds in the total financing mix, borrowing costs (I) increase, and increase more rapidly than the amounts borrowed. For example, increasing debt funds from $25 million to $30 million (+20 percent) could result in an increase in interest on the additional $5 million to 15 percent from the prior rate of 10 percent (+50 percent). Thus, while $R = 24\%$, the difference ($R - I$) will shrink. The reason the rate of interest would rise is that creditors are now providing relatively more funds than are owners (equity), and therefore, proportionately more of the risks of the business are being shouldered by the creditors. Creditors will require greater compensation in the form of higher interest rates (and perhaps controls over the business—an indirect cost).

Second, when the cost of debt financing rises—directly and indirectly—so will the cost of equity funds. The employment of leverage causes the *quantity* of earnings available to the owners to increase whenever leverage is employed successfully ($R > I$). However, as more debt is employed relative to equity funds, the *quality* of earnings can deteriorate.

Table 9-1 shows the return on shareholders' equity at book value as the result of differing rates of return on assets and capital structures (L/E). The assumption in the table is that debt costs 5 percent (I), and taxes on income are ignored.

TABLE 9-1

PERCENTAGE RETURNS FOR SHAREHOLDERS UNDER
ALTERNATIVE CAPITAL STRUCTURES*

Percent Rate of Return on Assets (R)	Liability/Equity Ratio (L/E)			
	0	½	1	2
−4	−4	−8	−13	−22
0	0	−2	−5	−10
4	4	3	3	2
5	5	5	5	5
7	7	8	9	11
9	9	11	13	17
10	10	12	15	20

*Assumes 5 percent interest rate (i) on debt.

Example:

$$\text{Rate of return on equity} = R + (R - I)L/E$$
$$= -4 + [(-4) - (+5)]\,2$$
$$= -4 + (-9)2$$
$$= -4 + (-18)$$
$$= -22$$

Note that when the return on assets equals the interest rate on borrowed funds (5 percent), the return to shareholders is independent of the degree of financial leverage—that is, L/E. On the other hand, if the rate of return on assets is greater than (less than) the interest rate, the stockholders' percentage return is increased (decreased) by leverage. Furthermore, the increased volatility of shareholder returns increases with the expansion of L/E, or the degree of financial leverage. Note that over the range of return on assets shown, the range of shareholder returns expands from the range (−4% to +10%) to (−22% to +20%) as we move from no leverage to a 2:1 ratio. This increase in variation or range can effect the P/E on the stock downward or increase the cost of equity capital. In addition, equity costs might increase, since the risk of bankruptcy is greater. With no leverage, a series of years of −4 percent returns on assets can injure a firm; however, with L/E of 2, a series of −4 percent returns on assets leads to −22 percent on equity and accelerates the risk of ruin to stockholders markedly.

The greater volatility of earnings (up *and* down) owing to increased leverage can, at certain levels of debt financing, cause the market to pay less per dollar of earnings. Suppose the quantity of earnings is increased 10 percent owing to expanded leverage, but the market pays 15 percent less for the earnings because of their lower presumed quality or stability. In effect, the result is that a lower price per share of stock is experienced. Thus we might say that the cost of equity capital has increased along with the higher interest cost of debt. In other words, earnings before and after taxes might increase through the expansion of borrowed capital, but the market might pay less for these increased earnings owing to a perceived (real or imagined) deterioration in the stability (quality) of these earnings. Lower stock prices suggest that shareholders are really *worse* off because of additional borrowings!

Finally, while the difference between R and I is decreasing as more debt is raised, and the improved earnings are worth less to stockholders, the likelihood that R will remain constant or increase as funds employed expand is questionable. R itself may become progressively more difficult to maintain (or improve) as a firm gets larger.

If it were not for the relationships noted—(1) higher I, (2) higher cost of equity (lower share prices), and (3) strain on R—we would observe many more firms than we do with debt pushed as close as possible to 100 percent of total funds.

The proportions of debt and equity financing in the total mix of funds can be measured in a variety of ways.[2] We shall simply relate debt to equity as:

$$\text{Debt:Equity} = \frac{\text{Total liabilities}}{\text{Equity}}$$

In our example, total company funds come to $50 million. Debt represents $25 million and equity $25 million. Thus the debt-equity ratio is 25/25, or 1. Translated into words, this means that the firm has $1 of debt for each $1 of equity capital. Suppose the $50 million had been split between $32 million in debt and $18 million in equity. The debt-equity ratio would be 32/18, or 1.77:1—in words, $1.77 in debt for each $1 in equity. The higher the debt-equity ratio, the greater the leverage being employed, and conversely, the lower the equity funds in a relative sense. Thus, larger amounts of debt relative to equity funds leads to increased leverage, or "trading on the equity."

The difference between the return on assets and the effective interest rate on borrowed capital yielded a percentage amount. We were originally concerned with an ultimate explanation of earnings in dollar form. To convert back:

$$\text{EBT} = (R)(A) - (I)(L) \tag{9.3}$$

$$= (\text{EBIT/Assets})(\text{Assets}) - (\text{Interest/Liabilities})(\text{Liabilities})$$

$$= \text{EBIT} - \text{Interest}$$

where:

A = assets
L = total liabilities

$$\text{EBT} = (.24)\,(\$50) - (.08)\,(\$25)$$

$$= \$12 - 2$$

$$= \$10$$

[2]Some authors use Debt/Total assets. This measure relates debt to total funds employed.

It is possible to recast Equation 9.3 to enable us to isolate and relate R, I, and L/E in the following manner: Since $A = L + E$ where E = equity, then:

$$EBT = (R)(L + E) - (I)(L)$$

and simplifying,

$$EBT = (RL) + (RE) - (IL)$$

To isolate $(R - I)$ and L/E, further simplification yields:

$$EBT = (RE) + (RL) - (IL)$$
$$= (RE) + L(R - I)$$

Dividing each element on the right side of the equation by E while simultaneously multiplying the entire right side by E maintains the integrity of the equation, so:[3]

$$EBT = \left[\frac{RE}{E} + \frac{L(R - I)}{E}\right]E$$
$$= [R + (R - I)L/E]\ E$$
$$= [.24 + (.24 - .08)\ 25/25]\ \$25$$
$$= (.24 + 16)\ \$25$$
$$= (.40)\ \$25$$
$$= \$10$$

We can now appreciate not only the importance of $R - I$ but the magnification of the difference depending upon L/E. In our example, if total assets ($50) had been divided into debt = $40 and equity = $10, and $(R - I)$ remained unchanged (a questionable assumption), then:

$$EBT = [.24 + (.24 - .08)\ 40/10]\ \$10$$
$$= [.24 + (.16)\ 4]\ \$10$$
$$= (.88)\ \$10$$
$$= \$8.8$$

With debt $40 and equity $10, EBT is only $8.8. With debt and equity each at $25, EBT was $10. However, if we relate EBT to equity (EBT/Equity), the answers are 8.8/10, or 88 percent, versus 10/25, or 40 percent. Stated in the latter form, we can visualize the point that when the difference $R - I$ is positive, larger values of L/E magnify the difference.

[3]Consider the following: $1 + 2 = 3$. If we divide and multiply by, say 2, we get $(\frac{1}{2} + 1)\ 2$, or $1\frac{1}{2} \times 2 = 3$.

In sum, at this juncture we have been able to define earnings before taxes as follows:

$$EBT = [R + (R - I)\, L/E]\, E \qquad\qquad (9.4)$$

Equity Financing and Earnings

Most firms obtain equity financing from (1) the issuance of new shares, and/or (2) retention of earnings.

The issuance of stock occurs through a cash sale or through an exchange for shares in another firm. The effect of issuing new shares depends primarily upon the relationship of the sale price to the asset value of outstanding shares. Asset value is determined in the following manner:

$$\text{Asset value per share} = \frac{\text{Assets}}{\text{Number of common shares}}$$

In our example, 5 million shares are assumed to be outstanding. The value of assets is $50 million. The asset value per share of stock is $10 ($50/5).

To see the earnings effect of new shares, let us assume we sell 1 million new shares at either $15, or $10, or $5 per share:

	New Share Price		
	$15	$10	$5
(1) Old asset base	$50.00	$50.00	$50.00
(2) Proceeds from sale of new shares	$15.00	$10.00	$ 5.00
(3) New asset base	$65.00	$60.00	$55.00
(4) Rate of return on assets	.24	.24	.24
(5) New EBIT (3 × 4)	$15.60	$14.40	$13.20
(6) EBIT/New shares (new total shares = 6 million)	$ 2.60	$ 2.40	$ 2.20

This exercise suggests that whenever new shares can be sold at a price in excess of asset value per share, earnings can be improved on a per-share basis. Earnings fall only if new shares are sold below asset value and/or if profitability declines. The level of EBIT before the assumed common-stock financing was $12.0 million, and the EBIT per share was $2.40. Notice that EBIT per share remains at $2.40 if new shares are sold at $10, but sales below $10 result in lower earnings per share than before the new financing and new shares sold at prices above $10 bolster earnings per share.

Even though we have been discussing the sale of new shares for cash, the same type of analysis is applicable to a merger in which the book value of assets per share received by the acquiring company exceeds the book value of the assets per share given to the stockholders of the acquired company. Furthermore, asset value per share can also be increased by retiring shares at a discount from existing book value. For example, assume that our hypothetical firm with an asset value per share of $10 is able to repurchase some of its shares in the open market at a price of $8 per share. Suppose sufficient cash is available to repurchase 1 million shares ($8 million). The new asset value per share will be $50 million less $8 million in cash, divided by 4 million remaining shares, or $10.50. This is an increase of 5 percent ($.50/$10). The ability to sustain a rate of return on assets (R) of 24 percent would cause earnings to be $42 million times .24, or $10,080,000. On a per-share basis this is $2.52 ($10,080,000/4 million), or a rise of 12 percent from the previous level of $2.40, corresponding to the percentage increase in asset value per share.

It is vital to remember that these examples of selling or exchanging stock above asset values or redeeming shares below asset values will influence earnings as a function of the ability of the company to maintain the level of the rate of return on assets (R = 24%).

The ability of the firm to maintain R = 24% is a prerequisite to improved earnings. This can occur under astute management, up to a point. If the ability to sustain (or improve) the return on assets (R) were possible regardless of the size of the firm (total assets), companies whose share prices exceeded asset values would find they could improve earnings per share almost without limit simply by selling more and more and more stock.

Earnings retention provides a basic source of earnings growth. Corporations in general tend to pay out about one-half of their earnings. The amounts retained increase the asset base. Our example company had earnings per share of $1.20 and paid a dividend of $0.84 per share. We can say:

$$\text{Dividend payout rate} = \frac{\text{DPS}}{\text{EPS}} = \frac{\$0.84}{\$1.20} = 70\% \qquad (9.5)$$

or, alternatively:

$$\text{Retention rate} = 1.00 - \text{Dividend payout (\%)} \qquad (9.6)$$
$$= 1.00 - .70$$
$$= .30, \text{ or } 30\%$$

The company's total earnings after taxes of $6 million was split into $4.2 million paid out and $1.8 million retained. The $1.8 million retained adds to the equity base and the total asset base. The maintenance of a return on assets of 24 percent, other things being equal, would add $.432 million to EBIT in the following year:

$$\text{Growth in EBIT} = \text{Retention rate} \times \text{Return on assets}$$
$$= .30 \times .24 = .072 = 7.2\%$$

or:

$$g = B \times R \qquad (9.7)$$

where:

B = retention rate (%)
g = growth rate of EBIT
R = return on assets

Retention and earnings growth are, once again, dependent upon maintaining the rate of return on assets.

EFFECTS OF TAXES

Our discussion so far has been in terms of earnings before taxes. The effects of taxes on income can be accommodated in our model by making the following transformation:

$$EAT = (1 - T) [R + (R - I) L/E] E \qquad (9.8)$$

where:

T = Effective tax rate = Tax expense/EBT

The notion $1 - T$ is really indicating what percentage of each $1 of income is available after satisfying Uncle Sam and other taxing authorities. Should $T = 60$ percent, we would say that 40 cents of every dollar of income is available after taxes ($1.00 − $.60). The lower the tax rate, the higher the percentage of income left over, and vice versa. The difference between a tax rate and an "effective" tax rate lies in the fact that not all income to the firm is taxed at the same rate. Hence the effective tax rate is apt to be different from what the rate schedule shows for the level of EBT.

Moreover, as we learned in Chapter 8, the income reported for tax returns may be different from the income shown on the reports to shareholders. For example, a firm may have ordinary operating income of $7 million, subject to a tax rate of 50 percent. Additional income of $3 million may be subject to lower capital gains rates of, say, 25 percent. The effective tax *rate* is the total tax relative to the total income to be taxed, or $4.25/$10, or 42.5 percent. Our example firm has an effective tax rate of:

$$T = \text{Tax expense/EBT} = 4/10 = 40\% \qquad (9.9)$$

EAT in the example becomes:

$$EAT = (1 - T) [R + (R - I) L/E] E$$
$$= (1 - .4) (\$10)$$
$$= \$6$$

EARNINGS AND DIVIDENDS PER SHARE

To convert EAT to a per-share basis, we need only divide it by the number of common shares outstanding:

$$EPS = \frac{EAT}{\text{Number of shares outstanding}} \qquad (9.10)$$

In general, then, in terms of our total model:[4]

$$EPS = \frac{(1-T)\,[R + (R-I)\,L/E]\,E}{\text{Number of common shares outstanding}} \qquad (9.11)$$

where:

  EPS = earnings per share
  T = effective tax rate (Tax expense/EBT)
  B = retention rate [or 1 −(DPS/EPS)]
  R = return on assets (EBIT/A)
  I = effective interest rate (Interest expense/Liabilities)
  L = total liabilities
  E = equity

Dividends per share can be calculated as:

$$DPS = (1-B)\,(EPS) \qquad (9.12)$$

The value of the model can now be appreciated in its fullest form. We can see that earnings per share and changes in earnings per share are a function of:

1. Utilization of asset base (turnover of assets)
2. Profit productivity of sales (margin on sales)
3. Effective cost of borrowed funds (effective interest rate)
4. Debt-equity ratio
5. Equity base
6. Effective tax rate

We have deliberately isolated the critical variables that determine earnings and in turn dividends. The final task we face is to (1) isolate how changes in specific variables affect earnings, and (2) examine the sustainability of each variable as a long-run influence upon earnings.

---

[4]This model and its enrichment are the result primarily of the work of Lerner and Carleton. See E. Lerner and W. T. Carleton, *A Theory of Financial Analysis* (New York: Harcourt Brace Jovanovich, 1966).

AN EXAMPLE: THE GROWTH COMPANY

Tables 9-2 and 9-3 show abbreviated financial statements for a company we have chosen to call the Growth Company. Table 9-4 is a summary of values for the key variables in our model for three years of data.[5]

The pattern of earnings over the three-year period indicates that earnings per share have grown 18 percent per year between 19X1 and 19X3. An impressive rate of growth indeed! The big question is, Is the growth rate transitory or is it sustainable? For example, has the growth been achieved through profitability rather than shifts in funds sources? The latter is not sustainable, while the former usually is. Let us take a closer look.

The return on assets has steadily improved, year to year. The primary source is improved profit margins in the face of slower asset turnover and almost stagnant sales. Such a profit-margin improvement is a healthy sign.

Increasing use has been made of debt financing relative to equity (although the retention rate on earnings has moved upward to increase the equity base). The upward movement of the effective rate of interest on borrowed funds shows the following changes in the spread between the return on assets and the effective interest rate $(R - I)$: 19X1, .109; 19X2, .119; 19X3, .109. In effect, increased return on assets between 19X1 and 19X3 (.126 to .138) has been negated by rising debt financing and the associated interest cost. The leverage provided (L/E) has increased. This makes the product $[(R - I)L/E]$ greater in 19X3 than in 19X1. The significance, however, is that earnings are more vulnerable to decline. The relatively fixed nature of I and the possible erosion of R is the key here!

Pre-tax earnings have been taxed at lower effective rates over time. What are the reasons? Is some revenue taxed at capital gains rates? Have differences occurred between reporting to shareholders and to the tax authorities? In

TABLE 9-2

THE GROWTH COMPANY: INCOME STATEMENTS FOR THE YEARS
ENDED DEC. 31, 19X1-19X3 ($ IN MILLIONS)

	19X1	19X2	19X3
Net sales	$117.0	$117.0	$116.0
Other income	1.0		3.2
Cost of sales	105.0	103.0	105.0
Earnings before interest and taxes	13.0	14.0	14.2
Interest expense	0.5	0.4	1.1
Earnings before taxes	12.5	13.6	13.1
Taxes	6.0	6.0	5.0
Earnings after taxes	6.5	7.6	8.1
Avg. shares outstanding (millions)	5.6	5.5	5.0
Earnings per share	$1.16	$1.38	$1.63
Dividends per share	.58	.65	.75

[5]The reader is invited to calculate several of the values in Table 9-4 to assure understanding of earlier materials.

general, lower effective rates of taxation, whatever the source, are not sustainable.

Increases in after-tax earnings per share are, in large measure, the result of a dwindling number of outstanding shares. The company could be buying back its own shares. Is it possible that reduced equity is being achieved by increasing debt to take its place?

The possibilities with respect to detailed analysis can be extended. We do not suggest that this company deliberately manipulated earnings. The point is that not all sources of improvement in earnings per share are desirable and/or sustainable. Mere earnings growth should not impress an analyst. The anatomy of earnings growth is the key!

Forecasting via the Earnings Model

Our emphasis thus far in the presentation of the ROI method has been to view it as a device for analyzing the effects of and interaction between the return a firm earns on its assets and the manner in which it is financed. However, this analytical device can be used as a forecasting tool. Once the analyst understands the inner workings of the firm's earnings-formation process, he can forecast the key variables, substitute the values into the model, and forecast EAT for the next period.

TABLE 9-3
THE GROWTH COMPANY: POSITION STATEMENT (ABBREVIATED),
DECEMBER 31, 19X1-19X3 ($ IN MILLIONS)

	19X1	*19X2*	*19X3*
Total assets	$103	$105	$103
Current debt	21	21	21
Long-term debt	9	8	17
Common-stock equity	73	76	65
Total debt and equity	103	105	103

TABLE 9-4
THE GROWTH COMPANY: SUMMARY DATA ON KEY FINANCIAL
VARIABLES, 19X1-19X3

Variable	*19X1*	*19X2*	*19X3*
Dividends per share	.580	.650	.750
Earnings per share	1.160	1.380	1.630
Return on assets:	.126	.133	.138
Margin	.111	.120	.122
Turnover	1.136	1.114	1.126
Effective interest rate	.017	.014	.029
Total liabilities/equity	.410	.380	.580
Equity ($ millions)	73.000	76.000	65.000
Number of shares (millions)	5.600	5.500	5.000
Effective tax rate	.480	.440	.380
Retention rate	.500	.530	.540

For example, assume that a firm's tax bracket is forecast to be 50 percent in 19X4, that 15 percent will be earned on its assets, and that it will pay an effective interest rate of 6 percent. Further assume that the firm will have $100 million of equity and $100 million of debt in its capital structure in 19X4. Then, if we substitute these values into the model, $EAT = (1 - T) [R + (R - I) L/E] E$, its forecast EAT will be as follows:

$$EAT = (1 - .5) [.15 + (.15 - .06) 100/100] \ \$100$$
$$= .5 [.15 + (.09) 1] \ 100$$
$$= .5 [.24] \ 100$$
$$= \$12$$

We can then subtract any forecast preferred dividends that will be paid, and divide the remainder by the projected number of outstanding common shares to arrive at EPS. This can then be multiplied by the projected P/E ratio to get the projected price. To continue our example, if our firm is expected to have 3 million shares outstanding and a P/E of 15 in 19X4, then EPS will be forecast at $4 ($12 million/3 million) and the price per common share at $60 (15 × $4). This can be translated to HPY by subtracting the beginning per-share price, adding dividends paid in 19X4, and dividing by the beginning price. If the price at the end of 19X3 is $50 and no dividends are expected during 19X4, then the projected HPY for 19X4 is 20 percent [(60 − 50)/50].

Market-Share-Profit-Margin Approach

The market-share-profit-margin approach emanates directly from the industry analysis. Once the industry forecast of market shares is completed, the analyst must next decide which firms are likely to be dominant factors, pacesetters, in the industry. If an investor has his choice, he will undoubtedly select a leader rather than a follower. Thus the next logical step for the analyst is to determine what share of the industry's total market the firm under analysis can reasonably be expected to achieve.

If the industry is established and has a track record of performance and stability, the analyst can probably make good use of the historical shares of the market attained by the competing firms. Industries such as autos, steel, oil, and copper have well-entrenched member firms. In a slightly more dynamic industry, such as household appliances, the analyst must translate the ability and aggressiveness of management relative to the competition into a forecast of market share. However, in an evolving and somewhat unstable industry, with new firms entering and leaving the market—such as the fast-food franchising industry—the analyst's job is considerably more difficult, perhaps even impossible, using this approach. He must attempt to start with those firms that have begun to establish their permanence in the industry; then he has at least a point of reference from which to depart. He can then subjectively determine the relative strengths and weaknesses of the firm's most pressing competition. These subjective opinions can be translated into estimates of the probable share of the market to be attained by both the firm under analysis and the competition.

Assume that the analyst is studying an industry that produces auxiliary swimming-pool equipment—items such as lounge chairs, pads, and beach umbrellas. Industry sales for 19X2 are $10 million, and the Danes Co. captured 10 percent of this market in 19X2, or $1 million in sales. The analyst forecasts a 20 percent increase in 19X3 sales for the industry because of a more favorable economic climate for leisure-time products. If he expects Danes Co. to increase its market share to 12 percent because of an aggressive campaign, what would its projected sales be? Industry sales will be $10 million plus the 19X3 increase of 20 percent ($2 million), for a total of $12 million. Danes Co. share is 12 percent; therefore, its sales will be 12 percent of $12 million, or $1.44 million.

With an estimate of sales for the company for the ensuing year, the analyst must next determine the most likely profit margin this firm can earn, given its manufacturing capacity, its total resources, and its projected level of sales. We define net-income profit margin as net income after taxes, divided by sales.[6]

The analyst must calculate the most likely net-income margin the firm is likely to achieve on each category of sales revenue. In the case of a predominantly one-product firm, the analyst multiplies the sales figure by the net-income margin to get the firm's profit from the predominating product.[7] For a multi-product firm, the analyst multiplies the sales of each division by the appropriate profit margin to obtain the various divisions' earnings, totals these, and arrives at the firm's total earnings. These earnings are then divided by the number of common shares outstanding (after deducting any preferred dividends), to get earnings per share.

Example. Danes's sales forecast for 19X3 is $1,440,000. If its net-income margin is forecast to be 5 percent and there are 100,000 shares of common outstanding, what would projected EPS be?[8]

1. Multiply projected sales by the projected margin to get total earnings. $1,440,000 \times 5\% = \$72,000$
2. Divide earnings by common shares outstanding (Danes has no preferred stocks). $\$72,000 \div 100,000 = \$.72/\text{share}$

Then the EPS is multiplied by the forecast P/E ratio to get the forecast price. The price at the beginning of the period is subtracted from the ending price to calculate the price change for the period. Then the annual dividend is added to the price change, and the sum is divided by the beginning price to calculate the holding-period yield.

---

[6]Throughout the ensuing discussion and text, we use the terms *net-income margin, net-income profit margin,* and *profit margin* interchangeably.

[7]The portion of sales arising from the other products of the firm, which are relatively unimportant compared to the predominant product, is often calculated merely by assuming a growth rate in the level of sales arising from these other products. This sales figure is multiplied by the appropriate profit margin, and this profit is added to the profit calculated above to arrive at the firm's total profit.

[8]Usually, estimates of net-income margins are based upon historical performance. If any changes in the mode of operation or market conditions have occurred, the analyst modifies the historical margins to incorporate these changes. The 5 percent figure for Danes reflects this procedure.

Example. If the P/E for the end of 19X3 is projected to be 20 and the price at the end of 19X2 was $10, what is the HPY for Danes Co.? Assume that a $.10 annual dividend is paid.

1. Multiply EPS by P/E. $.72 × 20 = $14.40
2. Subtract the beginning price from the ending price. $14.40 − $10.00 = $4.40 price change
3. Add dividend to price change and divide by beginning price.
$$\frac{\$4.40 + \$.10}{\$10} = \frac{\$4.50}{\$10} = 45\% \text{ HPY}$$

This approach involves forecasting only a few key variables, which are easier to get a handle on than the inputs required by the other traditional approaches, and thus it represents a realistic and practical method of forecasting. One last point is perhaps in order before proceeding.

Profit margins are apt to vary little over a very limited range of sales and operating capacity; however, they can vary drastically once the range of possible sales and capacity outcomes is broadened. In order to calculate a useful profit margin (for the relevant range), the analyst must understand the makeup and behavior of prices and costs of the firm in question. We refer, of course, to the relative importance to the firm of *fixed and variable cost.* In other words, we need first to appreciate the degree of operating leverage (the size of the fixed costs) the firm is employing before we can properly relate this information to sales and capacity figures. To facilitate this understanding, analysts frequently employ breakeven analysis and the adjunct breakeven chart.

BREAKEVEN ANALYSIS

A central concept in the breakeven analysis is the breakeven point. The breakeven point is a sales level at which total revenues equal total costs. To state the matter in its simplest form, a firm's total costs are made up of fixed costs plus linear variable costs. Fixed costs—for example, rent—are constant over large ranges of output over a finite time period.[9] Note in Figure 9-2, for example, that when total costs hit the *y*-axis, variable costs are zero and total costs equal fixed costs. On the other hand, variable costs—for example, materials—vary directly in proportion to output. The more items produced, the more variable costs increase. The aspect of breakeven analysis with which we are concerned here is the effect of high fixed costs versus low fixed costs on a company's profit margin, and how the profit margin changes about the breakeven point (level of sales).[10]

Figure 9-2 is a graphical depiction of a high-fixed-cost company; Figure 9-3, of a low-fixed-cost company. Observe that the breakeven point (in units) is higher for the high-fixed-cost company than for the low-fixed-cost company.

---

[9]All costs, given some wide dimensions, will be variable. Costs are fixed only over some "relevant" range.

[10]For the mechanics of breakeven analysis as used in an accounting sense, see James C. Van Horne, *Financial Management and Policy* (Englewood Cliffs, N.J.: Prentice-Hall, 1977), pp. 718-25.

FIGURE 9-2

BREAKEVEN POINT OF A HIGH-FIXED-COST COMPANY

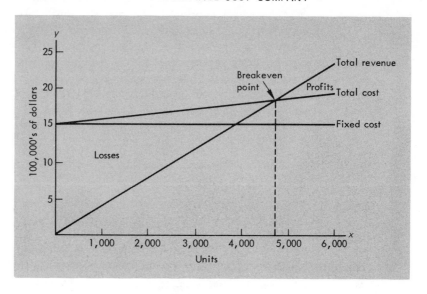

This is the general case. The high-fixed-cost company might be characterized as more capital-intensive (using larger amounts of equipment and machinery) than the low-fixed-cost company.

Generally, when a firm has high fixed costs, it also has lower variable costs. The significance of this fact can be seen by examining Figure 9-2. Below the breakeven point, large losses are sustained, and above the breakeven point, large profits are achieved. The losses get larger as the sales volume falls significantly below the breakeven point. Conversely, the profits get larger as sales move further and further above the breakeven point. Graphically this is depicted by the vertical distance between the total-revenue line and the total-cost line. This situation differs in degree rather than kind when one views the low-fixed-cost company illustrated in Figure 9-3.

Generally, when a firm has lower fixed costs, it has higher variable costs. Thus, while profits increase as sales move above the breakeven point and losses increase as sales fall below the breakeven point, the rate of increased profits and losses is substantially less than the rate for the high-fixed-cost company. In other words, profits and losses "explode" more rapidly in the case of the high-fixed-cost company than in the case of the low-fixed-cost company.

So we can see the importance that an analyst properly perceive (1) the type of firm (high or low fixed costs) he is analyzing, and (2) the level of sales volume the firm is likely to achieve during the forecast period; for these factors will greatly influence the net-income profit margin the firm will achieve. This problem becomes particularly acute as the projected sales volume of the firm approaches its breakeven point. A slight error in estimation in this region can have radical consequences for the success of investing in the firm's shares. This kind of analysis is helpful in determining the return on assets, R, if the analyst is using the earnings model discussed earlier in this chapter.

A breakeven chart for hotels and motels is illustrated in Figure 9-4. A room occupancy of 60.5 percent is required to cover both fixed and variable expenses. Most operating expenses, as well as rent, are semivariable in nature, so the fixed portion of those expenses is added to fixed charges which do not vary with changes in occupancy. Thus, at an occupancy level of 60.5 percent, total revenue would be \$10,333 per available room (\$170.80 × 60.5). Total expenses would include \$5,592 in fixed expenses and \$4,741 in variable expenses (\$10,333 × .459). Thus, revenues of \$10,333 and total expenses of \$10,333 leave zero profit at 60.5 percent of occupancy.

Independent Forecasts of Revenue and Expenses

The ROI method skirts the issue of specifically forecasting various categories of income and expenses. The approach we will discuss in this section differs on that score.

The independent forecasting of revenues and expenses, sometimes called the "scientific" method,[11] directly confronts the problem just outlined. The technique generally follows one of two main routes. The first and more specific approach is to forecast each and every revenue and expense item separately. For example, the analyst would separately forecast the sales of each division and

FIGURE 9-3
BREAKEVEN POINT OF A LOW-FIXED-COST COMPANY

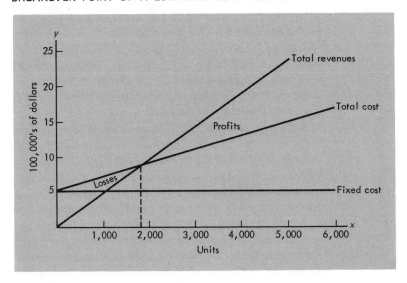

---

[11]This term is attributed to Benjamin Graham, David L. Dodd, and Sidney Cottle, in *Security Analysis* (New York: McGraw-Hill, 1962), p. 463.

each product line of the company, as well as each of the major expense items appearing on the firm's income statement. The advantage of this approach is that it forces the analyst to become intimately familiar with the inner workings of the business—both manufacturing operations and sales and administrative operations. The main disadvantage of this method is that for a company of any size, it is an extremely time-consuming and often tedious procedure; furthermore, there is always the danger that the analyst may become so involved with the detail that he misses some broader, but very fundamental, points of interest.

The second route is to take a broader-brush approach to the forecasting problem. Here the analyst hopes to overcome the pitfalls of the "scientific" method by analyzing the forecasting category totals rather than all the individual components. For example, he would look at the sales of the various divisions as totals, rather than attempting to forecast the sales of all the individual product lines of each division. He would forecast broad categories of expenses, such as administrative and sales expenses, rather than attempting to break these down finely into categories such as salaries, rent, and insurance. The advantage of this approach is that it avoids most of the problems of the specific approach and is more efficient. Also, it is perhaps more accurate per unit of time spent on the forecast, because generally there are over-and-under estimates of individual components that may be misleading when looked at separately, but that cancel out when they are added together.

When the analyst has completed his forecast of revenues and expenses by using either the specific or the broad approach just outlined, he merely subtracts expenses from the revenues, and he has his forecast of earnings. Then he deter-

FIGURE 9-4
BREAKEVEN ANALYSIS OF ALL HOTELS AND MOTELS

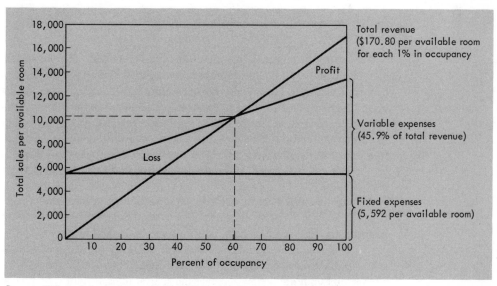

Source: *U.S. Lodging Industry, 1976* (Philadephia, Pa: Laventhal & Horwath, 1977).

mines the number of common shares that will be outstanding in the forecast period, and divides it into the forecast earnings (after deducting any preferred dividends) to get earnings per share. Next, the analyst would multiply this earnings-per-share figure by the estimated P/E ratio in order to arrive at his best estimate of price. Then he would subtract the price at the beginning of the period, add dividends, and divide by the beginning price to calculate the HPY.

Example. Danes Co. sales consist of two main divisions, one producing lounge chairs and pads, the other beach umbrellas and various other miscellaneous items. Our estimates call for $1.2 million in revenue from the lounge division and $240,000 from the umbrella division. These figures are based on advance orders and projected sales to new resort hotels and motels, as well as anticipated replacement orders. Manufacturing expenses are about 70 percent of total revenues; sales and administrative expenses and taxes are 25 percent of sales revenue. The other pertinent information about Danes is as previously noted. What is the projected HPY?

Revenues:	Lounge division	$1,200,000	
	Umbrella division	220,000	
	Total revenue		$1,440,000
Expenses:	Manufacturing	1,008,000	
	S&A	360,000	
	Total expenses		$1,368,000
	Net earnings		$ 72,000

As previously, EPS = $.72, and HPY = 45 percent.

The three approaches we have discussed represent the main lines and methodology traditionally employed by security analysts when performing a company analysis. These main approaches are not mutually exclusive; they are often combined and used to complement each other. Despite the fact that they have been used with much success by many analysts for some time now, it should be pointed out that they all possess some shortcomings. They are based to a large extent on subjective evaluations made at various stages of the analysis by the analyst or investor, and quite frequently involve his estimate of the most likely figure.

In statistics, this type of estimate, which attempts to zero in on *one* number, is called a *point estimate.* For example, a weatherman might estimate that the temperature will reach a high of 72° tomorrow; in this case, 72° is a point estimate. When these point estimates are made in security analysis, there is generally no formal statement about their reliability. That is, the reader of such a report does not know how accurate the analyst himself thinks the forecast may be, or, for that matter, how accurate the analyst thinks will be any of a range of point estimates he may have forecast. In addition, the output generated from such traditonal analyses is usually not directly usable in modern portfolio analysis. The approaches to be presented in the next chapter represent newer techniques that have been applied in the field of security analysis in an attempt to overcome these shortcomings.

Earnings-Model Projection for Holiday Inns

The starting point for the application of the earnings model to any company is to understand the relationships among the key variables for the particular firm. A good starting point for this analysis is to examine historical data. Table 9-5 contains this key financial data for Holiday Inns (HIA) for the period 1968-76. Table 9-6 contains the key variables for the earnings analysis for the 1973-76 period. The extreme right-hand column of Table 9-6 contains the average value for the variables for the 1973-76 period. Since these basic economic relationships are slow to change unless management by specific design takes steps to bring about a change, we will assume, for *purposes of illustration,* that those average values for 1973-76 persisted in 1977. However, we will use the 1976 values of debt and equity, on the assumption that they remained the same in 1977.[12] Thus, an estimate for 1977 is:

$$EAT = (1 - .399) \ [.1005 + (.1005 - .0550) \ .98] \ \$472$$

$$= (.601) \ [.1005 + (.0455) \ .98] \ \$472$$

$$= (.601) \ [\$68.482]$$

$$= \$41.158$$

Using a forecast of 30.6 million common shares outstanding in 1977 yields forecast EPS of $1.35. Assuming a P/E of 9, a beginning price of 12, and forecast dividend of $0.47 yields an HPY of 5.2 percent, which is calculated as follows:[13]

$$HPY = \frac{9 \ (\$1.35) - \$12.00 + \$.47}{\$12.00}$$

$$= \frac{\$12.15 - \$12.00 + \$.47}{\$12.00} = .052, \text{ or } 5.2\%$$

---

[12]In addition, we have used data that are restated to reflect pooling-of-interest figures throughout.

[13]For the time being, we ask the reader to go along with our assumption of a P/E of 9 and a dividend of $.47 for 1977, so that we can illustrate the HPY calculation for a one-year holding period, which is calculated one year forward from the time HIA is selling at 12. In Chapter 10 we will discuss procedures for arriving at an estimate of P/E and dividends per share.

TABLE 9-5

FINANCIAL DATA, HOLIDAY INNS, 1968-1976
($ IN MILLIONS EXCEPT WHERE NOTED)

	1976	1975	1974	1973	1972	1971	1970	1969	1968
Sales	965.60	912.20	981.10	878.00	768.50	702.60	602.50	529.10	396.50
EBIT	90.00	95.20	87.60	102.20	100.40	95.00	84.80	75.00	53.90
Interest	25.00	27.10	30.20	27.30	22.30	21.40	19.20	15.50	9.50
EBT	65.00	68.10	57.50	74.90	78.10	73.60	65.60	59.60	44.40
Taxes	25.40	26.70	24.80	28.50	36.10	33.00	28.60	27.60	18.70
EAT	39.70	41.40	32.60	46.40	42.00	40.60	37.00	32.00	25.70
No. of Shares	30.60	30.60	30.70	30.80	30.20	29.50	28.00	27.20	24.90
EPS (dollars)	1.29	1.36	1.06	1.50	1.38	1.36	1.15	1.15	1.01
DPS (dollars)	.39	.35	.32	.30	.28	.25	.23	.24	.16
Assets	936.00	930.00	961.00	910.00	864.00	764.00	677.00	575.00	442.00
Liabilities	464.00	486.00	536.00	505.00	492.00	432.00	428.00	371.00	281.00
Equity	472.00	444.00	425.00	405.00	372.00	332.00	249.00	204.00	161.00

This represents a *point estimate* of HPY, and based on this the analyst or investor needs to determine if investment in HIA is warranted. Note that there is no explicit statement of risk—that is, the chance that an HPY less than the expected HPY will materialize.

The fact that the ROI approach forces the analyst to become very close to the inner workings of the company is a decided disadvantage as well as an advantage, since it involves forecasting a number of key ratios and variables, which is very difficult to do. Thus, although in theory ROI is a very nice, neat approach, in practice it is a difficult one to implement with a high degree of accuracy.

Independent Forecast of Revenue and Expenses for Holiday Inns

Holiday Inns, Inc., is generally recognized as a leader in the lodgings industry. However, it has two other main operating divisions that constitute the balance of its business—the Products Division and the Transportation Division. In order to implement the independent forecast of revenue and expenses, it is necessary to forecast each division's revenue and expense contribution separately.

TABLE 9-6

EARNINGS ANALYSIS, HOLIDAY INNS, 1973-1976

	1973	1974	1975	1976	Avg. 1973-1976
DPS	$ .30	$ .32	$ .35	$ .39	
EPS	$ 1.50	$ 1.06	$ 1.36	$ 1.29	
Payout rate	20.0%	30.2%	25.7%	30.2%	26.5%
Tax rate	38.1%	43.1%	39.2%	39.0%	39.9%
Return on assets	11.23%	9.11%	10.23%	9.61%	10.05%
Profit margin	11.64%	8.92%	10.43%	9.32%	10.05%
Asset turnover (x)	.97x	1.02x	.98x	1.03x	1.00x
Interest rate	5.40%	5.63%	5.57%	5.38%	5.50%
Debt/Equity	1.25x	1.26x	1.09x	.98x	.98x
Equity ($ millions)	$405.00	$425.00	$444.00	$472.00	
No. of shares (millions)	30.80	30.70	30.60	30.60	30.60
Return on equity	11.38%	7.62%	9.32%	8.41%	
Book value per share	$ 13.15	$ 13.84	$ 14.51	$ 15.42	

LODGINGS (HOSPITALITY) DIVISION

The motel/hotel industry experienced considerable growth between 1964 and 1973. However, with the traumatic arrival of the energy crisis, it became obvious that this growth would slow down markedly. High interest rates would place a strain on the building of new capacity, since so much of the rapidly rising construction costs also required financing. Moreover, rising energy prices would no doubt put a damper on the amount of discretionary income available for travel. Sales of the industry have grown at a compound annual rate of 8 percent. However, the motel segment within that overall industry trend has grown at close to 12 percent compounded annually. The higher rate of growth for the motel area reflects a shift away from downtown areas; consumer desires for the more informal lodgings accommodations provided by the motel or motor-lodge type of facilities, both for family and business travel; and the continued increase of auto travel, facilitated by the use of modern highways and interstate turnpikes. A positive outlook for the lodgings industry is based in part upon the following: higher disposable income, which will allow more people from different income levels a higher frequency of travel; and more leisure time, as a result of longer vacation periods, possibly shorter workweeks, and the Monday holiday laws. Chain operations should continue to exert a very strong force in the future growth of the industry.

The chain operators, for reasons already cited, should fare better than the average non-chain-affiliated firm. The company's size, experience, marketing expertise, and financial capability place Holiday Inns in an excellent position within the industry over the next few years. For the industry as well as for Holiday Inns, 1977 was a pivotal year because of improving supply/demand relationships.

In building a forecast of revenues and expenses for this division, four main factors must be analyzed: the rooms available, the rates charged for these rooms, the occupancy rate of these rooms, and the amount of food and beverage consumed relative to room revenues. The rooms available are multiplied by the average room rate, and this figure is multiplied by the projected occupancy rate to obtain a forecast of revenue generated by lodgings operations. Then the food and beverage ratio is multiplied by the lodgings revenue to get food and beverage revenue. These two figures are added together to obtain the revenues of the division.

The process above represents a somewhat simplified version of the actual procedure. In actuality, consideration must be given to the type of rooms that are added—for example, a highway interchange motel, an inner-city motel, or a plush resort motel, perhaps in a foreign country. Each type of motel will have a different room rate and will take a different amount of time to achieve its "true" occupancy level.[14] During 1977, we estimated the occupancy rate to be

---

[14]Also, most inns are franchisee-owned rather than company-owned, and the revenue derived is different from that of the firm-owned motel. In 1976 the split was approximately 21 percent company-owned rooms and 79 percent franchisee-owned. Under the franchise arrangement, HIA receives an initial payment plus a royalty based on the revenue of the inn.

70 percent and the average revenue to be $23.50 per room. These figures compared with a 68 percent occupancy level and $22.17 average room revenue in 1976. All these factors were taken into account in building a forecast of lodgings revenue.

Using the blend of higher room rates and an improved occupancy-rate picture, it was assumed that Holiday Inns could potentially benefit from increased food and beverage sales relative to room revenues. While generally the hotel/motel industry has experienced food and beverage sales approximating 65-68 percent of room revenues, Holiday Inns' experience has been a somewhat poor 50 percent of room revenues. Management of Holiday, cognizant of this situation a few years ago, initiated a program to rectify the problem. Stated goals, although they are admittedly ambitious and will take several years to implement, set the desired proportion at 75 percent of room revenues. Even though this may not be an impossible target, let us assume that realistically the company can achieve a 52 percent proportion. Two of the steps taken to improve food and beverage sales are an effort to better the quality and image of the food-service operation, wherever possible providing a degree of uniformity of service; and the selective takeover of franchise food concessions, enabling the company to maintain better quality control. Assuming improvement in the company's food and beverage business, we projected a 5 percent rate of growth in this area. In 1976 food and beverage sales were about $148 million, or some 15 percent of revenues for the entire company.

As a result of better average room revenues, higher occupancy rates, and improved food and beverage sales, it was estimated that 1977 food and lodging revenues would reach $580 million, with expenses of $500 million. These figures compared with $539.4 million and $472.5 million, respectively, in 1976. Thus pre-tax profits as a percentage of revenues for the Lodgings Division were expected to improve to 13.7 percent in 1977 from 12.4 percent in 1976. Stated another way, Lodgings Division revenues should increase 11 percent, whereas profits should expand 20 percent. This is the result of operating leverage referred to earlier. This increase in contribution to pre-tax income stems in large measure from the two percentage points increase in occupancy levels and an improved average room revenue.

PRODUCTS DIVISION

In 1976 about 11 percent of Holiday's sales and almost none of its pre-tax income were derived from the Products Division. This group at one time consisted of three basic units: supply or distribution, manufacturing, and construction. The construction unit would build motel units; the manufacturing unit would produce furniture, carpets, and equipment for motel rooms and restaurants; and the supply division would provide such items as disposable products, furnishings, and kitchen equipment. Each activity was undertaken for company-owned inns, franchised units, and independents.

Holiday Inns decided to withdraw from the construction business in 1976. New units in the lodgings industry had turned down sharply because of both the energy crisis and high levels of interest rates. A further thinning out of activities in this area was anticipated with the selling off of manufacturing operations. (Write-offs due to abandoning construction activity were a major cause of the barely breakeven performance of the Products Division in 1976.)

For 1977 the Products Division was streamlined down to various supply and distribution activities. This type of business was expected to benefit from recent growth in hotel/motel refurbishing projects. Refurbishing activity by Holiday Inns as well as others was the result of attempts to upgrade existing facilities and services rather than construct new rooms.

We expected 1977 revenues for the newly reorganized Products group to gain about 5 percent over 1976 levels. This was based upon continued growth in the refurbishing business in the industry, which usually lags a rebound in the lodgings economy; some expansion of the division's market share; and the continued, less cyclical, growth of the disposables part of the supply business. We expected pre-tax margins, which were practically nil in 1976 due to write-offs and would likely have been about 2.5 percent, to expand modestly to about 3.6 percent. Overall, Products Division revenues were $105 million in 1976 and were expected to widen to $110 million in 1977. Pre-tax (operating) income of $0.6 million in 1976 was expected to be $4 million in 1977.

TRANSPORTATION DIVISION

The Transportation Division of Holiday Inns comprises Continental Trailways, which operates throughout most of the United States, and Delta Steamship, which carries cargo between the Gulf Coast, South America, Africa, and the Caribbean. Transportation accounted for approximately 33 percent of the company's 1976 revenues and 32 percent of pre-tax income, with Trailways representing some 75 percent of divisional revenues and 50 percent of divisional pre-tax income. This division has been a source of problems to the company since it joined Holiday Inns in 1968 (via merger). The prime difficulties seem to result from the very different nature of the transportation business. While transportation is a capital-intensive enterprise like the lodgings business, the similarities do not seem to extend much further. Operating buses and steamships is very different from running motels. In addition, transportation is highly unionized, a matter that has never been a key problem on the motel side. In short, HIA management, while exceedingly well equipped to select sites for and operate motels, was less suited to run buses and steamships and to deal with strong labor unions. As a result, HIA management has been continuously plagued by strikes in one or another of the Transportation units. Perhaps for these reasons, the investment community has penalized the P/E multiple awarded to HIA relative to those of other lodgings industry firms.

Continental Trailways, Inc.

Continental is the second largest intercity bus system in the United States (behind Greyhound). Operations include passenger service, package express, charter service, and tours. At present, buses are employed on a route structure of 68,000 miles that extends into most major population centers of the nation.

Passenger service, package express, and charter business contributed 60 percent, 17 percent, and 20 percent respectively of the bus-division sales in 1976. Passenger-service revenues are primarily the result of price, total bus miles traveled, and the bus occupancy factor (load factor). Inasmuch as the bus business is primarily a heavily fixed-cost operation, it is highly leveraged, and a small improvement in the load factor could mean a potentially significant increase in pre-tax income. Depreciation and terminal-facility costs are the primary cost factors, incremental sales gains are, therefore, highly profitable.

Management's concentrated effort to increase load factors and bus utilization is of prime importance. Part of the program to augment load factors took the form of fleet modernization. Currently, 88 percent of the buses in the fleet are of the luxury, "Silver Eagle" type, air-conditioned, with quieter motors, and seating forty-six people. Additionally, management has taken steps to improve terminal facilities—including modernization, added conveniences, and so on—all with the hope of competing effectively with other modes of transportation.

In addition to the aforementioned attempt at increasing load factors, better utilization of buses includes the promotion of the package-express business. This service provides shippers with predetermined schedules, delivery times, and destinations. The Silver Eagle bus type offers 30 percent more package-express capacity than do traditional buses. Holiday's package-express business has been growing at a 10-13 percent rate, and we expect this growth to continue. This is an important facet of the total bus division, since additional revenue can be generated with a relatively small increase in costs.

Continental's charter and tour service is another example of utilizing the bus system more effectively. One of the reasons for the acquisition of Continental Trailways was the synergistic potential of Holiday and Continental. Since weekend occupancy for Holiday, as well as for the industry, is typically low, tour business offering Holiday Inns accommodations could potentially improve the situation. To the extent that Holiday's marketing expertise can translate this potential into sales, improvement in this area is possible.

Intercity bus passenger rates are regulated by the Interstate Commerce Commission (ICC). While the ICC granted rate increases in 1976, Trailway's yield was up less, mainly as a result of discount fare promotions to encourage the use of buses for long-distance trips.

The number of revenue passengers on intercity buses is distinctly affected by employment and real disposable income in the demographic groups that constitute bus ridership (mostly lower-income and older persons); weather is a factor, as is the competition afforded by passenger-carrying railroads (e.g., Amtrak). A sharp falloff in 1975 and 1976 in traffic due to inflation and the unemployment situation suggested to us that profitability pressures on intercity bus operators would provide leverage for the ICC to approve additional fare increases. Such fare increases appeared even more likely due to increasing recognition of the energy-conservation aspects of intercity bus travel.

Overall, we expected that Trailways would contribute about $250 million to company revenues and $13 million in pre-tax profits in 1977. These numbers compared with $235 million and $15 million, respectively, in 1976. Thus, while we saw revenue increases of about 7 percent from bus operation, we expected profits to decline by about 14 percent.

Delta Steamship

Delta Steamship contributed approximately 8 percent of total revenues but 17 percent of pre-tax profits for the company in 1976. Delta is one of eleven companies operating vessels under the U.S. flag. The two principal trade routes serviced by Delta are from the Gulf Coast of the United States to the east coast of South America and the west coast of Africa. Shipments consist mainly of industrial tools, supplies, agricultural products, finished consumer goods, coffee, rubber, lumber, and ore. As is the case with Trailways, Delta is subject to labor stoppages, and it is therefore a difficult area to forecast.

Delta's results follow the economies of the United States, Brazil, Argentina, and the countries of the west coast of Africa. Profits had been fairly stagnant in the early 1970s until Delta introduced LASH container vessels. Because these ships do not have to dock to unload cargo, turnaround time has been speeded up, allowing more voyages to more ports, with increased flexibility in ship deployment as demand shifts among marketing areas.

Despite the negative aspects of the labor situation (there have been two major strikes in the past ten years), one positive factor deserves consideration. Under the Merchant Marine Act, a portion of Delta's earnings (up to 90 percent) can be deposited into a reserve fund for the purchase and reconditioning of vessels. These deposits are tax-free.

In 1977 we projected a 1 percent decline in revenues and about a 2 percent gain in pre-tax profits over 1976. We saw some falloff in total voyages and import restrictions but some offsetting cost efficiencies. Delta's revenues were expected to be about $80 million and its pre-tax income about $18 million in 1977. These figures compared with $81 million and $17.6 million, respectively, in 1976.

Earnings Recap for HIA

Table 9-7 summarizes our projections for the earnings of Holiday Inns for 1977.

Dividing the $47.6 million available for common by the forecast of 30.6 million shares yields as EPS of $1.55. We multiply this by the forecast P/E of 9 to obtain a forecast of price of $13.95. Using a beginning price of $12.00 and an estimated dividend for 1977, we get a holding-period yield (HPY) of 20 percent:

$$\frac{(\$13.95 + \$0.47) - \$12.00}{\$12.00} = .20$$

Because this company has several divisions in several different industries of an evolving nature, it is difficult to apply the market-share-net-income-margin approach to HIA in any meaningful fashion.

TABLE 9-7

HOLIDAY INNS, INC., OPERATING RESULTS,
ACTUAL 1976 AND FORECAST FOR 1977
($ IN MILLIONS, EXCEPT PER SHARE DATA).

	Actual 1976	Estimated 1977	Percent Change '77 vs. '76
REVENUES:			
Lodging (hospitality)	$539.4	$ 580.0	+ 11%
Products	105.0	110.0	+ 5
Transportation:			
Trailways	234.7	250.0	+ 7
Delta	81.1	80.0	− 1
Total	$315.8	$ 330.0	+ 4
Other revenues	5.4	5.0	− 8
Total revenues	$965.6	$1,025.0	+ 6
OPERATING EARNINGS:			
Lodging (hospitality)	$ 66.9	$ 80.0	+ 20
Products	0.6	4.0	+567
Transportation:			
Trailways	15.1	13.0	− 14
Delta	17.6	18.0	+ 2
Total transportation	$ 32.7	$ 31.0	− 5
Other income	2.0	2.0	
Total operating earnings	$102.2	$ 117.0	+ 14
Corporate expense	($ 9.2)	($ 11.0)	+ 20
Interest expense	(24.9)	(24.0)	− 4
Currency loss	(3.1)	−	−100
Earnings before taxes	$ 65.0	$ 82.0	+ 26
Taxes	$ 25.4	$ 34.4	+ 35
Earnings after taxes	$ 39.6	$ 47.6	+ 20
Common shares outstanding	30.7	30.6	
Earnings per share	$ 1.29	$ 1.55	+ 20
Dividends per share	$ 0.40	$ 0.47	+ 18

Reconciliation of Traditional Approaches

We have now utilized two traditional approaches to company analysis in conjunction with our analysis of Holiday Inns and the lodgings industry. It can be seen that our forecasts of EPS and HPY under the two approaches yielded different results. When this occurs, the analyst should not be alarmed. After all, many different variables are used in quite different ways in an attempt to forecast EPS. In practice, then, the analyst must recheck his assumptions and calculations in order to reconcile inconsistencies.

The sources of inconsistent results between the ROI method which yielded an EPS of $1.35 and our independent forecasts of revenue and expenses which led to an EPS estimate of $1.55 can be fairly easily traced. The ROI method utilized some "feel" for certain key variables (e.g., leverage, margins, etc.), which relied a great deal upon past averages. The independent forecast of revenues and expenses seems more reliable, since it is more susceptible to fine tuning. The latter method accounts more for the evolving "dynamics" of changing internal and external conditions facing Holiday Inns.

Pre-tax margins for the company should improve substantially due to the impact of operating leverage (profit changes greater than revenue increases). Our independent forecast for 1977 shows revenue gains of 6 percent over 1976, but profit margins will expand 14 percent! Long-term debt and interest expense and, therefore, financial leverage, is being reduced as a consequence of debt repayment and property sales. Foreign currency translation losses for Holiday Inns were about $3 million in 1976. However, reduction or conversion of debt in foreign currencies to U.S. dollar-denominated debt should cause little, if any, impact on earnings from currency translation in 1977. The effective tax rate was 39 percent in 1976. We expect this figure to rise nearer to 42 percent in 1977 due to changes in investment credits.

Summary

In this chapter we have shown how company information can be used to calculate holding-period yields. Three traditional techniques for the forecasting of revenues and expenses were examined—the return-on-investment approach, the market-share-net-income-margin approach, and the so-called scientific approach. It was noted that all three yield point estimates, with no statement of their likelihood of occurrence. In the ensuing chapter, newer, more sophisticated techniques will be analyzed.

Questions and Problems

1. What is the relationship between industry analysis and company analysis?

2. Assume that the return on assets of J. G. Company is forecast to be 20 percent. The effective interest rate is forecast at 9 percent, the tax rate at 50 percent, and the capital structure is expected to be $10 million. If J. G. is financed with 70 percent equity and 30 percent debt, what will be your forecast of EAT?

3. What are the advantages and disadvantages of the ROI technique as a forecasting device?

4. What potential uses do you see for the ROI approach other than as a forecasting device?

5. Discuss the market-share-net-income-margin approach to company earnings analysis.

6. Allgent Corp. has two divisions. The A division captures 10 percent of industry sales, forecast to be $50 million. The B division will capture 30 percent of its industry's sales, which are expected to be $20 million. Allgent's A division has traditionally had a 5 percent net-income margin, and the B division has had an 8 percent net-income margin. Allgent has 300,000 shares of common outstanding, which sell at $30. If you require at least a 20 percent, one-year HPY, and you expect the P/E to be 10 next year, would you purchase Allgent common at this time based on your one-year forecast?

7. How would you go about forecasting a firm's market share and net-income margin a year in advance?

8. How would you go about forecasting the earnings of the local pizza shop via an independent forecast of revenues and expenses?

9. In analyzing any company using each of the three traditional approaches to company analysis, would you expect your forecasts of HPY to be the same under all the methods? Why, or why not?

10. Determine the sales composition of Textron, Inc., for the year 1978 from sources such as Standard & Poor's, Moody's, *The Value Line,* or the firm's annual report. What would you expect the revenues for the various divisions to be in 1979, based on 1978 figures and your prediction of economic and industry conditions during 1979?

11. Following are data for Patten Products ($ millions):

1978		EST. 1979	
Assets	$600	Revenues	$660
Liabilities		CGS + Oper. exps.	594
Short-term	25	EBIT	66
8% Debentures ('84)	125	Interest	16
10% Bonds ('95)	50	EBT	50
Common stock ($5 par)	100	Taxes	20
Surplus	300	Dividends	5

a. Provide the following information for an analysis of earnings:
   (1) Asset turnover:
   (2) Effective interest rate:
   (3) Effective tax rate:
   (4) Financial leverage:
   (5) Dividend payout rate:
b. What growth rate of EBIT can be expected?

12. The following data pertain to the Souergrapes Corp.:

Shares outstanding (millions)	5.0
Effective tax rate	50%
Annual depreciation ($ millions)	$2.0
Total debt ($ millions)*	$60
Total stockholders' equity ($ millions)	$60
Last dividend (per share)	$0.72
Rate of return on equity	15%
EBIT/Assets	20%
Market price of stock ($)	$20
EAT/Sales	12.5%

*Current liabilities	$ 6.0
10%, 1st mortgage bonds (1985)	24.0
12%, Subordinated debenture bonds (2000)	30.0

a. What is the firm's implied growth rate of earnings? Do you think this rate is exceptional for firms in general? Why?
b. Suppose the data above persist into the near future and investors require a rate of return (discount rate) on this stock of 13 percent. Is the stock a "bargain" in theory? Explain.
c. Suppose $20 million in additional capital is to be raised and is evenly divided between 10 percent bonds and new shares sold at $20/share. EBIT/Assets continues at its present rate. What is the new earnings per share?

13. If a firm enjoys a positive difference between the rate of return on assets and the effective interest rate paid on borrowed funds, why shouldn't it push the mix of total funds acquired to the maximum limit of debt funds and minimize the financing that is done through equity sources?

14. In 1978 Scoville Corp. had assets of $600M, and EBIT of $90M on sales of $750M. In 1978 the company earned $3 per share and paid a dividend of $1.50. What rate of growth in EBIT is implied in these relationships?

CHAPTER TEN

COMPANY ANALYSIS: NEWER APPROACHES TO FORECASTING EARNINGS

In the preceding chapter we analyzed three traditional approaches to the forecasting of company earnings and holding-period yield. We observed that each of these techniques yielded a single estimate of earnings and HPY. In effect, a probability of 100 percent is attached to the outcome.

However, analysts are seldom so certain of the infallibility of their forecasts. Furthermore, modern portfolio analysis requires that we forecast not only the *expected return* but also the *expected risk* of an investment. In this chapter we will present four modern techniques of analysis: regression analysis, trend analysis, decision-tree analysis, and simulation. Collectively, they attempt to overcome the weakness of, while building their conceptual foundations on, the more traditional tools. These techniques are appealing for yet another reason— they are inherently useful, for they can be applied on a limited scale even by the investor who does not have a computer at his disposal.

We shall see that simulation, which can incorporate techniques such as trend and regression analysis, seems to be the superior technique in the areas of security and portfolio analysis. Simulation permits the analyst to uncover a distribution of alternative possible outcomes (returns) and their attendant risks that are associated with a particular investment opportunity. Let us now proceed with a discussion of these newer techniques of company analysis.

Regression and Correlation Analysis in Forecasting Revenues and Expenses

As explained in Chapter 7, regression analysis allows the user to examine the relationship between two variables in the case of simple linear regression, and the relationship of several variables in the case of multiple linear regression. Correlation analysis permits the user to test for the "goodness of fit" between these variables.[1] Many of the usages of regression analysis discussed earlier in conjunction with industry analysis can be translated to the company level. For example, many of the applications of regression analysis for end-use analysis and the regression on industry sales of economic variables such as GNP, disposable income, and indexes of industrial production can be adapted to company analysis by regressing the same variable against items such as company or division

---

[1] The reader is urged to review the portions of Chapter 7 in which these techniques were introduced.

301

CHAP. 10
*Company Analysis:
Newer Approaches
to Forecasting
Earnings*

sales. Furthermore, experience may have taught the analyst certain relationships not only between external economic variables and company sales but also between internal company variables and external industry variables. Also, relationships may exist among industry, economic, and firm variables and company expenses. These relationships can then be used to build rather sophisticated systems of regression equations.

One advantage of using regression analysis in this way over the methods discussed in the preceding chapter is that the point estimates that are derived by this method are based on a somewhat rigorous statistical and economic foundation. Furthermore, the analyst is forced to think through the various problems of the company and the various complex interrelationships between internal and external variables and company revenues and expenses.[2] Another advantage over more traditional approaches is that correlation analysis permits the analyst to have a very specific measure of the explanatory power of the regression equation; and thus he has a means for assessing the reliability of his point estimates. Correlation analysis tells the analyst how well the independent variable "explains" the dependent variable in the regression equation.

Trend Analysis

In conjunction with regression analysis, the technique of trend analysis can also be very useful. Frequently, trend analysis of time series utilizes regression analysis. For the sake of simplicity, we differentiate the two by referring to regression analysis when we are studying the degree of correspondence between two "real" variables, and we speak of trend analysis when we examine the behavior of an economic series over time (time series). Thus, in the case of trend analysis, we are looking at only one "real" variable (such as earnings), which is being regressed over time—that is, over a period of years. This is how the name *trend analysis* evolved.

Figure 10-1 illustrates trend analysis applied to a series of earnings per share of a company. The equation of the "fitted" straight line might then be used to forecast the next year's earnings. For example:

$$\text{Year } x \text{ EPS} = a + bx$$

where a and b have been calculated from the regression analysis and the underlying conditions will remain stable for the forecast period. Therefore, if 1966 = 1, 1967 = 2, 1968 = 3, and so on, the EPS for 1980 would be calculated as:

$$\text{Year } 15 = a + b(15)$$

Frequently analysts employ trend analysis by plotting the data on a special kind of graph paper, semilogarithmic or semilog paper, in order to reveal starkly

---

[2]In addition, it is possible that more stable, systematic relationships will be found between the company and some macroeconomic variable than will be found between the industry and the same macroeconomic variable.

FIGURE 10-1

TREND LINE FITTED TO EARNINGS PER SHARE

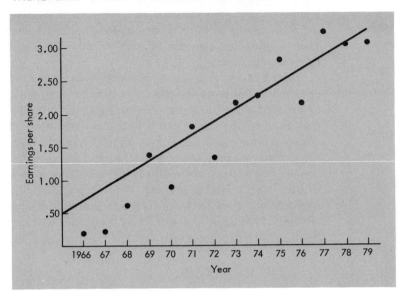

different growth rates. The advantage of plotting the information on semilog paper as opposed to plotting on arithmetic graph paper can be seen by examining Figures 10-2 and 10-3.

In an arithmetic graph, such as Figure 10-2, equal distances on an axis represent equal absolute quantities. In this example, each demarcation on the y-axis represents \$.10 of earnings per share. Because of this construction, Companies A, B, C, and D seem to have achieved identical patterns of growth in earnings per share between 1976 and 1979, since the trend lines are parallel.

However, if we examine the data carefully, we see that this is an illusion. Company A's earnings per share have increased from \$.10 to \$.20, or 100 percent during the period, Company B's earnings have increased from \$.30 to \$.40, or 33 1/3 percent, Company C's earnings have increased from \$.50 to \$.60, or 20 percent, and Company D's earnings have increased from \$.80 to \$.90, or 12 1/2 percent. Thus, even though their trend rates are parallel, their performances during the 1976-79 period have in fact been drastically different.

Semilogarithmic graphs attempt to overcome this optical illusion. In a semilogarithmic chart, one axis, usually the x-axis, is drawn as in the arithmetic graph. The difference lies in how the other axis, usually the y-axis, is constructed. Here, equal distance between demarcations represents equal percentage changes rather than equal quantities. Figure 10-3 depicts the same information as that in Figure 10-2, but this time on semilog paper. The reader can observe that when this is done, the four companies' trend lines are no longer parallel. In fact, the slopes of the four trend lines are radically different—as they should be. Thus the semilogarithmic graph clearly demonstrates the different growth

FIGURE 10-2
ARITHMETIC GRAPH FOR DEPICTING TRENDS IN
GROWTH RATES

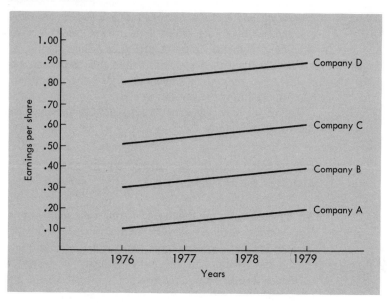

FIGURE 10-3
SEMILOGARITHMIC GRAPH FOR DEPICTING
TRENDS IN GROWTH RATES

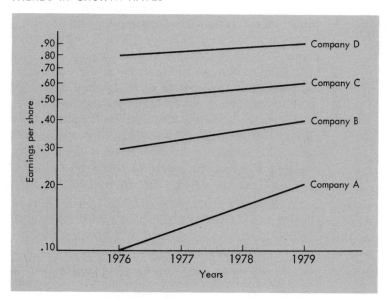

304

CHAP. 10
Company Analysis:
Newer Approaches
to Forecasting
Earnings

patterns in Companies A, B, C, and D and does so accurately. Here the different slopes clearly point out the difference in growth patterns of 100, 33 1/3, 20, and 12 1/2 percent. Generally, semilogarithmic graphs are very useful in comparing and visually demonstrating different growth rates among different companies. As a forecasting device, these trend lines can be used by merely extending them for the next period and then reading off the forecast on the *y*-axis. Clearly, this is a crude method that should be used only as an approximation, and only then when the underlying conditions are expected to remain stable during the forecast period.

Let us see how regression analysis and trend analysis can be applied to a forecast for Holiday Inns.

REGRESSION ANALYSIS AND TREND ANALYSIS APPLIED TO HOLIDAY INNS

We have already hypothesized in our economic and industry analyses that average hours worked per week, size of the U.S. population between the ages of 20 and 34, and disposable personal income were important variables in determining the revenues of the motel industry in general, and Holiday Inns in particular. In this section we attempt to investigate the possible validity of these hypotheses by regressing these variables against the sales revenue of the Food and Lodgings Division of Holiday Inns. The food and lodgings revenue figure is used because it is this figure that is hypothesized to be most influenced by these variables. Table 10-1 contains the values of these variables that were used in the regressions to be discussed below.

The procedure used was to collect data on these factors for the past several years, specifically 1967-76, since it was felt that the most relevant data would be the most recent. For if we want to use the coefficients of the fitted line to predict future values of the independent variable—HIA food and lodgings revenues—it is necessary to have (1) high correlation, (2) statistically significant results, (3) economically plausible relationships, and (4) stable underlying conditions. By the last, we mean that the environmental circumstances surrounding the behavior of the variables in the equation will be approximately the same in the forecast period as in the historical period used to calculate the coefficients.

In order to test the hypothesis that shorter workweeks mean more business to Holiday Inns, we regressed the average hours worked per week for private, nonagricultural workers against HIA revenues for food and lodgings. When this was done, we found the correlation coefficient was −.90. This figure is statistically significant,[3] indicating a high degree of negative correlation, since the limits of the values the correlation coefficient can take on are −1 to +1. In other words, the two series moved in opposite directions—exactly what had been hypothesized!

---

[3] Statistical significance can be determined from a simple test, such as a true-or-false test. The interested reader should consult any basic statistics text. Briefly, these tests tell the analyst if the observed relationship is meaningful in a formal, statistical sense—as it should be before he uses the regression equation as a forecasting tool.

TABLE 10-1

VALUES FOR INDEPENDENT VARIABLES IN REGRESSIONS

Year	Holiday Inn F&L Revenue (millions)	Disposable Personal Income (billions)	Auto Registrations (privately owned passenger cars) (millions)	Population Age 20-34 (millions)	Average Hours Worked/Week (private, non-agricultural)
1977E	??	$1,312.0	113.7	53.2	36.2
1976	$539.4	1,181.7	109.7	51.7	36.2
1975	525.7	1,080.9	106.7	50.2	36.1
1974	502.3	982.9	104.3	48.5	36.6
1973	467.0	901.7	101.2	47.0	37.1
1972	420.0	801.3	96.6	45.2	37.1
1971	360.4	742.8	92.2	43.9	37.0
1970	301.3	685.9	88.8	42.5	37.0
1969	253.0	630.4	86.4	41.2	37.7
1968	195.5	588.1	83.2	39.8	37.8
1967	159.9	544.5	80.0	38.4	38.0

Now the question is, How well can the "hours" figure predict HIA's food and lodgings revenues? It would seem in advance that even though the average work-week is important, it is not the *only* explanatory variable, and therefore, by itself would not be a particularly good predictor despite the high negative correlation. When we substituted into the regression equation resulting from the fitted line, we got:

$$1977 \text{ HIA F\&L revenue} = a + b \times (\text{Avg. hrs. worked, 1977})$$

Substituting values for a, b, and our forecast of average hours worked in 1977 yields:

$$\text{HIA F\&L revenue} = 7,874.31 - 202.40(36.2)$$

or, simplifying:

$$= \$547.43 \text{ million}$$

The 36.2 figure represents a forecast of the number of hours in the average workweek in the United States during 1977. It should be noted that this forecast is below the figure we arrived at for this division earlier, $580 million, using the revenue-and-expenses approach. This is not surprising, since the importance of the length of the average workweek is not all-pervasive. Let us now look at some other regressions.

To test if the size of the U.S. population between the ages of 20 and 34 was highly correlated with HIA F&L revenues, these variables were regressed against each other. The rationale behind this hypothesis is that this most mobile age group represents a potential market for the motel industry and Holiday Inns. The correlation coefficient of this regression equation was +.99 and, again,

306

CHAP. 10
Company Analysis:
Newer Approaches
to Forecasting
Earnings

highly significant statistically. In other words, these two series moved up together in a very significant fashion during the period 1967-76. Specifically, the
regression equation was:

$$\text{HIA F \& L revenue} = a + b \times (\text{Population, 20-34})$$

To forecast HIA food and lodgings revenues for 1977, the equation resulting
from a fitted least-squares regression line, and substituting the forecast value of
the independent variable, yields:

$$\text{1977 HIA F\&L revenue} = -1{,}112.43 + 33.27(53.2)$$

$$= \$657.53 \text{ million}$$

This figure is much higher than earlier forecast based on the length of the workweek. Again, we should point out that although the size of the population between the ages of 20 and 34 is important, it is not the *only* powerful explanatory
variable.

Disposable personal income is clearly going to be important to Holiday Inns.
Why? Because the more money people have available to spend, the more likely
they will travel and require the services of Holiday Inns. When disposable personal income (DPI) was regressed against HIA F&L revenue, a correlation coefficient of +.9741 was obtained. Also, the correlation coefficient was highly
significant statistically. Thus it was shown that these two series moved upward
together during the sample period in a very close fashion. Since DPI is an economic variable of broad impact, it was felt that it would be a fine predictor.
The equation used was:

$$\text{HIA F\&L revenue} = a + b(\text{DPI})$$

Substituting into this equation, we obtained:

$$\text{1977 HIA F\&L revenue} = -195.41 + 0.71(1312.0)$$

$$= \$736.1 \text{ million}$$

This is high compared with the $580 million figure forecast in Chapter 9. How-
ever, it was still felt that DPI is only one factor, and perhaps combining this
variable with another explanatory variable would yield an even better predictive
model.

So far we have tested Holiday Inns' food and lodgings revenues against
people likely to travel (population, age 20-34), available time (average hours
worked), and the discretionary income available to spend for travel (disposable
personal income). A fourth variable, privately owned passenger car registrations,
was also selected, since this variable is a good proxy for the available means of
travel. The correlation coefficient of this regression was +.994 and, again,
highly significant statistically. Specifically, the regression equation was:

307

CHAP. 10
Company Analysis:
Newer Approaches
to Forecasting
Earnings

HIA F&L revenue = $a + b$ (Auto registrations)

The resulting values for a and b and the forecast value of auto registration yields:

$$1977 \text{ HIA F\&L revenue} = -957.83 + 14.06(113.7)$$

$$= \$640.8$$

When a forecaster uses multiple regression analysis (regression analysis with more than one independent variable), he must strive to select independent variables that are *independent of each other*.[4] To achieve this, we used the following equation:[5]

HIA F&L revenue = $a + b$ (DPI) + c (Auto registrations) + d (Hours worked)

The correlation coefficient of this equation was .9979 and highly statistically significant. Since these factors together are so significant, one might expect them to be good predictors. Substituting values for a, b, c, and d, and forecasts of DPI, auto registrations, and hours worked, we got:

$$1977 \text{ HIA F\&L revenue} = -85.63 - .55(1,312) + 22.68(113.7) - 33.67(36.2)$$

$$= \$552.6 \text{ million}$$

This is below the figure in our earlier forecast. The fact is not surprising, because the equation in the multiple regression is a more complete "explanation" than that in the simple regression.

At this point, the analyst could attempt to build models through a similar procedure for the other divisions, or obtain forecasts using one of the other techniques for the other divisions, to get at total 1977 HIA revenue. He would then proceed to obtain expenses, EPS, P/E, and HPY. Again, however, no simple objective measure of risk is directly obtained.

TREND ANALYSIS

Now let us apply trend analysis to HIA. During 1967 a major change took place within Holiday: the acquisition of Continental Trailways and Delta Steamships. Thus, in establishing a base period for calculating our a and b values it is not meaningful to go back further than 1968, because before then HIA was a substantially different company. Thus we express the EPS for 1968 through 1976 over years 1 through 9 to get values for a and b. The reported EPS for 1967 through 1976 are as follows:

[4]When the independent variables are not independent of each other, complex statistical problems arise, and the results of the regression are suspect and not dependable for forecasting purposes.

[5]The variable, population (20-34), was discarded because it was the poorest predictor in the multiple regression. It did not add significantly to the coefficient of multiple correlation.

EPS FOR HOLIDAY INNS, 1967-1976

Year	EPS	Year	EPS
1967	$ .79	1972	$1.37
1968	1.08	1973	1.33
1969	1.13	1974	.89
1970	1.27	1975	1.37
1971	1.28	1976	1.28

The calculated a value was 1.018 and the b value was .0375. Now, to forecast 1977 EPS for HIA using trend analysis we need merely substitute into the following equation and solve:

$$\text{EPS } 1977 = \$1.018 + (.0375)(10)$$

$$= \$1.018 + .375$$

$$= \$1.39$$

The reader should note that this forecast assumes that the conditions that caused earnings growth in the 1968-76 period will be identical during 1977 and thus cause the same growth trend in 1977. To the extent that this assumption is not valid this forecast will prove inaccurate. Also note that again no simple objective measure of risk is obtained. The next two techniques attempt to overcome this objection by yielding both return and risk estimates.

Decision Trees

The traditional approaches to company analysis were criticized because they lacked an objective measurement of quality. That is, they were based to a large extent on subjective analysis and resulted in a point estimate, which did not carry along with it a formal measure of probability. Even though subjectivity has not been and cannot be removed entirely from the investment process, and the investor's or analyst's judgment will always be required, the newer techniques that have been presented thus far overcome the problem to some extent, because they are based upon formal statistical tools and often economic rationale as well.

Nonetheless, an important disadvantage still remains with these newer techniques: The output of the various regression models still yields a point estimate. Furthermore, this estimate of earnings, dividends, or price still does not carry a statement of the probability of actual occurence.[6] Techniques are available that attempt to overcome this last shortcoming.

Whenever alternative actions or probabilities exist in an investment environment, there should be some way of assessing the probabilities that the various

[6]However, the analyst can calculate—or have the program calculate—a standard error of the estimate, which can be used to determine the likelihood that a value within a range of values about the estimate will occur. See a basic statistics text.

309

CHAP. 10
Company Analysis:
Newer Approaches
to Forecasting
Earnings

outcomes will occur.[7] When a sequence of these decisions must be made, and the probability of a particular sequence's occurring is desired, the probabilities of occurrence of the various independent outcomes must be multiplied together. An example of two independent outcomes might be the temperature in Hawaii and the size of trout in a Rocky Mountain stream. Needless to say, the more alternatives that exist, and the more intermediate steps between the original decision and the final solution of a complex problem, the more complex these calculations become. Obviously, the expected value of each of the outcomes will be different, depending on the sequence of events that actually occurs. Decision-tree analysis is a technique aimed at formalizing and simplifying the procedure involved in the solution of such problems.

Perhaps a simple illustration will help clarify this technique. A decision tree contains within its branches *all* possible outcomes at a given stage of the decision-making process. Thus, when one adds up the probabilities of the end points of the branches, the sum will be 1, much as the probability of tossing heads or tails on a flip of a coin is 1. We say that the end points are collectively exhaustive. Since all specific outcomes are specified, we say they represent a discrete distribution—that is, a distribution in which only certain specific values are obtainable. However, even in the discrete case, a decision tree can become very cluttered, for the more discrete possible intermediate steps and outcomes, the more branches there will be.

Generally, when an analyst attempts to use a decision tree in conjunction with security analysis, he begins with a sales forecast. Thus, if sales can be at only one of three levels, such as $10 million, $11 million, or $12 million, there will be three initial branches with their associated probabilities of occurrence specified. However, should the analyst desire to refine his analysis significantly, such as by specifying all possible sales levels at $100,000 intervals between $10 million and $12 million, the number of initial branches, as well as of subsequent branches, will be significantly increased. Just to begin with, there would be twenty initial branches, as opposed to three in the former case.

Figure 10-4 is an example of the application of decision-tree analysis to security analysis. Assume that there are 1 million shares of stock outstanding. There are three key variables with subjectively determined probabilities that have been highlighted by the analyst based on his experience: sales (S), expenses (E), and P/E ratio (P/E). As seen in the partially completed tree, sales can be $12 million, $11 million, or $10 million, with probabilities of .2, .5, and .3

---

[7]There is a special branch of statistics whose purpose is to train the statistician in calculating these probabilities. For example, one such approach, the standard gamble, is explained in Robert Schlaifer, *Probability and Statistics for Business Decisions: An Introduction to Managerial Economics under Uncertainty* (New York: McGraw-Hill, 1959). The application of decision-tree analysis to security analysis is discussed in Jerome H. Buff, G. Gordon Biggar, Jr., and J. Gary Burkhead, "The Application of New Decision Analysis Techniques to Investment Research," *Financial Analysts Journal*, November-December 1968, pp. 123-28; and in a monograph prepared by the Research Department of Smith, Barney & Co., entitled *Risk-Adjusted Portfolio Performance: Investment Implications* (New York: Smith, Barney & Co., 1971).

FIGURE 10-4
A PARTIAL DECISION TREE APPLIED TO
SECURITY ANALYSIS

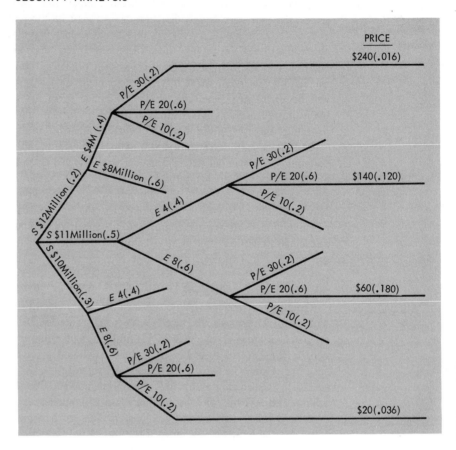

respectively; expenses can be either $4 million or $8 million, with probabilities of .4 and .6 respectively; and finally, the price-earnings ratio can be 30, 20, or 10, with probabilities .2, .6, and .2 respectively. Even in the simplified example, the inherent advantages and disadvantages of this technique can be seen.

We see that a complete set of possible outcomes (prices), together with their probabilities of occurrence, is generated from the analysis. This enables the analyst to set up a frequency distribution of prices for one period in the future. With current price and projected dividend, the analyst can calculate the frequency distribution of expected returns. Recall that the one-year holding-period yield is given by:

$$\text{HPY} = \frac{(P_1 - P_0) + D_1}{P_0}$$

311

CHAP. 10
*Company Analysis:
Newer Approaches
to Forecasting
Earnings*

where:

P_1 = price one year from now of one share of stock

P_0 = current price of the one share of stock

D_1 = dividends received on one share of stock one year from now

Figure 10-4 reveals that the maximum price of a share of this stock obtainable in one year is $240. The probability of this is about 2 percent. We also see that the minimum possible price will be $20, with a probability of about 4 percent. Two intermediate prices that are considerably more likely to occur are also given.

Let us trace the branches leading to a price of $140 and a probability of 12 percent. We see that sales of $11 million and expenses of $4 million are projected. Since we are assuming 1 million shares outstanding, EPS would be $7 [($11 million − $4 million)/1 million]. The P/E in this series of branches is 20. This leads to a price of $140 (20 × $7). To obtain the likelihood of this event, we must muliply together the probabilities associated with these levels of sales, expenses, and P/E. From the tree we see that these are .5, .4, and .6. When multiplied together, they come to .12, or 12 percent. The other branches can be completed by repeating this process.

When all other sequences of events (branches) are completed and the prices have been converted to HPYs, the analyst can calculate a measure of central tendency, such as the mean, and a measure of dispersion about the mean, such as the standard deviation. With all the work completed, the analyst and investor are in a much better position to make an informed judgment about the merits of this stock's purchase, since they have *measures of probable returns and risks,* rather than only a *point estimate of return.*

Analysts have also cited additional advantages:

1. Better investment decisions should result from a procedure that demands more intensive analysis. Breaking down investment uncertainties into manageable parts and analyzing them individually should lead to improved decisions when the parts are systematically combined.
2. Communication of investment ideas should be improved by the ability to express degrees of uncertainty more precisely, and by providing those taking investment action a deeper understanding of the thought processes behind the final recommendation.[8]

Let us apply this technique to Holiday Inns.

DECISION-TREE ANALYSIS APPLIED TO
HOLIDAY INNS

We have seen that if the analyst can determine possible values of key sequential variables with associated probabilities, he can use decision-tree analysis to calculate various terminal prices—that is, prices at the end of some holding

[8]Buff, Biggar, and Burkhead, "Application of New Techniques," p. 123.

312

CHAP. 10
Company Analysis:
Newer Approaches
to Forecasting
Earnings

period. These prices can then be used to calculate holding-period yields and their variability. Let us see how this was done for HIA.

First, after careful study of the economy, the lodgings industry, and Holiday Inns in particular, the analyst came up with values for sales, expenses, and P/E that he deemed possible for 1977, and he assigned to them the probabilities he thought most appropriate for each value. These are shown in Table 10-2.

TABLE 10-2
VALUES FOR DECISION TREE AND SIMULATION

Sales (in millions)	Probability	Expenses (in millions)	Probability	P/E	Probability
$1,025	.2	$ 975	.2	8	.4
1,030	.3	980	.3	9	.4
1,040	.3	990	.3	10	.2
1,050	.2	1,000	.2		

In addition, the analyst determined that there would be 30.6 million common shares outstanding during 1977. To estimate price, the analyst merely deducts an expense figure from a sales figure, divides by 30.6 to get EPS, and multiplies by a P/E to get a forecast of terminal price. Then the beginning price is subtracted from the terminal price, dividends added, and this sum divided by beginning price to arrive at an estimate of HPY. This process is repeated until all branches have been completed. There will be 48 end points in this example. How?

Well, we shall see. Table 10-3 shows a partial decision tree; let us trace out the top branch.

First, subtract expenses of $975 from sales of $1,025 to get income of $50. Divide by 30.6 shares to get EPS of $1.63. Multiply by a P/E of 8 to get $13.07, a forecast of terminal price. The probability is obtained by multiplying .2 × .2 × .4, the probabilities of achieving the given sales, expenses, and P/E figures respectively. The top line of Figure 10-5 shows these same calculations as performed on a computer.

Thus we see twelve end points for this one sales level. Obviously, each of the possible sales values has twelve end points, for a total of 48. Needless to say, it would be extremely time-consuming and tedious to draw out each branch and perform all these calculations manually, even for this simple tree. Two possible solutions to this dilemma are (1) to prepare the data in tabular form, or (2) to let the computer prepare the decision tree. Figure 10-5 shows the tabular output of a computer-projected decision tree. Note that the mean price is $14.38. The HPY of 23.7 percent can in turn be used to calculate a mean HPY and a variance of HPY.

Note that the mean price is $14.38. The yield per share (HPY) in each case is calculated by using a beginning price of $12.00 and an estimated dividend per share of $0.47 and whatever ending price per share is shown by the decision

313

CHAP. 10
Company Analysis:
Newer Approaches
to Forecasting
Earnings

tree. For example, the yield per share on line 1 of Figure 10-5 is calculated as:

$$\frac{\$13.07 - \$12.00 + \$0.47}{\$12.00} = .128$$

In summary, then, we see that decision-tree analysis is particularly useful when the number of sequential decisions (sales, expense, and P/E, for example) is limited, a manageable number of alternative outcomes are possible, and the analyst can assess the associated probabilities.

On the surface, decision-tree analysis seems to have done away with most of our objections to the other techniques of company analysis. Unfortunately, we should not celebrate too soon. In a real-world situation, there would be many possible alternatives, and many steps before we arrived at a final solution. Under these circumstances, the number of calculations and the plotting of a decision tree such as that in Figure 10-5 would be all but impossible (even this simplified example has proved somewhat arduous to handle).[9] Therefore we need another technique that does not require us to specify all the possible branches in our tree. The use of a computer would also help. Such a technique, which has only recently been considered in security analysis, is simulation.

TABLE 10-3
PARTIAL DECISION TREE FOR HOLIDAY INNS

Sales	Expenses	P/E	Price	Probability
	$975	8	$13.07	(.016)
		9	$14.71	(.016)
		10	$16.34	(.008)
	$980	8	$11.76	(.024)
		9	$13.24	(.024)
		10	$14.71	(.012)
$1,025	$990	8	$9.15	(.024)
		9	$10.29	(.024)
		10	$11.44	(.012)
	$1,000	8	$6.54	(.016)
		9	$7.35	(.016)
		10	$8.19	(.008)

[9] Furthermore, this example calculated prices only one year hence. If the analysis were extended to cover additional periods, the calculations would be increased tremendously. Part of the problems created stem from the assessment of additional probabilities several periods in advance.

Payoff matrixes are an alternative that is much easier to construct than the decision tree, but not as useful in sequential problems. For a very readable discussion of payoff matrixes, see Clifford H. Springer, Robert E. Herlihy, Robert T. Mall, and Robert I. Beggs, *Probabilistic Models* (Homewood, Ill.: Richard D. Irwin, 1968), pp. 214-60.

FIGURE 10-5

RESULTS OF COMPUTER-GENERATED DECISION TREE

	EARNING PER SHARE	PRICE PER SHARE	YIELD PER SHARE	PROBABILITY
1	1.63	13.07	0.128	0.016
2	1.63	14.71	0.265	0.016
3	1.63	16.34	0.401	0.008
4	1.47	11.76	0.02	0.024
5	1.47	13.24	0.142	0.024
6	1.47	14.71	0.265	0.012
7	1.14	9.15	-0.198	0.024
8	1.14	10.29	-0.103	0.024
9	1.14	11.44	-0.008	0.012
10	0.82	6.54	-0.416	0.016
11	0.82	7.35	-0.348	0.016
12	0.82	8.17	-0.28	0.008
13	1.8	14.38	0.237	0.024
14	1.8	16.18	0.387	0.024
15	1.8	17.97	0.537	0.012
16	1.63	13.07	0.128	0.036
17	1.63	14.71	0.265	0.036
18	1.63	16.34	0.401	0.018
19	1.31	10.46	-0.089	0.036
20	1.31	11.76	0.02	0.036
21	1.31	13.07	0.128	0.018
22	0.98	7.84	-0.307	0.024
23	0.98	8.82	-0.226	0.024
24	0.98	9.8	-0.144	0.012
25	2.12	16.99	0.455	0.024
26	2.12	19.12	0.632	0.024
27	2.12	21.24	0.809	0.012
28	1.96	15.69	0.346	0.036
29	1.96	17.65	0.51	0.036
30	1.96	19.61	0.673	0.018
31	1.63	13.07	0.128	0.036
32	1.63	14.71	0.265	0.036
33	1.63	16.34	0.401	0.018
34	1.31	10.46	-0.089	0.024
35	1.31	11.76	0.02	0.024
36	1.31	13.07	0.128	0.012
37	2.45	19.61	0.673	0.016
38	2.45	22.06	0.877	0.016
39	2.45	24.51	1.082	0.008
40	2.29	18.3	0.564	0.024
41	2.29	20.59	0.755	0.024
42	2.29	22.88	0.945	0.012
43	1.96	15.69	0.346	0.024
44	1.96	17.65	0.51	0.024
45	1.96	19.61	0.673	0.012
46	1.63	13.07	0.128	0.016
47	1.63	14.71	0.265	0.016
48	1.63	16.34	0.401	0.008

* *

MEAN

PRICE PER SHARE	14.3791
HOLDING PERIOD YIELD	0.237424

* *

Simulation

Since projecting HPY, even after much rigorous analysis, has been shown to require several key subjective decisions, it would seem to be less than prudent to make only one point estimate of holding-period yield. The judicious use of simulation as a technique allows the seasoned analyst to project a distribution of HPYs with associated probabilities of occurrence.

Simulation is a technique that systematically repeats the application of a rule or formula to a given set of data. Here we will be dealing with a special kind of simulation, Monte Carlo simulation. To use Monte Carlo simulation, all we need do is specify the probability distributions, either discrete or continuous, and the decision rule or formula that should be applied to the selected values of the variables.[10]

Monte Carlo simulation is named after the famous casino because of the procedure of selecting variables by chance (randomly). An example will help illustrate this point. Let us assume that we are attempting to forecast the price of a share of stock one year from now and its probability of occurrence, and that this estimate must be based on forecasts of sales, profit margins, net income, the number of shares outstanding, and P/E ratio.[11] Now that the variables have been enumerated, it is necessary to specify the probability distribution for each variable. This is done in Figure 10-6. For example, we can see that there is a 30 percent probability, in the analyst's judgment, that next year's sales will be $10 million.

After the probabilities are specified, the next step is to set up the formulas that are to be used. In this example, the formulas are:

$$\frac{\text{Sales} \times \text{Margin} (\%)}{\text{No. of shares outstanding}} = \text{Earnings per share} \qquad \textbf{(10.1)}$$

$$\text{Earnings per share} \times \text{P/E} = \text{Price per share} \qquad \textbf{(10.2)}$$

The computer program that has been written by or for the analyst will then randomly select numbers and match them against the corresponding values in Figure 10-6. One value of each variable will be selected; these variables are the same as in the decision-tree example.[12]

For example, the computer will select four numbers randomly and match each of the four against the distributions of sales, profit margin, shares out-

---

[10] A classic example of the application of simulation to a business problem is seen in David B. Hertz, "Risk Analysis in Capital Investment," *Harvard Business Review,* January-February 1964, pp. 95-106. An interesting application to security analysis is contained in David Whittall, "A Simulation Model for Estimating Earnings," *Financial Analysts Journal*, November-December 1968, pp. 115-18.

[11] This approach, and much of the ensuing discussion, draws from Ronald J. Jordan and Miles Livingston, "Simulation: An Application to Security Analysis," working paper (Storrs, Conn.: University of Connecticut, School of Business Administration, 1971).

[12] The expenses have been replaced with approximate net-income profit margins. Simulation can be used whenever decision-tree analysis can be applied; however, simulation is much more practical when there are many alternatives. In fact, if sufficient alternative values are specified, we would represent the data as a continuous distribution.

316

CHAP. 10
*Company Analysis:
Newer Approaches
to Forecasting
Earnings*

standing (in this case all values will be matched against 1 million shares because it is the only possible value), and P/E ratio. Assume that the random values so selected are $10 million, 33 1/3 percent, 1 million, and 20, respectively. Then these values would be substituted into equations 10.1 and 10.2. This would lead to, first, [$10 million × 33 1/3%)/1 million], or $3.33 earnings per share. Then EPS of $3.33 times a P/E of 20 yields a price of $66.60. This process is called one iteration.

The process is then repeated as many times as the analyst desires. It is generally repeated at least several hundred times, which takes only a few seconds of computer time. Thus, many prices and returns will have been generated. Next, probability measures can be calculated based on the distribution of these prices and returns.

At this point, the analyst has a calculated distribution of prices with a mean and a standard deviation. This information alone is extremely helpful, for these two statistics are necessary inputs for modern portfolio analysis. (This will be more evident to the reader in Chapter 17.) However, this is not the only information the simulation provides to the analyst. The distribution itself is very important. It can be portrayed graphically in a histogram (a bar graph) when the distribution is discrete, in a continuous curve when the distribution is contin-

FIGURE 10-6
PROBABILITY DISTRIBUTIONS OF KEY VARIABLES

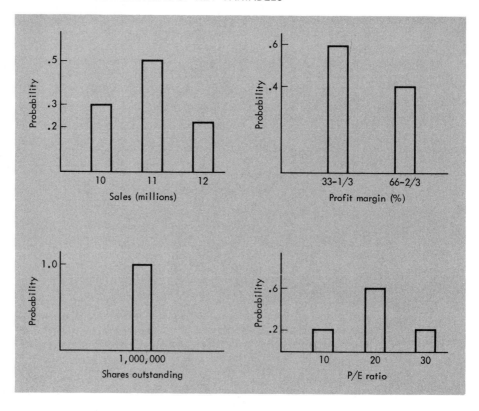

317

CHAP. 10
Company Analysis:
Newer Approaches
to Forecasting
Earnings

uous, or in tabular form as a frequency distribution. This allows the analyst to see directly by inspection in which ranges the most likely outcomes will be.[13]

The example just discussed can be made considerably more sophisticated and more accurate.[14] First, the model as it has been set up here implicitly assumes that the various distributions are entirely independent. This implicit assumption is made because we randomly selected values from the various distributions without regard to the other values that have been and will be selected from the other distributions. For example, we draw a value from the profit-margin distribution without regard to the value we have selected from the sales distribution. This can be somewhat unrealistic, because we might select a very low sales figure and a very high profit margin. This event is certainly unlikely to occur in reality, since low sales implies underutilization of facilities, which in turn implies lower profit margins. One way of overcoming this potential problem is to "constrain" the distributions so that the selection of certain values from one distribution is conditional upon the value of a previously selected value from another distribution. For example, if a low sales value has been randomly selected from the sales distributions, only a low profit margin can be selected from the profit-margin distribution. This is accomplished in the simulation program.

Another way of introducing more economic rationale into the simulation model is to generate possible values of key variables in the program itself via regression analysis. That is, generate values from a behavioral model that has been developed from past experience, and then select values randomly from this distribution of outcomes—outcomes that make economic sense. For example, experience may have taught us that obtainable margins are dependent on certain variables. These obtainable margins are generated from the regression that utilizes the "proven" explanatory variables, and then we select randomly from this internal (internal to the simulation) distribution. Thus Monte Carlo simulation provides much of the information the security analyst requires in terms of price forecasts and overcomes the objections to the other techniques.

At this point it would be helpful to apply simulation to Holiday Inns and observe the transition from theory to practice.

SIMULATION APPLIED TO HOLIDAY INNS

Fortunately, Monte Carlo simulation is a statistical technique that has considerably more flexibility than does decision-tree analysis. Simulation is able to handle processes that require many decisions and have large numbers of possible outcomes, because the computer has little problem in processing this vast amount of data. All the analyst must provide are the possible outcomes, their

---

[13]If the outcomes are normally distributed (which is very likely), techniques of statistical inference can be used in conjunction with the mean and standard deviation. The interested reader can refer to one of the statistics texts cited at the end of this chapter for a discussion of statistical inference.

[14]In addition, more decision variables (such as input costs, variable sales prices, etc.) can be introduced, and more alternative values of these variables can be hypothesized. These present more of a practical implementation problem than a conceptual problem.

318

CHAP. 10
Company Analysis:
Newer Approaches
to Forecasting
Earnings

associated probabilities, and the formula to be applied repeatedly. In other words, the inputs from the security analyst are the same as in decision-tree analysis, but the situations can be far more complex. You might think of Monte Carlo simulation as a way of handling a huge decision tree.

The formula used in our HIA example is to deduct expenses from sales, divide by the number of shares, and multiply this EPS by a P/E. Values for each of the variables (those contained in Table 10-2) are selected randomly by the computer and substituted into this formula. Thus there is no guarantee that the expected value or mean of the prices generated by the simulation will exactly equal the mean value for price of the decision tree—unless, of course, many hundreds of iterations are performed. However, for a fairly substantial number of iterations, the mean value of the simulation will converge on the "true mean" of the decision tree.[15] This is not necessarily a disadvantage of simulation, however, because (1) it may well be impossible to complete the decision tree because of its complexity, and (2) the values (mean and standard deviation) of the simulation will rapidly converge on the mean and standard deviation of the decision tree as the number of iterations increases.

For those who may not understand how these values are generated randomly, it may be helpful to think of a small wheel of chance with ten numbers—two are 1,025; three are 1,030; three are 1,040; and two are 1,050. This would represent the possible sales distributions for HIA in 1977 as perceived by the security analyst. Similar wheels are set for expenses and P/E's. The wheels are "spun" and one value wins on each wheel. These are combined via the given formula. This yields one price and completes one iteration.

When this process was repeated two hundred times, the distribution shown in Table 10-4 was obtained. The first probability column tells us the probability that a value will fall within a given interval. For example, there is only a 15.7 percent chance that a price between $12.50 and $13.00 will occur, given the input to the simulation, but there is a 33 percent chance that a price between $14.50 and $15.00 will occur. The mean of this distribution is $14.39, with a standard deviation of $1.26.[16]

The information is plotted in Figure 10-7. Again we can add the projected dividend of $0.47 to each projected price change and divide by the beginning price of $12.00 to obtain a distribution of projected HPY. This gives us a forecast of risk and return. If we do this using the mean value of the simulation, we get as our estimate of HPY:

$$\frac{\$14.39 - \$12.00 + \$.47}{\$12.00} = .24, \text{ or } 24\%$$

The top of Table 10-4 indicates that the holding-period yield is expected to be 24 percent, with a standard deviation of 10 percent. This would be the

---

[15]This is because all possible branches (with probabilities) have been traced out in the decision tree.

[16]Note how close the mean of the simulation is to the mean of the decision tree. This is because we have performed two hundred iterations. If we continued to increase the number of iterations, the means would eventually be equal.

TABLE 10-4
SIMULATION RESULTS FOR HOLIDAY INNS

	Mean	Standard Deviation
Earning per share	1.63	0.02
Price per share	14.39	1.26
Holding period yield	0.24	0.1

		Frequency Distribution of Values (%)		
Interval	Lower Limit	Prob. of Being Within Interval	Prob. of Less Than Value	Prob. of Greater Than Value
1	12	0	0	100
2	12.5	15.7	15.7	84.3
3	13	24.8	40.5	59.5
4	13.5	0	40.5	59.5
5	14	3.7	44.2	55.8
6	14.5	33.0	77.2	22.8
7	15	1.2	78.4	21.6
8	15.5	1.2	79.6	20.4
9	16	15.3	94.9	5.1
10	16.5	5.1	100	0

forecast of return and risk for Holiday Inns shares for a one-year holding period (in this case for 1977).

Problem Areas in Implementation of Newer Techniques

Thus far in this chapter, we have examined the newer analytical techniques of company analysis. However, we have not addressed some of the problems that face the security analyst or investor when he attempts to implement these tools. In this section we must face up to these difficult issues.

FIGURE 10-7
HISTOGRAM FROM HIA SIMULATION

```
                          RELATIVE FREQUENCY(%)
        INTERVAL
        LOWER LIMIT     0     5    10    15    20    25    30    35


        12              —
        12.5            —×××××××××××××××
        13              —×××××××××××××××××××××××
        13.5            —
        14              —××××
        14.5            —××××××××××××××××××××××××××××××××
        15              —×
        15.5            —×
        16              —×××××××××××××××
        16.5            —×××××
        17              —
```

319

REGRESSION ANALYSIS TO FORECAST
REVENUES AND EXPENSES

In order to implement regression analysis for the forecasting of revenues and expenses, it is necessary to develop plausible economic relationships between revenues and expenses of the firm and other economic variables, such as GNP, national income, some index of industrial production, per capita consumption of the firm's output, and so on. Generally, these relationships will be developed after examination of past data, the application of economic rationale to explain logical relationship, and the application and testing of these two items. After the initial testing has been completed, the analyst will undoubtedly find some relation between independent (influencing change) and dependent (affected by the influencing factors) variables that he feels will yield sufficiently good results correlatively. He may be willing to base his stock recommendation upon these relationships. When these relationships have been selected, monitored, and put in final form, the user will apply these various systems of equations to the analysis in order to generate forecasts of revenues and expenses.

Unfortunately for the investor or analyst, isolating key explanatory variables is a time-consuming process, and one requiring a thorough understanding of the firm's mode of operation as well as the structure and performance of its industry. But for those able to isolate these key relationships, the payoffs can be great—both in dollars and in personal satisfaction.

DECISION TREES

Decision-tree analysis, as we presented it earlier, attempts to enumerate the various possible combinations of events that culminate in the formation of share price and the probabilities of the various events occurring. Specifically, this can involve the forecasting of such things as revenues, expenses, shares outstanding, and P/E ratio, together with their probabilities of occurrence. This process necessitates that the analyst seek out all information he can get concerning these variables, and any others he wishes to add to the analysis, so that a more realistic set of outcomes and associated probabilities can be obtained. In addition to the price outputs that are generated in the specific decision-tree model we have discussed, it is possible with the proper statement of the end points of the branches of a decision tree to construct a cumulative probability distribution. That is, a distribution could take the following form (the values are hypothetical): There is a 30 percent probability that the share price of the firm in question will be at least $60, there is a 45 percent probability that the share price will be at least $50, and there is a 90 percent probability that the share price will be at least $25. In other words, as the combination of events becomes ever more pessimistic, the probability of accuracy of the final outcome increases. This is a very useful output of the technique, for it gives the analyst a "feel" for the underlying price-formation process.

Up to this point we have said very little about the problems of generating the necessary inputs to decision-tree analysis—or for that matter, simulation. Without going into great detail, let us introduce this required step in the implementation of decision-tree analysis.

First, it is necessary to know enough about the firm so that one can establish the possible outcomes that may occur. This information undoubtedly stems from insight into the workings of the firm in question and, perhaps more likely, insight into the workings of the industry or industries in which the firm is involved. With this understanding of the firm and its industry and a knowledge of historical sales volume, prices, revenues, and costs, the analyst is in an excellent position to estimate the likelihood of the various alternative outcomes. It is not at all unrealistic to expect this knowledge of the analyst. The research organizations of large brokerage firms and large financial institutions have been traditionally organized along industry lines, with a research analyst or group of analysts assigned to a specific industry—such as construction, shoes, and lodgings. This practice, in effect, creates industry experts whose sole job is to become intimately familiar with the inner workings of the industry and the firms comprising it. These industry experts keep on top of all the latest developments within the industry. In addition, they visit the various companies they follow and interview management personnel. The results of their activities, coupled with addresses by company officials at analysts' meetings, round out the analyst's main sources of information.

For those investors who are attempting to reach their own considered judgment, there is opportunity to receive this knowledge in the form of reports from the industry experts at a number of institutions, such as Standard & Poor's, Moody's, *The Value Line*, and a variety of brokerage firms. In addition, the *Wall Street Transcript* regularly publishes these addresses of speakers at the analysts' luncheon meetings, as well as brokerage reports on key corporations. With this variety of expertise assembled by surveying a number of sources, investors can reach a consensus opinion without doing all the legwork themselves. Furthermore, by knowing what constitutes good research (as we hope the readers of this book will be able to do), investors will be in a position to assess the quality of the research before they evaluate its recommendations.

Ultimately, then, analysts or investors using decision-tree analysis arrive at a forecast of a number of possible prices of the shares one period in advance, together with the probabilities of each outcome's occurring. In addition, these analysts or investors can construct a cumulative frequency distribution of price and holding-period yield that gives them an even firmer grasp on the range of the most likely outcomes one period in advance.

SIMULATION

Simulation can be thought of as a more sophisticated, more efficient approach to handling a sequential decision such as those handled by decision-tree analysis. Thus the problems noted above apply here as well.

322

CHAP. 10
*Company Analysis:
Newer Approaches
to Forecasting
Earnings*

The newer analytical techniques of regression analysis, correlation analysis, trend analysis, decision-tree analysis, and simulation are all interconnected in their attempt to get at an accurate forecast of earnings, dividends, P/E, price, and HPY. Simulation is different from the other of these techniques only in providing more information in the form of probabilities and accompanying frequency distributions. It draws from all the other methods in the process of achieving its goals.

Several key issues, however, still need to be confronted. How does the quality of a firm's management enter the analysis? Where does the all-important P/E come from? And how about the dividend payout ratio? These are the topics of the next several sections.

Management in Company Analysis

Before we can complete our company analysis and make a final decision or an investment action, we need to determine whether management is capable of carrying out its policies so that our expectations are fulfilled.

The future developments that will affect the variables we have discussed in the past several chapters will be in the hands of company management. So it is important that the analyst have faith in the ability of the management of a company he favors. Management should have clear-cut goals in mind, and strategies for achieving them. Obviously, among the key end points that will measure management's success will be the earnings per share, dividends, and share price. In order to assess the likelihood that management will achieve the desired end points of the analysis, the analyst can take a number of steps.

First, the analyst can look at past performance of management to see if his past expectations and management's past hopes have been fulfilled. Second, through interviews with management personnel, he can learn something about their backgrounds, experience, motivations, and outlook on such things as the firm's future research and development expenditures, plans for product improvement, marketing strategy, future competition, sales and profits. In the course of these interviews and his firsthand observations of the firm in operation, he must take note of management's ability to plan, to organize, and to select, motivate, and control personnel.[17]

In the realm of planning, the analyst should ascertain whether clear-cut corporate objectives have been specified. Organization comprises a well-outlined arrangement of duties, including who has what authority and what responsibility. Good personnel selection is management's knowledge of how to recruit, develop, and keep the right people for the right jobs—including the ability to motivate them to do their best in these jobs. Control involves a series of communication devices, such as budgets and reports, that permit management up and down the organization chart to keep tabs on corporate activities.

When this research is coupled with discussions with others who are familiar

---

[17]Townsend Hoopes, "Appraising Managements," and Harlow J. Heneman, "The Financial Analyst and Management," in Institue of Chartered Financial Analysts, *Readings in Financial Analysis* (Homewood, Ill.: Richard D. Irwin, 1970).

with the management of the company under analysis, the analyst can get an idea of how much faith he can place in management, and thus how likely it is that his forecast will be fulfilled. He will manifest his conclusion about management abilities in the P/E ratio he assigns to the firm's stock.

Determining A P/E Ratio

Thus far, our analysis has focused on determining a forecast of earnings per share. This was translated into price by applying the "appropriate" P/E ratio as multiplier. The forecast price was then a central figure in the HPY calculation. We now need to zero in on the critical questions, "What is an appropriate P/E ratio?" and "Where does it come from?"

The most commonly used P/E multiplier is defined as the closing price of the stock, divided by the reported earnings of the most recent twelve months. Thus, if the closing price of the stock was $50 and earnings for the last four quarters totaled $2, the P/E multiplier would be 25. Generally, the P/E is based upon the current price—that is, the closing price of the stock on the day the analysis is being conducted. Thus the P/E can change daily.

The multiplier, or P/E, is primarily determined by the riskiness of the firm and the rate of growth in its earnings. Low P/E's are associated with low earnings growth and high P/E's with high earnings growth. The Dow Jones Industrial Average, which represents a cross section of stocks with average risk and growth prospects, might sell in the 8-10 P/E range. IBM may sell at a P/E of 16 because of its high rate of earnings growth. Standard Oil of California may sell at a P/E of 7 because of below-average growth and above-average risk (that of the ever-present threat of takeover of the company's oil interests in the Mideast).

The analyst seeks various rules of thumb for selecting an appropriate price-earnings ratio that can be applied to a company's earnings to determine his valuation for its shares. The resulting price is compared with current market prices to assess bargains or overpriced stocks—at least, superficially. For example, if IBM is expected to earn $17 per. share and normally sells at a P/E of 16, the analyst might conclude that a fair price at present is $272. If the stock is currently selling for $260, some analysts might consider it undervalued. Should the stock sell for $280, it might be judged overpriced (overvalued).

ACTUAL AND "NORMAL" P/E

The determination of the current P/E on a stock must be followed by a standard of comparison, invariably taken from the historical record of the stock. The analyst may ascertain the median or *mean* P/E for a stock, its *range* over time, and the P/E relative to the "market" P/E (e.g., Dow Jones Industrial Average or Standard & Poor's 425 Stock Index). More weight can be given to the recent past. This provides boundaries within which the P/E should fall (assuming nothing has changed drastically) and indicates whether the stock is tending to sell at the upper limits of expectation (high end of P/E range) or lower limits (low end of range). Industry P/E's provide some guidelines; however, different

324

CHAP. 10
Company Analysis:
Newer Approaches
to Forecasting
Earnings

companies in the same industry frequently carry quite different P/E's.

Bing found that several techniques are favored by analysts in determining proper multiples. In the majority of cases, he found that analysts (1) used time horizons from one to three years, and (2) preferred to use several techniques in combination rather than sticking rigidly to one. Seventy-five percent of the analysts surveyed used "normal" multiplier rules of thumb under the following techniques:

1. They compared current actual P/E with what they considered normal for the stock in question.
2. They compared price times estimated future earnings (one to three years out) with what they considered a normal multiplier for the stock in question.
3. They compared the multiplier and the growth of earnings of individual stocks with industry group multiple and earnings growth.[18]

The lingering question is, of course, What is a "proper" or "normal" P/E? The question of a "normal" P/E for the market has been addressed by several sources. Cohen and Zinbarg estimate the P/E for the S&P 425 Industrial Price Index to range from 13 to 23, with a mean value of 17 for the decade 1962-72. The impact of inflation on earnings and the dividend payout ratio in recent years suggests to them a new range closer to 10-13 for the market P/E.[19]

The principal determinants of a standard P/E for a stock would be determined by the extent to which the following variables exceed or fall below S&P averages:

1. Expected five-year growth of earnings
2. Dividend payout ratio
3. Sales stability
4. Institutional ownership of stock (e.g., mutual funds, etc.)
5. Financial leverage (use of debt financing)

In practice, analysts frequently attempt to view the price-earnings ratio on a given stock in relation to the price-earnings ratio prevailing on some broad market index. The most common market gauge is Standard & Poor's 425 Stock Index. Once a sense of the relationship is attained, the analyst will attempt to estimate the P/E that will be applicable to the "market" over a forward period and derive a P/E for the stock based thereupon. In other words, how does the multiple (P/E) on the stock behave in relationship to the market?

The annual earnings per share for the stock is related to the high, low, and closing price of the stock for the year. Thus we get a P/E ratio based upon the high, low, and closing price for the year. The resulting P/E in each case is divided by the S&P 425 price-earnings ratio to determine a *price-earnings relative* (i.e., stock P/E relative to the S&P price-earnings ratio). Suppose the S&P price-earnings ratio was 10 and the calculated P/E for a stock was 15. The price-earnings relative would be:

---

[18] R. A. Bing, "Survey of Practitioners' Stock Evaluation Methods," *Financial Analysts Journal,* May-June 1971, p. 56.

[19] J. B. Cohen, E. D. Zinbarg, and A. Zeikel, *Investment Analysis and Portfolio Management* (Homewood, Ill.: Richard D. Irwin, 1977), pp. 245-55.

325

CHAP. 10
*Company Analysis:
Newer Approaches
to Forecasting
Earnings*

$$\frac{\text{Stock P/E}}{\text{S\&P Index P/E}} = \frac{15}{10} = 1.5$$

This in effect says that for the measurement period involved, the stock sold at a P/E that was one and one-half times the "market" P/E.

STATISTICAL ANALYSIS OF P/E's

Analysts equate normality with experience conditioned by recent history and intuition. The analyst's job remains essentially unstructured, and analytical approaches are highly individualist and eclectic, and therefore somewhat unstable. In an attempt to bring some scientific evidence to the problem of "normality" in P/E's, several studies have been conducted, using statistical techniques to achieve solutions. Correlation analysis has been prominent among these techniques. When using correlation analysis, the analyst selects factors or variables that he believes are the main influences on the price of stock. The aim of correlation analysis is to determine the nature and extent to which the variables chosen explain stock price.

Whitbeck and Kisor studied a number of stocks over the same time span. They speculated that differences in P/E's between stocks could be explained by (1) projected earnings growth, (2) expected dividend payout, and (3) the variation in the rate of earnings growth, or growth risk.[20] Bower and Bower used a similar approach for a different time period with another sample of firms. They used earnings growth and payout as variables but divided risk into subcomponents, including marketability of the stock, its price variability, and its conformity with the market (how it moved with the market).[21]

Whitbeck and Kisor applied their statistical technique to a cross section of 135 stocks in 1962 to explain differences in individual P/E's. They concluded that P/E is an increasing function of growth and payout and inversely related to the variation in the growth rate. In other words, higher P/E's were associated with higher growth and payout and less variation in the growth rate. Bower and Bower showed results similar to Whitbeck and Kisor's for a cross section of stocks over the period 1956-64. They saw the same positive effects of earnings growth and payout. However, their examination of risk was more detailed. They discovered that higher P/E ratios were associated with more rapid earnings growth and higher dividend payout; lower P/E's with less marketability, greater conformity to market price movements, and higher price variability.

Malkiel and Cragg studied the effects of historical growth of earnings, dividend payout ratio, and the stock's rate of return relative to the market in determining P/E. Earnings growth was found to have a positive effect on the P/E. The closer a stock's return followed that of the market, the more negative

[20] V. S. Whitbeck and M. Kisor, Jr., "A New Tool in Investment Decision-Making," *Financial Analysts Journal,* May-June 1963, pp. 52-62.

[21] R. S. Bower and D. H. Bower, "Risk and the Valuation of Common Stock," *Journal of Political Economy,* May-June 1969, pp. 349-62.

326

CHAP. 10
*Company Analysis:
Newer Approaches
to Forecasting
Earnings*

the P/E effect. The dividend payout effect was not clear; in some years, the higher the payout the higher the P/E, but this was not true for all years.[22]

P/E DIFFERENCES BETWEEN FIRMS AND INDUSTRIES

The main finding of these statistical studies of P/E's was that stable growth in earnings has strong positive effect on a firm's price-earnings ratio. Now let's look at specific firms to see if we can explain in some fashion the P/E's prevailing on these stocks.[23]

It is logical to assume that various industry groups would project an image of growth or lack of growth to the investment community. Therefore it should not surprise us that some groups will sport higher P/E's than others do. Table 10-5 contains data on average P/E's for selected industries for the years 1968-71. Two rather significant facts are apparent.

First is the relative consistency in the average level of price-earnings for these established industries over time—drugs have fluctuated only between 28 and 31, brewing between 22 and 25, and so on. Second, some industry groups have caught the fancy of Wall Street, and some have not. Note the huge difference in P/E level between toiletries and office equipment on the one hand and tobacco on the other. This variance is due in large part to the fact that the projected growth rates in earnings of the former industries is much higher than of the latter group.

But aside from the differences in average levels among industries and the consistency of P/E levels for many industries for a few years, it should be noted that large differences exist between firms in the same industry grouping. For example, Kresge and Woolworth appear to be similar operations, and certainly in the same industry. Yet Kresge's P/E is currently many times that of Woolworth's. The reason seems to be that Kresge's earnings have risen modestly but steadily for a number of years, while Woolworth's earnings have fluctuated erratically. The market appears to favor growth that is *somewhat predictable* as opposed to growth that furnishes recurring surprises. In the auto industry,

TABLE 10-5

SELECTED AVERAGE INDUSTRY PRICE-EARNINGS RATIOS, 1968-1971

	1971	*1970*	*1969*	*1968*
Brewing	22	22	23	25
Toiletries and cosmetics	36	29	28	31
Tobacco	12	11	13	15
Drugs	30	28	31	31
Office equipment and computers	38	35	37	42

[22]B. G. Malkiel and J. G. Cragg, "Expectations and the Structure of Share Prices," *American Economic Review*, 60, No. 4 (September 1970), 601-17.

[23]The examples of individual firms in this section come from John C. Perham, "The Riddle of the P/E Ratio," *Dun's Review,* September 1972, pp. 39-42.

327

CHAP. 10
Company Analysis:
Newer Approaches
to Forecasting
Earnings

General Motors usually has a higher P/E than either Ford or Chrysler, probably because of the leadership position GM holds in the industry. In addition, certain stocks, such as IBM, Xerox, Johnson & Johnson, Polaroid, Avon, and Coca-Cola, continue to support high P/E's compared to the market. This seems to be because of their impressive historical growth records, as well as the projected high, stable growth that is forecast to continue for some time into the future.[24] Where does all this leave us?

The business of selecting an appropriate P/E is one requiring *judgment*. The analyst must consider the state of the market and the specific industry group, and scrupulously evaluate *all* aspects of the individual firm. Only then can he make an informed decision.

Projecting Dividends

At this juncture we have gathered all the numbers we need to compute the projected HPY, except for the dividend. We already have the projected price, beginning price, and necessary tax and commission information. The starting point for the dividend calculation is the earnings projection, since dividends ultimately stem from earnings. The projected figure for earnings per share available to common is multiplied by the *payout ratio* (the percentage of EPS that is paid out as a dividend) to arrive at projected dividends.

This seems relatively simple; all we need is the payout ratio. Empirical studies have produced several interesting findings: (1) companies appear to have a predetermined payout ratio that they attempt to adhere to over the long run; (2) dividends are raised only if corporate management feels that a new, higher level of earnings can be supported in the future; and (3) managements are extremely reluctant to cut the absolute dollar amount of cash dividends.[25] We might apply these findings to the problem at hand—namely, projecting dividends.

First, we must keep in mind the evidence that firms have a long-run payout ratio. This means, for example, that on balance over time, a firm with a target payout of 50 percent is likely to pay out $1 in dividends if the EPS is $2; however, the *long-run average* need not be the figure decided upon in any one year[26]. The analyst must look at any trend in earnings, as well as at the absolute level of recent cash dividends. For example, suppose our firm with the 50 percent target payout had earnings of $.90 in 1974, $1.00 in 1975, $1.10 in 1976, $1.20 in 1977, and $1.40 in 1978, and had paid $.45, $.45, $.50, and $.50 in cash dividends during the first four of these years respectively. We must

[24]See Donald E. Fischer, "Performance of High and Low Price/Earnings Stocks," *Atlanta Economic Review,* Vol. 20, No. 6 (June, 1970), pp. 11-13.

[25]See John Lintner, "Distribution of Income of Corporations," *American Economic Review,* May 1956, pp. 97-113; John A. Brittain, *Corporate Dividend Policy* (Washington, D.C.: The Brookings Institution, 1966); and Eugene F. Fama and Harvey Babiak, "Dividend Policy: An Empirical Analysis," *Journal of the American Statistical Association,* December 1968, pp. 1132-61.

[26]The analyst can zero in on a target-payout ratio by computing the average payout over a number of recent fiscal years.

328

CHAP. 10
Company Analysis:
Newer Approaches
to Forecasting
Earnings

decide if management feels strongly enough about the growth rate in earnings (note that it rose between 1977 and 1978, from 9 percent ($.10/$1.10) to 17 percent ($.20/$1.20) to raise the absolute dollar dividend from $.50 to, say, $.65 or $.70. It appears that management will at least raise the dividend; the question is, How much? Will the payout again approach the 50 percent long-run target? (It has not been at that level since 1974.) If management is optimistic about future prospects, the $.70 dividend may well come about. Projecting dividends, much like projecting a P/E ratio, requires experience, insight, and sound judgment.

Forecasting P/E and Dividend for Holiday Inns

Now that we have discussed the theory behind the formulation of P/E ratio, dividend payouts, and dividends, it remains for us to arrive at a justification for the P/E and dividend we have used for HIA in our example in Chapters 9 and 10. The reader will recall that a dividend of $0.47 and a P/E of 9 were forecast for 1977 in Chapter 9. In Chapter 10, a forecast of 10 was the most optimistic of three possible P/E's used.

TABLE 10-6
HOLIDAY INNS, INC.: HISTORICAL DIVIDEND INFORMATION

Year	Dividends per Share	Dividend Payout Ratio	Average Dividend Yield*
1976	$0.39	30%	2.8%
1975	0.35	25	2.3
1974	0.32	30	4.0
1973	0.30	19	1.5
1972	0.28	19	0.6

*Dividend/Price using average of high and low price.
Source: Standard & Poor's *Stock Reports.*

Table 10-6 contains dividend data on Holiday Inns for 1972 through 1976.
During the 1967-71 period the company had an average dividend payout ratio of about 16 percent. This relatively low payout rate prevailed, since during these days of vigorously expanding earnings Holiday was also depending upon much needed internal financing to support additions to unit capacity. Since 1971 the concentration on internal operating improvements and reduced activity in terms of adding new capacity has apparently influenced the management to adopt a higher dividend payout. Extra pressure has come to bear upon Holiday for higher absolute dividends as the investing public has shifted interest dramatically toward requiring more of total expected return on the "front end." That is, many investors have expressed the sentiment that a "bird-in-the-hand (dividend) is worth more than something-in-the-bush (price appreciation)." Between 1967 and 1972 the average dividend yield on Holiday shares was a paltry 0.6

329

CHAP. 10
Company Analysis:
Newer Approaches
to Forecasting
Earnings

percent. Since 1972 a combination of lower share price and improved dividends has raised the yield well above the 2.5 percent level, on average.

Based upon the recent trend of quarterly dividends, and management pronouncements on the matter of dividend policy, it is realistic to assume that the annual dividend per share in 1977 will approach $0.47. This amount is also in line with what we perceive to be a new target-payout rate of the company in the area of 25-30 percent (30 percent of $1.55 estimated EPS is about $0.47).

TABLE 10-7
HOLIDAY INNS P/E RATIO: ABSOLUTE AND RELATIVE
TO MARKET, 1972-1976

	1972	*1973*	*1974*	*1975*	*1976*
P/E ratio range	40-26	29-7	17-4	12-4	16-8
P/E relative to S&P 425:					
High price	2.1	1.9	1.5	.9	1.0
Low price	1.6	.6	.6	.4	.8
Year-end closing price	1.6	.7	.6	.9	.8

Source: Standard & Poor's *Stock Reports*.

In Table 10-7 we see the P/E range for Holiday Inns during the 1972-76 period.

The slowdown in Holiday Inns' earnings growth rate commencing in 1971 and 1972 and the subsequent erratic nature of earnings in the 1974-75 period are reflected in Table 10-7. The P/E applied to Holiday's shares eroded relative to what investors were willing to pay for a dollar of market earnings. The average P/E (average of high and low) for Holiday had the following pattern from 1973 through 1976: 33, 18, 11, 8, and 12. It would appear from the P/E relatives that the P/E for Holiday using the year-end closing price will be in the range of 80 to 90 percent of the S&P 425 price-earnings ratio. Based upon our earlier examination of the economic outlook for 1977, we would predict that the S&P 425 Index price-earnings ratio for the year would be in the vicinity of 9 to 10. Thus a reasonable estimate for the P/E to use with our earnings forecast for Holiday might be in the 8 to 9 range.

Summary

In this chapter we have discussed several newer techniques of company analysis—regression analysis and the related tools of trend and correlation analysis, decision-tree analysis, and simulation. We have noted the strengths of these approaches as well as potential troublespots; however, on balance, we have concluded that they are superior to the more traditional techniques. In short, the newer methods have the strengths of the traditional methods while attempting to overcome their shortcomings.

1. What is the primary shortcoming of the traditional approaches to company analysis?

2. How should an analyst go about selecting variables to use in a regression during the company-analysis phase of his security evaluation procedures?

3. What variables do you think might "explain" the sales of a steel manufacturer? Why?

4. Differentiate between trend analysis and regression analysis.

5. Why are semilog graphs useful in plotting growth rates?

6. What are the pros and cons of using decision trees?

7. Prepare a decision tree for U.S. Steel, with no more than three branches at each stage of the tree.

8. What is simulation? Do you think it might be a useful technique in security analysis? Why? How would you simulate the data in your answer to Question 3? Would you expect the means of the end points of the decision tree and the mean value of the result of simulation to be equal?

9. If you were a junior security analyst in a conservative research department, how might you try to convince management to experiment with more modern techniques of company analysis?

10. What determines an appropriate P/E for the analyst to use? Why is this important?

11. What variables have been found to be useful in "explaining" P/E's?

12. Would you expect firms in the same industry to have approximately the same P/E's? Explain.

13. How might you forecast a firm's dividend for the next year? Forecast U.S. Steel's dividend for next year using this approach.

14. Based on your analysis of U.S. Steel performed above, what is your forecast of a one-year holding-period yield for U.S. Steel, beginning with yesterday's price?

CHAPTER
ELEVEN

OPTIONS

So far we have discussed risk and return on common stocks from the viewpoint of a direct commitment. But it is also possible to buy, sell, and even issue rights to a stock with price and time stipulations. These rights to buy and sell underlying securities are called *options*. Options are in reality "derivative" assets. Their value flows directly from the underlying common stock to which they are related.

The right to buy a security is referred to as a *call* option; the right to sell is a *put* option. There are two principal variants of call options—warrants and convertibles—which are distinguished by (1) the length of time during which they are exercisable, and (2) the reasons behind their origin.

Corporations issue call options against their own securities. Individual and institutional investors issue (write) and purchase put and call options in order to speculate in securities they do not own at the time or to hedge a position already established in a security. These speculative and hedging ingredients in options will be examined as our discussion unfolds.

Warrants

A *warrant* is a call option to buy a stated number of shares of stock at a specified price. The typical warrant has a period of several years during which it is exercisable. Warrants specify an option price that exceeds the current price of the common stock.

Warrants often originate in company reorganizations or are offered as inducements to potential investors to purchase bonds or preferred stocks offering terms less favorable than those the investors would otherwise require. But in return for accepting less favorable terms on the senior securities, such as a lower interest rate, the investor acquires an option on the possible appreciation of the common stock of the firm. He may then sell the warrants if he desires, since warrants are normally detachable from the senior security and may be traded separately.

VALUE OF A WARRANT

A warrant's value, theoretically, is determined by the market price of the associated common stock and the option price. The theoretical value of the warrant would equal:

$$\text{(Market price of common stock} - \text{Option price)} \times \text{Number of shares each}$$
$$\text{warrant entitles owner to purchase}$$

This formula yields a *theoretical* value of zero for any warrant on a common stock whose market price is below the option price (negative values are meaningless). But *actual* prices of warrants under these conditions are greater than zero. In fact, actual prices almost always exceed theoretical values. The difference between the actual price and the theoretical value is called the *premium*.

Warrant Premiums

The existence of premiums on warrants is partly due to the attractive leverage features that they offer. The lower price of warrants, which usually enjoy the same absolute change in value as the underlying common stock, enables them to return much higher profits as a percentage of investment. Suppose that warrants entitling their holder to purchase one share of AT&T at $52 are selling at $12, and that the AT&T common is selling at $48. The warrants have a theoretical value of zero $(48 - 52)$. As the AT&T common moves to $52, assume that the price of the warrant moves to $16. The holder of the common stock receives a holding-period yield of about 8 percent $[(52 - 48)/48]$. The holder of a warrant receives a 33 percent holding-period yield $[(16 - 12)/12]$. However, this leverage can also work against the warrant holder if the common moves downward.

If a stock has any potential for rising above the option price during the life of the warrant, then the warrant will become a valuable instrument, with its ability to generate high-percentage returns on investment. Thus, warrants on more volatile stocks, or stocks with higher probabilities of obtaining prices above the option price, will have higher premiums. Likewise, the longer the remaining period of the warrant, the higher the probability that the price of the common will exceed the option price, and thus the higher the premium.

The leverage effect leads one to expect a higher premium on a warrant whose associated common stock has a value that is a high multiple of the value of the warrant. Consider a warrant providing the holder the option to buy one share of stock at $10. Assume that the warrant and the stock trade on parity over time; that is, the warrant sells at its theoretical value, or a zero premium. The price relationships below are intended to depict behavior over six years:

	Period					
	1	*2*	*3*	*4*	*5*	*6*
Stock price	$12	$15	$30	$45	$90	$99
Warrant price	$2	$5	$20	$35	$80	$89
Stock warrant ratio	6	3	1.5	1.29	1.125	1.11

From period 1 to 2, the stock advanced 25 percent ($12 to $15) while the warrant jumped 150 percent ($2 to $5); from period 2 to 3, the stock advanced 100 percent (15 to 30) and the warrant climbed 300 percent (5 to 20); and so on. Notice how leverage is operating—and how it is gradually dwindling. In the first case, the warrant moved six times as much as the stock (150/25). From period 2 to 3, the warrant moved only three times as much as the stock (300/100). The stock-warrant ratio is a kind of leverage or magnification index. As it becomes smaller, the leverage effect is diminishing.

Potential warrant holders should note that as time goes on, the remaining option period decreases (if the warrant has an expiration date), and as the price moves upward significantly, the leverage effects are lessened. These changes, as well as changing expectations for the associated stock, can result in changes in the premium a warrant commands.

The existence of a positive premium on a warrant means that it will always be more beneficial for the warrant owner to sell his warrant, thus realizing its theoretical value plus its premium, than to exercise it. The reason is that in exercising it he would receive only the theoretical value. This also, however, shows that the premium associated with a warrant will shrink as its expiration date approaches, other factors remaining constant. On the expiration date, the actual value of the warrant will equal its theoretical value.

Warrant holders receive no dividends. The dividend on the common can affect the value of the warrant because this current income is forgone by the investor who chooses to hold a warrant rather than the common stock. A high dividend payout may also have an adverse effect on the price of a warrant, because if the dividends were not paid out but were retained, their reinvestment could cause the market price of the stock to rise.

These are some of the factors that are thought to determine the premiums on warrants. The most important is obviously the outlook for the underlying common stock. An investor's expectations in this regard should be the prime consideration in whether or not he purchases a warrant. The leverage effects mentioned are a two-edged sword, with the effects on the downside being severe. After the investor determines his expectations concerning the common stock, he must then look at the warrant, determine its premium, and consider what changes in the premium, if any, might take place. The change in the value of the warrant will be made up of changes in the value of the underlying common and in the premium that the market places on the warrant.

Table 11-1 gives examples of three warrants with different life spans.

The Tri-Continental warrants are shown in Table 11-1 primarily because they are among the few "perpetual" warrants in existence. These warrants have no nominal due date. Further, note that each warrant entitles the holder to acquire 3.7 shares of Tri-Continental common at a price of $6.30 per share. These warrants are selling at just about their theoretical value.

The Avco warrants are selling for about 56 cents each (9/16). No wonder! The common is at $15.63 and the warrant entitles the holder to buy the stock at $56.00. There may be a chance that Avco common will make it to $56.00 by 1993, but this is quite a gamble.[1]

The Textron warrants, like the Tri-Continentals, are selling at just about their

---

[1]For a discussion of speculating in warrants that are away from their theoretical value, see Donald E. Fischer, "Shorting Expiring Warrants," *Mississippi Valley Journal of Business and Economics*, Vol. 10, No. 2 (Winter 1974-5), pp. 73-83.

TABLE 11-1
EXAMPLES OF WARRANTS

	Tri-Continental Corp.	Avco Corp.	Textron Corp.
Expiration date	none	1993	1984
No. shares per warrant	3.7	1	1
Exercise price (per share)	$ 6.30	$56.00	$10.00 §
Market prices: (7/77)			
Common	$20.12	$15.63	$26.00
Warrant	51.25	9/16	16.25
Theoretical value of warrant*	$51.13	($40.37)	$16.00
Warrant % premium†	0.2%	‡	1.6%
Stock price/Warrant price	1.4‖	27.8	1.6

*[(Market price common − Exercise price) × No. shares per warrant].
†(Market price − Theoretical value)/Theoretical value.
‡Infinite.
§Increases to $11.25 from 5/1/79 through 5/1/84.
‖Warrant price adjusted to reflect number of shares per warrant ($51.25/3.7 = $13.85).

theoretical value. Notice one key difference here. The exercise price rises from $10.00 to $11.25 on May 1, 1979. Some interesting pressures could develop for the warrants in the vicinity of this date when the change in exercise price occurs.

Convertible Securities

Convertible bonds and convertible preferred stocks combine the basic attributes of common stocks and corporate bonds or preferred stocks in a single security. Because they may be exchanged for common shares, convertibles participate in the growth and appreciation potential of the underlying equities. Equally significant, their status as senior securities with the obligation to pay fixed interest or dividends gives convertibles those qualities of nonconvertible senior securities that reduce risk. All convertibles possess such dual stock/bond characteristics; the extent to which one or the other attribute is more influential varies from issue to issue, and even for a single issue over a period of time. Therefore, convertibles may satisfy a wide range of investment objectives.

BASIC FEATURES

The discussion that follows deals with convertible bonds. Analysis and selection of convertible preferred stock parallels the examination of convertible bonds with slightly less complication along certain lines.

The number of common shares for which a bond may be exchanged (converted) is established when the bond is issued, but this number is usually subject to adjustment in the event of stock splits or stock dividends of given amounts. The number of shares of stock per bond is referred to as the *conversion rate*. The stock value of the bond at any given point in time can simply be derived by multiplying the stock price by the conversion rate. For example, suppose a convertible bond can be exchanged for 20 shares of common stock. If the current market price of the common is $45, then the *conversion value* is $900 (20 × $45). The conversion value will change as the stock price changes.

The convertible bond will also have what is called an *investment value*. This is the theoretical value based upon the yield to maturity of similar issues having no conversion feature. For example, suppose a 6 percent convertible bond due in twenty-five years is convertible into 20 shares of common stock. The common is currently at $55. Thus the conversion value is $1,100 ($55 × 20). However, suppose similar-quality bonds due in twenty-five years but without a conversion option are yielding 6 percent to maturity. This suggests an investment value for our 6 percent convertible bond of $1,000. This investment value is often regarded as a support level for the convertible bond in a declining stock market. However, the investment value also declines if interest rates rise during this period, as they usually do.

The notion of conversion and investment values (or the stock value of the bond and the bond value of the bond, as it were) must be compared with the actual market price of the bond to determine the extent to which the market price exceeds these levels. Consider the following for our 6 percent convertible bond that can be exchanged for 20 shares of common stock:

Market Prices:
  Stock $55
  Bond $1,200
Conversion value: $1,100   ($55 × 20 shares)
Investment value: $1,000   (to yield 6%)

In absolute terms the bond sells $100 above its conversion value and $200 above its investment value. In relative terms we have:

$$\text{Premium over conversion value} = \frac{\text{Bond price} - \text{Conversion value}}{\text{Conversion value}}$$

$$\text{Premium over investment value} = \frac{\text{Bond price} - \text{Investment value}}{\text{Bond price}}$$

$$\text{Conversion parity price of stock} = \frac{\text{Bond price}}{\text{No. shares upon conversion}}$$

The *premium over conversion value* is 9.09 percent [($1,200 − $1,100)/ $1,100], suggesting that the stock must rise about 9.09 percent for the break-even point to be reached, or: [($55) + (.0909)($55) = $60]. The *conversion parity* of the stock tells us the same thing: $1,200/20 = $60. The bond will generally sell some distance above its conversion value, since investors know the leverage potential in holding the convertible bond and are looking ahead at the future price potential of the common.

The market price of a convertible bond will normally equal or exceed the conversion value of the bond. That is, negative conversion premiums are unlikely.

This will be guaranteed by arbitrageurs. Let us see why. Suppose a bond is convertible into 20 shares of common stock. If the common stock was selling for $55 and the bond was selling for $1,000, the bond would be selling for $100 less than its conversion value ($55 × 20 = $1,100). Traders would see a profit opportunity in the *simultaneous* placement of orders to buy a bond and short sell 25 shares of stock (or multiples of this arrangement). They would pay $1,000 for each bond and receive $1,100 by delivering 25 shares of common stock to cover the short position—a nice $100 profit for each bond purchased. A lot of simultaneous trades of this sort will have the effect of raising the price of the bond and lowering the price of the common until an equilibrium relationship exists where the bond's conversion value is at least equal to or less than its market value.

The *premium over investment value* is 16.67 percent [($1,200 − $1,000)/$1,200], suggesting that the bond could fall 16.67 percent if the stock declined significantly before it reached a kind of price "floor." Presumably, if the stock declined from $55 to, say, $40, the bond might cease falling at $1,000 even though its conversion value would be $800 ($40 × 20 shares). However, it is likely that the deterioration in the stock price implies certain fundamental changes in risk surrounding the company, which will also reflect upon the quality of the bond. Increased risk in the bond might alter the required "straight" yield from 6 percent to a higher level, suggesting a lower investment value. Thus the bond floor (investment value) is not necessarily a rigid value.

It is also important to contrast the *current yield* on the bond and the stock to determine the relative income advantage (disadvantage) of holding one or the other. Suppose the underlying stock, selling currently at $55, pays an annual indicated dividend of $1.65 per share. Thus:

$$\text{Current yield on stock} = \frac{\text{Dividend}}{\text{Price}} = \frac{\$1.65}{\$55.00} = 3\%$$

$$\text{Current yield on bond} = \frac{\text{Interest}}{\text{Price}} = \frac{\$60.00}{\$1,200.00} = 5\%$$

In this instance the current yield on the stock is 3 percent and the current yield on the bond is 5 percent. In effect, the outright holding of the bond provides a higher relative income yield than the outright purchase of the common stock. Alternatively, a $1,200 investment yields $60 per year in interest or $36 in dividends [($1,200/$55) × $1.65].

CONVERTIBLES ARE A COMPROMISE

Let us see where we are at this point:

Market Prices:
   Stock $55
   Bond $1,200
Conversion Rate: 20 shares per $1,000 (par) bond

Values:

Conversion:	$1,100
Investment:	$1,000
Parity:	$ 60

Premiums:

Conversion:	9.09%
Investment:	16.67%

Current Yields

Stock:	3.00%
Bond:	5.00%

The central question is, Why wouldn't someone interested in capital gain (with some risk) buy the common outright at $55 and why wouldn't someone desiring current income and safety of principal buy a nonconvertible bond yielding 6 percent? Why buy this "hybrid"?

The general answer seems to be, in this case, that the buyer of the convertible would be looking for some compromise vehicle that provides a blend of current income, safety of principal, and capital gain potential. How much of each an investor wants and where he will compromise on each can only be determined by assessing (1) the bond's conversion premium, (2) the bond's investment premium, and (3) the relative current yields on the stock and the bond.

At current prices, purchase of the convertible bond provides a current yield that is higher than holding the common (5 percent vs. 3 percent) but less than owning a nonconvertible issue (6 percent). Purchase of the common at $55 and a subsequent rise to, say, $66 would represent a 20 percent capital gain. Purchase of the bond at $1,200 would suggest a price of at least $1,320 (maybe slightly higher). This represents a capital gain of only 10 percent. Thus, from a capital appreciation standpoint, there is less potential with the bond than with the common (10 percent vs. 20 percent). Another compromise. From a safety-of-principal viewpoint, a 20 percent decline in the common from $55 to, say, $44 would suggest that the bond should fall to a level of only $1,000, or 16.7 percent (to its investment value). There is relatively more "downside" protection on the bond than on the stock.

Different mixes of yield, investment, and conversion premiums will thus appeal to different investment objectives. The extent to which one or another of these attributes is more influential varies from issue to issue, and even for a single issue over a period of time.

RISK OF CALL

The possibility of call must be considered when investing in convertible bonds. That risk increases as the price of the common stock moves above the conversion price. A corporation that calls a convertible security expects most holders to exchange their bond for common stock instead of accepting cash (the call price). Therefore, convertible bonds are unlikely to be called until the bond is selling well above the call price and probably at little or no premium above conversion value. To continue our example, suppose the 6 percent convertible bond is callable at $1,050 and that the common sells for $60. The conversion value of $1,200 ($60 × 20 shares) is above the call price. What would most bondholders do if a call were made: accept $1,050 in cash or $1,200 worth of common stock? The answer is obvious.

As the price of the common passes $52.50 (conversion value = call price = $1,050), it will be difficult to justify paying any premium over conversion value for the bond. This is true since any premium paid will be lost in a call. Suppose the common is at $60 and the bond is at $1,300. If a call is exercised at $1,050, $100 is lost, since the common stock you receive is only worth $1,200.

EXAMPLES OF THE CONVERTIBLE SPECTRUM

Table 11-2 shows pertinent data for three convertible bonds. They are each quite different in technical characteristics that make them compatible with specific portfolio goals.

Let us try to sort out the complicated set of parameters to judge the compatibility of each of these bonds to specific investment goals.

Able Corp.'s 4.75 percent bonds due in 1999 are selling at $146, which is very far above par. The price has been pulled up by the common, which has advanced sharply. The bond sells right on its conversion value and far above its investment value. Buying this bond at $146 is essentially a quasi-equity commitment, since the bond is vulnerable to call (at $103.60). Moreover, there is probably a lot of conversion taking place, since the stock provides better current in-

TABLE 11-2

		Able Corp.	Baker Co.	Charlie, Inc.
1.	Rating	A	Baa	Baa
2.	Coupon/Maturity	4.75%, '99	6 1/2%, '90	4 1/2%, '97
3.	Bond price (% of par)	146.00	86.75	63.00
4.	Yield to maturity	6.52%	8.20%	8.33%
5.	Current yield	3.25%	7.49%	7.14%
6.	Dividend yield	3.35%	4.50%	5.5%
7.	Stock price	$83.50	$14.00	$24.00
8.	Conversion rate (shares)	17.50	54.42	14.39
9.	Stock value of bond (% of par)	146.00	76.19	34.54
10.	Call price (% of par)	103.60	103.88	103.15
11.	Premium over conversion value	0.0%	13.9%	82.4%
12.	Investment value (% of par)	62.38	83.00	61.50
13.	Premium over investment value	57.3%	4.3%	2.4%

Key:
(3) = % of par (i.e. 146.00 = $1,460/$1,000 par bond)
(5) = (2)/(3)
(6) = Indicated common dividend/(7)
(9) = (7) × (8)
(11) = [(3) − (9)]/(9)
(12) = Price required to give equivalent yield to maturity on similar "nonconvertible" bonds

come than the bond (3.35 percent vs. 3.25 percent). The risk of price decline is similar to that of the common stock. In sum, the Able Corp. bonds are an example of a convertible that has just about "run its course."

The Charlie, Inc., 4½ percent bonds due in 1997 are diametrically opposite to the Able Corp. bonds. These bonds exemplify a convertible bond that has "fallen out of bed." It has an option of only remote value. The price of the stock has fallen drastically and taken the bond to a point just above its investment value. At the current level of the bond price, the stock would have to advance from $24 to $44 to reach conversion parity (hence the sizeable premium over conversion value). This bond offers a holder relative safety of principal (vis-à-vis the stock), and better current income (7.1 percent vs. 5.5 percent). Appreciation potential is strictly a long shot!

The Baker Co. 6½ percent bonds due in 1990 represent what many would call a true convertible bond. This bond has an interesting mix of current income, safety of principal, and appreciation potential versus the common. The Baker bond is clearly superior to the stock in the production of current income (7.5 percent vs. 4.5 percent). The bond sells at only about 14 percent above its stock value (conversion value) and at just about 4 percent above its worth as a nonconvertible bond (investment value). Clearly, there is better downside safety of principal than on the common and upside appreciation potential, though it is less than for an outright purchase of the common. Some would say that this is equivalent to "having one's cake and eating it too."

In the real world of investment opportunities, convertible bonds will take on shades of the income, safety of principal, and price appreciation potential exemplified by the three bonds above. The potential convertible bond investor must always assess the trade-offs and compromises in current income, safety of principal, and price appreciation that are inherent in a given bond. The outright purchase of straight (nonconvertible) bonds or common stock is a viable alternative.

Holiday Inns Convertibles

In 1969 Holiday Inns merged TCO Industries into its organization. As a part of the purchase price for TCO, Holiday Inns issued shares of Special Series A stock.

The most important feature of this special stock is that it is convertible into 1½ shares of common stock and is entitled to noncumulative stock dividends at an annual rate of $1.70 of market value of common per share. That is, the stock pays dividends not in cash but in common shares, with an annual cash equivalent of $1.70 in common-stock market value. Were Holiday Inns common to sell at, say, $15 throughout the year, the special shares would receive $1.70/ $15, or .1133 shares of common stock as a dividend. To be specific, $0.85 market-value equivalent is paid, based upon the price of HIA shares, May 1 and November 1 (every six months). The number of fractional shares received will depend upon the price of the HIA common at each semiannual period, but $1.70 in equivalent market value is to be received each year.

This is a somewhat unusual brand of security. Yet it is not uncommon in mergers to exchange convertible preference shares for the shares of the company being acquired, mainly for tax purposes. The inclusion of a stock rather than a cash dividend allows the former TCO holders to receive a dividend similar to what they were receiving before the merger, but it allows HIA to maintain its lower overall cash dividend on the common, which was about $0.10 at the time of the merger. Further, HIA is spared having to use valuable cash to pay dividends. The holders of special shares can receive the equivalent cash through sale of their stock dividends in the market.[2]

The conversion option provides 1½ shares of common for each special share. The shares are callable after five years from the date of issuance at $105 per share plus dividends. The redemption price may be paid in cash or common stock.

Recently the following prices generally prevailed on the common and the Special Series A stock: common, 14⅛; Series A, $23.50. The common paid a current annual dividend of $0.46; the Series A paid $1.70. Let us assume that as straight preference stock (without a conversion feature), this Series A should yield 9 percent. (The fact that dividends are noncumulative suggests that a somewhat higher yield might be appropriate.)

Thus the following is derived:

Conversion value of Series A = $21.19 ($14 1/8 × 1½)
Investment value of Series A = $18.89[3]

The Special A stock sells at an 11 percent premium over conversion value [$23.50 − $21.19)/$21.19] and a 20 percent premium over investment value [$23.50 − $18.89)/$23.50]. The Special A stock is selling functionally as a convertible. The only clear advantage to the Special A at these price levels is its greater aggregate dividend. Converted, the Series A shares would receive 1½ × $0.46, or $0.69 in equivalent common-stock dividends, instead of $1.70. Alternatively, the common stock yields 3.26 percent ($0.46/$14), while the Series A yields 7.23 percent ($1.70/$23.50).

There is currently no call risk on the Series A, since the call price of $105 per share exceeds the market price of $23.50 by a substantial amount.

The purchase of the Series A at $23.50 would require that the common reach $15.67 before conversion parity is reached. Should the common rise 50 percent (from $14⅛ to $21), the Series A share should rise at least 34 percent (from $23.50 to $31.50). There does not seem to be much relative advantage to the Series A on this score. However, should the common fall to, say, $7 (a 50 percent drop), the Series A would probably not fall below $18.89 (a 24 percent decline) because of the investment value floor. Clearly, there is better relative downside protection in the Series A shares. In addition, the Series A are a better

[2]Cash will be paid in lieu of fractional shares if desired; the holder can purchase enough fractional shares to make full shares; and fractional shares can be sold through special arrangements.
[3]A dividend of $1.70, to yield 9 percent, requires a price of $18.89 ($1.70/.09).

current income vehicle, yielding 7.23 percent; the common has a dividend yield of only 3.26 percent.

Put and Call Options

OPTIONS TERMINOLOGY

To ensure a proper understanding of the following discussion of put and call options, it is imperative that certain terms be made clear at the outset. A standard *option contract* allows the buyer to buy 100 shares of stock at a specific price during a specific period of time, regardless of the market price of that stock. A *call* is an option contract giving the buyer the right to purchase the stock. A *put* is an option contract giving the buyer the right to sell the stock. The *expiration date* is the date on which the option contract expires—the last day on which an option can be exercised. The *exercise* (or *striking*) *price* is the price at which the buyer of a call can purchase the stock during the life of the option, and the price at which the buyer of a put can sell the stock during the life of the option. Finally, the *premium* is the price the buyer pays the writer for an option contract. The term *premium* is often synonymous with the word *price*.

Elements of Option Quotations

Listed option *contracts* are standardized in size (100 shares) and *expiration dates* (generally at three-month intervals). Trading in listed call options was inaugurated in 1973. Prior to that time, options were purchased or sold in the over-the-counter market solely through dealers and were more or less the province of professionals.

The newspaper excerpt shown here, Figure 11-1, is from the *Wall Street Journal* of Wednesday, July 6, 1977. The first item listed in this excerpt is the name of the stock with the exercise (striking) price. This is followed by three double columns listing the volume and price for each of the three expiration dates that are available. The final figure is the closing price of the stock, which is given just for the reader's convenience. Thus the second line for "Avon" means that a call on Avon with the striking price of 45 that expires at the end of July closed at $4 ($400 per contract) and that there were 360 contracts traded (36,000 shares). The entry "Avon . . . p . . . 45" indicates a put option. Note that under the October and January columns for Avon/40 the symbol *b* appears. This means that the 40 exercise-price call is not available for those periods. This is because the price of the stock had fallen far enough from 50 that the directors of the Chicago Board (CBOE) decided not to offer it for April and July, preferring that investors trade in the 45 strike-price call that is nearer to the current price of the stock.

The Alcoa/60 call has an *a* in the column for July. This means that although the call is available, it was not traded that day due simply to a lack of interest on the part of buyers and sellers.

At the bottom of the illustration the total volume is given. This is the volume

342

FIGURE 11-1

Listed Options Quotations

Wednesday, July 6, 1977

Closing prices of all options. Sales unit usually is 100 shares. Security description includes exercise price. Stock close is New York Stock Exchange final price. p-Put option.

Chicago Board

		— Jul —		— Oct —		— Jan —		N Y
Option &	price	Vol	Last	Vol	Last	Vol	Last	Close
Alcoa	50	57	2¼	18	4	12	4¾	52½
Alcoa	60	a	a	14	⅜	49	1	52½
Am Exp	35	3	4¼	a	a	a	a	38⅞
Am Exp	40	73	3-16	16	1⅜	15	2	38⅞
Am Tel	60	98	2¾	53	3¼	38	3⅝	62⅝
Am Tel	65	50	1-16	55	½	398	1	62⅝
Am Tel	70	b	b	a	a	5	¼	62⅝
Atl R	50	91	10	21	10½	a	a	60
Atl R	60	304	11-16	113	2¾	79	4⅛	60
Avon	40	134	8⅞	b	b	b	b	48⅞
Avon	45	360	4	140	4½	68	5⅜	48⅞
Avon p	45	b	b	101	⅛	31	1½	48⅞
Avon	50	524	5-16	250	1 13-16	105	2 9-16	48⅞
Avon p	50	b	b	165	2⅞	29	3¾	48⅞
BankAm	20	a	a	a	a	1	4¾	23⅞
BankAm	25	16	1-16	32	⅝	204	1⅛	23⅞
BankAm	30	a	a	142	1-16	78	3-16	23⅞
Beth S	30	b	b	70	1 11-16	52	2⅜	30⅛
Beth S	35	a	a	132	⅜	42	¾	30⅛
Beth S	40	a	a	4	1-16	a	a	30⅛
Bruns	15	31	1-16	102	7-16	153	¾	13⅝
Bruns	20	15	1-16	a	a	a	a	13⅝
Burl N	40	a	a	3	10¼	b	b	50
Burl N	45	25	5¼	16	6⅛	1	7⅛	50
Burl N	50	41	9-16	22	2 11-16	12	3¾	50
Burrgh	50	35	11¼	28	12⅜	a	a	61⅜
Burrgh	60	295	1⅞	112	4¼	16	6⅛	61⅜
Burrgh	70	a	a	155	15-16	60	2	61⅜
Burrgh	80	a	a	56	⅛	b	b	61⅜
U A L	20	46	11-16	88	1 5-16	158	1 15-16	19⅛
U A L	25	8	⅛	94	⅜	136	⅝	19⅛
U Tech	35	17	5¾	1	6½	a	a	40½
U Tech	40	100	1⅜	49	2⅜	26	3⅜	40½
U Tech	45	17	⅛	100	¾	13	1⅛	40½
J Walt	30	5	4¾	a	a	a	a	34½
J Walt	35	10	11-16	18	1½	2	2	34½
Willms	20	25	3⅛	67	3¾	a	a	22½
Willms	25	219	¼	52	⅝	157	1⅛	22½

Total volume 96,694 Open Interest 1,890,853

Source: Reprinted with permission of the *Wall Street Journal*, © Dow Jones & Company, Inc., 1977. All rights reserved.

of call contracts and must be multiplied by 100 to find the number of single calls traded. This should be done to make the figures comparable with those published by the stock exchange. Thus on this day the CBOE traded 96,694 contracts representing 9,669,400 shares.

The open interest figure is the cumulative total of all the calls that have been sold to open short positions. When a call writer writes a call contract, the open interest figure goes up by one and will continue to reflect that contract until the contract expires, or until it is exercised, or until the writer closes out his position by purchasing an identical call.

Each stock in which options are traded may have a series of fixed option prices for options maturing at the end of the standard three-month interval.

Table 11-3 shows quotations of CBOE call options for the Ford Motor Company. Ford options are quoted at four different option or exercise prices ($40-$45-$50-$60) for each of three standard expiration dates (January-April-July). The exercise price of an option is set by the exchange when trading first begins in that option. For example, suppose today is February 1. All January options have just matured, and the CBOE will start trading in October options. If Ford is currently $46 per share on the NYSE, the exercise price for its October call option will likely be set at $45. This will be the only CBOE call option for Ford for October unless Ford stock makes a big move. If Ford stock dropped down to $42, for example, an additional class of Ford October options—such as Ford/40—could be established by the exchange. This new option would trade in addition to the Ford/45.

TABLE 11-3
HYPOTHETICAL OPTION QUOTATIONS

Options and Exercise Price	*Closing Prices for Options Expiring End of*			
	January	April	July	Stock Price
Ford 60	1/16	1/2	3/4	46 1/2
Ford 50	1/8	1 1/2	2 5/8	46 1/2
Ford 45	*	3 1/4	4 1/4	46 1/2
Ford 40	*	6 3/4	7 5/8	46 1/2

*Unavailable.

Examine Table 11-3. At the time the quotations were available, the price of Ford Motor Company common stock was $46.50 per share. Those exercise prices quoted at the left that are below the prevailing price of the common stock are referred to as being "in-the-money." This means that the options have some "intrinsic" value represented by the difference between the stock price and the exercise price. Therefore we know that the "intrinsic" value of the Ford/40 is $6.50, and for the Ford/45 it is $1.50 (regardless of the expiration date). Any difference between these "intrinsic" values and the price of the option is what is being paid for an expected rise in the price of the common that *may* lie ahead. This could be referred to as the "time" value of the option contract.

Those option contracts with an exercise price that exceeds the current market price of the stock are referred to as being "out-of-the-money." In effect, these options have no "intrinsic" value. The prices quoted for these options are what is being paid for any perceived "time" value.

OPTION PREMIUMS

The option premium at any given moment is a reflection of existing supply and demand, a consensus judgment of the option's current value. This delicate equilibrium can be rapidly tilted either higher or lower by any of a number of events or combinations of them.

In times of rising stock prices, there is generally increased interest in owning options to purchase stock but less interest in writing options. Other things equal, more would-be buyers and fewer would-be writers usually leads to an increase in option premiums. When stock prices are declining or weak, there is more interest in writing options but less incentive to buy them. Premiums thus tend to decline.

The current market price of the stock in relation to the exercise price of the option is a major factor affecting the option premium. For example, if a stock is currently selling at $40 a share, an option with an exercise price of $30 is obviously more valuable—and will command a higher premium—than an otherwise identical option with an exercise price of $50. In general, option premiums tend to move point for point with the price of the underlying stock only when the option is at parity, that is, when the exercise price plus the premium equals the market price of the stock. Prior to reaching parity, premiums tend to increase *less* than point for point with stock prices. There are two major reasons: first, because a point-for-point increase in the option premium would result in sharply *reduced leverage* for option buyers (the ratio between the premium and the price of the stock). Reduced leverage means reduced demand for the option. Second, a higher option premium entails increased capital outlay and increased risk—again reducing demand for the option. Declining stock prices also do not normally result in a point-for-point decrease in the option premium. This is because even a steep decline in the stock price in the span of a few days has only a slight effect on one major component of the option's total value, its time value.

As a wasting asset, if an option cannot be exercised at a profit by its expiration, it becomes valueless. Thus, as the expiration is approached, its time value decreases. All else being equal, the more time remaining until the expiration date, the higher the premium will be. The volatility of the underlying security is still another factor influencing an option premium. The option for a stock that traditionally fluctuates a good deal is likely to demand a higher premium than the option for a stock that normally trades in a narrow price range.

Option premiums must be sufficiently high to encourage investors to write options, rather than seek alternative investments that may involve less or no risk. Rising interest rates therefore tend to put upward pressure on option premiums, and declining interest rates normally lead to lower option premiums.

Looking at the various Ford options in Table 11-3, notice that for any standard exercise price (e.g., Ford/50), the market price of the option increases as the contract gets longer. For example, the Ford/50 due in April can be purchased for $1.50. This means $1.50 per share in the standard contract of 100 shares, or a total of $150. This $1.50 plus the exercise price of $50 brings the total to $51.50, or about a $5 premium above the current market price of Ford stock of $46.50. The premium of $5 is about 11 percent above the prevailing price of the stock ($5/$46.50). In effect, the dollar premium is calculated by adding the exercise price and the option price together and subtracting the market price of the stock. The premium for the Ford/50 for July is about $6.125, or 13 percent ($6.125/$46.50).

The percentage premium rises as the contract grows longer and also as the amount of cash the buyer must put up gets smaller. For example, look at the July Ford/40 and Ford/45. The Ford/40 sells at a 2½ percent premium and requires the buyer to put up $76.25 (7⅝ × 100 shares). The Ford/45 sells at a premium of 6 percent but requires the buyer to put up only $42.50 (4¼ × 100 shares). The cash required in the latter case is about half that of the Ford/40 option.

Most option prices are between 5 percent and 20 percent of the price of the stock, depending upon the stock's volatility as well as the particular terms of the option.

CBOE option contracts carry commissions based upon the option price, not the stock price, in accordance with regular NYSE commission schedules. There is a minimum commission of $25 each way (buy or sell), and option buyers are limited to owning no more than 1,000 calls (100,000 shares) on a single stock to prevent the use of call options to gain control of a firm.

WHY BUY OPTIONS?

The basic reasons underlying the motivation for buying call options can be illustrated quite clearly. Following are some hypothetical quotes for listed options available for shares of the GTX Corp.:

GTX CORP.

Expiration/Exercise Price	Price of Option (Premium)	Stock Price
Apr./15	7	21 1/2
Apr./20	2	21 1/2
Apr./25	1/2	21 1/2

The first reason may be too obvious—speculators get a hot tip on a stock but do not have the money to buy it. A call is cheaper in actual dollars. To buy an April/20 call option on GTX stock costs $200 (excluding commissions) versus $2,150 required to own 100 shares of the stock outright. The second reason is that an investor who wants to buy the stock might be afraid that it will decline in value. Buying a call rather than the stock will reduce his profit by the amount of the premium if the stock advances, but it will limit his loss to the amount of the premium if it declines sharply. In the case of GTX, if the stock were purchased outright at $21.50 and the shares declined to $18, the investor would lose $350 on the purchase of 100 shares. The maximum that could be lost on the purchase of an April/20 option is $200. While the judicious use of a stop order might reduce the loss potential through the outright purchase of common shares, one is never certain at what price a stop order will be executed.

Other investors want to take profits in a stock that they have held for a long time—either for tax purposes or simple profit-taking desires—but cannot separate themselves from their love affair with the stock that has made them so much money. A call can be bought with a percentage of the profits, although this is emotional, not intelligent, investing. A call can be bought for protection: A speculator has sold his stock short but wants to limit his loss should the stock advance. He could enter a stop order, but he then runs the risk of being whipsawed. A call would prevent that at least until expiration or the maximum loss can easily be identified. There are other more esoteric reasons for buying calls, but these are the basic ones, and the others are merely variations of these.

In summary, investors buy listed calls with the hope of selling the option at a higher price. This use is a speculation, and the buyer risks losing 100 percent of the price paid for the call. For his capital, the buyer gets an impressive array of risk opportunities. First, leverage is obtained. A small investment of hundreds of dollars in a call controls underlying stock valued in the thousands. Second, profit potential is relatively unlimited. Many times call-option prices double or triple in a week. These "quantum jump" potentials attract speculators. A third benefit is the fixed risk. The option buyer has peace of mind in knowing the limit of his loss and the knowledge that his loss can never exceed his total capital commitment. This is the speculative side of option buying.

In its simplest form, the put is used by the buyer as a safer way of betting on a decline in the stock than going short. The put increases in value as the underlying stock declines. If the buyer of the put was right about the prospects of the stock, he will get a much higher return on investment than if he had gone short. If he is wrong, he loses the entire price of the option. And if his timing was merely off, the limited loss may give him the courage to wait for the reversal to come. Of course, on the buy side, not all purchasers of puts are going to be speculating on a decline in the underlying stock. Some will be long-term investors who want to buy some insurance against a short-term or intermediate setback in appreciated stock they already hold.

WHY SELL OPTIONS?

Most calls are sold by conservative investors who want additional income. An investor may own a stock for which he paid $30 and is now $40. He does not want to sell it at this level, but if he could get five points more he would be willing to part with it. He can get these five points by selling a call, but his gain is limited to those five points. On the other hand, if the stock price declines, he has the $500 premium and still owns the stock which he would have kept anyway (although if the stock rises quickly to $45, the buyer might not exercise, waiting for higher prices, and then watch the price decline; this would prevent the seller from taking his profits). If a writer is particularly bullish on the stock, he can sell a straddle, thereby getting additional premium money for the put side which he does not expect to be exercised. However, he is committing himself to buy stock only if that stock is declining in price, a practice that can be quite dangerous. Of course, it is also possible to write puts on short positions. This writer would venture an opinion that an option-writing program is less profitable on a consistent basis than is warrant (and convertible bond) hedging, but much easier to explain to prospective clients, as well as simpler to manage. Many writers of options write them naked—i.e., without either owning or being short the underlying stock. This is dangerous if done for one or two stocks, but if an investor utilizes substantial amounts of capital and writes puts and calls on a largely diversified group of securities, the percentage gains work out well, since, as we have already seen, most short-term options are significantly overvalued. It should be pointed out that writing naked options well requires nerves of steel and substantial capital.

Writing puts is a sensible strategy for an individual who wants to accumulate a particular stock but believes a better buying opportunity will arise at a later date. With XYZ selling at $50, the investor writes a put at 50 for which he receives a premium of $500, or $5 a share. If the stock drops to 40, and the put is exercised, he must buy the stock at 50, which is offset by the premium received, so the effective purchase price is 45. This is better than 50, at which the decision was made, but worse than the 40 that could have been received if he had waited longer.

On the other hand, if the investor is wrong and the stock climbed immediately, the missed opportunity to buy at 50 is compensated by the income from the premium received.

Another investor, though, may believe the stock is going to rise. He writes the put hoping that the put will expire without being exercised and he will have made a profit from the premium without significantly encumbering any capital.

Option Positions and Strategies

This section deals with the analysis of option positions using graphs, which allows us to examine the risk-reward characteristics of any holding. These graphs facilitate a profit-loss analysis of any position. A specific set of stock and option terms and prices has been selected to make the examples comparable and permit the reader to combine two or more strategies. To simplify our analysis, the following basic assumptions have been adopted:

1. A call option is available with six months remaining until expiration. It has a striking price of $100. The current price of this call is $10.
2. It is possible to buy or sell a put analogous to the call with a striking price of $100. These puts are selling at $11.
3. The common stock the investor purchases or sells short or which underlies any options he may buy or write is selling at $95 a share.

Each investment position or strategy is depicted on a standardized graph. The profit-loss line on the graph shows the dollar profit or loss the investor will experience at each possible stock price approximately six months after the position is initiated. In the case of strategies involving options, one assumes that the options will expire in six months, so the price six months out is also the price of the stock when the option expires. Any two strategies can be compared at any stock price by transferring the profit-loss line from one graph to the other or by preparing a new graph and imposing both strategies on that graph.

Buy Short-Term Debt Securities

Our first graph (Figure 11-2) helps explain the use of the graphic technique. The vertical axis on the chart measures the dollar profit that the investor will realize by following this strategy. The horizontal axis lists possible prices for the hypothetical stock six months from the day the investment is initiated.

In the example illustrated here, the investor buys a short-term debt instrument paying 6 percent annually, or 3 percent over the six-month period. On a $95 investment, the interest income for six months is 3% × $95, or $2.85. As indicated by the horizontal profit-loss line, income is totally independent of the price of the security.

FIGURE 11-2
PURCHASE SHORT-TERM DEBT SECURITIES

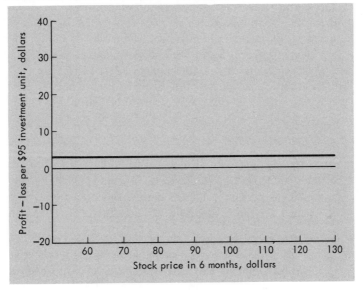

Buy Stock

In Figure 11-3, assume that the investor purchases 100 shares of common stock at a price of $95 per share. The profit or loss is exclusively a function of the price of the stock six months in the future. If the price of the stock falls to $75, the investor suffers a loss of $20 per share over the six-month period. If the price of the stock rises to $120, there is a profit of $25. The key feature of this strategy is that the investor's profit or loss bears a direct linear relationship to the price of the stock on the date the determination of return is made. If an investor is optimistic about the probable course of stock prices in general and the price of this stock in particular, this position would be favored. If the investor is not overly optimistic, a strict long position in the stock would probably be avoided.

FIGURE 11-3
PURCHASE STOCK

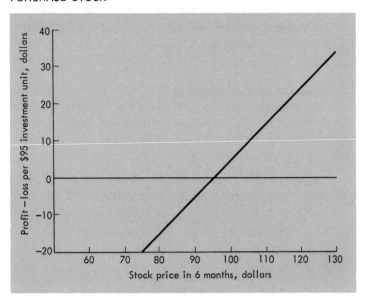

Sell Stock Short

The graph (Figure 11-4) depicting the short seller's position is the converse of the stock buyer's graph illustrated in Figure 11-3. For every point the stock rises, the buyer gains $1 per share and the short seller loses $1 per share. If the stock declines, the short seller profits to exactly the extent that the buyer loses.

Buy a Call

With the purchase of a call (see Figure 11-5), the profit-loss line is no longer a straight line passing through the price of the stock on the day the purchase was made. The purchase of a call with a striking price of $100 at a premium of $10 would result in the loss of the entire investment if the call expired with the stock selling below the striking price of $100 per share. In addition, the investor does not even begin to make money until the price of the stock exceeds the striking price plus the option premium paid for the call. In this case, $100 (striking price) plus $10 (option premium) equals $110 (breakeven point). However, if, for example, the price of the stock rises to $130 per share, the call buyer will have at least tripled his investment, since the call option is worth at least $30 ($130 − $100).

The key advantages and disadvantages of owning a call option should be evident. Although the buyer loses his entire investment if the stock sells below the striking price when the option expires, his maximum risk exposure is limited to the amount of the option premium. This is true regardless of how low the price of the stock may fall. On the other hand, the call buyer participates in any

FIGURE 11-4
SELL STOCK SHORT

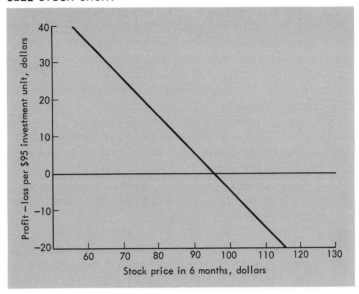

advance in the price of the stock above the striking price. Profit increases point for point, no matter how high the price of the stock may rise over the life of the option.

FIGURE 11-5
PURCHASE A CALL

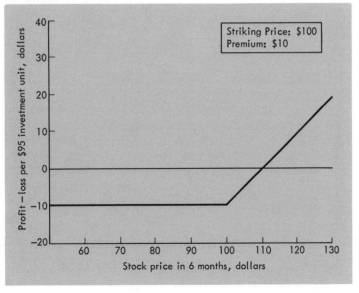

The graph in Figure 11-6 illustrates the position of the writer of a call option who does not own the underlying stock. Such a position is referred to as uncovered, or "naked." The uncovered writer gets to keep all of the call premium if the buyer of the option does not exercise it. The "naked" writing position will be profitable as long as the price of the stock does not rise above the writer's breakeven point: $100 (striking price) plus $10 (call premium) equals $110 (breakeven point).

The premium received by the option writer is available to him to invest in Treasury bills, reduce the debit balance in his margin account, or whatever.

The risk position of the "naked" call writer is such that he can never gain more than the amount of the call premium, yet his possible loss in the event of a runaway stock is substantial. The loss could easily be many times the amount of the option premium. In spite of this risk, "naked" writing can be an effective strategy when used intelligently.

If an investor feels strongly that a particular stock is going to decline but does not anticipate that the decline will be of such magnitude that a short sale will be highly profitable, he may elect to write "naked" calls. As long as his commitment in this case is not substantial relative to his resources, the profitability can be excellent, and the "naked" writing position can actually reduce the overall level of risk in the portfolio. The way in which this apparently high-risk strategy can reduce risk will be clear when we discuss option hedging shortly.

FIGURE 11-6
SELL OR WRITE A CALL

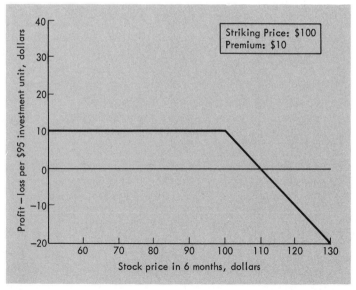

Striking Price: $100
Premium: $10

Purchase a Put

In some respects, the purchase of a put is the reverse of buying a call (see Figure 11-5). Unless the put buyer is able to sell or exercise his put at a time when the price of the stock is below the striking price, he can lose his entire investment. To the extent that the price of the stock drops, the buyer of a put participates point for point in any decline below the striking price. In the example in Figure 11-7, the put is profitable at any price below $89 (the striking price minus the option premium, or $100 − $11), neglecting the effect of commissions.

FIGURE 11-7
PURCHASE A PUT

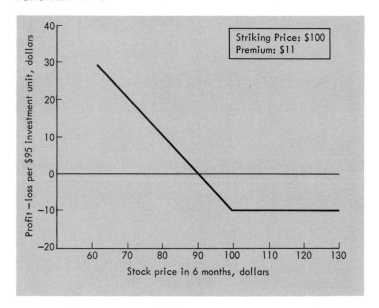

Sell a Put

Just as the writer of "naked" calls receives 100 percent of the premium if the stock is selling below the striking price when the call expires, the seller of "naked" puts receives 100 percent of the put premium if the stock is selling above the striking price when the put expires. The "naked" put seller's reward declines as the price of the stock falls below the striking price. In the example illustrated in Figure 11-8, the seller of the "naked" put actually begins to lose money when the stock price falls below 89.

The motivation of the writer of "naked" puts is usually different from that of the writer of "naked" calls. In general, the writer of "naked" calls sees this strategy as an alternative to short selling. A "naked" put writer is usually a potential investor in the underlying stock who would like the price of the stock to decline so that he can buy it more cheaply. He is not trying to profit from the

FIGURE 11-8
SELL OR WRITE A PUT

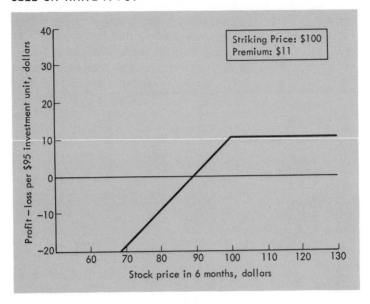

option premium itself. The writer's goal is to buy the stock at a lower net price. If the put is exercised, his cost on the stock is reduced by the amount of the put premium. The option premium is his consolation in the event that he does not get an opportunity to buy the stock.

Purchase the Stock and Sell a Call

This strategy is illustrated by the solid line in the graph (Figure 11-9) and is the classic posture of the covered call writer. The covered call writer buys 100 shares of the underlying stock and writes one call contract using the stock position as collateral. The call premium provides a degree of protection should the underlying stock decline during the life of the option. In return for this down-side protection, the covered writer's profit is limited, in this case to $15 per share over six months, no matter how high the stock price rises. At any stock price in excess of $110 per share, the writer would have been better off not to have written the call, as indicated in owning the stock without writing a call.

The reasons for writing covered options are diverse. An investor may have a long-term position in the underlying stock which, for tax reasons, he is reluctant to sell even though he is not optimistic about the near-term price action of the stock. Rather than incur a large tax liability, he writes options to partially insulate himself from what he feels is a significant downside risk. In the event that this investor's appraisal of the stock proves incorrect and it rises over the life of the option, he does not have to deliver his long-term low-cost stock. He can repurchase the option, terminating his writer's obligation and realizing an ordinary loss on the option.

FIGURE 11-9
PURCHASE THE STOCK AND SELL A CALL

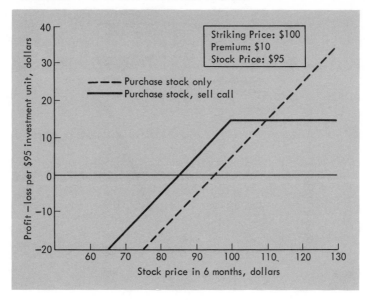

Some writers write calls only on stocks they feel positive about and are willing to hold. This tactic may seem odd, for by writing the option, these investors are precluded from obtaining more than limited profit if the stock rises as they anticipate. If the stock rises above the striking price, these writers are sure to earn the option premium. When earned consistently, option premiums can provide a highly satisfactory return. The major risk in adopting this strategy is that the premium may limit the return when the stock rises by substantially more than it reduces the loss when the stock declines.

Others will write covered options only when they feel the option premium is high relative to the fair value of the option. Such persons are usually relatively neutral toward the stock but can have a strong opinion that the option is overpriced.

Purchase the Stock and Sell a Put

The investor who sells a put on a stock he already owns will participate fully in any upside move due to his long position in the stock (see Figure 11-10). In addition, he will receive the amount of the premium paid by the buyer of the put. On the other hand, he doubles his leverage on the downside. For every point that the stock drops below the striking price, the value of this investor's position will drop by two points, one point from the decline in value of the stock he owns long and one point from the decline in value of the stock that will be sold to him by the holder of the put.

The reasons for an investor's adopting this strategy may seem somewhat obscure. Usually, this investor has a very positive attitude toward the underly-

FIGURE 11-10
PURCHASE THE STOCK AND SELL A PUT

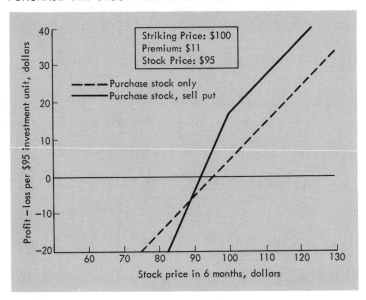

Striking Price: $100
Premium: $11
Stock Price: $95

- - - Purchase stock only
—— Purchase stock, sell put

ing stock. In fact, by selling the put he is expressing a willingness to double his position. By selling a put rather than simply purchasing the stock outright, the investor is trying to have the best of all possible worlds. If the stock rises as expected, he will participate in the rise through the increase in the value of his stockholding. The put will not be exercised, and the premium will be pure profit. If the price of the stock declines, he will find himself the proud owner of twice as much stock as he owned before. Thanks to the premium received for writing the put, his effective cost on the additional stock purchased will be $89 per share, a saving of $6 over the $95 market price at the time the transaction is initiated.

On the negative side, this strategy can be dangerous if an investor's resources are limited. The collateral value of his stock position will be declining at the time he is called upon to buy additional shares. Unless an investor's feelings on a stock are particularly strong, writing puts against a long position in the stock is probably not a sound strategy.

Spreads

Often, more than 25 percent of the total volume in the options market is made up of trades called "spreads." A "spread" is a trade involving the purchase of one option and the sale of another, both on the same stock. The person doing the "spreading" is hedging. Although spreads often become complicated, all are based on either of two patterns. If both options have the same exercise price, but one expires later than the other, we refer to this as a "time" spread. If both expire in the same month, but one exercise price is higher than the other, we have a "price" spread.

To illustrate the price spread, let us suppose we have three options on the same stock, expiring in the same month: one at an exercise price of 50, another at 60, and a third at 70. If these options have about three months to run, and the stock is now selling at 60, we might see these prices:

Option at 70	2
Option at 60	4
Option at 50	11

If you were bearish on the stock, you might find it attractive to sell the option at 50 and buy the option at 60. You would thus take in $1,100 from your sale, and pay out $400 on your purchase. The difference would be $700, which would be credited to your account. To make the trade, you must put up margin equal to the difference in the exercise prices. In this instance, it would be 10 points, or $1,000. But you need supply only $300 of your own funds, since the spread itself would give you a credit of $700. We speak of this as a "bearish" spread, since it becomes profitable as the price of the stock goes down. The best outcome would be if the stock declined to 50 or lower and both options expired worthless. Then you would keep the $700 as your profit. The worst outcome would be if the stock rose to 60 and if the option at 50, which you sold, were then exercised. In turn, you could exercise the option at 60, which you bought. The purchase and sale of the stock would show a loss of $1,000, since you would buy at 60 but sell at 50. However, you would still have the $700 you took in at the outset. So your net loss would be reduced to $300.

This "bearish" spread, where a profit is anticipated if the stock declines, generally involves buying the lowest-priced option (highest exercise price) and selling the most expensive option (lowest exercise price). In this case of a "vertical" spread we are dealing with options with the same expiration date.

"Bullish" spreads run in the opposite direction—you buy the most expensive option (lowest exercise price) and sell the cheapest option (highest exercise price). The spread will show a profit if prices rise. For example, let us assume the 60's are selling for 4 points and the 70's for 2. If you were bullish on the stock, you might buy the 60's. Or you might prefer the bullish spread, buying the 60's and selling the 70's. You would pay out $400 and take in $200, so your net cost would be $200. If the stock is selling above 70 at the expiration date, the option at 70 that you sold will then be exercised. In turn, you may exercise the option at 60 that you bought. But your profit can never be more than $1,000, less the net cost of $200 you paid at the outset. This is an attractive ratio of risk to reward; you stand to lose $200 or make $800.

Of course, it is also possible to enter into "horizontal" spreads. These are trades involving the purchase of one option and the sale of another, both on the same stock at the same exercise price. The purchase and sale, however, involve different expiration dates. In using horizontal, or time, spreads, it is generally useful to sell the option with the smallest premium (closest expiration date) and to buy the option with the larger premium (later expiration date).

The "price" spread is illustrated graphically in Figure 11-11. Specifically, this spread assumes that the investor buys the $10 option with the $100 striking price used in the previous graphs. To set up the spread, the investor writes an

FIGURE 11-11
CALL SPREAD

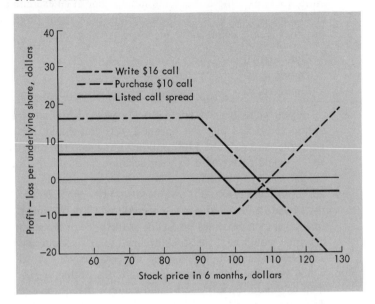

Stock price in 6 months, dollars

option having the same expiration date, but a striking price of $90, that is selling for $16, that is, $1,600 per 100-share contract. The unadjusted profit-loss line shows a fair profit if the stock declines and a loss if the stock rises.

Combinations of Put and Call Options

The simultaneous availability of puts and calls makes for some interesting combinations. Four basic kinds of options are a combination of puts and calls. A *straddle* is a put and a call on the same security at the same exercise price and for the same time period. A *strip* is two puts and one call at the same exercise price for the same period. A *spread* consists of a put and a call option on the same security for the same time period at different exercise prices. A *strap* is two calls and one put at the same contracted exercise price and for the same period.

The buyer of a straddle is betting the premium paid that the price of the option security will deviate (either up or down) from the exercise price. The writer of a straddle accepts this bet and implicitly asserts confidence that the security's price will not vary significantly before the option expires. The buyer of a strip is betting the price of some security will change from the exercise price, but the buyer believes that the security's price is more likely to fall than it is to rise. Since a strip is two puts and a call, the buyer evidently believes a decrease in the price of the option security is more probable than an increase. A strap is like a strip that is skewed in the opposite direction. The buyer of a strap evidently foresees bullish and bearish possibilities for the optioned security, with a price rise being more likely.

358

Purchase a Straddle

As illustrated by the graph in Figure 11-12, the buyer of a straddle is in a unique position. In our example a put is purchased at $11 and a call at $10. Like other option buyers, the straddle buyer can lose no more than 100 percent of the amount he invests in the straddle ($21); but he can lose that much only if the price of the stock on the expiration date of the options is exactly equal to the striking price ($100), or so close to it that sale or exercise of at least one side of the straddle does not justify the outlay of round-trip stock commissions.

Just as it is hard to lose the entire premium paid for a straddle, it can also be hard to make a profit. Even though the investor has paid substantial option premiums for both the put and call sides of the straddle, at least one of them is nearly certain to expire worthless. Consequently, the stock has to move substantially, either up or down, before the straddle buyer recovers his investment, let alone makes a profit. In the graph the breakeven point on the upside is $100 (striking price) plus $11 (put premium) plus $10 (call premium), or $121 (breakeven point). On the downside the breakeven calculation is similar: $100 (striking price) minus $11 (put premium) minus $10 (call premium) equals $79 (breakeven point).

Perhaps a more typical strategy of the straddle buyer would be to sell the "winning" position (whether put or call) at the point at which he thinks a price reversal is imminent, in the hope of selling the other position after the reversal has run its course.

FIGURE 11-12
PURCHASE A STRADDLE

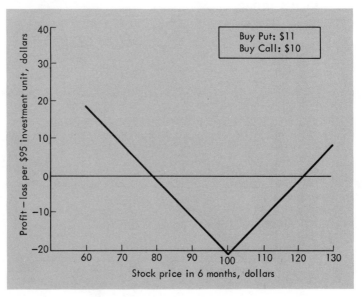

The purchase of a straddle is appropriate when the investor is convinced that a stock will make a dramatic move but is uncertain whether the move will be up or down. Once the stock price passes the breakeven point in either direction, the investor participates point for point in any further advance or decline in the price of the stock.

Sell a Straddle

Writing "naked" straddles is not a common strategy, though when used with care it can be very effective. Ordinarily the writer of a "naked" put or call has some thoughts about the direction a stock is likely to move during the life of the option. The seller of a "naked" straddle, on the other hand, is making a bet on the magnitude of the move. His point of maximum profitability is the striking price of the options that make up the straddle. At that price neither side of the option will be exercised. As the price of the stock on the expiration date moves away from the striking price, the profit to the writer of the uncovered straddle declines. In the example illustrated in the graph (Figure 11-13), the seller of the straddle will earn a profit over a $42 range of stock prices from $79 on the low side to $121 on the high side. In writing the straddle, he is betting that on the day the option expires, the stock will be selling within this range, hopefully close to the center of it.

Selling a "naked" straddle can be a sensible strategy when the investor feels strongly that the underlying stock will not move significantly in either direction over the life of the option.

FIGURE 11-13
SELL A STRADDLE

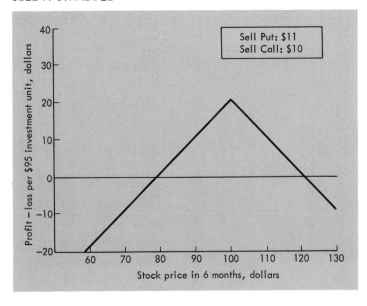

Sell Put: $11
Sell Call: $10

For orders totaling under $100 (which would be, for example, one contract of calls selling for less than $1 each) and for orders totaling over $30,000, there are no minimum commissions. It should be noted that firms differ widely here. The commission for selling a single contract of calls at 1/16 ($6.25 for the contract) could range from $1.00 at one firm to $3.00 at another. This is quite a difference when one considers that this is a range of from 16 percent to 48 percent of the price of the calls!

On all orders totaling between $100 and $30,000, the minimum commission that the exchanges permit their member firms to charge their clients is comprised of three parts. The first part is a fixed amount depending upon the total dollar amount of the transaction:

Amount Involved in the Order	Fixed Amount of Commission
$100-$2,499	$12
2,500-19,999	22
20,000-29,999	82

The second part is a percentage commission that is also a function of the total amount of money involved in the transaction:

Amount Involved in the Order	Percentage Commission
$100-$2,499	1.3%
2,500-19,999	0.9
20,000-29,999	0.6

The third part is a fixed amount for each option traded. For the first to tenth option covered by an order, this amount is $6 per option. For the eleventh option and over covered by the order, the rate is $4 per option. Finally, the exchanges add a surcharge of 10 percent of the total to arrive at the final commission charged to the customer.

The above rates are for orders covering more than one option. If the order should be for only one option, the rates are identical except that the third part of the commission is not charged. In addition, there is a minimum fee of $25 for any order, whether it be for one option contract or any number, provided of course that the total order is over $100. The commission for a single option contract may not be more than $65.

A Single-Contract Commission

Let us take the following as an example of the commission for a single option. If you sell or buy a call contract for $1,200—i.e., at $12 a call—you will pay a commission of $12 for the first part, plus the $15.60 (1.3 percent × $1,200) for the second part, for a total of $27.60 plus the 10 percent surcharge $2.76, giving a total commission of $30.36. If the amount of the option was less, so that the commission calculation yielded less than $25, the commission would still be at the minimum of $25.

Multiple-Contract Commissions

Now let us take an example of a trade involving a number of contracts. Let us assume that you want to buy a call on Holiday Inns that is currently trading at 1½, and you decide that you will buy 20 options. The amount of your order is obviously the premium per contract of 100 calls, $150 × 20, or $3,000. Therefore the first part of the commission is $22. The second part of the commission is 0.9 percent of $3,000, or $27. The third part, which is the fixed amount per option, is 10 × $6, or $60 for the first 10 options, plus 10 × $4, making $40 for the second 10 options. This comes to a grand total of $149 plus 10 percent ($14.90), which makes $163.90. Note that this is a commission of 5.4 percent of the total price, which is fairly steep. Compare it with the commission of $30.36 on the $1,200 call purchase described previously, which amounted to 2.5 percent of the total amount involved. The reason for this difference is that the premium for each call was so much smaller in the second transaction. As a general rule, the smaller the premium, the higher the percentage commission you will have to pay on a trade of a given total amount of dollars.

Margin Requirements

The minimum margin that must be maintained on a daily basis in the margin account of an uncovered writer of an option is the greater of 100 percent of the current market value of the option or $250. Margin is not required with respect to a covered writing position in an option. However, margin must be maintained with respect to the underlying stock position in the account in an amount equal to 25 percent of the current market price of the underlying stock or of the exercise price of the option, whichever is less. The New York Stock Exchange's rules require an uncovered writing transaction to be margined as if the option has been exercised. This means that 30 percent of the market value of the underlying stock must be maintained in the margin account. Many brokers impose more stringent requirements upon their option-writing customers.

Holiday Inns Call Options

Call options on Holiday Inns stock are traded on the Chicago Board (CBOE). In mid-September 1977 the following quotes were available:

	Nov.	Feb.	May	Stock Price
HIA/10	4	4 1/8	4 1/2	14
HIA/15	1/4	11/16	7/8	14

The HIA/10 contracts were already "in-the-money" by four points. That is, these options had an intrinsic value of $4. Any difference between the $4 value and the actual quote was what buyers were willing to pay for the time value of the options. The HIA/15 contracts were "out-of-the-money," since the striking price of $15 was above the market price of the stock. Any amount paid for the HIA/15 was purely for the time value perceived by traders. Note that the premium increases with the time to expiration for any specific striking price.

The November/15 was clearly the most speculative possibility in the set and the May/10 was the safest. The purchase of one November/10 contract would cost $17.20 (see p. 361). Since 100 shares are involved in a single contract, this suggests that the stock would have to advance a total of 34 cents per share to merely cover the commissions on the purchase and sale (commission paid going in and going out). Further, during the period between mid-September and late November, Holiday Inns would pay a dividend on its stock (payment date November 1). This dividend went to the option seller (writer) under CBOE rules. If Holiday Inns stock advanced to the $14\frac{3}{8}$ level before late November, the option buyer would begin to make money and see price leverage operating beyond that point. A dividend of about $0.12 per share would go to the writer (100 shares $\times$ $0.12 = $12.00). Would you buy or would you sell an HIA call? Which striking price is best? Which expiration date is optimal? What do you think?

Return and Risk in Options

The measurement of return and task in options is somewhat facilitated by the fact that, except for convertibles, options do not provide dividends or interest. The entire return comes from the difference between purchase and selling prices.

Consider an investor examining a call option that allows him to purchase one share of MNO Corp. common stock at a price of $10. The option has a limited life and will expire at the end of one year, the contemplated holding period. The current price of the option is $10, and the price of the common stock is $15. Almost all the prospect for returns hinges upon the future course of the price of the common stock. At the moment, although the option is priced at $10, its "theoretical" value is only $5, because paying $5 to acquire the option plus $10 extra in cash to obtain the stock would be equivalent to buying the stock outright at $15, the prevailing market price. Thus the stock would have to rise to $20 in one year just for the option buyer to break even.

Even if the stock and the option traded on a parity—that is, the option at $5 and the stock at $15, or any other combination of prices whose difference equals $10—the attraction of the option can be seen. For example, suppose the stock moves to $20 in six months. The option would have to move to at least $10. The reason is that if the option were at, say, $9, a speculator would buy it at that price and short the stock at $20. It will cost him $19 to replace the stock he sold for $20. Such a process, called arbitraging, will insure the proper spread. However, the movement of the stock to $20 and of the option to $10 in six months provides the following six-month HPYs:

$$\text{Stock HPY} = \frac{(\$20 - \$15)}{\$15} = \$5/\$15 = .333$$

$$\text{Option HPY} = \frac{(\$10 - \$5)}{\$5} = \$5/\$5 = 1.000$$

Of course, in reality the option is likely to sell at some premium over its conversion value. The size of the premium at any point in time will be related mainly to the following variables:

1. Price of the common stock and its volatility
2. Time to expiration of the option
3. Income differences between the option and equivalent common shares in terms of:
   a. Dividend income
   b. Transaction costs

Using probabilities and related decision tools we discussed in Chapters 9 and 10, it is possible to determine expected return for the underlying common stock and the option over the intended holding period. Similarly, the use of historical risk measures or projected volatility of return provides the analyst with the other dimension of the return-risk framework.

Summary

This discussion of the various options on common stocks has shown how they are similar and dissimilar. They are all dependent on the price movement, or expectations of price movement, of the associated common stock. They all vary in the length of time during which they are in effect—an important difference, since, in buying an option, the investor must predict not only a price movement but also the period within which the movement will take place.

The options discussed here give the investor varying amounts of leverage that are unobtainable by owning the common stock. They also offer somewhat more safety than the common, in that the investor need not put as much capital at risk to obtain the same reward. These features cause the options to sell at a premium, as a general rule. Thus it is important to know *why* the particular option sells at a premium, in order to tell if the premium is so high that it overshadows these attributes of the option. This trade-off between the premium demanded and the advantages gained by the option, along with the outlook for the associated common stock, determines whether an option is an attractive buy.

Questions and Problems

1. Consult Moody's manuals or Standard & Poor's *Stock Guide.* Determine data similar to those shown in Table 11-1 for the stock and warrants of Cott Corporation.

2. If a convertible bond is selling at its straight-bond or investment value, is the bond inherently a better investment than the common stock of the same company?

3. A convertible bond has the following characteristics: market price = 106, call price = 109, conversion price = 25, stock price = 28, bond value = 100. What is your assessment of this situation?

4. A convertible preferred stock has the following characteristics: dividend = $4.50, par value = $100, call price = $106, conversion rate = 4 shares, market price = $126. Equivalent straight preferreds are selling to yield 9 percent. The underlying common stock pays an annual dividend of $1.00 and sells for $28. Would you buy the convertible? Why?

5. KWIK Corp. has a 6 percent ($50 par) preferred stock outstanding that is callable at $53 and convertible into two shares of common stock. The preferred is selling for $60. The common is selling for $25 (and paying a $2 dividend). Straight preferreds are currently selling to yield 8 percent.

   a. Calculate the investment and conversion values of the 6 percent preferred stock.

   b. Assume the preferred sold at $47. How might a speculator capitalize on this fact, other things equal?

   c. If the preferreds were called at this time, what would most holders likely do? Why?

6. Archway Corp. has a $10 ($100 par) convertible preferred stock selling for $108. The preferred are convertible into two shares of common stock. The common stock is currently selling for $53. Nonconvertible preferred stocks of a similar quality are currently selling to yield 10 percent. If the common stock were to fall from $53 to $45, a decline of about 8 percent, about how much would the preferred decline? Why?

7. The Ford Motor Credit Corp. has a 4½ percent debenture (Bbb) (1996) outstanding that is convertible into Ford Motor stock at a price of $78⅛. The bonds are callable at 103.55 and have an investment value of 8.60 percent. Ford common currently sells for $55.50, with an indicated dividend of $4.00. The current price on the bonds is $750 ($1,000 par). Provide a systematic analysis of this bond. Indicate whether you would buy it *today* in light of the economic outlook and normal tests of attractiveness.

8. Assume Xerox (XRX) stock is currently at $100. It is now July 1. Three call options are quoted: XRX/Nov/110... $1; XRX/Nov/100... $10; XRX/Jan/90... $20. Ignoring commissions:

   a. List three reasons why the premium on the Jan/90 call is so much higher than the premium on the Nov/100 call.

   b. Suppose you purchased 100 shares of Xerox on June 1 at a cost of $95/share. You wrote (sold) one XRX/Jan/90 on July 1. Suppose that on January 15 Xerox stock was at $105.

   (1) Would the holder of the XRX/Jan/90 benefit from exercising the call? Why?

   (2) If the call were exercised on January 15, what is your tax status?

   c. Suppose you do not own Xerox shares. You simultaneously write one XRX/Nov/110 and buy one XRX/Nov/100. What is your annualized rate of return if Xerox stock closes in November at 115? (Ignore commissions and dividends.)

9. Assume Texas Instruments stocks is currently at $100. Two call options are quoted: TI/Nov/110... $1 and TI/Jan/90... $20. Ignoring commissions:

   a. Why is the premium on the January call so much higher than the premium on the November call?

b. Suppose you owned 100 shares of TI at a cost of $95/share. At what price would you begin to lose money if you wrote a call on the TI/Jan/90?

c. If you were short TI, would there be any advantage in buying a call? How so?

10. You wrote a call for HIA/Oct/10 for a premium of $1 in January. The option was written against stock held long at a cost of $12/share. Ignoring commissions, and assuming the call was exercised in early October, what is your tax status on HIA at the end of October?

11. Trace carefully the ramifications of purchasing a call on a warrant.

IV

BOND ANALYSIS

IV

Because of their fascination and preoccupation with the rewards associated with investing in common stocks, investors often lack an interest in or an understanding of fixed-income securities as an investment vehicle. The reasons behind the "second-string" role of fixed-income securities are not too difficult to sort out.

First, recent returns from investing in long-term bonds have not been impressive. For example, from the early 1960s to the early 1970s, long-term interest rates moved higher and higher—from 4½ to 9 percent—causing bond prices to undergo steady declines. The second reason is the nature of the beast. Bonds pay a fixed and unchanging income with the expectation that their price will not be subject to wide fluctuations. The rather straightforward type of analysis of bonds that centers on quality and safety certainly lacks the sex appeal of discovering the wonder stock of the future.

Notwithstanding the record of returns on bonds and the somewhat unglamorous nature of bond analysis, several factors make bond analysis a very challenging topic. First, stabilization, or even a moderate downward trend, in interest rates over the next decade would contribute to renewed enthusiasm for bonds as an investment medium. Second, regardless of the future trend of interest rates, trading in bonds has always been a path to more glamour and returns. Trading involves taking advantage of technical, seasonal, and cyclical factors in the bond markets. Third, in recent years the relative odds in the stock and bond markets have shifted noticeably. Whereas the long-term return on common stocks has averaged about 9 percent, long-term interest rates moved from the 4½ percent level in 1960 to near 9 percent in the late 1970s. This very tendency toward more equalization has contributed to a current surge in public participation in the bond markets. It is estimated that net purchases of bonds by individuals in 1970-71 alone equaled total net purchases over the entire eight-year period from 1962 through 1969!

With an eye to the validity of bonds as an investment medium, the next three chapters of the text discuss bond analysis. Preferred stocks are also discussed throughout, since their fixed-income nature provides close similarities to bonds.

Chapter 12 explores the nature and sources of systematic risk affecting bonds and preferred stocks. The impact of purchasing-power and interest-rate risk are noted. A substantial portion of the chapter is devoted to the underlying causes of changes in the overall level of interest rates and the structure of yields according to time.

Chapter 13 analyzes unsystematic risk in bonds and preferred stocks by examining and measuring business and financial risk bearing upon them. In addition, we note how changes in financial and business risk contribute to alterations in the risk premiums demanded by investors. Certain key nonrisk factors that influence yields are also probed.

The final chapter in this section, Chapter 14, examines historical risk-return experience on bonds and probes the problem of estimating future return and risk on a bond over a forward holding period.

CHAPTER TWELVE

BOND ANALYSIS: SYSTEMATIC RISK

**Holding-
Period
Yield on
Preferred
Stocks and
Bonds**
Bonds and preferred stocks are commonly referred to as fixed-income or fixed-dollar securities, since the annual interest or dividend income received from them is fixed by contract. The holding-period yield on preferred stocks is calculated in the same manner as that on common stocks. The basic difference is evident in the fixed nature of preferred dividends. Common-stock dividends are variable and may trend upward, whereas preferred dividends are generally set at a maximum but are relatively more certain.

The dividends paid on preferred stocks are frequently stated in dollar or percentage-of-par terms. A "$2 preferred stock" indicates the annual dollar dividend. Alternatively, a "4 percent preferred" with a $50 par value would also pay a $2 dividend, since the dollar value is the product of the dividend rate (percentage) multiplied by the par value.

The holding-period yield on bonds is defined much like that on stocks, except that interest payments rather than dividends are received. Interest is customarily paid semiannually, whereas dividends on stocks are paid quarterly as a rule. The nature of debt contracts is such that the interest payments on a bond issue are fixed and are more certain than dividends, either common or preferred. The holding-period-yield formula for bonds is:

$$\text{HPY} = \frac{(P_1 - P_0) + I}{P_0} \tag{12.1}$$

where:

HPY = holding-period yield
I = interest payments
P_0 = beginning price
P_1 = ending price

The single most important fact to observe about HPYs on fixed-income securities is that, since the annual income received is fixed in dollar terms, any shifts in required HPY must come from changes in price. This is not so in the case of common stocks, where dividends can fluctuate up and down and, it is hoped, will grow larger over time.

The same general categories of risk that influence common stocks also influence fixed-income securities, but there are differences in the degree of their impact. The primary sources of *systematic* risk in holding fixed-income securities are interest-rate and purchasing-power risk.

PURCHASING-POWER RISK

To a great extent, the return expected on U.S. government securities at any point in time will reflect the rate of inflation in the economy, since the rate on USGs embodies a riskless rate plus some compensation for purchasing-power risk. Governments are devoid of business and financial risk, owing to a monopoly status and taxing powers available to ensure that debt-servicing obligations are met.

Extensive studies of interest rates by the Federal Reserve Bank of St. Louis tend to indicate that the riskless rate of interest fluctuates around 3 percent.[1] If this is true, adding to this an allowance for the rate of price change (purchasing-power risk) might produce a fair approximation of the rate of interest on long-term government bonds.

The rate of price change is the annual percentage change in prices; we often refer to it as the change in the cost of living. If a price index begins the year at 100 and ends at 103, we say the rate of increase (inflation) is 3 percent [(103 − 100)/100]. If, from the second to third year, the index changes from 103 to 109, the rate of price change is said to be about 5.8 percent [(109 − 103)/103]. The rate of change in prices can also be downward (deflation).

The necessity to adjust the rate of interest for price changes can be seen in a simple example. Suppose you lend $100 today for a promise to be repaid $105 at the end of a year. The rate of interest is 5 percent. However, assume that prices over the next year are expected to advance 6 percent. Because of inflation, the $105 received at the end of the year has a purchasing power of only 94 percent of $105, or $98.70. You must charge 5 percent plus an inflation premium of 6 percent, or a total of 11 percent, to allow for inflation.

The rate of inflation experienced in the United States over long time periods prior to 1969 was on the order of 2-3 percent. The rate was 7 percent compounded per annum between 1972 and 1977.

The tricky part of the whole process is that long-term interest rates reflect both *expected* inflation and *uncertainty* about inflation. Rates of expected future inflation will not necessarily be the same as those experienced in the past, even the most recent past.

INTEREST-RATE RISK

Interest-rate risk can be identified as the truly overwhelming systematic risk associated with holding fixed-income securities. The impact of changes in the

---

[1]See Federal Reserve Bank of St. Louis, *Monetary Trends,* September 1969.

level and direction of interest rates carries the same kind of sweeping control over bond and preferred-stock prices that market risk does over common stocks. A study showed that about half the movement in the price of individual common stocks could be traced to a market influence. Although there have been no studies regarding the impact of interest-rate shifts on an average bond or preferred stock, one could speculate that the degree of influence is equal to if not greater than market risk in common stocks.

Interest rates may be viewed as the price of money. The U.S. government generally pays the lowest price or interest rate to borrow money because its promises are probably the most riskless in the world. In effect, the rate of interest it pays is the closest approximation of what we might call a "pure" or riskless rate.

Changes in the rate of interest required on governments result from shifts in supply and demand, just as in any other commodity. The effect is to cause the price on governments to shift. As the price of governments falls, for example, they become cheaper and relatively more attractive than other securities. Shifts out of other securities into governments tips the supply-demand balance and will eventually cause the prices of all securities to fall in concert. This trigger mechanism does not lead to instantaneous or equal price changes across the broad spectrum of securities; however, the eventual result is a decline in prices across a broad front. The effect upon debt securities is most noticeable, although equity prices are affected directly and indirectly, as pointed out in Chapter 5.

Let us assume an investor has a one-year holding period. Further, assume that bond interest is received at the end of the year. Yesterday he purchased a U.S. government security due in one year that pays $60 in interest and can be acquired for $1,000, or par value. His expected HPY is:

$$HPY = \frac{\$60 + (\$1,000 - \$1,000)}{\$1,000}$$

$$= \frac{\$60}{\$1,000} = .06, \text{ or } 6\%$$

He assumes, of course, that the security will be redeemed at par value at maturity in one year and that interest will be paid as promised. However, unexpected new government borrowing has just been announced in the press. Judging by the weak balance in the current supply-demand relationships for one-year governments, the interest on a new $1,000 security due in one year is expected to be 6½ percent, or $65.

The result of this event is that we have *old* government securities due in one year paying a fixed $60 per year per $1,000 par value; *new* governments will pay $65 per year per $1,000 par value. Those holding the 6 percent securities will have to accept less than $1,000 in order for potential buyers to prefer them equally to the 6½ percent securities. The desired 6½ percent HPY on the old securities is accomplished by the following price adjustment:

$$HPY = \frac{(P_1 - P_0) + I}{P_0}$$

$$.065 = \frac{(\$1,000 - P_0) + \$60}{P_0}$$

$$P_0 = \$995.29$$

This example has illustrated the fact that *rising interest rates on new securities cause the prices of outstanding securities to fall and their holders to suffer in two ways: First, if they are forced to sell before the security matures, they will suffer a loss in price. Second, at worst they can hold on until maturity, but they experience an "opportunity loss" in forgoing the higher rate now available on new securities of equal maturity and risk. Opposite effects result from falling interest rates.*

Let us examine how an analyst might go about forecasting the level and direction of change in interest rates.

Forecasting Interest-Rate Trends

Varied socioeconomic and political forces have an impact upon the level and direction of interest rates.[2] These forces tend to push rates up or down in harmony over a broad spectrum of fixed-income securities. In the process, however, two significant developments are watched closely by an investor. First, for securities in the same class, rates move in harmony but to differing degrees, depending upon term to maturity. Second, securities of different default-risk classes with similar terms to maturity also move in differing degrees.

Bonds and preferred stocks are often traded by speculators and money managers to take advantage of the very short-term, day-to-day or seasonal (month-to-month) fluctuations in yields. The skills required include keen insight into both random and predictable supply-demand relationships, courage, and, of course, impeccable timing. Our main concern is with forecasting interest rates over the medium term or business cycle.

The forecaster must be both a psychoanalyst and a value analyst. Interest rates are determined not only by what is currently happening but by what people think will happen. Let us turn our attention first, however, to the information that can be brought to bear upon value analysis.

ASSUMING AN ECONOMIC MODEL

The analyst must first develop an economic model for the year ahead that takes into account recent economic trends and known government policies. In Chapter 6

---

[2]This section draws heavily upon Sidney Homer, "Techniques for Forecasting Interest-Rate Trends," an address before the Chicago chapter of the American Statistical Association on June 14, 1966; and W. C. Freund and E. D. Zinbarg, "Sources and Uses of Funds," in *Financial Institutions and Markets,* ed. M. E. Polakoff (Boston: Houghton Mifflin, 1970), pp. 463-84.

we examined tools and techniques for assessing the economic outlook in terms of short-run forecasting. GNP model-building, indicators, and econometric models were seen to be powerful allies in assessing the level and direction of various measures of economic activity. The key is to determine what stage of the cycle the economy is in, where it is moving, and how fast.

The movement of the economy and of interest rates is of overriding importance in the purchase of fixed-income securities generally. An article of faith among most financial persons is the proposition that business recessions bring low interest rates (rising bond prices) and business booms bring high interest rates (falling bond prices). Therefore an outlook for an extended upward trend in interest rates would tend to augur against a commitment to bonds. However, an opportunity for capital gains lies in the possibility of a decline in interest rates subsequent to a bond or preferred-stock purchase.

Interest rates have typically turned at about the same time as industrial production. To the extent that this relationship prevails, interest rates could be classified as a coincident economic indicator. However, these relationships are not always consistent, and the determination of economic turning points is difficult (see Chapter 6). If the time to buy bonds was at the peak of economic activity, not before, and an analyst was good at picking these turning points, then bond investing would indeed be easy![3] Aside from the difficulties in forecasting economic (interest-rate) turns, another problem exists. Do fluctuations in business activity of less importance than booms or recessions promise correspondingly (if milder) increases or decreases in interest rates?

Sidney Homer, long recognized as the bard of the bond business, suggests an answer to this question. His work indicates that the correlation between bond yields and the business cycle

> . . .can only be relied upon in periods when cyclical forces are powerful, such as peaks of booms or recessions, and that at other times the bond market is capable of a wide variety of patterns which do not correlate with business trends and are influenced no doubt partly by long-term secular fundamentals and partly by transitory political or economic events. . . .[4]

C. C. Abbott found two long cycles in bond prices since 1874, each lasting about forty-six years. Within these cycles, he noted that periods of falling rates (rising prices) lasted about twenty-six years; periods of rising rates (falling prices) lasted about twenty years. This would suggest long cycles within which shorter undulations (seasonal, cyclical influences) take shape.[5]

The existence of short cycles and transitory effects on the way to a peak or

---

[3]It was long believed that business recessions meant falling interest rates and stock prices. But in the 1973-75 period, the recession brought the stock market down, and interest rates rose.

[4]Homer, "Techniques for Forecasting Interest-Rate Trends."

[5]C. C. Abbott, "Yes, But Rates Can't Act That Way," in Institute of Chartered Financial Analysts, *1972 Supplementary Readings in Financial Analyses* (Homewood, Ill.: Richard D. Irwin, 1972), pp. 67-79. Abbott thought the softening of rates in 1968 signaled the end of a long cycle. He was in error—at least temporarily.

toward a recession provides opportunities for respectable returns in fixed-income securities by gearing investment and speculative strategies to cyclical and transitory events. Obviously, if the long-term trend in interest rates is downward, long-term investing in bonds is desirable.

PRICES AND EMPLOYMENT

Business activity and interest rates are closely tied; however, there is divergence between their relative cycles. The early stages of economic recoveries sometimes bring bear bond markets, but often the bond market is little affected until late boom stages. Since interest rates really reflect the price of money, it helps to examine other relative prices, such as those for materials and labor—the latter from the viewpoint of employment.

The trend of prices and employment affects government policies in the areas of fiscal and monetary policy. Stable or soft prices accompanied by high unemployment enable monetary and fiscal policy to promote economic expansion without fear of inflation. Rapid economic growth under such conditions could mean stable or even declining bond yields. Conversely, low unemployment and rising prices would imply that any economic outlook predicting growth could bring rising bond yields.

SUPPLY AND DEMAND FOR CREDIT

Given the outlook for the economy and its components, it is necessary to look into where the money will come from. This stage of forecasting requires a systematic look at all the factors making up the supply of and demand for funds. The Federal Reserve has developed a system that accounts for this supply and demand, using the flow of funds through the varied sectors of the economy similar to that of the national income accounts. For those seeking a summary of these flows, as well as a one-year forecast, Salomon Bros., a large bond house in New York, publishes its *Prospects for the Credit Markets* each February.

The aim of flow-of-funds accounts and the Salomon Bros. research is to quantify the forces of supply and demand for funds in the economy, and to see (1) whether the balance of force lies in the direction of higher or lower interest rates, and (2) which segments (short and/or long term) will face more or less pressure. Imbalances detected between supply and demand indicate interest-rate effects: Unsatisfied demands place upward pressures on interest rates; excess supply tends to force rates down.

Table 12-1 is taken from *Prospects for the Credit Markets in 1977*. This is a summary table of supply and demand for credit. Similarly, the tables referred to inside Table 12-1 provide detail on specific aspects of the markets.

"Net Demand" represents demand for funds, both historically and forecast into the future one year. In this case, the years 1971-75 represent historical data (1976 is estimated, since refined data were not available at press time). The estimate of demand is shown for 1977. The numbers for each year show the net annual increase in demand in each important department of the capital

TABLE 12-1

SUMMARY OF SUPPLY AND DEMAND FOR CREDIT ($ BILLIONS)

	See Table	Annual Net Increases in Amounts Outstanding							Amounts Outstanding 12/31/76e
		1971	1972	1973	1974	1975	1976e	1977p	
Net Demand									
Privately Held Mortgages	II	44.3	68.8	68.7	42.8	38.5	61.3	69.5	760.1
Corporate Bonds	III	24.7	18.9	13.5	27.5	32.7	27.6	24.1	334.3
Domestically Held Foreign Bonds	III	0.9	1.0	1.0	2.2	6.3	9.3	10.4	34.2
Subtotal Long-Term Private		69.9	88.7	83.2	72.5	77.5	98.2	104.0	1,128.6
Business Loans	VIII	7.7	24.8	38.4	34.3	−14.5	−1.1	14.0	236.6
Consumer Installment Credit	VIII	9.3	15.6	19.7	9.0	6.9	16.0	21.0	178.2
All Other Bank Loans	VIII	7.7	11.0	7.4	3.2	2.8	10.0	12.0	89.4
Open Market Paper	VII	−0.1	1.6	8.3	16.6	−1.3	5.6	7.0	72.0
Subtotal Short-Term Private		24.6	53.0	73.8	63.1	−6.1	30.5	54.0	576.2
Privately Held Treasury Debt	V	19.0	15.2	−2.0	10.2	75.8	61.8	49.5	406.7
Privately Held Federal Agency Debt	VI	2.7	9.0	21.2	17.9	7.7	13.1	18.5	119.5
Subtotal Federal		21.7	24.2	19.2	28.1	83.5	74.9	68.0	526.2
State & Local Tax-Exempt Bonds	IV	16.4	14.1	13.3	11.9	16.9	17.8	19.0	228.6
State & Local Tax-Exempt Notes	IV	5.3	−1.3	0.8	2.6	−1.2	−4.1	−2.0	13.8
Subtotal Tax-Exempt		21.7	12.8	14.1	14.5	15.7	13.7	17.0	242.4
Total Net Demand for Credit		137.9	178.7	190.3	178.2	170.6	217.3	243.0	2,473.4
Net Supply*									
Mutual Savings Banks	IX	9.0	8.8	5.3	3.1	10.4	11.9	11.9	121.1
Savings & Loan Associations	IX	30.2	37.1	27.5	21.7	42.0	51.0	53.0	362.7
Credit Unions	IX	2.0	2.9	3.5	3.3	5.1	6.9	8.0	38.9
Life Insurance Companies	IX	7.2	8.8	10.0	10.3	15.2	18.0	18.6	228.1
Fire & Casualty Companies	IX	3.7	3.8	3.5	4.6	5.4	4.1	4.5	55.3
Private Non-Insured Pension Funds	IX	−1.7	−0.7	2.0	5.8	7.9	7.4	7.6	59.0
State & Local Retirement Funds	IX	3.6	3.1	3.4	8.0	7.0	8.8	9.0	82.3
Personal & Common Bank Trust Funds	IX	3.9	2.7	4.1	2.0	3.6	4.0	4.7	52.3
Foundations & Endowments	IX	1.7	−0.1	0.6	0.9	1.1	1.2	1.5	18.2
Closed-End Corporate Bond Funds	IX	0.2	1.2	1.1	0.2	0.0	0.0	0.0	2.8
Money Market Funds	IX	0.0	0.0	0.0	1.0	0.6	0.3	0.4	1.8
Municipal Bond Funds	IX	0.3	0.4	0.7	1.1	2.1	2.8	4.5	8.9
Open-End Stock Funds	IX	0.0	0.0	−0.2	−0.4	0.7	0.4	−0.3	8.0
Real Estate Investment Trusts	IX	2.3	4.1	5.6	0.2	−4.6	−4.6	−2.2	6.2
Finance Companies	IX	4.2	7.5	8.8	2.4	0.5	8.1	10.1	84.4
Total Non-Bank Institutions	X	66.6	79.6	75.9	64.2	97.0	120.3	131.3	1,130.0
Commercial Banks†	X	50.9	73.3	77.6	59.8	31.0	44.5	58.0	785.9
Business Corporations	XI	2.4	0.9	3.4	8.0	10.6	7.1	8.1	74.2
State & Local Governments	XI	−3.5	5.5	3.3	1.2	2.5	6.7	7.7	44.1
Foreigners	XI	26.4	9.1	2.1	10.9	4.5	14.2	15.7	100.4
Subtotal		142.8	168.4	162.3	144.1	145.6	192.8	220.8	2,134.6
Residual: Households Direct	XII	−4.9	10.3	28.0	34.1	25.0	24.5	22.2	338.8
Total Net Supply of Credit		137.9	178.7	190.3	178.2	170.6	217.3	243.0	2,473.4

*Excludes funds for equities, cash and miscellaneous demands not tabulated above.

†Includes loans transferred to non-operating holding and other bank-related companies.

Source: Salomon Brothers, *Prospects for the Credit Markets in 1977* (New York: Salomon Brothers, 1977).

market. "Net Supply" shows net annual acquisitions of various instruments by investor groups.

We can see which types of credit demand are dynamic or stable. In addition, we can see the appetites of particular investor groups over time. Large or small increases in total credit do not, in themselves, indicate tendencies toward higher or lower interest rates, because supply and demand will balance by definition. A small expansion in total demand can be the result of a shortage of funds (tight money = high rates) or insufficient demand (easy money = lower rates). Surplus supply (lower rates) or excessive demand (higher rates) can cause large total expansion. Homer suggests that large expansions in total credit implied rising interest rates in 1959 and 1965, but did not in 1961-63.[6] The surge in 1970 and 1971 did suggest higher rates; the increase in 1972 did not.

Freund and Zinbarg find that the clues to the level of interest rates to be found in forecasts of sources and uses of funds lie in two key areas. First, as these forecasts are being built, source by source and use by use, the first approximation ends with an imbalance between the two. Balance will ultimately be achieved between supply and demand as the analyst assumes, say, contracting demand through tightening in the markets for funds (higher interest rates). This iterative process of closing the gap provides insight into the probable direction of interest rates.[7] Salomon Bros. analysts reach the conclusions found in the verbal analysis of their tables through much of this kind of iterative process of getting supply and demand to balance.

Second, Homer suggests that the "Residual" category in Table 12-1 can help indicate the direction of rates.[8] This category includes individuals and miscellaneous investors, a group that appears to be sensitive to interest rates and is a marginal provider of funds. When demand exceeds supply, one way to induce this group to bring about a balance is for rates to rise sufficiently. Particularly good examples of periods of rising rates in tune with rising "residuals" are 1973 and 1974.

The sources of supply expand and contract to different degrees over time. Commercial banks play a key but volatile role. The major swings in funds supplied by savings institutions such as savings and loan associations directly affect the mortgage markets, their principal outlet for funds. Note, for example, the surge in real estate mortgages and the increase in funds in savings and loan associations in 1976. By contrast, note the small decrease in funds supplied by savings and loans in 1973, while mortgages stayed constant.

The details of the analysis could go on and on, but the point seems clear. Information on sources and uses of funds from the Federal Reserve accounts or in summary and forecast form from Salomon Bros. provide useful insight into the level of interest rates. It must all be considered, of course, against a backdrop of the outlook for the economy, and prices and employment in particular.[9]

---

[6]Homer, "Techniques for Forecasting Interest-Rate Trends."

[7]W. C. Freund and E. D. Zinbarg, "Application of Flow of Funds to Interest Rate Forecasting," *Journal of Finance,* May 1963, p. 237.

[8]Homer, "Forecasting Interest-Rate Trends."

[9]The reader is particularly encouraged to examine the analysis and many interesting tables of the latest *Prospects for the Credit Markets.*

Monetary policy, as used here, refers to government activities with respect to the cost and availability of credit. *Fiscal policy* refers to government taxing and spending activities.

The major goals of monetary policy are to help smooth out business cycles and promote economic growth, maintain price stability and full employment, and maintain external equilibrium in terms of balance of payments and the value of the dollar. These goals are fostered by the control of spending and investment, through influencing the cost and availability of funds through the banks. Fiscal policy influences credit markets through the manner in which government debt is managed, whether deficits or surplus are forecast for the year ahead, and how they will be handled. Without joining the heated debate over the role and effectiveness of monetary versus fiscal policy, let us trace the general effects of policy on interest rates.

Prospects of price inflation, balance-of-payments deficit, and pressure on the dollar would probably lead to restraint in monetary policy. Decelerated economic growth, business recession, and high unemployment could call for monetary ease and lower interest rates.

To tighten or loosen credit, the Federal Reserve System has generally influenced short-term rates of interest. These changes are gradually transmitted to longer-term rates. The Federal Reserve System (the "Fed") influences rates largely by buying and selling U.S. government securities in the market, an activity referred to as *open-market operations.* Buying and selling activity influences bank reserves and lending power. For example, monetary ease is achieved through buying governments and expanding bank reserves. Monetary restraint is achieved through sale of governments. To a lesser extent, the Fed can affect interest rates by adjusting the level of reserves required to back bank deposits (*reserve requirements*) and adjusting the rate at which it will lend money to banks (*discount rate*).

Of course, the goals of monetary policy are often conflicting. The balance between full employment and stable prices is delicate indeed. Low interest rates help promote economic growth by encouraging borrowing and spending. However, these same low interest rates place pressure on the dollar when balance-of-payments deficits exist for this country. That is, to settle accounts and make up the deficit, the United States would normally pay in either gold or IOUs. The nation to whom we owe money might prefer interest-bearing IOUs (for instance, Treasury securities) rather than non-interest-bearing gold. But if low interest rates prevail on U.S. obligations, then gold might be taken instead and converted to higher-interest IOUs in other countries. The balance-of-payments problem may suggest a level of interest rates somewhat above the one produced by the "real" influences in an analysis of supply and demand for credit. Also, the late 1970s have shown us the paradox of inflation along with high unemployment. These simultaneous problems would seem to indicate contrasting monetary policy: high interest rates to restrain inflation, but low rates to encourage economic growth and full employment.

Fiscal policy makes its mark on the credit markets and interest rates. Budget deficits or surpluses mean that additional borrowing is added to pressures in the markets for funds, or that additional funds are supplied through debt retirement. Moreover, government securities are maturing every day, and the manner in which they are replaced has an effect upon the credit markets. Of course, deficits need not be met by added borrowing; they can be reduced or eliminated by increased taxes. The consequences of this strategy may have reverse effects upon interest rates, depending upon whose taxes are raised and how taxpayers adjust to meet the payments.

These crosscurrents and conflicting effects of monetary and fiscal policy on the level and direction of interest rates are significant. For the domestic economy as a whole, we might think of monetary and fiscal policy as reacting to and influenced by (1) the economic outlook, (2) price and employment prospects, and (3) the natural forces of supply and demand in financing this outlook. When we expand the sphere of concern to include the international situation, political and economic (for example, balance of payments and the dollar), the influence of monetary and fiscal policy can move against the thrust of the other three forces. The investor must, therefore, look carefully at the probable effect of monetary and fiscal policy on the outlook for interest rates.

If projections suggest that interest rates are expected to move to a certain level, the question is whether all maturities and classes of securities will move in unison and to the same degree.

The Term Structure of Interest Rates

Interest-rate levels, direction, and patterns can be analyzed in three categories: short term, medium term, and long term. Short-term fluctuations are often called seasonal and last from a few weeks to a few months.[10] Long-term movements or secular trends can last from several business cycles to several decades. Medium-term or cyclical trends roughly coincide with trends of the business cycle.[11] Our discussion has concerned itself mainly with the last.

For a given bond issuer, such as the U.S. government, the structure of yields that is observed for bonds with different terms to maturity (but no other differences) is called the *term structure of interest rates.* In more everyday financial parlance, a diagram of the rates prevailing on a class of securities that are alike in every respect except term to maturity provides us with a *yield curve.* The most common portrait of yields plotted against time, or yield curve, is for marketable U.S. government securities.

The record of interest rates, when viewed according to term to maturity, suggests that at times short rates are above long rates, and vice versa. We want to explain the possible determinants of such changes in the term structure of interest rates. Figure 12-1 shows interest rates on governments by term to maturity

[10]Studies of seasonal factors suggest that they have a strong influence upon short-term rates and negligible effects on long-term rates. Between 1951 and 1960, Conrad found tendencies for highs in December and lows in June or July. See J. W. Conrad, *The Behavior of Interest Rates* (New York: National Bureau of Economic Research, 1966), pp. 53-54.

[11]Homer, "Forecasting Interest-Rate Trends," p. 23

FIGURE 12-1

YIELD CURVE FOR U.S. GOVERNMENT SECURITIES

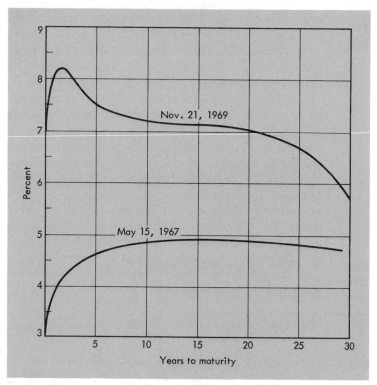

Source: Donald P. Jacobs, Loring C. Farwell, and Edwin Neave, *Financial Institutions,* 5th Ed. (Homewood, Ill.: Richard D. Irwin, 1972), p. 204.

at two different points in time. The first, May 15, 1967, is identified as a period of recessed business activity and interest rates. The other is a period of business boom and high interest rates. Why do these disparate configurations exist?

One of the most frequently noted behavior patterns concerning the term structure is the observation that, over the business cycle, short-term rates have a greater magnitude of variation than long-term rates have. Over the course of a complete cycle from recession to peak and back to recession, the level of rates will move upward and downward; however, the shorts will move more frequently and to a greater extent than the longs.

The lower curve (at May 15, 1967) is a classic upward-sloping configuration when interest rate levels were relatively low. In eighteen months, rates had tightened up considerably, as evidenced by the yield curve on November 21, 1969. The *level* of rates rose sharply and the *shape* of the yield curve turned downward (long rates below short rates). Notice the relative movements in short and long rates between the two dates. For example, very short-term rates (one year or less) moved up from around 3 percent to 7 percent. Very long rates (25 years) rose from just under 5 percent to around 6½ percent.

From an operational point of view, it is necessary for an investor to recognize that (1) short-term *rates* do fluctuate more violently than long-term rates over a business cycle, (2) long-term *prices* are apt to fluctuate more than short-term prices, (3) the shape of the curve at recession, recovery, and boom phases moves from upward to horizontal to downward sloping; the short end becomes progressively more shallow (differences between very short and three years' rates become narrow); and the long end tends to remain level as it rises or falls. Figure 12-2 shows the yield curve for governments over successive stages of a business cycle. Figure 12-3 shows a large number of positive and negative government yield curves through history. Note the negative (declining) curves of the early 1900s and the positively sloped curves of the 1940s and 1950s.

FIGURE 12-2

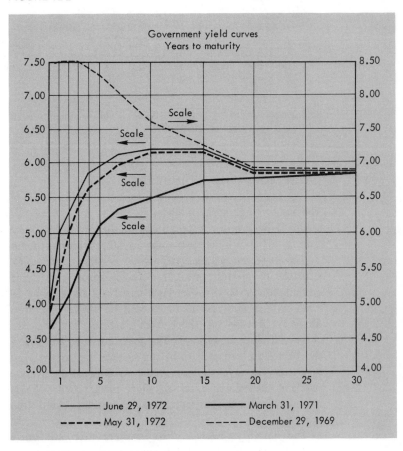

Source: Henry Kaufman et al., eds., *Bond Market Monthly Review* (New York: Salomon Brothers, June 1972), p. 5.

FIGURE 12-3

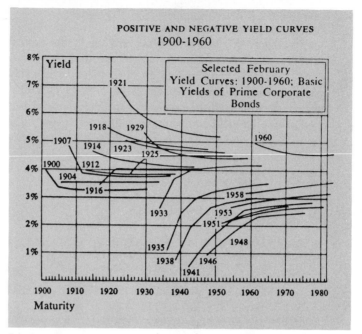

Source: From *A History of Interest Rates* by Sidney Homer, Rutgers University Press, New Brunswick, N.J., 1963.

CAUSES OF TERM STRUCTURE

The underlying cause of differing shapes and overall level in the yield curve seems to be investor expectations of the future course of interest rates. Controversy arises as to whether there are other important factors.

The *expectations theory* provides a very simple explanation of the term structure of interest rates. If expected future short-term rates are above the current short rate, then the yield curve will slope upward. That is, the rate on a bond with a two-year maturity will be above the rate on a one-year bond. Similarly, if expected short rates are below the current short rate, the yield curve will slope downward. The yield curve will be flat (horizontal) if future short rates are expected to be the same as the current short rate. Hence the rate of interest on any long-term security will equal the average of the current short rate and intervening expected short rates.[12] Other theories can be viewed as alternatives to the expectations hypothesis, based upon criticisms lodged against it.

The *liquidity-premium theory* argues that although expectations are important, the existence of risk aversion among investors (and speculators) will result in a preference for shorts over longs, since the principal value of shorts

[12]Actually, it will equal the *geometric* average.

is more certain than that of longs. More will be paid for shorts as a liquidity premium. This inherent aversion to risk requires that longs yield more than shorts. Liquidity premiums thus may modify the steepness of the slope of the yield curve caused by basic expectations.

The existence of downward-sloping yield curves might appear to negate the liquidity-premium idea. The implication is that the aversion to longs cannot cause long rates to be below shorts. The fairest explanation seems to be that downward-sloping curves are still explained by basic expectation of lower short rates; liquidity premiums may modify the steepness of the downward slope.

The *segmentation hypothesis* recognizes that risk aversion can lead to a preference for shorts *or* longs. Long-term securities have the risk of principal uncertainty, but shorts have the risk of income uncertainty. Some investors want to ensure a certain income return over time. Buying a succession of shorts subjects them to the uncertainty of short rates.

The segmentation theory recognizes that the supply and demand for funds is segmented in submarkets for those individuals and institutions that prefer to lend or borrow on one end of the time spectrum or the other. For example, institutions with long liabilities, such as pension funds and insurance companies, prefer long-term securities. Banks, with primarily short-term liabilities, prefer short-term investments. If the markets had just these two segments, the relative supply and demand for funds in each would, in the aggregate, explain the shape of the overall yield curve. But observed behavior suggests that investors often leave preferred maturities temporarily to take advantage of favorable yields in other maturity ranges. So it seems that, in practice, maturity leeway exists and is taken advantage of. This suggestion does not invalidate the segmentation hypothesis; it points up the possibility that premiums are needed to induce such shifting.

The *eclectic theory* of the yield curve suggests that investors have an expectation of a "normal" range of interest rates. They lack a precise way, or an inclination, to predict short rates well into the future. "Normal" ranges are perhaps determined by experience. If rates have varied in the recent past between 3 and 5 percent, investors might expect them to remain in that band. This "normal" range expectation can explain upward- and downward-sloping yield curves.

When short rates are high in the band, the yield curve will slope downward. When short rates are low, there is likely to be an upward-sloping curve. Suppose rates have ranged between 3 and 5 percent. Now they are 4½ percent. The highest they might go is 5 percent, but they may fall much of the way (although not all the way) down to 3 percent. The capital gains possibilities outweigh the loss possibilities. There is more to gain than to lose from buying long bonds. Prices on longs will be bid up and their yields will fall relative to shorts. With rates at the lower end of the band, there is more to lose with longs. Hence a preference for shorts will bid their prices up and their yields down relative to longs. The eclectic theory is an expectations theory; however, it does not require the heroic assumptions on the ability and willingness of investors to make precise forecasts of short rates well into the future.

Most empirical studies highlight the important role of expectations in explaining yield curves. A bias in recent years toward upward-sloping yield curves lends some support to the liquidity-premium hypothesis. Studies give some indication that liquidity premiums vary inversely with the level of interest rates, in keeping with the changing risk of capital loss. Tests of the segmentation theory are largely inconclusive.

Summary

The contractually fixed nature of interest on bonds and dividends on preferred stocks is such that any changes in required holding-period yields occur through market-price changes, which result from changes in systematic and unsystematic risk factors. Perceived increases (decreases) in risk lead to lower (higher) market prices.

Changes in interest rates are the most powerful forces affecting prices of fixed-income securities. This systematic risk factor is really two-dimensional: First, the level of interest rates may move up or down. Second, as the level of rates changes, securities that differ in maturity dates may not move up or down to the same extent; short-term rates may move above long-term rates, or vice versa.

Forecasting the level of interest rates requires insight into business activity, prices, and employment for the period ahead. Along with predicting the economic outlook and price and employment prospects, the analyst needs to gauge the natural forces of supply and demand in financing this outlook. Monetary and fiscal policy must be predicted as a force that will augment or upset projections of business activity, prices, and employment.

As the level of interest rates is forecast to move up or down (or remain relatively stable), the shape of the yield curve may change. The underlying cause of differing shapes in the yield curve seems to be investor expectations of the future course of interest rates. Even though there are other factors involved, it appears that if expected future short-term rates are above current short-term rates, then the yield curve will slope upward. Similarly, if expected short rates are below current short rates, the yield curve will slope downward. Alternative explanations serve to modify somewhat this rather simple explanation.

Questions and Problems

1. Assume that you loan a friend $200 at 6 percent interest. The loan plus interest is to be repaid at the end of one year. The level of consumer prices is expected to advance 4 percent during the year.

    a. How much money will you receive at the end of one year?

    b. What is the true purchasing power of the money you receive?

2. The current interest rate on quality corporate bonds is 7½ percent on a $1,000 instrument due in one year. Suppose one-year rates drop to 7 percent because of shifts in supply and demand. What should the price of the 7½ percent bond be to adjust to a 7 percent market?

3. Refer to Table 12-1. What specific sources or uses of funds can you identify as exhibiting (a) dynamic and (b) stable influences since 1971?

4. In analysis of sources and uses of funds, what is the pivotal role that has been attributed to the so-called residual category?

5. If the Federal Reserve wanted to ease credit and exert a downward influence on interest rates, in what ways might it act?

6. How can the goals of economic growth and equilibrium in the balance of payments suggest both lower and higher levels of short-term interest rates at the same time?

7. In what way(s) do fiscal and monetary policy (a) conflict and (b) complement each other in the credit markets?

8. What is the significance to an investor of a downward-sloping yield curve (long rates below short rates)?

9. Compare and contrast the expectations theory and the eclectic theory of the yield curve.

10. Is the existence of downward-sloping yield curves proof that the liquidity-preference idea is invalid? Why?

CHAPTER
THIRTEEN

BOND ANALYSIS:
UNSYSTEMATIC
RISK

In forecasting purchasing-power and interest-rate risk, what we are really talking about are expectations concerning the outlook for the price of commodities and of money. These major sources of systematic risk in fixed-income securities expalin why it is that the level and time shape of interest rates shift.

There are also unsystematic influences that create risk and explain why certain classes of fixed-income securities, such as governments and corporates, or different subgroups of corporates, may move in general harmony with systematic forces, but not in a parallel or synchronous fashion.

Investors must learn to react not to a single yield curve but to a whole family of them. The yield curve for corporates might have the same shape as that for governments on any given day, but it could be at a different level and less stable. There are different yield curves for each type of bond, and they change every day!

The analytical thrust of high-grade bond selection differs markedly from common-stock selection, although earning power is the fundamental basis of value for both. High-grade bond selection emphasizes continuity of income and protection against loss of principal, whereas common-stock selection emphasizes earnings and dividend growth and capital appreciation potential.

Losses in high-grade bonds arise from either of two factors: changes in the level of interest rates or impairment in quality. Market fluctuations due to interest-rate changes may be short run or long run, but in any event the original principal is recovered at maturity and the only loss is an opportunity cost in maximizing income.

An impairment in quality causes a greater loss in market value, which may become permanent in case of default. Quality impairment arises principally from a decline in earning power relative to the level of debt and fixed charges (or an increase in debt and fixed charges relative to earning power), which may portend future financial difficulties. Normally, a decline increases sensitivity to interest-rate changes, so that market price fluctuation is typically greater for lesser-quality bonds than for the highest-quality issues.

Secondary-quality bonds may improve in quality over time due to increased earnings and asset protection, or they may be paid at maturity despite underlying uncertainties. Such bonds will provide an extra return in capital appreciation in addition to interest. The task of analysis is to weight the risk or uncertainty of payment relative to the potential return, just as for common stocks.

Business and Financial Risk

Corporate bonds sell at higher yields than governments do, mainly because of business and financial risk. Within the generic group called corporate bonds, yield differentials or "spreads" will exist. Business and financial risk are absent from government bonds because of the monopoly status of the government and its ability to meet debt-servicing requirements through taxation. For corporates, the concepts of business and financial risk are generally combined in a single term, *default risk*.

Default in a legal sense is the failure of the issuer to meet the terms of the debt contract. In investment terms, default refers to the probability that the return realized will be less than promised, rather than to total loss. For example, if you buy an 8 percent bond for $1,000 to hold ten years to maturity, you expect $80 in interest each year and the return of principal at the end of ten years. Assume—an unlikely event—that interest payments are delayed ten years, at which time accumulated interest and principal are paid in full. You *realize* less than 8 percent because of the time value of money. The $1,800 ($800 interest plus $1,000 principal) you receive at the end of the tenth year provides a realized return of only about 6 percent.[1]

Default is a matter of degree, from the simple *extension* of time to make an interest payment, to legal *liquidation* of the debtor to settle accumulated interest and principal. An extension occurs when creditors voluntarily allow extension of maturity and/or postponement of interest payments. Liquidation may occur when a number of successive interest payments are missed owing to underlying problems of management. When it appears that the borrower has no hope of turning the situation around, liquidation proceedings are instituted. Creditors hope to recover some portion of the original principal advanced, plus back interest.

Between extension and liquidation, we have the practice called *reorganization*. A financial reorganization involves the issuance of new securities of the reorganized company for defaulted bonds. In such a case, the nature of interest and/or sinking-fund payments is such that the company cannot generate sufficient cash from operations to meet these requirements. So new securities with revised payment schedules, in amount and/or timing, replace the defaulted securities in the hope that the cash strain is relieved.

These varied degrees of default stem largely from inadequate liquidity and/or earnings. The former case is a manifestation of weak cash-flow management. The earnings problem results from some combination of (1) an inadequate revenue-operating cost relationship (business risk), and (2) too much borrowed capital (financial risk).

[1] $1,000 \times (1 + r)^{10} = $1,800$
$r = 6\%$

Bond-investment agencies evaluate the quality of bonds and rank them in categories according to relative probability of default. For the typical investor, this evaluation somewhat simplifies the task of assessing default risk. The principal rating agencies are Moody's Investors Service and Standard & Poor's Corporation.[2]

The bond categories are assigned letter grades. The highest-grade bonds, whose risk of default is felt to be negligible, are rated triple A (Aaa or AAA). The rating agencies assign pluses or minuses (e.g., Aa+, A−) when appropriate to show the relative standing within the major rating categories. Table 13-1 shows the ratings used by the two leading rating agencies, with brief descriptions of each. Table 13-2 shows more-detailed descriptions for the ratings of Standard & Poor's Corporation.

Not all bonds are rated by the agencies. Small issues and those placed privately are generally not rated. For those bonds that are rated, the competing services generally rank the same bond in the same rating category; seldom do they disagree by more than one grade.[3] Overall, the evidence indicates a close correspondence between rating category and subsequent default experience.[4]

Ratings, however, do not totally solve the investor's problem of default-risk discrimination between bonds. First, fully 90 percent of all rated bonds fall into the top four rating categories—not a very detailed distinction for making choices. Second, although the agencies seldom differ widely in their evaluation and classification, they do occasionally differ. Third, and of considerable importance, ratings are changed (up or down) slowly. Under constant review, they are altered only when the agencies deem that sufficient changes have occurred. Thus, letter grades assigned by rating agencies serve only as a general, somewhat coarse form of discrimination.

In the sections that follow, we will consider key factors that an analyst examines to verify and refine default ratings. The major factors include earnings power, cash flow, financial leverage, and liquidity.[5]

---

[2]Preferred stocks are also rated by the agencies, but not on a basis consistent with bond ratings. For example, Standard & Poor's preferred-stock ratings are not necessarily graduated downward according to the issuer's debt. Preferred ratings refer to relative security of dividends and prospective stability of yield.

[3]Louis Brand, former head of Standard & Poor's bond department, estimated that S&P and Moody's disagreed on ratings of about one in twenty utility bonds and one in ten industrial bonds. See H. C. Sherwood, "How They'll Rate Your Company's Bonds," *Business Management*, 29 (March 1966), 38-42ff.

[4]See W. B. Hickman, *Corporate Bond Quality and Investment Performance* (New York: National Bureau of Economic Research, 1958). Hickman concluded that the record of rating agencies between 1900 and 1943 was remarkably good.

[5]Fisher found that risk premiums on bonds were related to (1) earnings variability of the firm, (2) the length of time it was solvent, (3) the equity/debt ratio, and (4) the market value or marketability of its debt issue. In effect, companies of long standing, with relatively stable earnings, whose bonds are highly marketable and covered by a large equity cushion, sell at lower default-risk premiums than their counterparts with opposite traits. See L. Fisher, "Determinants of Risk Premiums on Corporate Bonds," *Journal of Political Economy*, 67 (June 1959), 217-37.

TABLE 13-1

RATINGS BY INVESTMENT AGENCIES

	Moody's
Aaa	Best quality
Aa	High quality
A	Higher medium grade
Baa	Lower medium grade
Ba	Possess speculative elements
B	Generally lack characteristics of desirable investment
Caa	Poor standing; may be in default
Ca	Speculative in a high degree; often in default
C	Lowest grade
	Standard & Poor's
AAA	Highest grade
AA	High grade
A	Upper medium grade
BBB	Medium grade
BB	Lower medium grade
B	Speculative
CCC-CC	Outright speculation
C .	Reserved for income bonds
DDD-D	In default, with rating indicating relative salvage value

EARNINGS COVERAGE

Heavy burdens of fixed-interest and preferred-dividend payments have led many companies into default and eventual bankruptcy. The degree of default risk is measured in two ways by analysts: (1) earnings-coverage ratios and (2) capitalization ratios. Each of these will be explored in turn.

Earnings coverage rests on income relative to charges on debt and preferred stock. The higher the income relative to charges, the lower the risk of default, other things being equal. This income-charges relationship is normally cast in ratio terms, Income/Charges.

Earnings and Charges—Bonds

The income referred to is generally EBIT (earnings before interest and taxes). Since interest is a tax-deductible expense, it is logical to compare it with earnings before taxes.[6]

The *level of income* used in the computation of earnings-coverage ratios deserves serious consideration. The most important consideration here is: What level of income will be most representative of the amount that will actually be available in the *future* for the payment of debt-related fixed charges? An average

---

[6]It is customary to exclude extraordinary and/or nonrecurring income from earnings. Such extraordinary items cannot be assumed to occur regularly or predictably.

TABLE 13-2

STANDARD & POOR'S CORPORATE BOND RATINGS

AAA	Bonds rated AAA are *highest grade* obligations. They possess the ultimate degree of protection as to principal and interest. Marketwise they move with interest rates, and hence provide the maximum safety on all accounts.
AA	Bonds rated AA also qualify as *high grade* obligations, and in the majority of instances differ from AAA issues only in small degree. Here, too, prices move with the long term money market.
A	Bonds rated A are regarded as *upper medium grade.* They have considerable investment strength but are not entirely free from adverse effects of changes in economic and trade conditions. Interest and principal are regarded as safe. They predominantly reflect money rates in their market behavior, but to some extent, also economic conditions.
BBB	The BBB, or *medium grade* category is borderline between definitely sound obligations and those where the speculative element begins to predominate. These bonds have adequate asset coverage and normally are protected by satisfactory earnings. Their susceptibility to changing conditions, particularly to depressions, necessitates constant watching. Marketwise, the bonds are more responsive to business and trade conditions than to interest rates. This group is the lowest which qualifies for commercial bank investment.
BB	Bonds given a BB rating are regarded as *lower medium grade.* They have only minor investment characteristics. In the case of utilities, interest is earned consistently but by narrow margins. In the cases of other types of obligors, charges are earned on average by a fair margin, but in poor periods deficit operations are possible.
B	Bonds rated as low as B are *speculative.* Payment of interest cannot be assured under difficult economic conditions.
CCC-CC	Bonds rated CCC and CC are *outright speculations*, with the lower rating denoting the more speculative. Interest is paid, but continuation is questionable in periods of poor trade conditions. In the case of CC ratings the bonds may be on an income basis and the payment may be small.
C	The rating of C is reserved for *income bonds* on which no interest is being paid.
DDD-D	All bonds rated DDD, DD and D are *in default*, with the rating indicating the relative salvage value.

Source: Standard & Poor's *Bond Guide* (New York: Standard & Poor's Corporation, June 1977), p. 6.

earnings figure encompassing the entire range of the business cycle, and adjusted for any known factors that may change it in the future, is most likely to be the best approximation of the average source of funds from future operations which can be expected to become available for the payment of fixed charges. Moreover, if the objective of the earnings-coverage ratio is to measure the creditor's maximum exposure to risk, then the proper earnings figure to use is that achieved at the low point of the enterprise's business cycle.

The *total charges* on bonds usually amount to the sum of the annual interest charges on all debts. Although a company may have several bonds outstanding with different priorities to income (and assets), such as mortgage bonds and debentures, we generally do not calculate a separate mortgage-bond coverage and debenture-bond coverage. Ability to meet interest payments on mortgage bonds but not debentures can put the company into bankruptcy. Then the mortgage bondholders are in jeopardy as well. The chain of bond priorities is only as strong as the weakest link.

Let us illustrate our *coverage-ratio* idea. The income statement of ABC, Inc., shows its EBIT to be $25 million. The company has outstanding a 6 percent, first-mortgage bond issue in the amount of $50 million. In addition, an 8 percent debenture-bond issue is outstanding in the amount of $25 million. Total interest payments would be $5 million (6 percent of $50 million, plus 8 percent of $25 million). Earnings coverage would be calculated as follows:

$$\text{Interest coverage on all bonds} = \frac{\text{EBIT}}{\text{Interest charges on all bonds}} \qquad (13.1)$$

$$= \frac{\$25 \text{ million}}{\$5 \text{ million}} = 5$$

The earnings coverage is said to be five times. The larger this ratio, the better. We must recognize, however, that the significance of this coverage is enhanced by gauging it (1) over a period of years, future as well as past, and (2) against some standard to ascertain whether it is high or low, good or bad.

The adequacy of the ratio must be related to the volatility and other characteristics of earning power. Coverage ratios in cyclically sensitive businesses such as autos, machinery, or chemicals should average higher than for more stable businesses such as food or drugs. If a company is to enjoy a high credit rating, it should show sufficient coverage so that even under the worst of foreseeable conditions, there is a cushion against unexpected adversity. Companies in this position will continue to enjoy adequate credit standing and have access to financial markets under even the most adverse conditions.

Debt-Service Analysis. The use of borrowed capital also typically requires cash outlays to discharge part or all of the principal of the debt in future years. Serial maturities or sinking funds are the typical contractual covenants that indicate cash requirements for this purpose. Although payments on debt principal may represent a regular flow of cash out of the company, they are not reflected on the income statement. Investor protection can be impaired by the inability of the issuer to meet sinking-fund or amortization requirements, since these are also legal obligations, just like regular interest. Therefore the analyst should make some determination of the issuer's capacity to cover total requirements, including both interest payments and annual debt reduction. Coverage of both is essential.

In this light, it is customary to determine *debt-service coverage* by the following:

$$\frac{\text{EBIT}}{\text{Interest charges on bonds} + [\text{Sinking-fund payments}/(1 - \text{Tax rate})]}$$

Since sinking-fund payments are not expenses but return of principal, they are not reported on the income statement. Hence they must be paid out of after-tax dollars. This is the reason for the mathematical setup in the denominator of the fraction. Thus, for a company in the 40 percent tax bracket to cover $300,000 for sinking-fund payments, $500,000 must be earned before taxes ($500,000 less $200,000 in taxes is $300,000). Hence, for ABC, Inc., let us assume that a 40 percent tax rate applies, and that the $25 million in 8 percent debentures calls for an annual sinking-fund payment of $300,000. Debt-service coverage could be calculated as:

$$\frac{\$25}{\$5 + [\$0.3/(1 - .4)]} = \frac{\$25}{\$5 + \$0.5} = \frac{\$25}{\$5.5} = 4.5$$

Earnings and Charges—Preferred Stock

Preferred-stock dividends are paid after interest. Recognition of this fact means that preferred dividend coverage must include in the total charges all prior interest. Preferred dividend requirements could be added to interest charges, if any, and this sum could be divided into earnings. However, complications arise.

Preferred dividends are paid after taxes, whereas bond interest is paid before taxes. Adding both together is like mixing apples and oranges. Either preferred dividends must be adjusted to a before-tax basis or interest payments must be adjusted to an after-tax basis. The former is preferable. At a tax rate of 50 percent, a corporation needs $2 in EBIT to pay $1 in preferred dividends; only $1 of EBIT is needed to pay $1 in interest, since interest is a pre-tax expense. In general, to adjust preferred dividends to a before-tax basis:

$$\text{Pre-tax preferred dividend requirement} = \frac{\text{Preferred dividends}}{1 - \text{Tax rate}} \quad (13.2)$$

In other words, at a 40 percent tax rate, a company has to earn $5 million before taxes to pay $3 million in preferred dividends [$3 million/(1 − .4) = $5 million].

After adjustment for the tax factor, earnings coverage on preferred dividends becomes:

$$\text{Preferred dividend coverage} = \frac{\text{EBIT}}{\text{Interest} + \text{Preferred dividend}/(1 - \text{Tax rate})} \quad (13.3)$$

Assume that ABC, Inc., has EBIT of $25 million and the balance sheet shows:

	(in millions)		
Current assets	$90	Current liabilities	$30
		6% first-mortgage bonds	$50
		8% debentures	25
Fixed assets	$140	8% preferred stock	25
		Common equity	100

Total interest was determined earlier to be $5 million. Preferred dividends are determined in dollars as 8 percent of $25 million, or $2 million. Assuming a tax rate of 40 percent, total charges are covered:

$$\text{Preferred dividend coverage} = \frac{\text{EBIT}}{\text{Interest} + [\text{Preferred dividends}/(1 - \text{Tax rate})]}$$

$$= \frac{\$25}{\$5 + (\$2/.6)} = \frac{\$25}{\$5 + \$3.33} = \frac{\$25}{\$8.33} = 3 \text{ times}$$

Note that where a company has both bond and preferred-stock financing, the coverage of the preferred is always lower than the coverage on the bonds.[7]

CAPITALIZATION

Financial leverage or risk can also be measured on the balance sheet. Capital from each of varied sources—debt, preferred stock, and common stock—can be related in percentage form to total funds. To the bondholder or preferred stock-holder, the greater the percentage of total funds that common stockholders provide, the better. Extending our ABC, Inc., example:

	(in millions)
6% first-mortgage bonds	$50
8% debentures	25
8% preferred stock	25
Common equity	100
Total long-term capital	**$200**

Capitalization ratios, at book value, can be stated as:

Long-term bonds	37.5%	(75/200)
Preferred stock	12.5	(25/200)
Common equity	50.0	(100/200)
Total	100.0%	

If the ABC bonds were being analyzed, the relevant capitalization ratio would consider preferred and common stock as junior in standing to bonds. In this case, a bondholder would note that his equity "cushion" is 62.5 percent (125/200) of total long-term funds. For preferred stockholders, the cushion is 50 percent (common equity). Bondholders and preferred stockholders desire a strong common-equity base to cushion their position.[8]

---

[7]The reader can see the fallacy in subtracting interest from EBIT and dividing the result by adjusted preferred dividends. The result is $20/$3.33 = 6 times. Recall that bond interest coverage was 5 times. Preferred dividends cannot be better protected than bond interest.

[8]At times, preferred stock has no par value or has a nominal value, such as $1 per share. Preferred stockholders would be entitled to more on liquidation of the company—say, $50 maximum per share. To compute capitalization ratios, it is appropriate to show preferred stock at liquidation value. Any difference between nominal value and liquidating value would come from a reduction of surplus accounts. The result is to lower the common-equity percentage of total funds.

Analysts often deduct intangible assets from common equity in calculating capitalization ratios. The result is a lower common-equity percentage of total capital. The reason lies in the fact that many intangible assets (patents, goodwill, franchises and so on) are placed on balance sheets at doubtful values. The removal of these amounts from the asset side of the balance sheet necessitates similar elimination from common equity. The resulting figure is called tangible net worth, or tangible common equity.

The rating services and analysts look at capitalization in alternative ways to the percentage breakdown of long-term capital shown above. The possibilities seem almost unending if we look again at the components and how they might be related:

Total assets	$100	Liabilities (debt)	$20
		Equity	80
		Total debt and equity	$100

Financial risk can be measured on the balance sheet by Total debt/Equity (20/80 = .25). This is interpreted as 25 cents of debt for every $1 of equity. The percentage breakdown, or capitalization ratios, would be Debt = .2, and Equity = .8. Debt is 20 percent of total long-term funds. A kind of asset-coverage relationship similar to the earnings-coverage idea is derived by relating assets to debt (Assets/Debt), or 100/20 = 5. Debt is covered five times by assets in the event that assets are liquidated now at book value.

LEASES

An analytical complication arises when a company leases some or all of its fixed assets. Instead of borrowing long-term funds to buy buildings and equipment, many companies lease them.[9] Financial analysts call this "off-balance-sheet" financing, referring to the fact that since leased facilities are not owned, their cost is typically not carried as an asset. More important, at most only current lease installments appear as a liability. In effect, two companies may be utilizing the same amount of fixed assets, one leasing and the other owning. They may generate identical profits, but they will show different debt outstanding and interest charges, as well as different earnings coverage and capitalization ratios.

Payments under a lease are designed to cover three basic ingredients required by the lessor or the landlord: (1) depreciation on the property, (2) interest expense on the borrowing, and (3) a profit margin. Only interest expense plus profit margin is analogous to bond interest.

Analysts attempt to make financial statements of companies comparable. When companies lease property, fixed charges and long-term debt must be adjusted upward. How? A rule of thumb is to assume that about one-third of a

---

[9]For analytical purposes, use of the alternative of borrowing rather than selling stock stems from the debt-like nature of most lease contracts.

lease payment represents interest payments.[10] Dividing this amount by prevailing rates available to the company on long-term debt at the time the lease was arranged in effect "capitalizes" the lease. This capitalization provides us a debt-value equivalent represented by the lease.[11]

Suppose ABC, Inc., makes lease payments of $4.5 million on a building. At the time of the lease arrangement, the company could have borrowed at 6 percent (the rate on its mortgage bonds). With the suggested rule of thumb:

$$\frac{1/3 \times \$4.5 \text{ million}}{.06} = \frac{\$1.5 \text{ million}}{.06} = \$25 \text{ million}$$

The $25 million is the equivalent amount of debt represented by the lease. When the building was built, if ABC had borrowed money at 6 percent rather than signing a lease agreement, annual interest expense would be $1.5 million higher than shown in the income statement, and long-term debt on the balance sheet would be greater by $25 million.

Revised coverage and capitalization ratios for ABC would be determined by adding back one-third of the lease payments to EBIT on the income statement. This has the effect of raising EBIT. Interest expense is then raised by $1.5 million. Thus:

$$\frac{\text{EBIT} + 1/3 \text{ lease payment}}{\text{Interest} + 1/3 \text{ lease payment}}$$

$$\frac{\text{EBIT (revised)}}{\text{Interest on bonds (revised)}} = \frac{\$25 + \$1.5}{\$5 + \$1.5} = \frac{\$26.5}{\$6.5} = 4.1$$

Our earlier bond coverage of five times has been reduced. Since defaults on lease payments have legal consequences, the revised coverage of 4.1 times adds meaning to our default-risk measurement using earnings coverage. Preferred-dividend coverage would have to be adjusted accordingly.

Lease (rental) payments would have to be reflected in a revised *debt-service*

---

[10] The inclusion of a portion of lease (rental) expense (deemed to be an interest factor representative of leases) is typically performed only for "financing leases." These are defined by the SEC as non-cancellable leases that (1) cover 75 percent or more of the economic life of the property, or (2) assure the lessor a full recovery of his initial investment plus a reasonable return. For years prior to 1973 it was necessary to rely on conventions such as capitalizing total lease rentals. Since 1973 the SEC has required that notes to the financial statements of annual reports show how these leases are capitalized. Generally these leases are capitalized at the present value of gross minimum rentals based on the interest rate implicit in the terms of the lease. The use of the one-third total net rental payments is an inexact method, but it is the best available for years prior to 1973 and is preferable to omitting rentals.

The interested reader should refer to the footnotes to the financial statements of Holiday Inns, Inc. (Chapter 8) to see how lease commitments are reported. FASB No. 13 goes into great detail on the subject of how leases are to be disclosed in financial statements.

[11] It would be best to use present-value calculations using the term to maturity of the lease. However, most financial data available to the investor do not include all the terms of lease contracts to make this refined calculation possible.

coverage ratio. The interest coverage computation included only that portion of leases (rentals) that is attributable to the interest factor. As a long-term observation, from a contractual point of view, the interest portion is indistinguishable from the principal portion (the remaining two-thirds, as it were). Consequently, debt-service coverage should account for the entire amount of leases (rentals), rather than only the interest portion. Thus:

$$\frac{\text{EBIT} + \text{Lease payments}}{\text{Interest} + \text{Lease payments} + [\text{Sinking-fund payments}/(1 - \text{Tax rate})]}$$

$$= \frac{\$25.0 + \$4.5}{\$5 + \$4.5 + \$0.5} = \frac{\$29.5}{10.0} = 2.95$$

Preferred dividend coverage would be revised as follows:

$$\frac{\text{EBIT} + 1/3 \text{ Lease payment}}{\text{Interest} + [\text{Preferred dividends}/(1 - \text{Tax rate})] + 1/3 \text{ Lease payment}}$$

$$= \frac{\$25 + \$1.5}{\$5 + \$3.33 + \$1.5} = \frac{\$26.50}{9.83} = 2.7$$

Similarly, revised capitalization ratios would recognize the added $25 million debt equivalent:

Long-term debt	$ 75.0	33.3%	(75/225)
Debt equivalent	25.0	11.1	(25/225)
Preferred stock	25.0	11.1	(25/225)
Common equity	100.0	44.5	(100/225)
	$225.0	100%	

The common-equity cushion was calculated earlier to be 50 percent.

The methods employed to adjust for leases are admittedly somewhat crude. Security analysts and accountants have grappled with the problem of widespread, adequate lease-disclosure standards for many years. More and more companies are providing some information on leases in footnotes to financial statements. We are still some way from having the kind of detail necessary to sound analysis, but at least the methods presented here are significantly better than making no adjustment for leases at all.

LIQUIDITY

Adequate earnings coverage does not mean that adequate cash will be on hand to make actual payments required on bonds and preferred stock. Companies rich with earnings can be cash-poor.

The amount of cash and working capital (current assets minus current liabilities) a company has will provide a good indication of its ability to ride out a general recession or a temporary decline in its particular industry, and still make interest, dividend, and sinking-fund payments. The size of its cash and working capital will also indicate its ability to finance improvements or expand sales volume without resorting to further borrowing.

The analyst is interested in (1) the size and (2) the character of a company's liquid position. Levels of cash and sources of cash should be examined. Stable or increasing cash positions are desired, generated mainly internally, rather than from outside sources such as bank borrowing. Analysts want to be certain that the company's dividend policy is in line with the industry. Over-liberal dividends weaken defenses against business downturns and benefit only common shareholders.

Liquidity connotes the ability to meet obligations as they mature and to sustain current operations. The liquidity position of a company may be thought of as a reservoir into which cash is deposited from revenues and cash flows out to pay obligations incurred for expenses and expansion. When the reservoir gets too low, it may be replenished in the first instance from liquidation of short-term financial assets or by borrowing in the capital market or from banks or by sales of equity. If these avenues are not available, a financial crisis develops. Often a weakness in one type of cash resource is quickly followed by weakness in the others. The bondholder's interest in the company's liquidity is directed toward the overall financial position and ability to meet debt maturities without recourse to a refunding operation in the capital market, which might happen to be congested at the time.

There are several key funds items of interest to the analyst as measures of basic cash flow in the business on a long-run basis. *Internal funds* are defined as retained earnings plus depreciation, the change in deferred taxes, and, where material, minority interest. Also where material, we remove undistributed earnings of unconsolidated subsidiaries accounted for by the equity method. In an extreme situation, dividends could be stopped to increase cash flow as defined, but usually the capacity to pay dividends is one evidence of financial strength and hence we use retained earnings. This is a conservative measure because it excludes other sources of funds, importantly, any increase in payables and accruals. *Funds used* are capital expenditures plus the change in receivables and inventories. There are other uses of funds, of course, but these are the principal expenditures necessary for the operation and growth of the business.

Companies that keep these two totals in balance seldom need to raise new capital. An occasional imbalance may be financed by temporary bank credit. Often the excess of funds used over internal cash flow may be funded steadily into debt while holding the debt ratio constant. However, sustained excesses of funds used over internal cash flow and a rising debt ratio can be a danger signal.

The bondholder is interested in appraising the company's ability to repay debt out of internal cash flow, in comparison with other uses of funds. This has been shown to be an important measure of credit quality and liquidity and is briefly defined as follows:

$$\frac{\text{Total debt}}{\text{Internal funds}}$$

It indicates the number of years required to retire all debt out of internal cash flow. Excluded from this calculation are other fixed obligations (leases), since these are retired via direct charges to expense or revenues.

While actual appropriation of all internal cash flow to debt reduction for several years would hamper the future growth of the business and be tantamount to liquidation, a high ratio of cash flow to debt—or a low number of years to pay—gives a company considerable flexibility in financing its business internally and/or externally and therefore is an indicator of credit quality.

The actual maturity schedule is also important to the bondholder. One possible measure of the ability to handle maturities would be the ratio of present internal cash flow to annual debt maturities, including sinking-fund requirements, for the next five to ten years. However, maturity schedules generally are highly variable from year to year, so that it is not useful to compute such a ratio. But a simple comparison of the maturity schedule with internal funds generation could indicate potential problems over the next few years. For a long-term measure, the ratio of debt to internal funds described above is useful here also. In effect, this ratio is another way of indicating that the level of earning power, as expressed in various ways, is the wellspring of credit standing and liquidity, and hence of bond safety.

Among the conventional tests of the adequacy of liquid resources are the current ratio (current assets/current liabilities), the cash ratio (cash/current liabilities), and working-capital adequacy (current assets minus current liabilites/long-term debt).

Expanding our data on ABC, Inc., will help to illustrate these tests of liquidity:

($ in millions)

Cash	$6.0	Current liabilities		$30.0
Total current assets	90.0	Long-term debt		75.0
Fixed assets	140.0	Preferred stock		25.0
		Common equity		100.0
Cash ratio		= 6/30	=	0.2
Current ratio		= 90/30	=	3.0
Working capital/long-term debt	=	60/75	=	0.8

Working capital/long-term debt (including lease equivalent) = 60/100 = 0.6

It is difficult to generalize about what constitutes high or low cash and working-capital ratios. A standard of 2 to 1 is often set for the current ratio. However, liquidity requirements are largely dependent upon the industry in question.

Net income is generally not a reliable measure of funds provided by operations that are available to meet fixed charges. The reason is, of course, that fixed charges are paid with cash or, from the longer-term point of view, with funds (working capital), while net income includes items of revenue that do not generate funds as well as expense items that do not require the current use of funds. Thus a better measure of fixed-charges coverage may be obtained by using as numerator funds obtained by operations rather than net income. This figure can be obtained from the statement of changes in financial condition, which is now a required financial statement and should, consequently, be generally available.

Under this concept the coverage ratio could be computed by dividing funds provided by operations by fixed charges (i.e., interest, sinking-fund, and lease payments).

THE SECURITY CONTRACT

Bond indentures and preferred-stock contracts spell out the legal rights of holders and the restrictions under which a company must operate once it has issued bonds and/or preferred stocks.[12] The many covenants of these lengthy and complex legal documents are designed to insure against the kind of bad housekeeping that may lead to default. These various thou-shalts and thou-shalt-nots specify what a company may do while it is among the living as well as what happens if it dies. *Analysts and investors should look to see that contracts contain certain protective covenants.*

Security contracts do not ensure rising sales and profit margins. However, they can attempt to (1) control the total amount of debt and preferred-stock financing relative to common equity—a prime source of default—and (2) protect priorities to interest or dividends and principal payments in the event of default.

Controls that attempt to minimize default risk and maximize recovery in bond issues are generally stated in the areas of sinking funds, collateral, additional funded debt, and dividend restrictions. Comfort seems to lie in knowing that principal will be recaptured on a regular payments schedule (sinking fund) and/or that certain assets are pledged to support principal (collateral). Further, current bondholders want to exercise a degree of control over the amount of debt permitted over future time periods (additional funded debt). Dissipation results when too many creditors vie for limited earnings and/or assets. Dividend restrictions protect future ability to generate interest payments.

Periodic repayment of principal between date of issuance and the final due date has several advantages to investors. First, it provides greater assurance that the company will not default than does the promise of payment of the total issue in one lump sum at a distant due date. Second, with preferreds, this buy-back method lends price support to a security that, unlike bonds, has no nominal maturity. Third, if earnings are steady, piecemeal retirement enhances earnings and asset coverage on the remaining principal. On the other hand, however, as interest rates fall, a sinking-fund buy-back can take from an investor a security with an attractive yield.

An annual sinking-fund payment is usually made on corporate bonds to provide funds to buy them back through the marketplace or random call. Less frequently, the funds are placed in an escrow account (at interest) to retire the

---

[12]For other details on features found in bond indentures and preferred-stock contracts, the reader may wish to review Chapter 1.

entire issue at once. Municipal bonds are normally divided into parts, each part having a different maturity date. This is a serial-maturity arrangement. The holder knows exactly when his bond is due (avoiding the chance aspects of sinking funds). Sinking-fund arrangements are designed to cope with investor fears of default risk. Serial bond issues are designed to match the repayment ability of the issuer.

Indentures normally provide for additional debt financing if certain tests are met. Added debt is given no more than an equal, and often junior, security position to debt previously issued. A common test to be met before new debt financing can occur is to relate net tangible assets to total old and new debt.[13] A rule might be that new debt can be issued only if, after the issue, net tangible assets amount to at least two and one-half times as much as current and proposed debt. Suppose a company has $100 million in net tangible assets and $25 million in long-term debt. Its ratio of net tangible assets to debt is 4:1. A proposed new long-term debt issue of $25 million would bring the ratio to 2½:1 (125/50).[14]

If additional debt is to be backed by collateral, it is common to provide equal or lesser standing to other lienholders. This feature is important when debentures (unsecured bonds) are used. Should mortgage bonds be sold subsequent to a debenture issue, it is common for debentures to be given equal and proportionate secured standing.

Dividend restrictions attempt to avoid excessive payout, which weakens the equity base and liquidity. In some instances, dividends may be limited to retained earnings subsequent to the issuance of a particular bond issue, or subsequent earnings plus some stipulated amount of accumulated earnings.

Owners of preferred stocks normally enjoy equal claim to assets and dividends behind bondholders. Rarely, a "prior" preferred receives first claim to income and assets; this might be called a "first" preferred. Preferred issues protect against issuance of subsequent debt and preferred stock of equal or greater rank by veto rights. In such a case, the votes of, say, two-thirds of the preferred holders are required to approve prior or parity securities *unless* total debt and preferred-stock charges are covered to a specified extent (maybe two and one-half times fixed charges), and/or common-stock equity is not less than preferred-stock equity after new preferred is sold (that is, common equity $\geq$ preferred equity).

It is standard for preferred-stock contracts to provide for cumulation of dividends. In other words, if dividends are missed, they must be made up before any dividends can be paid on common shares. Moreover, when a certain number of dividends are missed, preferred stockholders can elect a number of directors to prevent further difficulties. This voting right is contingent upon missing dividends and is relinquished when arrears are cleared up.

---

[13]Net tangible assets are net assets less intangibles, such as patents, copyrights, and goodwill.

[14]The reader may note that an asset-to-debt ratio is a sort of asset-coverage counterpart to the earnings-coverage ratio.

TESTS OF CORPORATE-BOND RISK:
A REVIEW EXAMPLE

Table 13-3 shows single-year data for Husky Industries. Table 13-4 is a summary of key tests of default risk bearing on the bonds and preferred stock of the company if they were being analyzed on the statement dates. This example is included to assist the reader in pulling together the many strands of analysis introduced so far.[15]

Key items to note are:

1. Extraordinary income (land sale) is included in revenues. Exclude $1.2 from EBIT as nonrecurring, leaving EBIT = $11. (Note: Income taxes of $4.7 include $0.3 from 25 percent tax on land sale of $1.2.)

TABLE 13-3
HUSKY INDUSTRIES, FINANCIAL STATEMENTS FOR THE YEAR 197X

Income Statement
for the year ended 12/31/7X
(in millions)

Net revenues*	$101.2
Cost of sales	78.0
Depreciation	10.0
Lease payments†	1.0
EBIT	12.2
Interest expense	2.2
EBT	10.0
Income taxes‡	4.7
EAT	5.3
Preferred dividends	1.2
Earnings available to common	4.1
Common dividend	2.1

Position Statement
12/31/7X (in millions)

Cash	$ 2.0	Current debt	$ 10.0
Other current assets (net)	60.0	4% 1st-mortgage bonds	10.0
Intangible fixed assets (net)	5.6	4½% debenture bonds §	40.0
Tangible fixed assets (net)	83.0	6% cumulative preferred	20.0
		Common stock ($1 par)	0.6
		Surplus accounts	70.0
Total assets	$150.6	Total debt and equity	$150.6

*Includes pre-tax long-term capital gains on sale of land, $1.2 million.
†Financial lease. Borrowing equivalent cost = 8%.
‡Tax rates on income: ordinary income = 50%; capital gains = 25%.
§Annual sinking fund of $2.4 million.

[15]To illustrate certain points, some statement items have been placed and/or combined in a manner contrary to good accounting practices.

2. Regarding lease payments, a net lease might assume that one-third the payment is equivalent to interest. Capitalized at a borrowing cost of 8 percent (.33/.08), this gives a long-term debt equivalent of $4.17. Add one-third of the lease payment to previously adjusted EBIT, and the interest portion to interest expense. EBIT = $11.33; Long-term debt = $54.17; Interest and lease payment = $2.53.

3. Pre-tax preferred dividend adjustments should use a tax rate of 50 percent, not the effective rate on the income statement (Income tax/EBT = 4.7/10.0 = 47%). (See item 1, p. 404.) Pre-tax preferred dividend is $1.2/.5, or $2.4.

4. Total tangible assets equal $145 ($150.6 minus $5.6). Tangible common equity is $65.0 ($70.6 minus net intangible fixed assets of $5.6).

TABLE 13-4
KEY MEASURES OF RISK IN FIXED-INCOME SECURITIES

Ratio	Calculation	Result
Coverage ratios:		
Interest coverage	[(11.0) + (0.3)] / [(2.2) + (.33)]	4.47
Preferred-dividend coverage	[(11.0) + (0.3)] / [(2.53) + (2.4)]	3.87
Debt-service coverage	[(11.0) + (1.0)] / [(2.2) + (1.0)]	3.75
Cash flow coverage	[(11.0) + (1.0) + (10.0)] / [(11.0) + (1.0) + (2.4)]	1.53
Capitalization ratios:		
Long-term debt	$50.00	.36
Debt equivalent for lease	$ 4.17	.03
Preferred stock	$20.00	.14
Tangible common equity	$65.00	.47
Liquidity ratios:		
Cash ratio	2/10	.20
Current ratio	62/10	6.20
Working capital: funded debt	52/54.17	.96

MUNICIPAL-BOND ANALYSIS

There are two principal types of municipal securities: general-credit obligations and revenue bonds. General-obligation bonds are backed by the full taxing power of the municipality. Revenue bonds, however, are backed only by the revenue of the specific project for which they were issued. A toll-road bond issue is an example of a revenue bond. Because of the greater risk of revenue bonds, they must provide higher yields to maturity.

Municipal securities, like corporates, are subject to default risk and are rated by Moody's and Standard & Poor's as to their probability of default.

General-Obligation Bonds

The general factors that must be considered in assessing default risk on municipals are the taxing base, existing debt in relation to this base, and the variability of tax revenues. Several common ratios can be used to judge the relative risk of default.

First, what is the amount of tax-dependent debt relative to the assessed valuation of taxable real estate? The wealth and income of a community can be measured roughly in terms of property values. The resulting ratio is a debt-to-property-value measure. Care must be taken in making comparisons, to ensure that assessment methods are standardized. Communities normally take market values of property and reduce them to assessed value by some percentage multiplier. One may assess property at 60 percent of market value, and another at 80 percent. High-quality bonds would normally fall in a range of 8-10 percent for debt to assessed value. In a sense, this measure is a rough equivalent of a debt-to-asset ratio for corporates. The reciprocal is an asset-coverage ratio.

Second, debt per capita is also measured. The number of residents of a community does not necessarily represent the number of taxpayers, so care must be taken not to use this ratio in isolation.

Third, debt service as a percentage of the community's budgeted operating expenses can be measured. Debt service refers to the sum of annual interest plus debt retirement. This ratio is a roundabout equivalent of interest-coverage ratios on corporates. Instead of using earnings or revenues as with corporates, however, it measures the community's burden in paying for debt service relative to other operating costs out of tax receipts.

Revenue Bonds

Revenue bonds bear risks similar to those of corporate bonds. Interest and principal must be paid from earnings, so earnings-coverage ratios become vitally important. The investor must assess the future revenue-generating ability of the project (toll road, sports stadium, or whatever).

DEFAULT RISK AND MARKET YIELDS

Figure 13-1 indicates the pattern of the structure of yields on governments, municipals, and corporates over time. The general correspondence of governments and various grades of corporates is in line with basic differences in underlying default risk and premiums.

The reader should be warned that default risk alone does not explain the differentials or spreads in yields. Identical agency ratings of quality can disguise differentials among industrial, finance, and electric and gas utility bonds, and even among issues within these categories.

Differences in taxation can be seen in the low levels of yields on municipals. Certain situations that exist with corporates provide different tax situations in the same rating category. Call features and differences in degree of marketability are other factors that are hidden in Figure 13-1.

Changes in Yield Differentials

Yields on different instruments do not move in lockstep. Differentials, or spreads, are altered when circumstances that caused them in the first place

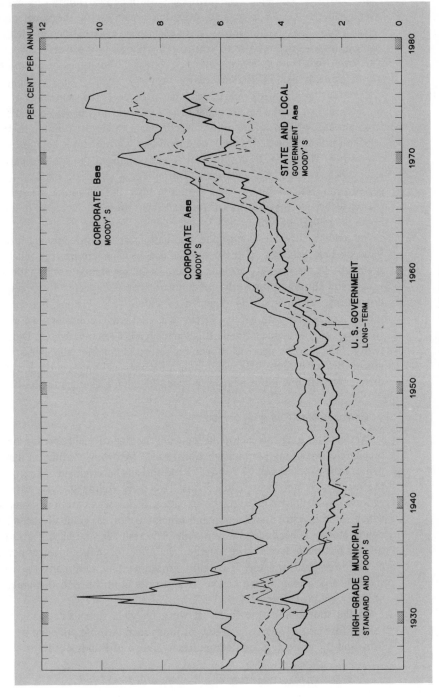

Source: Board of Governors of the Federal Reserve System, *Historical Chart Book 1977.*

change. Figure 13-2 depicts the historical pattern and variability of yield spreads. Average levels of AAA corporates over time are shown in the upper panel. The vertical lines show yield ranges during each year. Fluctuations of yields within given years are large relative to year-to-year changes in the average level of yield. The lower panel shows spreads between four different types of bonds. The size of the spreads has fluctuated greatly over the years. The variability of the differentials within many years is as large as or larger than the range of the level of rates shown in the upper panel. The shrinkage in the Aaa-Baa differential from about 2 percent in pre-World War II years to almost nothing in 1964 and 1965 is striking. This is the result of diminished worries about default or another depression. The Aaa-U.S. government spread shrank in the postwar period until after 1965, when it widened again. During these years, no hard evidence suggested that Aaa corporates had become more default-prone. There is some reason to believe that the spread resulted from dramatic increases in corporate-bond financing and diminished long-term-debt financing by the government.[16]

In general, although change and fluctuations are the rule in yield spreads, the basic cyclical behavior of these spreads can be characterized as follows: Risk premiums in the market for bonds fluctuate in a systematic way with the business cycle. During upturns, the premium for risk is expected to narrow; during downturns, the premium is expected to widen. In recessions, bondholders are mostly concerned with safety. Prices of higher-grade bonds are bid up relative to those of lower-grade bonds (high-grade yields fall relatively). During prosperity, less concern may be shown for safety and more willingness to bear a greater risk of default. The seeking out of higher-yielding securities will tend to drive down risk premiums relative to lower-yielding, higher-grade bonds.

Forces Behind Changing Spreads

Among the long-run factors influencing the size of yield spreads are (1) the breaking down of market imperfections, and (2) growing confidence that serious depressions can and will be avoided. Yield spreads have tended to narrow among the markets as borrowers and lenders have been willing to take advantage of various opportunities offering better rates. Strict segmentation of markets in which some investors participate and others do not has gradually been breaking down. Money is becoming more mobile. The result has perhaps been to narrow spreads but make levels more volatile. The effect of reduced fear of depressions is narrower-yield spreads. No doubt government commitments to economic stability and a long period of low default rates contribute to this greater sense of safety among lenders.

In the shorter run, the forces at work on yield spreads necessitate looking behind forecasts of sources and uses of funds such as those provided by Salomon Bros. and the more detailed Federal Reserve Flow of Funds Accounts.

---

[16] A. M. Wojnilower, "Yield Differentials," in *Financial Institutions and Markets,* ed. M. C. Polakoff (Boston: Houghton Mifflin, 1970), pp. 425-54.

FIGURE 13-2
YIELD DIFFERENTIALS

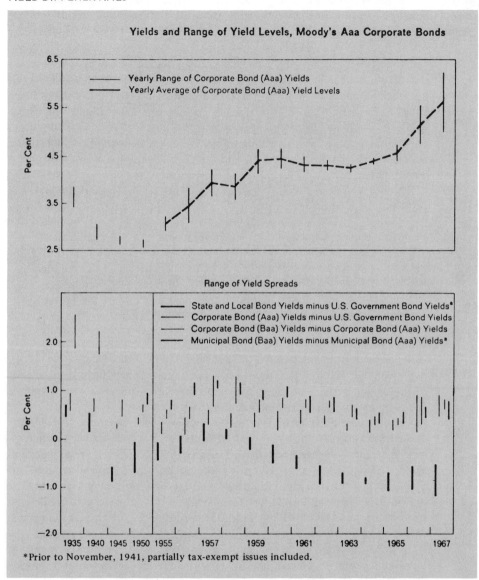

Sources: Board of Governors of the Federal Reserve System, *Banking and Monetary Statistics,* 1943; Board of Governors of the Federal Reserve System, *Supplement to Banking and Monetary Statistics,* Section 12, 1966; Board of Governors of the Federal Reserve System, *Federal Reserve Bulletin,* reprinted in A. M. Wojnilower, "Yield Differentials," in M. E. Polakoff, ed., *Financial Institutions and Markets* (Boston: Houghton Mifflin Co., 1970), p. 453.

Certain qualities inherent in bonds, common stocks, and preferred stocks have nothing in particular to do with risk in its traditional definition. Some of these factors result from *laws*, some from *terms in security contracts* and others from the way *securities markets* function.

Each of these factors might make a security desirable to some investors and not to others. The more desirable a particular factor or factors might be to an investor, the more he will pay for a security that bears it, other things being equal. Conversely, if an investor is neutral or can get along without a particular feature, he will not pay more to obtain it. Investors who are averse to a given quality in a security will be willing to buy it only at a lower price. In all cases, the change that results from a willingness or unwillingness to pay for a particular quality has an effect on a security's yield or return.

Three principal ownership qualities are of interest to us: marketability, call features, and taxation of returns.

MARKETABILITY

Differences in yield for various securities may result from differences in marketability. *Marketability* refers to the ability of the owner to convert to cash. This conversion process relies upon price realized and time required to sell the security. Price and time are interrelated, since it is often possible to sell a security quickly if enough price concession is given. For securities, marketability is the ability of the seller to sell a significant volume of the securities in a short period of time without significant price concessions (which include the matter of transaction costs). The more marketable a security, the greater the investor's ability to execute a large transaction near the quoted price.

Usually, marketability of a security is judged by the difference between the quoted bid and asked prices in relation to the level of prices, since the percentage difference depends upon the price level. For example, if we express bid-asked differentials as a percentage of the bid price, a $1 spread on a bid of $10 is 10 percent. The same $1 spread on a bid of $100 is only 1 percent. The bid price is the price the dealer stands ready to buy a security for; the asked price is the price he is willing to sell the security for. The smaller the spread, expressed as a percentage of the bid price, the more marketable the security.

Dealer spreads are like a retailer's markup: They must cover expenses, risk of loss, and a profit. In general, like any fast-moving merchandise, securities with a large volume of transactions carry narrower markups or spreads. Competition keeps dealers from taking larger markups than required by expense, risk, and a reasonable profit.

Investors find advantages in more marketable securities because the cost of buying and selling them is less. A highly marketable preferred stock might be quoted as 50 bid, 50½ asked. The ½-point spread is the markup. If you bought 100 shares for $5,050 and sold them again for $5,000, the service charge would be $50. (Of course, it is unlikely that the quotes would stay constant.) The cost of buying and selling the security is 1 percent of the bid price ($50/$5,000).

Consider another case where a preferred is quoted as 100 bid, 102 asked. If you purchased 50 shares at $5,100 and resold at the bid price for $5,000, you would pay a service fee of $100. This is double the dollar and percentage cost in the first example.

It is quite common for investors to refer to a stock or a bond as having a "thin" market. The connotation is that there is not much of the security for sale at the asked price, and not much sought at the bid price. If you place an order to buy or sell a relatively large block, it may be executed at a price materially different from the price of the last transaction. The converse is thought of as a "broad" market, in which one can sell large amounts at once with little or no effect upon the quoted price. Poorly marketable securities have thin markets. Buying or selling small blocks in a market dominated by large trades can lead to similar marketability problems.

The marketability of a security can be judged by observing the bid-asked spread over several different time periods. It is commonplace to assume that securities of small, unseasoned companies listed on the over-the-counter market have less marketability than those of large, seasoned companies listed on the New York Stock Exchange. This is only a generalization. Each case must be considered individually. Frequently, "thin" markets are referred to in regard to stocks that have small numbers of shares in active supply. Large percentages of shares might be held by family trusts, or the companies may be small and have few shares issued and outstanding.

Small investors who purchase bonds must assess marketability very closely. The bond markets are dominated by large institutional holders who tend to buy and sell in blocks in the millions of dollars. The bid-asked prices appearing in the financial press will most probably be for transaction sizes (in dollars) that reflect institutional supply and demand. For example, the latest quote on a corporate bond is 100 bid and 100¼ asked. Should you wish to buy or sell $2,000 worth, the dealer might quote you 99½ bid and 101 asked, because the published quotes reflect a market of transactions many times greater than yours. Yours is, in a sense, an odd-lot order.

One final comment is in order relative to the marketability of an issue. Certain liquidity problems or trading difficulties can be encountered as the bond gets older, that is, as it approaches maturity. These bonds typically begin to move into the portfolios of permanent investor types who tend to hold them to maturity.

Thus, differences in return (yield) between different securities are caused not only by differences in default risk but also by differences in marketability. The lower the marketability, the greater the yield an investor would demand, and vice versa.

Seasoned vs. New Issues

Bonds that have been outstanding for some time are generally referred to in the bond trade as "seasoned." The yields on older, "seasoned" issues will typically be below those on "new" issues, with the difference depending upon the level of interest rates. The yields on new issues frequently exceed those on seasoned issues of the same quality and maturity when interest rates are high. The reason for these higher yields is that underwriters do not want to hold the new issues in inventory because of the associated carrying costs and the danger of a further rise in the level of interest rates. Their behavior is such that they mark down the prices on new issues (higher yields) vis-à-vis seasoned issues. In addition, older, lower-coupon bonds tend to sell at a discount. Their inherent tax advantages and call protection cause their prices to be bid up (lowering yields). These tax and call advantages will be discussed shortly.

Overall, the spread between seasoned and new issues is a function of the level of interest rates and can vary anywhere from 0 to 50 basis points (seasoned issues are below new issues by this amount). The higher the level of interest rates, the larger will be the spread.

THE CALL FEATURE

Many issuers put terms in the contract giving them the right to redeem or call the entire outstanding amount before maturity, subject to certain conditions. Most corporate bonds and preferred-stock issues provide for a call feature, and some Treasury securities (governments) are callable. Generally, municipal securities are not callable; they are serial.

In the case of corporate bonds and preferred stocks, the call price is usually above the face or par value of the security and decreases over time. For example, an 8 percent, 25-year bond issue may be callable initially at 108 (108 percent of par). The call price might decline by ¼ percent per year (108, 107.75, 107.50, and so on). It is common for the initial call price to be the equivalent of one year's interest plus the par value of the bond.

The call feature modifies maturity and thereby affects a security's relative yield. The call feature is exercisable immediately or it is deferred for some time. The most widely used deferred-call periods are five years for public utility bonds and ten years for industrial bonds. During the deferment period, the investor is protected from a call by the issuer.

The issuer pays a premium for the option of calling the bonds before their nominal maturity. The option to call provides the issuer with flexbility. Should interest rates decline significantly, the issuer does not have to wait until maturity to refinance but can call the bonds and reissue others at a lower interest cost. The call may also be exercised to eliminate any protective covenants in the bond contracts that have become unduly restrictive.

The call feature does not come free. When interest rates are high and expected to fall, the call feature is likely to have significant value. Investors will be unwilling to invest in callable bonds unless yields are more than those of bonds that are noncallable or unless call is deferred, other things being equal. Borrowers are willing to pay a premium in yield for some sort of call privilege. When rates are expected to rise, the call feature has negligible value to the issuer. The spread between immediately callable and deferred call bonds may narrow close to zero.

Yield differentials are available for newly issued corporate bonds having similar ratings but immediate and five-year-deferred call. These are shown in Figure 13-3. The spread widens in periods of high interest rates, narrows in periods of low interest rates. High-interest period in 1959 and 1966-68 show a differential of about ½ percent (or 50 basis points, in the jargon of the bond analyst). During the 1963-65 period, no premium was evident. Overall, the evidence would suggest that the call privilege has the most value and cost to issuers when interest rates are high and expected to fall.

FIGURE 13-3
YIELD DIFFERENTIAL BETWEEN IMMEDIATELY CALLABLE
AND DEFERRED CALLABLE Aa PUBLIC UTILITY BONDS, 1958-68

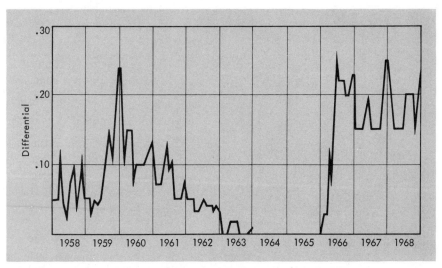

Source: James C. Van Horne, *Function and Analysis of Capital Market Rates* (Englewood Cliffs, N.J.: Prentice-Hall, 1970), p. 125. As reprinted from *An Analytical Record of Yields and Yield Spreads* (New York: Salomon Brothers).

About one-third of all governments have a call feature. The primary purpose is to obtain flexibility in new financing near the maturity date of an outstanding obligation. This contrasts sharply with the principal purpose of savings in interest cost attributable to corporate issues. The Treasury constantly replaces its debts as they mature, instead of paying them off. The market may or may not be "right" at maturity; so the Treasury places optional maturity dates on some bonds to provide flexibility in refinancing. For example, the terms of the 4¼ percent bonds of 1987-92 state that the call privilege may be exercised any time between 1987 and the final maturity in 1992. The bonds' life may be shortened no more than five years from the original maturity. In a thirty-year corporate with a ten-year-deferred call, the maturity could be shortened by twenty years.

Thus the threat of a call feature to an investor is dependent upon his expectations that interest rates will fall significantly during the life of the bond or preferred-stock issue. Accepting securities with immediate call privileges will tend to provide more return (yield) than accepting some deferral period. In periods of high interest rates, this can mean a difference of ¼ percent in yield. Whether the risk of call is worth the extra ¼ percent is principally a function of the outlook for interest rates and whether the issuer feels he will be able to refund the bonds at a profit (savings).

Another strategy for approaching the call-risk problem is to buy deep-discount bonds—bonds that sell well below par or face value.[17] The principal reason for this condition is that they bear coupon rates far below prevailing rates required in the market. Using bond-yield tables, it is possible to show that in a market where the returns on ten-year AAA bonds are 8 percent, a newly issued ten-year AAA bond with an 8 percent coupon would sell for 100, whereas an older bond with a 4 percent coupon, due in ten years, would sell at 73. The 4 percent bond provides most of its required return of 8 percent through appreciation in price at maturity.

If market rates fall to 6 percent, the 8 percent bond will move to 115, and the 4 percent bond to 85. But the 8 percent bonds are in danger of call, whereas the 4 percent bonds are still far below their probable call price. It is important to realize, however, that the deep discount aspects of bonds are really attractive on two counts: call protection and tax advantages. Since ordinary interest income is taxed at regular tax rates and long-term capital gains (increases in principal values) are taxed at lower capital gains rates, deep discount bonds possess tax-savings appeal.

Sinking Funds

Sinking funds have been designed to provide for the retirement of a certain portion of a bond issue through purchases by the issuing corporation at predetermined regular intervals. Nearly all industrial bonds have sinking funds. Although less frequently used by electric utilites in the past (less than 50 percent), investor pressure has built recently to force the increasing inclusion of a sinking fund in new utility issues.

The sinking fund provides two broadly defined benefits to an investor. The orderly retirement of debt by the corporation should provide the bond investor increasing credit safety, since the amount of debt outstanding is reduced and the pressure on the company to refinance a large amount of debt at maturity is moderated. A second important benefit is that the sinking fund provides an additional element of liquidity to the issue through regular purchase activity to meet sinking-fund requirements.

As a result, investors have traditionally held the notion that the existence of a sinking fund provided some extra value over and above what would be the bond's market value at any given point in time. Within the context of rising

---

[17]It is important to recognize the fact that a bond selling far below its face value is not necessarily in trouble.

interest rates over the last twenty-five years, the sinking fund has indeed provided extra value to the bondholder. The mere fact that a sinking fund shortens the average life of the bond and therefore provides the investor an opportunity to reinvest at a higher yield earlier has provided substantial incremental value.

However, when interest rates reach high levels, the existence of the sinking fund may actually reduce the relative value of the bonds, since the potential exists for bonds to be retired at par if rates subsequently fall and prices rise.

Since the sinking fund is placed in a bond issue largely for the benefit of the investor, the typical sinking-fund price is a *maximum* of par value plus any accumulated interest. Thus, if interest rates rise subsequent to the issuance of a bond, the bond will tend to fall below par. Since issuers are obliged to pay no more than the par value of the bond for sinking-fund purposes, they will generally satisfy the sinking-fund requirement by purchasing bonds in the open market. This injects demand into the market for the bonds and, depending upon the size of the sinking fund, provides support for the bond price. Should interest rates fall subsequent to the issuance of a bond, the bond will rise in price above par value. Again, since the maximum price to be paid for the bond for sinking-fund purposes is the par value, the question remains: What is the most equitable way to repurchase bonds if the required sinking-fund price is below the market price? Typically, bonds will be redeemed by random lot. That is, bonds are selected randomly by bond number, and a sufficient number are repurchased to satisfy the sinking-fund requirement. Thus, in a period of declining interest rates, the operation of a sinking fund injects a lottery risk into the holding of such bonds. You may have purchased a bond at, say, 102 only to see it called at 100.

Therefore the presence of a sinking fund in a bond issue is a mixed blessing. It may provide the bondholder with some peace of mind that there is a regular redemption schedule in place and provide some price support for the bond in a period of rising interest rates. However, if interest rates decline subsequent to the issuance of a bond, an investor may have his bond called away for sinking-fund purposes and be faced with a knotty problem of reinvestment at lower rates.

TAX FACTORS

Chapter 3 dealt with the broad question of taxes. Our present discussion will concern the tax effects primarily related to bonds and preferred stocks. In particular, we will explore the tax impact of (1) discount bonds, (2) municipal and government bonds, and (3) preferred stocks.

Discount Bonds

As we have noted, discount bonds are bonds selling below their par or face value. These bonds provide not only a large measure of call protection but also certain tax advantages. The most important tax we shall consider is, of course, the federal income tax. The differential impact upon yields arises because interest and dividends are taxed at ordinary rates, whereas gains on securities held more than twelve months receive the more favorable capital gains treatment in which only half the gain is taxable.

The greater the discount on a bond, the greater its capital gains attraction and the lower its yield relative to what it would be if the coupon rate were such that the bond sold at par. A simple example will illustrate the tax implications.

Consider the alternatives of buying two bonds of similar quality. The first can be bought for par with an 8 percent coupon to yield 8 percent to maturity. The second has a 4 percent coupon and sells at a discount sufficient to provide an added 4 percent in capital gains yield, so the total yield to maturity is also 8 percent. An investor in the 50 percent tax bracket would realize 4 percent after taxes on the par bond and 5 percent on the discount bond. This is because the entire return from the 8 percent bond is subject to ordinary tax rates (50 percent in this case); the other bond is subject to a 50 percent rate on the 4 percent coupon, but only half the capital gain of 4 percent is taxed. In other words, the tax on the 4 percent capital gain is 1 percent (.5 $\times$ ½ $\times$ 4%). After taxes, the investor is left with 3 percent plus the 2 percent from coupons.

The result of this example suggests that, in order for the high-coupon and the deep-discount bond to sell on an identical yield-to-maturity basis (after taxes), the 4 percent bond would have to be priced to yield 6.67 percent to maturity.[18] This rate, or course, is hypothetical, since other factors are involved. Par and deep-discount bonds of the same quality are purchased by people in various tax brackets that achieve different net yields. Also, the value of call protection in discount bonds bears on the issue.

Governments and Municipals

Unlike the case with all other categories of securities, interest income (but *not* capital gains) from state and local government securities is exempt from federal income taxes. This unique tax status accounts for the fact that municipal-bond yields are lower than those of other securities. Most states do not tax income from their own bonds, or income from bonds of their political subdivisions. Thus, from an overall tax standpoint, there are advantages to buying municipals issued in the state of residence of an investor.

Typically, municipal bonds will yield less than taxable bonds, depending on the level of interest rates. Since the tax exemption on municipal bonds applies only to the interest, discount and premium municipal bonds are less attractive than municipal bonds selling at par. Therefore, discount and premium municipal bonds will not sell at the same yield to maturity as municipal bonds selling at par.

Commercial banks are among the largest holders of municipal bonds, particularly at times when the demand for loans is soft. Investment in municipal bonds serves as a substitute when the demand for consumer and business loans is weak. When the level of interest rates is high, banks generally sell municipal bonds to meet loan demand. This has a tendency to force down the prices on

---

[18]The mathematics of these arguments will be developed in Chapter 14.

municipal bonds and therefore raises the level of rates. Thus, yields on municipal bonds during such periods will tend to rise faster than yields on taxables. That is, the spread between municipals and taxable bonds narrows. Conversely, when the demand for consumer and business loans falls, the reverse occurs. That is, banks tend to purchase municipal bonds, and this demand raises the price of municipal bonds and lowers their yields. The spread between municipal yields on taxable bonds widens.

In addition to the federal income tax, the federal tax on estates has an impact upon Treasury securities. The estate tax is levied on assets upon the death of the owner. Certain Treasury bonds, if owned by the deceased, are redeemable at par if the proceeds are used to pay federal estate taxes. These are referred to as "flower bonds." A $1,000-par government bond purchased at $800 would be worth $1,000 in settlement of estate taxes. For this reason, qualifying government bonds selling at discounts have a special attraction above and beyond the capital gains implications.

Figure 13-4 shows the yield distinction between high-grade governments and high-grade municipals over time. The spread in yields, or differential, has ranged from 100 to 150 basis points (1 to 1½ percent), owing almost entirely to the

FIGURE 13-4

YIELD DIFFERENTIAL BETWEEN LONG-TERM TREASURY BONDS
AND PRIME MUNICIPAL BONDS AFTER TAXES, 1950-68
ANNUAL AVERAGES[19]

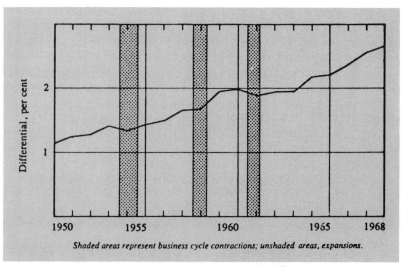

Shaded areas represent business cycle contractions; unshaded areas, expansions.

Source: James C. Van Horne, *Function and Analysis of Capital Market Rates* (Englewood Cliffs, N.J.: Prentice-Hall, (1970), p. 113.

[19]For a detailed historical perspective on the use of preferred stock see Donald E. Fischer and Glenn A. Wilt, Jr., "Non-Convertible Preferred Stock as a Financing Instrument, 1950-1965," *Journal of Finance*, Vol. 33 (September, 1968), pp. 611-24.

difference in taxation of these two categories of bonds under the federal income tax law.

Preferred Stocks

Federal tax laws provide that intercorporate dividends shall not be excessively taxed. One corporation receiving dividends from another and, in turn, paying dividends to its own shareholders could be faced with double taxation. Taxing the dividend to the ultimate shareholder would amount to triple taxation. To alleviate this chain of taxation, intercorporate dividends are taxed at very low rates.

A substantial portion of dividends received on preferred or common stocks held by corporations may be deducted when they compute their taxable income. Under existing federal income tax law, such investors (including, in certain cases, life insurance companies and mutual savings banks) are entitled to a deduction equivalent to 85 percent of dividends received on certain preferred-stock holdings. This deduction applies to income from all preferred issues other than issues of public utility operating companies; income from these is entitled to the 85 percent deduction only if such preferred stocks were issued for "new-money" purposes on or after October 1, 1942. New-money issues are those sold to raise funds for the first time, rather than to redeem existing financing. For corporations in the 48 percent tax bracket, with only 15 percent of such dividend income taxable, 7.20 percent of the dividends on such issues will be paid in taxes, thus providing an after-tax return equal to 92.80 percent of the dividend.

For financial institutions that have an effective tax rate of 25 percent, slightly more than 96 percent of the dividend on industrial or "new-money" utility preferred stocks is retained after tax (see table).

Table 13-5 shows how these calculations are made. To make similar calculations for effective tax rates other than 48 percent or 25 percent, substitute the appropriate effective tax rate in the first column and compute as shown.

TABLE 13-5
EXAMPLES: 9.00% DIVIDEND (OR YIELD)

Effective Tax Rate		% Dividend Subject		% of Dividend (or Yield) Paid in Tax		% Remaining After Tax		Dividend Rate (or Yield)	After-Tax Dividend (or Yield)
48%	X	15	=	7.20	thus	92.80	X	9.00%	8.35%
25%	X	15	=	3.75	thus	96.25	X	9.00%	8.66%

Source: *Preferred Stock Guide*, 1976 Edition (New York: Salomon Brothers, 1976), p. 4.

The following table, Table 13-6, indicates pre-tax yields and enables corporations to determine yield needed on interest-bearing obligations to equal the after-tax yield on 85 percent tax-exempt preferreds. For example, using the 48 percent tax-rate section, if a taxpaying institution were to purchase a preferred stock yielding 9.00 percent (see left-hand column), it would have to receive a 16.06 percent yield on a government or corporate bond or on a mortgage, or a 8.35 percent yield on a tax-exempt issue, in order to obtain the same after-tax yield as is received on the preferred issue on a 9.00 percent basis.

TABLE 13-6
PREFERRED STOCK EQUIVALENT YIELD TABLE

	Corporate Holders 48% Tax Rate	
	Yield Needed to Equal After-Tax Return on 85% Exempt Preferred	
Yield on Preferred Entitled to 85% Exemption	on Bonds, Mortgages* (100% Taxable)	on Tax Exempt Obligations†
7.50	13.38	6.96
7.75	13.83	7.19
8.00	14.27	7.42
8.25	14.73	7.66
8.50	15.17	7.89
8.75	15.62	8.12
9.00	16.06	8.35
9.25	16.50	8.58
9.50	16.96	8.82
9.75	17.40	9.05
10.00	17.85	9.28
10.25	18.29	9.51
10.50	18.73	9.74

*$\frac{\text{Yield} \times .928}{.52}$

†Yield × .928

Source: *Preferred Stock Guide*, 1976 Edition (New York: Salomon Brothers, 1976), p. 5.

Investing in Preferred Stocks. The small investor has been effectively priced out of the market for preferred stocks, because of the advantage taxable institutions have of excluding 85 percent of dividends received from income. Bond interest, other than that on municipals, is fully taxed. For institutional investors, the relative after-tax yields on high-quality corporate bonds and high-grade preferred stocks is obvious. A tax rate of 50 percent applied to an 8 percent bond and an 8 percent preferred stock gives an after-tax yield of 4 percent on the bond and 7.4 percent on the preferred stock. This is more than enough difference to overcome any perceived differences in risk.

Table 13-7 shows the yields on high-quality corporate bonds and preferred stocks over time. Preferreds generally yield *less* than bonds, with the average differential being about 35 basis points. The underlying causes are the tax anomaly and the diminishing supply of available preferred stocks. *For the small investor without the income tax exclusion on preferreds, it hardly seems worth taking more risk and getting a lower return than on bonds.*

From time to time, there is talk of a speculative strategy involving non-callable preferreds. There are about a dozen of these outstanding, mostly issues by industrial firms. The record shows that many noncallable preferreds have been retired at sizable premiums over market price. The small number still outstanding makes this type of speculation one with very long-shot possibilities.

TABLE 13-7
YIELDS ON HIGH-GRADE BONDS AND PREFERRED STOCKS,
1965-77

Year	*(1)* *Aaa* *Corporate* *Bonds*	*(2)* *Preferred* *Stocks*	*Spread* *(2) over (1)*
1965	4.49%	4.33%	−0.16
1966	5.13	4.97	−0.16
1967	5.51	5.34	−0.17
1968	6.18	5.78	−0.40
1969	7.03	6.41	−0.62
1970	8.04	7.22	−0.82
1971	7.39	6.75	−0.64
1972	7.21	7.27	+0.06
1973	7.44	7.23	−0.21
1974	8.57	8.23	−0.34
1975	8.83	8.38	−0.45
1976	8.43	7.97	−0.46
1977 (May)	8.04	7.65	−0.39

Source: *Federal Reserve Bulletin.*

Default Risk in Holiday Inns Long-Term Debt and Preferred Stock

Table 13-8 contains, in summary form, financial data and certain ratios applying to Holiday Inns. The information was gleaned from various sources, including the annual statements of the company (see Chapter 8 and its appendix).

TABLE 13-8
FINANCIAL DATA AND RATIOS RELATIVE TO DEFAULT RISK
BEARING UPON DEBT AND PREFERRED STOCK OF HOLIDAY
INNS, INC. ($ IN MILLIONS)

	1972	*1973*	*1974*	*1975*	*1976*
EBIT	$100.40	$102.20	$ 87.60	$ 95.20	$ 90.00
Interest	22.30	27.30	30.20	27.10	25.00
Interest coverage	4.50	3.70	2.90	3.50	3.60
Preferred dividends	0.40	0.30	0.20	0.00	0.00
Preferred dividend coverage	4.50	3.70	2.90	3.50	3.60
Depreciation and amortization	40.40	46.40	57.00	59.40	57.80
Cash flow (per share)	2.71	3.00	2.92	3.31	3.18
Cash	47.00	33.30	46.40	61.10	61.60
Current assets	155.00	152.90	178.10	177.70	180.60
Current liabilities	102.70	109.30	135.20	128.30	137.30
Cash ratio	.46	.30	.34	.48	.45
Current ratio	1.60	1.40	1.30	1.40	1.30
Working capital adequacy	.16	.12	.13	.16	.16

Interest coverage dropped significantly from 1972 through 1974 and then improved noticeably subsequent to 1974. The significance of the erratic nature of this coverage is that Holiday Inns faced rising borrowing costs during a period of eroding earnings (1972-74). The company was able to reverse the decline in interest coverage as interest rates eased and total debt was reduced (1975-76). The mortgage bonds of HIA (9½ percent bonds due in 1995) are rated Bbb. Since it is difficult to determine directly the standard for giving certain coverage relationships specific ratings, two things can be done in this regard. First, we shall examine some of the thoughts of Standard & Poor's on the Bbb rating. Second, in Figure 13-5 we will examine the yield at which HIA's 9½ percent bonds have traded in the recent past, relative to other Bbb-rated bonds.

FIGURE 13-5
HOLIDAY INNS, INC., 9½% DEBENTURE BONDS' YIELD
TO MATURITY, VARIOUS DATES

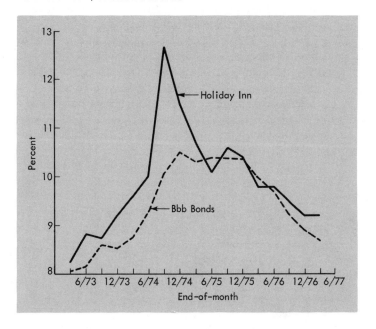

Standard & Poors suggests two specific tests that an issue of debt must pass in order to get a rating of Bbb or higher: a minimum cash flow/debt ratio of 25 percent, and a net tangible assets/debt ratio of over 200 percent. (Neither of these tests shows on our tabulation in Table 13-6, but these figures for HIA have been calculated separately.) The HIA 9½ percent mortgage bonds were offered in 1970. At the end of 1969, the cash flow/debt ratio for HIA was 26 percent and the net tangible assets/debt ratio was 256 percent. It is easy to see that HIA's bonds are close to the lower limit of the Bbb rating on these two measures. Of course, there are other tests that serve as the basis of the Bbb rating, many of them derived from the data in Table 13-6. The ratios calculated in the table are also utilized.

Figure 13-5 shows the yield to maturity each quarter between March 1973 and March 1977 for HIA 9½ percent bonds and S&P's index of Bbb-rated bonds. Notice that the HIA bonds sold at a higher yield than the class of bonds of which they are a part during 1972-74, suggesting that the HIA bonds, for any number of reasons, traded closer to the next lower rating (Bb), although they do tend to move in conjunction with Bbb bonds in general. Since 1974, Holiday Inn's 9½% bonds have yielded a return much closer to the Bbb average. This is due in large part to the improved coverage ratio noted earlier. Over the entire period, the Holiday Inns' bonds yielded about 50 basis points more, on average, than the rating class of which they were a part. One possible explanation of the higher yield than Bbb bonds in general is no doubt the small size of the issue ($30 million), which somewhat inhibits marketability and produces borderline ratios from a rating standpoint. Also, the yield on the HIA 9½ percent bonds is affected by a deferred-call option, which prohibits call prior to June 15, 1980, from money borrowed at an interest-rate cost less than 9.50 percent. The high coupon (9½ percent), with Bbb bonds moving down toward the 9 percent level, will no doubt serve as a damper or lid on price rises, owing to the possibility of call in 1980 at a call price at that time of 105. This bond issue also contains a sinking fund that began in 1976. At that time and through 1994, the company is required to redeem $2.25 million in bonds each year, with the option to retire more in a given year.

Preferred-dividend coverage has improved over time, mainly as the result of regular retirement of preferred shares for sinking-fund purposes. Preferred dividends have fallen from about $800,000 in 1967 to almost nil in 1977.

Summary

Yields differ on various kinds of bonds and preferred stocks. A rational way to view these differences is to isolate differences in risk associated with each. Market yields on U.S. government securities reflect compensation for the pure cost of lending or borrowing money without risk, plus compensation for purchasing-power risk. The structure of yields on corporates and municipals can be examined by differences in default risk and certain nonrisk variables influencing yield.

Investors are aided in assessing relative risks of default by established, independent rating agencies. However, the investor is well advised that these broad default ratings are only guides and provide, at best, a rough discrimination between bonds. Detailed analysis of the factors likely to contribute to default can pay handsome rewards. These factors mainly relate to asset and earnings coverage on bonds and preferreds.

Nonrisk factors influence yields as the result of tax laws, various features of security contracts, and the way in which securities markets function. Not all returns from securities are taxed in a similar manner. Municipal bonds and discount bonds possess unique tax appeal. Sinking-fund and call features represent advantages and disadvantages to investors. The cost and benefits of these contractual features must be weighed in an investment decision. Not all securities have active, broad markets. As a result, conversion back to cash may result in price concessions that detract from realized yield.

1. Refer to the ABC, Inc., example on page 394. What would interest coverage be if the first-mortgage and debenture bonds were considered separately—in other words, in order of risk priority?

2. Of what significance to investors are bonds that sell below par value?

3. Can you think of any advantages to the issuer of making periodic repayments of principal via a sinking fund? Are there disadvantages to the investor?

4. How would you go about analyzing an opportunity to purchase a few bonds of an issue that is currently in default? Locate a bonds issue quoted in the *Wall Street Journal* that is in default and analyze the prospects.

5. It has been argued that the loss to the federal government in income taxes because of the tax-exempt status of municipal bonds is greater than the savings in interest realized by issuing municipalities.

   a. How could this be so?

   b. What would the overall effects of abolition of tax exemption on municipal-bond interest after a specified date in time?

6. The table on page 419 indicates relative yields required by corporate holders of bonds and preferreds to achieve levels of indifference between them with respect to after-tax return. Prove that an 8 percent preferred entitled to 85 percent exemption provides the same after-tax yield as a taxable bond yielding 14.27 percent and a tax-exempt obligation yielding 7.42 percent.

7. What has been the historical behavior of bond-yield spreads in terms of cycles and trends? What investment strategies are suggested if these historical relationships hold in the future?

8. Mortgages are really bonds backed by real property that are retired monthly via sinking fund. Determine the present relationship between yields on 25-30 year Aaa corporate bonds and 25-30-year conventional home mortages. How do you explain the differences?

9. The following data are for Salt Lake Industries (tax rate = 50%):

Year	EBIT (thousands)
1979	$4,750
1978	4,500
1977	4,500
1976	4,250
1975	4,000

DEBT AND PREFERRED CAPITALIZATION (12/31/79)
(IN THOUSANDS)

Long-term debt:	
8% first-mortgage bonds (due 1987)	$25,000
6½% debentures (due 1996)	10,000
Preferred stock:	
$1.40 cumulative first preferred (par value $5/share).	2,000
7% noncumulative preferred	14,000

Analyze the default risk bearing upon the bonds and preferred stock in the greatest detail possible.

10. Obtain a recent edition of *Moody's Industrial Manual.* Examine the major contractual features of the following Aaa bonds: Texaco 5.75 percent (due 1997), and Exxon 6 percent (due 1997). How do you account for the fact that these two bonds of identical rating and maturity sell at differing prices over time?

11. Dairee, Inc., earned $50 million after interest, taxes, and preferred dividends in 1979. The company had an effective tax rate of 40 percent. Its capital structure consists in part of $12.5 million in 8 percent debentures and $5 million in 9 percent cumulative preferred stock. Calculate pre-tax coverage of interest and preferred dividends for 1979.

12. What kinds of protective covenants should a prospective bondholder look for in a bond contract?

13. The following information applies to Noll Products, Inc. ($ millions):

Revenues	$125
Operating expenses:	
Variable	25
Fixed	82*

*Includes depreciation of $10.5 million; tax rate = .4.

6% first-mortgage bonds (1990)	$ 50†
10% subordinated debentures (1998)	60†
$6 preferred stock ($50 par)	50
Common equity	600

†Combined sinking-fund payments of $6 million.

    a. What is the *debt-service* coverage for this firm?

    b. How safe are the preferred-stock holders' dividends (ignore sinking-fund payments on the debt)? Explain.

14. What two strategies might bond investors utilize in attempting to guard against the threat of a call feature?

15. A 7 percent preferred, entitled to 85 percent exemption, provides the same after-tax yield as a taxable bond yielding _____ and a tax-exempt obligation yielding _____ for a corporation in the 25 percent bracket.

BOND ANALYSIS: ESTIMATING RETURN AND RISK

We have been looking at systematic and unsystematic influences that create risk in holding fixed-income securities. It was observed that shifts in market assessments of these risk factors have a direct effect upon the level, term structure, and spread of interest rates. The importance of forecasting yield levels, structure, and spreads should be clear.

This chapter examines return-and-risk measures in bonds. We will examine historical return-and-risk experience in various classes of bonds over a broad sweep of time, take up return-risk calculations for several specific bonds, and probe the problem of estimating return and risk on a bond over a forward holding period. We shall see the use of interest-rate forecasts in this process.

Bond Returns and Prices

Adverse reactions to increased risk bearing upon bonds will normally cause investors to demand higher yields. Positive reactions to reduced risks should lead to lower bond yields. However, since interest payments on bonds are fixed by contract, the prices of these securities bear the brunt of the necessary adjustments to reflect altered expectations of yields. Thus, should higher yields be demanded in the market, bond prices will fall; lower yields lead to rising bond prices.

This inverse movement of yields and bond prices is not as simple as it appears on the surface. For any specific change in the level of yields, the resultant change in a bond's price is sensitive to (1) the length of time to maturity, (2) the size of the bond's coupon rate, and (3) whether the change in yield is upward or downward. Understanding these factors is prerequisite to estimating return and risk over a forward holding period.

TIME-ADJUSTED YIELD ON BONDS

To enable us to better appreciate the responsiveness of bond prices to changes in required returns, or yields, let us review and expand upon the notion of bond valuation and yields introduced in Chapter 4.

As long as a bond is not expected to go into default, the expected return is made up of annual interest payments plus the price to be recovered at maturity

426

or sooner. Take an example of a five-year bond with a principal value of $1,000, bearing a nominal rate of interest (coupon) of 6 percent. Assume that an investor wishes to purchase this bond for a rate of 6 percent. What should he be willing to pay for a series of five $60 interest payments and a lump sum of $1,000 at the end of the fifth year?

The present value of the interest-payment stream of $60 per year for five years is as follows:

$$P = \$60/(1 + .06) + \$60/(1 + .06)^2 + \$60/(1 + \$60/(1 + .06)^3 + \$60/(1 + .06)^4 + \$60/(1 + .06)^5 = \$253$$

The present value of the principal at maturity (end of year 5) is $1,000/(1 + .06)^5 = \$747$. The total value of the bond is thus $253 + $747, or $1,000. In other words, a $1,000 bond is worth $1,000 today if the nominal rate and the required rate of interest are equal. The $1,000 value is a composite of $253 of interest payments and $747 of principal.

In general, what a bond is worth can be determined thus:

$$V = \sum_{n=1}^{N} \frac{I_n}{(1+i)^n} + \frac{P_N}{(1+i)^N} \tag{14.1}$$

where:

V = value of bond
I = annual interest ($)
i = required rate of interest (%)
P = principal value at maturity
N = number of years to maturity

It is easy to see that although bonds carry a promise to maintain a constant-dollar interest payment to maturity, I, and pay a fixed principal at maturity, P, the number of years to maturity, N, and the required rate of interest, i, can vary.

Suppose new five-year bonds are offered at 7 percent. Outstanding 6 percent bonds will continue to pay $60 per $1,000 by contract. The advance in interest rates will cause the price of the outstanding bond to fall:

$$P = \$60/(1 + .07) + \$60/(1 + .07)^2 + \$60/(1 + .07)^3 + \$60/(1 + .07)^4 + \$60/(1 + .07)^5 + \$1,000/(1 + .07)^5$$
$$= \$959$$

Had new five-year bonds been offered at 5 percent, or less than the outstanding 6 percent bonds, the price of the 6 percent bonds would have risen to $1,044. (See Table 4-5, page 88, for a quick bond-table answer.) A basic principle concerning bonds is that *prices move inversely to interest rates.*

An *approximate* method for determining yield to maturity, which does not weigh the returns for time, is given by:

$$Y = \frac{I + \dfrac{1,000 - M}{N}}{\dfrac{P + M}{2}}$$

where:

Y = approximate yield to maturity
I = annual coupon interest ($)
P = par value of bond = $1,000
M = market price of bond
N = number of years during which bond will remain outstanding

This equation is roughly accurate, as we see in a test of our $959 figure:

$$.07 = \frac{\$60 + \dfrac{\$1,000 - M}{5}}{\dfrac{\$1,000 + M}{2}}$$

$$.07 = \frac{\$60 + \$500 - .5M}{\$500 + .5M}$$

$$\$957 = M$$

The distortion between approximate and time-adjusted yield calculations increases as the maturity (N) increases.

This equation says, in effect, that the approximate yield to maturity is equal to the average annual return divided by the average annual investment in the bond.

Extracts from a book of bond tables can be found in Table 4-5, on page 88. Bond tables are used by analysts to determine exact per annum yield to the maturity date according to equation 14.1. The table is constructed for a given coupon rate (in this case, 6 percent). From the table one can determine the bond price (V) necessary to achieve a particular per annum yield (i) or, given a price in the market (V), the associated per annum yield (i). For example, a required yield per annum to maturity of 4 percent for a five-year, 6 percent bond indicates a price of 109, meaning 109 percent of par. For a $1,000 par bond, price is thus $1,090. The same 4 percent for a 25-year maturity suggests a price of between 130 and 132.

The Volatility of Bond Prices

High-grade bond prices react to a given change in yield as a function of maturity, the coupon rate, and the general level of yields from which the change occurs. All other things being equal, with the same percentage change in yield, the *volatility* of the price of a bond *increases*

1. as the maturity lengthens (the longer the maturity, the greater the bond price volatility).
2. as the coupon rate declines (the lower the coupon, the greater the price volatility).
3. as the yields rise (the higher the yield level from which a yield fluctuation starts, the greater the price volatility).

Before attempting to explore the structural forces that create these three determinants of volatility, let us look at Table 14-1, which illustrates the volatility effect of these three variables: maturity, coupon, and the starting level of yields.

The first section of Table 14-1 illustrates the relationship between price changes and maturity. The example being used assumes a 6 percent coupon bond with a face value of $100. Notice that when the required yield is 6 percent, the bond price is 100 regardless of the number of years to maturity. As the required yield moves away from the coupon rate, notice that prices move in an inverse direction. For example, for a bond with a one-year maturity and a 6 percent coupon, if the required yield is 4 percent, the suggested bond price is 102. Similarly, if the required yield is 8 percent, the suggested bond price is 98.

For a given difference between the coupon rate and required yield, the longer the term to maturity, the greater the accompanying price change. For example, if rates move from 6 percent to 7 percent, the price of the bond will move to 99 if the maturity is one year; at the forty year maturity the price would fall to 87. Note that the *percentage* decline in price is 1 percent at one year [(99)-100]/100 and 13 percent at forty years [(87)-(100)]/100.

The relationship between price changes and the coupon rate is illustrated in the second section of Table 14-1. All the examples in this table assume a constant 20-year maturity bond. A 20-year bond with a 4 percent coupon will sell at 68 if the required yield is 7 percent. If interest rates rise to 8 percent, the bond will fall in price to 60. The same 4 percent coupon bond would rise to 87 if interest rates fell to 5 percent. Looking at the entire second section of Table 14-1, it is obvious that the greatest price volatility occurs in the lowest coupon bonds.

The relationship between price changes and the level of rates is illustrated in the third section of Table 14-1. Using a 6 percent, 20-year bond throughout this table illustrates the price effects of a 10 percent change from the original yield level in each case. If the original yield is 7 percent, the suggested price for a 6 percent, 20-year bond is 89. If interest rates rise 10 percent to 7.7 percent, the new bond price is 83. This represents a 7.3 percent decline in the bond price. Looking at the entire third section of Table 14-1, it becomes apparent that price volatility is greatest when interest rates change from a high level of yields versus a lower level of yields.

TABLE 14-1
VOLATILITY OF BOND PRICES

1. Price Changes and Maturity

Face = $100   Coupon = 6%

Required Yield	Years to Maturity			
	1	*10*	*15*	*40*
4%	102*	117	123	140
5	101	108	110	117
6	100	100	100	100
7	99	93	91	87
8	98	86	83	76

2. Price Changes and Coupon (20-year maturity)

	Interest Rates Rise			Interest Rates Fall		
Coupon	*7%*	*8%*	*% Change*	*7%*	*5%*	*% Change*
4%	68*	60	−11.3	68	87	+28.7
5	78	70	−10.5	78	100	+27.1
6	89	80	−10.0	89	112	+25.8
7	100	90	−9.8	100	125	+25.1
8	110	100	−9.5	110	137	+24.4

3. Price Changes and Level of Rates

6%, 20-year bond. Basis point change of 10% from original yield in each case.

	Interest Rates Rise				Interest Rates Fall			
Original Yield	*Price*	*New Yield*	*New Price*	*% Change*	*Price*	*New Yield*	*New Price*	*% Change*
4%	127*	4.4	121	−4.9	127	3.6	134	+5.3
5	112	5.5	106	−5.8	113	4.5	120	+6.3
6	100	6.6	93	−7.0	100	5.4	107	+7.3
7	89	7.7	83	−7.3	89	6.3	96	+8.1
8	80	8.8	74	−8.0	80	7.2	87	+9.0

*All prices are rounded for simplification. Thus, percentages will not correspond exactly.

Effect of Interest-Rate Change on Income

We have had a rather elaborate discussion of the inverse relationship between interest rates and bond prices. The lesson learned was that greater price changes, percentagewise, occur in bonds with longer rather than shorter maturities for any given change in interest rates. Now it is time to judge the relative size of interest-rate changes on short-term versus long-term securities.

Shorter-maturity debt securities have a greater degree of interest-rate risk than do longer-term securities, for two reasons. First, by definition, they mature in a shorter period of time and will require more frequent reinvestment at whatever rates prevail. Second, short-term interest rates fluctuate more widely than long-term interest rates. This means more marked changes in the yield obtainable upon reinvestment of funds.

Short-term interest rates are subject to relatively wide fluctuations during a business cycle. Figure 14-1 indicates short- and long-term rates on various debt securities over time. Figure 14-2 shows the short- and long-term rates on governments. The relative amplitude and frequency of fluctuation is obvious.

The reasons why short-term rates are so sensitive and volatile are easy to trace. First, the demand for short-term funds by businesses and individuals during a business cycle rises dramatically during the expansion phase and falls substantially during contraction. These normal market pressures can turn off and on rather suddenly, and rates will advance or decline briskly. Long-term rates also fluctuate cyclically; however, the relatively stable supply-demand relationship for long-term funds leads to less cyclical variation.

In sum, in terms of total HPY, changes in interest rates cause greater instability in the income component of shorter-term securities and greater instability in the price-change component of longer-term securities.

Historical Return and Risk in Bonds

TRENDS AND CYCLES IN INTEREST RATES

The decade of the 1960s produced an ebullient, rising stock market. The Dow Jones Industrial Stock Average rose from 566 to nearly 1,000. In contrast, from the early 1960s to mid-1970, a long decline occurred in bond prices—the most devastating of a series of setbacks that have dominated the secular bear bond market of the postwar years. Figure 14-3 depicts the scenario of rising interest rates following World War II. This pattern of advancing yields can be translated into vivid examples of deteriorating bond prices. For example, a 30-year corporate bond purchased in 1954 for $1,000 and a yield of 3 percent would, by mid-1970, have been worth $570 in a market where yields had risen to 8¼ percent. From the early 1960s to mid-1970, prices retreated 43 percent for long-term government bonds, 47 percent for corporates, and 49 percent for municipals, and long-term interest rates were carried to their highest levels in a century!

This paints a rather bleak picture of a bear market in bonds that has lasted almost a quarter of a century. Hidden in this secular downturn in bond prices (rising yields) are the rallies and upturns that have occurred, mostly during business recessions.

Despite the secular rise in interest rates since World War II, the fixed-income markets have presented numerous opportunities to active, flexible investors willing and able to take advantage of turns in the market.

FIGURE 14-1
LONG- AND SHORT-TERM INTEREST RATES

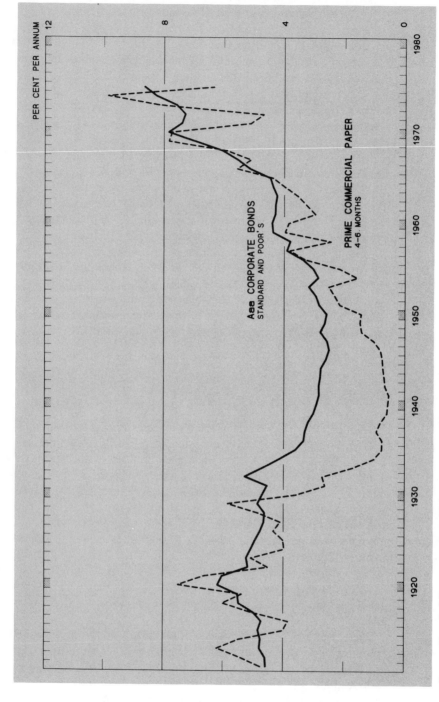

Source: Board of Governors of the Federal Reserve System, *Historical Chart Book 1972.*

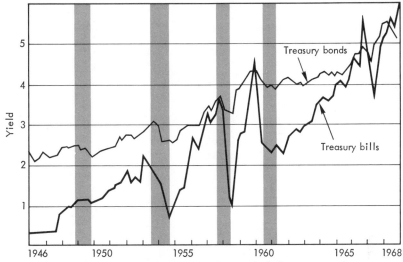

Shaded areas represent business cycle contractions; unshaded areas, expansions.

Source: Municipal & Government Manual (New York: Moody's Investor
Service, Inc.) as reprinted in James Van Horne, *Function and Analysis of
Capital Market Rates* (Englewood Cliffs, N.J.: Prentice Hall, 1970), p. 77.

RETURN AND RISK IN INDIVIDUAL BONDS

To display the calculations of return and risk in holding bonds, we use two
bonds—the first of longer standing in its presence in the market, the second not
very old.

The calculations of return (HPY) and risk (standard deviation) are identical to
those performed earlier on common stocks. The bonds are bought and sold each
year at beginning-of-the-year prices. Interest payments are received at the end of
the year.

The prices of Standard Oil of California 4⅜ percent bonds due in 1983 are
shown in Table 14-2. The bonds are rated Aaa, the highest given by the rating
services. Annual returns are indicated, along with rates on Aaa bonds in general.
Notice the falling price of the Standard Oil bonds as Aaa interest rates rose over
the 1965-73 period. The average one-year holding-period yield over the period
was 4.6 percent, with a standard deviation of 8.1 percent.

Holiday Inns has some outstanding 9½ percent debentures, rated Bbb and due
in 1995. Historical one-year holding-periods yields, shown in Table 14-3, were
calculated from specific months in given years to the corresponding month one
year later. The average HPY for the twenty-two one-year holding periods calculated is 9.3 percent. The standard deviation of these returns is 11.7 percent
(range in returns is −20.4 to +31.7 percent).

FIGURE 14-3
YIELDS OF PRIME LONG CORPORATE BONDS SINCE 1900

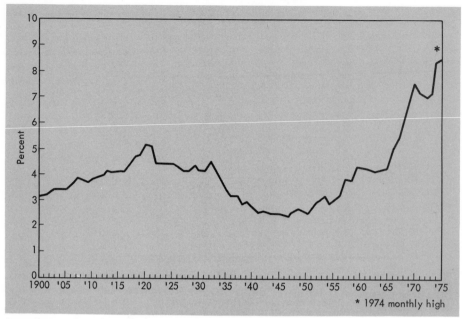

* 1974 monthly high

Annual averages based on Durand basic 30-year yields.
Source: Salomon Brothers, *1975 Annual Review of the Bond Market* (New York: Salomon Bros., 1976).

TABLE 14-2
PRICES AND HOLDING-PERIOD YIELDS ON STANDARD OIL OF CALIFORNIA 4 3/8% BONDS DUE IN 1983

Year	AAA Rates	Beginning-of-Year Price	Annual Interest	Holding-Period Yield (%)
1959	4.27%	$1,000.00	$43.75	—
1960	4.28	990.00	43.75	3.4
1961	4.21	1,010.00	43.75	6.4
1962	4.18	1,028.75	43.75	6.2
1963	4.14	1,020.00	43.75	3.4
1964	4.32	1,002.50	43.75	2.6
1965	4.45	962.50	43.75	0.4
1966	5.12	807.50	43.75	(11.6)
1967	5.49	896.25	43.75	16.4
1968	6.12	775.00	43.75	(8.6)
1969	7.03	701.25	43.75	(3.9)
1970	8.04	701.25	43.75	4.4
1971	7.39	800.00	43.75	20.2
1972	7.21	811.25	43.75	6.8
1973	7.44	817.50	43.75	6.1
1974	8.57	780.00	43.75	0.8
1975	8.83	778.75	43.75	5.4
1976	8.43	790.00	43.75	7.1
1977	8.04	880.00	43.75	16.9

RETURN AND RISK ON CLASSES OF BONDS

The expression of bond yield in terms of annual holding-period yields enables us to view return and risk in holding bonds much the same way as we did for common stocks in Chapters 4 and 5. It will be instructive to view the influence of historical trends and cycles in interest rates on HPYs and the variability of HPYs in bonds.

Wilbur calculated one-year HPYs for high-grade bonds over the period 1900-57. His calculations were made assuming that bonds with maturities of from one to twenty-five years were purchased each year and held one year. His conclusions were roughly that one-year HPYs achieved on long-term bonds were marginally better than those achieved by buying bonds with one- to three-year maturities. However, the standard deviation of HPYs on the long-term bonds suggested that these yields were more than twice as risky as HPYs for one- to three-year bonds. In sum, if a potential bond buyer in 1900 with a one-year holding period knew what we know now, he would have been well advised to invest in bonds with two- to five-year maturities at the beginning of each holding period. He would have received the same returns, on the average, as on longer-term bonds—and with less risk.[1] Of course, we never know if the past will repeat itself.

In another study, Soldofsky and Miller examined annual HPYs and their standard deviation for long-term governments, several corporate-bond rating categories, and several classes of preferred and common stocks over the period 1950-66.[2] These securities were also analyzed in relation to certain subperiods within this time frame. Over the entire period, 1950-66, several observations were clear. First, returns on governments and corporate bonds in general are extremely unimpressive. Governments averaged returns in the vicinity of $1\frac{2}{3}$ percent, whereas corporates averaged between $1\frac{1}{2}$ and 2 percent in this period. This is far below rates paid on savings accounts! Except for Baa corporates, HPYs and risk in corporates—as expected—decrease as ratings increase (for instance, from A to Aaa). The higher return and risk on governments, however, does not seem to fit expectations. Intuitively we assume that governments bear less risk and, therefore, provide lower returns than corporates. Soldofsky and Miller suggest that this apparent contradiction may be due in part to reduced default risk associated with corporates during the general economic prosperity in the period 1950-1966. Except for speculative issues, preferreds exhibited equal or less return but greater risk than Ba corporate bonds.

The relative return and risk on these various fixed-income classes exhibit different patterns over subperiods displaying varying traits of economic expansion and contraction, as well as important upward and downward movements in interest rates.

---

[1]W. L. Wilbur, *A Theoretical and Empirical Investigation of Holding Period Yields on High Grade Corporate Bonds* (Ph.D. dissertation, Graduate School of Business Administration, University of North Carolina at Chapel Hill, 1967).

[2]R. M. Soldofsky and R. L. Miller, "Risk Premium Curves for Different Classes of Long-Term Securities, 1950-1966," *Journal of Finance*, 24 No. 3 (June 1969), 429-45.

TABLE 14-3

**END-OF-QUARTER PRICES AND ONE-YEAR HPYs ON
HOLIDAY INNS 9 1/2 PERCENT DEBENTURES DUE IN 1995**

Year/Quarter	End-of-Quarter Price	One-Year HPY*
1970/1	—	—
2	—	—
3	100	.174
4	104.5	.139
1971/1	108	.125
2	103.5	.164
3	107.9	.116
4	109.5	.117
1972/1	112	.096
2	111	.047
3	110.9	.055
4	112.8	.003
1973/1	113.3	(.042)
2	106.7	(.014)
3	107.5	(.204)
4	103.0	(.090)
1974/1	99.0	.007
2	95.7	.092
3	76.1	.317
4	84.2	.211
1975/1	90.2	.186
2	95.0	.122
3	90.7	.208
4	92.5	.210
1976/1	97.5	—
2	97.1	—
3	100.1	—
4	102.4	—

*Calculated from qtr./year shown to qtr./year one year later; e.g.:

$$\frac{\text{Price (Sept. '71)} - \text{Price (Sept. '70)} + 9\ 1/2\%}{\text{Price (Sept. '70)}}$$

$$= \frac{(107.9 - 100) + 9.50}{100} = \frac{17.40}{100} = .174$$

**Active
Bond
Portfolio
Management**

Many bond buyers find it difficult to justify buying a bond and holding it to maturity. At some point in the future, interest rates will be different, up or down; yield differentials between varying maturities and/or quality segments will be changed. Moreover, the issuer of the bond may have improved or reduced its quality. And so on. Furthermore, certain provisions such as call features and refundability may adversely impact the bond price some time in the future.

Various techniques are available for actively managing—i.e., improving—a bond portfolio. There are a number of ways of changing, or switching, from securities of one *coupon* to another, one *quality* level to another, and one *yield* level to another, both within and between various types and categories of fixed-income securities. Another name for this switching activity is *swapping,* which simply consists of selling one fixed-income security to purchase another. While swaps are oriented toward portfolio *improvements,* not all swaps will achieve this in-tended objective of upgrading the investor's holdings, since swaps involve risks as well as rewards.

REASONS BEHIND SWAPS

Swaps are generally undertaken in order to gain an increased amount of current income, an increased yield to maturity, or both. A second motivating factor behind swapping is to seek improved price appreciation potential in the event of an upward or a downward change in interest rates. This type of maneuver, in-volving such tactics as investing in short-term securities if interest rates are ex-pected to rise and lengthening the maturity of one's investments if interest rates are expected to fall, is basic to fixed-income investing.

A third reason for swapping is to purchase a certain security at a historically attractive yield relative to other similar issues or groups of issues. If and when the security that the investor bought moves back to its historical relationship with other issues, the investor may "reverse swap" back into his original invest-ment or its equivalent. This type of swap usually necessitates having, or obtain-ing, knowledge of current and previous yield patterns for several types of securities. Additional reasons for swapping also exist. The investor may wish to establish a loss to offset capital gains or income on his tax return, or he may wish to upgrade the quality or improve the marketability of his holdings, to name just two reasons.

Swapping between various fixed-income securities may also result in disadvan-tageous investment results. If the investor guesses wrong about the price move-ment of the security that he switches into relative to the price performance of the security he sold or other issues, the swap may result in lessened interest in-come or even a capital loss greater than might have been experienced otherwise. While the investor may believe a certain security has become less expensive rela-tive to another security and that in time the security will regain its comparative value, this does not always turn out to be the case. In some instances the "temporarily" cheaper security may take longer than expected to regain its relative investment value, and occasionally the cheaper security may never again sell on a basis similar to its former patterns. To avoid this, the investor should always think carefully about the *underlying causes* regarding an out-of-the-ordinary yield relationship and whether these causes will soon be eliminated or continue for a long time. An apparent bargain may be relatively cheap be-cause its fundamental components of value have been temporarily or perma-nently impaired, and it is up to the investor to determine *beforehand* whether a security is priced accurately or represents true value.

Knowledge of historical yield spreads between several types and categories of fixed-income securities can be obtained through performing reviews of his-torical and current yield spreads between a very broad range of securities. It is vital to concentrate primarily on present and future trends in the yields of various types of fixed-income securities, both on an absolute basis and rela-tive to each other. The critical decisions rest on whether a swap should be done *within* a specific category of securities or *between* one category and another.

MAJOR TYPES OF SWAP TRANSACTIONS

Swaps between Equivalent Securities Having Different Prices

One of the simplest and most fundamental types of swaps involves the sale of a fixed-income security and the purchase of a lower-priced security of the same or a very similar issuer that is equivalent in coupon, quality, and maturity. Often these swaps are carried out between similar securities of the various operating subsidiaries of the Bell Telephone System, or between various government agencies having similar degrees of safety. For example, the investor might execute the following transaction:

	Price		Yield to Maturity, %
SELL: 25-year maturity, 8% bond A at	100	=	8.00
BUY: 25-year maturity, 8% bond B at	99	=	8.10
GAIN in yield to maturity			0.10

The swap from A bonds to B bonds generates a gain of 10 points in yield to maturity and enables the investor to free up $10 per $1,000 bond for any desired use. An additional benefit of this type of swap comes about if the newly purchased security begins to trade on a basis similar to that of the security that was originally owned. If, after six months, interest rates have fallen, to 7¾ percent for securities such as the ones above, and if both the A bonds and the B bonds trade in line with these new yield levels and with each other, the original bond would have gained about 3 points in price (from 100 to 103), while the newly purchased bonds would have experienced a larger price gain, of 4 points (from 99 to 103). If the two bonds begin to trade on an equivalent basis while general yield levels remain the same or trend upward, the newly purchased bonds will still perform better.

A number of swap opportunities of this type arise when a new issue, even though it is the equivalent of seasoned issues already outstanding, declines in price after the underwriting syndicate has disbanded. In this case the investor could sell his existing holding and purchase the equivalent security at a lower price (higher yield to maturity).

Swaps between Securities with Different Coupons

This type of swap is done between securities of similar maturity and quality, but whose coupon rates are different. The coupon level of a security can exert an influence on its yield, owing to differences in the tax treatment of income as compared with capital gains. Thus, low-coupon taxable securities tend to trade at a slightly *higher* price (lower yield to maturity) than would normally be indicated by the yield tables, and low-coupon tax-exempt securities tend to trade at a slightly *lower* price (higher yield to maturity) than yield tables would suggest. Even so, because of expectations about interest rates and other factors, a low-coupon issue may become more or less attractive than similar higher-coupon issues when evaluated strictly from a yield standpoint. This presents opportunities to switch into or out of low-coupon issues from high-coupon securities.

There are two additional primary motivations behind swaps between similar securities having different coupons. The first is to increase or decrease the tendency toward wide price fluctuations in an environment of changing interest rates. By switching from a high-coupon security to an otherwise similar low-coupon issue, the investor can increase the possible capital gain that will occur if interest rates fall, and by swapping from a low-coupon issue to a similar high-coupon issue, the investor can limit somewhat the price decline that happens when interest rates increase. Second, an investor might switch from a low-coupon security to a similar high-coupon issue in order to increase current income. For instance, the investor might do the following:

	Price		Yield to Maturity, %
SELL: 20-year, A-quality 4% T bond at	60	=	8.00
BUY: 20-year, A-quality 7% T bond at	90	=	8.00

From the above example it can be seen that the investor's annual interest income is increased to $70 per $1,000 bond from $40 per $1,000 bond, yet to do this he must put up additional funds if he desires to own the same number of bonds. If, instead, the investor wishes to merely maintain the dollar amount of his investment, he coud buy a smaller number of the 7 percent T bonds after selling the 4 percent T bonds. For example, if the investor owned forty of the 4 percent bonds, he could use the proceeds of these bonds (40 bonds × $600 per bond = $24,000), on which the total income was $1,600 per year, to purchase almost twenty-seven bonds ($24,000 ÷ $900 per bond = 27 bonds), on which the total income is $1,890 per year. Thus, even without investing additional capital, the investor is able to increase his annual interest income by 18 percent, or $290 per year. However, the investor should remember that this advantage is balanced somewhat by the fact that the face value of twenty-seven bonds ($27,000) will be received at maturity rather than the face value of the forty bonds ($40,000) which would be obtained by retaining his original holdings.

On the other hand, if the investor desires to reduce his current annual income and receive a larger portion of his total yield to maturity in the form of a capital gain, a switch from higher-coupon securities to lower-coupon issues might be in order. This maneuver can also free up funds, because when the investor *sells* the 7 percent T bonds and buys the same number (not the same dollar amount) of the 4 percent T bonds, he would, at a 8 percent overall interest rate level, have $300 per $1,000 bond left over for additional investments or other uses.

Swaps between Securities with Different Quality Ratings.

These swaps require a sense of timing, a knowledge of historical versus current yield spreads, and most importantly, an ability to forecast future interest rate movements and possible credit-rating changes. For example, the normal yield pattern for a certain type of fixed-income security (such as a utility issue, an industrial security, or a general obligation tax-exempt security) may show that an A-rated issue has generally averaged 75 basis points more in yield than a triple-A-rated issue of equal coupon and maturity during the past several years. If the A-rated security happens to move up in price so that it now yields only 50 basis points more than the AAA-rated security, the investor can usually profit by selling the A-rated issue and buying the AAA-rated bond. After this swap transaction has been executed, the investor can then *swap back* into the A-rated security from the AAA-rated issue when the yield spread between the two securities has widened to well in excess of its normal 75-basis-point differential, perhaps to a 100-basis-point spread.

Let us assume that the normal yield differential between AAA and A securities is 75 basis points, but the existing spread is 50 basis points:

	Price		Yield to Maturity, %
SELL: 30-year, A-rated, 8% XXX bonds	94.6	=	8.50
BUY: 30-year, AAA-rated, 8% ZZZ bonds	100	=	8.00
Basis point *differential* = 50 basis points		=	0.50
Additional *money needed* for the trade = $54 per $1,000 bond.			

At some point in the future, the yield differential between AAA and A securities has moved above normal to 100 basis points:

	Price		Yield to Maturity, %
SELL: 30-year, AAA-rated, 8% ZZZ bonds	100	=	8.00
BUY: 30-year, A-rated, XXX bonds	90	=	9.00
Basis point *differential* = 100 basis points		=	1.00
Money generated from the trade = $100 per $1,000 bond.			

Thus, swapping from the A-rated security into the AAA-rated security and back again when the normal yield spread has been exceeded produced a net gain of $46 per $1,000 bond in the example above. Similar relative gains can be achieved even in periods of changing interest rates. This type of swap can also be done in reverse. That is, if the investor expects interest-rate spreads between A and AAA securities to return to a 75-basis-point level from an existing level of 100 basis points, he should buy the A-rated bonds at a lower price (100-basis-point higher yield) than the AAA-rated bonds, and then swap back into the

AAA-rated bonds when their price is higher relative to the A bonds (at or below the normal 75-basis-point higher yield).

Several important caveats must be kept in mind when doing swaps between different quality ratings of the *same type* of securities or between the same or different quality ratings of *different types* of securities. First, the average differential between two groups of issues during the past several years may not necessarily be experienced again during the investor's own investment time horizon. Second, related to this phenomenon is the possibility that yield spreads owing to quality differences may continue to widen when they are expected to narrow, and vice versa. Third, a particular issue may trade differently from others within its own quality-rating category because of liquidity factors or because it is about to be upgraded or downgraded in its quality ranking. Fourth, success in swapping between securities of different quality ratings is not simple to achieve, and it demands that the investor have or obtain information about historical yield spreads. Sometimes the investor may concentrate too much on yield differentials due to quality rankings when instead he should be aware of broad emerging interest-rate trends or the credit risks involved in investing in lower-quality securities.

As was mentioned earlier, during periods of easier monetary conditions (lower interest rates), differences in yields because of quality considerations tend to narrow, while during stringent monetary conditions (higher interest rates), investors tend to place more emphasis on quality differences between various fixed-income securities, causing yield spreads between high-quality and low-quality issues to widen. Generalizing from the above comments, when yield differentials between similar high-quality and low-quality securities are expected to *widen,* investors may wish to swap from low-quality securities to higher-quality issues. On the other hand, when yield spreads are expected to *narrow* between high-quality securities and low-quality issues, it may be more beneficial to switch out of the higher-quality securities into lower-quality issues, while keeping possible credit risks in line with the investor's own guidelines.

Knowledge of the effect of maturity, coupon rate, and the general level of yields as they affect bond price volatility is of critical importance to investors.

Expectation of higher yields for those who seek to avoid or minimize prospective volatility suggests that they should invest in short-term instruments and plan to reinvest later on in the higher-yielding long-terms they anticipate. The danger in this policy is, of course, the high risk of yield loss if yields turn counter to one's prediction and move downward.

Those who expect substantially lower yields over the long term should, of course, seek maximum volatility, and maximum yield protection. For both of these reasons, they should favor long-term low-coupon bonds, provided the yield sacrifice is not too large.

On the other hand, some investors may expect moderately higher yields but may not be able to accept either the long-term yield risks or the lower current yields entailed in buying short-term instruments. Such investors can consider high-coupon premium bonds having several years of remaining call protection. These bonds often provide solid yield advantages, which together with their lower volatility makes them a fair price in yield hedge against moderate yield increases. On the other hand, if yields drop, the investor will have purchased a handsome yield over at least the period of call protection.

Return-Risk Estimates

Holding-period yields on fixed-income securities over any forward period will be sensitive to the outlook for the level, structure, and spread of interest rates. These important concepts absorbed the bulk of our work in Chapters 12 and 13. We observed that the systematic forces of purchasing-power and interest-rate risk might suggest higher or lower *levels* of interest rates. Any change in level, however, might lead to dissimilar changes across the *time* spectrum of interest rates. Additionally, unsystematic forces can cause securities of the same maturity to alter or maintain their yield *spreads*.

These observations must be coupled with the simple arithmetic of time-adjusted yield and bond tables. In this chapter we observed that changes in required yields have an opposite effect upon prices. That is, bond prices move opposite to yields. However, for any given change in yields, *percentage* price changes are least for shorter maturities and higher coupon rates. Further, an equal increase or decrease in yields from the same starting point results in capital gains that are greater than capital losses.

Estimating return and risk on specific bonds requires a procedure not unlike that undertaken with common stocks. We begin with a forecast of the market. In the case of bonds, the market for debt securities is best represented as a starting point by yields on government bonds. A forecast of government interest rates over the holding period will take into account the systematic forces of purchasing-power and interest-rate risk.

Assume that long-term governments are currently yielding 5 percent. At the end of a holding period of one year, rates likely to prevail on governments and the related subjective probabilities are these:

Gov't. Yields, End of Period	Probability
4.50%	.10
4.75	.20
5.00	.40
5.25	.20
5.50	.10

The second step is to estimate, for the bond to be analyzed, its yield to maturity one year hence. The question to answer is, Given the probability distribution of government yields shown above, what would be the effect on yield to maturity and price of the bond being examined? This is where yield spreads enter into the analysis. The analyst should look at historical and expected spreads between governments and the rating class of the bond being examined. Recall that spreads tend to widen and narrow like an accordion under certain economic conditions.

Let us apply the second step to a hypothetical 7 percent Aa bond due in eighteen years. The bond is currently selling at 112. Present-value or bond tables will indicate that this bond has a time-adjusted yield, or yield to maturity, of about 5.91 percent. Let us assume that if government yields move across 5 percent in one year, the spread between governments and Aa's—which is currently 5.91-5.00 percent, or 91 basis points, in a bondman's vocabulary—will narrow to 75 basis points; a fall in governments below 5 percent will cause the spread to widen to 100 basis points. Armed with this information, we may estimate yield to maturity on our Aa at the end of the one-year holding period.

(1) Gov't Yields, End of Period	(2) Aa Spread	(1) + (2) Aa Yield, End of Period	 Aa Price, End of Period
4.50%	1.00	5.50%	116
4.75	1.00	5.75	113½
5.00	.91	5.91	112
5.25	.75	6.00	110½
5.50	.75	6.25	108

Given the anticipated yields to maturity, it is necessary to look up the bond's projected price in each case from a bond table. The coupon is known (7 percent) and the number of years to maturity is now one year less (17). Thus, for an end-of-period yield assumed to be 5.50 percent for the Aa bond, this is a *decline* from the present 5.92 percent. We will expect the bond price to *rise*, since the interest income is fixed. Bond tables indicate that the price will rise from 112 to 116.

We are, of course, interested in translating these yield-to-maturity changes into holding-period yield (HPY). Thus, assuming a $1,000-face-value bond and, therefore, interest of $70 and a price at the beginning of the holding period of 112 (or $1,120), if yield to maturity should fall from 5.92 percent to 5.50 percent, HPY will be:

$$\text{HPY} = \frac{\$70 + (\$1,160 - \$1,120)}{\$1,120}$$

$$= \frac{\$70 + \$40}{\$1,120}$$

$$= \frac{\$110}{\$1,120}$$

$$= .0982, \text{ or } 9.82\%$$

Once yields are estimated and end-of-period bond prices are estimated, probability estimates must be applied to arrive at an *expected* HPY:

(1) Ending Price	(2) Estimated HPY	(3) Probability	(2) X (3) Expected HPY
116	9.82	.10	0.982
113½	7.14	.20	1.428
112	6.25	.40	2.600
110½	5.35	.20	1.070
108	2.59	.10	0.259
			6.339

Of course, the expected HPY of 6.34 percent is sensitive to the forecast of the level and spread of interest rates and the probability distribution. Larger probabilities of rates below current yields to maturity will result in higher expected bond prices and, therefore, higher expected HPY. Similarly, larger probabilities assigned to yields above existing rates will alter eventual HPYs downward. Such nonsymmetrical distributions are likely when the analyst believes that the band of probable rates over the holding period tends toward relatively lower or higher levels of rates.

Variability of return as measured by the standard deviation of returns is an appropriate risk measure with bonds as it was with common stocks. This can be accomplished objectively by witnessing past one-year holding periods on the Aa bonds in question. Such historical variation serves as the basis for estimating risk. Subjective determination of future variation, tempered by past experience, is the best approach.

The mathematics of bond tables can now be appreciated when we look at the effects of changes in interest rates upon bonds that differ in coupon and maturity. Let us assume we are examining the behavior of Aa bonds, and the yield curve is basically flat from five years out to thirty years. Thus, Aa bonds yield 5.91 percent from five through thirty years. Assume that the curve remains flat and the *level* of yields *drops* to 5.50 percent. The absolute and percentage *price rises* will be sensitive to coupon and maturity as follows:

1. A five-year bond will rise from 100 to 107, a 7 percent rise; 25-year bonds will climb from 100 to 120, a 20 percent increase.
2. Using a 25-year maturity, a 3 percent coupon bond would rise from 62 to 66, an increase of 6 percent; a 7 percent coupon bond would rise from 114 to 120, a 5.25 percent increase.

Of course, this example assumed a flat yield curve that did not change its shape as interest-rate levels fell. Further, default-risk spreads were not altered or even considered for other classes of bonds (Aaa, A, and so on).

Summary

The fixed nature of interest payments on bonds suggests that bond prices must bear the brunt of the necessary adjustments to reflect altered expectations of yields. In the main, bond prices move opposite to interest rates, with greater absolute price changes associated with bonds of longer maturities. In addition, percentage gains or losses in bond prices are different as a function of coupon rates on bonds.

Historically, the long period following World War II witnessed a long bear market in bonds as interest rates went through a pronounced secular rise. However, within this secular fall in bond prices (rise in interest rates) were shorter periods of seasonal and cyclical influences that afforded handsome capital gains to flexible bond investors.

Holding-period yields on bonds can be forecast after careful estimates have been made of the outlook for the level, structure, and spread of interest rates. This chapter examined holding-period yields historically for several individual bonds as well as classes of bonds. Based upon certain assumptions about the level, structure, and spread of interest rates, and using our knowledge of the mathematics of bond yields, we were able to estimate return and risk for a hypothetical Aa bond.

Questions and Problems

1. Using the approximation method for determining yield to maturity, what is the yield to maturity on a 10 percent, 20-year bond, selling for 110?

2. Using present-value tables and Equation 14.1, determine:

a. The present worth of a bond where $P = \$1,000$, $I = \$80$, $N = 40$, and $i = .10$.

b. Assume the same data as above, except that $N = 5$. Determine the present worth of the bond.

c. How do you account for the effect of merely reducing the life of the bond in part b above?

3. a. Set up the equation for determining the rate of interest (i) implied by a 4 percent, ten-year bond selling at $790 (principal at maturity is $1,000).

b. Solve the equation for the implied rate of interest. Can you see any advantages to yield tables such as Table 4-5?

4. Look up the present quotes on both the Standard Oil of California $4\frac{3}{8}$ percent bonds due in 1983 and the Holiday Inns 9½ percent debentures due in 1995. Calculate the yield to maturity on each bond. Explain the difference, if any, between your calculated yields to maturity and HPYs found in Tables 14-2 and 14-3.

5. Prove the entry in Table 4-5 that states that the return on a 6 percent bond due in three years and selling at 90 is about 10 percent.

6. Under what specific circumstances would continuous reinvestment in one-year bonds yield superior total income relative to a one-time purchase of a 25-year bond?

7. You are interested in buying some bonds. The *Wall Street Journal* lists two bonds for a company you are very much interested in:

UVM, Inc.   4s 86 ...   70
UVM, Inc.   10s 86 ...   110

a. What would you be willing to pay for the "4s 86" if you required a return of 10 percent on bonds of this quality/maturity?

b. Based upon the combination of coupon, price, and maturity, each of these bonds actually yields 8.5 percent to its maturity. Suppose this return was satisfactory to you. What are *two* advantages of buying the "4s 86" vis-à-vis the "10s 86"? The major disadvantage?

8. Outline the broad steps to be taken in estimating risk and return on a Aaa bond to be purchased today and held for one year.

9. An investor has engaged in the following transactions:

   (1) Sell: 8%, 20-year, A-rated, Gas Co. bond. Price = 95¼
       Buy: 8%, 20-year, AAA-rated, Electric Utility bond. Price = 100

   (2) Sell: 7½%, 20-year, AAA-rated, Food Co. bond. Price = 95
       Buy: Treasury bills, 90-day maturity. Price = 98½

   (3) Sell: 8.10%, 10-year, AA-rated, Drug Co. bond. Price = 100¼
       Buy: 8.90%, 8-year, AA-rated, Chemical Co. bond. Price = 100

   For each of these "swaps," what are the apparent underlying motivations and the associated risks?

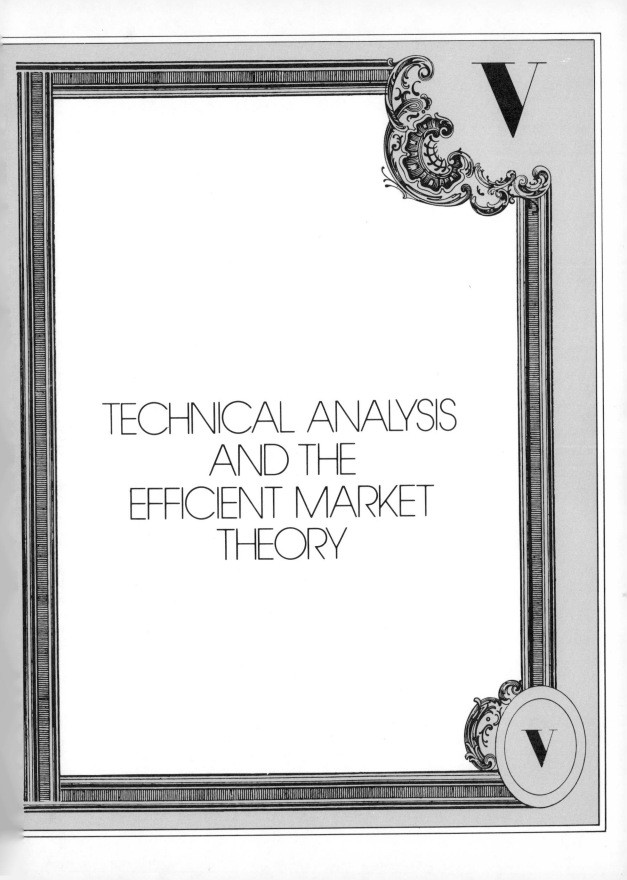

TECHNICAL ANALYSIS AND THE EFFICIENT MARKET THEORY

The approach to security analysis presented thus far is generally called *fundamental analysis.* The technique is based on the premise that the analyst needs to consider the major factors affecting the economy, the industry, and the company in order to determine an appropriate investment decision. In this section, we will discuss two different approaches to investment decision making.

Chapter 15 contains a discussion of a number of rather mechanical indicators of the stock market, individual security prices, and price behavior. Technical analysis in its truest form examines historical price and volume information.

Among the market indicators we will discuss are the Dow Theory, advances and declines, and the list of most-active stocks. Among the volume indicators we will review are short-selling statistics, odd-lot trading statistics, and odd-lot short sales. We will also look at mutual-fund activity, confidence indicators, the credit balance theory, and several charting approaches including point-and-figure and bar charting.

The theory of efficient markets, the subject of Chapter 16, in essence refutes technical analysis. The efficient market hypothesis, sometimes called the theory of random walk, states that historical price and volume information is of no use in predicting future price movements of either individual securities or groups of securities.

More specifically, we will discuss three main forms of the efficient market hypothesis. The weak form of the efficient market hypothesis says that the current prices of stocks already fully reflect *all* the information contained in the historical sequence of prices. The semi-strong form of the hypothesis goes still further. It states that the current prices of stocks not only reflect all informational value of historical prices, but also reflect all *publicly available information* about the corporation being studied. The strong form goes the farthest by saying that all information is useless to the investor for purposes of earning consistently superior investment returns. Empirical tests and results of tests of various forms of the efficient market hypothesis will be presented.

The chapter ends with a reconciliation of the theory of random walk and fundamental analysis, as well as a discussion of the investment implications of this theory, in both the selection of individual stocks and the construction of portfolios.

FIFT

TECHNICAL
ANALYSIS

Fundamentalists forecast stock prices on the basis of economic, industry, and company statistics. The principal decision variables ultimately take the form of earnings and dividends. The fundamentalist makes a judgment of the stock's value within a risk-return framework based upon earning power and the economic environment.

In this chapter we will examine an alternative approach to predicting stock price behavior. This approach is called *technical analysis*. Technical analysis is frequently used as a supplement to fundamental analysis rather than as a substitute for it. Thus, technical analysis can, and frequently does, confirm findings based on fundamental analysis.

The technician does not consider value in the sense in which the fundmentalist uses it. The technician believes the forces of supply and demand are reflected in patterns of *price* and *volume* of trading. By examination of these patterns, he predicts whether prices are moving higher or lower, and even by how much. In the narrowest sense, the technician believes that price fluctuations reflect logical and emotional forces. He further believes that price movements, whatever their cause, once in force persist for some period of time and can be detected.

Thus, technical analysis may be used for more than a supplement to fundamental analysis. Fundamental analysis allows the analyst to forecast holding-period yield and the riskiness of achieving that yield, but these figures alone do not necessarily prompt a buy or sell action. Technical analysis, however, may be useful in *timing* a buy or sell order—an order that may be implied by the forecasts of return and risk. For example, the technical analysis may reveal that a drop in price is warranted. Postponement of a purchase, then, if the technical analysis is correct, will raise the forecast HPY. Conversely, a sell order might be postponed because the charts reveal a rise in the price of the security in question.

The technician must (1) identify the trend, and (2) recognize when one trend comes to an end and prices start in the opposite direction. His central problem is to distinguish between reversals within a trend and real changes in the trend itself. This problem of sorting out price changes is critical, since prices do not change in a smooth, uninterrupted fashion.

The technician views price changes and their significance mainly through price and volume statistics. His bag of tools, or indicators, helps him measure price-volume, supply-demand relationships for the overall market as well as for individual stocks. Technicians seldom rely upon a single indicator, as no one indicator is infallible; they place reliance upon reinforcement provided by groups of indicators.

The remainder of this chapter concentrates upon some of the major technical indicators employed to assess the direction of the general market and the direction of individual stocks.[1]

Market Indicators

The use of technical "indicators" to measure the direction of the overall market should precede any technical analysis of individual stocks, because of the systematic influence of the general market on stock prices. In addition, some technicians feel that forecasting aggregates is more reliable, since individual errors can be filtered out.

First, we will examine the seminal theory from which much of the substance of technical analysis has been developed—the Dow Theory—after which, other key indicators of market activity will be examined in turn.

DOW THEORY

Around the turn of the century, Charles H. Dow formulated a hypothesis that the stock market does not perform on a random basis but is influenced by three distinct cyclical trends that guide its general direction. By following these trends, he said, the general market direction can be predicted. Dow classified these cycles as primary, secondary, and minor trends. The primary trend is the long-range cycle that carries the entire market up or down. The secondary trend acts as a restraining force on the primary trend, tending to correct deviations from its general boundaries. Secondary trends usually last from several weeks to several months in length. The minor trends are the day-to-day fluctuations in the market. These have little analytic value, because of their short duration and variations in amplitude. Primary and secondary trends are depicted in Figure 15-1.

The basic proposition in the Dow Theory is relatively simple. A bull market is in process when successive highs are reached after secondary corrections, and when secondary upswings advance beyond previous secondary downswings. Such a process is illustrated in Figure 15-1. The theory also requires that the secondary downswing corrections will be of shorter duration than the secondary upswings. The reverse of these propositions would be true of a bear market.

The classical Dow Theory utilizes both the industrial average and the transportation average in determining the market position. When both averages are moving in the same direction, valid indicators of a continuing bull or bear market are implied.

---

[1]An excellent source of much of the raw data for various indicators is found in the "Market Laboratory" section of *Barron's*, a weekly publication of Dow Jones, Inc.

FIGURE 15-1

REPRESENTATION OF DOW THEORY

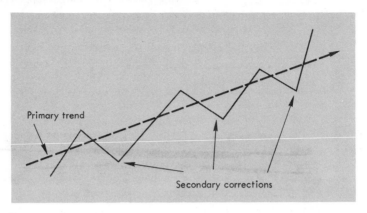

PRICE INDICATORS

The two variables concerning groups of stocks or individual stocks that technicians watch with the most interest are the behavior of prices and the volume of trading contributing to and influenced by changing prices.

It was amply noted earlier that the change in a security's price is probably *the* most important component in the total rate of return resulting from holding a security. This fact has not escaped the technician any more than it has the fundamentalist. In examining the influence of the market on stock prices in general, technicians particularly note certain signals, or price indicators: price advances versus declines, new highs versus new lows, and the price patterns of the "most active" stocks.

Advances and Declines

Looking only at the popular stock averages such as the Dow Jones Industrial Average (DJIA) can often be misleading. A relatively few stocks may be moving ahead while the majority of stocks either are making no progress or are actually moving down. The average may be behaving contrary to the larger population of stocks.

The basic idea behind the measurement of advances and declines is to determine what the main body of stocks is really doing. Comparison of advances and declines is a means of measuring the dispersion, or breadth, of a general price rise or decline. The phrase often used is "breadth of the market."

Many measures could be used. The most common is to calculate the daily net difference between the number of New York Stock Exchange stocks that advance and the number of those that decline. This net difference is added to the next day's difference, and so on, to form a continuous cumulative index. The index is plotted in line form and compared with the DJIA. For example:

	Advances	Declines	Breadth (Cumulative Advances Less Declines)
Monday	1000	400	+600
Tuesday	650	800	+450
Wednesday	500	1100	−150
Thursday	900	700	+ 50
Friday	1200	400	+850

The technician is more interested in change in breadth than in absolute level. Further, breadth is compared with a stock-market index, such as the DJIA. Normally, breadth and the DJIA will move in unison. The key signals occur when there is divergence between the two. When they diverge, the advance-decline line will show the truer direction of the market. The DJIA cannot move contrary to the market as a whole—at least, not for long. The longer the resistance, the greater the expected reversal. During a bull market, if breadth declines to new lows while the DJIA makes new highs, a peak in the averages is suggested. This peak will be followed by a major downturn in stock prices generally. Breadth can also be used to detect recovery. The advance-decline line will begin rising as the DJIA is reaching new lows.

Figure 15-2 is a monthly plot of cumulative net advances and the DJIA. The important feature to note is cycle-to-cycle breadth versus DJIA, and not the trend. Like other indicators, this one has been useful as a leading indicator at times. At other times, such as the early 1970s, this method was of little value.

New Highs and New Lows

A supplementary measure to accompany breadth of the market is the high-low differential or index. The theory is that a rising market will generally be accompanied by an expanding number of stocks attaining new highs and a dwindling number of new lows. The reverse holds true for a declining market.

The number of New York Stock Exchange stocks making new highs for the year minus the number making new lows is averaged for a five-day period. A moving average smooths out erratic daily fluctuations and exposes the trend. Such a high-low index would normally move with the market. Again, divergence from the market trend is a clue to future price movements.

The Most-Active List

Most major weekly market newspapers in the United States publish the twenty most active stocks for the week. By itself, this segment of the market is at first glance relatively useless, since the makeup of the list changes from week to week. However, these issues taken as a whole represent only 1 percent of the total issues traded but account for almost 15 percent of the total volume. Viewed in this way, the list tends to have a recognizable pattern if certain dimensions are assigned.

The number of issues each week showing a net gain cannot exceed twenty, nor can they exceed twenty for a net loss. Since random variations often occur

FIGURE 15-2
NET ADVANCES VS. DJIA

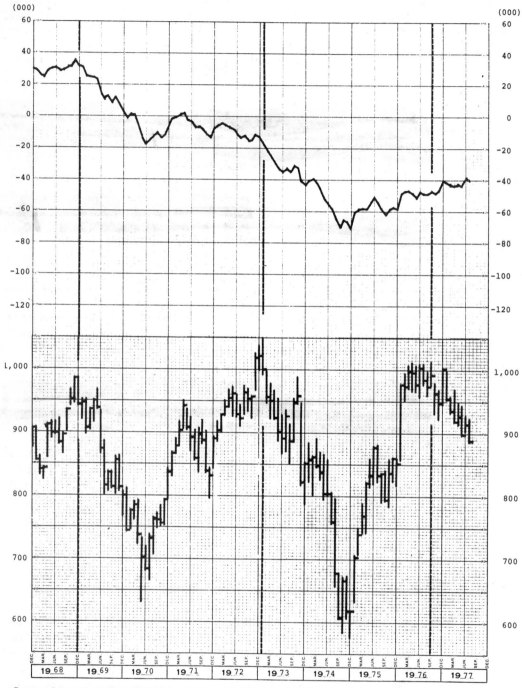

Source: *Long-Term Technical Trends* (Boston: Stone & Mead, 1977).

in the stock market, an additional time dimension of several weeks will tend to smooth an otherwise erratic curve. If three weeks of activity are added together to act as a stabilizer, then the upper and lower limits of the most-active list become +60 and −60.

When plotted on a three-week basis, the twenty most active stocks oscillate within a certain range. The maximum three-week upside plurality during the period 1962-69 was +51. The lowest net weekly plurality has been −52. One low point occurred on June 20, 1961, and was followed by a 350 gain in the Dow Jones Industrial Average over a 190-week period.

Figure 15-3 provides some interesting insights. On February 11, 1966, the Dow closed at 989.03, with the most-active indicator at +15. During the following thirty-four weeks, the DJIA lost 245 points. On October 7, 1966, the Dow closed at 744.32, with the most-active indicator at −47. This condition was

FIGURE 15-3
MOST ACTIVE STOCKS VS. DJIA

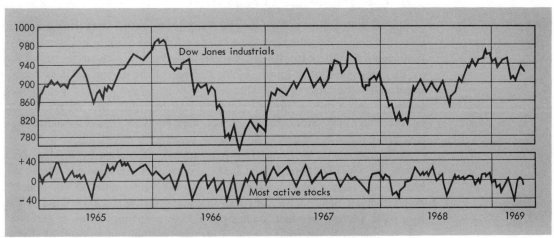

Source: F. R. West, "New Market Tool, "Barron's, 49, No. 17 (April 28, 1969), 5.

reminiscent of the indicator's position just before the 1962 upturn. The Dow climbed over 200 points, to 960, during the next fifty weeks. Perhaps one of the most interesting things about the twenty-six-week decline from 934 was the way in which the bear market terminated: The most-active list showed signs of bullishness as the market drew closer to its bottom.

The experience of the past decade has shown that the most-active indicator should approach −50 following a long and continuous decline that results in a selling climax, but in the case of an eroding decline, the indicator should move toward zero while the market continues to decline. In a bull market, the conditions are reversed, and oscillations around +35 are indications of strength in a rising market. A warning signal is flashed when the market continues to rise in the face of subsequent declines in the indicator.

VOLUME INDICATORS

Volume changes are believed by most technicians to be prerequisite to any change in price. Volume is a function of the demand for and supply of stocks and can signal turning points for the market as well as for individual stocks.

A Dow Theory tenet is that during bull markets, volume increases with price advances and decreases with price declines. In a major downward price trend, the reverse will hold true; volume will generally increase as prices decline and dwindle on price rallies. Further, volume generally falls in advance of major declines in the stock price averages and rises sharply during market bottoms. Thus, forecasting price changes requires examination of the trend of price changes as well as fluctuations in volume of transactions.

The financial press publishes daily data on upside and downside volume, and the technician can look closely at volume generated when the market was rising or falling during a given trading day. These data provide insight that is not available when net figures are utilized.

New York and American Exchange Volume

The American Stock Exchange has long been identified as listing smaller, more fledgling companies than those listed on the New York Stock Exchange. It is estimated that three-fourths of the shares traded on the ASE are accounted for by the public, and three-fourths of the trading volume on the NYSE is institutional. Therefore American Exchange is, rightly or not, viewed as a market for more speculative securities. Many technicians regard the relative volume on the New York Stock Exchange and the American Stock Exchange as a measure or index of changes in the trend of prices.

Daily volume on each exchange is compared most often by dividing ASE volume by NYSE volume. ASE volume in excess of NYSE volume is rare, so the index would assume values between zero and 1.00. Values closer to 1.00 indicate that activity is high on the American (more speculative stocks) relative to the New York (more investment-grade stocks). High percentage values in excess of .60 are thought to represent a zone of high speculation and an eventual change in trend from bullish to bearish as speculative excesses bring about a collapse. Percentage values below .30 are considered healthy and representative of buying opportunities. Historically, when the index has gone above 60 percent, the market top was generally reached several months later.

Short Selling

Around the twentieth of each month, the ASE and NYSE make public the number of shares of key stocks that have been sold short. Recall that short selling refers to selling shares that are not owned. The seller has behaved in this way because he feels the stock will fall in price. He hopes to purchase the shares at a later date (cover his short position) below the selling price and reap a profit.

As a technical indicator, short selling is called *short interest*. The theory is that short sellers must eventually cover their positions. This buying activity increases the potential demand for stock. In effect, short interest has significance for the market as a whole, as well as for individual stocks.

Monthly short interest for the market can be related to average daily volume for the preceding month. Thus, monthly short interest divided by average daily volume gives a ratio. The ratio indicates how many days of trading it would take to use up total short interest. Historically, the ratio has varied between one-third of a day and four days.

In general, when the ratio is less than 1.0, the market is considered weak or weakening. It is common to say that the market is "overbought." A decline should follow sooner or later. The zone between 1.0 and 1.5 is considered a neutral indicator. Values above 1.5 indicate bullish territory, with 2.0 and above highly favorable. This market is said to be "oversold." The most bullish effect would occur when the market is turning up and the short-interest ratio is high.

Figure 15-4 shows the short-interest ratio over a period of years in conjunction with the DJIA. It does not seem to be too revealing at market highs, but does give good clues of important lows when it reaches the 1.7-2.0 range.

Data are now being made public regarding short selling by stock specialists. Specialists are permitted to use short selling as one of their tools to promote orderly markets in the stocks they specialize in. Increasing and high levels of specialist short selling tend to signal important market tops. Conversely, low levels of specialist short selling tend to signal market bottoms.

Odd-Lot Trading

The small investor more often than not buys fewer than 100 shares of a given stock—an odd lot—and such buyers and sellers are called *odd lotters*. Many find reason to watch the buying and selling activities of the odd lotters very closely.

Odd lotters try to do the right thing most of the time; that is, they tend to buy stocks as the market retreats and sell stocks as the market advances. However, technicians feel that the odd lotter is inclined to do the wrong thing at critical turns in the market.

If we relate odd-lot purchases to odd-lot sales (purchase ÷ sales), we get an odd-lot index. An increase in the index suggests relatively more buying; a decrease indicates relatively more selling. During most of the market cycle, odd lotters are selling the advances and buying the declines. During advances, the odd-lot index is falling. However, at or near the market peak, the index begins to rise as odd lotters sell proportionately less. The volume of odd-lot purchases increases noticeably just before a decline in the market. Similarly, during declines, the index is rising. Just before a rise in the market, the volume of odd-lot sales increases greatly and the index begins to fall.

Figure 15-5 shows the ratio of odd-lot purchases to sales as compared with the DJIA. A declining trend in the purchases-to-sales line is a sign of technical deterioration. A rising trend is a sign of improvement.

Odd-Lot Short Sales. The presumed lack of sophistication on the part of odd lotters is often further verified by looking at their activities in short selling. A

FIGURE 15-4

SHORT INTEREST VS. DJIA

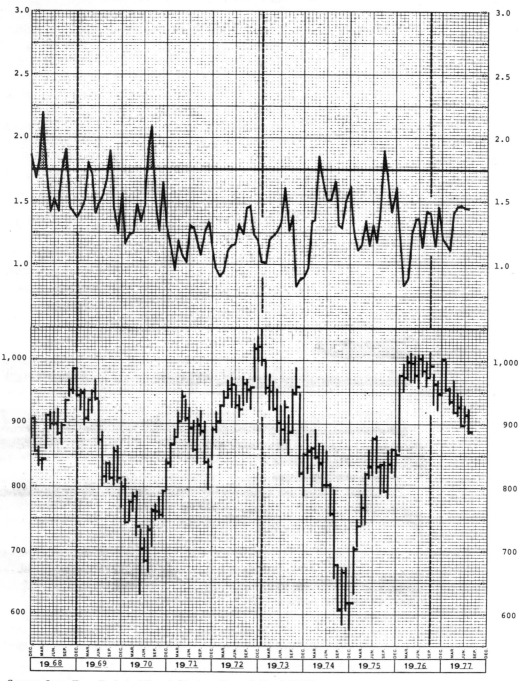

Source: *Long-Term Technical Trends* (Boston: Stone & Mead, 1977).

FIGURE 15-5

ODD-LOT INDEX VS. DJIA

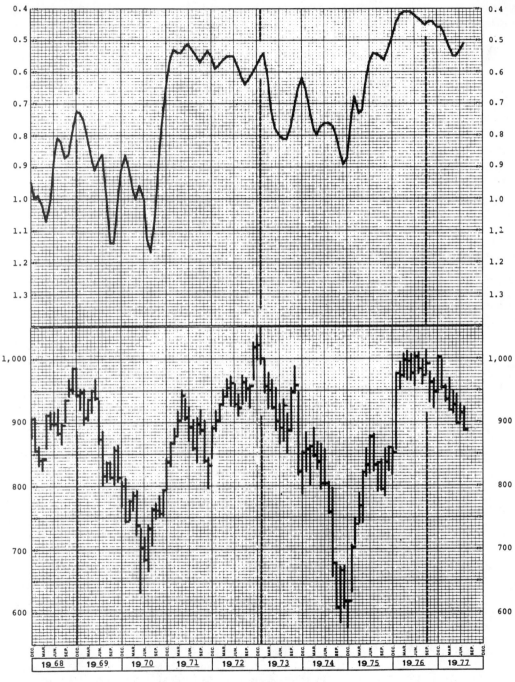

Source: *Long-Term Technical Trends* (Boston: Stone & Mead, 1977).

459

ratio can be calculated by dividing odd-lot short sales by total odd-lot sales. This short sales/sales ratio is gauging the speculative activities of the man on the street, who, as a speculator, is presumed to be more wrong than the average odd lotter. Odd-lot short sellers tend to increase their short sales sharply near the bottom of a declining market. As soon as the market turns around, they tend to lose faith and reduce their short sales noticeably. An increasing ratio of short sales to sales suggests increasing bearishness; a falling ratio indicates decreasing bearishness.

Normally, a short-sale ratio of 0.5 percent suggests high optimism. A ratio over 3 percent suggests high pessimism.

OTHER MARKET INDICATORS

The number of indicators technicians use to predict changes in the trend of the overall market is almost limitless.[2] In the following paragraphs we will try to capture the essence of some other popular market indicators.

Mutual-Fund Activity

Mutual funds represent one of the most potent institutional forces in the market, and they are a source of abundant data that are readily available. The cash position of funds and their net subscriptions are followed closely by technicians.

Mutual funds keep cash to take advantage of favorable market opportunities and/or to provide for redemption of shares by holders. It is convenient to express mutual-fund cash as a percentage of net assets on a daily, monthly, or annual basis. In theory, a low cash ratio would indicate a reasonably fully invested position, with the implication that not much reserve buying power remains in the hands of funds as a group. Low ratios (on the order of 5-5½ percent) are frequently equated with market highs. At market bottoms, the cash ratio would be high to reflect heavy redemptions, among other things. Such a buildup of the cash ratio at market lows is an indication of potential purchasing power that can be injected into the market to propel it upward.

Another mutual-fund indicator that is monitored quite closely is net subscriptions (subscriptions to new shares, less redemptions of existing shares). Like the odd-lot statistics, this indicator measures public sentiment and the outlook for the stock market. The trend to more or less buying moves in tandem with the odd-lot purchase-to-sale ratio. The sales-redemption differential narrows considerably prior to market advances. In effect, market advances are preceded by a relative shift toward redemptions. Shifts toward relative buying (sales of new shares) tend to precede market declines.

---

[2]Many who are cynical about technical analysis cite elaborate efforts to tie market movements to sunspot activity (lunacy and speculation) or the length of women's skirts (hemline theory), and the use of various aspects of the occult, including tarot-card reading, palmistry, and so on.

Credit Balance Theory

Typically, investors receive credit balances in their accounts at their brokerage houses when they sell stock. At this point the investor has two choices: He can either have the credit balance forwarded to him or leave the credit balance in the account. However, these balances frequently earn no interest. Thus the only reason for maintaining the credit balances in the account would be for purposes of reinvestment of these funds in the very near future.

Figures on these credit balances at brokerage houses are published regularly in the financial press and in such publications as the *Federal Reserve Bulletin.* It is thought that a build-up in these cash balances represents large reservoirs of potential buying power. In effect, investors are leaving the credit balances in their brokerage firm accounts because they anticipate a drop in prices and thus a buying opportunity. Conversely, a drop in credit balance suggests that prices will go up. Because an increase in prices was expected, investors have already used up their credit balances. However, technicians feel that investors in general as their actions get reflected in credit balances are usually wrong. That is, the investors are buying stocks when they should be selling them and selling stocks when they should be buying. As such, the credit balance theory is a contrary opinion theory.

In other words, technicians suggest that a wise investor will buy stocks as credit balances are rising and sell stocks as credit balances are dropping. In short, technicians say the wise investor should do the opposite of what the credit balances are doing.

Confidence Indicators

Two indicators of confidence have been popular with market analysts. One is based upon *Barron's* ratio of higher- to lower-grade bond yields. The other compares Standard & Poor's low-priced and high-grade common stocks.

The *Barron's* indicator divides high-grade bond yields by the relatively higher yields of low-grade bonds. A rise in the index indicates a narrowing of the spread between high- and low-grade bonds. In a previous chapter we saw that narrowing yield spreads were indicative of boom times or rising stock markets; so a fall in the index would imply widening yield spreads and recessed conditions in the economy and markets. The assumption behind the value of the index is that "smart" money moves from high to low quality, or vice versa, in anticipation of major market shifts, and such a move causes yield spreads to change. To the extent that this is true, *Barron's* confidence index is a leading indicator of the economy and the stock market.

The S&P confidence indicator measures low-priced common stocks and high-grade common stocks. Speculative stocks are assumed to be closely identified with low-priced shares. Thus we have a low- and high-grade stock indicator much like *Barron's* low- and high-grade bond indicator. When the market is advancing, investors are willing to take greater risks and buy speculative (low-priced) stocks. During market declines, quality (in high-grade stocks) is sought. The index (low-priced/high-grade) would fall prior to a market peak as confidence wanes and speculative stocks are changed for high-quality shares. A rise in the index would signal revival from a market bottom.

After the technical analyst has forecast the probable future performance of the general market, he can turn his attention to individual stocks. Let us examine a few of the tools used for the technical analysis of individual common stocks.

As in forecasting the market, the technician believes that understanding historical price-volume information of individual securities is the key for determining their probable future performance. Technical analysts believe that history repeats itself, and thus, historical trends and patterns will be repeated through time. They seek to detect an evolving key trend or pattern in supply and demand conditions of the stock in question. The techniques that have evolved are aimed at detecting shifts in underlying supply and demand conditions as reflected in changes in volume and, consequently, prices. In this section we will discuss representative approaches in two broad categories of tools—those looking only at price, and those looking at price-volume relationships.

PRICE ANALYSIS APPROACHES

Point-and-Figure Charting

Charting represents a key activity for the technical analyst. It provides visual assistance to him in detecting evolving and changing patterns of price behavior. The two oldest and most widely used charting procedures are point-and-figure charting and bar charting. These lie at the core of many technical schemes for individual stock analysis.

Perhaps the most baffling form of stock analysis, in the mind of the average investor, is the technique of point-and-figure charting.[3] The major features of this method of charting a security are that (1) it has no time dimension, (2) it disregards "small" changes in the stock price, and (3) it requires a stock to reverse direction a predetermined number of points before a change in direction is recorded on the chart.

A simple illustration will demonstrate the plotting technique quite easily. For stocks priced above 50 and below 100, the plotting increments are often one point, although the user may elect any increment he desires. All fractions are then discarded, so that 51 7/8 becomes 51. On a sheet of graph paper, the closing price of the stock being charted is recorded with an X. If the price at the close of the next trading day is within the plotting increment, no additional X can be entered. (We are assuming that the chart only records closing-price information, to the exclusion of intraday activity.) Only when the stock price

---

[3]One reason for this is the great number of variations on the basic point-and-figure approach. We present only one representative approach.

moves into another plotting increment are changes recorded. Therefore a stock may move upward several points over a fairly long period with only a small amount of plotting. For example, if a stock moved from a price of 50 in small increments to a price of 53 over a three-month period, only four X's will have been made on the chart, as in Figure 15-6(a).

Obviously, if no additional parameters were assigned, only one vertical line of X's would develop. A *reversal spread* is used to prevent this. A reversal spread is the number of points (dollars) an issue must fall from its immediately previous high, or rise from its immediately previous low, to develop a new vertical column. When this occurs, a new column is started to the right. These reversal spreads are assigned according to the volatility of the issue. In the example, if the reversal spread were three points, and if the stock had gone from 50 to 60 without ever closing three points below the high for the column, the chart would look like Figure 15-6(b). However, if the stock developed a downtrend after reaching 60 and hit 56½ on a close, a new column would be started, and all the points from 60 to 56 would be filled in, as in Figure 15-6(c). The stock is now in a downward cycle and will remain classified as such until a three-point reversal occurs, as in Figure 15-6(d), which shows that the stock moved from 40 to 43.

By ignoring the time element, we can see the forces of supply and demand at work in Figure 15-7(a), where the equilibrium price of the issue seems to be between 45 and 50. At any price above 50, the sellers move in, and at any price below 45, the buyers move in and clear the market. If the stock suddenly moves to 55, we are aware that this is outside the realm of the stock's normal trading range and some form of unusual activity is taking place.

Over the years, point-and-figure adherents have observed various formations that occur before major price movements. One such formation, for example, is the *triple top*, as illustrated in Figure 15-7(b). A triple top occurs when a stock reaches its third consecutive high at the same price level. A buy signal is given when the stock surpasses the third high. A time element should be noted somewhere on the chart for each high, since the shorter the period from the first to the third high, the greater the underlying strength.[4]

Another key formation to point-and-figure chartists is the *congestion area*. A congestion area is formed on the chart by the lateral movement of X's. This comes about by a series of brief rallies and reversals, such as in Figure 15-7(a), that preclude the establishment of lengthy vertical columns. The width of the congestion area gives the technician some insight into the probable size and direction of a move by the stock to a "price target." Unfortunately, it is difficult to pinpoint when this target will be hit.[5]

A substantial number of patterns and corresponding rules have been developed by point-and-figure proponents over the years. These patterns can take con-

---

[4]See Ernest J. Staby, *Stock Market Trading* (New York: Cornerstone Library, 1970), pp. 28-30.

[5]Daniel Seligman, "The Mystique of Point-and-Figure," *Fortune*, 65, No. 3 (March 1962), 113-15 ff. See also Robert A. Levy, "The Predictive Significance of Five Point Chart Patterns," *Journal of Business,* July 1971.

FIGURE 15-6
SAMPLE POINT-AND-FIGURE CHARTS

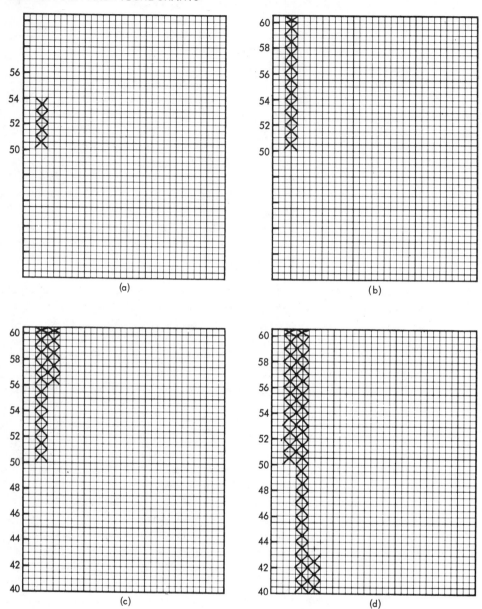

(a)

(b)

(c)

(d)

FIGURE 15-7
SAMPLE POINT-AND-FIGURE CHARTS

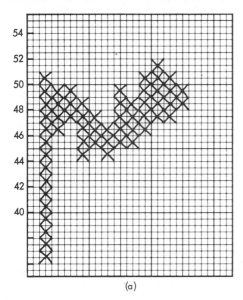

(a)

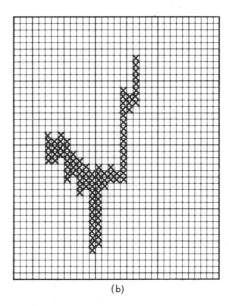

(b)

siderable periods of time to evolve on the chart, particularly when large plotting increments (several points) and reversal spreads are used. To the extent that large numbers of investors adhere to the basic tenets of point-and-figure charting, the prophesies of the charts may very well be self-fulfilling.

Bar Charting

Point-and-figure charts have a measure scale only on the vertical axis (no time dimension). Bar charts contain measures on both axes—price on the vertical axis, and time on the horizontal axis. The horizontal axis can be marked off in any dimension the analyst wishes—days, weeks, or months. On bar charts, rather than just plotting a point on the graph at a point in time, the analyst plots a vertical line to represent the range of prices of the stock during the period. That is, if the analyst were plotting daily data, the top of the vertical line would represent the high price of the stock during the day, and the bottom of the line would represent the low price of the stock during the same day. A small horizontal line is drawn across the bar to denote the closing price at the end of the time period. Generally, bar charts contain, at the bottom, volume information for the same period that the price information covers. The *Wall Street Journal* publishes bar charts of the three Dow Jones Averages—industrials, transportation, and utilities—each day.

Bar chartists, like point-and-figure chartists, have found key patterns to look for in determining the most probable price action of a stock. Typical patterns are illustrated in Figures 15-8 and 15-9. Figure 15-9 contains interpretations of certain of these patterns.

FIGURE 15-8
TYPICAL GRAPHIC PATTERNS USED IN TECHNICAL
MARKET ANALYSIS

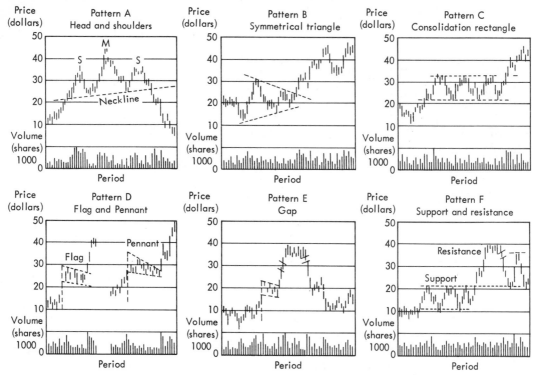

Source: Sidney M. Robbins, *Managing Securities* (Boston: Houghton Mifflin, 1954), p. 502.

Figure 15-10(a) presents a bar chart for Holiday Inns, from the Mansfield Stock Service. This service also provides bar charts of industry groupings. Figure 15-10(b) contains an explanation of the vast amount of information contained in the charts of this service.

The 200-Day Moving Average

One of the most reliable and easily read technical indicators available to investors is the 200-day moving average of a security. The technique for computing the average is simple. The closing prices of the stock market observation are added up for the most recent 200 days it has been traded. This sum is divided by 200. The objective is to obtain a relatively simple and smooth curve for the issue. Random variations and erratic price changes tend to cancel out, and a general underlying trend becomes visible. For those who see this as a maze of adding-machine tape, the entire process for 744 major issues can be obtained each week from the Trendline Market Service.

In his book, Joseph E. Granville listed eight basic rules for using the 200-day moving average, in a chapter on "The Grand Strategy of Stock Trading":

FIGURE 15-9
FIVE STANDARD CHART PATTERNS

MARKET EQUAL TO SUM OF ITS PARTS

In the fall of 1969, Alan R. Shaw, Harris, Upham & Company vice president, took on a herculean task. He wanted to examine the price behavior of all the stocks on the New York Stock Exchange to determine the technical position of each stock. Doing so, he felt, would enable him to get a picture of where the market stood. Accordingly, he designed five typical chart patterns which could best describe the price behavior of most stocks and proceeded to place all the N Y S E stocks into one of these five categories. Over a period of six weeks, all the stocks were arranged by pattern and listed in the firm's weekly market letter. (At the time, more stocks fell into the second category than in the others.)

The five patterns are shown and described below. They have been arranged so that the most vulnerable pattern with the least upside potential appears first. Then, progressing to more favorable patterns, the one most favorable is at the bottom. It should be noted that all stocks will usually fit one of these patterns no matter what kind of market we are in.

Five Standard Chart Patterns

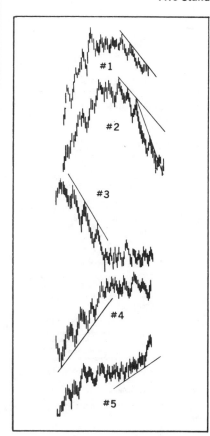

Chart Pattern #1

Stocks with vulnerable trends and/or possible downside potential.

Chart Pattern #2

Stocks with less vulnerability that appear to have reached possible lows, but need consolidation.

Chart Pattern #3

Stocks that have declined and experienced consolidation, and could do well in a favorable market.

Chart Pattern #4

Stocks that have performed relatively well but are currently in "neutral" trends.

Chart Pattern #5

Stocks in established uptrends and/or with possible upside potential.

Source: Yale Hirsch, *The 1971 Stock Trader's Almanac* (Old Tappan, N.J.:
The Hirsch Organization, 1970), p. 37.

FIGURE 15-10a
BAR CHART OF HOLIDAY INNS, INC., STOCK

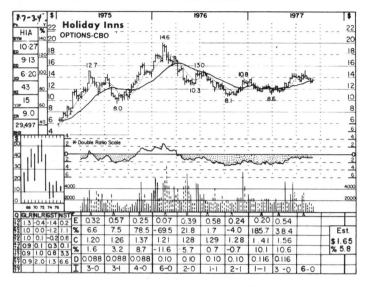

FIGURE 15-10b
INFORMATION CONTAINED IN MANSFIELD STOCK SERVICE CHARTS

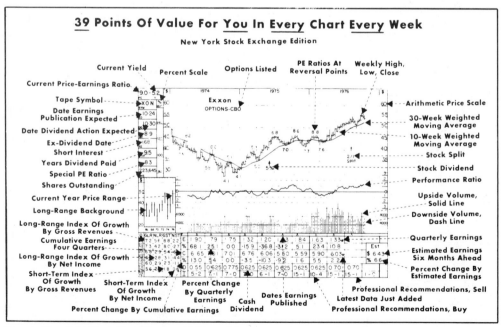

Source: Mansfield Stock Chart Service, 26 Journal Square, Jersey City, N.J. 07306.

1. If the 200-day average line flattens out following a previous decline, or is advancing, and the price of the stock penetrates that average line on the upside, this comprises a major buying signal.

2. If the price of the stock falls below the 200-day moving average price while the average line is still rising, this is also considered to be a buying opportunity.

3. If the stock price is above the 200-day line and is declining toward that line, fails to go through and starts to turn up again, this is a buying signal.

4. If the stock price falls too fast under the declining 200-day average line, it is entitled to an advance back toward the average line and the stock can be bought for this short-term technical rise.

5. If the 200-day average line flattens out following a previous rise, or is declining, and the price of the stock penetrates that line on the downside, this comprises a major sell signal.

6. If the price of the stock rises above the 200-day moving average price line while the average line is still falling, this also is considered to be a selling opportunity.

7. If the stock price is below the 200-day line and is advancing toward that line, fails to go through and starts to turn down again, this is a selling signal.

8. If the stock price advances too fast above the advancing 200-day average line, it is entitled to a reaction back toward the average line and the stock can be sold for this short-term technical reaction.[6]

Obviously, these rules are only a guideline to assist the analyst in using the 200-day moving average as an indicator for individual securities. For the person who is trading in speculative issues, the technique gives signals based on trends or changing trends in the price of the security in question. See Figure 15-11 for an example of this type of chart. Here the smooth line represents the 200-day moving average.

Relative Strength

A more recent approach to technical analysis of price has been proposed by Robert Levy.[7] His method is called *relative-strength analysis.* A basic tenet of this technique is that certain securities perform better than other securities in a given market environment and that this behavior will remain relatively constant over time. Generally, this technique is used in conjunction with either (1) the stocks of individual companies or industries or (2) portfolios consisting of stocks and bonds.

When the stock application is used, the analyst calculates ratios for the returns (over time) of the stock to those of its industry group, returns of the stock to those of the general market, and returns of the industry group to those of the general market.[8] These ratios are then plotted over time to see the relative

---

[6] Joseph E. Granville, *A Strategy of Daily Stock Market Timing for Maximum Profit* (Englewood Cliffs, N.J.: Prentice-Hall, 1969), pp. 237-38.

[7] Robert A. Levy, "Relative Strength as a Criterion for Investment Selection," *Journal of Finance*, December 1967, pp. 595-610.

[8] Both Moody's and Standard & Poor's services provide industry averages that can be used to calculate industry performance.

FIGURE 15-11

SAMPLE 30-WEEK MOVING AVERAGE STOCK CHART

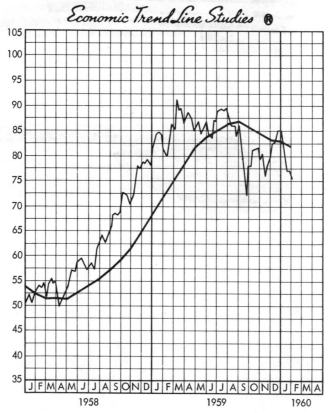

Economic TrendLine Studies ®

Source: From the book, *A Strategy of Daily Stock Market Timing for Maximum Profit*, by Joseph E. Granville, © 1960 by Prentice-Hall, Inc. Published by Prentice-Hall, Inc., Englewood Cliffs, New Jersey.

strengths. Technicians using the relative-strength approach have observed that those firms and industries displaying greatest relative strength in good markets (bull) also show the greatest weakness in bad markets (bear). These "relatively strong" firms could well have high betas.

When the stock-bond approach is used, the analyst opts for a higher proportion of stocks in the portfolio (relative to bonds) as the market moves upward, and a higher proportion of bonds (relative to stocks) as the market moves downward. In other words, he selects the security type with the most relative strength in the prevailing market. Levy has tested this procedure of switching between stocks and bonds and has concluded that the returns earned by a portfolio utilizing this technique outperform portfolios managed in a more naive manner— that is, by the "buy-and-hold strategy" of purchasing securities and then merely holding them regardless of any changes in the economic environment.[9]

[9]Robert A. Levy, "Random Walks: Reality or Myth," *Financial Analysts Journal*, November-December 1967, pp. 69-77.

PRICE-VOLUME ANALYSIS APPROACHES

Resistance-Support Charts

Earlier we discussed two well-known types of charts—point-and-figure and bar charts. There is a much newer variety of chart, whose avowed purpose is to detect resistance (areas of supply) as a stock's price goes up, and support (areas of demand) as a stock goes down. The chart is constructed to show, in a series of horizontal lines, the levels at which the stock in question has traded in the past. The levels are determined regardless of the volume at which the stock traded, but rather at those levels at which the stock traded most often—the more often, the longer the horizontal line. The hypothesis is that popular levels (longer lines) encountered by the stock in an upward move present resistance; and conversely, popular levels (longer lines) encountered by the stock in a downward move provide support. A specimen of this chart form is shown in Figure 15-12.

Price-Volume Bar Charting

When we discussed the role of bar charting, we saw that the emphasis of technicians using this chart form was generally on price behavior; however, we noted that volume information is often included on bar charts. Chartists, following the seminal Dow Theory, believe that volume goes with the price trend—that a volume increase with an upward move in prices is good, and a volume increase with a downward move in prices is bad. Furthermore, if volume decreases during a price drop, this is good (a drying up of supply), and if volume decreases during a price rise, this is bad (a drying up of demand). These statements represent traditional technical folklore. It would be interesting to test the statistical validity of these views.

Ying has conducted an empirical study of price-volume relationships. His results were:

1. A small volume is usually accompanied by a fall in price.
2. A large volume is usually accompanied by a rise in price.
3. A large increase in volume is usually accompanied by either a large rise in price or a large fall in price.
4. A large volume is usually followed by a rise in price.
5. If the volume has been decreasing consecutively for a period of five trading days, then there will be a tendency for the price to fall over the next four trading days.
6. If the volume has been increasing consecutively for a period of five trading days, then there will be a tendency for the price to rise over the next four trading days.[10]

Ying's conclusions seem to provide support for the traditionally held view, with

---

[10]Charles C. Ying, "Stock Market Prices and Volumes of Sales," *Econometrica*, July 1966, p. 676.

FIGURE 15-12
SAMPLE RESISTANCE & SUPPORT CHARTS

NEW INVENTION: RESISTANCE & SUPPORT CHARTS

Basically, there are two kinds of stock charts in use today: the *bar chart* and the *point-and-figure chart*. The more widely known bar chart is a graphic representation on a grid, of a stock's past price action on either a daily, weekly or monthly basis. Vertical bars show a stock's high, low and closing prices. (Some charts may show closing prices only). The volume of shares traded also appears as vertical lines at the bottom of the chart. Chart services such as *Trendline* and *Mansfield* fall into this category.

P & F charts came into being about 75 years ago. Adherents to this system of charting ignore the elements of time and volume and concentrate solely on price action. These are the charts that show strange-looking columns of X's moving to the right, corresponding to prices marked along the side of the chart. A stock moving in price from $40 to $50 without changing directions would appear as a column of ten X's. On a subsequent decline to $45, five corresponding X's would be entered in the next column on the right, and so on. Two well known P & F chart services are *Paflibe* and *Chartcraft*.

Early in 1970, a new kind of chart was introduced by Chart Service Institute (450 New England Bldg., Winter Park, Florida 32789) headed by Samuel F. Sipe, creator of the new chart. Its name, *Resistance & Support Charts,* implies just what it attempts to do—show where a stock moving upward may meet resistance (supply) and where a declining stock may find support (demand). Here are several samples:

Sample Resistance & Support Charts

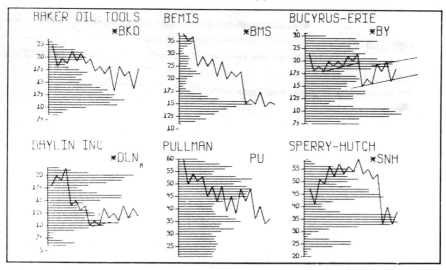

Many years of each stock's price movements were fed into a computer. The resulting horizontal lines drawn by the computer show at what levels in the past the stock has traded most often—irrespective of time and the volume of shares traded. Short lines, little activity; longer lines, greater activity. Superimposed over the horizontal lines is a graph of the stock's most recent action with little wiggles eliminated.

In theory, a stock might decline more swiftly through the shorter lines—where few investment decisions were made in the past—and find support at a cluster of long lines —where many investment decisions were made and may be made again. Conversely, a rising stock might move up through an area of short lines quite handily till it bumped into a "ceiling" of resistance at a group of long lines.

The charts appear to be useful by themselves. They could also serve as an adjunct to the other two kinds of charts. They are worth investigating.

Source: Yale Hirsch, *The 1971 Stock Traders Almanac* (Old Tappan, N.J.: The Hirsch Organization, 1970), p. 25.

one notable exception—number 5. That is, declining volume seems to be associated with price declines and thus would not be a bullish indicator.[11]

Other Tests,
Conclusions
and Summary

A number of tests have been conducted to obtain statistically reliable estimates of the worth of various technical trading strategies. Many of these tests fall into a body of literature called the random-walk theory. These will be discussed in some detail in Chaper 16.

Here we will report in a general fashion their key conclusions.[12] First, with respect to tests of mechanical trading rules (procedures that are strictly followed regardless of economic circumstances) and price-volume relationships, the results have been inconclusive because of different findings of different researchers using different procedures and different samples. Attempts to reconcile these differences have been difficult. Tests of possible relationships between price and short interests have been more conclusive. Generally, no significant relationship between stock prices and short interests were found. Finally, tests of odd-lot and advance-decline theories have detected very tentative and unconvincing results regarding their validity. Thus, in summary, these tests have given less than overwhelming support to the various technical theories examined to date, while at the same time not supporting random walk unequivocally.[13] There are several reasons for this.

First, some have questioned whether the tests have been performed on technical theories as they are actually used in practice.[14] To the extent that the tests accurately reflect the practice, the results may have some meaning. To the extent that they do not, the results and their implications are of dubious value. Second, only selected phases of technical analysis have been rigorously tested, and then only one at a time. It is possible that yet untested technical procedures will prove to have greater usefulness than those already examined. Furthermore, technicians very infrequently use only one indicator at a time, but rather use several in conjunction with one another.[15] Thus it is possible that tools found lacking when tested one at a time are useful when combined. This

---

[11]We are aware of at least one trading system that refines the analysis even further. It looks at *each* transaction in the stock and weights the direction of price changes (upticks and downticks) between transactions by the number of round lots associated with the price change (trade).

[12] This section draws heavily from a fine, nonmathematical review of tests of technical analysis by George E. Pinches, "The Random Walk Hypothesis and Technical Analysis," *Financial Analysts Journal*, March-April, 1970, pp. 104-10.

[13]Technical analysis should be thought of as an adjunct to fundamental analysis, not as its replacement.

[14]It should be pointed out that the same technical theories are often applied differently by different technical analysts. Therefore the success of the strategy is often dependent on the man rather than the method alone.

[15]Commercial investment services exist which combine numerous technical indicators into a composite index or diffusion index. There are problems, however, such as which indicators to select, how to combine them, and then how to weight them in the index. Finally, the validity of the index needs to be tested.

has not yet been empirically investigated. Random-walk theorists, however, feel that they have gathered sufficient evidence to relegate technical analysis to a position comparable to reading a crystal ball.

Questions and Problems

1. Explain the relationship of a basic law of economics and an underlying premise of technical analysis.

2. Dr. Knowitall of the Psychology Department at a large midwestern university claims he has a sound theoretical argument in favor of technical analysis. What do you think that argument is?

3. Assume that you are a statistician. Like every good statistician, you are extremely concerned with good sampling techniques. Comment on technical analysis from this point of view.

4. Since you are the top technical analyst in your firm, your boss has turned to you for an answer to a difficult question. He wants to know which one single indicator you think is the best, and why you think so. What is your answer?

5. What is the alleged purpose of technical market indicators? Why is this important?

6. What is meant by "breadth of the market"? How is it measured?

7. Explain (a) the logic behind, and (b) the method of measuring, either Barron's confidence indicator or odd-lot trading.

8. If short selling indicates that the investor expects the price of the shorted security to decline, why does the technician become optimistic as the short interest goes up?

9. What is the basic premise of analysts who use the odd-lot trading index?

10. If a stock sells for 60 and moves in the following pattern over a ten-day period—60, 60¼, 60¾, 60½, 61, 61½, 63, 62¼, 61¾, 60½—how many X's would be plotted if the investor used point-and-figure charting with a one-point chart and a three-point reversal spread?

11. If the investor used bar charting and the data in Question 10, how many bars would there be in his chart? Why is this different from the number of X's in Question 10?

12. Compare and contrast bar charting and point-and-figure charting.

13. What general price-volume relationships do researchers use to predict the trend of the market?

14. What implications, if any, do Levy's findings using the relative-strength criterion have for a buy-and-hold strategy?

15. Suppose the stock market has been declining. A technician is looking for signs of an upturn in the market. What sorts of reading should he or she be expecting from (a) breadth of the market, (b) volume of trading, (c) odd-lot trading, (d) short selling?

CHAPTER SIXTEEN

EFFICIENT MARKET THEORY

The primary aim of the text thus far has been to systematize the vast amount of publicly available information, both objective fact and subjective feeling, into a valuation framework so that one can reach a buy, sell, or hold decision. The methodology employed up until the preceding chapter is generally categorized as fundamental analysis, or fundamentalism. The more mystical approach discussed in Chapter 15 is called technical analysis. Our objective in this chapter is to review briefly these two approaches and then present yet a third theory of stock price behavior, one that had its origin in a voluminous body of literature generally lumped together under the label of the theory of random walk. In the process, we will explore this theory and explain the various statistical measures that have been employed to test its appropriateness or inappropriateness. Finally, we will discuss implications of random walk for both fundamental and technical analysis.

Fundamental and Technical Analysis

The reader will recall that in the fundamental approach, the security analyst or prospective investor is primarily interested in analyzing factors such as economic influences, industry factors, and pertinent company information such as product demand, earnings, dividends, and management, in order to calculate an intrinsic value for the firm's securities. He reaches an investment decision by comparing this value with the current market price of the security.

Technical analysts, or chartists, as they are commonly called, believe that they can discern patterns in price or volume movements, and that by observing and studying the past behavior patterns of given stocks, they can use this accumulated historical information to predict the future price movements in the security. Technical analysis, as we observed in the preceding chapter, comprises many different subjective approaches, but all have one thing in common—a belief that these past movements are very useful in predicting future movements.[1]

---

[1] The reader is encouraged to read, for an excellent treatment of the bar-chart and the point-and-figure approaches to technical analysis, Daniel Seligman's two excellent and somewhat cynical articles, "Playing the Market with Charts," *Fortune,* 65, No. 2 (February 1962), 118, and "The MYstigue of Point-and-Figure," *Fortune,* 65, No. 3 (March 1962), 113.

In essence, the technician says that it is somewhat an exercise in futility to evaluate accurately a myriad of detailed information as the fundamentalist attempts to do. He chooses not to engage in this type of activity, but rather to allow others to do it for him. Thus, after numerous analysts and investors evaluate this mountain of knowledge, their undoubtedly diverse opinions will be manifested in the price and volume activity of the shares in question. As this occurs, the technician acts solely on the basis of that price and volume activity, without cluttering his mind with all the detail that he feels is superfluous to his analysis. He also believes that his price and volume analysis incorporates one factor that is not explicitly incorporated in the fundamentalist approach— namely, the psychology of the market.

Random Walk

Can a series of historical stock prices or rates of return be an aid in predicting future stock prices or rates of return? This, in effect, is the question posed by the random-walk theory.

The empirical evidence in the random-walk literature existed before the theory was established. That is to say, empirical results were discovered first, and then an attempt was made to develop a theory that could possibly explain the results. After these initial occurrences, more results and more theory were uncovered. This has led then to a diversity of theories, which are generically called the theory of random walk.

A good deal of confusion resulted from the diversity of the literature; and only recently has there been some clarification of the proliferation of empirical results and theories.[2] Our purpose here is to discuss briefly the substantive differences among these theories; however, in the rest of this chapter, we will not be concerned with these distinctions, but rather we will deal with an impressionistic stereotype that will represent the substance if not the detail of this random walk model, perhaps more properly called the efficient market model.

The Efficient Market Hypothesis

It is advantageous to view the random-walk model or hypothesis as a special case of the more general efficient market model or hypothesis. In fact, one might more readily understand the distinctions and variations of the various forms of the more general efficient market hypothesis by viewing this hypothesis and its variations as lying on a continuum, with the so-called random-walk model at one end. In the following paragraphs we will briefly consider the three generally discussed forms of the efficient market hypothesis—namely, the weak form of the efficient market hypothesis, the semistrong form, and the strong form.

[2]Much of the material in this section was adapted from Eugene F. Fama, "Efficient Capital Markets: A Review of Theory and Empirical Work," *Journal of Finance*, 25, No. 2 (May 1970), 383-417; and Eugene F. Fama, "Random Walks in Stock Market Prices," *Financial Analysts Journal*, 21, No. 5 (September-October 1965), 55-59.

Weak Form

The weak form says that the current prices of stocks already fully reflect all the information that is contained in the historical sequence of prices. Therefore, there is no benefit—as far as forecasting the future is concerned—in examining the historical sequence of prices. This weak form of the efficient market hypothesis is popularly known as the random-walk theory. Clearly, if this weak form of the efficient market hypothesis is true, it is a direct repudiation of technical analysis. If there is no value in studying past prices and past price changes, there is no value in technical analysis. As we saw in the preceding chapter, however, technicians place considerable reliance on the charts of historical prices that they maintain.

In later sections of this chapter we will analyze statistical investigations of this weak form of the efficient market hypothesis.

Semistrong Form

The semistrong form of the efficient market hypothesis says that current prices of stocks not only reflect all informational content of historical prices but also reflect all *publicly available knowledge* about the corporations being studied. Furthermore, the semistrong form says that efforts by analysts and investors to acquire and analyze public information will not yield consistently superior returns to the analyst. Examples of the type of public information that will not be of value on a consistent basis to the analyst are corporate reports, corporate announcements, information relating to corporate dividend policy, forthcoming stock splits, and so forth.

In effect, the semistrong form of the efficient market hypothesis maintains that as soon as information becomes publicly available, it is absorbed and reflected in stock prices. Even if this adjustment is not the correct one immediately, it will in a very short time be properly analyzed by the market. Furthermore, even while the correct adjustment is taking place, it will not be possible for the analyst to obtain superior returns on a consistent basis. Why? Because the incorrect adjustments will not take place in a consistent manner. That is, sometimes the adjustments will be overadjustments and sometimes they will be underadjustments. Therefore an analyst will not be able to develop a trading strategy based on these quick adjustments to new publicly available information.

Tests of the semistrong form of the efficient market hypothesis have tended to provide support for the hypothesis.[3]

---

[3]See, for example, Eugene F. Fama et al., "The Adjustment of Stock Prices to New Information," *International Economic Review,* 10, No. 1 (February 1969), 1-21. Also see Myron S. Scholes, "The Market for Securities: Substitution vs. Price Pressure and the Effects of Information on Share Prices," *Journal of Business,* 45, No. 2 (April 1972), 179-211; Ray Ball and Phillip Brown, "An Empirical Evaluation of Accounting Income Numbers," *Journal of Accounting Research,* 6 (Autumn 1968), 159-78; and Ronald J. Jordan, "An Empirical Investigation of the Adjustment of Stock Prices to New Quarterly Earnings Information," *Journal of Financial and Quantitative Analysis,* 7, No. 4 (September 1973), 609-20.

Strong Form

To review briefly, we have seen that the weak form of the efficient market hypothesis maintains that past prices and past price changes cannot be used to forecast future price changes and future prices. In the paragraphs that follow we will review many of the tests that have been conducted to test the weak·form of the efficient market hypothesis, more commonly known as the random-walk theory. We have examined the semistrong form of the efficient market hypothesis, which says that publicly available information cannot be used consistently to earn superior investment returns. Several studies that tend to support the semistrong theory of the efficient market hypothesis were cited. Finally, the strong form of the efficient market hypothesis maintains that not only is publicly available information useless to the investor or analyst but *all information* is useless. Specifically, no information that is available, be it public or "inside," can be used to consistently earn superior investment returns.

The semistrong form of the efficient market hypothesis could only be tested indirectly—namely, by testing what happened to prices on days surrounding announcements of various types, such as earnings announcements, dividend announcements, and stock split announcements. To test the strong form of efficient market hypothesis, even more indirect methods must be used. For the strong form, as has already been mentioned, says that no type of information is useful. This implies that not even security analysts and portfolio managers who have access to information more quickly than the general investing public are able to use this information to earn superior returns. Therefore, many of the tests of the strong form of the efficient market hypothesis deal with tests of mutual fund performance. Shortly, we will review some of the findings of these tests of mutual-fund performance and in Chapter 20 we will examine them in greater depth.

Tests of the trading of specialists on the floor of the stock exchanges and tests of the profitability of insider trading suggest that the possibility of excess profits exists for these two very special groups of investors who can use their special information to earn profits in excess of normal returns.[4]

The strict form of the efficient market hypothesis states that two conditions are met: first, that successive price changes or changes in return are independent; and second, that these successive price changes or return changes are identically distributed—that is to say, that these distributions will repeat themselves over time. In a practical sense, this seems to imply that in a random-walk world, stock prices will at any time fully reflect all publicly available information, and furthermore, that when new information becomes available, stock prices will instantaneously adjust to reflect it. The reader will note that the random-walk theorist is not interested in price or return levels, but rather in the changes between successive levels.[5]

---

[4]See James H. Lorie and Victor Niederhoffer, "Predictive and Statistical Properties of Insider Trading," *Journal of Law and Economics,* 11 (1968), 35-53; and Scholes, "Market for Securities." It should be emphasized that these two examples of market inefficiencies represent very minor inefficiencies when compared with the market as a whole.

[5]Oftentimes one will read in the random-walk literature of percentage changes in the prices or returns themselves.

The more general efficient market model, when interpreted loosely, acknowledges that the markets may have some imperfections, such as transactions costs, information costs, and delays in getting pertinent information to all market participants; but it states that these potential sources of market inefficiency do not exist to such a degree that it is possible to develop trading systems whose expected profits or returns will be in excess of expected normal, equilibrium returns or profits. Generally, we define *equilibrium profits* as those that can be earned by following a simple buy-and-hold strategy rather than a more complex, mechanical system.[6] Thus we see that the random-walk model represents a special, restrictive case of the efficient market model.

THE EFFICIENT MARKET HYPOTHESIS AND MUTUAL FUND PERFORMANCE

It has often been said that large investors such as mutual funds perform better in the market than the small investor does because they have access to better information. Therefore it would be interesting to observe if mutual funds earned above-average returns, where these are defined as returns in excess of those that can be earned by a simple buy-and-hold strategy. The results of such an investigation would have interesting implications for the efficient market hypothesis.

As we shall see in Chapter 20, researchers have found that mutual funds do not seem to be able to earn greater net returns (after sales expenses) than those that can be earned by investing randomly in a large group of securities and holding them. Furthermore, these studies indicate, mutual funds are not even able to earn *gross* returns (before sales expenses) superior to those of the naive buy-and-hold strategy. These results occur not only because of the difficulty in applying fundamental analysis in a consistently superior manner to a large number of securities in an efficient market but also because of portfolio overdiversification and its attendant problems—two of which are high bookkeeping and administrative costs to monitor the investments, and purchase of securities with less favorable risk-return characteristics. Therefore it would seem that the mutual fund studies lend some credence to the efficient market hypothesis.

EMPIRICAL TESTS OF RANDOM WALK

Over the years an impressive literature has been developed describing empirical tests of random walk.[7] This research has been aimed at testing whether successive or lagged price changes are independent. In this section we will review briefly some of the major categories of statistical techniques that have been employed in this research, and we will summarize their major conclusions. These

[6]We will defer our discussion of such mechanical systems to a later section of this chapter.

[7]For an excellent collection of many of the early random-walk studies, see Paul H. Cootner, ed., *The Random Character of Stock Market Prices* (Cambridge, Mass: M.I.T. Press, 1967).

techniques generally fall into two categories: those that test for trends in stock prices and thus infer whether profitable trading systems could be developed, and those that test such mechanical systems directly.

Simulation Tests

Note Figures 16-1 and 16-2. These graphs were produced a few years ago as part of an interesting experiment performed by Harry Roberts. The

FIGURE 16-1

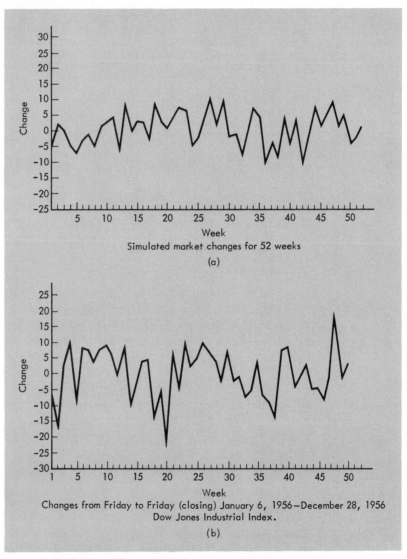

Simulated market changes for 52 weeks

(a)

Changes from Friday to Friday (closing) January 6, 1956—December 28, 1956
Dow Jones Industrial Index.

(b)

Source: Harry Roberts, "Stock Market Patterns and Financial Analysis: Methodological Suggestions," *Journal of Finance*, March 1959. Reprinted from *An Introduction to Risk and Return from Common Stocks* by Richard A. Brealey by permission of the M.I.T. Press, Cambridge, Massachusetts. Copyright 1969 by the Massachusetts Institute of Technology.

FIGURE 16-2 (a)
SIMULATED AND ACTUAL MARKET LEVELS

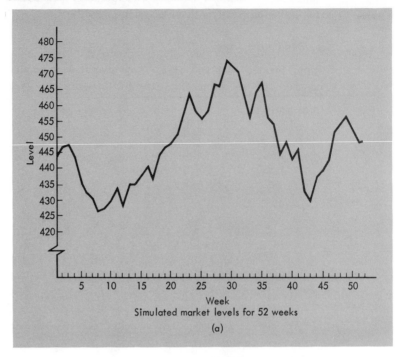

Simulated market levels for 52 weeks

(a)

essence of this experiment was to examine the appearance of the actual level of the Dow Jones index expressed both in levels and in terms of weekly changes, and to compare these graphs with a simulated set of graphs.[8] A series of price changes was generated from random-number tables and then these changes were converted to a graph (Figure 16-1 and 16-2) depicting levels of the simulated Dow Jones index.

The reader will note the similarity between panels (a) and (b) of Figure 16-1, and also the similarity between panels (a) and (b) of Figure 16-2. Both figures reveal the "head-and-shoulders" pattern that is often referred to in the chartist literature. Since these very similar patterns were observed, between the actual and the simulated series, the inference is that the actual results may well be the result of random stock price movements.

Serial-Correlation Tests

Since the random-walk theory is interested in testing for independence between successive price changes, correlation tests are particularly appropriate.

---

[8] Harry Roberts, "Stock Market Patterns and Financial Analysis: Methodological Suggestions," *Journal of Finance,* March 1959, pp. 1-10.

FIGURE 16-2 (b)
SIMULATED AND ACTUAL MARKET LEVELS

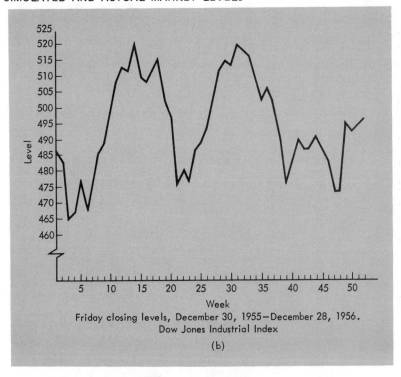

Friday closing levels, December 30, 1955—December 28, 1956.
Dow Jones Industrial Index

(b)

Source: Harry Roberts, "Stock Market Patterns and Financial Analysis:
Methodological Suggestions," *Journal of Finance*, March 1959. Reprinted
from *An Introduction to Risk and Return from Common Stocks* by
Richard A. Brealey by permission of the M.I.T. Press, Cambridge, Massachusetts. Copyright 1969 by the Massachusetts Institute of Technology.

These tests check to determine if price changes or proportionate price changes in
some future period are related. For example, we are interested in seeing if prices
in a period $t + 1$ are correlated to prices in the preceding period, period t. If in
fact prices are correlated, points plotted on a graph will tend to lie along a
straight line. Figures 16-3(a) and 16-3(b) depict such a relationship. Figure
16-3(a) implies that, on average, a price rise in period t is followed by a price rise
in period $t + 1$; Figure 16-3(b) implies that, on average, a price decline in period
$t + 1$ follows a price rise in period t; the former, then, implies a correlation
coefficient of close to +1, the latter a correlation coefficient of close to −1.
Figure 16-3(c), which does not appear to demonstrate any linear relationship in
the scatter diagram, implies close to a zero correlation coefficient. In other
words, the correlation coefficient can take on a value ranging from −1 to +1; a
positive number indicates a direct correlation, a negative value implies an inverse
relationship, and a value close to zero implies no relationship.

Table 16-1 reports the findings of one such test of serial correlation. As can

FIGURE 16-3
SCATTER DIAGRAMS TO "OBSERVE" CORRELATION

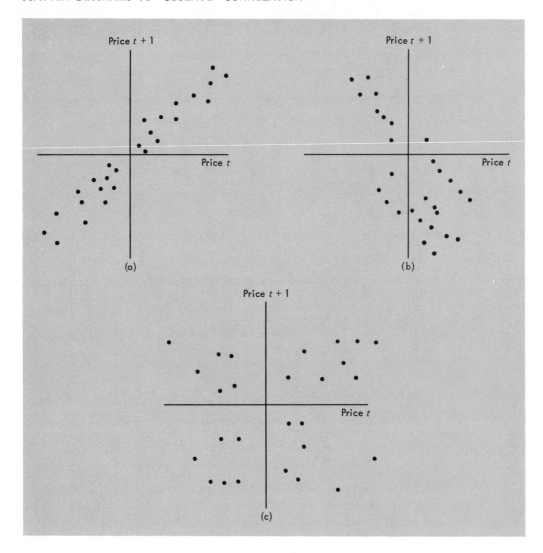

be seen in this table, no large departure from zero was found in these particular serial and lagged serial correlation coefficients in daily prices of the Dow Jones stocks. Similar results have been found using series of commodity prices, other individual stocks' prices, and price indexes.

Runs Tests

There is a potential problem, however, when one uses a correlation coefficient to evaluate the possibility of independence in a particular series. This

TABLE 16-1

CORRELATION COEFFICIENTS BETWEEN DAILY PRICE CHANGES
AND LAGGED PRICE CHANGES FOR EACH OF THE DOW JONES STOCKS

| | | | | | Lag, Days | | | | | |
Stocks	1	2	3	4	5	6	7	8	9	10
Allied Ch	.02	−.04	.01	−.00	.03	.00	−.02	−.03	−.02	−.01
Alcoa	.12	.04	−.01	.02	−.02	.01	.02	.01	−.00	−.03
Am Can	−.09	−.02	.03	−.07	−.02	−.01	.02	.03	−.05	−.04
Am T&T	−.04	−.10	.00	.03	.01	−.01	.00	.03	−.01	.01
Am Tob	.11	−.11	−.06	−.07	.01	−.01	.01	.05	.04	.04
Anacond	.07	−.06	−.05	−.00	.00	−.04	.01	.02	−.01	−.06
Beth Stl	.01	−.07	.01	.02	−.05	−.10	−.01	.00	−.00	−.02
Chrysler	.01	−.07	−.02	−.01	−.02	.01	.04	.06	−.04	.02
duPont	.01	−.03	.06	.03	−.00	−.05	.02	.01	−.03	.00
E Kodak	.03	.01	−.03	.01	−.02	.01	.01	.01	.01	.00
Gen Elec	.01	−.04	−.02	.03	−.00	.00	−.01	.01	−.00	.01
Gen Fds	.06	−.00	.05	.00	−.02	−.05	−.01	−.01	−.02	−.02
Gen Mot	−.00	−.06	−.04	−.01	−.04	.01	.02	.01	−.02	.01
Goodyr	−.12	.02	−.04	.04	−.00	−.00	.04	.01	−.02	.01
Int Harv	−.02	−.03	−.03	.04	−.05	−.02	−.00	.00	−.05	−.02
Int Nick	.10	−.03	−.02	.02	.03	.06	−.04	−.01	−.02	.03
Int Pap	.05	−.01	−.06	.05	.05	−.00	−.03	−.02	−.00	−.02
Johns Man	.01	−.04	−.03	−.02	−.03	−.08	.04	.02	−.04	.03
Owens Ill	−.02	−.08	−.05	.07	.09	−.04	.01	−.04	.07	−.04
Proct G	.10	−.01	−.01	.01	−.02	.02	.01	−.01	−.02	−.02
Sears Ro	.10	.03	.03	.03	.01	−.05	−.01	−.01	−.01	−.01
St Oil Cal	.03	−.03	−.05	−.03	−.05	−.03	−.01	.07	−.05	−.04
St Oil NJ	.01	−.12	.02	.01	−.05	−.02	−.02	−.03	−.07	.08
Swift Co	−.00	−.02	−.01	.01	.06	.01	−.04	.01	.01	.00
Texaco	.09	−.05	−.02	−.02	−.02	−.01	.03	.03	−.01	.01
Un Carbide	.11	−.01	.04	.05	−.04	−.03	.00	−.01	−.05	−.04
Unit Aire	.01	−.03	−.02	−.05	−.07	−.05	.05	.04	.02	−.02
US Steel	.04	−.07	.01	.01	−.01	−.02	.04	.04	−.02	−.04
Westg El	−.03	−.02	−.04	−.00	.00	−.05	−.02	.01	−.01	.01
Woolworth	.03	−.02	.02	.01	.01	−.04	−.01	.00	−.09	−.01
Averages	.03	−.04	−.01	.01	−.01	−.02	.00	.01	−.02	−.01

Source: R. Brealey, *An Introduction to Risk and Return from Common
Stock* (Cambridge, Mass: M.I.T. Press, 1969), p. 13, from Eugene F. Fama,
"The Behavior of Stock Market Prices," *Journal of Business*, January 1965,
pp. 34-105.

problem arises because correlation coefficients can be dominated by extreme
values. That is, an extremely large or extremely low value or two in the series
can unduly influence the results of the calculation used to determine the
correlation coefficient. To overcome this possible shortcoming, some researchers
have employed the runs test.

Runs tests ignore the absolute values of the numbers in the series and observe
only their sign. The researchers then merely count the number of runs—consecutive sequences of signs—in the same direction. For example, the sequence
−−−+0+ has four runs. Next, the actual number of runs observed is compared
with the number that are to be expected from a series of randomly generated
price changes. It has been found that when this is done, no significant differences
are observed. These results further strengthen the random-walk hypothesis.

Filter Tests

The empirical tests of random walk we have examined thus far have been aimed at testing directly whether successive price or return changes are in fact independent—or in statistical terms, that their serial-correlation coefficients are not statistically significantly different from zero. If this is so, then an inference can be made that stock price changes appear to be random, and therefore it would be extremely difficult to develop successful mechanical trading systems. Now we will discuss briefly another set of tests that examine the random-walk hypothesis from a different, but more direct, approach. Categorized as filter tests, they have been developed as direct tests of specific mechanical trading strategies. In other words, no inferences about such strategies need be made, for the approach is to examine directly the validity of specific systems.

One such test is based on the premise that once a movement in price has surpassed a given percentage movement, the security's price will continue to move in the same direction. Thus the following rule, which is similar to the famous Dow Theory:

> If the daily closing price of a security moves up at least X%, buy the security until its price moves down at least X% from a subsequent high, at which time simultaneously sell and go short. The short position should be maintained until the price rises at least X% above a subsequent low, at which time cover and buy.[9]

As the reader has undoubtedly observed, the selection of a high filter will cut down his number of transactions and will lead to fewer false starts or signals, but it will also decrease his potential profit because he would have missed the initial portion of the move. Conversely, the selection of a smaller filter will ensure his sharing in the great bulk of the security's price movement, but he will have the disadvantage of performing many transactions, with their accompanying high costs, as well as often operating on false signals.

As Table 16-2 shows, only when the filter was at its smallest did this mechanical procedure outperform a simple buy-and-hold strategy, and even then, only before transactions costs were considered. Similar tests of various other trading systems have yielded similar results, thus giving additional validity to the random-walk hypothesis.

Distribution Patterns

It is a rule of statistics that the sum or the distribution of random occurrences will conform to a normal distribution. Thus, if proportionate price changes are

[9]R. A. Brealey, *An Introduction to Risk and Return from Common Stocks* (Cambridge, Mass: M.I.T. Press, 1969), p. 25. Adapted from Eugene F. Fama and Marshal E. Blume, "Filter Rules and Stock Market Trading," *Journal of Business,* 39 (January 1966), 226-41.

randomly generated events, then their distribution should be approximately normal. When such a test was conducted, only very slight deviations from normality were noted.[10] See Figure 16-4 for verification of this point. The differences, as can be seen, are, first, the appearance of a greater than normal number of extremely large and extremely small values; and second; a more peaked distribution—that is, a deficiency of medium-sized changes. This type of distribution is a member of the stable Paretian family. Generally, the small differences between these two distributions are overlooked in empirical work.

WHAT THE RANDOM-WALK MODEL SAYS

Our generalization of the random-walk model, then, says that previous price changes or changes in return are useless in predicting future price or return changes. That is, if we attempt to predict future prices in absolute terms using only historical price-change information, we will not be successful.

Note that random walk says nothing more than that successive price changes are independent. This independence implies that prices at any time will on the average reflect the intrinsic value of the security. (Often the reader will find this intrinsic worth referred to as the present value of the stock's price, or its equilibrium value.) Furthermore, should a stock's price deviate from its intrinsic value because, among other things, different investors evaluate the available information differently or have different insights into future prospects of the firm, professional investors and astute nonprofessionals will seize upon the short-term or random deviations from the intrinsic value, and through their active buying-and-selling of the stock in question will force the price back to its equilibrium position.

WHAT THE RANDOM-WALK MODEL DOES NOT SAY

It is unfortunate that so many misconceptions of the random-walk model exist. It is, in point of fact, a very simple statement.[11]

The random-walk model says nothing about relative price movements—that is, about selecting securities that may or may not perform better than other securities. It says nothing about decomposing price movements into such factors as market, industry, or firm factors. Certainly, it is entirely possible to detect trends in stock prices after one has removed the general market influences or other influences; however, this in no way would refute the random-walk model, for after these influences have been removed, we will in fact be dealing with

[10]Eugene F. Fama, "The Behavior of Stock Market Prices," *Journal of Business,* 38 (January 1965), 34-105.

[11]Material in this section is in part adapted from C. W. J. Granger, "What the Random Walk Model Does NOT Say," *Financial Analysts Journal,* May-June 1970, pp. 91-93.

TABLE 16-2

AVERAGE ANNUAL RATES OF RETURN PER STOCK

Value of x	Return with Trading Strategy	Return with Buy-and-Hold Strategy	Total Transactions with Trading Strategy	Return with Trading Strategy, After Commissions
0.5%	11.5%	10.4%	12,514	−103.6%
1.0	5.5	10.3	8,660	− 74.9
2.0	0.2	10.3	4,784	− 45.2
3.0	−1.7	10.3	2,994	− 30.5
4.0	0.1	10.1	2,013	− 19.5
5.0	−1.9	10.0	1,484	− 16.6
6.0	1.3	9.7	1,071	− 9.4
7.0	0.8	9.6	828	− 7.4
8.0	1.7	9.6	653	− 5.0
9.0	1.9	9.6	539	− 3.6
10.0	3.0	9.3	435	− 1.4
12.0	5.3	9.4	289	2.3
14.0	3.9	10.3	224	1.4
16.0	4.2	10.3	172	2.3
18.0	3.6	10.0	139	2.0
20.0	4.3	9.8	110	3.0

Source: R.A. Brealey, *An Introduction to Risk and Return from Common Stocks* (Cambridge, Mass.: M.I.T. Press, 1969). From Fama and Blume, "Filter Rules and Stock Market Trading," *Journal of Business*, January 1966, pp. 226-41.

relative prices and not with absolute prices, which lie at the heart of the random-walk hypothesis.

In addition, it should be reemphasized that the empirical results came first, to be followed by theory to explain the results; therefore, discussions about a competitive market, or instantaneous adjustments to new information, or knowledgeable market participants, or easy access to markets, are all in reality not part of the random-walk model, but rather possible explanations of the results we find when performing our empirical investigations.

Also, there seems to be a misunderstanding by many to the effect that believing in random walk means that one must also believe that analyzing stocks, and consequently stock prices, is a useless exercise, for if indeed stock prices are random, there is no reason for them to go up or down over any period of time. This is very wrong. The random-walk hypothesis is entirely consistent with an upward or downward movement in price, for as we shall see, the hypothesis supports fundamental analysis and certainly does not attack it.

IMPLICATIONS OF RANDOM WALK FOR TECHNICAL AND FUNDAMENTAL ANALYSIS

The random-walk theory is inconsistent with technical analysis, or chartism.[12] Whereas random walk states that successive price changes are independent, the

[12]Specifically, random walk denies that a technical approach can be consistently successful over a long period of time.

FIGURE 16-4

DISTRIBUTIONS OF DAILY PRICE CHANGES OF SIX STOCKS,
SUPERIMPOSED ON A NORMAL DISTRIBUTION

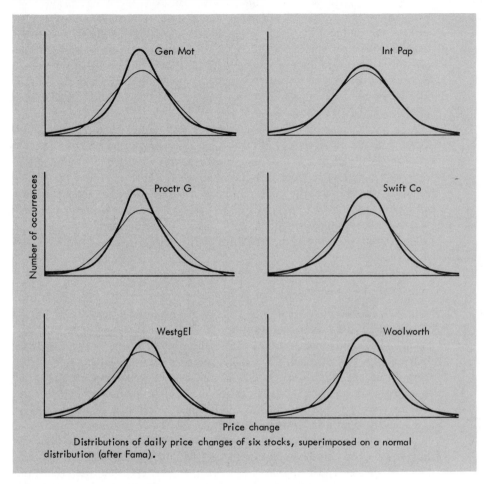

Distributions of daily price changes of six stocks, superimposed on a normal
distribution (after Fama).

Source: Eugene F. Fama, "The Behavior of Stock Market Prices," *Journal
of Business,* January 1965, pp. 34-105. Reprinted from *An Introduction to
Risk and Return from Common Stocks* by Richard A. Brealey by permission of the M.I.T. Press, Cambridge, Massachusetts. Copyright 1969 by
the Massachusetts Institute of Technology.

chartists claim that they are dependent—that is, that the historical price behavior
of the stock will repeat itself into the future, and that by studying this past
behavior the chartist can in fact predict the future. Random walk, through the
statistical testing discussed earlier in this chapter, directly opposes this line of
reasoning and relegates technical analysis to a curious position of mysticism,
seemingly completely unfounded on any substantive facts. The technicians,
however, deny the findings of researchers in this area by saying that the
statistical procedures employed in the literature of the past were too simple
to detect complex, historical price relationships.

The relationship between random walk and fundamental analysis is a bit more complex. First, random walk implies that short-run price changes are random about the true intrinsic value of the security. Thus we can see that it is the day-to-day or week-to-week price changes, and consequently return changes, that are random, and not the price levels themselves. Consequently, it is entirely possible while believing in random walk to believe also in the existence of an upward or downward drift in prices of individual securities over a longer period. In other words, random walk says nothing about trends in the long run or how price levels are determined; it speaks only of the phenomenon of short-run price-change independence.

As a result, what the random-walk theory really says to the fundamentalist operating in a random-walk world is that his fundamental analysis must be truly *exceptional* so that he can seize upon opportunities when security prices differ somewhat significantly from their intrinsic value. This means that the fundamentalist can be successful only in those instances when he either *possesses superior insight into the company's future prospects or possesses inside information.* It is clear even under random walk that such superior fundamental analysis will lead to superior profits for the astute security analyst or investor.

Functions of Astute Investors and Analysts in a Random-Walk Market

In a random-walk market, then, the functions of the analyst are (1) to determine the risk-return characteristics of stocks in the hope of occasionally coming across situations where his expectations differ markedly from those of the market as a whole, and (2) to make these risk-return combinations available to investors and investment counselors so they can construct portfolios with appropriate risk-return characteristics for their needs. The implications for the investor are (1) to plan on buying and holding the selected securities until he sees adequate reason for revising his portfolio, and (2) under normal conditions, to buy a well-diversified portfolio whose returns are likely to parallel those of the market. The former implication arises because of the empirical findings discussed already, and the latter because of the difficulty of outperforming the market portfolio in an efficient market.

Empirical Results of Technical Analysis

To date, little empirical work has been conducted in the area of technical analysis—certainly not nearly as much as has been done on random walk. What little has been done is not conclusive, nor are the results as consistent as those found in the random-walk literature. Most, if not all, chartist theories tested to date have yielded results that are not very reassuring to the chartist.

These negative chartist results can perhaps be defended. It is argued that the tests of various trading strategies that have been carried out thus far do not adequately simulate the behavior of the technical analysts that we meet in actual practice. The tests have been too simple, because they have been of one trading system or technical tool at a time, rather than testing various methods concurrently and then somehow weighing the results of the various tools and reaching a consensus decision.[13]

As for the empirical results of random walk, the chartists are not as concerned, for they state that either the tests employed are too simple or they are inappropriate. This latter reason refers to the point that most of the statistical methods employed in the random-walk literature assume that a linear relationship exists. If that assumption is inappropriate, then the methods and thus the results are also inappropriate.

Summary

There are three broad theories concerning stock price movements. The fundamentalists believe that by analyzing key economic and financial variables, they can estimate the intrinsic worth of the security and then determine what investment action to take. The technical or chartist school maintains that fundamental analysis is unnecessary; all that has to be done is to study historical price patterns and then decide how current price behavior fits into these. Since the technician believes that history repeats itself, he can then predict future movements in price based on the study of historical patterns. The random-walk school has demonstrated to its own satisfaction through empirical tests that successive price changes over short periods, such as a day, a week, or a month, are independent. To the extent that this independence exists, the random-walk theory directly contradicts technical analysis; and furthermore, to the extent that the stock markets are efficient in the dissemination of information and that they have informed market participants and the proper institutional setting, the random-walk school poses an important challenge to the fundamentalist camp as well.

If the markets are truly efficient, then the fundamentalist will be successful only when (1) he has inside information, or (2) he has superior ability to analyze publicly available information and gain insight into the future of the firm, and (3) he uses (1) and/or (2) to reach long-term buy-and-hold investment decisions.

The empirical evidence in support of the random-walk hypothesis rests primarily on statistical tests, such as runs tests, correlation analysis, and filter tests. The results have been almost unanimously in support of the random-walk hypothesis, the weak form of the efficient market hypothesis.

The technician has done very little if anything to defend any of the chartist theories against the onslaught of random walk. All chartists have done is to claim that their various systems work. In the future, if their theories are to have widespread acceptance in the academic community, it will be necessary for them to test and demonstrate that their methods can consistently outperform a simple buy-and-hold strategy. The fundamentalist needs also to show that his efforts in analyzing securities are successful enough—that is, earn enough more profit than does a simplified strategy—to justify his expenditure of time and effort.

[13]An excellent summary and review of the literature in this area can be found in George E. Pinches, "The Random Walk Hypothesis and Technical Analysis," *Financial Analysts Journal,* 26, No. 2 (March-April 1970), 104-10.

1. Discuss in abbreviated fashion the essence of fundamental and of technical analysis.

2. How do technicians and random-walk advocates differ in their view of the stock market?

3. What connection is there between the efficient market hypothesis and the studies of mutual-fund performance?

4. Explain the implications of the serial-correlation tests for (a) the random-walk theory, (b) technical analysis, and (c) fundamental analysis.

5. What are the implications of filter tests for (a) the random-walk theory, (b) technical analysis, and (c) fundamental analysis?

6. What sequence of events might bring about an "efficient market"?

7. Does the random-walk theory suggest that security price levels are random? Explain.

8. How is technical analysis generally regarded in the academic literature? Why? What do technical analysts have to say about this?

9. According to random-walk theorists, what does a chartist (technician) need to succeed in the stock market? A fundamentalist?

10. Mr. Elf Gnome is a well-known technical analyst (and authority on tarot). He shares an office with Randy Wok, MBA, who has recently joined the firm from Farout U. The market has been bearish for some time. Elf is keenly watching his charts for a signal of a rally on the upside.

    a. Which *three* of the more *reliable* technical indicators might Elf be watching closely? What *signal* would he expect to see from each that would suggest a reversal?

    b. Wok, amused by Gnome's antics, cried "Rubbish!" Why might he not trust Gnome's indicators? What might Gnome offer as a logical retort?

PORTFOLIO ANALYSIS:
SELECTION
AND
MANAGEMENT

VI

VI

Thus far we have dealt with the investment environment and the valuation of individual securities. The final section of the book deals with portfolio management.

The observed behavior of most investors suggests that they prefer to hold groups of securities rather than a single security that seems to offer the greatest expected return. The implication is that return is not the only feature of securities that concerns investors; they also seek to avoid risk.

The expected return on a portfolio is directly related to the returns on its component securities; however, it is not possible to know portfolio risk merely through knowing the riskiness of individual securities. Risk is not only individual but also interactive between securities.

The risk-return output of security analysis is the raw material for portfolio management. The remaining four chapters of this book deal systematically with problems of analyzing and selecting portfolios, revising them over time, and evaluating their performance in line with stated goals. Chapter 17 deals with modern methods for *analyzing* portfolios and packaging securities in such a way as to achieve diversification of risk. In Chapter 18 we examine both traditional and newer methods available to assist investors in *selecting* the best portfolio from those available, given the way in which they trade off risk and return. Chapter 19 provides an in-depth treatment of some well-known techniques for *revising* portfolios over time, as economic conditions alter and the prospects for individual securities change. The primary techniques discussed include the varied forms of formula planning.

The concluding chapter in the text, Chapter 20, explores the ways in which the performance of a portfolio might be *evaluated* over time. Performance evaluation in an empirical sense has reached its widest application in the area of investment companies. We take this opportunity to examine investment companies as an alternative to do-it-yourself portfolio management by looking at the performance results of these managed-money alternatives.

CHAPTER SEVENTEEN

PORTFOLIO ANALYSIS

Individual securities, as we have seen, have return-risk characteristics of their own. Portfolios, which are combinations of securities, may or may not take on the aggregate characteristics of their individual parts.

Portfolio analysis considers the determination of future risk and return in holding various blends of individual securities. In this chapter we shall analyze the range of possible portfolios that can be constituted from a given set of securities. We will show how the "efficiency" of each such combination can be evaluated.

**Traditional
Portfolio
Analysis**

Traditional security analysis recognizes the key importance of risk and return to the investor. However, direct recognition of risk and return in portfolio analysis seems very much a "seat-of-the-pants" process in the traditional approaches, which rely heavily upon intuition and insight. The results of these rather subjective approaches to portfolio analysis have, no doubt, been highly successful in many instances. The problem is that the methods employed do not readily lend themselves to analysis by others.

Most traditional methods recognize return as some dividend receipt and price appreciation over a forward period. But the return for individual securities is not always over the same common holding period, nor are the rates of return necessarily time-adjusted. An analyst may well estimate future earnings and a P/E to derive future price. He will surely estimate the dividend. But he may not discount the values to determine the acceptability of the return in relation to the investor's requirements.

In any case, given an estimate of return, the analyst is likely to think of and express risk as the probable downside price expectation (either by itself or relative to upside appreciation possibilities). Each security ends up with some rough measure of likely return and potential downside risk for the future.

Portfolios, or combinations of securities, are thought of as helping to spread risk over many securities. This is good. However, the interrelationship between securities may be specified only broadly or nebulously. Auto stocks are, for example, recognized as risk-interrelated with rubber stocks; utility stocks display defensive price movement relative to the market and cyclical stocks like steel; and so on.

This is not to say that traditional portfolio analysis is unsuccessful. It is to say that much of it might be more objectively specified in explicit terms.

Why Portfolios?   You will recall that expected return from individual securities carries some degree of risk. *Risk* was defined as the standard deviation around the expected return.[1] In effect, we equated a security's risk with the variability of its return. More dispersion or variability about a security's expected return meant the security was riskier than one with less dispersion.

The simple fact that securities carry differing degrees of expected risk leads most investors to the notion of holding more than one security at a time, in an attempt to spread risks by not putting all their eggs into one basket.[2] Diversification of one's holdings is intended to reduce risk in an economy in which every asset's returns are subject to some degree of uncertainty. Even the value of cash suffers from the inroads of inflation. Most investors hope that if they hold several assets, even if one goes bad, the others will provide some protection from an extreme loss.

DIVERSIFICATION

Efforts to spread and minimize risk take the form of diversification. The more traditional forms of diversification have concentrated upon holding a number of security types (stock, bonds) across industry lines (utility, mining, manufacturing groups). The reasons are related to inherent differences in bond and equity contracts, coupled with the notion that an investment in firms in dissimilar industries would most likely do better than in firms within the same industry. Holding one stock each from mining, utility, and manufacturing groups is superior to holding three mining stocks. Carried to its extreme, this approach leads to the conclusion that the best diversification comes through holding large numbers of securities scattered across industries. Many would feel that holding fifty such scattered stocks is five times more diversified than holding ten scattered stocks.

Most people would agree that a portfolio consisting of two stocks is probably less risky than one holding either stock alone. However, there is disagreement over the "right" kind of diversification and the "right" reason. The discussion that follows introduces and explores a formal, advanced notion of diversification

[1] Standard deviation is a risk surrogate, not a synonym for risk. For a review of some aspects of risk, see Fred D. Arditti, "Risk and the Required Return on Equity," *Journal of Finance*, March 1967, pp. 19-36.

[2] The reader should note that some advocate a concentration philosophy. This point of view stresses "putting all your eggs into one basket and keeping a sharp eye on the basket." See, for example, Gerald M. Loeb, *The Battle for Investment Survival* (New York: Simon & Schuster, 1965).

conceived by the genius of Harry Markowitz.[3] Markowitz's approach to coming up with good portfolio possibilities has its roots in risk-return relationships. This is not at odds with traditional approaches in concept. The key differences lie in Markowitz's assumption that investor attitudes toward portfolios depend exclusively upon (1) expected return and risk, and (2) quantifications of risk. And risk is, by proxy, the statistical notion of variance, or standard deviation of return. These simple assumptions are strong, and they are disputed by many traditionalists.[4]

Effects of Combining Securities

Although holding two securities is probably less risky than holding either security alone, *is it possible to reduce the risk of a portfolio by incorporating into it a security whose risk is greater than that of any of the investments held initially?* For example, given two stocks, X and Y, with Y considerably more risky than X, a portfolio composed of some of X and some of Y may be less risky than a portfolio composed exclusively of the less risky asset, X.

Assume the following about stocks X and Y:

	Stock X	Stock Y
Return (%)	7 or 11	13 or 5
Probability	.5 each return	.5 each return
Expected return (%)	9*	9†
Variance (%)	4	16
Standard Deviation (%)	2	4

*Expected return = (.5)(7) + (.5)(11) = 9
†Expected return = (.5)(13) + (.5)(5) = 9

It is clear that although X and Y have the same expected return, 9 percent, Y is riskier than X (standard deviation of 4 versus 2). Suppose that when X's return is high, Y's return is low, and vice versa. In other words, when the return on X is 11 percent, the return on Y is 5 percent; similarly, when the return on X is 7 percent, the return on Y is 13 percent. Question: Is a portfolio of some X and some Y in any way superior to an exclusive holding of X alone (has it less risk)?

Let us construct a portfolio consisting of two-thirds stock X and one-third

[3] Harry M. Markowitz, *Portfolio Selection: Efficient Diversification of Investments* (New York: John Wiley, 1959). Competing portfolio models are found in Henry A. Latané, "Investment Criteria—A Three-Asset Portfolio Balance Model," *Review of Economics and Statistics,* 45 (November 1963), 427-30; and Jack Hirschleifer, "Investment Decision under Uncertainty: Application of the State-Preference Approach," *Quarterly Journal of Economics,* 80 (May 1966), 252-77.

[4] Many other assumptions underlying portfolio analysis and the math to carry it off are still in dispute. For a look at how practitioners view some aspects of the Markowitz approach, see Frank E. Block, "Elements of Portfolio Construction," *Financial Analysts Journal,* May-June 1969, pp. 123-29.

stock Y. The average return of this portfolio can be thought of as the weighted-average return of each security in the portfolio; that is:

$$E_p = \sum_{i=1}^{N} X_i E_i$$

where:

E_p = expected return to portfolio
X_i = proportion of total portfolio invested in security i
E_i = expected return to security i
N = total number of securities in portfolio

Therefore:

$$E_p = (2/3)(9) + (1/3)(9) = 9$$

But what will be the range of fluctuation of the portfolio? In periods when X is better as an investment, we have $E_p = (2/3)(11) + (1/3)(5) = 9$; and similarly, when Y turns out to be more remunerative, $E_p = (2/3)(7) + (1/3)(13) = 9$. Thus, by putting part of the money into the riskier stock, Y, we are able to *reduce* risk considerably from what it would have been if we had confined our purchases to the less risky stock, X. If we held only stock X, our expected return would be 9 percent, which could in reality be as low as 7 percent in bad periods or as much as 11 percent in good periods. The standard deviation is equal to 2 percent. Holding a mixture of two-thirds X and one-third Y, our expected and experienced return will always be 9 percent, with a standard deviation of zero. We can hardly quarrel with achieving the same expected return for less risk. In this case we have been able to eliminate risk altogether.

The reduction of risk of a portfolio by blending into it a security whose risk is *greater than* that of any of the securities held initially suggests that it is not possible to deduce the riskiness of a portfolio simply by knowing the riskiness of individual securities. It is vital that we also know the interactive risk between securities!

The crucial point of how to achieve the proper proportions of X and Y in reducing the risk to zero will be taken up later. However, the general notion is clear. The risk of the portfolio is reduced by playing off one set of variations against another. Finding two securities each of which tends to perform well whenever the other does poorly makes more certain a reasonable return for the portfolio as a whole, even if one of its components happens to be quite risky.

This sort of hedging is possible whenever one can find two securities whose behavior is inversely related in the way stocks X and Y were in the illustration. Now we need to take a closer look at the matter of how securities may be correlated in terms of rate of return.

A CLOSER LOOK AT PORTFOLIO RISK

The risk involved in individual securities can be measured by standard deviation or variance. When two securities are combined, we need to consider their interactive risk, or *covariance*. If the rates of return of two securities move together, we say their interactive risk or covariance is positive. If rates of return are independent, covariance is zero. Inverse movement results in covariance that is negative. Mathematically, covariance is defined:

$$\text{cov}_{xy} = \frac{1}{N} \sum_{t=1}^{N} [(x_t - E_x)(y_t - E_y)] \qquad (17.2)$$

where the probabilities are equal and:

cov_{xy} = covariance between x and y
x_t = return on security x
y_t = return on security y
E_x = expected return to security x
E_y = expected return to security y
N = number of observations

Using our earlier example of stocks X and Y:

	Return	Expected Return	Difference
Stock X	7	9	−2
Stock Y	13	9	4
			Product −8
Stock X	11	9	2
Stock Y	5	9	−4
			Product −8

Covariance = ½[(7−9)(13−9) + (11−9)(5−9)] = ½[(−8) +(−8)] = $\frac{-16}{2}$ = −8

Instead of squaring the deviations of a single variable from its mean, we take two corresponding observations of the two stocks in question at the *same point in time*, determine the variation of each from its mean, and multiply the two deviations together. If whenever x is below its average, so is y, then for those periods each deviation will be negative, and their product consequently will be positive. Hence, we will end up with a covariance made up of an average of positive values, and its value will be large. Similarly, if one of the variables is relatively large whenever the other is small, one of the deviations will be positive and the other negative, and the covariance will be negative. This is true with our example above.

The *coefficient of correlation* is another measure designed to indicate the similarity or dissimilarity in the behavior of two variables. We define:

$$r_{xy} = \frac{cov_{xy}}{s_x s_y}$$

where:

r_{xy} = coefficient of correlation of x and y
cov_{xy} = covariance between x and y
s_x = standard deviation of x
s_y = standard deviation of y

The coefficient of correlation is, essentially, the covariance taken not as an absolute value but relative to the standard deviations of the individual securities (variables). It indicates, in effect, how much x and y vary together as a proportion of their combined individual variations, measured by $s_x s_y$. In our example, the coefficient of correlation is:

$$r_{xy} = -8/[(2)(4)] = -8/8 = -1.0$$

If the coefficient of correlation between two securities is -1.0, then a perfect negative correlation exists (r_{xy} cannot be less than -1.0). If the correlation coefficient is zero, then returns are said to be independent of one another. If the returns on two securities are perfectly correlated, the correlation coefficient will be $+1.0$, and perfect positive correlation is said to exist (r_{xy} cannot exceed $+1.0$).

Thus, correlation between two securities depends upon (1) the covariance between the two securities, and (2) the standard deviation of each security.

PORTFOLIO EFFECT IN THE TWO-SECURITY CASE

We have shown the effect of diversification on reducing risk. The key was not that two stocks provided twice as much diversification as one, but that by investing in securities with negative or low covariance among themselves, we could reduce the risk.[5] Markowitz's efficient diversification involves combining securities with less than positive correlation in order to reduce risk in the portfolio without sacrificing any of the portfolio's return. In general, the lower the correlation of securities in the portfolio, the less risky the portfolio will be. This is true regardless of how risky the stocks of the portfolio are when analyzed

[5]The approach adopted in this section was suggested in Fred Weston and Eugene Brigham, *Managerial Finance*, 6th ed. (New York: Holt, Rinehart & Winston, 1978), pp. 355-56.

in isolation. It is not enough to invest in *many* securities; it is necessary to have the *right* securities.

Let us conclude our two-security example in order to make some valid generalizations. Then we can see what three-security and larger portfolios might be like.

In considering a two-security portfolio, portfolio risk can be defined more formally now as:

$$S_p = \sqrt{X_a^2 S_a^2 + X_b^2 S_b^2 + 2X_aX_b\,(r_{ab}S_aS_b)} \qquad (17.3)$$

where:

S_p = portfolio standard deviation
X_a = percentage of total portfolio value in stock X
X_b = percentage of total portfolio value in stock Y
S_a = standard deviation of stock X
S_b = standard deviation of stock Y
r_{ab} = correlation coefficient of X and Y

Note: $r_{ab}S_aS_b = \text{cov}_{ab}$

Thus we now have the standard deviation of a portfolio of two securities. We are able to see that portfolio risk (S_p) is sensitive to (1) the proportions of funds devoted to each stock, (2) the standard deviation of each stock, and (3) the covariance between the two stocks. If the stocks are independent of each other, the correlation coefficient is zero $(r_{ab} = 0)$. In this case, the last term in Equation 17.3 is zero. Second, if r_{ab} is greater than zero, the standard deviation of the portfolio is greater than if $r_{ab} = 0$. Third, if r_{ab} is less than zero, the covariance term is negative, and portfolio standard deviation is less than it would be if r_{ab} were greater than or equal to zero. Risk can be totally eliminated only if the third term is equal to the sum of the first two terms. This occurs only if (1) $r_{ab} = -1.0$, and (2) the percentage of the portfolio in stock X is set equal to $X_a = S_b/(S_a + S_b)$.

To clarify these general statements, let us return to our earlier example of stocks X and Y. In our example, remember that:

	Stock X	Stock Y
Expected return (%)	9	9
Standard deviation (%)	2	4

We calculated the covariance between the two stocks and found it to be -8. The coefficient of correlation was -1.0. The two securities were perfectly negatively correlated.

What happens to portfolio risk as we change the total portfolio value invested in X and Y? Using Equation 17.3:

Stock X %	Stock Y %	Portfolio Standard Deviation
100	0	2.0
80	20	0.8
66	34	0.0
20	80	2.8
0	100	4.0

Notice that portfolio risk can be brought down to zero by the skillful balancing of the proportions of the portfolio devoted to each security. The preconditions were $r_{ab} = -1.0$ and $X_a = S_b/(S_a + S_b)$, or $.666 = 4/(2+4)$.

Changing the Coefficient of Correlation

What effect would there be using $a = 2/3$ and $b = 1/3$ if the correlation coefficient between stocks X and Y had been other than -1.0? Using Equation 17.3 and various values for r_{ab}, we have:

r_{ab}	Portfolio Risk
−0.5	1.34*
0.0	1.9
+0.5	2.3
+1.0	2.658

$$*S_p = \sqrt{(.666)^2 (2)^2 + (.334)^2 (4)^2 + (2)(.666)(.334)(-0.5)(2)(4)}$$
$$= \sqrt{1.777 + 1.777 - (.444)(4)} = \sqrt{1.777} = 1.34$$

If no diversification effect had occurred, then the total risk of the two securities would have been the weighted sum of their individual standard deviations:

$$\text{Total undiversified risk} = (.666)(2) + (.334)(4) = 2.658$$

Since the undiversified risk is equal to the portfolio risk of perfectly positively correlated securities ($r_{ab} = +1.0$), we can see that favorable portfolio effects occur only when securities are not perfectly positively correlated. The risk in a portfolio is less than the sum of the risks of the individual securities taken separately whenever the returns of the individual securities are not perfectly positively correlated; also, the smaller the correlation between the securities, the greater the benefits of diversification.

In general, some combination of two stocks (portfolios) will provide a smaller standard deviation of return than either security taken alone, so long as the correlation coefficient is less than the ratio of the smaller standard deviation to the larger standard deviation.

$$r_{xy} < \frac{s_a}{s_b}$$

Using the two stocks in our example:

$$-1.00 < \frac{2}{4}$$

$$-1.00 < +.50$$

If the two stocks had the same standard deviations as above but a coefficient of correlation of, for example, +.70, there would have been no portfolio effect, since +.70 is not less than +.50.

Graphic Illustration of Portfolio Effects

The various cases where the correlation between two securities ranges from -1.0 to $+1.0$ are shown in Figure 17-1. Return is shown on the vertical axis and risk is measured on the horizontal axis. Points A and B represent pure holdings (100 percent) of securities A and B. The intermediate points along the line segment AB represent portfolios containing various combinations of the two securities. The line segment identified as $r_{ab} = +1.0$ is a straight line. This line shows the inability of a portfolio of perfectly positively correlated securities to serve as a means to reduce variability or risk. Point A along this line segment has no points to its left. That is, there is no portfolio composed of a mix of our perfectly correlated securities A and B that has a lower standard deviation than the standard deviation of A. Neither A nor B can help offset the risk of the other. The wise investor who wished to minimize risk would put all his eggs into the safer basket, stock A.

The segment labeled $r_{ab} = 0$ is a hyperbola. Its leftmost point will not reach the vertical axis. There is no portfolio where $S_p = 0$. There is, however, an inflection just above point A that we shall explain in a moment.

The line segment labeled $r_{ab} = -1.0$ is compatible with the numerical example we have been using. This line shows that with perfect inverse correlation, it is possible to reduce portfolio risk to zero. Notice points L and M along the line segment AGB, or $r_{ab} = -1.0$. Point M provides a higher return than point L, while both have equal risk. Portfolio L is clearly inferior to portfolio M. All portfolios along the segment GLA are clearly inferior to portfolios along the segment GMB. Similarly, along the line segment APB, or $r_{ab} = 0$, segment BOP contains portfolios that are superior to those along segment PNA. Markowitz would say that all portfolios along all line segments are "feasible," but some are more "efficient" than others.

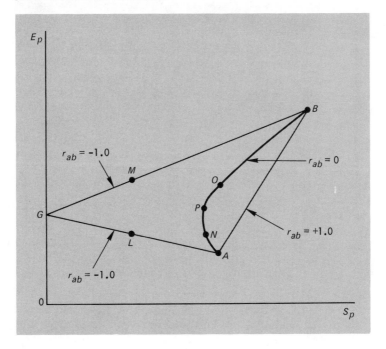

THE THREE-SECURITY CASE

Figure 17-2 depicts the graphics surrounding a three-security portfolio problem. Points *A, B,* and *C* each represent 100 percent invested in each of the stocks A, B, and C. The locus *AB* represents all portfolios composed of some proportions of A and B, the locus *AC* represents all portfolios composed of A and C, and so on. The general shape of the lines *AB, AC,* and *BC* suggests that these security pairs have correlation coefficients less than +1.0.

What about portfolios containing some proportions of all three securities? Point *G* can be considered some combination of A and B. The locus *CG* is then a three-security line. The number of such line segments representing three-security mixtures can be seen from Figure 17-3, where any point inside the shaded area will represent some three-security portfolio. Whereas the two-security locus is generally a curve, a three-security locus will normally be an entire region in the E_p, S_p diagram.

Consider for a moment three portfolio points within the E_p, S_p diagram in Figure 17-3. Call the portfolios $P1, P2,$ and $P3$. If we stop to think for a moment, the number of three-security portfolios is enormous—much larger than the number of two-security portfolios. Faced with the order of magnitude of portfolio possibilities, we need some shortcut to cull out the bulk of possibilities that are

FIGURE 17-2
THREE-SECURITY PORTFOLIOS

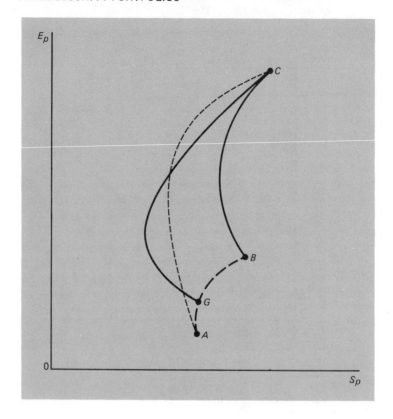

clearly nonoptimal. Looking at portfolios $P1$ and $P2$, we might observe the fact that since $P2$ lies to the left of and below $P1$, $P2$ is probably more appealing to the conservative investor, and $P1$ appeals to those willing to gamble a bit more. Would a rational investor select $P3$? We think not, since it involves a lower return than $P2$ but has the same risk. Thus we say that a portfolio is "inefficient" or dominated if some other portfolio lies directly above it in the risk-return space.

In general, an efficient portfolio has either (1) more return than any other portfolio with the same risk or (2) less risk than any other portfolio with the same return. In Figure 17-3 the boundary of the region identified as the curve LC dominates all other portfolios in the region. Portfolios along the segment AL represent inefficient portfolios, since they show increased risk for lower return. Each point on the segment AL is dominated by a more efficient portfolio directly above it on segment LC.

The actual determination of risk and return on various three-security portfolios such as $P1$, $P2$, and $P3$ requires that we extend our earlier formulas for two-asset portfolios.

FIGURE 17-3
REGION OF PORTFOLIO POINTS WITH THREE SECURITIES

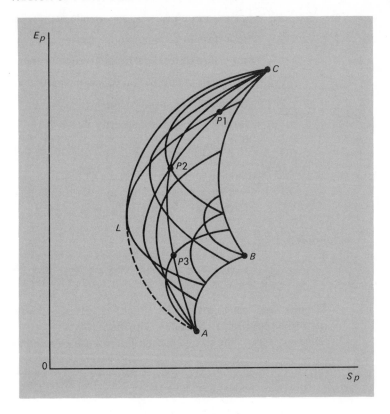

Risk-Return in a Three-Security Portfolio

The three-security case uses the same formulation for expected portfolio return indicated earlier in Equation 17.1:

$$E_p = \sum_{i=1}^{N} X_i E_i$$

The portfolio standard deviation depends as before upon the standard deviations of return for its components, their correlation coefficients, and the proportions invested.

$$S_p^2 = \sum_{i=1}^{N} \sum_{j=1}^{N} X_i X_j \, r_{ij} S_i S_j \tag{17.4}$$

where:

S_p^2 = portfolio variance; $\sqrt{S_p^2}$ = portfolio standard deviation

X_i = proportion of total portfolio invested in security i

X_j = proportion of total portfolio invested in security j

r_{ij} = coefficient of correlation between securities i and j

S_i = standard deviation of security i

S_j = standard deviation of security j

N = total number of securities in the portfolio

$\sum\limits_{i=1}^{N} \sum\limits_{j=1}^{N}$ = double summation sign means N^2 numbers are to be added together. Each number is obtained by substituting one of the possible pairs of values for i and j into the expression.

For $N = 2$:

$$S_p^2 = X_1 X_1 r_{1 \cdot 1} S_1 S_1 + X_1 X_2 r_{1 \cdot 2} S_1 S_2 + X_2 X_1 r_{2 \cdot 1} S_2 S_1 + X_2 X_2 r_{2 \cdot 2} S_2 S_2$$

The first and last terms can be simplified. Clearly, the return on a security is perfectly (positively) correlated with itself. Thus, $r_{1 \cdot 1} = 1$, as does $r_{2 \cdot 2} = 1$. Since $r_{2 \cdot 1} = r_{1 \cdot 2}$, the second and third terms can be combined. The result is:

$$S_p^2 = X_1^2 S_1^2 + X_2^2 S_2^2 + 2 X_1 X_2 r_{1 \cdot 2} S_1 S_2$$

Since $r_{ij} S_i S_j = \text{cov}_{ij}$, we can simplify further to:

$$S_p^2 = \sum_{i=1}^{N} \sum_{j=1}^{N} X_i X_j \text{cov}_{ij} \tag{17.5}$$

Example. Consider the following three securities and the relevant data on each:

	Stock 1	Stock 2	Stock 3
Expected return	.10	.12	.08
Standard deviation	10	15	5
Correlation coefficients:			
Stocks 1,2 = .3			
2,3 = .4			
1,3 = .5			

Question: What are portfolio risk and return if the following proportions are assigned to each stock? Stock 1 = .2, stock 2 = .4, and stock 3 = .4.

The portfolio return would be as per Equation 17.1:

$$E_p = \sum_{i=1}^{N} X_i E_i$$

or:

$$E_p = (.2)(.10) + (.4)(.12) + (.4)(.08) = (.10)$$

Using the formula for portfolio risk (Equation 17.5) and expanding it for $N = 3$, we get:

$$S_p^2 = X_1^2 S_1^2 + X_2^2 S_2^2 + X_3^2 S_3^2 + 2X_1 X_2 r_{1 \cdot 2} S_1 S_2 + 2X_2 X_3 r_{2 \cdot 3} S_2 S_3 + 2X_1 X_3 r_{1 \cdot 3} S_1 S_3$$

Substituting the appropriate values, we have:

$$S_p^2 = (.2)^2 (10)^2 + (.4)^2 (15)^2 + (.4)^2 (5)^2 + (2)(.2)(.4)(.3)(10)(15) +$$
$$(2)(.4)(.4)(.4)(15)(5) + (2)(.2)(.4)(.5)(10)(5)$$
$$= 4 + 36 + 4 + 7.20 + 9.6 + 4$$
$$= 64.8$$
$$S_p^2 = 8.0$$

What we have just done, through a process that is somewhat arduous (particularly without a calculating machine), is to calculate return and risk on a portfolio consisting of certain proportions of stocks 1, 2, and 3. This portfolio is simply one of many three-security combinations that would make up our risk-return space or diagram. Although we found that a portfolio consisting of 20 percent of stock 1 and 40 percent each of stocks 2 and 3 had an expected return of 10 percent and a standard deviation of 8.0, is it possible that a portfolio of different weights lies (1) directly above or (2) directly to the left of our example portfolio? Remember, if another portfolio met conditions (1) or (2) relative to our example portfolio, it would dominate, or be more efficient.

TRACING OUT THE EFFICIENCY LOCUS

Figure 17-4 is intended to enunciate the dilemma of determining efficient portfolios. Our example three-security portfolio is identified among a mass of feasible portfolios in the risk-return diagram. We can see that it is inefficient, since there are other portfolios that (1) exceed its return at the same level of risk (e.g., portfolio A), and (2) have lower risk for the same level of return (e.g., portfolio D).

FIGURE 17-4

FEASIBLE PORTFOLIOS IN A RISK-RETURN SPACE

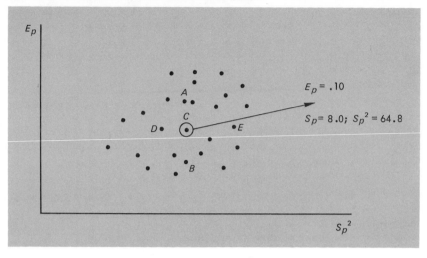

Harry Markowitz devised an ingenious computational model designed to trace out the efficiency locus and to identify the portfolios that make it up. In other words, he produced a scheme whereby large numbers of feasible portfolios could be ignored completely where they were dominated by more efficient portfolios.

In the calculations, Markowitz used the techniques of quadratic programming.[6] He assumed that one could deal with N securities or fewer. Using the expected return and risk for each security under consideration, and covariance estimates for each pair of securities, he is able to calculate risk and return for any portfolio made up of some or all of these securities. In particular, for any specific value of expected return, using the programming calculation he determines the least-risk portfolio. With another value of expected return, a similar procedure again yields the minimum-risk combination.

Figure 17-5 depicts the process. For return level E_i, the programming calculation indicates that point L_i is the least-risk portfolio at that level of return. Since no portfolio points lie to the left of L_i, it is the most efficient portfolio at that level of return. The locus of points from A to B is the end result of the tracing process. We have our efficiency locus, or so-called *efficient frontier*. The line AB divides the space between portfolios that are "possible" and those that cannot be attained ("impossible").

[6]For the interested reader, a graphic approach to the solution of the efficient frontier can be found in J. F. Weston and W. Beranek, "Programming Investment Portfolio Construction," *Analysts Journal* (May 1955), pp. 51-55.

FIGURE 17-5

SCHEMATIC SHOWING MARKOWITZ EFFICIENCY CALCULATION

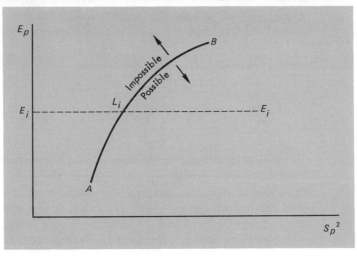

THE *N*-SECURITY CASE

Most real-world portfolio-analysis problems involve portfolios larger than three stocks, chosen from a universe of securities that itself is quite large. In dealing with two-stock portfolios drawn from a modest universe of three-stock candidates, the number of possible portfolio combinations is not overwhelming. Neglecting the proportions devoted to each security, the possible two-stock combinations from stocks D, E, and F are DE, DF, and EF. Now let us gauge the changes brought about by attempting to draw two-stock portfolios from an expanded universe of five candidates, D, E, F, G, and H. The possible combinations are DE, DF, DG, DH, EF, EG, EH, FG, FH, and GH. The mere addition of two new stock candidates causes the number of possible portfolios to rise from three to ten. In general, the number of possibilities increases far more rapidly than does the number of stocks to be considered. Mathematical analysis and the computer go a long way toward culling out the bulk of possible portfolios on the ground that they are clearly nonoptimal. The time required to calculate and discriminate by hand ten-stock portfolios, with varying percentages devoted to each security, taken from the almost two thousand stocks on the New York Stock Exchange alone boggles the mind!

The movement from three- to *N*-security portfolios not only highlights the enormousness of the calculation problem and the assistance provided by the Markowitz algorithm; it also points up the expansion of the data bits required for fundamental analysis. The inputs to the portfolio analysis of a set of *N* securities are (1) *N* expected returns, (2) *N* variances of return, and (3) $(N^2 - N)/2$ covariances. Thus the Markowitz calculation requires a total of $[N(N + 3)/2]$ separate pieces of information before efficient portfolios can be calculated and identified. To use the Markowitz technique for portfolios of the following size, we need the corresponding pieces of information (estimates):

Number of Securities	Bits of Information
10	65
50	1,325
100	5,150
1,000	501,500

It is easy to see that the Markowitz model is extremely demanding in its data needs and computational requirements. The intractable nature of these demands upon estimating time as well as computer time (and their related dollar costs) has perhaps limited the extent to which the Markowitz technique has been used directly for portfolios of any size. Further efficiencies in programming and computer technology will no doubt lower some of the impediments.

THE SHARPE INDEX MODEL

William Sharpe, who among others has tried to simplify the process of data inputs, data tabulation, and reaching a solution, has developed a simplified variant of the Markowitz model that reduces substantially its data and computational requirements.[7]

First, simplified models assume that fluctuations in the value of a stock relative to that of another do not depend primarily upon the characteristics of those two securities alone. The two securities are more apt to reflect a broader influence that might be described as general business conditions. Relationships between securities occur only through their individual relationships with some index or indexes of business activity. The reduction in the number of covariance estimates needed eases considerably the job of security-analysis and portfolio-analysis computation.[8] Thus the covariance data requirement reduces from $(N^2 - N)/2$ under the Markowitz technique to only N measures of each security as it relates to the index. In other words:

No. of Securities	Markowitz Covariances	Sharpe Index Coefficients
10	45	10
50	1,225	50
100	4,950	100
1,000	499,500	1,000
2,000	1,999,000	2,000

[7]W. F. Sharpe, "A Simplified Model for Portfolio Analysis," *Management Science*, 9 (January 1963), 277-93.

[8]One study in 1967 showed that, using then-current computers, a 150-security Markowitz calculation took ninety minutes to run, at a cost of $600.

However, some additional inputs are required using Sharpe's technique, too. Estimates are required of the expected return and variance of one or more indexes of economic activity. The indexes to which the returns of each security are correlated are likely to be some securities-market proxy, such as the Dow Jones Industrial Average or the Standard & Poor's 500 Stock Index. (The use of economic indexes such as gross national product and consumer price index was found by Smith to lead to poor estimates of covariances between securities.)[9] Overall, then, the Sharpe technique requires $3N + 2$ separate bits of information, as opposed to the Markowitz requirement of $[N(N+3)]/2$.

Sharpe's single-index model has been compared with multiple-index models for reliability in approximating the full covariance efficient frontier of Markowitz. The more indexes that are used, the closer one gets to the Markowitz model (where every security is, in effect, an index). The result of multiple-index models can be loss of simplicity and computational savings inherent in these shortcut procedures. The research evidence suggests that index models using stock price indexes are preferable to those using economic indexes in approximating the full covariance frontier. However, the relative superiority of single versus multiple-index models is not clearly resolved in the literature.[10]

Risk-Return and the Sharpe Model

Sharpe suggested that a satisfactory simplification would be to abandon the covariances of each security with each other security and to substitute information on the relationship of each security to the market. In his terms, it is possible to consider the return for each security to be represented by the following equation:

$$E_i = a_i + b_i I + c_i$$

where:

E_i = return on security i

a_i = intercept of a straight line or "alpha" coefficient

b_i = slope of straight line or "beta" coefficient

I = level of index (market)

c_i = error term with a mean of zero and a standard deviation which is a constant (e_i).

In other words, the return on any stock depends upon some constant (a), plus

---

[9]Keith V. Smith, "Stock Price and Economic Indexes for Generating Efficient Portfolios," *Journal of Business,* 42 (July 1969), 326-36.

[10]See K. J. Cohen and J. A. Pogue, "An Empirical Evaluation of Alternative Selection Models," *Journal of Business,* 40, No. 2 (April 1967), 166-93; and B. A. Wallingford, "A Survey and Comparison of Portfolio Selection Models," *Journal of Finance and Quantitative Analysis,* June 1967, pp. 85-106.

some coefficient (*b*), times the value of a stock index (*I*), plus a random component (*c*). Let us look at a hypothetical stock and examine the historical relationship between the stock's return and the returns of the market (index).

Figure 17-6 shows the historical relationship between the return on a hypothetical security and the return on the Dow Jones Industrial Stock Average (DJIA). If we mathematically "fit" a line to the small number of observations, we get an equation for the line of the form $y = a + bx$. In this case the equation turns out to be $y = 8.5 - .05x$.

FIGURE 17-6
SECURITY RETURNS CORRELATED WITH DJIA

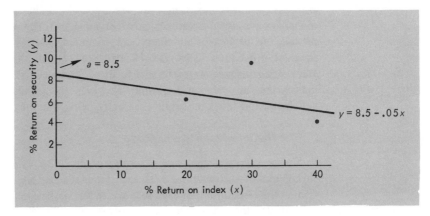

The equation $y = a + bx$ has two terms or coefficients that have become commonplace in the modern jargon of investment management. The "*a*" or intercept term is called by its Greek name "alpha". The "*b*" or slope term is referred to as the "beta" coefficient. The alpha value is really the value of *y* in the equation when the value of *x* is zero. Thus for our hypothetical stock when the return on the DJIA is zero the stock has an expected return of 8.5 percent ($y = 8.5 - .05(0)$). The beta coefficient is the slope of the regression line and as such it is a measure of the sensitivity of the stock's return to movements in the market's return. A beta of +1.0 suggests that, ignoring the alpha coefficient, a 1 percent return on the DJIA is matched by a 1 percent return on the stock. A beta of 2.5 would suggest great responsiveness on the part of the stock to changes in the DJIA. A 5 percent return on the index, ignoring the alpha coefficient, leads to an expected return on the stock of 12.5 percent (2.5 times 5 percent). While the alpha term is not to be ignored, we shall see a bit later the important role played by the beta term or beta coefficient.

The Sharpe index method permits us to *estimate* a security's return then by utilizing the values of *a* and *b* for the security and an estimate of the value of the index. Assume the return on the index (*I*) for the year ahead is expected to be 25 percent. Using our calculated values of $a = 8.5$ and $b = -.05$ and the estimate of the index of $I = 25$, the return for the stock is estimated as:

$$R_i = 8.5 - .05 \ (25)$$

$$R_i = 8.5 - 1.25$$

$$R_i = 7.25$$

The return on the security in question will be 7.25 percent if the return on the index is 25 percent, and if a and b are stable coefficients.

For portfolios, we need merely take the weighted average of the estimated returns for each security in the portfolio. The weights will be the proportions of the portfolio devoted to each security. For each security, we will require a and b estimates. One estimate of the index (I) is needed. Thus:

$$E_p = \sum_{i=1}^{N} X_i \ (a_i + b_i I) \tag{17.6}$$

where all terms are as explained earlier, except that E_p is portfolio return, X_i is the proportion of the portfolio devoted to stock i, and N is the total number of stocks.

The notion of security and portfolio *risk* in the Sharpe model is a bit less clear on the surface than are return calculations. The plotted returns and some key statistical relationships are shown below.[11]

Year	Security Return	Index Return
1	6%	20%
2	5	40
3	10	30
Average	= 7	30
Variance from average	= 7	100
Correlation coefficient	= −.189	
Coefficient of determination	= .0357	

Notice that when the index return goes up (down), the security's return generally goes down (up). Note changes in return from years 1 to 2 and 2 to 3. This reverse behavior accounts for our negative correlation coefficient (r).

The *coefficient of determination* (r^2) tells us the percentage of the variance of the security's return that is explained by the index (or market). Only about 3.5 percent of the variance of the security's return is explained by the index; some 96.5 percent is not. In other words, of the total variance in the return on the security ($\doteq 7$), the following is true:

Explained by index = 7 × .0357 = .25

Not explained by index = 7 × .9643 = 6.75

[11]It should be noted that such a small number of observations makes results prone to considerable error. The modest number of obervations is simply an illustrative convenience.

Sharpe noted that the variance explained by the index could be referred to as the *systematic risk.* The unexplained variance is called the residual variance, or *unsystematic risk.*

Sharp suggests that systematic risk for an individual security can be seen as:

$$\text{Systematic risk} = b^2 \text{ times (Variance of index)}$$

$$= b^2 s_I^2 \tag{17.7}$$

$$= (-.05)^2 (100)$$

$$= (.0025)(100)$$

$$= .25$$

$$\text{Unsystematic risk} = (\text{Total variance of security return}) \text{ minus (systematic risk)}$$

$$= e^2 \tag{17.8}$$

$$= 7.00 - .25$$

$$= 6.75$$

Then:

$$\text{Total risk} = b^2 s_I^2 + e^2$$

$$= .25 + 6.75 \tag{17.9}$$

$$= 7.0$$

And porfolio variance:

$$S_p^2 = \left[\left(\sum_{i=1}^{N} X_i b_i \right)^2 S_I^2 \right] + \left[\sum_{i=1}^{N} X_i^2 e_i^2 \right] \tag{17.10}$$

where all symbols are as above, plus:

S_p^2 = variance of portfolio return

S_I^2 = expected variance of index

e_i^2 = variation in security's return not caused by its relationship to the index

Table 17-1 demonstrates the calculation of the key statistics we have discussed in the preceding paragraphs.

Portfolio Analysis: An Expanded Example

We shall use an example to show how efficient portfolios might be constructed using the ideas of Markowitz and Sharpe. What follows is concerned with generating the efficient frontier. In Chapters 18 and 20 we will extend the

TABLE 17-1

CALCULATION OF ALPHA, BETA, AND RESIDUAL VARIANCE,
THE PALMER COMPANY

X = S&P 500 annual rate of return $\qquad$ n = number of observations

Y = Palmer Co. annual rate of return

Year	X	Y	XY	X^2	Y^2
1	.123	.1564	.0192	.0151	.0244
2	−.100	.1161	−.0116	.0100	.0135
3	.237	.5300	.1256	.0561	.2809
4	.108	.2944	.0318	.0116	.0867
5	−.083	.1277	−.0106	.0069	.0163
6	.028	.3103	.0087	.0008	.0963
7	.142	.5355	.0760	.0202	.2867
8	.173	.6008	.1039	.0299	.3610
9	−.130	.2736	−.0356	.0169	.0748
	$\Sigma X = .498$	$\Sigma Y = 2.9448$	$\Sigma XY = .3074$	$\Sigma X^2 = .1676$	$\Sigma Y^2 = 1.2406$
	$\bar{X} = .0553$	$\bar{Y} = .3272$			

Formulas:

Beta (the slope of the line):

$$b = \frac{n\Sigma XY - (\Sigma X)(\Sigma Y)}{n\Sigma X^2 - (\Sigma X)^2} = \frac{(9)(.3074) - (.498)(2.9448)}{(9)(.1676) - (.248)} = \underline{+1.03}$$

Alpha (the intercept of the line):

$$a = \bar{Y} - b\bar{X} = .3272 - [(1.03)(.0553)] = \underline{+.27}$$

Residual variance (unsystematic risk):

$$e^2 = \frac{\Sigma Y^2 - a\Sigma Y - b\Sigma XY}{n} = \frac{(1.2406) - (.27)(2.9448) - (1.0315)(.3074)}{9} = \underline{.0142}$$

Correlation coefficient (an estimate of the extent to which the rate of return on the stock is correlated to the rate of return on the market):

$$r = \frac{n\Sigma XY - (\Sigma X)(\Sigma Y)}{\sqrt{n\Sigma X^2 - (\Sigma X)^2}\sqrt{n\Sigma Y^2 - (\Sigma Y)^2}} = \frac{(9)(.3074) - [(.498)(2.9448)]}{\sqrt{[(9)(.1676)] - (.248)}\sqrt{[(9)(1.2407)] - (8.672)}}$$

$$= +.73$$

Coefficient of determination (the percentage of variation in the stock's rate of return explained by the variation in the market's rate of return). It is the square of the correlation coefficient:

$$r^2 = (.73)^2 = .53$$

example to include selection of a "best" portfolio and the monitoring of performance over subsequent time periods.

Listed in Table 17-2 are sixteen common stocks. Let us assume that these stocks have emerged from the security-analysis stage as candidates for portfolios. A uniform holding period was used in estimating risk and return for each stock. Specifically, each stock was examined as a possible holding for a one-year period. Our task here is to discover the efficient combination of these stocks.

TABLE 17-2

SIXTEEN STOCKS FOR PURCHASE OVER A ONE-YEAR
HOLDING HORIZON

1. General Electric	9. Burroughs Corporation
2. Dover Corporation	10. Continental Oil
3. Budd Company	11. Black & Decker
4. CIT Financial	12. Ethyl Corporation
5. Florida Power and Light	13. Associated Spring
6. Maytag Corporation	14. Foxboro Corporation
7. Pfizer	15. Xerox
8. Ingersoll-Rand	16. Mobil Oil Corporation

DATA NEEDED FOR EACH STOCK

Under the Markowitz system of portfolio analysis, we need three bits of information for each stock: (1) expected return for the holding period, (2) expected risk for the holding period, and (3) expected covariance for each pair of stocks. The Sharpe simplification would require (1) and (2), and for (3), covariance estimates for each stock relative to the market (index).[12] In addition, for the Sharpe model we need to estimate the return and variance on the index for the holding period.

For each of the sixteen stocks listed in Table 17-2, the regression coefficients (a, b) and the residual variance (e^2) were calculated from historical data. Historical annual rates of return on each stock were regressed against Dow Jones Industrial Average annual rates of return for a ten-year period. Table 17-3 shows

TABLE 17-3

XEROX CORP., PRICE, DIVIDEND, AND RATE-OF-RETURN
DATA

Year	Average Price per Share*	Dividend per Share	Holding Period Yield†
1	$ 3.50		
2	8.00	$.02	1.291
3	8.50	.04	.067
4	19.36	.07	1.286
5	33.50	.13	.737
6	51.36	.18	.539
7	65.50	.28	.281
8	85.25	.37	.307
9	93.00	.48	.096
10	97.68	.57	.057
11	90.50	.60	(.067)

*Yearly high plus yearly low, divided by two.

†E.g.: $E = \dfrac{(P_2 - P_1) + D_2}{P_1} = \dfrac{(8.00 - 3.50) + .02}{3.50} = 1.291$

[12] Markowitz data requirements for sixteen stocks would be 152, and Sharpe 50.

the rates-of-return data by year for Xerox shares. Figure 17-7 is a plot of Xerox rates of return compared with the DJIA, along with the equation for the line of best fit ($y = a + bx$).

Operations similar to those performed for Xerox common stock were completed for the remaining stocks in Table 17-2. Table 17-4 shows the a, b, and e^2 data for all sixteen stocks.

The most crucial input before beginning to generate efficient portfolios was an estimate of the return and risk on the index (DJIA) for the holding period (one year ahead). The return on the DJIA was estimated by projecting an estimated level of the index one year ahead plus expected dividends on the index. The return was estimated at 10.12 percent (.1012), with a risk (variance) of 2.27 percent (.0227).

These two estimates, return and risk on the DJIA, serve as the focal point for estimating return and risk for each stock and, therefore, portfolios of stocks. Recall that, using the Sharpe method, return and risk estimates for portfolios are

FIGURE 17-7
RATES OF RETURN ON XEROX STOCK VS.
DJIA RETURNS

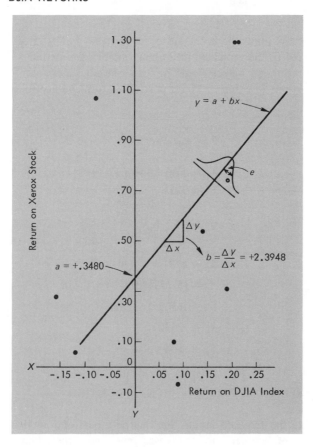

TABLE 17-4

STOCK PORTFOLIO CANDIDATES—a, b, and e² FOR SHARPE MODEL (USING DJIA AS THE INDEX)

Stock Name	a	b*	e²
General Electric	.0086	.3869	.0249
Dover Corporation	.2269	.7946	.0360
Budd Company	.0603	.2345	.0627
CIT Financial	.0450	.6807	.0416
Florida Power and Light	.0143	.6474	.0131
Maytag Corporation	.1848	.1317	.0354
Pfizer	.1454	.1384	.0291
Ingersoll-Rand	.0273	.5944	.0044
Burroughs Corporation	.1221	−.1338	.0197
Continental Oil	.0183	.7696	.0011
Black & Decker	.1952	−.0181	.0125
Ethyl Corporation	.1855	1.2873	.0747
Associated Spring	.1470	−.3971	.0502
Foxboro Corporation	.0098	.9149	.0781
Xerox	.3480	2.3948	.1238
Mobil Oil Corporation	.1475	.3879	.0071

*These betas are calculated using annual data for only ten years. This leads to several "negative" betas which are not likely in reality. The calculations would be more accurate using monthly or quarterly data.

built by using the a, b, and e^2 estimates for portfolios for individual stocks applied to the projected return-risk variables for the index. Let us examine what the return-risk values would be for a one-stock portfolio, using Xerox data and Equations 17.6 and 17.10 for portfolio return and portfolio risk:

$$E_p = \sum_{i=1}^{N} X_i (a_i + b_i I) \tag{17.6}$$

$$E_p = 1.00 \,[.348 + (2.3948)\,(.1012)]$$

$$E_p = .5902$$

$$S_p^2 = \left(\sum_{i=1}^{N} X_i b_i\right)^2 S_I^2 + \sum_{i=1}^{N} (X_i^2 \, e_i^2) \tag{17.10}$$

$$S_p^2 = b_i^2 S_I^2 + e_i^2 \text{ (since } X_i = 1.00)$$

$$S_p^2 = (5.735)\,(.0227) + .1238$$

$$S_p^2 = .1302 + .1238$$

$$S_p^2 = .2540$$

$$S_p = .504$$

GENERATING THE EFFICIENT FRONTIER

Using the required inputs, the Sharpe model and an IBM 360-65 computer, a series of "corner" portfolios was generated rather than an infinite number of points along the efficient frontier. The traceout of the efficient frontier connecting corner portfolios is shown in Figure 17-8. Table 17-5 shows the stocks and relative proportions invested at several corner portfolios. Point 1 is the first corner portfolio.

Corner portfolios are portfolios calculated where a security either enters or leaves the portfolio. Corner portfolio 1 is a one-stock portfolio. It contains the stock with the greatest return (and risk) from the set— in this case, Xerox. Notice in Table 17-5 that the return of 59 percent (.590) and the standard deviation or risk of 50.4 percent (.5040) for corner portfolio 1 (Xerox) correspond to the earlier calculations shown to arrive at these figures.[13] The computer program proceeds down the efficient frontier finding the corner portfolios. Corner portfolio 2 is introduced with the appearance of a second stock, Dover Corporation. Typically, the number of stocks increases as we move down the frontier until we reach the last corner portfolio—the one that provides the minimum attainable risk (variance) and the lowest return. To better understand what is happening between any two successive corner portfolios, examine numbers 9 and 10. Between these two, Budd Company stock makes its initial appearance.

The actual number of stocks entering into any given efficient portfolio is largely determined by boundaries, if any, set on the maximum and/or minimum percentage that can be devoted to any one security from the total portfolio. If

FIGURE 17-8
EFFICIENT FRONTIER CONNECTING "CORNER" PORTFOLIOS

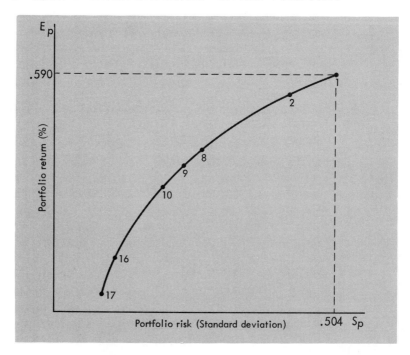

---

[13] The reader is invited to prove the expected return and standard deviation for corner portfolio 2, using Equations 17.6 and 17.10.

TABLE 17-5
SELECTED CORNER PORTFOLIOS

Security	Corner Portfolio Number					
	1	2	9	10	16	17
General Electric					.0485	.0508
Dover Corporation		.4320	.0785	.0607		
Budd Company				.0164	.0281	.0287
CIT Financial					.0060	.0059
Florida Power and Light					.0276	.0276
Maytag Corporation			.0895	.0833	.0608	.0608
Pfizer			.0764	.0824	.0734	.0734
Ingersoll-Rand					.1251	.1251
Associated Spring			.0668	.0699	.0797	.0797
Xerox	1.000	.5680	.0198	.0049		
Burroughs Corporation			.1130	.1336	.1567	.1567
Black & Decker			.2963	.2704	.2130	.2130
Ethyl Corporation			.0112	.0082	.1781	.1781
Mobil Oil Corporation			.2483	.2700		
Expected return	.5900	.4682	.1924	.1799	.1436	.1424
Expected standard deviation of return	.5040	.3356	.0602	.0561	.0511	.0510

these percentages (weights) are free to take on any values, the efficient frontier may contain one- or two-security portfolios at the low or high extremes. Setting maximum (upper-bound) constraints assures a certain minimum number of stocks held. The efficient frontier in Figure 17-8 had no constraints placed upon weights.

Summary

Investors are concerned not only with expected return on their investments but also their riskiness. However, knowing the riskiness of individual securities does not make it possible to deduce the riskiness of a portfolio of those securities. Using the ideas of Markowitz and others, we learned that portfolios are packages of securities that are constructed by knowing the return and risk on individual securities and also the *interactive* risk that exists *between* securities.

Our discussion in this chapter proceeded logically from the construction of feasible portfolios of two securities to bigger portfolios from a large universe of securities. We noted that some portfolios dominate others in that they provide either (1) the same return but lower risk, or (2) the same risk but higher return. These criteria distinguish portfolios that are feasible (possible) from those that are more "efficient."

The growing complexities of considering interactive risk in large populations of security candidates call for shortcuts in method. The ideas of Sharpe in simplifying the portfolio-analysis process were introduced. Finally, sixteen candidate stocks for analysis were packaged into feasible and efficient portfolios, using the Sharpe methodology and a large, highly efficient computer.

1. Can you think of any reasons for portfolios other than to minimize risk?
2. Stocks R and S display the following returns over the past two years:

Year	Stock	Return
19X3	R	10%
19X3	S	12
19X4	R	16
19X4	S	18

   a. What is the expected return on a portfolio made up of 40 percent R and 60 percent S?
   b. What is the standard deviation of each stock?
   c. What is the covariance of stocks R and S?
   d. Determine the correlation coefficient of stocks R and S.
   e. What is the portfolio risk of a portfolio made up of 40 percent R and 60 percent S?

3. Consider a third security, T, along with stocks R and S in question 2. Its return over the past two years was: 19X3, 16%; 19X4, 10%. Would this security provide any advantages in combination with stock R? with stock S? with stocks R and S together?

4. Stocks Y and Z display the following parameters:

	Stock Y	Stock Z
Expected return	15	20
Expected variance	9	16
Covariance$_{yz}$ = +8	+8	

Is there any advantage in holding some of Y and some of Z? Why?

5. Write out the expressions for expected return and standard deviation for the case of four securities.

6. Distinguish between a "feasible" and an "efficient" portfolio in the Markowitz sense.

7. How many inputs are needed for a portfolio analysis involving sixty securities if covariances are computed using (a) the Markowitz technique, or (b) the Sharpe index method?

8. Shown below are the returns on Xerox and the Standard & Poor's 500 Stock Index for the years 1966-70.

Year	Return on Xerox	Return on S&P 500
1966	.29	(.10)
1967	.31	.24
1968	.10	.11
1969	.06	(.08)
1970	(.07)	.03

    a. Plot the returns on Xerox vs. the S&P 500.

    b. Calculate the regression equation for the returns you have plotted (i.e. alpha, beta and residual variance) and draw the line on your graph.

    c. Indicate (1) total variance for Xerox, and (2) the proportions that are explained and not explained by the S&P 500.

    d. How do your answers to b and c compare to the a, b, and e^2 calculated in Table 17-4?

9.   The return on Xerox for 1971 was .177. The S&P return was .14. Would the return on Xerox for 1971 be suggested by your regression equation in 8b above? Why or why not?

10.   Refer to the sixteen-stock example in Table 17-4.

    a. Which stock would most likely be selected by an aggressive investor wishing to hold a single security and expecting the DJIA return next year to be (1) .10; (2) −.10?

    b. The last column in Table 17-4 shows the unexplained variance (risk) for each of the sixteen candidate stocks. What significance, if any, is there to stocks with the largest unexplained variances (e^2).

    c. Which stock would a defensive investor place all his money in if he wanted to minimize his risk when the DJIA was expected to decline 10 percent?

11.   Show that the portfolio return and variance for corner portfolio 2 in Table 17-5 are .468 and .336, respectively.

12.   Stock L has a standard deviation of 5 and stock M has a standard deviation of 15. The coefficient of correlation of the returns of stocks L and M is +.40. Is it possible to produce a portfolio of these two stocks that has a smaller standard deviation of return than either security taken alone? Why or why not?

13.   Following are data for several stocks. The data result from correlating returns on these stocks versus returns on a market index:

Stock	a	b	e^2
MNO	−.05	+1.6	.04
PQR	+.08	−0.3	.00
LUV	.00	+1.1	.10

    a. Which *single* stock would you prefer to own from a risk-return viewpoint if the market index were expected to have a return of +.10?

    b. What does the e^2 value for PQR imply? The a value for LUV?

PORTFOLIO
SELECTION

This chapter is concerned with the question, How should an investor go about selecting the one best portfolio to meet his needs? Or, more explicitly, how should an investor go about selecting which securities to purchase and how many dollars to invest in each?

First, we shall explore the more traditional means employed to provide investment counsel and portfolio selection, such as is preeminent among portfolio managers at the present time. Next, we will examine newer selection techniques suggested by Markowitz and others. The traditional and newer techniques will be compared to see how they interface and how each can help improve the other.

Traditional Portfolio Selection

Traditionally, portfolio selection has been viewed as an art form, perhaps even a craft. Portfolio men are builders. Much of their work has its roots in a kind of life-cycle, interior-decorator approach.

Security-portfolio selection must be preceded by attention to financial planning. Needs must be analyzed and provision made for such things as emergency savings, adequate insurance, and home ownership. For many people, basic living expenses, savings, insurance, and shelter costs absorb most, if not all, income and resources. For these people, direct securities investing may never be a practical reality. Others frequently plunge into the securities markets before paying proper attention to financial-planning prerequisites. The question of appropriate portfolio selection would presume that an investor had his financial house in order first.

As a kind of financial interior decorator, the portfolio manager picks securities to match the needs and objectives of the investor. For example, widows and retired persons will own bonds and other securities with good, safe income. Young persons in the early years of work will opt for capital growth rather than income. Quite frequently, portfolios are constructed according to whether they stress (1) income, (2) some income and modest appreciation, or (3) appreciation.

The approach to traditional portfolio building has strong roots in the ideas of Sauvain.[1] His approach recognizes several basic tenets: First, investors prefer larger to smaller returns from securities. Second, the way to achieve this goal is to take more risk. Third, the ability to achieve higher returns is dependent upon (1) the investor's judgment of risk, and (2) his ability to assume specific risks. Spreading money among many securities can reduce risk.

As components of risk, the theory recognizes specific types of risk and nonrisk factors bearing upon return—namely, interest-rate risk, purchasing-power risk, financial risks (including business, financial, and market risk), and nonrisk variables such as taxation and marketability. Portfolios are presumably constructed by employing securities associated with varying degrees of risk and nonrisk factors.[2]

The financial interior-decorator approach would follow a general sequence of steps. First, it is necessary to establish the minimum income an investor must have to avoid hardship under the most adverse economic conditions. Family and economic factors are the principal ingredients in the projection of nonsecurity income and expenses. Economic factors take into account the family balance sheet (assets and debts) and income statement (income and expenses). Family factors affect income and expenses through such variables as the number of dependents and their ages and health. Income-expense differentials establish the minimum income required from investments.

Second, the larger the principal in relation to the minimum investment income required, the greater the risk of loss of income that can be tolerated. Of course, one must plan for changes in principal available, changes in income from other sources, and changes in minimum expenses. Take two contrasting situations. In both, the principal amount is $100,000 and future expenses are forecast at $20,000 per year. Salary income is $18,000 in one case and only $8,000 in the other. In the former situation, the income "gap" is $2,000; the latter case has a gap of $12,000. A portfolio of $100,000 would have to yield 2 percent in the first case ($2,000/$100,000), and 12 percent ($12,000/$100,000) in the second. If good-quality bonds yield 8 percent, in the first example only $25,000 of principal is needed to provide the required income. This means that $75,000 can be invested at greater risk. The latter case requires (1) increasing outside income, and/or (2) reducing expenses, and/or (3) using some of the principal (assuming that additional principal is not forthcoming). Thus the future budgeting of nonsecurity income and expenses tells us the *degree of risks of principal or income the portfolio can tolerate.* Quality bonds and common stocks with generous, stable yields provide income with minimum risk to principal. The greater price volatility associated with stocks in general over bonds can be tolerated when required portfolio income is not substantial relative to principal available.

Third, the more nearly investment income generated at current rates of yield

---

[1] H. Sauvain, *Investment Management* (Englewood Cliffs, N.J.: Prentice-Hall, 1973).

[2] Our discussion emphasizes personal portfolio selection. Institutional portfolios are selected along similar lines. Basic security types are dictated very much by laws and regulations in addition to debt-equity ratios and term structure of debts.

on high-grade bonds meets the minimum investment-income requirements projected on an inflation basis, the greater is the ability to risk loss of purchasing power of investment income. It is necessary to see that nonsecurity income (such as salary) and expenses may rise at different rates as price-level changes occur. Should expenses rise more rapidly than nonsecurity income, income from fixed-income securities will make the investor vulnerable to rises in the price level. This would suggest a need for some defense against inflation, in the form of securities that provide larger dollar income at a higher price level. More relative emphasis might be placed upon convertible securities that can be purchased at modest premiums over investment and conversion value. The greater the need for inflation protection, the more the emphasis moves to straight common-stock commitments.

Overall, in this decision-making process, an investor would be assessing the kinds of risk and degree of each type that he can tolerate. In addition, the importance of nonrisk factors such as marketability and taxation would be assessed after the risk factors. The fundamental risk factors bear upon income and principal in constant (price-level-adjusted) dollars. Financial risk can be minimized by commitments to top-quality bonds. These securities, however, offer poor resistance to inflation. Stocks provide better inflation protection than bonds but are more vulnerable to financial risk. Good-quality convertibles may bridge the financial-risk-purchasing-power-risk dilemma. The problems associated with interest-rate risk suggest that maturity is of major concern. Short-term fixed-income securities offer greatest risk to income; long-term fixed-income securities offer greatest risk to principal.

What we emerge with from this approach is a series of *compromises* on risk and nonrisk factors after an investor has assessed the major risk categories he or she is trying to minimize. The final answer will be in terms of relative portfolio weights assigned to classes of securities—that is, bonds (quality, maturity), stocks (income, cyclical, growth), and hybrids (convertibles). The specific securities chosen will be the more attractive in each class as judged by security analysis. Not uncommonly, the dollar amounts devoted to each security or class of securities will be a simple equal allotment.

AN EXAMPLE OF TRADITIONAL PORTFOLIO SELECTION

Shown below is an illustration of portfolio construction along the lines discussed. The case involves making appropriate adjustments to a portfolio already in existence. The case and the accompanying "school" solution were taken from an examination for Chartered Financial Analysts. The answer provided was considered an acceptable approach to designing an investment plan for a widow with dependent children.[3] This solution was published several years ago. A solution today might be very different considering the investment environment.

---

[3]C. Stewart Sheppard et al., *Investment Management Decision Making* (Homewood, Ill.: Richard D. Irwin, 1970), pp. 228-29. The reader is referred to past CFA examinations published in the *Financial Analysts Journal* (various dates) for similar cases involving individuals in varied family and economic circumstances.

Mr. Jones, a professional man, has just died of a heart attack at age 55. He did not qualify for Social Security. He left an estate, after all taxes, of $230,000, $30,000 of which is in cash and $200,000 in securities, purchased recently on the advice of friends, as follows:

	Approximate Market Value
Stocks:	
International Business Machines Corp. (IBM)	$ 60,000
Polaroid Corporation	40,000
Sperry Rand	25,000
Bonds:	
St. Louis, Missouri, G.O.,* Aa 4 3/4s, 1989	
(par value $23,000)	21,000
Tenneco 6 1/4s, 10/1/92, B-rated convertible debentures;	
conversion price 30; market price of common 28 7/8;	
yield to maturity 5.58 (par value $50.00)	54,000
	$200,000

*General obligations.

The market price of these securities approximates cost.

In addition to the $230,000 as above, Mrs. Jones was left a comfortable home, subject to a $10,000 mortgage, with monthly payments of $150 remaining for ten years. She has a fully paid new automobile. Mrs. Jones also has $6,000 in Series E, U.S. savings bonds, which she has held since her marriage during the Korean War.

Mrs. Jones is 53 and enjoys good health. She has four daughters, ages 13, 15, 17, and 18. The girls are expected to attend college. Mrs. Jones has a college education, and if she obtained a teaching certificate, which would require attending college for one semester, she would be able to earn about $6,000 annually by teaching part-time in the public schools for nine months each year.

Living costs of the Jones family have been approximately $30,000 annually in the past. They live in a midwestern city of approximately 60,000 population. It is estimated that attendance at a state university for each girl will run about $2,500 per academic year.

Mrs. Jones has worked out a rough estimate of current monthly expenses on a pared-down basis. These amount to $1,500 per month, excluding income taxes.

Mrs. Jones strongly desires to leave the estate intact for her children and grandchildren.

Question

Design an investment plan, and show how you would implement this plan, with specific suggestions as to individual security issues or types of securities. Your investment plan should carry Mrs. Jones through her retirement years.

Suggested Solution

The first step in designing an investment plan for Mrs. Jones is to consider her present state of affairs:

1. Four dependents—ranging in ages from 13 to 18—all want to attend college.
2. Mrs. Jones is in good health and has medical insurance.
3. Mrs. Jones expects to work and thereby supplement her annual income by $6,000.
4. Minimum investment-income requirements:

Minimum-expense budget	$1,500/mo.	$18,000/yr.
Income from other sources	500/mo.	6,000/yr.
Amount required from investments	$1,000/mo.	$12,000/yr.

This shows her "normal" expense requirements; it does not take into consideration the amount she will require for college expenses once her daughters begin college. I have assumed that all four girls will go to college for four years. The first will begin in the fall of this year. College expenses for Mrs. Jones will be as follows (assuming $2,500 per year per daughter):

Year	Annual Amount	No. of Daughters in School	Age of Mrs. Jones
1	$2,500	1	53
2	5,000	2	54
3	7,500	3	55
4	7,500	3	56
5	5,000	2	57
6	5,000	2	58
7	2,500	1	59
8	2,500	1	60
9	2,500	1	61

Thus her minimum-expense budget will reach a peak of $25,500 ($18,000 normal expense and $7,500 college expense) by year 3. It will return to $16,200 by year 11. Thus her income requirements from her investments will be as follows:

Year	Normal Expenses	No. of Dependents	College	Income from Teaching	Required from Investments
1	$18,000	4	$2,500	$6,000	$14,500
2	18,000	4	5,000	6,000	17,000
3	18,000	4	7,500	6,000	19,500
4	18,000	4	7,500	6,000	19,500
5	18,000	3	5,000	6,000	17,000
6	18,000	2	5,000	6,000	17,000
7	18,000	2	2,500	6,000	14,500
8	18,000	1	2,500	6,000	14,500
9	18,000	1	2,500	6,000	14,500
10	18,000	—	—	6,000	12,000
11	16,200	—	—	6,000	10,200

Inflation should also be considered. I have assumed that the effects of inflation on Mrs. Jones's plans will be partially offset by an increase in her teaching salary.

Now we must consider Mrs. Jones's assets:

	Market Value
Stocks	$125,000
Bonds	75,000
U.S. savings bonds	6,000
Cash	30,000
Total	$236,000

Summary of Mrs. Jones's needs:

1. Income from investments must range from $14,500 in year 1 to a peak of $19,500 in year 4, and level off at $10,200 from year 11 until Mrs. Jones retires in year 14 at the age of 65.
2. She expects all girls to attend college.
3. The mortgage on her home will mature in year 11, reducing her need for income from investments to $10,200.
4. When Mrs. Jones retires in year 14, I assume that her Social Security and teacher's pension will provide her about $250 monthly; then, at that time her money needs will be as follows:

Minimum-expense budget	$16,200
Income from other sources	3,000
Minimum income from investments	$13,200

Based on her income requirements, Mrs. Jones's needs would be comfortably met by liquidating her persent holdings and investing the proceeds in high-quality current-coupon corporate bonds, which are now yielding about 7½ percent. Thus:

$$\$236,000 \times 7.5\% = \$17,700$$

This would cover her expenses in the next two years and enable her to save almost enough to cover her needs for the following two years. Thereafter, she would be home free.

I have not suggested tax-exempts for Mrs. Jones, because considering her expenses and exemptions, she does not appear to be in a high enough tax bracket to warrant tax exemption.

Now, the plan above is one extreme; it would meet her immediate needs, but I don't suggest it because it would provide her no protection against inflation—purchasing-power risk.

Rather, I would suggest the following: Aim for a balanced portfolio consisting of high-grade bonds and high-grade stocks, such as the following:

	Amount	Percent	Est. Income
Current-coupon bonds	$120,000	51	$9,000 @ 7½%
Common stocks	110,000	47	3,300 @ 3%
Cash	6,000	2	300 @ 5%

I would sell the St. Louis, Missouri, G.O.'s and put this money into a higher-yielding, taxable current-coupon bond. In her tax bracket, municipals would not be attractive. I would probably keep the Tenneco 6¼ convertible debentures for the present—the current yield is reasonably attractive and the conversion premium is only about 12 percent—but I would consider this part of the equity portfolio. I would also sell the U.S. savings bonds and purchase current-coupon corporates.

I would divide my common-stock participation between growth stocks and income stocks, approximately as follows:

Growth stocks	40%	$ 44,000
Income stocks	60%	66,000
		$110,000

I would diversify the growth stocks over five names and the income stocks over seven names—thus providing some diversification, but not overdiversifying. I would sell Polaroid and IBM down to an $8,500 position and add names such as Eastman Kodak, Merck, and International Telephone to the list of growth stocks. I would sell Sperry Rand—I don't believe it offers enough quality for Mrs. Jones.

For the income stocks, I would use some utilities, oil stocks, and food stocks and make use of convertible debentures.

Now, in order to make up the difference in income between the $14,500 to $19,500 Mrs. Jones will require over the next few years and the approximately $12,600 this portfolio will generate, I suggest Mrs. Jones draw from the principal of the account. I have provided $6,000 cash that she can draw on to satisfy the gap for the next couple of years. By that time the portfolio should have appreciated sufficiently so that she can draw the funds she needs over the next several years without reducing the fund significantly below the initial amount.

This program accomplishes the following:

1. It enables Mrs. Jones to meet her current needs in the next few critical years, when her expenses will reach their peak.
2. It enables her to maintain a high standard of living without seriously dissipating her capital.
3. It will enable her to leave the funds essentially intact when she passes away—in fact, depending on the success of the common-stock selection, the portfolio might show some fine gains.
4. It provides her protection against long-term inflation.

Naturally, as Mrs. Jones gets older and her needs change—particularly when she reaches retirement—this policy should be reviewed. At retirement, the bond portion of the account may have to be stepped up to offset her loss of income.

Any investment policy should be subject to constant, objective review as the needs of the client change.

A New Look at Risk and Investor Preferences

Our examination of the theory behind Markowitz-type diversification re-revealed the substance behind the determination of an efficient frontier, or locus of portfolio opportunities. The issue now is, How should investors (analysts) choose a "best" option on the efficient frontier?

Our central vehicle for attacking this problem is the satisfaction an investor receives from investment opportunities. Our assumption has been that risk-return measures on portfolios are the main determinants of an investor's attitude toward them. We need to look closely at the manner in which risk affects preference.

Utility functions, or indifference curves, are normally used to represent someone's preferences. Let us invent a set of preferences or indifference curves for a hypothetical investor, as displayed in Figure 18-1. For the moment, we will make no pretense that this indifference "map" depicts any real investor any of us may know. This investor (call him M) has indifference curves that are parallel to one another and linear. The higher a curve, the more desirable the situations lying along it. Each curve carries equal satisfaction along its length. We have

FIGURE 18-1
INDIFFERENCE MAP FOR HYPOTHETICAL INVESTOR

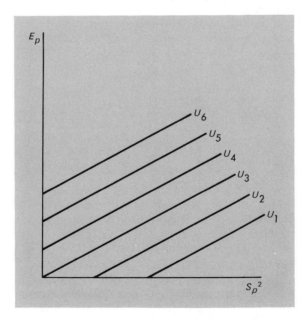

labeled the indifference (utility) curves from 1 to 6 in order of increasing desirability. M's problem is to find the feasible portfolio tangent to the best attainable (highest) indifference curve (line). If we combine the efficient frontier with the family of indifference curves, as in Figure 18-2, we can see how M might solve his problem. Point *B* is his "best" portfolio, since (1) it is efficient, and (2) at that point, the frontier will be tangent to the indifference curve (line).

Since most investors would be expected to seek more return for additional risk assumed, utility or indifference curves (lines) are positively sloped. Figure 18-3 depicts a set of indifference curves (lines) for a risk lover. His indifference curves are negative sloping and convex toward the origin. With the risk averter, the lower the S_p^2 of his portfolio, the happier he is; the risk lover is happier the higher the level of S_p^2.[4]

The degree of slope associated with indifference curves will indicate the degree of risk aversion for the investor in question. A sort of aggressive versus conservative risk preference is shown in Figures 18-4 and 18-5. The conservative investor (Figure 18-4) requires large increases in return for assuming small increases in risk; the more aggressive investor will accept smaller increases in return for large increases in risk. Both dislike risk, but they trade off risk and return in different degrees.

FIGURE 18-2
INDIFFERENCE MAP AND EFFICIENT FRONTIER FOR
HYPOTHETICAL INVESTOR

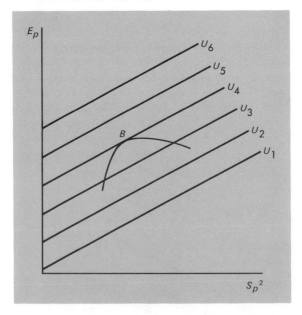

[4]It might be noted that if an efficient frontier were drawn on Figure 18-3, the only point of tangency with the risk lover's indifference curves would be at the upper-right point of the frontier. This point contains one security and follows the risk lover's maxim or putting all one's eggs into a single basket.

FIGURE 18-3
RISK-LOVER INDIFFERENCE CURVES

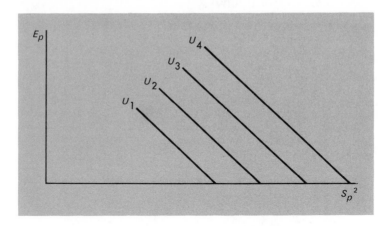

Although differences may occur in the slope of indifference curves, they are assumed to be positive sloping for most rational investors. A more important question is whether indifference curves are curves and not straight lines as depicted so far.

Does different utility accrue to given increments of return? For example, the utility received from $100,000 may or may not be worth twice that received

FIGURE 18-4
RISK-FEARING INVESTOR'S INDIFFERENCE CURVES

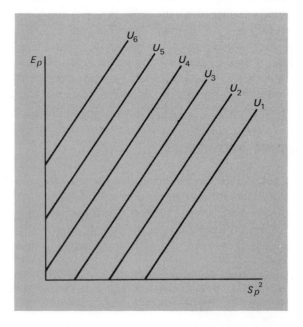

FIGURE 18-5

LESS-RISK-FEARING INVESTOR'S
INDIFFERENCE CURVES

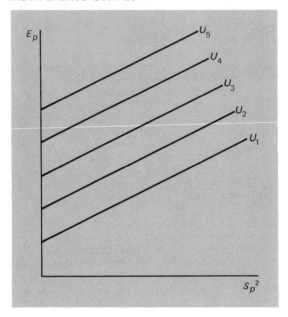

from $50,000. In effect, in Figure 18-6 we can see three different slopes to an indifference or utility curve (line). Curve *A* depicts increasing marginal utility, curve *B* constant utility, and curve *C* diminishing marginal utility. While constant marginal utility (straight line) would suggest that, say, doubling return doubles utility (satisfaction), increasing marginal utility means that increasingly larger satisfaction is to be found from the same increase in return. Increasing marginal utility would suggest the case of the inveterate gambler who is, in fact, a risk lover. Curve *C*, diminishing marginal utility, is probably identified with the way most investors behave. In sum, constant marginal utility of return means that an investor is risk-neutral; decreasing marginal utility means that he is risk-averse; increasing marginal utility suggests that he likes risk.

BORROWING AND LENDING

We have yet to introduce borrowing and lending as strategies available to the investor.[5] Lending is best thought of as an investment in a riskless security. This security might be a savings account, Treasury bills, or even high-grade commercial paper. Borrowing can be thought of most easily as using margin. In Markowitz's analysis, borrowing would be equivalent to *issuing* a riskless security.

[5] The development of capital-market theory is traceable largely to William Sharpe, "Capital Asset Prices: A Theory of Market Equilibrium under Conditions of Risk," *Journal of Finance*, September 1964, pp. 425-42.

FIGURE 18-6
VARIOUS MARGINAL-UTILITY CURVES

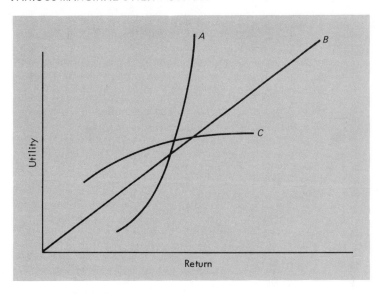

Borrowing and lending options transform the efficient frontier into a straight line. Figure 18-7 shows the standard efficient frontier *ABCD*. Assume that an investor can lend at the rate of $E_L = .05$, which represents the passbook rate on a savings account. We view such an investment as riskless ($S_p^2 = 0$), since the principal amount on deposit can be retrieved at any time without loss. Hence the point E_L represents a risk-free investment ($E_p = .05; S_p^2 = 0$). The investor

FIGURE 18-7
EFFICIENT FRONTIER WITH INTRODUCTION OF LENDING

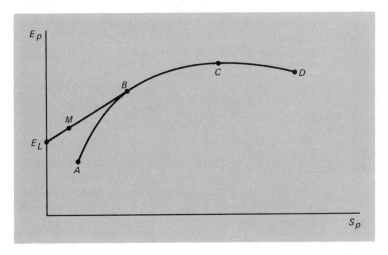

could place all or part of his funds in this riskless asset. If he placed part of his funds in the risk-free asset and part in one of the portfolios of risky securities along the efficient frontier, what would happen? He could generate portfolios along the straight-line segment $E_L B$.

Let us examine the properties of a given portfolio along the straight-line segment $E_L B$. Consider point B on the original efficient frontier $ABCD$ where, say, E_p = .10 and S_p = .06. If we placed one-half of available funds in the risk-less asset and one-half in the risky portfolio, B, the resulting combined risk-return measures for the mixed portfolio, M, can be found from Equations 18.1 and 18.2:

$$E_p = XE_r + (1 - X)E_L \qquad (18.1)$$

where:

E_p = expected return to portfolio

X = percentage of funds invested in risky portfolio

$(1 - X)$ = percentage of funds invested in riskless asset

E_r = expected return on risky portfolio

E_L = expected return on riskless asset

and:

$$S_p = XS_r \qquad (18.2)$$

where:

S_p = expected standard deviation of the portfolio

X = percentage of funds invested in risky portfolio

S_r = expected standard deviation on risky portfolio

For our example, the risk-return measures for portfolio M are:

$$E_p = (\tfrac{1}{2})(.10) + (\tfrac{1}{2})(.05) = .075$$
$$S_p = (\tfrac{1}{2})(.06) + (\tfrac{1}{2})(.00) = .03$$

The result indicates that our return and risk have been reduced. All points between E_L and B can be similarly determined using Equations 18.1 and 18.2. As stated, the locus of these points will be a straight line.

Introduction of the possibility of borrowing funds will change the shape of our efficient frontier in Figure 18-7 to the right of point B. In borrowing, we consider the possibilities associated with total funds invested being enlarged through trading on the equity.

Consider three cases. If we assume that X is the percentage of investment wealth or equity placed in the risky portfolio, then where $X = 1$, investment wealth is totally committed to the risky portfolio. Where $X < 1$, only a fraction of X is placed in the risky portfolio, and the remainder is lent at the rate E_L. The third case, $X > 1$, signifies that the investor is borrowing rather than lending. It may be easier to visualize this by rewriting Equation 18.1 as follows:

$$E_p = XE_r - (X - 1)E_B \qquad (18.3)$$

where all terms are as in 18.1 and the new term, E_B, is the borrowing rate. For simplicity, the borrowing rate and lending rate are assumed to be equal ($E_L = E_B$), or 5 percent. The first component of Equation 18.3 is the gross return made possible because the borrowed funds, as well as the original wealth or equity, are invested in the risky portfolio. The second term refers to the cost of borrowing on a percentage basis. For example, $X = 1.25$ would indicate that the investor borrows an amount equal to 25 percent of his investment wealth. This is equivalent to a margin requirement of 80 percent ($X = 1/$Margin requirement). His *net* return on his investment wealth would become:

$$E_p = (1.25)(.10) - (0.25)(.05) = .1125$$

The associated risk would become:

$$S_p = XS_r = (1.25)(.06) = .075$$

Hence the levered portfolio provides increased return with increased risk.

SEPARATION THEOREM

The introduction of borrowing and lending has given us an efficient frontier that is a straight line thoughout. Figure 18-8 shows the new efficient frontier, $E_L BG$. Point B now represents the optimal combination of risky securities. The existence of this combination simplifies our problem of portfolio selection. The investor need only decide how much to borrow or lend. No other investments or combination of investments available is as efficient as point B. The decision to purchase B is the investment decision. The decision to buy some riskless asset (lend) or to borrow (leverage the portfolio) is the financing decision.

These conditions give rise to what has been referred to as the *separation theorem*. The theorem implies that all investors, conservative or aggressive, should hold the same mix of stocks from the efficient set. They should use borrowing or lending to attain their preferred risk class.[6] This conclusion flies in the face of more traditional notions of selection of portfolios. Traditional

---

[6]W. F. Sharpe, *Portfolio Theory and Capital Markets* (New York: McGraw-Hill, 1970), p. 70.

FIGURE 18-8

EFFICIENT FRONTIER WITH INTRODUCTION OF BORROWING
AND LENDING

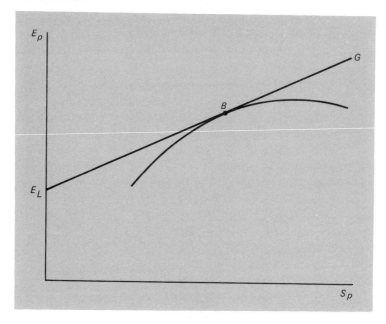

portfolio-building rules would construct certain types of portfolios for conservative clients and others for investors who are more daring. This analysis suggests that both types of investors should hold identically risky portfolios. Risk levels are then achieved through financing.

Portfolio Selection Example

Our example in Chapter 17 is extended here. Figure 17-8 was a traceout of the efficient frontier. Figure 18-9 introduces borrowing and lending, which makes the efficient frontier a straight line. The borrowing and lending rate of 5 percent is the one-year rate on Treasury securities.[7]

The optimal stock portfolio is corner portfolio 9.[8] Corner portfolios to the left of 9 (10 to 17) can be made more "efficient" by choosing 9 plus partial lending. Portfolios to the right of 9 (1 to 8) are similarly dominated by 9 plus some amount of borrowing.

The desired risk level would be achieved through lending or borrowing (the financing decision). The translation of security proportions for corner portfolio

---

[7]Many would use the higher rate on high-grade commercial paper.

[8]The "best" portfolio is probably the market itself. However, transaction costs may effectively prevent its use. The optimal portfolio may well lie between 8 and 9, or 9 and 10. This can be determined mathematically. Since we avoided introducing this mathematical solution, portfolio 9 is an approximation of the optimal stock portfolio.

FIGURE 18-9

EFFICIENT FRONTIER WITH BORROWING-LENDING LINE

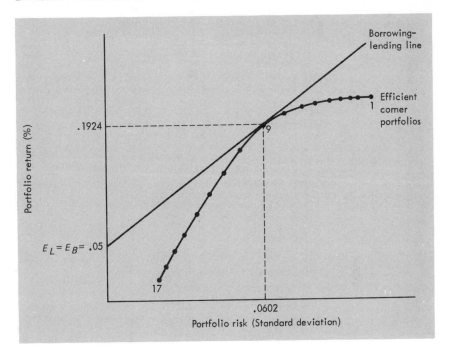

9 into actual dollars and numbers of shares is shown in Table 18-1. A hypothetical sum of about $1 million was assumed. The total is slightly more, because of certain rounding operations.[9]

Significance of Beta in the Portfolio

Sharpe notes that proper diversification and the holding of a sufficient number of securities can reduce the unsystematic component of portfolio risk to zero by averaging out the unsystematic risk of individual stocks. What is left is systematic risk which, because it is determined by the market (index), cannot be eliminated through portfolio balancing. Thus the Sharpe model attaches considerable significance to systematic risk and its most important measure the *beta coefficient* (b).

According to the model the risk contribution to a portfolio of an individual stock can be measured by the stock's beta coefficient. The market index will have a beta coefficient of +1.0. A stock with a beta of, for example, +2.0 indicates that it contributes far more risk to a portfolio than a stock with, say, a

[9] Some proportions were modestly altered to enable purchase of round lots as nearly as possible. The savings in transaction costs (brokerage fees) and resulting increased return should be weighed against any added risk.

TABLE 18-1

STOCK PORTFOLIO FOR ONE-YEAR HOLDING PERIOD

Company	(1) Stock Price	(2) No. Shares	(3) Proportions*	(4) Market Value [(1) × (2)]	(5) Beta†
Associated Spring	32 5/8	2,100	.067	68,000	−.397
Burroughs Corp.	128 1/2	880	.113	113,080	−.134
Black & Decker	73 1/2	4,000	.296	294,000	−.018
Dover Corp.	49 1/4	1,600	.079	78,800	.794
Ethyl Corp.	23	500	.011	11,500	1.287
Maytag	34 7/8	2,600	.090	90,675	.132
Mobil Oil Corp.	55 3/4	4,500	.248	250,875	.388
Pfizer	38	2,000	.076	76,000	.138
Xerox	116	170	.020	19,720	2.395
			1.000	1,002,650	.196

*Proportions are those shown for corner portfolio 9 in Table 17-5.

†Beta coefficients are taken from Table 17-4. The portfolio beta is the weighted average of the betas of the component securities (proportions multiplied by respective betas and summed), or 196.

beta of +.05. Stocks with negative betas are to be coveted, since they help reduce risk beyond the unsystematic level.

Since efficient portfolios eliminate unsystematic risk, the riskiness of such portfolios is determined exclusively by market movements. Risk in an efficient portfolio is measured by the portfolio beta. Table 18-1 indicates the beta coefficients of each stock in the portfolio that was chosen from the efficient frontier. The beta for the portfolio is simply the weighted average of the betas of the component securities. Corner portfolio 9 has a beta less than +.2, which suggests that is has a sensitivity far below the +1.0 attributed to the market. If this portfolio is properly diversified (proper number of stocks and elimination of unsystematic risk), it should move up or down about one-fifth (.2) as much as the market. Such a low sensitivity or beta suggests a conservative portfolio. Should the market move up over the holding period, corner portfolio 9 will be expected to advance only modestly. However, a market decline should find this portfolio falling in value only slightly.

BETA IN STOCK SELECTION

It is easy to see the central role played by the beta coefficient in the determination of expected return and risk for stocks as well as portfolios.

Some analysts have proposed using beta coefficients to approach the problem of stock selection. In this approach, the outlook for the market is assessed. Portfolios are constructed by optimizing beta coefficients in line with the market outlook. For example, if the market is expected to advance in the future, portfolios would be constructed containing stocks with beta coefficients that give maximum return. Such stocks would also carry high risks when the beta coefficients are large. A beta of +1.0 would indicate a stock with "average" volatility relative to the market. A beta of +2.0 would mean that if the market return was forecast as 10 percent, the stock would have an estimated return of 20 percent (excluding the value of alpha).

Should the outlook suggest a market decline, stocks with large positive beta coefficients might be sold short. Stocks with negative betas would provide resistance to the market downtrend. Suppose the forecast is for a 10 percent decline in the market. A stock with a beta of +2.0 would provide a negative return of 20 percent if held long. If the stock is sold short, a gain of 20 percent is suggested. Should the 10 percent market decline be forecast, a stock with a beta of −1.0 would provide a return of +10 percent [−1.0 x −.10]. Unfortunately, stocks with negative betas are scarce.

These approaches to stock selection are valid under two key assumptions. First, it is necessary to forecast the timing and direction of market moves with reasonable accuracy. Second, the historical measure of beta must persist at roughly similar levels during the forecast period.

Under the first assumption, the continuous tailoring of portfolio volatility in order to capitalize on anticipated market moves can operate *against* the investment-return objectives of the portfolio. This is especially the case if the timing and direction of the forecast market moves are not consistently correct.

The second assumption is equally important. Whereas the variability of market returns is able to explain roughly 75-95 percent of the variability of the returns of most portfolios, owing to the averaging effects that are achieved by diversification, the market is able to explain only 15-65 percent of the volatility of most individual securities. As a result, the statistical significance of the estimated coefficients is suspect in the cases of some common stocks. Moreover, questions have been raised on the stability of these coefficients during short- to intermediate-term periods, and this is the time horizon of interest to most portfolio managers.

Table 18-2 contains a volatility analysis of several securities taken from a group of fifty-six examined in a study by Smith, Barney & Co. The beta coefficients are computed for two adjacent time periods, January 2, 1968-November 3, 1969, and November 3, 1969-October 1, 1971. Both periods encompassed rising and falling stock markets.

For example, in reviewing the volatility performance of the first security, Allegheny Power System, we note that its beta coefficient increased significantly from one time period to the next. However, the market was able to explain only 12 percent of the stock's volatility during the initial time span. An increase in the stock's responsiveness to market moves accompanied the increase in its volatility, as evidenced by the ability of the market to explain nearly 44 percent of the stock's variability during the latter period.

One noteworthy observation from the Smith, Barney analysis of fifty-six stocks is the number of sizable shifts in the values of the volatility coefficients between the two time periods. Coefficients for twelve of the issues remained reasonably stable, twenty-eight increased significantly, and sixteen declined notably. The sampling of securities is by no means large enough to draw any firm conclusions concerning the stability of beta factors. However, the Smith, Barney study tends to suggest caution in the use of beta coefficients in stock selection.

This stationariness or lack thereof of betas is of significant concern to the investor who wishes to make predictive decisions using beta coefficients. Levy

TABLE 18-2

MARKET VOLATILITY ANALYSIS OF SELECTED COMMON STOCKS

Security	11/03/69 - 10/01/71		01/02/68 - 11/03/69	
	Beta	% Variation Explained by S&P 500	Beta	% Variation Explained by S&P 500
Allegheny Power System	1.10	43.9%	.54	12.3%
Allied Stores	2.01	68.3%	1.16	31.3%
American Airlines	2.49	55.0%	1.63	31.6%
American Cyanamid	.47	12.1%	1.26	65.1%
American Investment	2.51	55.3%	1.01	21.3%
American Tel. & Tel.	.77	47.8%	.46	25.2%
Atlantic Richfield	1.64	54.5%	1.87	34.1%
Bausch & Lomb	2.38	35.0%	2.22	54.9%
CMI Investment	1.63	35.0%	2.23	25.2%
Coastal States Gas	.68	29.4%	1.19	28.5%

Source: G. Gordon Biggar, Jr., *Risk-Adjusted Portfolio Performance: Its Investment Implications* (New York: Smith, Barney, & Co., 1971), p. 37.

has written on this matter and concluded that beta coefficients are fairly un-predictable for individual securities. In the same study, however, Levy sug-gested that portfolio betas were somewhat stationary for small portfolios and very stable over time for large portfolios.

"Adequate" Diversification

Many traditional approaches to diversification stress that the more securities one holds in a portfolio, the better. Markowitz-type diversification stresses not the number of securities but the right kinds; the right kinds of securities are those that exhibit less than perfect positive correlation.

An unfortunate fact is that nearly all securities are positively correlated with each other and the market. King noted that about half the variance in a typical stock results from elements that affect the whole market (systematic risk).[10] The upshot of this is that risk cannot be reduced to zero in portfolios of any size. The one-half of total risk that is not related to market forces (unsystematic) can be reduced by proper diversification, but once unsystematic risk is reduced or eliminated, we are left with systematic risk, which no one can escape (other than by not buying securities).

Thus, beyond some finite number of securities, adding more is expensive in time and money spent to search them out and monitor their performance; and this cost is not balanced by any benefits in the form of additional reduction of risk! Evans and Archer's work suggests that unsystematic risk can be reduced naively by holding as few as ten to fifteen stocks.[11] (In fact, risk can be in-

---

[10]B. F. King, "Market and Industry Factors in Stock Price Behavior," *Journal of Business* 39, No. 1 (January 1966), 139-90.

[11]John L. Evans and S. H. Archer, "Diversification and the Reduction of Dispersion: An Empirical Analysis," *Journal of Finance*, December 1968, pp. 761-69.

creased by duplicating within industries.) This results from simply allowing unsystematic risk on these stocks to average out to near zero. With Markowitz-type diversification, risk can technically be reduced below the systematic level if securities can be found whose rates of return have low enough correlations. Negative correlations are ideal.

**Portfolio
Selection:
Old Versus
New**

The Markowitz and the more traditional views of portfolio selection both take risk and return into account. Markowitz attempts to quantify risk more precisely. Portfolio selection in the traditional sense involves selection by class of security (bond, stock) and diversification by maturity (bonds), by industry, or by subgroup (income, cyclical, growth stocks).

The logical extension of Markowitz-type diversification is to treat the investment and financing decisions separately. In other words, return is achieved from current income *and* capital gains. Further, every class of investor might hold the same stock portfolio. A preferred risk class would be achieved through borrowing or lending. The purist version of the traditional theme might have a widow exclusively in bonds for required income. The thought that (1) some return (income) for the widow might be through capital gains, or that (2) *any* stocks would be held at all, is where the old and new ideas of portfolio selection seem to part company.

As always, the old and the new learn from each other. The newer notions of Markowitz and others are beginning to find their way into some of the thinking of portfolio managers. Portfolio theorists are modifying newer techniques as empirical testing and real-world practices are merged into the process. The result, it is hoped, will be to make portfolio analysis and selection less of an art and somewhat more of a science.

Summary

Chapter 17 suggested to us that there are "feasible" or possible portfolios and "efficient" portfolios. Efficient portfolios are those that dominate others by having (1) similar risk but higher return, or (2) similar return but lower risk. In portfolio analysis we are concerned primarily with developing efficient portfolios. But how does one select the one "best" portfolio from a group of efficient portfolios?

The process of portfolio building has traditionally had its roots in a kind of life-cycle or interior-decorator approach. Knowledge of the investor's needs, objectives, and financial planning are paramount considerations around which the "best" available securities are combined to maximize return.

But since most investors hold more than one security, we know that risk as well as return must be a consideration in constructing securities portfolios. Diversification attests to a concern that investors exhibit toward risk. While investors like return and dislike risk, the central question concerns how investors "trade off" return against risk.

Investors seek to maximize the expected utility of money or return, and they act as if additional amounts of money or return have decreasing *marginal* utility. This notion is entirely plausible when we observe that an extra $20 means less to a millionaire than it does to most readers of this book.

Building upon the notion of utility and utility curves, we chose a single portfolio from those efficient portfolios available to our hypothetical investor in Chapter 17. The idea of the separation of the investment decision from the financing decision (the separation theorem) was introduced in the selection process.

Finally, the significance of the beta coefficient in the areas of stock selection and portfolios was discussed, as well as the appropriate number of securities necessary to achieve adequate diversification.

**Questions
and
Problems**

1. A portfolio-selection scheme was offered for Mrs. Jones, using traditional techniques.

    a. What alternatives exist to permit her to avoid the tightness in her budget?

    b. Can you conceive of an alternative strategy to avoid drawing upon the principal of her portfolio?

    c. How would modern portfolio-selection techniques provide a solution to her problem of which stocks to own and what percentage of her portfolio should be devoted to stocks?

2. As an investment adviser, describe an appropriate investment program for the following:

    a. An associate's parents, ages seventy-three and seventy-five, have $60,000 to invest. They have pension income in the amount of $6,000 annually, although they have been accustomed to an income of $14,000. This sum and their home, owned free and clear, are their only assets.

    b. An unmarried career woman is approaching forty, has no dependents, and has a secure and well-paying job as an advertising art director which is supplemented by an attractive retirement program. She saves $2,000 to $2,500 every year but is bored with talk about investments and the stock market. She has just inherited $100,000.

3. A widow in her seventies and in good health comes to you for advice about her investments. Her husband left her a portfolio that consists mostly of low-yielding "growth" stocks that are now at prices that approximate their adjusted cost. She has found that the income available is not nearly enough to help her maintain a comfortable standard of living. She needs $25,000 income before taxes from her investments. The current market value of the portfolio is $400,000, and its current yield is 2.3 percent.

    Since she will need this higher income for perhaps the next ten years, you have suggested that she place at least half of the portfolio in high-yielding straight corporate bonds.

    a. List the assumptions you made regarding the investment environment and the widow's situation in order to consider the immediate investment of one-half of the portfolio in bonds a *prudent* decision.

    b. Describe the types of investments you would select for the remainder of the portfolio that is not invested in high-yielding straight corporate bonds.

    4. Using the notion of corner points and the efficient frontier developed earlier, show on a risk-return diagram that the "best" portfolio (corner point) for a risk lover would be corner point 1.

    5. Prepare a table indicating the values of X in Equation 18.3 for margin requirements of 80, 75, 65, and 50 percent.

    6. The borrowing-lending rate is 7 percent. The optimum portfolio of risky securities (corner point 9) has an expected return of 19 percent and an expected standard deviation of 6 percent.

    a. What is the portfolio return and risk if 20 percent of available funds are placed in a riskless security and 80 percent is invested in the securities in corner portfolio #9?

    b. If the margin requirement is 60 percent, what is the portfolio return and risk if the securities in corner portfolio #9 are purchased to the full limit of the margin requirement?

    7. Determine from your broker what the present interest rate is on margin accounts. Also determine the prevailing rate on one-year Treasury securities. Are they identical? What does this fact reveal about the borrowing-lending line and the "best" stock portfolio?

    8. The "best" stock portfolio can be discovered graphically at the point of tangency between the efficient frontier and the borrowing-lending line, or at that corner point that maximizes $\theta = (E_p - E_L)/S_p$ where E_p = expected return on the portfolio; S_p is the expected standard deviation on the portfolio, and E_L = lending rate.

    a. Show that corner point 9 provides a higher value for θ than corner point 10 in Table 17-5.

    b. Determine the riskless rate at which θ is the same for corner points 9 and 10.

    9. The sixteen candidate stocks in the sample problem in the chapter led to a "best" portfolio shown in Table 18-1.

    a. Why do you suppose that Black & Decker and Mobil account for over half the total portfolio?

    b. How would we go about assessing the trade-off between transaction-cost savings and changes in portfolio return and risk by making Burroughs and Xerox purchases in round lots of 900 and 200 shares, respectively?

    10. In what ways are corner portfolios 16 and 17 better for a risk-averse person than the placement of all funds in the least-risk stock, Associated Spring (see Table 17-5)?

    11. Refer to the diagram on the next page.

    a. Which portfolios shown are "feasible" (possible)?

    b. Which portfolio would a risk-lover choose? Why?

    c. Which portfolio would an irrational investor choose? Why?

    d. Which portfolios shown are "efficient"? Why?

    e. Which portfolio is better, B or C, if $E_B = .12$, $S_B = .06$, $E_C = .10$, $S_C = .05$, and the riskless rate = .05?

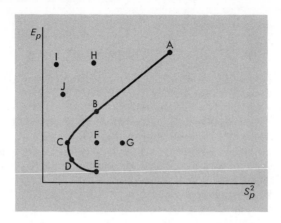

12. Refer to the following diagram:

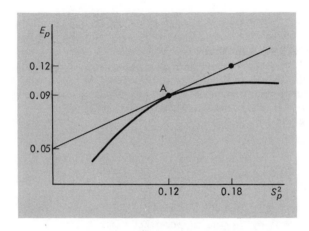

a. Suppose 80 percent of funds were placed in portfolio A and 20 percent of funds were placed in the riskless security. What is the return and risk on such a portfolio?

b. The margin requirement is 40 percent. What is the portfolio return and risk if portfolio A is purchased and margined to the limit?

PORTFOLIO REVISION TECHNIQUES

Timing has long been a problem that has challenged investors. Buying at prices that are too high limits the return that can be obtained. Likewise, selling out at low prices will often result in losses. But stock prices do fluctuate, and the natural tendencies of investors often cause them to react in a way opposite to one that would enable them to benefit from these fluctuations. Ideally, investors should buy when prices are low, and then sell these securities when their prices rise to higher limits of their fluctuations. But investors are hesitant to buy when prices are low for fear that prices will fall lower, or for fear that prices won't move upward again. When prices are high, investors are hesitant to sell because they want to maximize their profits, and feel that the price may rise further. It requires discipline to buy when stock prices are low and pessimism abounds, and to sell when stock prices are high and optimism prevails!

Most investors have the discipline to carry out such a course of action *if* they know the course of the future fluctuations. But these fluctuations have proved very difficult, if not impossible, for most investors to forecast. Mechanical portfolio-management techniques have been developed to ease the problem of timing and minimize the emotions involved in investing. These techniques are referred to as *formula plans.*

Formula plans assume that stock prices fluctuate up and down in cycles. Empirical evidence does seem to show that cycles exist and that cycles are closely related to movements in economic activity.[1] Formula plans further assume that investors cannot forecast the direction of the next fluctuation. If an investor merely buys a stock and remains indifferent to fluctuations in its price, he is merely ignoring them. Formula plans are an attempt to exploit these fluctuations and make them a source of profit to the investor. This chapter will examine (1) constant-dollar-value, (2) constant-ratio, and (3) variable-ratio formula plans, as well as well as another mechanical investment plan, dollar averaging.

---

[1]Richard A. Brealey, *An Introduction to Risk and Return from Common Stocks* (Cambridge, Mass.: M.I.T. Press, 1969), pp. 31-32.

Formula plans are efforts to make the decisions on timing automatic. They consist of predetermined rules for *when* purchases and sales will be made and *how large* the purchases and sales will be. Formula plans eliminate the emotions that surround timing decisions, such as pessimism and optimism, since the rules and plan of action are predetermined. The rules will often call for specified action that is contrary to what the investor would otherwise do, and contrary to what the majority of the investors in the market are doing. The *selection* of a formula plan and the determination of the appropriate ground rules cause the investor to consider and outline his investment objectives and policies. The *implementation* of a formula plan relieves the pressures on the investor to forecast fluctuations in stock prices.

Formula plans are not, however, a royal road to riches without any weaknesses. First, as an effort to solve the timing problem of investing, they make no provisions for *what securities* should be selected for investment. Such selection is made by analyzing securities within the E-I-C framework. Second, a formula plan by its very nature must be inflexible, thus imposing the necessary action on the investor. This inflexibility makes it difficult to know if and when to adjust the plan to new conditions present in the investment environment. Third, formula plans need a long period to work optimally, and the longer the period required, the more risk there is of substantial changes in the investment environment or in the investor's position. Finally, some formula plans do not free the investor from making forecasts but only require that he make forecasts of a different kind.

BASIC GROUND RULES

Formula plans call for the investor to divide his investment funds into two portfolios, one aggressive and one conservative (defensive). The aggressive portfolio, usually consisting of stocks, must be more volatile than the conservative portfolio, which often consists of bonds because stability is its most important requirement. The volatility of the aggressive portfolio should ensure that it rises more rapidly and to a greater extent than the conservative portfolio in times when the fluctuation is upward, and that it falls more quickly and more severely when the fluctuation is downward. Generally, the larger the difference between the movements of the two portfolios, the larger the profit the formula plan can yield.

The pursuit of this maximum difference in the movement of the two portfolios is one of the major reasons that high-grade bonds have been advocated as the optimum investment for the conservative, defensive portfolio. High-grade bonds have a high degree of safety and stability, and they also provide steady current income. But in addition, bonds' prices are apt to fall during periods of prosperity, owing to rising interest rates, while stock prices are rising. The opposite situation is likely to appear in unfavorable economic climates. This opposite movement of the two portfolios would be advantageous to formula plans that specify predesignated rules for the transfer of funds from the aggressive into the conservative portfolio as the value of the aggressive portfolio rises. These formula plans also designate that funds be transferred from the conservative to the aggressive portfolio when the value of the aggressive portfolio falls. This automatically causes the investor to sell stocks when their prices are rising and to buy stocks when their prices are falling. If the prices of bonds are moving in the opposite direction to the prices of stocks, this will yield higher profits than if the conservative portfolio's value remains completely stationary.

The facts available from observation, however, show that the fluctuations of stock prices and bond prices do not run in opposite directions at all times. The turning points of trends in stock prices and interest rates do not always coincide, and to the extent that they do not, the bond and stock prices will be moving in the same direction; therefore, the difference between their movements, which the formula plan capitalizes on, will be less than if the conservative portfolio's value had remained stationary. The existence of this coincident movement in bond and stock prices, which sometimes decreases the profits under a formula plan, has led some writers to advocate the use of cash or a savings account for the funds in the conservative portfolio. The stationary value of cash or a savings account would yield a bigger difference between the movements of the two portfolios.

STOCK PORTFOLIO

Common stocks are nearly always recommended as the appropriate investment medium for the aggressive portfolio. The selection of the appropriate common stocks is, as stated earlier, not dealt with by the formula plan. The securities that are most appropriate for use in a formula plan are in general no different from those appropriate for investment otherwise, with the one possible exception of *volatility*.

Since maximum profits result from formula plans when the difference between the fluctuations of the two portfolios is the largest, one would expect that the more volatility in the aggressive portfolio, the better. The amount of volatility that any person using a formula plan will seek will depend on his risk-and-return preferences. If the investor seeks a higher level of capital safety and more current income from the aggressive portfolio, he will, of course, choose less volatile stocks than will the investor who is willing to bear more risk in seeking higher capital growth and less current income. The investor employing the formula plan more conservatively will still benefit from its use.

Along with volatility, investors in formula plans must also seek *quality* and *growth* in the stocks they choose. Even though the formula plan seeks to profit from the fluctuations in a stock's price, the investor is taking an ownership position in the stock, and if the general trend that is expected (aside from the fluctuations that the formula plan seeks to exploit) is level or upward, it is better for the investor than if the trend is downward. Also, as we shall see, the formula plan requires that stocks undergo complete price cycles in order to obtain the most favorable results. Stocks of inferior quality or with negative growth trends may never rebound from downward fluctuations.

As one can see, the selection of securities for formula planning may be more difficult than ordinary security selection, since the optimum security has all the qualifications of any otherwise acceptable investment and also a higher degree of volatility than other securities. To select securities with higher levels of volatility, investors must use the past history of a stock's movement compared with the movement of various indexes as a measure. This measure of volatility is actually a beta value, as mentioned in Chapter 17. Even though there does seem to be empirical evidence that the volatility of a stock will tend to persist over time,[2] the volatility characteristic of a stock in the past may or may not materialize in the future. When the aggressive portfolio contains many stocks, however, the volatility of the portfolio as a whole is much more predictable than it is for individual stocks.

Three basic types of formula plans will be discussed here. They are all different in their provisions for transferring funds from an aggressive to a conservative portfolio, or vice versa. The prespecified provisions work automatically to force the investor to sell stocks as their value rises and to buy stocks as their value falls. Each of these plans has many modifications, but if the basic plan is grasped, the modifications are easily understood. The different basic plans are closely related. Some overcome disadvantages of the others while adding complexity and sometimes other shortcomings.

Constant-Dollar-Value Plan

The constant-dollar-value plan specifies that the dollar value of the stock portion of the portfolio will remain constant. Thus, as the value of the stocks rises, the investor must automatically sell some of the shares in order to keep the value of his aggressive portfolio constant. If the prices of the stocks fall, the investor must buy additional stock to keep the value of the aggressive portfolio constant. By specifying that the aggressive portfolio will remain constant in dollar value, the plan also specifies that the remainder of the total fund will be invested in the conservative fund. The constant-dollar-value plan's major advantage is its simplicity. The investor can clearly see the amount that he needs to have invested. However, the percentage of his total fund that this constant amount will represent in the aggressive portfolio will vary at different levels of his stock's values.

The investor must choose predetermined action points—sometimes called *revaluation points*. The action points are the times at which the investor will make the transfers called for to keep the constant dollar value of the stock portfolio. Of course, the portfolio's value cannot be *continuously* the same, since this would necessitate constant attention by the investor, innumerable action points, and excessive transaction costs. In fact, the portfolio will have to be allowed to fluctuate to some extent before action is taken to readjust its value. The action points may be set according to prespecified periods of time,

---

[2]Brealey, *Risk and Return,* pp. 42-46.

percentage changes in some economic or market index, or—most ideally—percentage changes in the value of the aggressive portfolio.

The timing of action points can have an important effect on the profits the investor obtains. Action points placed too close together cause excessive costs that reduce profits. If the action points are too far apart, however, the investor may completely miss the opportunity to profit from fluctuations that take place between them. For example, assume that action points are set by the percentage change in the value of the aggressive portfolio, such as whenever the value changes by 20 percent. The investor will make no changes, no matter how many fluctuations take place, if the fluctuations are within a range of plus or minus 20 percent of the last valuation of the portfolio. So the setting of action points in this formula plan involves the trade-off between costs and profitability.

The constant-dollar-value plan does not require forecasting the extent to which upward fluctuations may reach. A forecast of the extent of downward fluctuations is necessary, however, since the conservative portfolio must be large enough so that funds are always available for transfer to the stock portfolio as its value shrinks. This step requires a knowledge of how low stock prices might go. Then the required size of the conservative portfolio can be determined. If the investor can start his constant-dollar fund when the stocks he is acquiring are not priced too far above the lowest values to which they might fluctuate, he can obtain better overall results from a constant-dollar-value plan.

Examples will help to clarify the implementation of formula plans. All the plans discussed will be examined as they apply to a single common stock over an identical and complete cycle, thereby facilitating comparison of the plans under various conditions. Although the examples refer to the investment in one stock, the concepts are identical for a portfolio of many stocks, as the portfolio's total value changes. The stock or portfolio of stocks can be changed whenever the investor finds a selection that he feels more appropriately meets his requirements. But the value of investment is regulated by the formula plan. The example covers a full cycle because this is the most appropriate test of the formula plans. A full cycle includes both an upward and a downward fluctuation and ends at the beginning price. We will use fractional shares and ignore transaction costs to simplify the examples.

EXAMPLE OF CONSTANT-DOLLAR-VALUE PLAN

An investor with $2,000 for investment decides that the constant dollar value of his stock portfolio will be $1,000. The remaining $1,000 of his fund at this time makes up the conservative portfolio. He purchases 40 shares of stock selling at $25 per share. He also determines that he will take action to revalue the fund each time its value reaches 20 percent above or below the constant $1,000 value. Table 19-1 indicates the positions and actions of the investor during the cycle of the stock's price. Also shown is the value of a comparative strategy, where $2,000 is invested only in stocks—80 shares at $25—that are simply held. Column 1 of the table shows various prices of the stock during one cycle of fluctuation. Notice the revaluation actions (represented by boxed areas) taken

TABLE 19-1

EXAMPLE OF A CONSTANT-DOLLAR-VALUE FORMULA PLAN

(1) Stock Price Index	(2) Value of Buy-and-Hold Strategy (80 Shares × Col. 1)	(3) Value of Conservative Portfolio (Col. 5 − Col. 4)	(4) Value of Stock Portfolio (Col. 7 × Col. 1)	(5) Total Value of Constant-Dollar Portfolio (Col. 3 + Col. 4)	(6) Revaluation Action	(7) Total Number of Shares in Stock Portfolio
25	$2,000	$1,000	$1,000	$2,000		40
22	1,760	1,000	880	1,880		40
20	1,600	1,000	800	1,800		40
20	1,600	800	1,000	1,800	Buy 10 Shares at 20*	50
22	1,760	800	1,100	1,900		50
24	1,920	800	1,200	2,000		50
24	1,920	1,000	1,000	2,000	Sell 8.33 Shares at 24	41.67
26	2,080	1,000	1,083	2,083		41.67
28.8	2,304	1,000	1,200	2,200		41.67
28.8	2,304	1,200	1,000	2,200	Sell 6.95 Shares at 28.8	34.72
25	2,000	1,200	870	2,070		34.72

*To restore the stock portfolio to $1,000, $200 is transferred from conservative portfolio and used to purchase ten shares at $20 per share.

when the price fluctuated to 20, 24, and 28.8, since the value of the stock fund became 20 percent greater or less than the goal of a constant $1,000 value. Notice, also, that the investor using the constant-dollar-value formula plan has increased the total value of his fund to $2,070 after the complete cycle, while the buy-and-hold strategy yielded only $2,000.

Constant-Ratio Plan

The constant-ratio formula plan specifies that the ratio of the value of the aggressive portfolio to the value of the conservative portfolio will be held constant. This automatically forces the investor to sell stocks as their value rises, in order to keep the ratio of their value to the conservative portfolio constant. Likewise, as the value of stocks falls, the investor is forced to transfer funds from the conservative portfolio to purchase common stocks.

Since, under this plan, the aggressive portfolio is kept at a constant proportion of the total value of the fund, there will always be funds in the conservative portfolio to be transferred to the aggressive portfolio to purchase stocks if the stocks continue to fall in value. This means that, unlike the constant-dollar-value plan, the constant-ratio plan requires no forecast of the lowest level to which stock prices might fluctuate. The constant-dollar-value plan does, however, call for a consistent level of aggressiveness in transfer to and from the stock portfolio; the very nature of the constant-ratio relationship causes the purchase of stocks to become *less aggressive* as the prices continue to fall, since the constant ratio is applied to a total fund that is *decreasing* in value. Likewise, the constant-ratio plan calls for less aggressive sales as the prices of stocks go up. This is because the total value of the fund grows, and the constant ratio allows a larger dollar value for the stock portfolio.

This phenomenon of the constant-ratio plan—that the most aggressive sales of stocks take place just above the middle range of a fluctuation and the most aggressive purchases just below the middle range of fluctuation—causes it to function suboptimally when the fluctuations of stock prices are characterized by relatively long swings upward and downward. To perform more optimally, as the variable-ratio plan does, a formula plan should sell more aggressively as the stock prices fluctuate further and further above the middle range of the fluctuation and buy more aggressively as the prices move lower and lower below the middle range of the fluctuation. To implement the more optimal strategy, however, requires forecasting a great deal more about the fluctuations that will take place. But decreasing the dependency on forecasts was one of the alleged attributes of formula plans, and the constant-ratio plan calls for no forecasting at all.

The constant-ratio plan will result in higher profits than either the constant-dollar-value plan or the variable-ratio plan during a sustained rise or a sustained fall by itself, since the ratio automatically puts the investor into a more optimal position (that is, larger investment during a rise and lower investment during a fall). However, over the entire cycle of a fluctuation (both up and down), the constant-ratio plan performs less satisfactorily than the other two plans. This is because the constant-ratio plan calls for funds to be transferred into and out of the stock portfolio most aggressively near the median of the fluctuation rather than near its turning points.

The selection of action points for a constant-ratio plan is subject to the same considerations as under the constant-dollar-value plan. Here the action point is determined by the percentage that we allow the constant ratio to fluctuate within before we readjust to its value. If we allow the range of fluctuation of the ratio to be very small, then we will be forced to make many and smaller transactions. If we allow the range of fluctuation of the ratio to be quite large, we will have fewer transactions, but we will not benefit from fluctuations that are too small to cause adjustment action to take place.

EXAMPLE OF A CONSTANT-RATIO PLAN

Our example of a constant-ratio plan divides an initial $2,000 fund into equal portfolios. The starting point and other information are the same as in the previous example. The ratio set is:

$$\frac{\text{Value of stock portfolio}}{\text{Value of conservative portfolio}}$$

Equal allotment gives a ratio of 1.00. A constant-ratio plan that placed one-third in the stock portfolio would yield a ratio of .33/.66, or 0.50. The portfolios will be revalued when the ratio of the value of the stock portfolio to the conservative

TABLE 19-2
EXAMPLE OF CONSTANT-RATIO FORMULA PLAN

(1) Stock Price Index	(2) Value of Buy-and-Hold Strategy (80 Shares X Col. 1)	(3) Value of Conservative Portfolio (Col. 5 − Col. 4)	(4) Value of Stock Portfolio (Col. 8 X Col. 1)	(5) Total Value of Constant-Ratio Portfolio (Col. 3 + Col. 4)	(6) Ratio (4):(3)	(7) Revaluation Action	(8) Total Number of Shares in Stock Portfolio
25	$2,000	$1,000	$1,000	$2,000	1.00		40
23	1,840	1,000	920	1,920	.92		40
22.5	1,800	1,000	900	1,900	.90		40
22.5	1,800	950	950	1,900	1.00	Buy 2.22 Shares at 22.5*	42.22
20.25	1,620	950	854	1,804	.90		42.22
20.25	1,620	902	902	1,804	1.00	Buy 2.37 Shares at 20.25	44.59
20	1,600	902	891	1,793	.99		44.59
22.4	1,792	902	992	1,894	1.10		44.59
22.4	1,792	947	947	1,894	1.00	Sell 2.01 Shares at 22.4	42.58
24.6	1,992	947	1,043	1,990	1.10		42.58
24.6	1,992	995	995	1,990	1.00	Sell 1.95 Shares at 24.6	40.63
27.0	2,160	995	1,095	2,090	1.10		40.63
27.0	2,160	1,045	1,045	2,090	1.00	Sell 1.85 Shares at 27.0	38.78
28.8	2,304	1,045	1,117	2,162	1.07		38.78
27.0	2,160	1,045	1,045	2,090	1.00		38.78
25	2,000	1,045	967	2,012	.93		38.78

*To restore the ratio from .90 to 1.00, total value of the fund, $1,900, is simply split in two equal segments of $950; and $950/$950 = 1.00. The $50 transferred from the conservative portfolio will buy 2.22 shares at the prevailing price of $22.50.

portfolio becomes plus or minus .10 from the desired ratio of 1.00.

In Table 19-2 the offset rows, shown in boxes, exhibit the actions taken to readjust the value of the portfolios to reobtain the desired ratio. For example, when the stock reaches $27, funds are transferrred from the aggressive portfolio into the conservative portfolio by selling stocks. Notice that this constant-ratio plan calls for more transactions than the constant-dollar-value plan did, but this plan's purchases and sales are less aggressive. Therefore the constant-ratio plan yielded a smaller increase in total value after the entire cycle, $2,012. It did, however, outperform the buy-and-hold strategy after the complete cycle.

Variable-Ratio Plan   The variable-ratio formula plan specifies that the ratio of the value of the aggressive portfolio to the value of the conservative portfolio will decrease as the value of the aggressive portfolio rises, and increase as the value of the aggressive portfolio decreases. This forces the selling of stocks and the buying of bonds as stock prices rise, and the buying of stocks and selling of bonds as stock prices fall.

The plan specifies a predetermined schedule of the appropriate proportions for various levels of stock prices. If the plan is started at a price that is considered a median around which future fluctuations will move, then the appropriate proportion for the aggressive portfolio would be the proportion of the total fund that the investor can risk in common stocks. From this median proportion, the complete schedule can be determined by the investor. The plan, therefore, calls for a forecast as to whether the current price is a true median. It also requires forecasts of the range of fluctuations both above and below the median to establish the varying ratios at different levels of stock prices. If these forecasts of the range of fluctuations are not correct, the investor may find himself completely in stocks while the prices continue to fall or completely out of stocks while the prices continue to rise, if his schedule of ratios allows either portfolio to become 100 percent. Clearly, variable ratios demand more forecasting than the other formula plans discussed.

Varying the ratio causes the purchases and sales of stocks to become more aggressive as the prices move further below or above the median of their fluctuation. This enables the investor using the variable-ratio plan to profit more from the fluctuations that formula plans are designed to exploit than he can with the other plans. The more extensive forecasts that must be made to implement variable-ratio plans seem to be their only disadvantage. The dependency on forecasting means that incorrect forecasts subject the investor to more risk.

There are many variable-ratio plans that allow for the norm, and thus the whole schedule of ratios, to be changed when new conditions evolve in the investment environment. The most common of these variations is one that calls for the norm to be adjusted along a growth trend that is anticipated for the common stock. This enables the plan to exploit fluctuations around the long-term trend more efficiently, since this growth component of the value change is anticipated by the changing norm. Changing the norm requires even more forecasting.

Other variable-ratio plans call for the ratios to vary according to economic or market indexes rather than the value of the stock portfolio. Some use moving averages of indicators. This means that the indicator that is chosen is considered a better forecaster of the true trend of stock prices than the stocks in the aggressive portfolio. As more and more of these variations of variable-ratio plans are introduced, increased complications are injected. Beyond a point, it might become questionable as to whether the highly complicated variable-ratio plan is more satisfactory or yields higher profits than the extensive analysis and forecasting that it was supposed to replace.

EXAMPLE OF A VARIABLE-RATIO PLAN

Our example of a variable-ratio plan assumes that the investor forecasts that the present price of $25 is the median price, and therefore the initial division of the total fund will be into two equal portfolios. The stock-portfolio value is 50 percent of the total portfolio. The plan further states that if the value of the stock portfolio rises 20 percent from the median, the appropriate percentage of the total value of the fund for the stock portfolio will be 30 percent. Likewise, if the value of the stock portfolio decreases by 20 percent from the median, its appropriate percentage of the total fund's value will be 70 percent. Again, other facts are the same as in the original example.

In Table 19-3, notice that action was taken to readjust the value of the portfolios at $20 and $25, since they are 20 percent shifts from the median. For example, at $20, funds were transferred from the conservative portfolio into the stock portfolio to achieve a new ratio (70 percent). The profits under this plan are $116 after the complete cycle. The higher profits relative to other plans discussed are due to the more aggressive purchases and sales of shares during the cycle, even though there were fewer trades. It should be noted that fluctuations of less than 20 percent from the median were ignored.

Modifications of Formula Plans

There are many modifications of basic formula plans. The most common modification is to *delay action points*. If the investor feels that the trend that has caused the action point to be reached is going to continue, then he can increase his profits by waiting until the trend continues before he takes his action to revalue the portfolio according to the provisions of the plan. This requires forecasting whether or not the trend will continue, and it therefore goes against the unemotional and automatic advantages associated with the nature of formula plans. Many other modifications represent similar efforts to put more flexibility into formula plans. As stated earlier, the inflexibility of formula plans

TABLE 19-3
EXAMPLE OF VARIABLE-RATIO FORMULA PLAN

(1)	(2)	(3)	(4)	(5)	(6)	(7)	(8)
Stock Price Index	Value of Buy-and-Hold Strategy (80 Shares × Col. 1)	Value of Conservative Portfolio (Col. 5 − Col. 4)	Value of Stock Portfolio (Col. 8 × Col. 1)	Total Value of Variable-Ratio Portfolio (Col. 3 + Col. 4)	Value of Stock as % of Total Fund (Col. 4 ÷ Col. 5)	Revaluation Action	Total Number of Shares in Stock Portfolio
25	$2,000	$1,000	$1,000	$2,000	50%		40
22	1,760	1,000	880	1,880	47%		40
20	1,600	1,000	800	1,800	44.5%		40
20	1,600	540	1,260	1,800	70%	Buy 23 Shares at 20	63
22	1,760	540	1,386	1,926	72%		63
25	2,000	540	1,576	2,116	74.5%		63
25	2,000	1,058	1,058	2,116	50%	Sell 20.7 Shares at 25	42.3
26	2,080	1,058	1,100	2,058	53%		42.3
28.8	2,304	1,058	1,218	2,276	54%		42.3
25	2,000	1,058	1,058	2,116	50%		42.3

gives them some of their best attributes, but it can also be a disadvantage. Whether or not the investor feels he needs the inflexibility will determine how appropriate modifications are for his use.

It is difficult to generalize on the effectiveness and usefulness of formula plans. Some plans used have often been greatly modified, or they have been used over periods that have not permitted fair tests of their worth. The intrinsic worth of formula plans lies in their taking the investment decision-making process outside the emotions of the investment environment. However, investors must make their predetermined plans on the basis of certain assumptions. They assume that stock prices will fluctuate, and they base this assumption on historical data. The level of success that formula plans achieve will be dependent on the closeness to which actual future behavior resembles the pattern that the formula plan anticipates. Formula plans are, therefore, possibly useful in some cases, but they are not a foolproof method for achieving profits.

Dollar-Cost Averaging

Another mechanical investment technique, which is not technically a formula plan, is dollar averaging. It is very similar to formula plans in that it forces investors to make trades automatically that they might otherwise be averse to making. Dollar averaging requires that investors invest a constant-dollar sum in a specified stock or portfolio of stocks at periodic dates, regardless of the price of the stocks. This technique is especially appropriate for investors who have periodic sums to invest or who are otherwise in the process of *building a fund*. The formula plans discussed earlier dealt with the investment of an *already-accumulated fund*.

Dollar averaging helps the investor avoid buying securities at high levels. If dollar averaging is executed over a complete cycle of stock prices, the investor will obtain his shares at a lower average cost per share than the average price per share of the stock over that same period. This phenomenon results from the fact that the constant-dollar sum purchases more shares at lower prices than at higher prices.

Dollar-averaging plans can vary according to the length of intervals between investments. The size of the dollar sum invested must be large enough to keep the percentage of commission costs relatively low if possible, and this may require the intervals between investments to be fairly long. For best results from the plan, however, the shorter the interval the better. The shorter interval makes it less likely that the investor will miss the opportunity to purchase stocks at low prices resulting from downward fluctuations.

The capacity of the dollar-averaging plan to achieve a lower average cost per share works most dramatically shortly after the program is started, when the fund is still small. As the program continues for long periods of time and the total fund becomes very large, the incremental addition of each new investment at various prices is averaged over many shares, and the effect on the average cost per share is greatly diluted. This is the reason that it is sometimes better for an investor to switch to one of the other formula plans when his fund becomes large.

TABLE 19-4

EXAMPLE OF CHANGING EFFECTS OF DOLLAR AVERAGING
AS FUND SIZE INCREASES

Date	Dollar Value of Investment	Total Value of Investment	Price of Stock	No. of Shares Purchased	Total Shares	Avg. Cost per Share
1/69	$1,000	$1,000	$50	20	20	$50
1/70	1,000	2,000	40	25	45	44.4
•	•	•	•	•	•	•
•	•	•	•	•	•	•
•	•	•	•	•	•	•
•	•	•	•	•	•	•
1/79	1,000	11,000	50	20	220	50
1/80	1,000	12,000	40	25	245	48.2

Table 19-4 shows purchases of shares in the lower range of a fluctuation of the same size (50 to 40). However, as the total size of the fund grows, the new shares purchased lowers the average cost per share by a smaller amount (from 50 to 48.2, versus from 50 to 44.4). As the total size of the fund becomes even larger, this effect will become even smaller.

Dollar averaging does not aid the investor in selecting the appropriate securities. As with formula plans, the investor must still seek quality and growth potential to obtain the best possible results. The fact that dollar averaging enables investors to acquire the shares below their average price is not as important as the growth of the value of the shares over the long term (see Table 19-5). Dollar-averaging programs are generally considered most useful over long terms, such as five to fifteen years, periods enabling stock prices to complete numerous cycles and to achieve the long-term growth that is anticipated. Higher volatility leads to higher profits in a dollar-averaging plan over entire cycles, but advocating high volatility seems questionable, particularly concerning the application of dollar averaging for savings plans, in which investors would seek low levels of risk. Dollar averaging is not advocated for use by anyone who might need to withdraw funds from his investment program on short notice. Such a situation can lead to losses if the investor has to liquidate his holdings at low prices. If an investor can meet these

TABLE 19-5

EXAMPLE OF DOLLAR-COST AVERAGING

Installment (1)	Regular Investment (2)	Price of Stock (3)	Shares Purchased (2)÷(3)=(4)	Total Shares Owned Σ(4)=(5)	Total Amount Invested Σ(2)=(6)	Total Value of Investment (3)(5)=(7)	Average Price per Share [Σ(3)]÷(1)=(8)	Average Cost per Share (6)÷(5)=(9)
1	$1,000	$25	40	40	$1,000	$1,000	$25	$25.0
2	1,000	20	50	90	2,000	1,800	22 1/2	22.2
3	1,000	20	50	140	3,000	2,800	21 2/3	21.4
4	1,000	30	33 1/3	173 1/3	4,000	5,200	21 3/4	23.0
5	1,000	25	40	213 1/3	5,000	5,320	24	23.5
6	1,000	30	33 1/3	246 2/3	6,000	7,400	25	24.3
7	1,000	30	33 1/3	280	7,000	8,400	25 5/7	25.0

requirements, dollar averaging can obtain favorable results if the proper stocks are chosen and timing of liquidation is successful.

DOLLAR-COST AVERAGING WITH HIA SHARES

Table 19-6 displays the results of a hypothetical dollar-cost-averaging program using Holiday Inns stock. The example assumes quarterly investments of $250 from December 1973 through March 1977. For the period considered, the average cost per share is lower than the average market value of a share in March 1977. As indicated in our earlier explanation of dollar-cost averaging, these favorable results are a function of the cycle in HIA shares over the period under consideration and the somewhat modest total investment of only $3,500.00.

TABLE 19-6
DOLLAR-COST AVERAGING WITH HOLIDAY INNS STOCK

(A) Install- ment Number	Install- ment (Quarter ending)	(1) Regular Invest- ment	(2) Price of Stock	(3) Shares Pur- chased (1) ÷ (2)	(4) Total Shares Owned Σ (3)	(5) Total Amount Invested Σ (1)	(6) Total Value of Invest- ment (2) × (4)	(7) Average Price per Share Σ (2) ÷ (A)	(8) Average Cost per Share (5) ÷ (4)
1	December 1973	$250.00	$13.13	19.0	19.0	$ 250.00	$ 250.00	$13.13	$13.13
2	March 1974	250.00	12.13	20.6	39.6	500.00	480.00	12.63	12.62
3	June 1974	250.00	11.00	22.7	62.3	750.00	685.00	12.08	12.03
4	September 1974	250.00	7.50	33.3	95.6	1,000.00	717.00	14.58	10.46
5	December 1974	250.00	5.13	48.7	144.3	1,250.00	740.00	12.22	8.66
6	March 1975	250.00	10.63	23.5	167.8	1,500.00	1,784.00	9.92	8.93
7	June 1975	250.00	13.13	19.0	186.8	1,750.00	2,453.00	10.37	9.36
8	September 1975	250.00	10.63	23.5	210.3	2,000.00	2,235.00	10.41	9.51
9	December 1975	250.00	14.38	17.4	227.7	2,250.00	3,274.00	10.85	9.88
10	March 1976	250.00	17.13	14.6	242.3	2,500.00	4,150.00	11.48	10.31
11	June 1976	250.00	14.38	17.4	259.7	2,750.00	3,734.00	11.74	10.58
12	September 1976	250.00	12.00	20.8	280.5	3,000.00	3,366.00	11.76	10.69
13	December 1976	250.00	13.13	19.0	299.5	3,250.00	3,932.00	11.86	10.85
14	March 1977	250.00	11.38	22.0	321.5	3,500.00	3,659.00	11.83	10.88

Summary

The mechanical investment plans discussed in this chapter are valuable to some investors in aiding their investment timing, but they do not help the investor in the selection of appropriate securities. The plans force investors to sell stocks as their prices rise and to buy stocks as their prices fall. The success of formula plans is determined by the closeness to which the pattern of the securities held approximates the pattern anticipated by the formula plan. Dollar averaging seems most appropriate for the investor accumulating an investment fund who might otherwise purchase stocks only at inflated prices.

Questions and Problems

1. It has been said that formula plans aid the investor in overcoming his emotional involvement with the timing of purchases and sales of stock. Why is this said?

2. Do formula plans aid the investor in selecting appropriate securities? If so, how? If not, what do they do?

3. What are some disadvantages of formula plans?

4. Since the defensive portfolio will probably have a low yield, how does it aid the investor using a mechanical formula plan?

5. What kind of security do you think you would select for your aggressive portfolio, and why?

6. What are the strengths and weaknesses of the constant-dollar-value plan? Constant-ratio plan? Variable-ratio plan? Which do you prefer? Why?

7. How are action points chosen?

8. If you were using a constant-dollar-value plan and started with a conservative portfolio worth $2,000 and a stock portfolio consisting of 40 shares of a $50 stock, at what points up and down would you first take action in both portfolios? Assume that you have set your action points at 10 percent above and below the $2,000 initial value of the stock portfolio.

9. Is dollar-cost averaging a formula plan? What exactly is it?

10. Why is it believed that the average cost per share of shares purchased under a dollar-cost-averaging plan will be lower than the average price per share of the same stock during the period of the plan's usage? Is this always true?

11. At what point in the building of a portfolio is the impact of dollar-cost averaging greatest? Why? Prove this by making up an example of your own.

CHAPTER TWENTY

MANAGED
PORTFOLIOS
AND PERFORMANCE
MEASUREMENTS

In this chapter we will discuss various types of managed portfolios, looking at broad categories as well as at differences among portfolios in each category. To do this, we will need to specify measures of portfolio performance. These will include the relative merits of return criteria and risk criteria, the adherence of the portfolio's management to publicly stated investment objectives, or some combination of these factors. Finally, we will examine sources of information on various types of managed portfolios.

Classification of Managed Portfolios

INVESTMENT COMPANIES

Closed-End Companies

A closed-end investment company is so named because its basic capitalization is limited, or "closed." That is, these firms sell shares much as a regular industrial company does. Closed-end firms can also use leverage by selling senior securities— bonds and preferred stocks. Instead of using proceeds from the stock sale to purchase land, equipment, and inventory, the closed-end investment company uses the proceeds to purchase securities of other firms.

The closed-end company is different from the open-end company in how its shares are traded after the initial offering.[1] The closed-end companies' shares are traded on organized exchanges, like those of any other company. Thus, when an investor buys shares in a closed-end investment company, he must generally buy them from another person. The buyer pays the normal commission on such a purchase.

The shares of a closed-end company can sell above or below the net asset value of the shares. *Net asset value* is the total market value of the fund's portfolio minus any liabilities, divided by the total number of shares outstanding. Reasons that closed-end investment companies sell at a discount are the investor's attitude concerning the abilities of the fund's management, lack of sales effort (brokers earn less commission on closed-end fund shares than on

---

[1]When the closed-end company desires to raise more capital, it can do so just as any other company can, through the sale of additional shares.

566

CHAP. 20
*Managed Portfolios
and
Performance
Measurements*

open-end fund shares), the riskiness of the fund itself, or the riskiness associated with the lack of marketability of the fund's shares because of a thin float
(that is, a small number of shares outstanding).[2]

Dual Funds

The dual fund is a special type of closed-end investment company. As its
name implies, it has two types of stock: income shares and capital shares. When
the investor purchases shares in a dual fund, he specifies which class of stock he
wants. The holders of the capital shares receive all the capital gains earned on all
the shares of the fund. The holders of the income shares receive all the interest
and dividends earned on all the shares of the fund. Thus it can be seen that the
investments of the dual fund's managers are divided into securities that promise
a sizeable dividend return and securities that promise substantial capital appreciation. The income investor enjoys leverage to the extent that he receives income on all the shares owned by the fund, and conversely the capital investor
enjoys leverage to the extent that he receives capital gains on all the shares
owned by the fund.

Potential problems can arise if management is unable to balance its investments properly. That is, if too large a share of the portfolio is invested in stocks
with large capital gain potential, there is likely to be too little dividend income
earned. Conversely, as too large a share of the portfolio is invested in high-
dividend-yielding securities, there is likely to be little capital appreciation.[3]

Open-End Companies

The open-end investment company, more commonly referred to as a mutual
fund, is characterized by the continual selling and redeeming of its shares. In
other words, the mutual fund does not have a fixed capitalization. It sells its
shares to the investing public whenever it can at their net asset value per share,
and it stands ready to repurchase these shares directly from the investment public
for their net asset value per share. In the case of a "no-load" mutual fund, the
investment company sells its shares by mail to the investor. Since no salesman is
involved, there is no sales commission (load). In the case of a "load" fund, the
shares are sold by a salesman. His entire selling commission (load) is added to the
net asset value, and a portion of the investor's equity is removed as the "load" at
the beginning of the contract to purchase shares. This process is called "front-
end loading," and thus the name "load fund." The load charge or commission
is generally about 8 percent of the sale price.

In addition, both the closed-end and open-end funds charge a management

---

[2]For an interesting discussion of closed-end investment company discounts, see Eugene
J. Pratt, "Myths Associated with Closed-End Investment Company Discounts," *Financial
Analysts Journal,* July-August 1966, pp. 79-82.

[3]See John P. Shelton, Eugene F. Brigham, and Alfred E. Hofflander, Jr., "An Evaluation
and Appraisal of Dual Funds," *Financial Analysts Journal,* May-June 1967, pp. 131-39; and
James A. Gentry and John R. Pike, "Dual Funds Revisited," *Financial Analysts Journal,*
March-April 1968, pp. 149-57.

567

CHAP. 20
*Managed Portfolios
and
Performance
Measurements*

fee to defray the costs of operating the portfolios—including such expenses as brokerage fees, transfer costs, bookkeeping expenses, and analysts' salaries. In the case of a load fund, a share with a net asset value of $10 would cost $10.80 if the load fee was 8 percent. If this fund were a no-load, the cost would be only the $10 net asset value. In the newspaper listings of mutual-fund shares, therefore, the bid and asked prices are equal for the no-load shares; the load funds have higher asked prices.

Mutual funds state specific investment objectives in their prospectuses. For example, the main types of objectives are growth, balanced income, and industry-specialized funds. Growth funds typically possess diversified portfolios of common stocks in the hope of achieving large capital gains for their shareholders. The balanced fund generally holds a portfolio of diversified common stocks, preferred stocks, and bonds with the hope of achieving capital gains and dividend and interest income, while at the same time conserving the principal. Income funds concentrate heavily on high-interest and high-dividend-yielding securities. The industry-specialized mutual fund obviously specializes in investing in portfolios of selected industries; such a fund appeals to investors who are extremely optimistic about the prospects for these few industries, and are willing to assume the risks associated with such a concentration of their investment dollars.

Money Market Funds

In 1974 and 1975 high yields prevailed in U.S. government securities, particularly in issues of short-term maturities. In addition to government securities of short-term duration, similar high returns prevailed in other types of short-term issues known as *money market instruments*. Frequently, large dollar amounts are required as minimum purchases for these types of issues. For example, the minimum dollar amount of U.S. Treasury bills that can be purchased is $10,000. Therefore, because of these high yields and because of the often-times large initial investment required, substantial interest developed in mutual funds that invested entirely in such issues. Total net assets of these money market funds amounted to close to $4 billion in early 1977.

These money market funds represent still another variety of open-end company which the mutual fund industry has brought to the investor's attention. The industry has continually been on the lookout for new types of funds to market.

Municipal Bond Funds

Municipal bond funds invest in a portfolio consisting entirely of tax-exempt bonds. Therefore the earnings that are passed on to the investor are totally tax free to the investor. Prior to 1976, because of the existing tax laws in the United States, these municipal bond funds took the form of so-called *unit trusts*. These unit trusts do not make continuous offerings as do the open-end funds. The units can either be purchased as new funds are formed or they can be purchased in the over-the-counter market after the initial offering of these units is com-

568

CHAP. 20
*Managed Portfolios
and
Performance
Measurements*

pleted. Normally these units sell on issuance at $1,000 per unit plus accrued interest. The interest on these units is usually paid monthly. The portfolio comprising the unit trust is fixed; that is, it is purchased before the units are sold to the public.

The Tax Reform Act of 1976 changed the previous tax law and allowed an open-end type of company such as a municipal bond fund to pass its income on to the shareholder in a tax-free manner. This permitted municipal bond funds that are set up as regular open-end companies to come into existence. The only difference between the municipal bond fund and the traditional stock open-end company is the portfolio composition. Namely, the portfolio of the municipal bond fund is comprised totally of tax-exempt municipal bonds. At the end of 1976 there was close to $7.5 billion of municipal unit trusts outstanding. Within a short time after the passage of the Tax Reform Act of 1976, there were as many as sixteen municipal bond funds on the market with sales in excess of $550 million. Table 20-1 lists the available tax-exempt unit trusts. Statistics on these unit trusts are not included in industry totals of the mutual fund industry because the unit trusts are considered different than the normal managed investment company. Statistics on the traditional managed investment companies are given later in this chapter.

Index Funds

Partly because of the overall poor performance of managed funds, and the market in general during the late 1960s and early 1970s, and because of a growing awareness of the efficient market hypothesis and the random-walk theory as outlined in Chapter 16, a new type of fund has become increasingly popular. This new type of fund is called an *index fund.* An index fund consists of a portfolio designed to reflect the composition of some broad-based market index. It does so by holding securities in the same proportion as the index itself. Frequently these index funds are constructed along the line of the S&P 500 Index—that is, the portfolio of the index fund is constructed in exactly the same proportion with respect to dollars involved as the S&P 500 Index. Therefore, by definition, the index fund is constructed to have a beta of 1.0 with respect to the S&P 500 Index if that is the index being emulated. In fact, an ideal index fund would be one holding all available common stocks in exact proportion to their outstanding market value. However, such an ideal fund would actually be impossible to construct and manage. Therefore it is hoped that an S&P 500 Index Fund will be a good surrogate for this ideal type of fund.[4]

There are two other main reasons for the growing interest in index funds. First, the expenses involved in administering index funds are considerably lower than those involved in handling a truly managed portfolio because the construction of the index-fund portfolio is entirely based upon maintaining proportions of the index being followed. As such, there would be considerably lower transaction costs involved because fewer purchases and sales of securities would take place. Furthermore, there would be much less need for expensive batteries

---

[4]Walker R. Good, Robert Ferguson, and Jack Treynor, "Investors' Guide to the Index Fund Controversy," *Financial Analysts Journal,* November-December 1976, pp. 27-36.

TABLE 20-1

TAX-EXEMPT BOND FUNDS (UNIT TRUSTS) OFFERINGS, 1961-1976

	Year First Offered	Series Offered in 1976		Total Series Offered	
		Number	$ Amount (millions)	Number	$ Amount (millions)
American Tax-Exempt Bond Fund	1974	9	32.5	15	59.4
California Tax-Exempt Bond Fund	1972	—	—	2	11.0
Cardinal Tax-Exempt Bond Trust	1975	5	25.9	7	35.9
F&M Tax Exempt Bond Fund	1973	—	—	3	10.5
First Trust of Insured Municipal Bonds	1974	10	146.8	21	210.8
Harris Upham Tax Exempt Fund	1973	—	—	6	47.5
E. F. Hutton Tax Exempt Fund:					
California Series	1970	—	—	7	40.0
National Series	1970	5	125.0	28	335.0
New York Series	1970	—	—	6	29.0
Michigan Fund Tax-Exempt Municipal Investment Trust	1972	—	—	2	11.0
Michigan Municipal Bond Fund	1974	—	—	1	3.5
Michigan Tax Exempt Bond Fund	1968	—	—	11	40.3
Michigan Tax Exempt Bond Fund:					
Insured Series A	1975	—	—	1	4.0
Multiple Maturity Tax-Exempt Bond Trust	1975	3	31.8	4	54.3
Municipal Bond Fund (The)	1972	10	175.5	34	394.5
Municipal Investment Trust Fund	1961	16	740.0	123	3,430.0
Municipal Investment Trust Fund:					
Intermediate Series	1976	7	147.0	7	147.0
National Municipal Trust	1973	5	64.5	17	159.0
National Municipal Trust Special Trusts:					
Discount Series	1976	1	4.5	1	4.5
Intermediate Series	1976	1	8.5	1	8.5
Nuveen Tax-Exempt Bond Fund:					
Long-Term Series	1961	13	481.5	92	1,611.0
Medium-Term Series	1976	2	32.0	2	32.0
Paine Webber Municipal Bond Fund	1966	—	—	3	23.1
PBT Tax-Exempt Bond Fund	1972	—	—	6	24.5
Pennsylvania Insured Municipal Bond Trust	1975	2	28.0	4	49.0
Pennsylvania Fund Tax-Exempt Municipal Investment Trust	1972	—	—	1	5.0
Quaker State Investment Trust, Pennsylvania Municipal Tax-Exempt Trust	1964	—	—	1	3.0
Tax-Exempt Environmental Bond Fund (The Monthly Income Series	1973	—	—	1	25.0
Tax-Exempt Income Fund	1965	—	—	4	19.2
Tax Exempt Municipal Trust:					
National Series	1975	8	118.0	13	141.0
New York Series	1975	—	—	1	10.0
Tax Exempt Securities Trust	1975	6	190.0	10	225.0
Texas-Southwestern Municipal Bond Fund	1973	—	—	1	5.0
Dean Witter Tax-Exempt Trust	1974	11	111.0	23	205.5
Totals		114	2,462.5	459	7,414.0

of security analysts and portfolio managers. Thus the overall administrative expenses would also be reduced. Second, with the passage of the new pension reform law, the investment trust laws surrounding the liability of portfolio managers of pension funds have changed with regard to the risk and return of the portfolio they manage. A discussion of the main changes as they affect portfolio managers is the subject of our next section.

PENSION-FUND MANAGEMENT AND ERISA

A *pension-fund* is a plan whereby an employer puts aside funds to provide for periodic payments to employees after they retire. Pension-fund assets represent an extremely large and fast-growing pool of institutional capital. At the end of 1975 the Securities and Exchange Commission estimated that pension-fund assets exceeded $400 billion. Of this amount, over one-half consisted of private pension-fund reserves. The remainder consisted of funds of various governmental agencies.

In 1974 the federal government passed the Employee Retirement Income Security Act, ERISA. This act has many far-reaching ramifications. Here we are primarily concerned with the impact on pension-fund institutional managers. Many critics have stated that this complex piece of legislation will greatly influence the behavior of institutional portfolio managers, and especially pension-fund managers. This act creates a federal standard for the legal fiduciary responsibility of the pension-fund manager. It expressly states that the fiduciary must act with care, skill, prudence, and diligence under the circumstances then prevailing that a prudent man acting in a like capacity and familiar with such matters would use in the conduct of an enterprise of a like character and with like aims. The act goes on to say that the fiduciary will be personally liable to make good to the plan any losses resulting from the breach of these responsibilities. The courts have ruled thus far that the fiduciary must produce a reasonable income and must preserve the capital of the fund. In fact, the preservation of capital is the key responsibility. It seems logical, therefore, that an index fund might well be sought after by pension-fund managers in order to escape liability under ERISA. This is because the pension-fund manager might argue that his fund did as well or no worse than the market as a whole performed over the period in question.

TRUST AGREEMENT

Commercial banks frequently offer their services as trustees for the management of an individual's portfolio. The fee charged for this service is generally a percentage of the size of the fund, decreasing with the size of the portfolio.

Generally, the trustee exercises complete discretion over the investments of the fund in a very conservative manner. Complete discretion means that the trustee selects which stocks to buy, at what prices, and the quantity he thinks appropriate, on his own, without consulting the person whose money he is managing. The legal statutes generally apply a "prudent-man" rule to judge whether proper management has occurred.

A special type of trust, which has become popular, is the common trust. Common trusts are essentially similar to mutual funds, except that the minimum investment in a common trust is substantially higher than that required in a mutual fund. In a common trust administered by a bank, the monies of a number of investors are commingled and are used to purchase a diversified port-

571

CHAP. 20
*Managed Portfolios
and
Performance
Measurements*

folio of securities. A basic advantage of the common trust is that there is more of a personal relationship between the bank and the investor. Furthermore, a common trust is an alternative available to smaller investors, since it requires less cost and principal investment than the usual trust arrangement does.

PROFESSIONAL INVESTMENT COUNSEL

The investor who uses a professional investment counsel hires the services of either a bank or an outside investment consultant to advise him on his investment policy. Typically, the investor discusses his objectives with the counsel, and as a result the investment counselor suggests alternative investment possibilities to the client. (In some cases, the counselor may even have total discretion.) The range of services can vary considerably under this type of arrangement, and consequently, so do the costs; however, the minimum cost of such a personal service is so high as to preclude this investment route for the typical small investor.

**Alleged
Advantages
of Managed
Portfolios**

Frequently, investors feel insecure in managing their own investments, because they consider themselves inadequate to perform this delicate task successfully. Oftentimes the investor feels he lacks the education, background, time, foresight, resources, and temperament to carry out the proper handling of his portfolio. When this occurs, the logical step is to turn the job over to a professional portfolio manager. Most often the source chosen takes the form of a mutual fund, or open-end investment company.

The main reasons for selecting an open-end investment company involve the management, diversification, and liquidity aspects of this organization form. Management trained in the ways of security analysis devotes full time to the carrying out of the fund's investment objectives as specified in its prospectus. This permits a constant monitoring of the securities comprising the portfolio. Furthermore, large amounts of money entrusted to the fund enable it to diversify its investments across industry and security types (that is, common stocks with various prospects, preferred stocks, and bonds) to an extent not possibly achieved by the average investor. This diversification evolves as a result of the stated objectives of the fund.

In Table 20-2, we see that 40 percent of the total assets held by mutual funds are in the hands of only twenty-one funds, or 3 percent of the number of funds. Funds specializing in growth and in growth and income common stocks hold 58 percent of the assets, and another 9 percent are held by those that stress common stocks with maximum capital gains. The investor can shop for a fund whose objectives are most in line with his own.

Finally, open-end companies represent a liquid type of investment. That is, shares can be readily converted into cash, for the company stands ready to redeem its outstanding shares.

TABLE 20-2

CLASSIFICATION OF MUTUAL FUNDS BY SIZE AND TYPE
(AS OF DECEMBER 31, 1976)

Size of Fund	Number of Funds	Combined Assets ($000)	% of Total
Over $1 billion	7	$11,811,000	21.8
$500 million-$1 billion	14	9,838,800	18.2
$300 million-$500 million	21	8,124,300	15.0
$100 million-$300 million	77	13,879,100	25.7
$50 million-$100 million	72	5,050,300	9.3
$10 million-$50 million	192	4,676,700	8.6
$1 million-$10 million	146	683,800	1.3
Under $1 million	27	10,500	0.1
Total	556	$54,074,600	100.0

Type of Fund	Number of Funds	Combined Assets ($000)	% of Total
Common stock:			
Maximum capital gain	111	$ 5,065,300	9.4
Growth	159	15,799,600	29.2
Growth and income	90	15,576,100	28.8
Specialized	13	362,500	0.7
Balanced	22	4,711,100	8.7
Income	95	7,738,800	14.3
Bond & pfd. stock	8	638,400	1.2
Money market	42	3,624,000	6.7
Tax-free municipal bonds	16	558,800	1.0
Total	556	$54,074,600	100.0

Source: *Investment Companies* (New York: Arthur Wiesenberger Services, 1977).

Let us examine the record to determine if these alleged advantages have in fact accrued to investors. Since most of the theory surrounding performance measurement, as well as the actual empirical work that has been conducted, has been connected with mutual funds, we will place our emphasis in this area. However, it should be noted that the notion of performance measurement is not something applicable only to open-end investment companies. Performance evaluation is necessary in *all* kinds of portfolios, whether individually or professionally managed.

Management-Performance Evaluation

We are interested in discovering if the management of a mutual fund is performing well. That is, has management done better through its selective buying and selling of securities than would have been achieved through merely "buying the market"—picking a large number of securities randomly and holding them throughout the period?

573

CHAP. 20
*Managed Portfolios
and
Performance
Measurements*

One of the most popular ways of measuring management's performance is by comparing the yields of the managed portfolio with the market or with a random portfolio. The portfolio-yield formula parallels the holding-period-yield formula for stocks that was presented in Chapter 4, and is:

$$\frac{NAV_t + D_t}{NAV_{t-1}} - 1 \qquad (20.1)$$

where:

NAV_t = per-share net asset value at the end of year t

D_t = the total of all distributions—both income and capital gains—per share during year t

NAV_{t-1} = per-share net asset value at the end of the previous year

Thus, if $NAV_t = \$11$, $D_t = \$1$, and $NAV_{t-1} = \$10$, the yield will be:

$$\frac{11 + 1}{10} - 1 = \frac{12}{10} - 1 = 1.2 - 1 = .2, \text{ or } 20\%$$

The two yields (managed portfolio and unmanaged portfolio) calculated by Equation 20.1 are then compared. The portfolio with the highest one-year holding-period yield is by this criterion deemed the better portfolio.[5]

This evaluation implies something about the management of the various portfolios under examination. In Table 20-3, we see the returns on a sample of thirty-nine mutual funds during the period 1951-60. It is of interest that fewer than half these sample funds were able to earn returns in excess of the 14.7 percent earned by the market (as measured by the New York Stock Exchange Average). In addition, note how inconsistent the funds' relative rankings were from year to year. However, merely measuring and comparing the returns on a managed and unmanaged portfolio is not enough.

First, if the managed portfolio did better than the unmanaged portfolio, the investor in the mutual fund should not rejoice too soon. He had to pay a management fee as well as suffer a reduction in equity equal to the loading charge (in the case of a load fund). So he must determine if the excess return is sufficient to cover these added expenses he has incurred by purchasing a mutual fund rather than purchasing a diversified portfolio on his own and paying the commissions (assuming he has this option). Second, the investor must determine the relative riskiness of the portfolio under analysis. It is entirely possible that the managed portfolio has achieved higher returns than the market or the un-

---

[5]This is the general formula used by the Arthur Wiesenberger Services, New York, N.Y. Representative reproductions from this excellent investment service will be presented in a later section of this chapter.

TABLE 20-3
YEAR-BY-YEAR RANKING OF INDIVIDUAL FUND RETURNS

Fund	Return on net (1)	1951 (2)	1952 (3)	1953 (4)	1954 (5)	1955 (6)	1956 (7)	1957 (8)	1958 (9)	1959 (10)	1960 (11)
Keystone Lower Price	18.7	29	1	38	5	3	8	35	1	1	36
T. Rowe Price Growth	18.7	1	33	2	8	14	15	2	25	7	4
Dreyfus	18.4	37	37	14	3	7	11	3	2	3	7
Television Electronic	18.4	21	4	9	2	33	20	16	2	4	20
National Investors Corp.	18.0	3	35	4	19	27	4	5	5	8	1
De Vegh Mutual Fund	17.7	32	4	1	8	14	4	8	15	23	36
Growth Industries	17.0	7	34	14	17	9	9	20	5	6	11
Massachusetts Investors Growth	16.9	5	36	31	11	9	1	23	4	9	4
Franklin Custodian	16.5	26	2	4	13	33	20	16	5	9	4
Investment Co. of America	16.0	21	15	14	11	17	15	23	15	15	15
Chemical Fund Inc.	15.6	1	39	14	27	3	33	1	27	4	23
Founders Mutual	15.6	21	13	25	8	2	20	16	11	13	28
Investment Trust of Boston	15.6	6	3	25	3	14	26	31	20	29	20
American Mutual	15.5	14	13	4	22	14	13	16	25	25	4
Keystone Growth	15.3	29	15	25	1	1	1	39	11	13	38
Keystone High	15.2	10	7	3	27	23	36	5	27	25	11
Aberdeen Fund	15.1	32	23	9	25	9	7	10	27	7	30
Massachusetts Investors Trust	14.8	8	9	14	16	9	15	20	18	32	28
NYSE Market Average*	14.7										
Texas Fund, Inc.	14.6	3	15	9	32	23	26	5	27	37	7
Eaton & Howard Stock	14.4	14	9	4	17	20	15	13	37	29	17
Guardian Mutual	14.4	21	26	25	34	31	29	13	20	15	2
Scudder, Stevens, Clark	14.3	14	23	14	19	27	15	29	9	15	30
Investors Stock Fund	14.2	8	28	21	22	27	20	23	5	29	23
Fidelity Fund, Inc.	14.1	21	26	25	34	31	29	13	20	15	23
Fundamental Investment	13.8	14	15	31	16	9	11	31	18	25	30
Century Shares	13.5	14	28	35	25	3	20	23	31	34	2
Bullock Fund Ltd.	13.5	29	9	21	19	14	9	20	34	34	20
Financial Industries	13.0	26	15	31	13	19	29	34	20	9	35
Group Common Stock	13.0	38	8	25	27	27	33	8	20	34	17
Incorporated Investors	12.9	14	13	37	6	3	13	37	11	18	39
Equity Fund	12.9	14	27	21	32	31	33	13	31	18	23
Selected American Shares	12.8	21	15	21	31	23	20	23	15	32	30
Dividend Shares	12.7	32	7	14	34	20	32	4	37	37	11
General Capital Corp.	12.4	10	28	9	38	35	39	23	34	13	23
Wisconsin Fund	12.3	32	26	4	37	35	38	10	34	18	7
International Resources	12.3	10	37	39	22	35	1	37	39	1	11
Delaware Fund	12.1	36	23	25	27	39	26	29	9	23	30
Hamilton Fund	11.9	38	28	9	34	35	36	10	31	18	17
Colonial Energy	10.9	10	15	35	39	20	4	36	20	39	10

*The NYSE market average represents what a tax-exempt investor could have expected to earn by randomly picking (for example, with a dart) a large number of stocks listed on the NYSE and holding them 10 years while reinvesting the dividends. The data were published by L. Fisher and J. Lorie. "Rates of Return on Investments in Common Stock," *Journal of Business*, January 1964, pp. 1-21.

Source: Eugene F. Fama, "The Behavior of Stock Market Prices," *Journal of Business*, January 1965 (Chicago: The University of Chicago Press, January 1965), p. 93.

managed portfolio by taking on considerably more risky investments. It is not surprising under such circumstances for higher returns to occur, for higher returns *should* go along with higher risks. Only after the relative risks of the portfolios have been considered is a comparison of returns meaningful.

SHARPE'S PERFORMANCE MEASURE FOR PORTFOLIOS

William Sharpe has attempted to get a summary measure of portfolio performance.[6] His measure properly adjusts performance for risk. The Sharpe Index is given by:

$$S_t = \frac{\overline{r}_t - r^*}{\sigma_t} \tag{20.2}$$

where:

S_t = the Sharpe Index

$\overline{r}_t$ = the average return on portfolio t

r^* = the riskless rate of interest

σ_t = the standard deviation (risk) of the returns of portfolio t

Thus the Sharpe Index measures the risk premiums of the portfolio (where the risk premium is the excess return required by investors for the assumption of risk) relative to the *total* amount of risk in the portfolio.

Graphically, the index, S_t, measures the slope of the line emanating from the riskless rate outward to the portfolio in question. (See Figure 20-1.) Thus the Sharpe Index summarizes the risk and return of a portfolio in a single measure that categorizes the performance of the fund on a risk-adjusted basis. The larger the S_t, the better the portfolio has performed. For example, assume that portfolio A has an average return of 10 percent with a standard deviation of 2 percent, and portfolio B has an $\overline{r}_B$ of 12 percent and σ_B of 4 percent. Further assume that $r^* = 5$ percent. Then the Sharpe Index (by Equation 20.2) for A equals:

$$\frac{.10 - .05}{.02} = 2.5$$

and for B:

$$\frac{.12 - .05}{.04} = 1.75$$

Thus A ranked as the better portfolio because its index is higher ($2.5 > 1.75$), despite the fact that portfolio B had a higher return ($12\% > 10\%$). The Sharpe Index and the Treynor Index, which we are about to discuss, have yielded very similar results in actual empirical tests.[7]

---

[6]William F. Sharpe, "Mutual Fund Performance," *Journal of Business, Supplement on Security Prices,* January 1966, pp. 119-38.

[7]*Ibid.,* p. 129.

FIGURE 20-1

GRAPHICAL REPRESENTATION OF TREYNOR INDEX, T_n

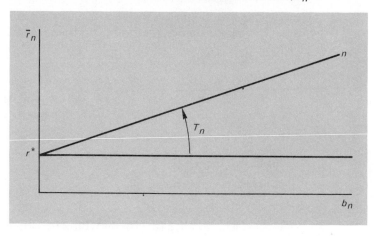

TREYNOR'S PERFORMANCE MEASURE FOR PORTFOLIOS

A key to understanding Treynor's portfolio-performance measure is the concept of a characteristic line.[8] In Figure 20-2 we see the graphical representation of a characteristic line of an ideal mutual fund.[9] More accurately, this linear representation is an approximation of what is probably more frequently a curvilinear relationship. This curvilinear representation is the dashed line in Figure 20-2. If a line were added to this graph that intersected the origin at a 45° angle, it would represent a portfolio return that was equivalent to the return of the market portfolio. The ideal fund lies above and to the left of the imaginary 45° line. Its return is at all times superior to the one earned on the market portfolio. When the market portfolio earns a low or negative return, the ideal portfolio still earns a positive return; and when the market portfolio earns a positive return, the ideal fund earns an even higher return. To put it more succinctly, the *characteristic line* relates the market return to a specific portfolio return without any direct adjustment for risk. This line can be "fitted" via a least-squares regression such as that involving a single index of a market portfolio. The Sharpe model we discussed in Chapter 17 was a single-index idea.

The slope of the characteristic line is the beta coefficient, a measure of the portfolio's systematic risk. Some people view systematic risk as a type of volatility measure. Thus, by comparing the slopes of characteristic lines, the investigator gets an indication of the fund's volatility. The steeper the line, the more systematic risk or volatility the fund possesses. Treynor has proposed

---

[8] Jack L. Treynor, "How to Rate Management of Investment Funds," *Harvard Business Review*, January-February 1965, pp. 63-75.

[9] This discussion parallels a comment on Treynor's paper that appears in Kalman J. Cohen and Frederick S. Hammer, *Analytical Methods in Banking* (Homewood, Ill.: Richard D. Irwin, 1966), pp. 374-78.

FIGURE 20-2

TREYNOR'S CHARACTERISTIC LINE OF AN IDEAL FUND

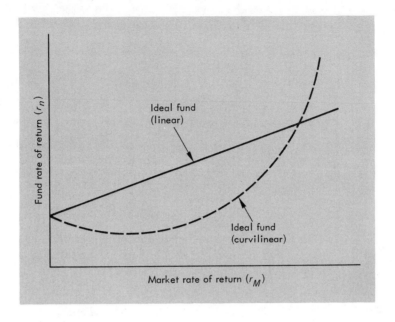

incorporating these various concepts into a single index to measure portfolio performance more accurately. This index is given by the following equation:

$$T_n = \frac{\bar{r}_n - r^*}{b_n} \qquad (20.3)$$

where:

T_n = the Treynor Index

$\bar{r}_n$ = the average return on portfolio n

r^* = the riskless rate of interest

b_n = the beta coefficient of portfolio n

Thus the Treynor Index measures the risk premium of the portfolio, where risk premium equals the difference between the return of the portfolio and the riskless rate. This risk premium is related to the amount of *systematic* risk assumed in the portfolio. So the Treynor index sums up the risk and return of a portfolio in a single number, while categorizing the performance of the portfolio. Graphically, the index measures the slope of the line emanating outward from the riskless rate to the portfolio under consideration. This is shown in Figure 20-3.

Note the differences in the axes of Figures 20-1 and 20-2. For example, if we

577

FIGURE 20-3
GRAPHICAL REPRESENTATION OF THE SHARPE INDEX, S_t

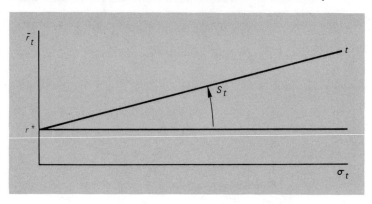

assume the same two hypothetical portfolios, A and B, from the previous section, and furthermore assume that the beta coefficients are .5 and 1.0, then the Treynor Index (by Equation 20.3) for A equals:

$$\frac{.10 - .05}{.5} = .10$$

and for B:

$$\frac{.12 - .05}{1.0} = .07$$

Again portfolio A performed better than B. Both the Sharpe and Treynor Indexes ranked A higher than B despite B's higher return.

JENSEN'S PERFORMANCE MEASURE FOR PORTFOLIOS

The Treynor and Sharpe Index Models provide measures for ranking the *relative performances* of various portfolios, on a risk-adjusted basis. Jensen attempts to construct a measure of *absolute performance* on a risk-adjusted basis—that is, a definite standard against which performances of various funds can be measured.[10] This standard is based on measuring the "... portfolio manager's *predictive ability*—that is, his ability to earn returns through successful prediction of security prices which are higher than those which we could expect, *given* the

---

[10]The discussion in this section closely parallels the development found in Michael C. Jensen, "The Performance of Mutual Funds in the Period 1945-1964," *Journal of Finance,* May 1968, pp. 389-416.

579

CHAP. 20
*Managed Portfolios
and
Performance
Measurements*

level of riskiness of his portfolio. . . ."[11] In other words, we are attempting to determine if more than expected returns are being earned for the portfolio's riskiness.

A simplified version of his basic model is given by:

$$\bar{R}_{jt} - R_{Ft} = \alpha_j + B_j (\bar{R}_{Mt} - R_{Ft}) \tag{20.4}$$

where:

$\bar{R}_{jt}$ = the average return on portfolio j for period t

R_{Ft} = the riskless rate of interest for period t

α_j = the intercept that measures the forecasting ability of the portfolio manager

B_j = a measure of systematic risk

$\bar{R}_{Mt}$ = the average return of a market portfolio for period t

The reader should note the similarity between this model and the basic Sharpe and Treynor models. An implication of forms of the Sharpe-Treynor Model is that the intercept of the line is at the origin. In the Jensen Model, the intercept can be at any point, *including* the origin. For example, in Figure 20-4, the upper line represents a case of superior management performance. In fact, α_j = a positive value represents the average superior extra return accruing to that particular portfolio because of superior management talent. The line $\alpha_j = 0$ indicates neutral performance by management; that is, management has done as well as an unmanaged market portfolio or a large, randomly selected portfolio managed with a naive buy-and-hold strategy. The lower line, α_j = a negative value, indicates inferior management performance, because management did not do as well as an unmanaged portfolio of equal systematic risk. This situation could arise in part because portfolio returns were not sufficient to offset the expenses incurred in the selection and managing process. Figure 20-5 shows an application of the Jensen approach that has been reported by a major Wall Street brokerage firm.[12]

**Empirical
Tests of
Mutual-Fund
Performance**

We have thus far examined various proposals that have been put forward for mutual-fund performance evaluation. In this section we will examine the results of a number of key empirical tests that have been conducted, to answer such questions as "Can mutual funds do better for me than I can do by myself?" "Are the management and selling fees that mutual funds charge worth the

---

[11]*Ibid.*, p. 389.

[12]G. Gordon Biggar, Jr., *Risk-Adjusted Portfolio Performance: Its Investment Implications* (New York: Smith, Barney & Co., 1971).

FIGURE 20-4

GRAPHICAL REPRESENTATIONS OF JENSEN'S MEASURE OF
MANAGEMENT ABILITY

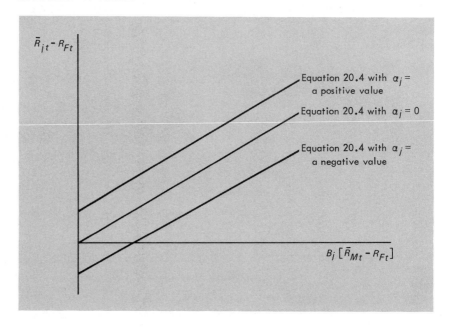

price?" and "Do managed funds adhere to their stated investment objectives?"

We have already seen in Table 20-3 that the answer to the first question above is negative. That is, mutual funds contained in this particular sample did not, on the average, outperform the returns that could be earned by following a naive strategy over the sample period. Because of the growing importance of investment companies in the United States, the Securities and Exchange Commission engaged the Wharton School of Finance and Commerce to conduct a study of mutual funds.[13] The investigation found no relationship between the performance of the mutual funds studied and the management fees and sales charges that these funds levied. "The fact that the analysis does not reveal a significant relation between management fees and performance indicates, in other words, that investors cannot assume the existence of higher management fees implies that superior management ability is thereby being purchased by the funds...."[14] The study reached a similar conclusion with regard to sales charges.[15]

[13]Irwin Friend, F. E. Brown, Edward S. Herman, and Douglas Vickers, *A Study of Mutual Funds,* prepared for the Securities and Exchange Commission by the Wharton School of Finance and Commerce, Report of the Committee on Interstate and Foreign Commerce, 87th Cong., 2nd sess., August 28, 1962.

[14]Friend et al., *op. cit.,* "Summary and Conclusions," as reprinted in Hsiu-Kwang Wu and Alan J. Zakon, *Elements of Investments* (New York: Holt, Rinehart & Winston, 1965), p. 384.

[15]This latter conclusion would seem to imply that the investor might be better advised to invest in a no-load fund than in a load fund.

FIGURE 20-5

ILLUSTRATION OF AN APPLICATION OF THE JENSEN APPROACH
CONDUCTED BY SMITH, BARNEY & CO.*

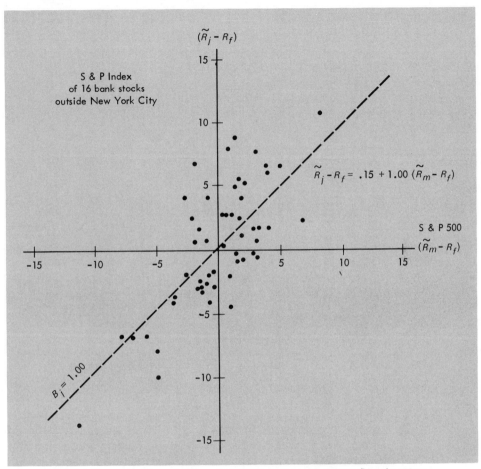

*Scatter diagram comparing the volatility of monthly investment returns (less the return on Treasury bills R_f) of the S&P Index of 16 Bank Stocks Outside New York City (vertical axis) and the S&P 500 Stock Index (horizontal axis) during the period January 1967-September 1971. The slope (B_j) of the dashed line measures the degree of volatility of the S&P Bank Stock Index in relation to that of the S&P 500.

Source: G. Gordon Biggar, Jr., *Risk-Adjusted Portfolio Performance: Its Investment Implications* (New York: Smith, Barney & Co., 1971), p. 20.

Jensen concluded that the funds in his study ". . .were *on average* not able to predict security prices well enough to outperform a buy-the-market-and-hold policy, but also that there is very little evidence that any *individual* fund was able to do significantly better than that which we expected from mere random chance. . . ." The reader can observe this by noting the preponderance of negative alphas in Figure 20-6. Here we see the frequency distribution of the alphas. These are the intercept values by which Jensen measures the ability of professional fund management. It should be noted that this distribution is skewed

FIGURE 20-6

FREQUENCY DISTRIBUTION OF ESTIMATED INTERCEPTS

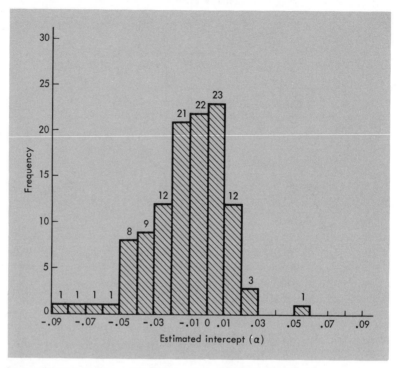

Source: Michael C. Jensen, "The Performance of Mutual Funds in the Period 1945-1964," *Journal of Finance*, May 1968, pp. 389-416.

to the left. This indicates the preponderance of alphas less than zero—an indication of negative management worth.[16] Sharpe reached a similar conclusion by comparing the Sharpe Index, the ratio of risk premium to risk, of a number of mutual funds with that of the Dow Jones Industrial Average.[17] Perhaps these findings are in part responsible for the growing popularity of funds, such as the Stagecoach Fund, that are constructed in the same proportions as some market index, such as the S&P 500 (an index fund). These funds would perform as well as the market.

The Securities and Exchange Commission as part of its Institutional Investor Study found some evidence that, in its sample, mutual funds outperformed the market by very small amounts. The SEC study was carried out on a risk-adjusted basis. However, a perhaps more enlightening finding of this same study was that there was no consistency with respect to which funds provided the investor with superior performance. Specifically, during the five-year period 1960-64 the least

[16]Jensen found that the funds earned (net of expenses) "about 1.1% less per year (compounded continuously) than they should have earned given their level of systematic risk...." Jensen, "Performance of Mutual Funds," p. 405.

[17]Sharpe, "Mutual Fund Performance," p. 125.

583

CHAP. 20
*Managed Portfolios
and
Performance
Measurements*

volatile funds in the sample tended to provide the strongest performance, while during the five-year period 1965-69 the more volatile funds in the sample provided the best performance. Thus the mutual funds in this study demonstrated a considerable lack of consistency in terms of which type of funds provided superior performance on a regular basis.[18]

In general, empirical investigations have found that fund managers are able to assess properly the risks and potential returns associated with alternative investment opportunities and have thus been able to meet their investment objectives fairly well.[19]

Extended Example of Portfolio Measurement

In Chapters 17 and 18 we introduced a population of sixteen stocks from which feasible portfolios were generated. A single "best" portfolio was chosen for holding, unmanaged, for a one-year period. Table 20-4 is a listing of the stocks in the portfolio chosen, along with the subsequent price results for the individual stocks, the entire portfolio, and the Dow Jones Industrial Stock Average, or market portfolio. Table 20-5 is a portfolio of stocks chosen at random.[20] This random portfolio was selected to duplicate the identical number of stocks in the so-called best portfolio. Equal dollar amounts were invested in each stock chosen at random, and the total dollar value of the portfolio was about $1 million. Table 20-6 shows the total dollar value of the "best," market, and random portfolios at month-end over the period.

Armed with the raw performance information for a (1) "best" portfolio, (2) market portfolio, and (3) naively selected portfolio, we want to see whether or not and by how much the "best" portfolio outperformed either of the others over the one-year time horizon in question.

The one-year returns on the three portfolios are:

"Best":	20.61%
Market (DJIA):	3.93
Random:	(8.48)

Without any adjustment for risk differences in the various portfolios, it would appear at first blush that the random portfolio is the worst performer and that the "best" portfolio outperformed the market by 20.61 versus 3.93 percent, or a

---

[18]*Institutional Investors Study Report of the Securities and Exchange Commission* (Washington, D.C.: Government Printing Office, 1971), Vol. II.

[19]However, the actual volatility of the portfolio proved to be a better appraisal of the funds' ultimate performance than did the words of management as expressed in their prospectuses. See Irwin Friend, Marshall Blume, and Jean Crockett, *Mutual Funds and Other Institutional Investors* (New York: McGraw-Hill, 1970), p. 150; and Donald E. Farrar, *The Investment Decision under Uncertainty* (Englewood Cliffs, N.J.: Prentice Hall, 1962), p. 73.

[20]Random portfolios are generated quite easily by using a table of random numbers. If such tables are not conveniently available, one could remove the New York Stock Exchange quotations from the *Wall Street Journal* and, blindfolded, throw a dart the appropriate number of times to select stocks. Random and market portfolios are most inexpensive to choose.

TABLE 20-4

PORTFOLIO PERFORMANCE—MARKET VALUE ($ IN HUNDREDS)

Security	Initial Value	Six Months Later	One Year Later
Associated Spring	$ 680	$ 619	$ 651
Burroughs Corporation	1,130	1,344	1,605
Black & Decker	2,940	3,220	4,200
Dover Corporation	788	904	912
Ethyl Corporation	115	124	122
Maytag	906	1,027	991
Mobil Oil Company	2,508	2,458	2,481
Pfizer, Inc.	760	837	· 845
Xerox Corporation	197	213	254
Total Portfolio	$10,026	$10,747	$12,061
DJIA	891.14	890.20	926.25

TABLE 20-5

RANDOMLY GENERATED PORTFOLIO—MARKET VALUE
($ IN HUNDREDS)

Company	Price	Shares	Initial Value	Six Months Later	One Year Later
Cincinnati Gas & Electric	25 1/2	4,400	$ 1,122	$1,149	$1,017
Collins & Aikman	24 1/8	4,600	1,109	1,408	1,035
Esterline Corp.	14 1/8	7,900	1,116	800	750
GF Business Equipment	9 1/4	12,000	1,110	1,080	1,035
Ideal Basic Indus.	18	6,200	1,116	1,023	1,054
Interstate Stores	14 3/4	7,500	1,106	862	628
Jaeger Machine Co.	6 5/8	17,400	1,109	1,218	1,500
Lane Bryant	29	3,800	1,102	1,306	997
Stone Container Corp.	10 1/2	10,800	1,113	850	1,134
			$10,000	$9,698	$9,152

TABLE 20-6

COMPARATIVE PORTFOLIO PERFORMANCE

Month	DJIA	"Best"	Random
Start	891.14	$10,026	$10,004
+1	858.43	9,881	9,696
+2	898.07	10,041	10,035
+3	887.19	9,965	9,666
+4	839.00	9,784	9,162
+5	831.34	9,645	8,804
+6	890.20	10,747	9,698
+7	902.17	10,828	10,084
+8	928.13	11,429	10,453
+9	940.70	11,125	10,147
+10	942.28	11,415	10,006
+11	960.72	11,962	9,820
+12	926.25	12,061	9,152

585

CHAP. 20
*Managed Portfolios
and
Performance
Measurements*

difference of 16.68 percent. The random portfolio behaved so dismally that it is safe to assume it did not beat the market or the selected portfolio on any basis adjusted for risk. Therefore we will analyze the random portfolio no further.[21] But let us see the Sharpe, Treynor, and Jensen approaches to portfolio evaluation in action on the other two portfolios.

Pertinent data for analytical purposes is contained in Table 20-7. During this period we have calculated monthly percentage value changes of the "best" portfolio and the Dow Jones Industrial Average.

TABLE 20-7
DATA ON A MANAGED PORTFOLIO

Month	Monthly Percentage Value Changes on Portfolio (MPV)	Monthly Percentage Value Changes on Dow Jones Industrials (MPVDJI)	Treasury Bill Rate (TBR)
1	−.0145	−.0368	.004075
2	.0163	.0462	.003450
3	−.0076	−.0121	.003508
4	−.0182	−.0543	.003225
5	−.0142	−.0091	.003300
6	.1143	.0709	.002533
7	.0076	.0134	.002458
8	.0554	.0288	.002491
9	−.0265	.0135	.002766
10	.0260	.0016	.002558
11	.0480	.0196	.002783
12	.0083	−.0358	.002808
$\bar{X} =$	.016241	.003825	.002996
$\bar{\sigma} =$	.040275	.036152	.000509

The reader should note that in our calculation of the various returns for both the managed and market portfolios, aggregate price appreciation (or depreciation) was the only input. The equation used for the calculation was:

$$R = \frac{V_{t+1} - V_t}{V_t}$$

where:

R = return

V_t = aggregate value at the beginning of the period

V_{t+1} = aggregate value at the end of the period

Dividends were *not* taken into consideration. The purpose of this section is merely to illustrate the implementation of the models, and with this in mind the imperfections of the data are inconsequential.

[21]Actually, under the Sharpe and Treynor formulas, the random portfolio shows a negative index value, owing to an average monthly return that is negative. Further, using the Jensen technique, the random portfolio has an annualized alpha of −12.5 percent.

586

CHAP. 20
*Managed Portfolios
and
Performance
Measurements*

The Treasury bill rate (TBR) is also shown in Table 20-7. The Treasury bill rate is in fact the riskless rate. For illustrative purposes, we are using the Dow Jones Industrial Average as a surrogate for the market portfolio.

SHARPE MODEL

At this juncture, let us compute the Sharpe Index (Equation 20.2) of the managed portfolio. The only inputs necessary for the Sharpe Model are:

1. r_t = the average return on the portfolio
2. r^* = the average riskless rate
3. $\bar{\sigma}_t$ = the standard deviation of the return on the portfolio

For this particular example, the imputs become $\overline{MPV}$, $\overline{TBR}$, and $\bar{\sigma}_{MPV}$, respectively. Their values can be extracted from Table 20-7. Please note that these are monthly rates. Simply substituting these values into the model, we find the Sharpe Index value to be:

$$S_t = \frac{\overline{MPV} - \overline{TBR}}{\bar{\sigma}_{MPV}} = \frac{0.016241 - (0.002996)}{0.040275} = 0.328864$$

TREYNOR MODEL

The Treynor Model (Equation 20.3) has the same numerator as the Sharpe Model. Therefore this portion of the index computation requires no further elaboration. The denominators, however, differ. Both involve a measure of risk; Sharpe uses total risk, σ_t, whereas the Treynor Index uses systematic risk, b_n (the beta coefficient of portfolio t). Determining the b_n value is a matter of performing a simple regression procedure using MPV as the dependent and $MPVDJI$ as the independent variable. The equation resulting from this procedure is:

$$MPV = 0.01308 + 0.8263(MPVDJI)$$

where:

α = .01308

b_n = .8263

All the necessary inputs for the Treynor model are now available. Simply substituting the data into the equations, with MRP representing the monthly return on the portfolio, yields:

$$T_n = \frac{\overline{MRP} - \overline{TBR}}{b_{MPV: MPVDJI}} = \frac{0.016241 - (0.002996)}{0.8263} = .016029$$

JENSEN MODEL

The implementation of the Jensen Model (Equation 20.4) using the data available in Table 20-7 requires a four-step operation. First, we must determine the difference between the monthly return on the portfolio and the respective Treasury bill rate ($MPV - TBR$) for each month individually. Next, we must find the difference between the monthly return on the Dow Jones Industrials and the respective Treasury bill rate ($MPVDJI - TBR$). Third, we must fit a regression line using the first difference ($MPV - TBR$) as the dependent and the second ($MPVDJI - TBR$) as the independent variable. This procedure gives us the excess return—that is, the return earned by both portfolios that is in excess of the risk-free rate; in other words, the reward for the assumption of risk. The equation for such a line is:

$$(MPV - TBR) = .01256 + .83042(MPVDJI - TBR)$$

where:

$\alpha = .01256$

$b = .83042$

The fourth and final step is simply to convert alpha, α, from a monthly to an annual basis. The reader will recall that α is the measure of bonus performance owing to superior portfolio management. Since in this regression we have used monthly data, α is stated as extra monthly return. To convert this to an annual basis, we merely need to multiply this figure by 12, to get 15 percent. ($12 \times .01256 = .1507$). This 15 percent then represents the additional return provided by investing in the managed portfolio rather than the market portfolio.

Mutual Funds as an Investment
Before we leave the subject of mutual funds, several closing remarks are in order. The fact that many of the studies just cited concluded that mutual funds have not performed very admirably does not lead to the seemingly obvious conclusion that mutual funds represent a bad investment outlet. What the studies concluded were that *on average,* mutual funds included in the various samples did not perform better than a market portfolio or a large randomly selected portfolio bought and held by the investor; however, exceptions to these summary conclusions were found in all cases.[22] Therefore, profitable investment opportunities existed in both the load and no-load areas. Furthermore, it is *impossible* for many investors to assemble a large, diversified portfolio of the kind that seems to do better than or as well as the managed portfolios, because

---

[22]It is interesting to note that the mediocre performance of mutual funds in general was apparently accomplished with considerably varying portfolios. For an interesting discussion of this, see Lawrence J. Marks, "In Defense of Performance," *Financial Analysts Journal,* November-December 1962, pp. 135-37.

of capital limitations. Indeed, mutual funds may represent the only opportunity many investors have for investing in an intelligent, diversified fashion in the securities of U.S. corporations.[23]

Sources of Investment-Company Information

One of the best sources of investment-company information available to the investor is Wiesenberger's *Investment Companies,* issued annually. Figures 20-7, 20-8, and 20-9 show the types of information provided by this service. Figure 20-7 is typical of the pages that capsulize information about individual funds. As can be seen, the summary contains a history of the fund, statement of objectives, something about its portfolio composition, key statistical data, and the result of a hypothetical $10,000 investment in the fund over a ten-year period. Figure 20-8 shows the performance of net asset value on a yearly basis and on a cumulative basis for a number of growth funds. (The formula utilized was given in Equation 20.1.) Figure 20-9 examines the price volatility of these same growth funds. (The explanation of the volatility measure is contained in the table.)

It is interesting to note that the Wiesenberger Service appears to recognize the importance of both return and risk considerations; however, these measures are presented separately, as can be seen in Figures 20-8 and 20-9, but are not brought together in a summary measure as has been done by others, such as Sharpe and Treynor. In fact, the volatility factor that the Wiesenberger Service calculates might be thought of as a crude measure of the beta factor in Equation 20.4.

Forbes, an investment magazine published twice a month, annually rates the performance of investment companies. Its system attempts to incorporate in a summary measure both return and risk considerations. Basically, the approach used is to compare the fund's performance with that of the general market during periods of rising and falling markets. Funds that perform exceptionally well on a consistent basis when compared with the market in up markets receive an A+ rating; those that do not do as well receive ratings down to a possible low of D−. In a similar fashion, *Forbes* compares the relative performance of individual funds with the market portfolio in declining markets. Thus each fund receives two ratings—one in up markets, and one in down markets.

From these ratings, the investor gets a rough indication of the potential risks of investing in a given fund, both when investment conditions are favorable and when they are unfavorable. Furthermore, an investor can choose a fund whose performance is in line with his risk preferences. For example, the investor who is very risk-averse will prefer a fund that has performed consistently well in both kinds of markets (probably betas of one or less). On the other hand, a less risk-averse person or a more aggressive investor might prefer a fund that has done exceptionally well in up markets, even if it means assuming exceptional risk should a down market occur (betas greater than one). Needless to say, it is an ideal portfolio whose performance excels in both rising and falling markets.

---

[23]The reader will recall the advantages of proper Markowitz diversification, as explained in Chapter 17. In addition, it should be pointed out that mutual funds may in fact over-diversify, as pointed out in Chapter 18.

FIGURE 20-7

SAMPLE PAGE FROM WIESENBERGER'S *INVESTMENT COMPANIES*

TEMPLETON GROWTH FUND, LTD.

Templeton Growth Fund was incorporated in Canada in 1954. It is a diversified investment company under the U.S. Investment Company Act of 1940. For several years shares of the fund were not offered in the United States, but became available to U.S. investors again in 1974. The fund's investments are diversified among the securities issued by different companies and governments. No more than 5% of total assets may be invested in any single company.

The fund's primary objective is long-term capital growth. The investment policy is flexible and investments may be made in all types of securities issued by companies or governments anywhere. At the end of the 1976 fiscal year the fund had the major proportion of its investments in the U.S., Japan and Canada, with smaller holdings in The Netherlands and Australia.

At the close of 1976, the fund had 88.7% of its assets in common stocks, of which a significant proportion was concentrated in five industry groups: chemicals & drugs

(10.2% of assets), real estate (10.1%), oil & gas (7.7%), food & beverage (7%), and health care (5.4%). The five largest individual common stock investments were Mitchell Energy & Development (6.8% of assets), Royal Dutch Petroleum (4%), Kao Soap (3.6%), Gulf Oil (3.4%), Trane Co. (2.9%). The rate of portfolio turnover during the latest fiscal year was 11% of average assets. Unrealized appreciation was 27% of calendar year-end assets.

Special Services: An open account arrangement serves for accumulation and automatic dividend reinvestment. Dividends are invested at net asset value. Minimum initial investment is $500 except under payroll deduction or other plans calling for regular monthly investments. Payments may be made by way of pre-authorized checks. A withdrawal plan is available for owners of $10,000 or more of shares; withdrawals may be of any amount monthly or quarterly.

Statistical History

| | | | | | — % of Assets in — | | | | | | | |
| | AT YEAR-ENDS | | | | | | | ANNUAL DATA | | | | |
Year	Total Net Assets ($)	Number of Share-holders	Net Asset Value Per Share ($)	Offer-ing Price ($)	Yield (%)	Cash & Equiv-alent	Bonds & Pre-ferreds	Com-mon Stocks	Income Div-idends ($)	Capital Gains Distribu-tion ($)	Expense Ratio (%)	Offering Price ($) High	Low
1976	42,844,213	3,500	12.03	13.15	0.9	7	4*	89	0.12	0.11	1.00	13.15	9.28
1975	19,796,132	1,900	8.39	9.20	1.5	7	9*	84	0.143	0.03	0.99	9.36	6.88
1974	13,500,000	1,700	6.23	6.82	1.6	13	9*	78	0.115	0.15†	1.07	8.85	6.66
1973	16,700,000	1,500	7.33	8.03	0.7	22	7	71	0.06	0.795†	0.93	10.53	7.69
1972	16,900,000	750	8.95	9.79	0.8	22	12	66	0.07	0.149	1.18	9.79	6.00
1971	7,900,000	650	5.47	5.98	1.3	13	20	67	0.076	0.09	1.30	5.98	5.09
1970	6,600,000	550	4.64	5.07	1.5	26	18	56	0.076	—	1.16	5.61	4.78
1969	7,200,000	500	5.03	5.50	1.3	28	11	61	0.071	—	0.98	5.50	4.61
1968	6,200,000	500	4.27	4.66	1.1	22	13	65	0.05	—	1.08	4.71	3.40
1967	4,800,000	515	3.14	3.44	1.5	16	8	76	0.05	—	1.02	3.67	3.06
1966	4,600,000	550	2.81	3.07	1.2	23	12	65	0.038	—	1.09	3.46	2.99

Note: Figures adjusted for 5-for-1 stock split in 1971. Total net assets are in Canadian dollars; other figures in U.S. dollars.
* Includes a substantial proportion in convertible issues.
† Includes $0.115 representing 1½% stock dividend in 1974 and $0.685 representing 8% stock dividend in 1973.

Directors: John M. Templeton, Pres. and Treas.; James W. Bradshaw; Robert M. Fowler; William F. James; Archibald D. Russel; Dr. John M. Templeton, Jr.; Henry A. Wilmerding; Dennis O. Yorke.

Investment Adviser: Templeton Investment Counsel Ltd. Compensation to the Adviser is at an annual rate of ½ of 1% of average daily net asset value, paid quarterly.

Custodian: Registrar and Transfer Agent: New England Merchants National Bank, Boston, MA 02106, and The Chase Manhattan Bank, N.A., Tokyo 100, Japan.

Distributor: Securities Fund Investors, Inc., 50 No. Franklin Turnpike, Hohokus, NJ 07423 is the principal underwriter. Moss, Lawson & Co. Ltd., 48 Yonge St., Toronto, Canada, is the exclusive distributor in Canada.

Sales Charge: Maximum is 8½% of offering price; minimum is 0.5% at $1 million. Reduced charges begin at $10,000 and are applicable to subsequent purchases on a permanent basis. Minimum initial purchase is $500.

Dividends: Income dividends and capital gains, if any, are paid annually.

Shareholder Reports: Issued semi-annually. Fiscal year ends April 30. The 1976 prospectus was effective in August.

Qualified for Sale: In all states, except AK, ID, NV, NM, WV, and WY.

Address: 145 King Street West, Toronto, Ontario M5H 2J3.

Telephone: (416) 364-4672.

An assumed investment of $10,000 in this fund, with capital gains accepted in shares, is illustrated below. The explanation on page 153 must be read in conjunction with this illustration.

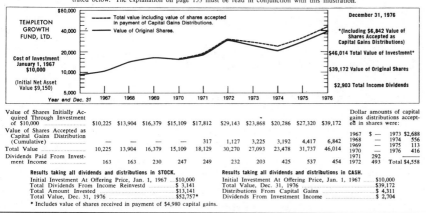

Value of Shares Initially Acquired Through Investment of $10,000	$10,225	$13,904	$16,379	$15,109	$17,812	$29,143	$23,868	$20,286	$27,320	$39,172
Value of Shares Accepted as Capital Gains Distribution (Cumulative)	—	—	—	—	317	1,127	3,225	3,192	4,417	6,842
Total Value	10,225	13,904	16,379	15,109	18,129	30,270	27,093	23,478	31,737	46,014
Dividends Paid From Investment Income	163	163	230	247	249	232	203	425	537	454

Dollar amounts of capital gains distributions accepted in shares were:

1967	$ —	1973	$2,688
1968	—	1974	556
1969	—	1975	113
1970	—	1976	416
1971	292		
1972	493	Total	$4,558

Results taking all dividends and distributions in STOCK.

Initial Investment At Offering Price, Jan. 1, 1967	$10,000
Total Dividends From Income Reinvestd	$ 3,141
Total Amount Invested	$13,141
Total Value, Dec. 31, 1976	$52,757*

* Includes value of shares received in payment of $4,980 capital gains.

Results taking all dividends and distributions in CASH.

Initial Investment At Offering Price, Jan. 1, 1967	$10,000
Total Value, Dec. 31, 1976	$39,172
Distributions From Capital Gains	$ 4,311
Dividends From Investment Income	$ 2,704

Source: *Investment Companies 1977* (New York: Wiesenberger Investment Companies Service).

FIGURE 20-8

APPROXIMATE PERCENT CHANGE IN NET ASSETS PER SHARE.

	Approximate Per Cent Change in Net Assets per Share RECORDS FOR INDIVIDUAL YEARS									
	ANNUAL RESULTS									
	1976	1975	1974	1973	1972	1971	1970	1969	1968	1967
I. GROWTH FUNDS										
A. Maximum Capital Gain										
Acorn Fund	64.4	30.4	−27.5	−23.7	8.6	31.2				
Afuture Fund	19.3	63.5	−42.0	−35.2	19.1	67.5	−26.8	−16.7		
Alpha Fund	22.7	22.1	−27.7	−31.9	27.4	28.1	− 9.0	− 8.4		
American General Venture Fund	25.3	86.8	−40.9	−38.8	28.8	61.1				
American Investors Fund	34.8	17.9	−29.7	−15.3	10.7	4.3	−29.3	−29.3	10.8	45.9
American National Growth Fund	37.8	38.0	−16.2	−37.1	3.0	28.3	− 1.4	−13.8	20.7	53.6
Centennial Capital Special	25.6	34.7	−30.4	−45.4	23.5	32.4				
Chase Frontier Cap. Fd. of Boston	8.0	15.1	−35.2	−46.5	17.9	30.7	−23.3	−14.1		
Chase Fund of Boston	10.5	36.5	−36.2	−31.2	5.6	29.5	−24.8	−17.1	20.6	81.6
Chase Special Fund of Boston	18.6	19.5	−33.9	−33.3	0.5	28.3	− 8.8			
Columbia Growth Fund	30.5	41.0	−22.4	−25.5	5.9	36.2	−13.5	− 2.9	37.9	
Comstock Fund	34.0	64.3	−16.8	−17.1	− 0.9	12.5	−17.4	−18.9		
Constellation Growth Fund	23.2	39.2	−26.2	−16.3	5.8	2.0	−48.5	− 6.5	16.1	
Contrafund	36.7	40.3	−14.2	−10.4	16.4	9.1	10.6	−15.9	16.4	
Delta Trend Fund	29.5	31.4	−37.7	−33.8	− 7.9	21.4	−19.0	−14.9		
Directors Capital Fund	14.1	26.0	−19.8	−32.7	11.0	31.6				
Dreyfus Leverage Fund	24.9	25.8	−26.3	−15.4	12.6	28.8	0.6			
Eaton & Howard Growth Fund	12.0	32.6	−45.2	−33.6	23.4	27.5	−11.6	− 7.0		
Eaton & Howard Special Fund	19.2	26.8	−40.6	−32.3	3.8	28.2	−21.7	−33.7		
Edie Special Growth Fund	6.8	40.1	−32.1	−40.4	16.5	34.3	− 1.7			
Enterprise Fund	14.8	33.6	−30.5	−20.5	6.4	23.5	−26.1	−25.9	44.3	116.9
Equity Growth Fund of America	16.3	17.7	−26.9	−22.0	1.9	17.4	− 4.5	−13.5	26.0	60.2
Evergreen Fund	48.8	60.1	−21.4	−26.2	10.1					
Explorer Fund	16.8	22.8	−35.0	−26.2	21.1	24.6	−25.7	−11.7	16.7	
Fairfield Fund	33.4	40.2	−25.6	−28.2	5.2	20.2	−17.1	−29.3	7.2	67.8
Financial Dynamics Fund	31.1	38.2	−34.8	−15.3	17.4	13.6	−40.0	−16.6	33.0	
First Investors Discovery Fund	34.2	41.5	−36.5	−37.7	− 3.4	15.5	−19.3			
First Investors Fund for Growth	18.3	24.6	−29.6	−29.7	6.5	29.8	−15.1	− 3.2	2.1	34.8
44 Wall Street Fund	46.5	186.1	−52.2	−46.8	− 5.4	71.8	6.6			
Founders Growth Fund	7.4	30.1	−21.9	−24.9	16.2	24.5	− 7.4	−28.2	17.2	68.5
**Founders Special Fund (1969)	16.9	0.7	−19.9	−19.1	−25.2	35.5	21.1	**	**	**
Franklin DynaTech Series	22.0	31.8	−33.4	−35.2	16.0	25.5	−20.0	−27.4		
Fund of America	20.9	14.8	−27.4	−17.8	10.1	6.0	−12.8	−16.5	6.0	50.3
Hamilton Growth Fund	26.9	45.9	−31.7	−30.1	5.4	16.0	−19.7	−10.8		
IDS New Dimensions Fund	14.7	28.3	−34.7	−28.4	27.1	48.5	−19.3	−12.8		
IDS Progressive Fund	16.1	31.1	−37.9	−28.3	11.2	44.1	−20.6			
Independence Fund	16.3	20.9	−27.0	−10.4	23.7	27.8	−43.0	−26.3	9.4	67.0
Industries Trend Fund	20.9	24.5	−21.3	−25.6	24.0	17.5	− 4.4	−15.1	18.7	40.6
ISI Growth Fund	12.5	13.0	− 4.4	− 7.8	16.3	8.5	−27.1	−18.3		
Ivest Fund	14.5	30.6	−33.5	−32.1	11.7	21.5	− 4.5	− 7.9	− 2.2	47.4
Janus Fund	20.2	13.4	− 6.9	−16.0	33.9	41.5				
Kemper Summit Fund	33.3	56.4	−33.9	−27.5	6.9	25.9	− 0.9			
Keystone S-4	32.5	36.8	−44.0	−40.5	13.0	35.2	−21.1	−20.8	21.1	66.0
Lexington Growth Fund	47.5	46.1	−23.3	−43.6	13.6	27.2	−16.8			
Lord Abbett Developing Growth	19.5	38.9	−35.6							
Magellan Fund	37.5	44.3	−28.1	−42.1	31.6	33.5	−15.8	−16.5	39.4	103.8
Mathers Fund	43.7	55.4	−29.7	−36.8	15.8	19.4	2.0	− 6.0	26.8	92.4
Neuwirth Fund	17.7	24.1	−22.0	−30.3	− 2.7	25.4	−20.2	−17.3	90.1	
New York Venture Fund	20.6	22.9	−20.1	−24.0	22.2	28.0	−26.3			
Nicholas Fund	22.7	47.7	−33.4	−52.7	28.1	85.5	−24.4			
Oceanographic Fund	12.1	1.4	−16.5	−11.5	8.8	17.5	− 7.5	−26.8		
Omega Fund	50.0	12.8	−19.9	−18.1	43.8	21.0	−24.6	−18.8		
Oppenheimer A.I.M. Fund	19.5	29.1	−32.5	−21.9	12.5	33.4	9.3			
Oppenheimer Fund	15.7	27.0	−25.2	−24.7	10.0	18.1	2.0	−16.0	22.1	37.2
Oppenheimer Special Fund	48.9	92.0	−16.3							
Oppenheimer Time Fund	32.5	58.5	−44.1	−43.8	21.8					
Pace Fund	27.8	34.2	−15.4	−42.5	18.0	43.6	−35.7			
Partners Fund	30.9	17.9	− 3.2	−26.5	− 8.4	13.5	− 8.6	−13.8		
**Pennsylvania Mutual Fund (1972)	49.0	121.1	−46.0	−48.5	− 3.4	5.7	−53.8	−28.1	67.9	**
Pilgrim Fund	28.0	45.3	−31.0	−39.7	10.4	26.7	− 4.9	−13.7	9.4	60.6

** This symbol, when appearing at the left of a fund name, indicates a change of management or policy occurred in the year shown in parentheses. When ** appears under a column heading, it indicates that figures have been omitted because the fund, while in existence throughout the period, was not readily available for purchase by the public, or that a complete change of policy makes earlier figures not meaningful.

Source: *Investment Companies 1977* (New York: Wiesenberger Investment Companies Service).

Summary

In this chapter we have examined a number of alternative types of managed portfolios available to the investor. These have included closed-end investment companies, open-end investment companies or mutual funds, dual funds, money

FIGURE 20-8 (cont.)

With Capital Gains (Reinvested) and Income Dividends (Added Back)

FOR PERIODS OF TWO TO TEN YEARS ENDED DECEMBER 31, 1976

	2 years from 1/1/75	3 years from 1/1/74	4 years from 1/1/73	5 years from 1/1/72	6 years from 1/1/71	7 years from 1/1/70	8 years from 1/1/69	9 years from 1/1/68	10 years from 1/1/67	Funds 10 Years Old % Change in Net Asset Value†	Total Income††	Funds Less Than 10 Years Old % Change in Net Asset Value†	Total Income††
I. GROWTH FUNDS													
A. Maximum Capital Gain													
Acorn Fund	112.5	52.7	16.1	25.9	64.4							54.7	9.7
Afuture Fund	95.0	13.2	— 26.6	— 12.5	46.3	7.1	— 10.8					— 11.0	0.2
Alpha Fund	49.2	7.0	— 27.1	— 8.8	19.3	8.3	— 0.7					— 10.4	9.7
American General Venture Fund	134.0	38.4	— 15.3	9.0	75.7					75.7	0		
American Investors Fund	58.4	10.6	— 6.4	3.6	8.1	— 23.6	— 45.9	— 39.7	— 11.3	— 17.6	6.3		
American National Growth Fund	87.9	54.0	— 3.8	— 0.9	27.0	24.6	7.0	29.1	98.0	68.4	29.6		
Centennial Capital Special	68.8	15.3	— 37.1	— 22.3	3.1							— 1.6	4.7
Chase Frontier Cap. Fd. of Boston	24.3	— 19.7	— 57.0	— 49.3	— 33.7	— 48.9	— 56.1					— 58.2	2.1
Chase Fund of Boston	50.5	— 5.1	— 34.7	— 31.0	— 10.3	— 32.5	— 43.5	— 31.5	25.1	6.6	18.5		
Chase Special Fund of Boston	41.3	— 6.8	— 37.8	— 37.4	— 19.2	— 26.1						— 30.8	4.7
Columbia Growth Fund	82.6	40.5	4.5	10.7	50.6	30.2	26.1	88.4				70.7	13.7
Comstock Fund	118.9	79.4	48.0	45.6	62.0	32.3	7.0					— 4.7	11.7
Constellation Growth Fund	70.7	24.8	4.8	10.9	13.2	— 41.8	— 45.6	— 36.8				— 39.8	3.0
Contrafund	90.3	61.0	42.9	65.6	78.7	94.6	61.0	86.6				61.0	25.6
Delta Trend Fund	69.6	5.0	— 30.4	— 35.9	— 21.6	— 36.5	— 45.3					— 50.4	5.1
Directors Capital Fund	43.0	12.8	— 24.1	— 15.8	10.9							1.0	9.9
Dreyfus Leverage Fund	56.2	14.1	— 3.5	8.5	39.8	39.7						27.2	12.5
Eaton & Howard Growth Fund	48.3	— 18.9	— 46.1	— 33.4	— 14.4	— 24.0	— 29.3					— 34.9	5.6
Eaton & Howard Special Fund	50.6	— 10.7	— 39.5	— 37.1	— 18.2	— 35.5	— 57.1					— 61.9	4.8
Edit Special Growth Fund	49.4	0.8	— 39.8	— 29.6	— 5.3	— 6.8						— 14.1	7.3
Enterprise Fund	52.6	4.9	— 16.6	— 11.1	10.1	— 18.8	— 39.8	— 13.1	88.7	57.5	31.2		
Equity Growth Fund of America	36.2	— 1.1	— 22.9	— 21.3	— 7.0	— 11.1	— 23.0	— 3.4	55.5	36.9	18.6		
Evergreen Fund	138.2	87.3	38.2	52.0								51.5	0.5
Explorer Fund	43.3	— 7.4	— 31.6	— 17.1	3.4	— 23.1	— 31.8	— 19.8				— 28.7	8.9
Fairfield Fund	85.6	36.7	— 2.1	2.9	23.5	2.0	— 27.8	— 22.6	29.7	18.4	11.3		
Financial Dynamics Fund	80.4	16.0	— 1.6	15.4	30.7	— 21.8	— 34.5	— 12.8				— 22.3	9.5
First Investors Discovery Fund	89.8	19.5	— 25.5	— 28.1	— 16.7	— 32.7						— 34.4	1.7
First Investors Fund for Growth	47.0	3.1	— 27.4	— 22.8	0.3	— 14.8	— 17.6	— 15.7	13.7	7.8	5.9		
44 Wall Street Fund	316.1	98.7	5.6	0	71.7	83.0						83.0	0
Founders Growth Fund	39.4	7.2	— 19.7	— 6.6	16.2	7.1	— 23.1	— 9.8	52.0	26.1	25.9		
**Founders Special Fund (1969)	17.0	— 7.1	— 24.6	— 5.5	28.0	55.1	**	**	**			33.8	21.3
Franklin DynaTech Series	60.2	6.1	— 31.2	— 20.0	0.6	— 19.4	— 41.4					— 45.9	4.5
Fund of America	37.9	— 1.1	— 18.6	— 10.0	— 4.1	— 16.4	— 30.0	— 26.1	11.1	— 8.2	19.3		
Hamilton Growth Fund	84.3	25.1	— 12.7	— 7.9	6.7	— 14.3	— 23.4					— 29.9	6.5
IDS New Dimensions Fund	46.9	— 4.5	— 31.6	— 13.1	29.1	3.9	— 9.3					— 15.6	6.3
IDS Progressive Fund	51.5	— 6.7	— 33.0	— 24.9	8.3	— 13.9						— 23.0	9.1
Independence Fund	40.1	1.5	— 9.0	12.4	43.6	— 18.4	— 39.7	— 33.6	11.5	0.1	11.4		
Industries Trend Fund	49.9	15.6	— 14.4	6.1	24.6	18.5	— 0.3	19.1	68.8	40.3	28.5		
ISI Growth Fund	26.4	19.7	10.5	27.8	38.1	0.1	— 18.2					— 31.7	13.5
Ivest Fund	49.3	— 1.1	— 32.8	— 24.6	— 8.0	— 12.0	— 18.9	— 20.6	17.1	4.6	12.5		
Janus Fund	36.0	24.6	3.9	39.1	96.8							79.8	17.0
Kemper Summit Fund	107.4	34.8	— 2.8	3.9	30.8	29.0						17.2	11.8
Keystone S-4	81.2	1.5	— 39.6	— 31.7	— 7.6	— 27.1	— 42.1	— 34.7	8.6	4.1	4.5		
Lexington Growth Fund	115.0	63.8	— 8.2	4.2	32.4	10.0						6.9	3.1
Lord Abbett Developing Growth	65.9	6.4										5.1	1.3
Magellan Fund	97.5	41.3	— 18.2	7.6	43.5	20.7	0.8	40.6	186.6	175.2	11.4		
Mathers Fund	137.8	63.6	— 4.3	10.7	32.3	34.6	26.5	60.4	208.4	175.3	33.1		
Neuwirth Fund	45.9	13.8	— 20.7	— 22.9	— 2.5	— 21.4	— 34.9	23.6				9.5	14.1
New York Venture Fund	47.4	16.7	— 11.4	8.2	38.4	1.9						6.4	8.3
Nicholas Fund	80.9	20.2	— 43.1	— 27.2	35.0	2.0						0.6	1.4
Oceanographic Fund	13.0	— 5.5	— 16.3	— 9.4	6.9	— 1.7	— 27.5					— 34.9	7.4
Omega Fund	69.2	31.6	7.7	55.0	85.8	37.7	11.5					0.6	12.1
Oppenheimer A.I.M. Fund	53.7	2.7	— 19.7	— 9.7	20.5	31.7						21.4	10.3
Oppenheimer Fund	46.5	7.5	— 19.0	— 10.6	5.8	7.9	— 9.3	10.7	53.6	31.5	22.1		
Oppenheimer Special Fund	185.1	138.8										136.5	2.3
Oppenheimer Time Fund	110.7	17.9	— 33.8	— 19.4								— 19.8	0.4
Pace Fund	71.5	45.1	— 16.4	— 1.5	41.4	— 9.1						— 9.1	0
Partners Fund	52.9	55.5	14.1	4.5	18.5	7.8	— 7.0					— 19.2	12.2
**Pennsylvania Mutual Fund (1972)	229.4	77.7	— 8.4	— 11.6	— 6.5	— 56.8	— 69.0	— 47.9	**			— 47.9	0
Pilgrim Fund	85.4	27.1	— 23.3	— 15.4	7.3	2.1	— 11.9	— 3.5	55.0	44.1	10.9		

† Including value of shares accepted as capital gains distributions.
†† As a per cent of asset value at the beginning of the period.

market funds, municipal bond unit trusts and funds, index funds, pension funds, ERISA, trust agreements, common trusts, and professional investment counsel. We discussed the characteristics of these alternative investment opportunities, as well as the alleged advantages of such professionally managed portfolios. We analyzed a number of alternative measures of performance evaluation, including

FIGURE 20-9
PRICE VOLATILITY OF MUTUAL FUND SHARES

PRICE VOLATILITY OF MUTUAL FUND SHARES

Because of varying investment objectives and portfolio policies, it is normal for the prices of some mutual fund shares to reflect rises and declines in the general stock market to a greater degree than do others. The relationship between percentage changes in a fund's asset value per share and the corresponding fluctuations in a broad index of common stock prices provides a measure of a fund's relative "volatility."

In the table below, price changes of leading funds—adjusted for capital gains distributed—are related to changes in the New York Stock Exchange Index of all common stocks listed on the Exchange, to provide a rough indication of volatility. The results are expressed as "factors." A volatility factor of 1.00 would mean that adjusted asset value of a fund experienced a percentage change equal to that of the NYSE Common Stock Index between the same dates; a lower factor indicates a smaller rise or decline; a factor above 1.00 shows an advance or decline in excess of the index.

The percentage changes in the NYSE Common Stock Index (composite) during the eight periods shown below were as follows:

April 28, 1971 to November 23, 1971	−14.1%
November 23, 1971 to January 11, 1973	+32.0%
January 11, 1973 to August 24, 1973	−17.3%
August 24, 1973 to October 26, 1973	+10.6%
October 26, 1973 to October 3, 1974	−45.1%
October 3, 1974 to July 15, 1975	+55.8%
July 15, 1975 to October 1, 1975	−14.2%
October 1, 1975 to December 31, 1976	+31.7%

Volatility is not a measure of management performance. It can be used chiefly in estimating the relative extent of risk in declining periods and of gain potentials in shorter-term rising markets. Management performance, in contrast, is a long-term concept. Chapter XI discusses this aspect of investment company selection.

	Declining Period 4/28/71 to 11/23/71	Rising Period 11/23/71 to 1/11/73	Declining Period 1/11/73 to 8/24/73	Rising Period 8/24/73 to 10/26/73	Declining Period 10/26/73 to 10/3/74	Rising Period 10/3/74 to 7/15/75	Declining Period 7/15/75 to 10/1/75	Rising Period 10/1/75 to 12/31/76
NYSE Common Stock Index (Composite)	1.00	1.00	1.00	1.00	1.00	1.00	1.00	1.00
I. GROWTH FUNDS								
A. Objective: Maximum Capital Gains								
Acorn Fund	1.35	0.95	1.57	2.15	1.04	1.19	1.27	2.14
Afuture Fund	0.34	1.44	0.82	1.82	1.31	1.50	0.93	0.94
Alpha Fund	0.64	1.38	1.40	0.65	1.02	0.85	1.34	1.00
American General Venture Fund	2.74	3.18	2.17	2.53	1.31	2.38	1.72	1.58
American Investors Fund	1.61	1.04	1.49	2.38	1.03	1.25	1.60	1.10
American National Growth Fund	1.13	0.64	1.82	1.52	0.89	0.97	1.04	1.53
Chase Frontier Capital Fund of Boston	1.37	1.41	2.46	1.86	1.18	0.91	1.36	0.26
Chase Fund of Boston	1.13	0.83	1.52	1.25	1.19	1.09	0.91	0.34
Chase Special Fund of Boston	0.91	0.65	2.42	2.19	1.11	1.10	1.02	0.57
Columbia Growth Fund	0.77	0.85	1.69	2.02	0.84	1.01	1.08	1.30
Comstock Fund	1.01	0.19	1.29	1.62	0.78	1.68	1.18	1.53
Constellation Growth Fund	2.46	1.08	1.10	1.60	0.90	1.14	1.34	1.06
Contrafund	1.12	0.94	0.76	1.77	0.88	1.39	0.96	1.17
Delta Trend Fund	1.45	0.32	2.10	1.76	1.13	1.24	1.21	0.99
Directors Capital Fund	1.29	1.18	1.31	0.93	1.03	0.70	0.61	0.48
Dreyfus Leverage Fund	0.98	1.14	1.08	1.23	0.90	0.85	0.70	0.73
Eaton & Howard Growth Fund	0.86	1.61	1.32	0.84	1.38	1.38	1.41	0.49
Eaton & Howard Special Fund	1.35	0.80	1.86	2.29	1.20	1.06	1.39	0.58
Edie Special Growth Fund	0.55	1.08	1.53	1.07	1.20	1.21	1.38	0.47
Enterprise Fund	0.86	0.63	1.40	1.60	0.95	0.85	0.96	0.65
Equity Growth Fund of America	1.05	0.46	1.24	1.14	1.02	0.92	1.28	0.77
Explorer Fund	1.31	1.46	1.17	1.10	1.06	0.96	1.52	0.51
Fairfield Fund	1.66	0.94	1.83	1.50	1.00	1.22	1.01	1.44
Financial Dynamics Fund	1.49	1.08	1.16	1.36	1.05	1.46	1.23	0.89
First Investors Discovery	1.71	0.84	2.03	0.69	1.15	1.80	1.75	1.34
First Investors Fund for Growth	0.71	0.77	1.72	1.59	1.05	1.07	1.20	0.81
First Multifund of America	1.16	0.99	1.10	0.80	0.53	0.44	0.80	0.58
44 Wall Street Growth Fund	0.52	1.26	2.54	3.82	1.39	3.22	1.88	2.15
Founders Growth Fund	0.84	0.98	1.06	0.42	0.81	0.69	0.96	0.37
Founders Special Fund	0.98	0.68	0.98	0.33	0.48	0.22	1.15	0.43
Franklin DynaTech Series	1.28	1.04	1.74	1.42	1.08	0.97	1.45	0.98
Fund of America	1.21	0.63	1.25	1.25	0.98	0.72	0.93	0.76
Hamilton Growth Fund	1.36	0.73	1.13	0.96	1.16	1.29	0.92	1.06
Hartwell Growth Fund	0.83	0.58	1.76	1.12	0.98	1.12	1.06	0.95
Hartwell Leverage Fund	0.85	0.02	1.22	2.66	1.04	1.48	1.23	2.73
Herold Fund	0.68	0.58	1.94	1.21	1.06	1.11	0.83	0.67
IDS New Dimensions Fund	0.62	1.77	1.26	0.92	1.21	1.23	1.23	0.63
IDS Progressive Fund	0.45	1.01	0.99	0.79	1.25	1.05	1.01	0.55
Impact Fund	1.41	1.13	1.42	1.28	0.97	0.85	1.09	1.15
Independence Fund	0.73	1.40	0.73	1.23	0.94	0.75	0.81	0.61
ISI Growth Fund	1.36	1.24	1.05	1.12	0.27	0.53	0.87	0.11
Ivest Fund	1.04	0.93	1.48	0.98	1.23	1.30	1.06	0.56
Janus Fund	0.55	1.97	0.66	0.60	0.51	0.34	0.98	0.88
Kemper Summit	1.08	0.86	1.57	1.66	1.10	1.34	0.89	1.15
Keystone Apollo Fund	0.76	1.30	2.03	1.54	1.20	1.33	1.18	0.47

Source: *Investment Companies 1977* (New York: Wiesenberger Investment Companies Service).

FIGURE 20-9 (cont.)

PRICE VOLATILITY OF MUTUAL FUND SHARES (Continued)

	Declining Period 4/28/71 to 11/23/71	Rising Period 11/23/71 to 1/11/73	Declining Period 1/11/73 to 8/24/73	Rising Period 8/24/73 to 10/26/73	Declining Period 10/26/73 to 10/3/74	Rising Period 10/3/74 to 7/15/75	Declining Period 7/15/75 to 10/1/75	Rising Period 10/1/75 to 12/31/76
NYSE Common Stock Index (Composite)	1.00	1.00	1.00	1.00	1.00	1.00	1.00	1.00

I. GROWTH FUNDS (Cont'd)

A. Objective: Maximum Capital Gains (Cont'd)

Keystone (S-4) Special Common	1.19	1.25	1.97	1.74	1.35	1.49	1.59	1.21
Lexington Growth Fund	1.37	1.18	2.10	1.30	0.96	1.20	1.27	1.87
Lexington Research Fund	1.22	0.88	1.29	1.06	0.86	0.86	0.50	1.01
Mathers Fund	1.32	1.12	1.63	0.97	1.10	1.37	1.26	1.64
Mutual Shares Corporation	0.78	0.29	0.69	1.00	0.22	0.79	0.65	1.91
Naess & Thomas Special Fund	0.91	1.26	1.04	1.03	0.68	0.77	1.15	0.87
Neuwirth Fund	1.23	0.56	1.53	1.92	1.02	0.82	0.90	0.69
New York Venture Fund	1.22	1.53	1.48	1.50	0.86	0.82	1.25	0.91
Nicholas Fund	0.29	2.07	2.18	1.47	1.35	1.54	1.30	1.02
Oceanographic Fund	1.25	0.85	1.33	2.22	0.69	0.60	0.87	0.10
Omega Fund	1.08	2.30	1.57	1.22	0.65	0.86	1.07	1.36
Oppenheimer AIM Fund	1.15	1.13	1.29	1.45	1.08	0.96	1.30	0.96
Oppenheimer Fund	0.90	0.67	1.24	1.25	1.05	0.93	0.96	0.64
Oppenheimer Time Fund	—	0.63	2.11	2.15	1.34	1.62	1.67	1.57
Pace Fund	0.84	1.50	2.38	2.05	0.97	1.17	1.03	1.34
Partners Fund	1.54	0.30	1.33	1.01	0.38	0.49	0.87	1.04
Pennsylvania Mutual Fund	2.74	0.49	2.35	2.33	1.39	2.62	1.26	2.00
Pilgrim Fund	0.70	0.91	1.90	1.35	1.04	0.94	0.94	1.17
Pilot Fund	1.14	0.81	0.96	1.33	0.81	1.07	1.07	0.67
PLITREND Fund	0.99	0.77	1.03	1.14	1.10	0.95	0.94	1.16
Polaris Fund	0.78	1.38	1.99	1.47	1.16	1.36	1.21	0.48
Putnam Equities Fund	0.62	1.53	1.45	1.18	1.01	1.59	1.47	1.02
Putnam Vista Fund	0.88	1.99	1.19	1.12	1.10	1.49	1.47	0.93
Putnam Voyager Fund	0.86	2.34	1.00	1.43	1.08	1.64	1.47	1.32
Rainbow Fund	2.70	0.61	2.45	0.68	1.00	0.50	0.99	1.23
Redmond Growth Fund	0.28	1.03	1.73	1.73	1.17	0.85	1.13	0.81
Research Equity Fund	1.42	1.19	1.06	0.88	0.98	0.69	1.45	0.62
Revere Fund	1.40	0.60	1.95	0.42	0.99	0.50	1.29	1.12
Rowe Price New Horizons	CT	0.95	1.79	0.89	1.27	1.26	1.39	0.58
Schuster Fund	1.27	0.51	1.55	0.76	1.14	1.06	1.42	1.11
Scudder Development Fund	0.36	2.15	1.63	1.23	1.39	1.60	1.63	1.21
Scudder Special Fund	0.98	0.87	1.52	0.91	1.15	0.87	1.28	1.03
Security Equity Fund	1.08	0.98	1.43	1.83	0.94	1.07	1.25	1.24
Security Ultra Fund	0.50	1.35	1.99	1.58	1.06	1.71	1.62	1.96
Selected Special Shares	1.37	0.39	1.35	1.35	0.86	1.03	1.07	0.58
Sequoia Fund	0.71	0.62	1.24	1.20	0.75	1.14	0.85	2.45
Sherman, Dean Fund	2.54	0.20	0.60	0.49	0.64	1.59	1.34	0.69
Sigma Capital Shares	1.42	1.12	1.82	1.47	1.12	1.46	1.29	1.44
Smith, Barney Equity Fund	0.66	1.19	1.42	1.71	0.94	0.82	0.87	0.61
Spectra Fund	1.51	0.89	2.29	1.33	1.18	1.18	1.08	1.01
Steadman American Industry	1.12	0.43	1.64	1.70	0.89	0.54	1.04	0.08
Tudor Hedge Fund	1.14	1.65	1.91	1.71	0.79	0.92	1.31	1.20
Twentieth Century-Growth	0.88	2.60	1.68	3.22	1.17	1.53	1.41	2.46
Union Capital Fund	0.72	1.55	2.03	1.58	0.99	1.25	1.01	1.12
United Vanguard Fund	0.93	0.50	1.38	0.93	1.28	1.30	1.50	0.90
Value Line Leveraged Growth	—	—	—	2.11	1.20	1.82	1.74	1.70
Value Line Special Situations	2.25	0.36	2.07	1.46	1.04	1.42	1.49	1.65
Vance Sanders Special Fund	0.84	1.02	1.60	1.82	1.14	1.23	1.20	1.23
Weingarten Equity Fund	0.43	1.26	1.46	1.66	1.15	1.51	1.20	0.66
AVERAGES	1.10	1.05	1.53	1.42	1.01	1.15	1.18	1.03

I. GROWTH FUNDS

B. Objective: Long-Term Growth—Income Secondary

Allstate Enterprises Stock Fund	0.61	1.63	1.14	1.05	1.19	1.46	1.28	0.52
AMCAP Fund	0.94	1.00	1.88	2.09	1.11	1.45	1.24	1.15
American Birthright Trust	0.48	0.38	0.28	0.52	0.06	0.22	0.53	0.98
American General Capital Growth Fund	0.84	0.98	1.46	1.04	1.06	0.85	1.21	0.67
American Growth Fund	0.84	0.51	0.66	0.81	0.83	0.84	1.03	1.01
American Leaders Fund	0.21	0.09	0.77	0.88	0.88	0.78	0.55	0.70
Anchor Growth Fund	1.15	0.53	2.27	1.29	1.10	1.01	0.93	0.60
Armstrong Associates	1.18	0.94	1.77	0.69	1.01	1.26	0.91	1.83
Audax Fund	0.66	1.28	1.82	1.10	1.07	1.43	1.27	0.81
Axe-Houghton Stock Fund	0.99	0.67	0.86	1.05	0.61	0.60	0.69	0.65
Beacon Investing Corp.	1.16	0.53	1.45	0.61	0.91	0.69	0.70	0.56
Berkshire Capital Fund	0.70	0.74	1.34	1.03	0.90	0.65	0.82	1.21
BLC Growth Fund	0.65	1.22	1.02	1.17	1.07	1.08	1.26	0.97
Brown Fund of Hawaii	0.97	1.37	1.69	0.67	1.04	1.45	1.08	0.88
Capital Fund of America	1.32	0.57	1.24	0.92	1.13	1.07	1.06	0.83

CT   Counter Trend.

the Sharpe, Treynor, and Jensen approaches. Then we reported the results in summary fashion of a number of key empirical studies of mutual fund performance. Finally, we concluded with a survey of key sources of information on investment companies.

Questions and Problems

1. Distinguish between closed-end and open-end investment companies.

2. What are the alleged advantages of professionally supervised portfolios? Have empirical tests offered support for these contentions?

3. How can one measure the holding-period yield on a market portfolio?

4. Many people advocate mutual funds for small investors. They suggest that the best strategy for small investors is to buy shares in a good mutual fund and put them away. What do you think of this advice?

5. What is the essential difference between the Sharpe and Treynor Indexes of portfolio performance? Which do you think is preferable? Why?

6. How can the elements of the Sharpe Index be calculated?

7. What is a characteristic line? How can it be determined?

8. What is the meaning of the alpha value in the Jensen Model?

9. What are the implications, if any, of the results of studies of mutual-fund performance for the random-walk theory?

INDEX